D1599099

WILLIAM CARLOS WILLIAMS
MAN AND POET

For Brother
EDGAR
in memoriam

and for Sons
WILLIAM ERIC and *PAUL*

WILLIAM CARLOS WILLIAMS

NATIONAL
POETRY
FOUNDATION
UNIVERSITY OF MAINE AT ORONO

Man and Poet

Edited
with an introduction by
Carroll F. Terrell

Published by

The National Poetry Foundation
University of Maine at Orono
Orono, Maine 04469

Printed by

The University of Maine at Orono
Printing Office

Library of Congress No. 83-61211
ISBN 0-915032-57-0 (cloth)
ISBN 0-915032-58-9 (paper)

PREFACE

The *Man and Poet* series was conceived as an instrument to bring to the attention of a wider public a few great American poets who have been neglected in the tradition. Of course, the truly great will be found and assigned their deserved place in time: Dante was found and appropriately honored in Europe and America although it took more than five hundred years. Chaucer and Shakespeare were eventually found. The series can only nudge the public in the right direction and make basic materials as an introduction easily available. With William Carlos Williams, the situation is a little different. Certainly, he was grossly neglected for all of his fifty most productive years. When he was stingily represented in anthologies, the selections were mostly taken from his most mediocre and uncharacteristic verse. But the situation began to change shortly after his death in 1963. From then and until 1975, a great deal of excellent basic scholarly work was done. With Emily Wallace's model bibliography and a number of compilations of critical works, scholars began to have the tools to work with. James Laughlin's New Directions started to provide us the *sine qua non*: editions of all of Williams' work in paperback. Then in 1975 Theodora Graham started the *William Carlos Williams Newsletter* (now *The Review*) with precisely the needed mission and tone: although it is a small publication it is one of the brightest and most solid journals available. In that year also Paul Mariani's *William Carlos Williams: The Poet and His Critics* provided the means for new scholars to approach Williams efficiently. Since 1975, the record of work done is amazing. I expected the annotated bibliography, 1974-1982, for this volume could be done in 75 pages. Although Professor Brogunier who did the work warned me, I would not back down from the original design: do it completely and don't cut corners. He didn't: thus the final result which is 133 pages.

It is clear that William Carlos Williams has finally come into his own and doesn't really need nudges in any direction. Thus the tone of this volume is commemorative and memorial in honor of

Williams' centennial year, as is the tone of the Centennial conference to be held August 23-26, 1983. The book does establish one precedent: it will be on sale at that conference even though half of its contents will be papers delivered at the time. In order to pull off a trick of this magnitude, it is clear that I'm much indebted to a lot of people, to begin with the writers who were coerced to get their work in enough ahead of time to make it possible.

I am much indebted, also, to William Eric and Paul Williams and their wives Mimi and Betty for their help with the conference as well as the book. John Dollar, the primary force behind the creation of the William Carlos Williams Center for the Performing Arts (the most amazing monument to a poet in the nation), was an enthusiastic aid and abettor as was Edith Heal Berrien, a long time friend of Williams.

The help of a number of people here at Orono I am delighted to acknowledge: my colleagues Burton Hatlen and Paul Bauschatz; then Fred Round, Dana Carson, James Guevara, Helen Smith, Tony Guay, Don Fuller, Arthur Dutch, Don Fogg, and John Merrill, all dedicated workers at the University Press, without whose help I couldn't get anything out on schedule. Then my own office staff: Nancy Nolde, Marie Alpert, Julie Courant and Marilyn Emerick. I'm indebted, too, to a few graduate students, in particular Dirk Stratton, a jack of all editorial trades, and Steve Boardway who did the index fast. And finally to a few other students who have worked willingly and late: Kate Woznik, Linda Burns, Julie Hatlen and Barbara Ramsay-Strout. As you can see, this book is the product of a team effort—and a great team it is.

CFT
Orono,
June 10, 1983

TABLE OF CONTENTS

CARROLL F. TERRELL

INTRODUCTION

Celebration is the tone of this book, the kind of celebration which takes place after a hard game is won and the fans tear onto the field and tear down the goal posts. Most early critics of Williams' work wrote in a defensive and querulous tone, as if they were voices crying out in some lonely wilderness. But not Pound who always wrote with the conviction of some delphic oracle in the teacher-like tone of his early note on *The Tempers* reprinted here. And not Kenneth Burke whose perceptions and convictions were never altered by what anyone else might think. Now that the game is won, our attitudes can conform to some of Pound's early observations: "Gloom and solemnity are entirely out of place in even the most rigorous study of an art originally intended to make glad the heart of man." He underlined the point by immediately quoting the delightful definition of Laurence Sterne: "Gravity, a mysterious carriage of the body to conceal the defects of the mind" [*ABCR*, 13]. We can say with Pound also: This "book is not addressed to those who have arrived at full knowledge of the subject without knowing the facts." We can even endorse his "private word to teachers and professors," also a preamble to *The ABC of Reading*: "I am not idly sowing thorns in their path. I should like to make even their lot and life more exhilarating and to save even them from unnecessary boredom in classroom." We can endorse it because it applies so much to Williams' work of a lifetime as well as to the intent and tone of this book, which

> proceeds from a firm conviction that the only way to keep the best writing in circulation, or to 'make the best poetry popular', is by drastic separation of the best from a great mass of writing that has been long considered of value, that has overweighed all curricula, and that is to be blamed for the very pernicious current idea that a good book must be of necessity a dull one.

And,

> A classic is classic not because it conforms to certain
> structural rules, or fits certain definitions (of which its author had
> quite probably never heard). It is classic because of a certain eter-
> nal and irrepressible freshness
>
> [pp. 13-14]

The reader will note that here an old story is restated. To most
discriminating readers Williams' poetry is now known to be among
the few classics produced in this century. It has taken a long time
to establish this fact because he created his own forms, structures,
and definitions which did not conform to rules established in earlier centuries.

II

The book contains a variety of material, starting with memories and tributes of other poets and friends in the section called
"Dove Sta Memora" and in some of the pieces in the section entitled "The Man." An underlying affection for a most remarkable
personality is everywhere present. And that's what matters, as we
read in *The Cantos*:

> nothing matters but the quality
> of the affection—
> in the end—that has carved the trace in the mind
> dove sta memoria
>
> [76/457]

The materials are organized under various headings on the grounds
that some organization is better than none, even though it is clear
that the man cannot be separated from his work. Subordinate organization is mostly alphabetical by the author's last name. Since
this is the kind of book one dips into and consults, I will give cues
in this introduction showing how some of the pieces lead almost as
if by design into others.

First, Philip Booth captures, as only a poet can, a memorable
moment during a reading by Williams. We see several aspects of
the poet's use of syntax in the poetic line while at the same moment we see the poet as a several-sided persona, ranging from a
deadly serious mood to one of Aristophanic-like humor. This
piece evokes memories for me because the one time I met Williams
and heard him read was about that same time [1950] in the Boston area. As I recall, it must have been at a regional meeting of
either the MLA or the CEA. He was vigorous enough to show complete recovery from his first cerebral incident. I remember clearly
how he repeated one sentence, again and again, in a tone of great

urgency: "You must understand if you change the poetic line, you change civilization." My reaction then was to say to myself, "What can he possibly mean?" and finally to conclude, after he'd said it a number of times, "He's got it backwards. What he really means is that if you change civilization, that change will eventually be reflected in the poetic line." So goes the arrogance of youth armed with ignorance! More than ten years had to pass before it dawned on me that he was right and had said exactly what he meant to say. I don't remember anything he read, but I do remember thinking that he wasn't reading well, that he wasn't at all doing justice to his own work. After the reading I gathered with a lot of others to shake hands, but I don't remember anything he said. I can only hope the crowd was large enough so that it would be impossible for me to explain his speech to him. Somebody once defined "positive" as "being mistaken at the top of one's voice."

Hayden Carruth, poet and editor, gives a glimpse of Williams in another seldom-mentioned role, as revealed by a young doctor who had once been a WCW medical protege. The doctor's neat explanation of *aphasia* becomes an ironic and deadpan lead into a note that justifies his title, "The Agony of Dr. Paterson." This, I don't want to think about. For a person to whom words meant so much, it's too horrible to think about. It ironically correlates with Pound's awful ten years of suffering silence. Then, one of Canada's greatest living poets, Ralph Gustafson, recalls meeting Williams along with a bevy of other notables at the Gotham Book Mart, which makes one feel like "those were the days." Robert Creeley then recalls his two visits to 9 Ridge Road, the first in the Spring of 1954. The few pages included here are conflated from taped interviews I had with Creeley in the Fall of 1982 while he was occupying the Lloyd H. Elliott Chair at Orono. The section concludes with an engaging scene: we are allowed to listen in on Allen Ginsberg teaching Williams to one of his classes.

The section entitled "The Man" includes memories by John Dollar of Williams as a social creature among his friends in Rutherford and the memories of Edith Heal Berrien, who worked with him on *I Wanted to Write a Poem*. Then we have an account by Mary Barnard of Charles Abbot's work in establishing The Poetry Archive at Buffalo which has become a model for similar collections started elsewhere. But the Williams' collection there is special because of his years of friendship with Abbott and their close cooperation. Mary Barnard speaks with authority because she started working with Abbott as early as 1939.

But the *pièce de résistance* here is the several pieces son William Eric Williams has done in recent years for the *WCW Review* collected under the title "Life With Father." Here a father, hero, doctor and friend comes to life.

As with other volumes in this series a good deal of space is given to young and promising scholars who, in this most difficult age of "publish or perish," need a hearing. But with the articles herein, they clearly deserve it. Kerry Driscoll with the fresh approach of the young senses the design of *Yes, Mrs. Williams* in a way none of the older critics ever has. If there is no excuse, there is at least a reason

Critics have always had difficulty with great works of art which break completely with the traditions they are trained in. Van Gogh and Picasso, creators of totally new traditions, could not be properly judged by the old and therefore had to be found wanting. So with great poets such as Whitman, Pound, and Eliot. It took ten years for critics to deal with *The Waste Land* because the references had to be to the poem itself. So, with much of the work in both prose and poetry of Williams. *Yes, Mrs. Williams*, a book 30 years in the making, has had to define itself, as has most of Williams' work in other modes, as the complex, economical, bit of art that it is.

Pound once said that you could tell who is talking by the noises they make. Williams devotes the first part of the book to his own complex reactions to his mother. The rest of the book is made up of a selection of verbatim quotes from his mother talking and his reactions to her: an extraordinary portrait emerges which could never have been contrived by any other means. Tangential things also emerge: a strong sense of family, Williams' changing attitude towards his own commitments to his art, his friends, and his work. Near the end we have this juxtaposition, mother first, Williams in italics:

> As Papa used to say, "Why don't you make a list, Monday this, Tuesday that, and so on, for the week." No, I couldn't do that. Perhaps it is a fault, I am too restless. In fact all my life I have reproached myself that I haven't a *parti pris*. The same in cooking.

> Sometimes they would send a girl into the country—on business and she would not return. The negroes would catch them and eat them—so they would believe.

> *Thank God for modern poetry, for poetry—alive that is. It is the only thing that gives any satisfaction, the only thing in the world worth living for (a painter might say the same about painting)—and Ezra Pound, thank God, is doing his part.*
>
> *Well, either he had to burst or go ahead because that's the only thing he's doing.*

Such gists become "luminous details" in the Poundian sense: they force the reader to think and therefore get him off dead center. What appears to be a *non sequitur* is not except that there are at least 5 steps in a train of thought before one can get to the response, "Thank God...."

William Eric's foreword to the 1982 paperback adopts the same technique: by indirections we find directions out. And by implication we have the strong sense of family which the United States seems to have lost. He starts by asking the question, "how does this multilingual Francophile *señora* married to our Anglophile traveling man citizen of Great Britain rate a book about herself?" He answers by giving examples of letters home from both William Carlos and his younger brother Ed. The first, dated Feb. 7, 1904, speaks loud and clear.

> Dear Mama,
>
> Today I spent part of the afternoon at Uncle's [Irving Wellcome's]. He had a big pile of old photographs which he had just taken out of a trunk and I was looking them over. As I was glancing from one picture to another I came upon a young girl of about twenty leaning on some old book. She was a beauty in fact she was such a girl as I have often dreamed of but never seen. I fell in love right away. She was not only beautiful for anyone could read her fine character through and through by looking into her eyes. She is as near my ideal as I have ever gotten. Mamy it was you. Now I can realize the popularity that must have been yours. I can see you flying across the ballroom in Paris with music softly playing and swaying dancers on every side. Oh it must have been great. That little picture has made me fall in love with you all over again. How coarse all the girls I know seem beside you. . . .
>
> Love to you to Papa and to Ed. Your son.
>
> Willie

William Eric comments in part

> She was my Nana Williams. She was small, gentle, and pleasantly scented. There was about her an aroma of Florida Water, lilac powder, and if lace and silk exude an essence that must have been the other element that completed the bouquet. She carried herself as tall as her five feet and an odd inch or two would permit, her back very straight, the neck and chin rigidly squared by the whale-bone-supported lace collar and dickey that she habitually affected. Her speech was staccato, her language often punctuated with Spanish exclamations and French adages. *"Pas de correspondance pour La Bastille,"* and *"Petit à petit l'oiseau fair son nid,"* for example. *"Madre de Dios," "Ai, Toledo,"* and other Spanish expletives rattled off in what I am told was perfect Castilian, the "R's" particularly having impressed me, the crescendo and decrescendo like summer thunder.

Then we have another letter from son William dated 26 October 1915:

Dearest Old Silly Mommy,

Of course you're a failure—what good would you be if you didn't think yourself a failure? It's the fineness of your appreciations alone that makes you discontented with yourself. You *are*—you exist, you feel, you aspire, you love and you hate—the deep inexplicable burning in your innermost heart is real—it isn't a sham—it isn't false—therefore how can you really dare to tell me you are a failure? Of course you wish you had painted great pictures—you wish you had followed your voice—you wish for self-confidence, happiness, pleasure—and when you have these last things you can't enjoy them.

In spite of everything you cannot free yourself—you fail to soar up into the sort of being you wish to be—therefore you call yourself a failure.

Mother dear—I also wish to do great works of art—to write great good poems—to help the poor and the unhappy—I also wish to be happy myself—but young as I am who shall say that I will not be a failure.

Mother that does not bother me in the slightest degree—it never has. I want to succeed of course but—so long as I can live a passionate life—full of striving, full of eager attempts to the whole extent of the power that is in me I shall say that I have really lived—that I have been really worthy of you—yes of you for you are to me perfect—say what you please—I cannot explain it.

Dear Mother you are perhaps my dearest possession. life is to be lived, Mother not to be eaten.

Be good now and come home to me soon.

Your son that loves you dearly,

Willie

Towards the end of the foreword, we have a few letters home from Willie's brother, Edgar. Says William Eric: "[Here is] a horse of a completely different color. No introvert he.... He, too, cared about Mamma but in a much more earthy way...":

Oct. 16, 1905

Dear Ma:

Do I like homemade cakes and jellies? Well I guess, yes!! . . .

Ed

This card had a drawing of Ed "burning the midnight oil." Other cards underline the point: listen to the noises they make including the different tone of those to his brother [Bill] he called "Bo":

Oct. 26, 1905

Dear Folks:
The box came this morning. Gee! it's great! There's no use talking, nothing can beat the home production. . . .

Love from Edgar

Nov. 4, '07

Dear Bo:
. . . Tell Mama to send my allowance. . . . I'm sending some football goods prepaid because I'm *busted*.

Ed

A hand-drawn postcard to "Bo":

Greasy Grind! Was ist los? Write a fellow!
Ed

To Bo:

Nov. 27, 1911

I surely am having one swell time. Paris is *won*derful. Aunt Eliza sends her love. I have an awful crush on her. *Gosh* I'm having a fine time. Honest to John.

Ed

Mon dieux comme c'est beau! J'aime mon vieux Paris.

William Eric's comment appears at first sight to be a comment on Edgar. But it's more than that: it's also a comment on the whole sense of family, and finally a comment on *Yes, Mrs. Williams* the book. For William Eric, understanding exactly what his father was doing, carries on by doing the same:

> Edgar was the quintessence of the All American Boy, who loves Mom's cooking, is always broke, plays football and sends home his dirty uniforms, has a crush on an older woman (who is not his mother), uses the current American slang expletives, moans about his college work schedule, but shows no lovey-dovey, mushy sentimental emotion, thank you. In later years, the family grapevine would have it that Ed was his mother's favorite. While living at 9 Ridge Road, Nana enjoyed no more effective tranquilizer than a visit from Edgar, who would drop out of the commuter parade while hoofing it up Park Avenue homeward bound to 131 West Passaic from the Rutherford railway station, one or two evenings a week.

Thus we can see how astute young Kerry Driscoll's brief piece, "The Mythos of Mother or *Yes, Mrs. Williams*," is. Coming to the work without a vast impedimenta in the canons of critics, she reacts to the work directly and intelligently.

Another young scholar, Jonathan Mayhew, tunes an acute ear to Williams' poetic line: he listens, feels, and hears without letting a burden of theory becloud the cadence of the line. Thus he is what the poet wanted most: a reader who would stop talking and listen. Eliot dug up a word to describe a process which this

young man avoids: "obnubilation." [TSE, *Selected Essays*, p. 14].
Robert Basil has the same direct approach. In "Imagination and
Despair in Williams" he explores various ways in which the "noth-
ingness" of fancy and abstract thought is a kind of "being" in itself. His ideas form an analog to Sartre's ideas out of the Angst
tradition starting with Kierkegaard, but with a refreshingly direct
response to Williams' images, gists, and cadences. He finds a despair in the poet but discriminates it from earlier formulations:
here is no romantic agony.

In "Bidding for Fame...", Rod Townley gets at one essence
of Williams by measuring his poetic practices against those of Wallace Stevens. He shows how the personal persona of each, being
different, must dictate different results: both were poets endowed
with great gifts; both by a lifetime of dedication and discipline
created work of a different kind though not necessarily of a different magnitude; if Stevens had a "rage for order" (and he did),
and Williams had a rage to express existent disorder (and he did),
it follows that they could not warm up to each others work (as
they didn't), at least in their early years. Rod's assignment was to
take a careful new look at *Collected Poems 1921-1931*. That he
does with knowledge and style. His piece articulates with the
memories of Roberta Chester who, living nearby in Passaic, went
to ask Williams what he thought about Wallace Stevens. She was
19 when she made her visit in 1959, but his words still echo
clearly in her mind—perhaps because she was a little shocked
when she heard them.

Thomas Schaub, a young man from Berkeley, explores some
ramifications of realism (certainly the most chameleon word in the
canon of critics) as understood by Williams at different times and
as practiced by Sorrentino in his eight novels. Elements of the
frustration of all appear as Sorrentino's ideas about Williams' ideas
slip and slide, decay with imprecision, because, at bottom, all, including Schaub, are aware that we live in a world of illusions and
that external reality must exist in the mind of the beholder (writer) before he can write about it, even if he breaks his toe upon
Berkeley's rock in the process.

In "Driving and Writing," Roy Miki, a young man from Canada, explores other dimensions of the difficulty. Here we are
given a metaphor of moving through a real but changing world
which the poet must improvise ways of catching, so to speak, on
the fly. Towards the end of his exploration he underlines the universality of the problem for all artists by giving illustrations from
Juan Gris and Gaudier-Brzeska, both of whom wrestled with the

seen and imagined world. Gris said the painter doesn't know what the appearance of his painting will be until it's finished. Then it becomes clear "that the subject does not materialize in the appearance of the picture, but that the subject, in materializing, gives the picture its appearance." Gaudier said he derived "his emotions solely from the arrangement of surfaces" which meant the planes and lines that defined them. With a nod to Gaudier, Williams said, "In using words instead of stone I accept 'plane' to be the affirmation of existence, the meeting of substances, whether it be stone meeting air or a sound of a certain quality against another or against silence." But no net of words will catch any of these artists, including Williams, any more than Williams could catch the landscape of people and things flying past his moving car. So Miki must conclude: "Rather, by allowing all the surfaces of the text to assert their particularity, Williams allows them to meet in an interchange that is an 'affirmation of existence.'"

With a neatness of coincidence rather than design, Neil Baldwin explores Williams struggling with several kinds of realism and reality in his prose trilogy, a work forty years in the making. Slowly objective reality gives way to emotional realities through the three novels until in the last, *The Build-Up,* natures change in a building crescendo. When Joe Stecher, the central character, loses all the Stecher family had fought for, he wins by losing. Misunderstanding what the reality of American freedom was really about, he touches bottom and reaches his lowest ebb. But, says Baldwin, he has "to lose daughters to marriage, son to death, wife to avarice, and country to jingoism, before he can experience the most exhilarating freedom of all." That was a kind of defeat, but as Hemingway had said, "The only victory is in defeat."

With the nicest of art and in a most delightful way, Anne Janowitz places Williams squarely in the old American tradition of tinkering with things and inventing contraptions to make them work. Whitman, who says he is "Bluff'd not a bit by drain-pipe, gasometers...installed amid the kitchen ware," only carried on Emerson's idea: "Machinery and Transcendentalism agree well." They both followed Ben Franklin's recommendation that society contrive "new mechanical inventions for saving labour...and all philosophical experiments that let light into the nature of things." Williams approaches poetic forms in the same way. Says he: Just as an "automobile or kitchen stove is an organization of materials...poems are mechanical objects made out of words to express a certain thing." He tinkered with *Paterson* for thirty years and more, but he was tinkering with a more and more clearly defined purpose and conviction: one thing you can't tinker with is things

as they are. While Stevens in the late 20s was being impelled to
a rage for order, Williams was defending "The Simplicity of Disorder" and recording it. Out of such a conviction a final dilemma
followed: how to bring *Paterson* neatly to a climax and a close.
But nothing in life comes neatly to any such thing. A staged drama
may but not life. So *Paterson* must flow on as a sort of slice of
life; the truth must not be tinkered with!

The reflections of the young British scholar, Diana Surman,
form a bright counterpoint to those of her American colleagues.
In "Towards the Crystal: Art and Science in Williams' Poetic,"
she explores some of the same qualities in the man and his world
as the others do but from a different angle of vision. Not only was
Virginia Woolf right in saying that on or about December 1910
human nature changed, but it has been changing rapidly ever since,
trying to keep pace with the astonishing discoveries of science.
The discovery of the x-ray may have given man a look into the
core of the crystal—or all matters—but it did not give him a look
into the heart of the matter. She ends her piece with lines from
"The Simplicity of Disorder," echoing some of the concerns noted
by Janowitz, and says it anticipates "The Desert Music."

Thus are we given a neat transition to the combined work of
a young American, E.P. Walkiewicz in collaboration with a senior
scholar, Hugh Witemeyer. Their piece, "Desert Music: Carlos Williams in the Great Southwest," leaves discussion of the poetic line
to some of the larger and dramatic issues facing America. WCW's
visit to the great Southwest including a trip across the Rio into
Mexico gave him some vital images to reflect upon. If America is
a melting pot, and it is, the interaction of Indian, Spanish, native,
and puritan, does in fact dramatize an intransigent polarization.
But in spite of poverty, poor diet, disease, and a lack of even the
elementary amenities the bourgeois white man considers essential,
the people there seemed to Williams to be happier, more vital, in a
word fuller than the predatory invaders who have taken over their
land and started the long process of bulldozing it into deathlike-
mediocrity and poisoning it with chemicals. Williams found both
the desert land and its people full of music...only partly tamed—
still swift and proud—even with eyes cast down upon the earth—
whence their strength seemed to come. The bridge over the river
thus became a symbol which reminds one of Pound's last page
in *The Cantos*, where he heard "The farfalla gasping/as toward
a bridge over worlds" and pleads for the human race "To be men
not destroyers."

From here we go to the reflections of major poets in the
Williams traditions and two of his most astute readers. Denise

Levertov in "The Ideas in the Things" finds that there is a lot more in WCW's famous phrase "than he is commonly credited with even today." As if by plan, her piece carries on from the ideas expressed in "Desert Music." In a detailed reading of "A Morning Imagination of Russia" she shows a similar social split at work in the revolution: a peasantry full of life close to the earth forming a sea around a walled-off bourgeosie who were empty inside. But it's an old-time human story: the more one gathers up treasure on this earth to support one's ego, the less ego there is to support, there is nothing inside at all. Ron Loewinsohn, in "The Sources of SOUR GRAPES: Williams and the Religion of Art" gives a close reading of this critical transitional volume between the earlier work of *Al Que Quiere* and the more mature work to come after. He approaches the poetry with a discriminating sensory apparatus (tasting, savoring, smelling) with the same kind of gusto Williams approached life with. Cid Corman on *Spring and All* does somewhat the same although his piece is written from a distance, in a more commemorative mood.

Then we come to Marjorie Perloff and when we do we get right down to business. In "To Give a Design...," she rolls up her sleeves, says to all who have written about Williams in the critical tradition (including Williams himself), "Come now, let's be reasonable and let's make sense!" That the "visual prosody" of Williams as it relates to the revolution in the visual arts of the time became a process of slow development is the ground she stands on. Says she, "How this process took place and how the resulting visualization of the 'poetic page' has changed one concept of the lyric—this is my subject." So it is, but before she's finished it becomes much more than that. It becomes in effect a rap on the table and a call to order.

III

Ezra Pound's 1928 retrospective examination of Williams as a novelist and writer of prose is a fascinating look at impressions made sixty years and more ago. The judgments made then appear to be valid now. But the piece has other interests: it shows Pound's growing frustration with difficulties both he and Williams contended with for the rest of their lives. One was and is the need for "a dissociation of ideas" if constructive dialog is to take place. In other places, he often said a thinker deserved to have his thoughts examined one at a time. When one comes to "omnibus" emotional words such as "communism" or "socialism," one has a cluster of ideas entangled in a kind of verbal glue:

such words include ideas and practices concerning a form of government, a legal system, a monetary system, an economic system, an attitude toward human rights, a political ideal, a system of dealing with enemies real and imagined, plus a lot more. Unless one can dissociate the ideas and examine them one at a time, one will not have dialog; one will have only Eliot's "obnubilation" in another context. And that's only part of the problem: one must see each of these ideas operating in a particular time and place involving particular problems. In our time El Salvador, for instance. But as Pound complained in his 1928 piece, one can't even try to sort such things out without censure, particularly with orthodoxies involving religion: "We are still so generally obsessed by monism and monotheistical backwash, and ideas of orthodoxy that we ...can hardly observe a dissociation of ideas without thinking a censure is somehow therein implied." The outlook is still bleak. Politicians still go around screaming "communism" in one hemisphere and "economic imperialism" in another; the media go on cheering and nobody really knows what anybody else is talking about—if anything. Williams created new forms in his prose; critics had only orthodoxies built on examination of past practices to go on. Such orthodoxies could not be used as effective measurements. The points Pound makes deserve hammering home because both he and Williams were victims of them all their lives.

IV

Bruce Comens has done a lot of thinking about the importance of the visual arts to Williams and to his work, both prose and poetry. He gives us the results of that thinking in "Williams, Botticelli, and the Renaissance" along with a detailed reading of several poems, including "The Birth of Venus," "The Botticellian Trees" and "Song." Although he probably finds a lot more there than Williams consciously thought he put there, he reports his hunting and finding with such a niceness of art that it's a pleasure to read. Towards the end, as he reflects on what he had done, Comens gives us some astute conclusions: "All we can retrieve from the sea of particulars is an empty shell, formally beautiful but lacking the real significance that can be obtained only by adhering more closely to the processes of life." Yes, indeed! And what is more, a number of apparent truths can add up to a lie. But all is not lost: "The semantic crisis occasioned by the positioning of 'lie' enacts the crisis that such emptiness will create: unless beauty is informed by love, and unless form and content are fused by love, art will lie and man will live a lie." Williams would certainly concur: in fact, the statement appears to be the story of his life.

As an approaching climax, we have Gilbert Sorrentino's reflections on Williams' use of language in his short fiction, in particular the ways he tried to solve the unsolvable in "The Knife of the Times." Sorrentino, not only a major poet in his own right but also an innovative writer of fiction who has faced similar problems, knows what he is talking about. The question is, how can one get unstated and repressed emotional states stated in prose: again, indirections must be the key. In this story we have a lesbian relationship that two women can neither understand, accept, nor resolve. Says Sorrentino: "The reality of their predicament is unrecognized by them because they have no language with which to plumb it other than one that connotes the spurious: their words have both invented and stranded their lives." The two women seemed to believe they were faced with a choice. They chose not to be lesbians or to be lovers. One, more than the other, kept making the choice for twenty years, but the choice, of course, changed nothing. Sorrentino explores the various strategies Williams deploys to get to the emotional tragedy and does so in the way only an expert technician can. As a technical expert himself, Sorrentino can recognize and point to the technical expertise of others.

One of the most interesting pieces in the book is written by Dr. Richard Zbornik who faced the choice Williams faced 50 years earlier. Says Zbornik: "I was attending Cincinnati Medical School, not sure about being a doctor or a writer, and along came Williams saying maybe I could do both. Not only that, but the poetry was alive—the things you heard in the street—and humane. I feel no compatibility with the 'learned poets'—the T. S. Eliots and Allen Tates. Here was a man who said it didn't have to be that way, and a doctor as well." So he wrote to Williams. The record he gives us of what took place thereafter includes some not wholly predictable results.

Truth to Zbornik has a matter-of-factness about it, we'd expect, and so does realism. But such reflections in the book at large lead us to another chameleon word: romanticism. When Williams began to sweat Keats out of his system, he supposedly left, not only Keats' way of writing, but also his romantic conceptions about art and life behind him. Thus, with "The Wanderer" of 1914, we have the new Williams. But Norman M. Finkelstein in "Beauty, Truth and 'The Wanderer'" asks us to pause a bit and think this assumption over. According to him, a touch of Keats remained with Williams all his life. His arguments are convincing enough to open up a number of questions which will engage critics for a long time. Perhaps we have here a question of degree.

Some of his evidence seems to suggest that they both had "a touch of the poet" and that the line where we cross to "a touch of Keats" may be hard to find.

The work of Chris Collins, New York University School of Poetics, and Marilyn Kallet, University of Tennessee, underline the recent changes of tone and attitude in recent criticism of Williams' work. The old defensiveness and argumentativeness is gone. Collins in "The Moving Eye in Williams' Early Poetry" explores the psychological and psychic factors in ones physical, eye-object, response to a poem, which is, like a painting, an object in a field of vision. The call for such a detailed study has been around ever since Pound took elaborate pains to distinguish the "moving image" from "the stationary image" and on these grounds was led to reject "Amygism" and establish the premises of Vorticism. In "Conversation as Design in 'Asphodel, That Greeny Flower,'" Kallet explores the vital role Floss played in Williams' art and life: a role always pervasive but even obtrusively dominant in the latest work. Both of these young scholars stimulate new lines of thought and bring us closer to the man and the poet.

But the real climax of the book is the detailed, meticulous work of Joseph Brogunier, a long-time Williams fan and scholar. His 133-page annotated bibliography of the works about Williams from 1974 through 1982 will be a most helpful tool to all scholars, new and old, who want to review the situation of where we are. The extraordinary variety of the work reinforces the impression we already have of Williams as a most complicated, multifaceted, and intensely human being of many moods and convictions: a sort of twentieth century Balzac. A number of times while I was working on the materials of the book and reading much of Williams over again, in particular the *Autobiography* and the work of William Eric, I was reminded of Balzac. Since I haven't taught Balzac for a dozen years, the association must have some relevance or I'd never have thought of it. Read William Eric's description of his father eating fruit [p. 59]. Now listen to Balzac's friend Gozlan:

> . . . his lips quivered, his eyes shone with happiness, his hands twitched with pleasurable anticipation at sight of a pyramid of beautiful pears or peaches. . . . He was magnificent in his flamboyant, Pantagruelian way; he had removed his cravat and his shirt collar was open; with a fruit knife in his hand he laughed, drank, and carved into the juicy flesh of a large pear. . . .*

---

*Stefan Zweig, *Balzac* (New York: Viking Press, 1946), p. 113.

And what about Balzac's enthusiasm in describing himself? Says he, in a letter to the Duchess d'Abrantes:

> In my five-foot two-inches there is compressed every imaginable contrast and contradiction. If anyone likes to call me vain, extravagant, stubborn, frivolous, inconsistent in my thinking, dandified, careless, indolent, lacking in due reflection and not sufficiently painstaking, without perseverance, loquacious, tactless, ill-bred, rude, subject to odd changes of mood, he will be no less right than anyone else who says that I am thrifty, modest, and courageous, tenacious, energetic, carefree, industrious, steadfast, taciturn, full of refinement, and courtesy, and always cheerful. It can be asserted with equal truth that I am a poltroon or a hero, a clever fellow or an ignoramus, extremely talented or stupid. Nothing will surprise me. I myself have finally resolved to believe that I am merely an instrument, the plaything of circumstance [p. 114].

Zweig makes a judgment which in many ways concurs with our judgment of Williams and in some details Williams' judgment of himself:

> He possessed the childlike good-nature that we generally attribute to giants, and nothing could shake it. Though he was aware that his colleagues were embarrassed in his all too massive presence and that they whispered to one another behind his back at his lack of style and a hundred other malicious calumnies, he had a friendly word for each of them, and mentioned them all somewhere or other in his *Comedie Humaine*. He was too magnanimous for enmity, and nowhere in his writings is there to be found a polemic against an individual [p. 113].

Perhaps we have here the reasons why Williams' work in toto can be conceived as the *Comedie Humaine* of our century. But most important of all, he was also a great poet whose lifelong ambition was to change the poetic line and thereby change civilization. We are pleased to note that this book, in addition to the many others listed in "The Testament," proves that his lifelong ambition has been realized.

DOVE STA MEMORA

Portrait of Williams around 1925.

ALLEN GINSBERG

*WILLIAMS IN A WORLD OF OBJECTS**

Accuracy. Williams' accuracy. The phrase "clamp your mind down on objects" is his. The phrase "no ideas but in things" is his. Does everybody understand what that means? . . . It means, "no *general* ideas in your poetry." Don't put out any abstract ideas about things, but present the things themselves that gave you the ideas. Let's try and understand what Williams is trying to say and then we'll propose a different theory. [Here are three lines from "Dance Russe"] :

> And the sun is a flame-white disc
> in silken mists
> above shining trees,—

Now he is being very fair there. He is just telling you what you can see. He's not laying a trip on you about the sun in general. Here he puts your eyes on the sun in one specific kind of day so that you can see it with your own eyes. He is saying "just put down the details of the things you see in front of you." If you can't begin there, what good are any ideas. Begin with what the sense offers. If you can't do that, you'll have to go to astronomy. But astronomy is based on observations of some kind.

   Suppose a dying man! If you can't *see* the dying man in front of you, you can't see what is wrong with your behavior toward him. Here is not a *change* of ideas; it's a change of *directive stance*. Once understood, Williams phrase becomes a basic building block:

---

*In the fall of 1976, Ginsberg was teaching a course about 20th century poets in which Williams became the central topic a number of times. The sessions were recorded on the old-fashioned reel-to-reel tapes. Allen provided me with several of the tapes where Williams and Pound were central to his talks and discussions. These pages are excerpted from them with only slight editorial interventions: the kind that fills in what voice and gesture would make clear. Interpolated phrases are put in brackets. The first was made on November 16th and the second, November 25th. When he reads the same poem in the second class, a cross reference has been made. I contrived the title "Williams in a World of Objects" as being inclusive of what's said and to provide for various indexing needs. —C.F.T.

for a system maybe, or a reference point; for a complete system in itself or usable with other systems. But until the phrase [no ideas but in things] is understood in itself, there is no common ground to begin with. In the lines from the poem, what's the one common ground we begin with? We've got the sun, an orange ball going down over the maple tree, or the sun just as we see it. How artfully can we describe what we see, so that it is common ground, where everybody is in the same place, so that one can use it like a reference point. It may be fictional but it is the common ground. If we don't have any reference point in the physical world, then what have we got? Here's one common reference point at least: everybody's breathing. That's where Buddhism starts—at that one place and moves from there. Starts at one place that everybody can locate: the tip of the nose where everybody is breathing in and out. Start close to the nose. That is a reality where everybody is or can be: we must begin where we are.

Williams got into this because *reality* had become so confusing in the twentieth century, and poetry had got so freaked out that it was strange: he didn't know what poetry was! He didn't know what anything was! But he knew where his nose was and could begin there. He gave up all ideas [meaning abstractions] and started with things themselves. Naturally everybody sees things differently: The word is not The Thing. The word "word", a concept in itself, is an abstraction, an idea. The entire world is fictional. "Words themselves are ideas!": There is a little double-dealing in that phrase. But, everybody can come down to the same place and begin there: the one place where *everybody* can be. There is only one place where everybody can be.

STUDENT: Isn't it weird that he started with something that is so susceptible to change—and not being what it seems to be? Actions like jumping?

RESPONSE: Jumping is more abstract. The question is, Where are we going to begin? [The answer is] let's begin with what we can see in front of us. Williams was looking for a place where everybody could begin together in poetry because everything was new; a new continent, newly discovered, newly invaded with European ideas plastered all over it. He was trying to clean up the slate and start all over again. That's why he wrote a book called *In the American Grain*, trying to reach American history, to see what fresh planet we'd come upon. "The natural object is always the adequate symbol": That's Pound's way of saying the same thing: "Don't bother with abstractions." In other words, no poetry but in "for instances," no ideas but in things. He would say you could include feelings, but you'd have to deal with them as observed things and not get lost. It is very similar to the process of meditation: paying attention to the breaths, wandering off into a daydream, and then becoming unconscious of the mind moving into the daydream, of the breaths, and then you could describe the thought you had but you no longer are obsessed by it or lost in it. Don't lose perspective. There is always the home base to touch back on. He's saying let's fill with *our* attention the things that other people can see and fill with *their* attention. Then we can both check our consciousness, one against another, and see where we are, like triangulating the stars.

Here's two short poems:

GOODNIGHT

In brilliant gas light
I turn the kitchen spigot
and watch the water plash
into the clean white sink.
On the grooved drain-board
to one side is
a glass filled with parsley—
crisped green.
                              Waiting
for the water to freshen—
I glance at the spotless floor—:
a pair of rubber sandals
lie side by side
under the wall-table
all is in order for the night.

Waiting, with a glass in my hand
—three girls in crimson satin
pass close before me on
the murmurous background of
the crowded opera—
                                        it is
memory playing the clown—
three vague, meaningless girls
full of smells and
the rustling sounds of
cloth rubbing on cloth and
little slippers on carpet—
high-school French
spoken in a loud voice!

Parsley in a glass
still and shining
brings me back.
I take a drink and
yawn deliciously.
I am ready for bed.

He brings us through the whole process.

The mundaneness is interesting, to me, because it sees so clearly that it becomes crisp in meaning, still and shining. The water glass suddenly is a totemic object. It becomes a symbol of itself, of his investment in his attention in that object: *it* becomes a symbol of itself also.

Because he sees it so clearly, he notices what about the object that shines, what's particular about the object that could be written down in a word—he sees the object without association. That's characteristic of visionary moments: you get supernatural visions by giving up supernatural visions; just looking at what is in front of you. You are not superimposing another idea or another image on the image that's already there.

The poem, *Thursday*, shows that he really is a Buddhist:

> I have had my dream—like others—
> and it has come to nothing, so that
> I remain now carelessly
> with feet planted on the ground
> and look up at the sky—
> feeling my clothes about me,
> the weight of my body in my shoes,
> the rim of my hat, air passing in and out
> at my nose—and decide to dream no more.

When I discovered this poem, I realized its thematic Buddhism: the practice we were doing and the pragmatic practice had intersected and there was a common ground. Williams had arrived at the same place that everybody else was studying and got there early and on his own: it reconfirmed my feelings that he was some kind of a saint of perception.

This is a beginning: to understand his basic principle and then extend it as we have to. Well, you can be mindful of generalizations if you are mindful of the particulars out of which you draw: *No ideas but in facts*!

II

Williams is the clearest and simplest and most direct when trying to tie the mind down, to bring the imagination down to earth again and put all of his intensity and all of his energy into seeing what is actually there, what anybody can see in the light of day: no imagination except what he's conscious of as daydreams while looking directly at people, cars, horses, bushes, maple trees, or Rutherford, New Jersey. He's a doctor. Let's start with a couple of his early sketches:

Late for Summer Weather

He has on
an old light grey fedora
She a black beret

He a dirty sweater
She an old blue coat
that fits her tight

Grey flapping pants
Red skirt and
broken down black pumps

Fat Lost Ambling
nowhere through
the upper town they kick

their way through
heaps of
fallen maple leaves

still green—and
crisp as dollar bills
Nothing to do. Hot cha!

Proletarian Portrait

A big young bareheaded woman
in an apron

Her hair slicked back standing
on the street

One stockinged foot toeing
the sidewalk

Her shoe in her hand. Looking
intently into it

She pulls out the paper insole
to find the nail

That has been hurting her

Williams was a friend of Reznikoff's. They were practicing the same poetics together trying to get it to boil down to the direct presentation of the object that they were writing about with no excess words. They composed their poems out of the elements of natural speech, their own speech, as heard on the porch or in talk over the kitchen table. Poetry that would be identical to spoken conversation that you could actually hear as regular conversation and not recognize it as poetry at all unless you suddenly dug that there was something going on, curiously sharp and fresh that was smart people talking.

Here's the doctor, maybe out on a call:

The Young Housewife

At ten a.m. the young housewife
moves about in negligee behind
the wooden walls of her husband's house.
I pass solitary in my car.

Then again she comes to the curb
to call the ice-man, fish-man, and stands
shy, uncorseted, tucking in
stray ends of hair, and I compare her
to a fallen leaf.

The noiseless wheels of my car
rush with a crackling sound over
dried leaves as I bow and pass smiling.

So, what's the use of being so flat and prosaic? Or, what's the purpose of trying to make poetry out of the objects seen under the aspect of ordinary minds? Generally we don't see ordinary objects at all. We are filled with daydream fantasy so that we don't see what is in front of us. We are not aware of what is close to the nose, and we don't even appreciate what everyday tables and chairs have to offer in terms of service for food or a place to sit; in terms of the centuries of maturing that it took to give us a place for the food. Zeroing in on actuality with the ordinary mind and abandoning any thought of heaven, illumination; giving up any attempt to manipulate the universe to make it better than it is; but, instead, coming down to earth and being willing to relate to what is actually here without trying to change the universe or alter it from the one which we can see, smell, taste, touch, hear and think about. Williams' work as a poet is very similar to Zen Buddhist mindfulness practice, because it clamps the mind down on objects and brings the practitioner into direct relations with whatever he can find in front of him without making a big deal about it; without satisfying some ego ambition to have something more princely or less painful than what already *is*.

Williams was good friends with extraordinary people: Pound, H.D., Marianne Moore. They all knew each other at the University of Pennsylvania I believe. But Williams was a square. He always thought Pound was a little cranky and crazy. Williams was kind of naive; square but inside he was such a humane man. Since he learned to deal with what was around him he learned to sympathize, empathize. His growth was totally self-made, totally natural. He had the idea of going in that direction very early and just kept working at it. He had the idea[about poetry] and thought about working on it, like going through medical school. Going through poetry and developing his focus was just like going through medical school. He deliberately stayed in Rutherford, New Jersey, and wrote poetry about the local landscape, using local language. He wanted to be a provincial from the point of view of really being there where he was; really knowing his ground. He wanted to know his roots, know who the iceman and fishman were; know the housewife; he wanted to know his town—his whole body in a sense. A strange idea; he might have got it from some literary sources like Guy de Maupassant; Keats might have given him some hints.

He was dealing with actual birth rather than literary birth, actual eyes, hair, etc. He was somebody no different from ourselves, actually, somebody you don't have to worry about pulling a fast metaphysical trick on you and declaring another universe. That's the whole point; dealing with *this* universe. And that was a fantastic discovery: that you can actually make poetry by dealing with this universe instead of creating another one.

ROBERT CREELEY

A VISIT TO AN IDOL *

While Bob Creeley was still in Majorca, in February 1951, he wrote to Williams and Pound for the first time. Says he: "obviously, I loved these two people, and I was awed and hopeful that I would get some response. Just starting to be an editor, I thought I had a legitimate question—to ask for something, you know. Both of them answered generously . . . if anything brightly and specifically." But it wasn't until the spring of 1954 that he made his first visit to Nine Ridge Road. In the meantime, Williams and Creeley had written often, and Bob had returned to the states and taken up his work at Black Mountain. In response to a request to visit, WCW had said to come out. Bob had just fallen in love with Cynthia Holman,—on the rebound from a parting of the ways with his first wife, so he and Cynthia trekked out to Rutherford together.

* * * * * * *

C: We went out by bus armed with directions as to how to find the house. We were walking through a small place, with a sort of '30s old-fashioned small-town feeling: a block with a drugstore and what not—sort of wandering much as Williams describes his seeing Cummings, *you know*, looking in the windows, etc.† In any case, we found the house with no

---

*These pages are taken from taped interviews I had with Bob Creeley during the fall of 1982, while he was occupying the Lloyd H. Elliott Chair at Orono. The dialogue has been conflated for brevity and to catch nuances the spoken word carries, but no changes of intent or meaning have been made.—CFT

†In the *Autobiography*, WCW describes the Cummings visit thus:

Once during that time, when I was alone with mother, E. E. Cummings came out to see me. It was a Sunday morning, a very quiet day, no one on the streets. I had given him specific instructions how to get here, so that when it got to be nearly one o'clock, knowing his reputation for indifference to conventional order, I went out to look for him. I shall not forget the impression I got of a lone person meandering up a deserted Park Avenue stopping at every store window to look in at the shoes, ladies' wear, now and then a bank window perhaps, or at an Easter card, or a brace and bit in Dow's hardware store [pp. 258-259].

remarkable difficulty and rang the doorbell. Moments later the door opens and *there* is Doctor Williams! It was like some incredible moment of epiphany for me. You know, this man that I literally revered was suddenly, physically, right *there*. He was also a doctor so he must have, yes he *must* have seen the effect he was having on this younger man. I think I must have gone white or something. He said, "Are you all right?" I said, "Yes, I'm fine. I'm just extremely, you know." I was sort of mumbling, saying, "I'm very moved by meeting you." And, he said, "well, come in." Then Floss came up and moments later they brought us both into the house. Then, while Floss and Cynthia were talking, Williams took me upstairs. He said, "Would you like to look around a bit?" I said, "yes," but I was very shy of leaning on him or asking him to show me this or show me that. In any case, he immediately took me upstairs and showed me his typewriter. I remember this wild, old machine. It seems to me it was something like a big Royal: a solid, great office machine that was in an old-fashioned wooden desk, made so you could drop the typewriter below the surface of the desk out of sight. I'd read a lot about his writing situation. Here was the physical instrument. Here was the way he said it worked and so on. He could drop it, pull it out, and drop it as patients came and went.

T: Did he walk around a lot? Was he nervous? Did he—fidget, did he . . .

C: No. I had the sense of a very intense person but not nervously intense: one of high energy, so to speak, which was remarkable because by this time he'd had at least two of the strokes. There was some slight sense of paralysis in his right side. They generously invited us to stay over for dinner. They had something like roast beef and Floss asked me if I would mind helping Bill cut up his meat? Then he had this sort of wild business. Because I had come from a situation with very small children I preceded to cut up his meat accordingly. Watching, he said, "I'm not a damned baby! You don't have to cut it this tiny—practically puree it!" The paralysis was a partial motor thing but physically, he certainly looked together.

T: Let's go back to the scene in the study. Did he invite you to sit down or . . .

C: Yes. And he showed me various things in the study. He showed me where his paper stock was and said, "I'm still using the paper my father-in-law gave me." He opened a closet and there was a great stack of paper. He also had manuscripts in there. I'd been asking him shyly if he had anything that might serve the *Black Mountain Review*. I didn't want to ask for materials that were primary. Pound had given me wise advice some time before that. He pointed out that any time I asked a writer such as Williams or himself or Wyndham Lewis, let's say, for primary manuscripts, I had to realize that I was cutting into the possible income of that writer. In other words, if I asked for something the *Hudson Review* would pay money for and I couldn't, then I was in effect asking them to subsidize me. So I was leery of doing that. But he told me he had a carbon copy of *Tituba's Children*, the opera text, and said if I were interested maybe I could do something with that. I took it with me, but I never was able to publish it. The *Black Mountain Review* didn't last long enough to do it.

T: Now back to the scene: I see you sitting in the chair, leaning back, and Williams at the desk there, talking.

C: Yes, we talked about a lot of things. We looked out the window for instance into the backyard which was a classic small, in-town backyard. There was a fairly battered summer house at the left end which was adjacent to other backyards. I remember Williams saying that he had always hoped to use that summer house as a place for summer theater productions. It was impressive to look at this modest area and recognize how he had transformed it in his mind into a center for community drama. And then the garden. Although the season wasn't appropriate, you could see the care with which he dealt with that garden.

T: How long did you talk?

C: The conversation upstairs must have been a half hour, possibly a little longer.

T: Did he get up during that half hour and go places . . . ?

C: Yes. He had that kind of physical compactness that I associate with Picasso. Their heads were similar, giving one a sense of extraordinary energy compacted. Once I happened to see Picasso. I didn't at first sight recognize him, but he was extremely attractive. He was then quite old, but he had this extraordinarily intense look and manner. Williams had very much the same characteristic. They both had a curious physical intensity which wasn't nervous but almost like an animal energy: I mean very alert, very . . . .

T: Yes. I get that impression reading him. Did he repeat himself?

C: Not that I recall. While we were upstairs he described his habits as a writer. It wasn't that he was defending them or rehearsing them in some nostalgic manner, but it was a curious instant intimacy, a sort of feeling he conveyed that he was telling me these things that he'd only tell to a friend who'd understand.

T: I remember hearing him read once where he repeated a number of times the line, "You must understand that if you change the poetic line you change civilization." Did he talk about that?

C: I think he paid me the compliment of thinking I understood that. Or if I didn't I probably wouldn't be there. Also, he knew my association with *Origin* and the *Black Mountain Review*, which had just published its first issue, and he also knew of the small books we had begun to publish. For example he liked Larry Eigner's *From the Sustaining Air* a lot. He was fascinated by that particular book. He was having more difficulties with Olson: he couldn't get hold of the line. At that point, he couldn't quite place what Olson was doing.

T: You talked about other poets?

C: Yes, several. There was a wild reference to Pound at one point in the conversation. Wild and paradoxical. He obviously had complex feelings about Pound who, on the one hand, was the friend of his life who most signally and singularly determined his own habits as a writer, but who, on the other hand, gave him a very strong sense of competition. He also had a wild imagination about the convenience of Pound's situation at the time. Here was he, himself, an ill doctor with all the dilemmas of time and money dogging him still. Then there was Pound in an almost comfortable situation with the Library of Congress just down the street and all of the freedom anyone could want to write and do his work. I couldn't quite agree that St. E's was that comfortable but . . .

T: In '54 it must have been that love/hate relationship which was always difficult to deal with.

C: Yes. Pound was absolutely the person closest to his imagination as a writer but he was equally the person whom he most measured his own authority by. So, he could see that he was low paid.

T: On another tack, what about the house?

C: Oh, I remember the household. And Floss. Floss I liked on the instant. She was a woman that I could instantly recognize. She was very much like dear persons in my own reality, such as my mother. She wasn't motherly, but she was a lovely, direct, a sort of no-funny-stuff person. She had humor. She wasn't simply a humorless watchdog: she was very wry and canny.

T: Did she bustle around?

C: Not so much bustle. She was very direct and forthright. She had this air of very real competence. She was really tough. They told me a lovely story later when we were in the kitchen. This was just prior to the meal. Just before we sat down to eat, she said it was an unimaginable house when both mothers-in-law were living upstairs. If it wasn't one yelling for something, it was the other. Then they got into competition about who would have the most authority over the young couple: a young couple in their sixties. He said, sometimes they literally would be down in the kitchen with their arms around each other trying to survive. He said one time his mother-in-law got irritated with him over something he had done or said, so she just cuffed him. He said, "She literally knocked me right across the room."

T: Did you talk about his health?

C: He did say something to me that was extremely moving, *a propos* the strokes or old age literally. He said that people qualify. There's always a sense around of old age as a foolish time of fruition, during which you can feel a life well-lived or think about things done: your accomplishments, etc. But he said it isn't like that at all. In fact, it's a physical impediment. You find your abilities to physically do things becoming more and more impeded. You reach for something and your grip isn't sufficient. It really is not fun or comfortable at all. So, *that* I took to heart. That was true information. Old age is not a pleasure.

T: The strokes had made it worse?

C: Floss told me about the strokes. She was quite outspoken. Before the last one, Bill had gone up to have a nap. She was doing some things down in the kitchen or some other part of the house. Then she suddenly intuited or thought that he'd been sleeping at lot longer than he usually does. On impulse she went upstairs to see if he was all right and discovered that he had had another stroke. His breathing was stertorous and his color was very poor, so she happily got help instantly. I think it was her son. But, she said, remarkably this stroke had actually moved the clot or whatever it was and left him better than before.

T: William Eric was there?

C: At least available. He had his practice in his father's office. So, happily they got him resuscitated and discovered that actually this stroke had been paradoxically benign: he survived it actually with some improvement. That is of his general state. But she said it was a sad fact that each time he did go to bed (he knew it and so did she), there was always the chance he'd not wake up. Since he didn't die until '63 he had a terribly existential situation all those years. I didn't get the sense of a man who is rushing to get his work done before he dies, but I did have the sense of a man who is intensely engaged as a writer with the physical world.

PHILIP BOOTH

WILLIAM CARLOS WILLIAMS–AN OPEN THANKSGIVING

It must have been in the winter of '48-'49 that I first heard Dr. Williams read: to maybe thirty people at the 92nd Street Y. Some ten years later I heard him after his stroke read "Of Asphodel . . ." at Wellesley, where the full-house audience gave him long silence before long applause. In the years between I'd listened to his part of Lloyd Frankenberg's remarkable anthology/record, "Pleasure Dome," and as I'd read and reread Williams I began to hear how his poems come off the page.

I've never understood Williams' defense of his "variable foot," but I'm certain I hear the strengths of his sense of measure, whether the line is stepped or not. From the beginning, he tuned his lines to how he kept hearing American speech; whenever I heard him his own voice was harsh, sharply uneven, almost sexual in its energies. Whether his subject is the misery of an Elsie or his own joy in bowing to a young housewife, his total attention to his subject (as if he were listening to one of his patients) genuinely informs the pressure of his lines and the pace at which they let words release their import.

Paterson says how long, and in how many ways, Dr. Williams attended to words, to the American language made up of them. But it's the earlier poems which most openly demonstrate how the words are weighted or lightened by the line, and how the line takes its shape and pace from the nature of the words. A prime example is surely the second stanza of "To a Poor Old Woman," where the poem opens to immediate joy in the various ways the plums "Taste good / to her" and "taste / good to her." Only as he here presents the immediacy of her tasting can the poem finally come down, and around, to the solace given her by the simple fact of "munching a plum on / the street." The doctor's attention is notably on *her* response–on her response as he gives voice to it. No less is true in "To Waken An Old Lady." Different as its jagged measure may be, there is Williams' familiar attention to where the voice is inclined to pressure or release this word or that, and to how such events lighten or weigh the line and so tip the poem's balance. The fulcrum in "To Waken . . ." is, of course, the syntactic interjection of a harshly natural question: "— / But what?" What question can be asked, what prescription given, to waken her? Again the attention is clinically particular yet emphatically human. In finding words for how his subjects fall the poet finds voice for how his own words rise. Just as in the so-called "Red Wheelbarrow," the poem's moves toward resolution depend on the very problem the poem initially poses.

Tactically as well as emotionally, Williams began to write each poem by making a start out of particulars. And those particulars included, however intuitively he came to them, syntax as well as measure. Williams has long since proven to be one of the Old Masters at making a poem new. The primitive syntax of "To a Poor Old Woman" has by now become a modernist cliché; so has such an interjectory question as shapes "To Waken An Old Lady," insofar as such a question makes for immediacy of voice. Williams' sense of measure has for years been measured and remeasured, but practically no critical attention has been paid to Williams' highly individual syntax. I hear the poems' syntax as being as important as their prosody; both tactical factors are primary elements of how openly a Williams poem validates itself.

I don't presume to be able to define the varieties of his syntax; I mean now only to point to it, given the pleasure I take from how strongly it works. Consider, for instance, the interjection "Let Us See, let us see!" in "Waiting," a poem in which the first strophe is syntactically commonplace, but acute in how its lines counteract the plainness of statement. "Let us see, let us see!" looks to be an interjection plain and simple, save only as doubling multiplies it tonally. But given the culminating question of the poem, as these words introduce it, they retroactively seem (beyond mere interjection) to be a petition for insight. Casual as such syntax appears to be, it is part of how the poem opens itself to a variety of emotional possibilities. I marvel at the still greater openness, and emotional complexity, of that remarkably unnoticed poem "A Portrait in Greys," where the misery of the speaker becomes, in the intricate syntax of the whole final sentence, subordinate to his (or, I would guess, *her*) concern for the subject of the portrait: the person whose emotions she cannot fully engage. Again, a series of questions move the poem toward its climax, questions in which the syntactic energy and rhythmic torque are each part of the other:

> Must I be always
> moving counter to you? Is there no place
> where we can be at peace together
> and the motion of our drawing apart
> be altogether taken up?

I marvel and I am, in all senses, moved. What a joy Williams is, even in this poem's intense misery. He realizes it! Always beyond self-pity, he realizes emotion *through* the poem, realizes it and releases it for sharing. Not only is Williams more unself-conscously open to experience than most poets, he opens his poems to every possibility of letting a reader experience them. His poems clearly invite a reader to share. He *wants* to share, to let the poem open our own emotion even as his emotion is given voice in the process of making the poem. Measure and syntax make his voice vitally present on, and beyond, the page; he makes a gift of how the experience gets said. And how broad and deep the experience is. What life there is to the poems! What vital fire in "Portrait of the Author." And not only in such famous field-and-weed poems as "Queen-Ann's-Lace" and "Great Mullen," what marvellous taste (beyond any mere bitterness) in *Sour Grapes*. Who among us has been at once so open and so resilient?

The particulars of measure and syntax inform, literally inform, every Williams poem, yes, from its very beginning. But behind and within such particulars there's a generosity, an essential humanity, that no medical school or poetry workshop can presume to teach. To read Williams closely is to learn useful tactics, of course. But to read him well is most of all to meet in the poems some fine part of one's self, to immediately experience not only one man's life, or one physician's city, but something close to the nature of a place, maybe even a country where democracy might actually be practiced.

Large-scale abstractions weren't Dr. Williams' stock-in-trade; democracy, as such, was seldom his explicit subject. But his concern and his practice were as open as his poems. In his reading at the Y in the late 'Forties, he spoke more than indirectly, and not without harsh humor, of the practice of poetry in this particular country. Dr. Williams was already sixty-five, and still widely unknown. In the awkwardness of the notably small audience, and his own awkward readings from Lorca, Dr. Williams after a while gave himself pause by asking for questions. Someone, without intending irony, asked what he saw as "the function of the poet in America." He drew back, startled, half-embarrassed that he'd seemed to ask for such asking.

Then he said, "Who was it—wasn't it Aristophanes who marched naked at the—what, you know—Pan-Athenaic Festival? That was how the old Greeks treated their poets: a poet at the head of the parade." He thought a while, building to a grin, and to what still are, in effect, the energies of his poems: "But the function of a poet in America? *Imagine me*, on the Fourth of July, walking down the Main Street of *Pat*erson, *bare*ass!"

HAYDEN CARRUTH

THE AGONY OF DR. PATERSON

Except for one lovely, ebullient luncheon in Chicago, about 1949, I never met William Carlos Williams, and except for five or six letters in response to my reviews and essays about his work, letters which said nothing not said elsewhere in his published writing, I never corresponded with him; so I cannot add much of substance to this memorial occasion. But I can recount one personal experience that may nevertheless have value.

In 1961 and 1962, and in fact until a couple of months after Williams died on 4th March 1963, I had a job that many other young writers would have envied. I was hired part-time by New Directions, the publishing firm, to put the files of back correspondence, from 1936 until the time I was working, into proper order for shipment to a library where they would be permanently deposited. It was a huge mass of material, as anyone who has worked in a publishing office can imagine; I'd guess now something like 40 or 50 filing cabinets crammed full of letters from authors, translators, editors, agents, designers, foreign representatives, etc., hundreds and hundreds of people connected with literature during the years in question and especially, of course, with avant-garde American literature. Much of this was ordinary and tedious stuff. Some was contemptible, so contemptible that in my mind certain writers became disqualified from any consideration, whether or not they had written the masterpieces they thought they had. (With one possible but unlikely exception, they hadn't.) But the files contained plenty of wonderful reading, too, and the file for Williams was among the best. Remember, New Directions was and is the publisher of everything Williams had written and wished to keep in print (with the exception of one book done by another firm), and for practical purposes, since Williams most of the time had faith in his own work, this meant everything he had written: poems, stories, novels, essays, everything. His file contained thousands of letters. I think the only one bigger than his was Ezra Pound's.

It was understood that I would respect the confidentiality of my job, and I did. I took no notes, made no xeroxes. I cannot remember a single significant phrase from all the letters I read. But I retain a strong impression of styles, attitudes, personalities. Williams wrote his letters quickly, almost always on the typewriter. He wrote, not volubly, but with a direct, forceful fluency that made his meanings perfectly clear, and he did not turn aside from humor, including sometimes remarks about his contemporaries set down in savored malice. For years the letters continued this way. Then he had his first stroke. He recovered. Then he had his second. His third. I don't know how many there were.

A characteristic letter from the earlier years of his final illness would contain a few peculiar errors, words repeated or transposed, nothing important, and since he obviously did not bother to reread his letters most of the time he may have been unaware of them. But the letters degenerated more and more quickly in the last years. Sometimes he would get no further than:

dea de de dea dea dea de dea dea dear

repeated across the page, and the sheet would be rumpled and torn where he had grabbed it out of the typewriter in exasperation. Often the rest of the letter was written by his wife, Flossie, in blue ink, her hand firm and businesslike. I could not understand what was happening in these letters. Aphasia seemed a reasonable symptom of a damaged brain, the tongue and brain being so closely connected; but a typewriter is a machine, one can go back and x-out one's mistakes, and this stammering in typescript seemed unaccountable to me; I did not even know what to call it. All I knew was that these letters from the late 50s and early 60s seemed to me among the most woeful things I had ever encountered, and I could not look at them without tears streaming down my face.

Some years later I had what would normally be the misfortune to spend Memorial Day weekend in a campground at Yosemite. My son was about four years old then, and he struck up a friendship with another boy of his own age whose family was "camped" a few tentsites away. When we were leaving—packing, cleaning up, loading the car—the father of my son's friend came over and introduced himself. It was one of those coincidences that make life truly, frighteningly mysterious. The young man had not only known Williams but had been his protege; not a literary protege, however, though he had read the poems, but a medical protege. My memory is hazy now, but I believe the young father, who was then a practicing doctor in San Francisco, had actually lived in the Williams household for a while and had been helped financially by Williams during medical school. I asked him to explain to me those final letters. We knelt; he took a stick and drew an oval in the dust, then divided it into squares, and pointed to four squares near the left-center. These control language functions, he said, though I can't quote him verbatim. This square controls the ability to speak, this the ability to understand speech, this the ability to write, and this the ability to read. Williams, he said, had been stricken in all four "squares." (Obviously he was simplifying, accommodating himself to my ignorance.) *Aphasia*, he said, is the term for all neuro-linguistic disorders.

I was grateful to the young doctor, and I wrote down his name and address in my pocket notebook, which of course vanished before long into wherever it is that pocket notebooks go. I know that my gratitude was not just for information given, however, but more for being shown that Williams was as much a physician as a poet and probably more a human being than either.

In *Paterson* the river is a river. Williams would have insisted on that. But to my mind one cannot avoid its symbolic functions, and one shouldn't. The river is also time, and the falls in the river are the present moment that divides the past, which is flowing away toward the sea, from the future, which is flowing toward us from the plain above and the distant mountains. More than this, the falls are noisy, the present moment is vocal. Hence the river is the stream not only of time but of language, and the falls are the present poem dividing "literature" below from the inchoate imagination above. And the poem never ceases; it is free, spontaneous, infinitely variable, like the falling water, and like William Carlos Williams in his marvelous fluency.

Imagine the agony when, in the here and the now, the voice and the poem and the falls were blocked. I think most of us have become aware that the termination of life has commonly become a far more difficult and protracted business than it was in the millenia before super-medicine. We know also that Death likes to hit us in our most painful and vulnerable areas; my own family has recently been terrorized by an especially dreadful instance. Why should Williams have escaped the common lot? No reason at all. But I am writing here as a poet and presumably for other poets and people close to poets. In Williams the death of language before the death of the man seems to me — — —

but I have no prose to express it.

RALPH GUSTAFSON

MEETING THE GREAT MAN

I had got into Verticalism with my poem "Mythos" and was to be published along with Masson, Kay Boyle, and Milosz in Eugene Jolas' *Vertical*; my poem "Flight into Darkness" was just to appear alongside Ezra Pound's "Canto Proceeding (72 circa)" in Dunstan Thompson's spectacular *Vice Versa*. That October (29th) 1940, I met William Carlos Williams. What a few days!

The cause of all this and where? At Frances Steloff's Gotham Book Mart on 47th Street, New York City. Where else? Who else? Through Frances I was to meet Cocteau, Edith and Osbert Sitwell, Sam Putnam, Anais Nin, Auden setting up a mike to a gramophone, Charles Henri Ford in his stocking feet in the Mart's show window, Horace Gregory on a ladder, Jose Garcia Villa putting commas in between each word of a poem, Oscar Williams with his anthology in a paper grocery-bag with more of his poems in it than Milton's, e.e. cummings who told me "Thank God there's someone else who can write a good love poem," what other name shall I drop with a thud? Gertrude Stein? No, just missed her; William Shakespeare? Unfortunately (or fortunately) no; Horatio Alger? I must have. William Carlos Williams? Gee, yes! as he used to say.

That was at the old Gotham Book Mart, the original down the street west at number 51, not that present fairly commodious Mart at 51—the original one on 47th Street, that long room over-crowded of course with tables of books and shelves and outside at the back that postage-stamp garden with its portable garage for more books and one place to sit and footage for poets, publishers and lovers if they stood vertical and those endless wonderful stupendous book parties that went on outside and flowed in inside. One afternoon—that big afternoon—no one was there but Frances doing something ineffable at her desk and me doing what could be done about books with little available cash and

turning to the stunning array of latest little magazines to see if
some one of the lot might be seeking just the poem I had just written—in *he* walked in professional suit and glasses and no hat and
not looking like a doctor—or did he? the impression was of greyness—William Carlos Williams. I suppose he wanted a book. Or did
he want a publisher? At one time he thought Frances Steloff
would know of a good publisher who would take his work. W.C.
Williams in need of a publisher! Anyway, I didn't know at the
time and would have been dumbfounded if I had known. I mean,
about poetry. I was sophisticated enough by then to know that
prose had a chance in the markets of the world. The proof was in
my hand: WCW's novel "In the Money", just published by New
Directions (of course), the second novel in WCW's trilogy: "White
Mule" had appeared three years before (1937) and "The Build-
Up" was still to come.

Frances brought me over as a Canadian poet working for the
British Information Service. WCW asked if I was a spy? In the context of my other thoughts I took it solemnly. My thoughts were
of him himself and poetry. I saw the comedy behind the bifocals.
I said No, self-consciously. I didn't have to ask him to inscribe
"In the Money." He remarked that he really wasn't, and with
pleasure wrote in the book. Not just an autograph. He wrote for
me my name. He didn't ask how to spell it. Everyone asks how to
spell my name. Perhaps WCW didn't because of his dash of
Danish blood (though I am half Swedish)—at least Pound says
that Williams was "half Danish."

I also had an untoward thought as WCW signed my "In the
Money": how could he sustain living in New Jersey? I had been
through Newark—as quickly as I could. Perhaps Rutherford
was different, that house at 9 Ridge Road? Anyway, there was
his friend Ezra Pound living it up, putting his lever under the
world and Yanking, writing non-square poems in Europe, and
here was WCW living it flat in New Jersey and writing square
prose.

Of course there is no idea but in things—all things. I realized
it then; have always realized it. In poetry there never has been
ideas except in things and never will be; even Plato needed a
cave to get his idea over. Poets have been writing in metaphoric
concrete images since Beowulf—so what's so new about that
phrase in WCW's "A Sort of Song"? The poem was not to appear
until four years after what I am writing about, but it
added nothing previous when it did appear and was declared
great shakes.

But that was then of no matter. The cat had put its hind foot into the empty flower pot ten years before and the barrow had been wheeled out to the chickens eleven years before that.

He looked in a hurry, did WCW that afternoon. Harrassed and hurried. But he took his time in the transaction of the book and Frances Steloff's introductory good kindness. There was nothing medical or obstetrically clinical about that warmest of interested smiles, nothing but delight that the commonalty of poetry had come down from the north into his purview. Never mind in what brief time all this occurred; the warmth was founded and was to last as long as his cat and wheelbarrow.

Had I published a book of poetry? I had. Two. But I didn't say so. Both are awful. Thank the Muse that I shut up about them. I said that I had a collection of poems ready for a publisher. A damn hard position to be in, was what he said to that. But that is only a point of view from the outside, he added. The center in the self is what determines poetry. Keep that protected, he said. And good luck.

The book was to be "Flight into Darkness" named after that poem in *Vice Versa* and was to be published four years later with as prestigious an imprint on its spine as you could get, Pantheon Books—Kurt and Helen Wolff's first book of poems on their lists—I had a letter from Helen about it just the other day. I could with some justice have sent it to William Carlos Williams. I didn't. The reason in me is that incurable habit of overambitious efface-ment and genuine unwishing to trouble anyone. Out of his very nature, WCW would have welcomed the book and provided usable praise. Everyone has a generous quote of his own from WCW and exploited it. Pound would have said burn the book, read Douglas.

What I wanted to say to WCW that afternoon, I wrote that night in a poem. I had learned to shut up; when I met Charlie Chaplin I said, "You are my hero." I still wince. I have learned to accept my nature; twice I could have said to Rachmaninoff, "Thank you"; once when we both were waiting for a bus on the corner of 57th Street and Sixth Avenue; once when we were alone together in Carnegie Hall, he was coming down the stairs and I was going up; I pressed to the side and let the great man escape communism. To satisfy myself about WCW I wrote some true verses.

For William Carlos Williams

It was one of those immortal wounds
Mister Frost talks about

a poem

sixteen words
it was made of

concerning the value
of a 1923 wheel
barrow

I was struck dumb
anything modern
could last
so long

THE MAN

The Williams family around 1899.

WILLIAM ERIC WILLIAMS

LIFE WITH FATHER *

FOOD

Dad enjoyed eating. For him it was a pleasurable necessity. He was
neither gourmet nor gourmand, but ate with relish and gusto what
was served him. Soup was blown and "supped." The soft boiled
egg in the morning was eaten from the shell in an egg cup, and the
last trace of white was scraped down to the amniotic membrane
before it was put aside. The ingestion of celery was a jam session,
with the masseter and temporal muscles at the sides of the face,
rhythmically rising and falling, setting the tempo. A rib bone was
to be chewed clean. A seafood dinner of steamers and lobster was
a full symphony. Each clam stripped, washed in the broth, dunked
in butter, and engorged, to be followed by the bits of white muscle
painstakingly scraped from each shell, and the last shred chased
by the cup of broth, which was drained to the sandy dregs. The
lobster was crushed, dismembered, stripped, picked and sucked
down to the most distal segment of the hindmost appendage.
Only a cup of shards remained to be returned to the kitchen. Each
leaf of an artichoke was repeatedly flensed, leaving only shreds
of the cellulose supporting structure to be discarded. At the end
the cleaned heart of the plant, submerged in the residual of the
melted butter, was impaled and mouthed with a final flourish.
His attack on an apple was an explosion. His strong functional
teeth were buried like a mechanical clam shell in the meat of the
fruit, and as the juices jetted laterally like the squirt of a disturbed
piss-clam, a wedge was ripped out, including a portion of the core,
and the whole joyously masticated as he wiped the cidery froth
from his chin on the back of his forearm. He was a vigorous and

*Reprinted from four numbers of *The William Carlos Williams Newsletter* (later *Review*)
with permission of the author: (1) "Food," *WCWN* (Fall 1979) © 1979 William Eric
Williams; (2) "The House," *WCWN* (Spring 1979) © 1979 William Eric Williams; (3)
"Cars," *WCWN* (Fall 1977) © 1977 William Eric Williams; (4) "The Physical," *WCWR*
(Spring 1982) © 1982 William Eric Williams.

happy trencherman, and yet not lacking in decorum. Quite regularly he bit the inside of his cheek at the peak of the feast.

Mom was and still is a good cook. Her kitchen was efficiently administered, and the food was respected and tastefully prepared. At all meals the table was nicely set. Serving dishes came from the kitchen piping hot, their savory steam providing us a preview of their contents. The job was well done, and I think Mom knew it. No need for hyperbole on Dad's part. Yet I feel the onus of the daily prospect of three square meals for an adult male and two growing boys was lightened for her by his wordless gustatory approbation. Was this perhaps a subtle form of lovemaking?

Smell and taste, those symbiotic senses triggered by the receptors imbedded in the lining of nose and mouth were actively working partners. His was a big nose, capable of sampling a more than generous aliquot of his environment. He pointedly smelled everything. A new book, a mushroom, a cow, a urine sample, the air about him and his own armpit were sampled olfactorily and thus given an added dimension. Isolated in a strange place, I think his first action in orienting himself would be to smell it. Charles Lamb would have understood. And smell's Siamese twin, taste, never was permitted to lose its tone. There were moments when we stood aghast at his temerity in tasting. A simple walk in the countryside became a laboratory session for the taste buds. We tasted the buds and twigs of the wild cherry, sassafras, birch and witch hazel. We dug and pulled to obtain the thumb-sized morsel in the heart of the common pasture fern that dots New England's pastures. The white, crisp, nutty slip of embryonic tissue was adequate reward for the time and energy expended. We sampled the sap of the maple in spring and found it wanting. We hacked off and chewed the gum of the spruce. Besides the traditionally edible wild berries, we sampled the barberry, wintergreen berries, bunch berries, shad or service berries, rose hips and the beautiful red fruit with the black umbilicus that adorns the yew in the fall. Granted almost everything we tried was known to be the natural food of some bird or beast. But there were times when Dad alone did the sampling. At Hilldale, Mom's Uncle Elinar's farm outside of Wilmington in Vermont, we gathered milk pails full of mushrooms. These were taken back to the house and studied with the help of a book on the subject. We knew most of the poisonous ones on sight, but while in the field we'd occasionally come upon a stranger, and Dad would peel the top and take a nip from the edge of the spore-bearing cap. This would be diced daintily between the incisors and ingested. Just a sample, you understand, the theory being that it wasn't an Amanita, and the other poisonous varieties were for the most part only emetic and would merely induce vomiting. He stubbornly maintained that he was one of those for whom the emetic Russula was non-poisonous. Yet on at least one occasion when Mom, with considerable reservations, cooked him an assorted batch of his gatherings, he was shortly thereafter compelled to vomit.

But acute indigestion, at least after his marriage, was not a chronic problem. In general he had an ironclad gut that mangled, absorbed and excreted everything that came its way in uncomplaining routine. In his bachelor days, on the other hand, he had been subject to frequent digestive disorders, and Mom attributes them to the diet in his parents' home. His mother was certainly an adequate cook, but her culinary background was strictly West Indian, and her dietary staples were beans and rice. His English father demanded his ration of beef, but cooked beyond recognition with the last trace of blood purged, leaving a colorless, flavorless and, at least for Dad, indigestible residue. His description of the table spread for the house staff during his internship in New York is certainly no prescription for a griping belly. Whether organic or psychosomatic, his complaints were cured by marriage and Mom's home cooking. In the years I lived with him and shared his table, the only digestive aids I knew him to take were an occasional slug of rhubarb and soda for over indulgence, and a rare ounce of castor oil for the usual indication.

Butter as an adjunct to any meal is a recognized staple in our country. But to Dad the meal was planned around the butter dish. A dash in the egg shell along with the salt to lace the flavor. A copious smear on all bread products to lubricate the track. An ear of corn swam in the stuff. A mound of mashed potatoes was cratered with a yellow oleaginous lake. Baked potato skins became butter sandwiches. Butter was the last item removed from our table, because the dessert, no matter what its character, just might be improved by a touch of butter. "Just leave the butter please, Lucy." His addiction was a standing family joke. I suppose Dad suffered during the days of rationing in 1917 until his fairy godmother took a hand. While driving one day on an outlying street he came upon a packing case in the middle of the road. Considering it a traffic hazard, he stopped, lifted it into the back of the car and continued on his way. Exploration later at home revealed enough oleomargarine to feed a battalion for a week. Judicious doctoring with salt and food coloring yielded a product sufficiently like butter so that we were able to prevent Dad's having withdrawal symptoms until the real stuff was obtainable again.

I suppose it's axiomatic that where there is good food there is good booze. There was always liquor available at 9 Ridge Road, but except for parties at New Year's Eve or other festive occasion, it was used most temperately. Cocktails in the evening before dinner (martinis, except for occasional frozen Daquiris in very hot weather) were the standard fare. Dad's limit was usually one. Wine at meals was for guests and special occasions. During prohibition there was good grain alcohol available on prescription, and Flossie transmuted it into good gin with juniper drops and charcoal filters. Patients from the Italian colony in Lyndhurst would settle an old account by bringing crates of grapes and crushing them in a hugh hogshead in the basement. Eventually there evolved gallons of purple wine in bottles of assorted sizes and ancestry. At Flossie's mother's place at Monroe there was Nannie's special home brew that would hit the ceiling in the dining room when uncapped at the table. In France the folks enjoyed walking tours of the Burgundy and Champagne countries with Bill and Sally Bird, sampling as they went.

Roy, the bootlegger, was a regular caller at Ridge Road, bringing everything from scotch to applejack. He later ran a clam-bar in Nutley on the river bank, and would show up every New Year's day about noon with a sack of oysters over his shoulder. After a slug of beef tartare and some black coffee he'd open as many oysters as Mom wanted (usually several dozen) and then take off for the next friend's house. No charge. I suppose it was he who brought into the house a pint flask of whiskey labeled "Panther Piss," the label displaying a lascivious looking panther with lolling tongue and a tremendous reproductive organ dangling below and dripping golden drops of "piss." It sounded as if the property would have gone up like a neglected still if you lit a match, but I never saw my father intoxicated, and I don't believe there was ever an hour in all the years he practiced medicine that he was incapacitated by alcohol. His attitude was that booze was a good ice-breaker and destroyer of inhibitions, but beyond that a poison and a stealer of precious time. He resented the fact that liquor could make one sleepy in the acute phase, and later incapable of doing one's thing in the hangover stage. Time was too precious to him to risk losing any of it in an alcoholic stupor. Consequently he was very moderate in his imbibing, enjoying the flow and camaraderie induced by alcohol when taken in moderation, but saving his pagan indulgence for the food that accompanied it.

THE HOUSE

The house at 9 Ridge Road was a gift from Pa Herman. His wedding present of two thousand dollars provided the down payment. He held the $6,000 mortgage for the balance, and semi-annually Mom and Dad made payments to him of 5% interest. In turn he made semi-annual gifts of these amounts to Mom at Christmas and on her birthday. The property was left to them in his will. It's a sizable frame structure, clapboard finish, which had a gingerbready front porch that was removed in the 1920s. Two red brick chimneys on the south and east sides served the two furnaces and the fireplace in the living room. The structure stands on the south boundary line of the lot, with ample front, back and north side yards. Over the years its color has been predominantly a light mustard shade. Six feet above the street level on a terraced plane, it has been a buttress against the advance of commercial progress into our neighborhood. The front door opens to the west, where the 102 Bus from Hackensack to Newark guns its motors for the climb up Ridge Road, and where until the twenties trolley cars made a similar run over the tracks in the middle of the red brick paved Park Avenue. The family have never used this entrance much. The back door opens to the east in an angle formed by the meeting of the house and office walls. It catches the first rays of sun in the morning, and the five wooden steps descending to the yard have over the years been our late winter and early spring bleachers for sun bathing and backyard bloom surveillance. This has always been the family entrance. From the foot of the stairs a thirty-foot walk of flat field stones leads straight ahead to the garage. No masterpiece of masonry, but a labor of love for which Dad hauled the rocks from hither and yon over a period of several years.

Through the back door one enters a small hallway. To the right and down two steps is the office. Straight ahead was the old icebox, whence came the ice-cold plums of the poem. To the left is the door to the kitchen. Across the kitchen and through a swinging door is the dining room, a square chamber, relieved on the east wall by an alcove containing the sideboard. Above it hangs an Audubon print, "The Great Blue Heron." Dad rescued the picture in pieces from the garret of a friend, and Mom found an understanding old German picture framer who restored it to its present condition. She vividly recalls unwrapping the tattered old print in his New York shop, and his exclaiming, "Ach, mein Gott, ein genuine Audubon; sure I fix 'im for you." In the center of the room is the Stickley oak dining table "made in Ohio," the matching black leather-seated chairs standing around the walls. Suspended dead center from the ceiling was a six-sided, rose-glass-paned chandelier, with a six inch skirt of strings of rose-colored beads hanging within two feet of the table top. On occasion, when Dad attacked the far side of the roast, arm and chandelier would collide, bringing down a shower of beads that bounced indiscrimimately into sugar bowl, fruit salad and mashed potatoes. Dad always sat facing the two windows in the south wall, with Mom to his left, me to his right, and my brother directly opposite. Dad's back was toward the front hall, whence the telephone could be brought on its extension cord and placed at his right elbow for convenience at meal times. Thus the mood, pace and flavor of our meals was often determined by conversations with the hospital or sick patients—i.e., rupture of membrane, frequency of contraction, and rectal findings in delivery cases; or frequency, amount, consistency and color of vomitus and stools in gastro-enteritis. Also to his right the early American corner cupboard, with a brick-colored earthenware Mexican jug on the top. In the early twenties Charlie Demuth gave the folks one of his delicate floral watercolors, *Pink Lady Slippers*, in appreciation for food, lodging and medical care in the early stages of his diabetes. They later bought *Tuberoses*, and the two hang there in the dining room to this day, rubbing elbows with works of Hank Niese, Harriet Gratwick, and Eyvind Earle (Mom's nephew).

Continuing clockwise to the right through double sliding doors is the wasp-waisted living room, a thirty foot expanse created by joining the old front and back parlors. Straight ahead to the west are five windows through which over the years we have watched the changing commercial scene along Park Avenue. Far up the block to the left is the Public Library, and in succession coming closer were Wahler's Candy Store, the Presbyterian Parish House, Sing Lee's Laundry, Bobby Stuart's optometry office, Park Hardware, a First National Store, Park Cleaners, Davenport Drug, Korwan's Jewelry, Probst's Butcher Shop, the Mayflower Bakery, Benowitz Hardware, Handler's Bakery, Borschnecks' Flower Shop, Zimmerman's Haberdashery, and finally the old city hall containing the police station and post office. They have provided a characterless stretch of commercial fronts with an equally unexciting row of second floor apartments above them.

On the south wall is the red brick fireplace, Mom's desk on one side and a hand-wound Victrola on the other. For perhaps the past twenty-five years the fireplace has been handsomely sandwiched between ceiling-high bookcases, with breast-high cupboards beneath. An austere Charles Sheeler water color of tulips hangs dead center on the chimney. Here there was once a chin-high mantle, with a centrally placed glass-enclosed thirty-day clock. At Christmas we kids hung our stockings there, beneath the decor of holly, ground pine and cones, with miniature reindeer and woodcarvings of peasant figures peeping through. This wall served as the backdrop for Charles Sheeler's wedding to Musya Sokolova, with a "piece-of-the-justice" (to quote Musya's mis-quotation of "justice of the peace") officiating. Here too Mom and Dad often sat on a two-sectioned couch, doing a crossword puzzle, reviewing correspondence, or reading. In front of them sat the copper-bound sea chest brought from China by Captain Rude years ago and given to Dad apparently just because he liked him. The north wall for years was dominated by a grand piano, and the intervening floor space has seen a parade of couches, tables, chairs and rugs in styles from horsehair and wicker through Windsor spindles to modern sectionals. Around the remaining walls is a mélange of paintings, the majority of which are water colors done by Dad's brother Edgar. Some have been there so long they spell a large part of my definition of home. A handsome portrait in oil of a golden-haired young woman was done by Raquel Hélène Hoheb, Dad's mother. Charlie Demuth's *End of the Parade—Coatesville, Pa.* has a wall to itself, as does Marsden Hartley's pastel of what Dad was wont to refer to as Marsden's "breasts" (*Mountains in New Mexico*).

Through the living room and again exit clockwise to the right is the front hall. This completes the pattern of the ground floor. A strictly utilitarian room—coat closet, telephone stand and chair, a large blanket chest built by Dad's good friend Russell Robinson during the Depression. Over the telephone stand is a big and fascinating print of Brueghel's *Children's Games*. To the right above the light switch hangs a copy of Ben Shahn's *Paterson*, done by the artist very informally and quickly at Roosevelt while Mom and Dad looked on. The left or north wall consists of the front door and the stairway to the second floor. A six-by-twelve foot mural covers the wall back of the landing half way up the stairs. It is a scene done by Eyvind Earle, looking down York Avenue on the east side of Manhattan from the 23rd floor of the Cornell Medical Center. Included is the East River, with Turtle Bay in the background beneath the span of the 57th Street Bridge.

From the landing one bears right up the last seven steps to the second floor. It is a duplicate of the ground floor. A large central hall, with built-in linen closet and drawers straight ahead. Overhead center the light cord. On the left wall a bookcase jammed with books, and the top littered with family pictures and assorted memorabilia. Framing the linen closet are two bedrooms, the one to the left the nursery when we boys were kids, that to the right Mom and Dad's. Continuing right on the west wall another bedroom and full right coming north a short passage out to the sleeping porch, later enclosed to become Dad's mother's room. Against the rail that guards the stairwell in this upper hall stood her sewing machine, from whose drawers Smokey the cat would steal a spool of thread in the dead of night. While the house slept she wove her maze of thread around, over and under the downstairs furnishings to catch our feet and challenge our imaginations in the morning.

The door frame leading left into the passage to the bathroom contained a chinning bar when we boys were tads. Dad was concerned about our physical fitness, and the three of us did our daily dozen chins, with a few "skin-the-cats" and "skim-the-milks" thrown in. It was installed about five feet eight inches from the floor, which was high enough for us boys to need a stool to reach it, but just low enough so that Dad's brow met it squarely on a trip to the bathroom in the dark. I distinctly recall his vehement "Jesus Christ" startling me from my sleep on more than one occasion when someone had forgotten to take it down. In later years when Paul and I were teenagers and staying out nights, that upper hall was the final obstacle to our getting to bed undetected. I won't say invariably, but I'll bet nine out of ten times the sneak from the head of the stairs to our bedroom doors was interrupted by Dad's voice from his bed—"Did you have a good time?"

Capping it all is an undivided attic full of steamer trunks, furniture, pictures, chests of old clothing and the assorted bric-a-brac and impedimenta of a small army of ancestors now dead, and of friends who have left things in trust and never returned. The family has never moved, so the attic contents have never had to be drastically reduced. It was a big barn of a place, unheated, without insulation and drafty in winter. A large gym mat once occupied the center of the floor, and there were a medicine ball, boxing gloves and a punching bag. In the twenties Dad stapled sheets of insulation between the rafters, then closed off the space under the eaves and created an eight-foot ceiling with sheets of beaver board. It became his studio, with the desk, typewriter, file and general literary storage area at the east end. On the wall at the opposite end, framing the window to the west, were two life-sized full length caricatures, "La Mère Prudente" and "Le Père Tranquil" done in water color by Dad's brother Edgar. The thirty-five-foot north and south walls are plastered to this day with cartoons, posters, children's drawings, primitive paintings, letters, postcards and menus. The south wall features a four-foot graph of the course of the New York Stock Exchange from 1928 to 1932. Alongside, with what intent let the reader decide, is pasted a tiny clipping from an unknown periodical. It reads:

> I'm just a little prairie flower
>   Growing wilder hour by hour
> Nobody even cultivates me
>   I'm wild.

In the center of this wall is a chest-high shelf, six feet long and slightly inclined like the old school desks, where he could stand and write. I recall his discussing the desirability of having facilities for writing in different bodily attitudes (sitting, reclining, standing), because the changes gave refreshment.

The heavy black-stained wooden typing desk with the hinged foldaway top holding the typewriter is the central feature of the east end of the room. For ten years he worked here, with a coal stove in winter to make the temperature bearable, and fans in summer to temper the heat. An extension line was run up there and a phone installed. The light is a pull-cord overhead lamp, the flooring the original unfinished boards without carpeting. He sat on an adjustable, backless, screw-type stool while typing, and was a two-fingered, hunt-and-punch typist to his dying day. The sound of his typing when I was a youngster always gave me the impression that he was beating hell out of the machine. And this impression was fortified (on days when things didn't go right) by the scream of the roller as page after page was torn out, balled up, and pitched in the general direction of the wastebasket. Sometimes complete frustration drove him out into the yard to lose himself in sweaty garden labor for a couple of hours.

And it all sits on a fullsized, unfinished cellar, where the cat stepped delicately into the flower pot on top of the jam closet. But for us who lived here it was important as the focus of the coal-furnace-heat cycle. Winter mornings began between 6 and 7 AM when Dad went down to shake the furnace. The rattling of the iron grates in the furnaces was transmitted throughout the house. This was followed shortly by the sound of the coal shovel dug into the coal bin, and the chunks of anthracite tossed onto the residual hot coals from the previous day's fires. It was a daily ritual and our unofficial reveille. After school Paul and I were responsible for hauling the ashes from the pits out to the garbage cans. The cycle was completed by the coal truck that made monthly deliveries, running a steel chute through the cellar window into the coal bins beneath the dining room. The truck bed was tilted upward and the coal rattled and roared down the chute, making conversation impossible when delivery was made at meal time.

CARS

It was just prior to my birth that my father acquired his first automobile. He had started his practice of medicine in Rutherford with a bicycle as his sole means of conveyance. I don't think he ever qualified as a horse-and-buggy M.D., although like all the young blades in his time he probably had been "checked out" in a horse-powered rig. Anyway, 1913-1914 saw him at the wheel of his own Ford, and there began the classic man-auto duel that has been so often and so well told.

Winter mornings meant kettles of hot water poured into the radiator, then setting the magneto and gas before starting the cranking ritual. Running from the front bumper to the driver's seat to try to nurse that little spark of engine ignition before she stalled, and without flooding; skinning the knuckles; sweating to the point he had to come in the house and change his clothes down to the skin before starting out on his calls; cursing not just a little—all were part of the morning routine. Then covering the hood with a blanket when on a house call to preserve some heat to ease the next engine turn over. At times being snowed in when on an overnight maternity call, and not even trying to get started, but walking home and digging out later.

Summertime it was easier to get going but there were more flats. Jack it up, pull off the shoe, peel out the tube, find the leak and patch it. Then pump. Always a bucket in the car for overheating, hauling water from the nearest horse trough, brook, spring, or bog.

And so it went, as Dad gradually worked up the scale in opulence, first from a Ford to a Dodge, and later to a Buick (1927). Dad was never a car nut. A car was owned and maintained to serve its owner. Gas it, oil it, wash it, and when it wore out, get a new one. He was not his own mechanic. He trusted his serviceman and depended on him. No sentimentality about a car he owned.

I guess the nearest and dearest to his heart of all the cars he owned was a second-hand Buick, a two-door custom-built coupe that had enjoyed the blandishments of a rich old lady from Montclair for a couple of years before Dad took over. It had less than ten thousand miles on it and was the biggest, loudest and most powerful thing he had ever had on the road. A solid layer upon layer of baked paint finish, black, such as they were still putting on cars in the thirties. (And, believe me, a stinker to Simonize. Never could get it completely free of streaks.) But Dad enjoyed warming it up, and then just racing her for a minute to hear her growl. But a bloody truck to drive when you got going over fifty and were on a round-topped macadam road full of pot-holes. And those shocks, wow! When you took her from Ruther-ford to Vermont or Buffalo, you had done a day's work.

Dad was no milktoast on the road. Mom was continually imploring him, "Bill, please slow down," or "Bill, please don't race that fool driver." Dad was a competitor, easily aroused by someone driving faster than he, or by someone showing the least sign of negligence or disrespect on the road. They had to be passed and put in their proper places. Coming down Route 17 on a Sunday night, returning from the farm in Monroe (Mom's folks' place) was a nightmare even in the twenties and thirties. Three or four hours to do the forty-five miles. A suicidal trek down that three lane slaughterhouse. Everyone tired and angry. Everyone fighting to get one car ahead. Angry, shouting. Windows rolled down and fists shaking. On these trips Dad was not detached and thinking beautiful thoughts to knock out on the typewriter at his next opportunity. No sir, he was right in there racing and cussing and fist shaking with the rest of them. Mom would be nervous and irritated, but we kids loved it and urged him on, if not vocally, at least in spirit.

When we boys were perhaps eight and ten years old in the middle 1920s, Dad had one of his Dodges which was just broken in, and had had the 500-mile check-up. It had never been opened up wide and we were curious as to just how fast this machine could get over the ground. Five of us kids (Bill and Jim Black, Ick Platts and my brother Paul and I) were packed onto the seats. Dad taxied her out West Passaic to Jackson Avenue and turned South down the river toward Newark. This was a speed trial, and we glued our eyes to the speedometer. Dad put the gas pedal to the floor, and somewhere between the Cooper Lumber Yard and the old Rutherford Avenue Bridge across the Passaic River we hit 45 miles an hour. He was as thrilled as we were. We yelled our approval, and talked of it for weeks after.

But I guess the classic auto experience of his life was the trip from West Haven, Connecticut, to Rutherford on the September day of the big hurricane in 1937. Dad had gone up to 201 Ocean Avenue to pick up his mother who always summered there in a cottage a few feet from the shore of Long Island Sound. The mass news media had not yet learned the art of precipitating general public hysteria at the approach of every major weather change. And who had a radio in the car to pick up bulletins? No weather forecaster had warned of the storm. I remember the day well because it was the opening day of my second year in medical college in New York City. The opening ceremonies were being conducted in the amphitheater on York Avenue, and because of the heat the tall windows on each side of the hall were opened to allow some ventilation. The winds accompanying the storm made such a moaning, whistling and groaning in the openings that the windows were perforce closed to make the speakers audible. Our consequent discomfort was intense. The streets of Manhattan later that afternoon were littered with ruptured umbrellas, and quantities of signs blown off the faces of buildings.

And at about this same hour Dad started out the oyster-shell paved drive from the cottage in West Haven, probably a little after noon. It was hot and windless. Little breakers from the sound were making their normal "slap-slushhhhhh" on the beach at the foot of the jumbled stone wall in front of the cottages. Things went well for the first hour or so, but as they came closer to the city, there began to be trees across the road, and heavy rain made the visibility a little sticky. Grounded power lines flashed and smoked where they shorted on the wet ground, and branches and leaves flew horizontally across the line of vision.

What do you do in the middle of a hurricane with an old lady over ninety seated beside you, her impedimenta stacked about her? You just keep on going and hope for the best, which is just what they did. At every obstacle thrown or blown into their path they turned right or left, according to the passability of the road. They saw practically no one. In one town Dad spoke to a policeman who had no constructive suggestion, so they kept going. Later he couldn't recall exactly which towns they passed through, but with cars all along their way pinned under trees, pulled off onto the shoulder or otherwise rendered hors-de-combat, they somehow won through to the George Washington Bridge and home to Rutherford. Seven or eight hours to make what normally was a two to three hour trip. That evening he recounted to Mom that his mother, born and raised in the hurricane belt of the West Indies, had remarked at the height of the storm, "Why, it's almost like a hurricane!"

Dad's cars played a big part in his trips with Mom. They took them off the beaten path—to places like Tapahannock on the Rapahanock one night where the girl in the restaurant apologized because all she could cook for them was fresh shad roe. Or the run from Bangor to Island Falls up in Aroostook County where in the early twenties absolutely everything was unpredictable, from the condition of the road to the availability of the next gasoline pump, food and lodging. And trips across the Canadian border from Island Falls to smuggle back a few fifths of booze in the knickers that were the thing for the men out camping in Maine in the twenties. Dad was forever finding dandy stones for his path from the house to the garage, which stands today just as he finally completed it. Those stones were slung in the back of the car whenever and wherever they were found—at the farm in Monroe, on the shore at West Haven, at Garrett Mountain, at Cranberry Lake while visiting the Spences. And much of the landscaping of the property at 9 Ridge Road was done with trees and shrubs pulled up from spots as widely separated as the Cedar Swamps out in the Rutherford meadows, and the Mohawk trail between Greenfield and North Adams. Hemlocks from three different states separate the back and side yards. Shad bushes from Great Notch have done well, but the swamp azalea and blueberry bushes (which were doomed where they grew because of the ditching done by the mosquito commission to allow tide waters into the cedars) couldn't make it in our yard either.

There was always a wet newspaper or burlap-wrapped bundle of wild things in the car when he and mother returned from a trip. Ferns, mosses, wild orchids, ginger, trillium, wild violets in variety, trailing arbutus, wild geranium were healed into a protected spot until they could decide just where in the yard they would be most likely to survive. There was a daily ritual arm-in-arm circuit of the yard, usually early in the morning before leaving for the hospital, as he and mother inspected and planned the plantings. They shared a love of growing things, and from the appearance of the first snowdrop in late February until the last 'mums and wild asters gave up the ghost in late November, the garden was a major item of activity and conversation at our house.

And there was deviltry, too. Like the night the annual Williams, Spence, Wagner and Dugdale progressive dinner was progressing from the Spence house at 23 Lincoln Avenue to our house on Ridge Road. It seemed appropriate to the New Year's Eve mood to deviate from the customary route and take a short cut on the sidewalk down Park Avenue along the west side of the Presbyterian Church. A member of the local constabulary interrupted the frolic about halfway down the block, but in keeping with the holiday mood, and on recognizing Dad, he advised him to get back on the road and wished him a Happy New Year. Similarly on another occasion, driving in reverse from the Dugdale's on West

Passaic to the Spences'. Or charging the little thank-you-m'am
bridge on the Molly Start Trail about a mile east of Wilmington
up in Vermont. This was a ritual we kids loved and anticipated
with glee. The simple little arch over Beaver Brook when crossed
at any speed over thirty miles an hour would toss the back wheels
of the car up in the air like a bucking bronco, and of course we
young ones would fly up and hit the roof over the rear seat. What
fun!

And then there was Bobby. Dad had brought him home in
his pocket one night, a gift from a patient whose bitch had spawned
a litter of little mongrel terrier pups. The one Dad pulled out from
under the stove was a little white long-tailed male. We never had a
sweeter pup. He was everyone's friend, from the sergeant on the
desk at police headquarters across the street on whom Bobby
made a daily social call, to all the kids in the neighborhood who
frequented our yard. And Bobby loved Dad's car. He would go
along for the ride, whether invited or not. Often Dad would leave
in a hurry, jump into the car and be off to a delivery or other
urgent call. On arrival, there was Bobby, having somehow hung
onto the running board all unbeknownst until discovered at their
destination. And at Hilldale up in Vermont, driving over to
Raponda for a swim on a summer's afternoon, Bobby would hop
on the running board as we pulled away. This was a narrow dirt
road with bushes growing close on both sides. The pup would
take a beating from the wild cherry branches and blackberry stalks
that slapped him as we went by. About every other trip the
torture would get the best of him, and he'd look ahead for the
next branch that was about to clip him and close his teeth on it.
Of course, the car kept going, and unless Bobby let go promptly
he was pulled off into the ditch, only to pick himself up on his
four feet as the rolls and somersaults induced by the momentum
of the car had ceased. Lost in the dust cloud behind the car, we
could hear him better than we could see him as he tore along
behind, yipping his head off.

THE PHYSICAL

He was about five feet nine inches tall, shoe size 8D, hat size 7¼,
shirt size 15½-32, waist 32 to 34, with good posture in both standing and sitting positions. His weight fluctuated between 150 and
160 pounds and was well distributed. The shoulder girdles were
well developed and the pectorals completely concealed the rib

cage. His abdomen was flat, his legs just missed being skinny. He consciously walked with his toes slightly inverted, a custom encouraged in those days. To walk Indian style was to walk well.

His gait was purposeful. You felt he had a goal in mind as he strode along. This you can feel in the photo, well published, Dad in his old Panama, leaving the "old" Rutherford library, doubtless headed for the post office, which he habitually visited a half dozen times a day, getting off copy to publishers and letters to aspiring writers seeking advice. His arms were generously muscled, and I recall as a tad his ability to throw a walking stick high up into a hickory or chestnut tree to bring down a shower of nuts for us kids. His hands were spade-like, "a ditch-diggers's hands," he used to say, with blunt tipped fingers and calloused palms. He was always clean shaven. I can't seem to recall more than a single day's beard on his face, until in his late years his illnesses crippled him, and he made do with an electric shaver. The unruly jet black hair epitomized in his self portrait gradually gave way to baldness and an encircling halo of gray at the periphery of his skull. His eyes were dark brown, always searching, looking not only at you, but into you; not impolitely, but in an interested kind of way. I know it made my eldest, Emily, uncomfortable to be under his gaze when she was a toddler. There was nothing distinguished about his mouth, just a horizontal opening in his face paralleling the lower edge and completing the square of his moderately protuding chin. His dominating facial feature of course was his nose, which he recognized and early on glorified in his own poem "Smell!"

> Oh strong-ridged and deeply hollowed
> nose of mine! what will you not be smelling?
> . . . .
>
> Must you taste everything? Must you know everything?
> Must you have a part in everything?

It was his most characteristic facial feature, with the dromedary hump half way down the "strong ridge." A snapshot taken by his brother Ed in the arena at Fiesole around 1910 shows a classic Barrymoresque profile, the office girl's romantic hero. These physiognomic features were spaced appropriately on a weathered skin of slightly olive hue, peppered liberally in later years, particularly on the brow and temples, with pigmented nevi.

He grew up in a time when walking was in. He and his father and brother walked hundreds of miles for the fun of it. Penny postcards bearing Edgar's sketches of landmarks along their route to Lake George and beyond document their ability as hikers. They

walked from Rutherford to West Haven, Connecticut, by a cir-
cuitous route that took them through the northwestern part of
the state, stopping at inns and farmhouses along the way for
meals and bed. Dad himself between 1900 and 1910 would take
a trolley out of town 6, 8, or 10 miles and then walk back, observing and later recording at home in his card file the various fauna
and flora observed. He knew how to walk, and enjoyed it. He
could, as his father so aptly put it in his West Indian patois, "put
foot."

He knew and enjoyed the use of tools. Snapshots in the
family album show him down in a hole in the backyard chopping
the roots of a massive oak stump. This was in 1916, with me in
my white play suit equally involved in moving dirt. He made all
the foundation plantings in front of 9 Ridge Road, and he and
Mom together constructed a three hundred square foot rock
garden along the north wall of the house. He double dug and
planted a half dozen rose beds in the backyard over the years, the
final one remaining to this day and blooming in season. At the
Hermans' (Mom's parents) farm in Monroe, New York, he did
haying, gardening and road repairs, and later with me and Paul
built a dam down in the woods to create a pond that would
attract wildlife. At Hilldale, at Mom's uncle's place in Wilmington,
Vermont, he used a scythe to cut the millet that was fed to the
cows each evening in the summer months. Up there he shared in
the annual chore of burying the rocks that heaved up in the lane
from the main road every spring. And the cutting of wood with a
two-man saw, wedges and splitting axe was a daily routine at both
farms. He knew the smaller hand tools as well, having been indoc-
trinated in carpentry by his father, who was an able craftsman in
the shop. Rake, hoe, saw, scythe, pickaxe, sledge hammer, clip-
pers, mower, he used them all knowledgeably, but I think the
shovel family were his favorites. The gardening fork and spade
were his constant companions in the yard when making his rounds.
He definitely related to dirt. With a fork one can dig it, move it,
aerate it, cultivate it or scarify it. And all these things he did, in
an old pair of oxfords, sleeveless undershirt, and his other companion, the old fedora. The sweating body smeared with dirt gave
respite to that seething brain.

Dad enjoyed baseball as a player and as a spectator. He
pitched and played third; his brother Edgar was the catcher. In
fact Edgar played semi-pro summers in New England to bolster
the exchequer while studying at Boston Tech. He was a good man
with the bat. I recall a Sunday sitting in the old splintery, pitch-
oozing bleachers, watching the Unitarians play St. Mary's. Dad

and Ed were the battery for the Unitarians, and Ed had been having a ball slapping pitches to all fields. The St. Mary's pitcher, name of Meany, became understandably peeved, and the next time Ed came to bat, he threw a high hard one at his head. Before he could pick himself out of the dirt, Dad was half way to the mound with fire in his eye and curses on his tongue. Both benches emptied and the protagonists were squelched. But Dad's sensitivity and complete involvement in the game as player and/or spectator would manifest itself years later when he would be unable to sit and listen to, or watch on TV, a tense situation. In the ninth inning with two out, tie score, bases jammed and full count on the batter, he would have to excuse himself from the room and get the details later verbally. Carl Hubbell was his hero, particularly his feat of striking out the American League's "murderers' row" in the All Star game of 1937. He also got a chuckle from the Giants' Moore calmly reaching across the plate and stroking the ball to left on a pitch intended for an intentional pass. Frankie Frisch was his favorite commentator of all the sports announcers. "Oh, those bases on balls."

His involvement in tennis is strictly hearsay. Mom recalls a match in Paris in the early twenties on a neighborhood court in the vicinity of the residence of Ford Madox Ford. William Carlos Williams and Harold Loeb vs. Ford and Ernest Hemingway. Feeling ran high, because Loeb was Hemingway's financial crutch in those days, and furthermore had swiped Hemingway's girl; and Dad and "Hem" shared little other than their male attire and the purposeful juggling of words. Despite Hemingway's frequent interjections of "You have nothing" and "I'll wipe you off the court," neither team could win two successive games and end the match. Like so many amateurs, neither could break the other's service. The match ended with Hem's quitting the court complaining of his knee having given out.

The killer sports never interested Dad. He never owned a gun or fishing rod. Paul and I, on the other hand, have always been avid fishermen. On occasion Dad would accompany us, particularly when we went to the point east of the cottage at West Haven on Long Island Sound, fishing for conners and blacks off the rocks, or dunking speering under bobbers attached to long bamboo poles when the snapper blues were running off Woodmont. I guess his kicks came from being with us boys and sharing in our triumph with each catch. I recall a late September day with half a gale blowing and white caps making the water off the beach at Oyster River a solid blanket of foam. At my insistence we ventured out in a flat bottomed row boat. The tide was coming in, I had a bucket of clams and a rod, the sky was gray and we were closing the cottage for the season. Dad pulled that leaking, unmanageable tub back and forth across the mouth of the river a dozen times, the two of us bracing our bare feet on the opposing seats, licking the spray off our lips, the brine running in rivulets off our chins and elbows, and puddling on the seats beneath us. To a fisherman it was heaven, and to Dad at the oars it was a challenge. Crabs stole the bait, weeds weighted the line. It became a comedy of frustration. We agreed on a last pass across the river mouth. I like to think it was a lunker striper. We never saw him. The rod tip was under water, the mid-section of the rod rattattatting on the gunwale. I instinctively jumped up and reared back. Thud, thud, thud. Three magnificent heaves on the line and he was gone. I toppled over backwards, flattening Dad. The two of us, with oars on top, tangled in the bow with the remainder of my gear.

On the last day of camp (Camp Roosevelt, near Island Falls, Maine) on Lake Mattawamkeag in August 1924, a fellow Rutherfordian camper lacked a fifth variety of fish to complete his qualifications for his camp letter. Jack Holbrook was a little bigger and older than I, one of my heroes I guess, and I enticed Dad to row us out to Devil's Wall. This was a jagged ridge of rock that jutted above the surface a couple of miles down the lake. It was a bass paradise, with weed beds each side of the wall ending at a sharp drop off into deep water. Any kid could catch a bass on practically every cast. In fact Bill Sewell used to take groups of parents who lodged in his cabins down there in his motorboat. Hell, even our mothers caught bass. But not Jack. Dad rowed us down there, made a couple of loops around Devil's Wall, and then rowed back to camp. Jack sat tensely gripping his rod, refusing all my advice about changing lures, checking for weeds on the hook, etc. He caught nothing.

When we beached the boat next to the bateau in front of camp, Jack disconsolately reeled in his line. As the lure came to the side of the boat there hove into view a big blob of weeds. Dejectedly Jack started to clean the mess off the hooks, when lo and behold in the center of the weeds appeared a bass. Barely ten inches long (the required size to qualify), drowned like a pickle in a barrel, it had been dragged for God knows how many miles. We were all ecstatic, and Jack got his letter.

Dad and Edgar learned the basics of fencing while attending school in Europe. He kept up with this sport in college where he fenced on the team. Returning to Rutherford to practice medicine, he occasionally had the opportunity to go to a club in New York City with a couple of local buffs of the sword. I can recall his canvas suit and the head piece with the wire visor which he would on occasion don, perhaps for my amusement, pantomiming the feints and lunges of combat on the old mat in the attic. Two of his foils are still there, gathering dust in a corner. Although I was taken along to watch the workouts at the club in the city, I was never really enchanted, and never got the urge to participate. My idea of dueling was Doug Fairbanks in "Robin Hood" or "The Black Pirate." These middle-aged civilians in dueling garb, dancing back and forth on the narrow strip of matting, shouting things in French, filling the air with metallic scrapings and crashes, and finally admitting to being stabbed by shouting "touché," just never turned me on.

In the 1940s, with Dad in his 60s, there began a friendship with Prof. Charles Abbott at the University of Buffalo. How this came about I am not sure; probably it was initiated by Charles and fostered by Dad through a sense of appreciation for the attention it brought him. A kind of TLC. I first drove the folks up there in the spring of 1946 and they stayed on for a couple of weeks as the guests of Charles and Theresa on the Gratwick estate some miles east of Pavilion, New York, well south of Buffalo. This is an idyllic site on a ridge sloping south and east, the land part wooded and the rest largely cultivated and pasture. It was obviously a wealthy man's country abode, with a central manor house and scattered about, several satellite residences where once had resided the farmer, coachman, butler, etc. In the postwar, post-depression times of the 40s, maintenance of house and grounds wasn't quite up to Gratwick standards, but the evidences of former glory were everywhere, in the walled garden with the esplaniered fruit trees; the sunken garden with the central lily pond, and surrounding wall of elms; the Venetian garden with the canaliculi dividing the flower bed; the built-in pool, tennis courts, greenhouse, stables and pond, all joined by a maze of paths and roadways surrounding and leading inevitably to the central manor house. All formality of design and borders was lost to the encroaching weeds and brush that had insinuated their way into the plantings. Wood-chucks burrowed, feasted, bred and reproduced prolifically in the jungle, and what remained of the lawns was well-fertilized and close cropped by wandering sheep. Centrally located but lost in the herbage was a small stone chapel with multi-faceted walls fenestrated by narrow, unglazed windows starting at head height and extending up into the gloom overhead. A small lectern, niches in the walls for candle holders, a few hymnals and a couple of stone benches completed the furnishings. Capacity about 12. The services family conducted, short, intimate, featuring readings from various classical authors.

The folks occupied an apartment over the stables near the main gate, neighboring the house of the Abbotts, which, as I recall, had once been the residence of one of the leading functionaries on the place. Here Mom could prepare breakfast, served at a table overlooking the hen yard, where an old gander ruled the roost, trumpeting and honking at man or beast with the temerity to trespass on or near his domain. The surrounding hedge abounded with birds, robins nesting, catbirds, warblers, cardinals, sparrows and the chatterbox wrens, and beyond was Charles' vegetable garden, precisely planted and immaculately maintained. Fresh herbs, salad greens, cherry tomatoes, berries and tender young root crops, all less than a stone's throw from the kitchen door, planted in an elongated oval, framing a central patch of grass. This was one of Charles' sancta, which I quite innocently defiled one warm hazy morning by weeding and cultivating thoroughly from end to end, supposing all the while that I not only was getting a workout and a tan, but was being a bit of a good old boy and doing Charles a helluva favor. Unfortunately, this was a Gratwick farm no-no. Verboten! Defundu! No one, but no one, touched Charles Abbott's garden. So when he returned from Buffalo that evening I was well off in the fields with my rifle, potting woodchucks. Fortunately I am a bit of a garden buff myself, and if I do say so, I'd done a damn good job. And Charles did the sporting thing, not only forgiving me my trespasses after his inspection found no damage done, but granting me license thereafter to have at his precious garden when, if and as the urge should strike me.

Beyond the Abbott home was an old tumbled down greenhouse and pigeon loft, where Bill Gratwick conducted his tree peony culture. He of course was owner, boss, manager and resident factotum. His peony business was ostensibly the only source of income on the estate, and at that time was in its formative years. The greenhouse benches held the grafted seedlings which had been painstakingly bred in the field rows of wild Chinese tree peony stock. Pollination was accomplished early on a windless morning at a time when the field plants were full of maturing but unopened peony buds. The green bud is carefully peeled open to reveal the reproductive parts, specifically the pistil, which is then fertilized with the pollen of some distinguished blossom whose characteristics the nurseryman wishes to perpetuate, the pollen having been previously collected from ripe flowers into papers folded snugly against chance pollen particles windborn in the air. This one accomplishes by dipping a camel's hair brush in the pollen, transferring it to the female organ. The bud is then closed and further shielded by applying a covering bag which is tied over the bud and the terminal stem with twine. This ritual Dad and I shared in, and saw the benches full of the resulting potted grafts, developing toward the day when it would be apparent from the flower whether the whole procedure had been worthwhile. And so Dad's involvement in the growing led to his becoming the Poet Laureate of the Tree Peonies, riding to the sunken garden on a tractor, in the absence of a chariot, and there receiving the honorary award.

Indeed the developing, embryonic forms of the young peony plants were a fit subject and challenge for the artist. The tender, waxy cotyledons, peeling in sensuous whorls from the central phallus, and the anlages of divisions to form branches, suggested the parts of bodies in intimate embrace. It was Dad's challenge to capture in words this process of creation, from moment of conception to the final divine fruition, while the painter in residence, Nassos Daphnis, did the same in his own medium.

Paul and I have always shared a little act, pantomiming a characteristic attitude of Dad's. It consists of complete detachment from reality, with eyes unfocused, gait automatic, all receptors turned off. The musical accompaniment is a tuneless whistling evoked by tootling the gently exhaled breath between tongue and hard palate. This we aped, but still respected, as an indicator that something profound was taking place. As far as we know he was never aware of what was happening behind his back. You might say it was his cloud nine. Poet busy creating.

Actually these detached moments were rather rare. Typically in the presence of others, Dad was alert and dynamic, interested in people, a two-way conversationalist, willing to listen as well as to speak his own opinion. In a group he was always involved, not one to drift into a corner, unless of course the subject failed to interest him, or the conversation was dominated by a dogmatic bore. At these times he was quite capable of excusing himself and walking out—or simply taking a cat nap. In a mixed social gathering of neighborhood friends he was a catalyst. People were glad to see him. The men knew he enjoyed a smutty story, but respected him for his fairness and slowness to judge. The women were titillated by his presence, their color rising a little when he addressed them, and were on occasion excited to bizarre acts of aggression, like the time Louise Wagner tried to comb his hair with a garden rake.

So how to sum up? How to put a caul over this many-tentacled animal and put him on display? He was an average physical sample of homo sapiens living in an average suburban community who was distinguished from his neighbors because he happened to be a physician. The fact that he was an artist created not even a riffle on the surface on the pond that was Rutherford in the first half of the twentieth century. Furthermore, few other than some close intimates realized what boundless energy he possessed and how generous he was in spending it on his patients, his art and his fellow artists, or rather those who aspired to become fellow artists. His sleep requirement was minimal, and he apparently derived as much refreshment from a quick forty winks on the living room couch as you and I might from half a night's sleep. He needed physical work for an outlet, and there was about him an aura of tension, an invisible halo of potential that demanded a constant outlet. Yet he remained approachable. There was nothing obtrusive in his manner. People seemed to sense that here was a nice guy who, far from being offended, welcomed human contact. How else explain the little whore who grabbed his arm affectionately and suggested, "Wanna come home with me, Pop?" Mother, Paul, Dad and I were strung out somewhere between the old Astor and the Paramount. Paul was escorting Mom up ahead, I was next in line and Dad was sweeper. I heard her invitation and turned to see Dad smile and point up ahead with the remark, "I'm flattered, sweetheart, but maybe I'd better ask my wife." She too smiled, arched her eyebrows and with a rather philosophical move veered off into the crowd. A human guy who had something for everyone. "Human" by definition is imperfect. What he had for some was positive and perfect, and what he had for others could be negative and imperfect. But he wasn't a neutron. His vibes touched everyone who came in contact with him, attracting some and repelling others. His was a physical being that mattered.

MARY BARNARD

WILLIAM CARLOS WILLIAMS AND THE POETRY ARCHIVE AT BUFFALO

These pages are excerpted from *Assault on Mt. Helicon: A Literary Memoir*, to be published in 1983 by the University of California Press.

The Poetry Collection at the Lockwood Memorial Library was the first of its kind, so far as I know; that is, it was the first archive set up for books, manuscripts and letters of modern and in most cases still living poets. (Chronologically the Collection began with Yeats's first volume, and Yeats was still living when the Collection began to take shape.) It was also the first to solicit working manuscripts that showed the process of composition. It would be difficult to say which of these two aspects of the Collection excited the most ridicule. The English were the first to double up with laughter; there was even a cartoon in *Punch*. To the English the joke was all the better because the manuscripts were to be collected in a city with the barbarous name of Buffalo. They found the whole idea simply hilarious and have not yet stopped poking fun at the quaint American notion of what constitutes a scholarly archive. While attempting to put myself to sleep last night with an English detective story, I came upon this: "American universities have fallen on hard times. Most of them have stopped buying second-rate authors' cast-off underwear." Honor Tracy has written a whole novel about an impecunious writer who was busy manufacturing a "working manuscript" of his last book. Ah well, yes. We were asking for papers that would otherwise have gone into the trash basket.

The idea that it was part of a university's business to collect materials for research into the work of modern poets was as strange (not to say scandalous) to most American professors, including those on the University of Buffalo campus, as it was to the British. No self-respecting scholar would think of wasting his time on living writers. Charles Abbott himself believed that the

Collection would come into its own "perhaps in a hundred years." The scholars would begin to come when we were long gone, he said, but the time to collect materials was the present. He was collecting for posterity. Living poets would one day be dead, the present would have become the past, the scholars would eventually become interested, and by that time the materials they needed would be much more difficult and expensive to obtain. This was surely true. The fifty dollars we paid for Williams's little pamphlet called simply *Poems* (Rutherford, 1909) seemed fantastic even to me, but thirty-five years later the same book sold at auction for sixteen thousand.

I began my work as the first curator of the Collection forty-three years ago, on August 8, 1939. Charles Abbott had recently returned from England with a plentiful supply of letters and manuscripts not yet catalogued and filed. The book collection was still in the Librarian's study. Besides cataloguing and filing the accumulation of letters and manuscripts, I was supposed to write letters, and in some cases my personal and professional correspondence overlapped. It must have been in a Christmas letter to William Carlos Williams, whom I had first met in 1936, that I mentioned the manuscripts we hoped to get from him. He replied cordially on January 8, 1940, saying,

> ...thank you for a friendly letter and I wish you might be filing away scripts of mine as you should be if I had any to send you. I have a lot of junk lying around which I can bale up and dump on your lap if you want it but I can't imagine that it will be of use to anybody. Anything you want, ask for it. It's yours—with one or two exceptions, such as the script of the second volume of White Mule, now in the writing. I've promised that.

A few months later, in the spring of 1940, Williams arrived in Buffalo to give a lecture and reading. He and Flossie, like other visiting poets, stayed with the Abbotts at Gratwick Highlands, the first of the many visits they were to make there over the next twenty years. Visiting poets and household crises, I was to learn, were apt to go hand in hand, but Mrs. Abbott reported that she found the Williamses, following hard on the heels of the Wyndham Lewises, "very restful." For a while we had feared they would be there together, a possibility I didn't like to contemplate. In a letter to my parents, I said:

> One new complication is that the Lewises are going to stay until next Tuesday or Wednesday, which means the Abbotts will be entertaining them and the Williamses at the same time. I should think the Williamses would be very easy to entertain, but how Wyndham and William will hit it off at the same dinner table is another question. They're both friends of Ezra's, but that would give me qualms as quick as aything. I'm pretty

sure Williams wouldn't take offense—or at least would have too much respect for his host to take offense—at anything Lewis would say, but Lewis is awfully touchy and likely to fly off the handle at something Williams is most likely to say—because he's impetuous and certainly doesn't weigh well his words before he speaks, though he's willing to laugh almost anything off, himself.

As it turned out, I needn't have worried, since the Lewises left early, but I was also nervous about the lecture. This was the first time I had ever heard Williams perform in public. His coming had been partly my doing, and I was on edge about how the evening would turn out. He had read a few poems one evening when I was at Rutherford, probably when I was there with Fred Miller, and I had not thought he did them justice by any means. Mrs. Williams apparently felt that he did not read well, because she said, "Oh, no!" when he offered to read to us. I knew that he had done very few public lectures or readings up to that time, although on this trip he was appearing at Penn State, Dartmouth and Middlebury. My chief concern, however, was whether anyone would show up. At this time the Buffalo Public Library contained not a single volume of his work, poetry or prose, and interest in modern poetry (by anybody) was almost non-existent on the University of Buffalo campus outside the second floor of the library. All in all, I was afraid the audience would be limited to a handful of people who would wonder why he was there. Again I need not have worried. My next letter home reported that the evening was a success:

The lecture was good. I was afraid he'd be nervous, which he was, and that that would make him stiff, as it does some people, instead of natural, but he very successfully got rid of his own nervousness and the audience's stiffness by being very natural indeed and he had everybody laughing at least half the time I should think. The crowd was respectable, and certainly seemed to like him. When he mentioned quitting—drawing to a close, some girl behind me whom I didn't know, said "Oh, no, no!" very fervently. Most of the time he read from his poems. At the end, instead of asking whether there were any questions, as they usually do Mr. Abbott said anyone with questions should come up and ask them personally. He won't do it again. A group of students, a large group, and I'm sure not from U.B. (never saw any of them before and I can't imagine where on earth they came from) literally mobbed him and wouldn't leave. Mr. Abbott told me enthusiastically that he thought the lecture was "swell" and Dr. Williams inquired whether he had disgraced me and Mrs. Williams invited me to be sure and come to see them next time I came to N.Y. Which I would like to do, but I wonder when I'd squeeze it in.

My trips to New York were not so frequent as I would have liked, but were combined with library business so that I had a little expense money and a longer time to stay. The library business eventually took me out to Rutherford again, not just for an after-noon call, but for a visit of several days. One segment of the Collection that had become my own particular domain was composed of little magazines: *The New Freewoman*, and its successor *The Egoist*, *transition*, *Broom*, *The Little Review*, *Others*, *Exile*, *Blast*, *This Quarter*, and a great many more. Some were intermittent, most were short-lived, and all our runs were gap-toothed. Filling in the gaps became my responsibility. I soon realized that if we attempted to supply the missing issues from book catalogues the prices would bankrupt us. I suggested, therefore, that when I went to New York for a week-end, I might take an extra day and see what I could find on Fourth Avenue. My first tour of second-hand bookstores, though brief, was so profitable that from that time on I combined magazine-hunting with pleasure every time I went to New York. It was dirty work, but fun. For the only time in my life I experienced the collector's itch. If we had six issues of a magazine that ran for seven issues, the thought of that missing number 4 or 5, or whatever it was, plagued me until the run was complete.

When I was in search of defunct little magazines, I was haunted by the thought of all that I had seen in the Williams attic the first time I went out to Rutherford. We proposed to the doc-tor that he sell us the lot, but he said that he wanted to go through them and keep any issues in which he had published stories or poems, and he saw no hope of getting around to it soon. With the entry of the United States into World War II and the mobilization of doctors, that hope receded still further. Finally a solution was found: *I* was to do the job. Naturally, I was delighted. I looked forward both to the work and the week-end I would spend at 9 Ridge Road.

One very hot Saturday afternoon in June of 1942 I went to Rutherford, taking my suitcase, and moved into one of the spare bedrooms. (Bill was in the Navy, in California, and Paul was work-ing for Republic Steel in Canton, Ohio.) My next letter home had a full report on the week-end. I wrote that after I had washed off the grime,

> we had a delicious dinner with chicken and trimmings, and sat out in the back yard admiring the roses until the mosquitoes got bad, and then came in and drank iced lemonade with stalks of mint in it until bedtime. It was terribly hot until morning, and I kept tossing around thinking how hot it would be in the at-tic, but a cool breeze blew up around seven o'clock. There were windows in each end of the attic, with the breeze sweeping through, so I didn't suffer...All day Sunday I worked in the attic.

In the morning I sorted magazines and books. There's an enormous amount of material, and it was all scattered. Vol. I, No. 1 in a book case, Vol. I, No. 2 in a trunk, Vol. I, No. 3 in a desk drawer, another copy of Vol. I, No. 3 under a table, and so on and so on. I sorted one magazine from the other, books from magazines, and things we were interested in from the things we weren't. It was dirty, but I had fun. After lunch the doctor came up with me, and we both sorted, and he began to get out letters. By that time I was down to making lists, so I wrote and he read letters to me. If the lists are right, it's a miracle, because I was so interested in the letters. As for giving them to us, first he would, and then he wouldn't, and then he didn't know. I think what finally threw a monkey wrench into the business, was Mrs. Williams' putting her foot down, with the result that I came away with only two letters, but very good ones, one from Pound about 1907, one from H.D. when she was working on the *Egoist* in 1916. We may get others later.

The magazines are less important, but I found a lot of things we need. The duplicates I know he'll let us have. Some of the others we may get, and in any case, I know about a lot of magazines I didn't know about before—what's in them, and what we need. That information in itself is so hard to get. Monday I finished my lists and did some more rooting around in the grime, turning up things I had missed the first time.

I worked at a big table by the window at the front end of the house. From that window I looked down to the sidewalk. On Monday, every time I glanced out I saw the same scene: a baby carriage, empty, was sitting in front of the house; another baby carriage (occupied) was approaching; another was just rolling away out of sight around the bend of the street. It went on all day long. On Monday morning the Williamses suggested that instead of going back to New York, I should remain in Rutherford and commute until time to return to Buffalo. They were so cordial that I gave in easily, and stayed on for several more nights. Monday evening we had a blackout that lasted about twenty minutes. Williams had to rush for the schoolhouse, which served as first aid station, and Mrs. Williams and I went upstairs and watched for a searchlight display which didn't happen.

At Christmas time that same year I paid a call on Bill and Flossie and, to my surprise, came back to Buffalo with a big carton of letters. Writing of this event, I said:

I think we now have most of the Williams letters. He said he might as well give them to us, because if he died, well, Flossie would be interested for a while, but then (so-and-so) or (so-and-so) might come around and carry them off, and he'd rather we had them. Besides, I think I've sold him on the idea that having his things in our library is just like having a private secretary. I've looked up and copied several things he couldn't find, have an order to do another one, and he is even thinking of sending us

all his magazines, with poems he would like to anthologize checked
for me to copy and compile. It seems that's why he's holding
them, and he'll *never* get around to it without help.

I believe I was mistaken in thinking that we already had most
of the Williams letters at that time. Others came later. Besides giving us manuscripts, letters and magazines, by the time I left Buffalo in 1943 Bill had also filled in two of the worst gaps in our
book collection by selling us his copy of Pound's first volume,
A Lume Spento ("I'll buy a War Bond!" he said), and finding a
Rutherford friend who was willing to sell us his copy of Bill's
Poems, 1909. Of course none of us had any idea of the fantastic
prices those books would some day bring.

EDITH HEAL BERRIEN

MEMORY IS A SORT OF RENEWAL

"Memory is a sort of renewal," William Carlos Williams said in *Paterson II*. This little line might have served as an epigraph for our meetings during the poet's seventy-third year in the making of the little book, *I Wanted to Write a Poem*. I had walked through the big front door of 9 Ridge Road, always open to friends and poets, with a selfish request. I needed a subject for an essay required by Columbia for the M.A. I was working for. (Flossie said ruefully that people were always getting Ph.D.s and M.A.s with Bill doing all the work.) When I told Bill what I wanted, an account of the writing experience of a lifetime, a sort of notebook by recall of a writer in the act of being a writer, he said, "You're going to make me work."

I call him "Bill" because our acquaintance dated back to informal occasions in the little town of Rutherford where we both lived, at parties where he willingly read his poetry for us, and at mutual birthday celebrations where Flossie baked the cake. There was a dinner party with Flossie's admirable beef stew where my husband, Stephen Berrien, presented her with a silver tray he had won at a golf tournament. This brought a letter from Bill (copied here without the typographical errors!)

Dear Steve:

It was very nice of you to want to celebrate our cooperation in what we are cooperating in: our success or successes in our joint efforts, Edith's and mine. The silver tray is a useful decoration, when our titled acquaintances call they can leave their cards on it or go to hell—which is what you intended from the first. But since we have few titled acquaintances we'll serve canapes on it when the occasion arises. Meanwhile it will represent for us your excellence at a sport which is, I know, dear to your heart but doesn't mean a damned thing to me which brings us together as it should be with gentlemen.

Affectionately,
Bill

His letters were typed at a rolicking rate, without regard to typos in spelling and punctuation gone wrong. I was told that Ezra Pound followed the same pattern. On the other hand, his poetry was written and rewritten to the perfection he expected of it. He offers a lesson in craftsmanship. People who have seen his originals in the Lockwood Library at Buffalo have noted the many revisions, first jotted down on prescription blanks, followed by the normal pruning process, getting rid of redundancies in the line in the attempt to make it go faster.

While he believed in spontaneity—he wrote when he read my novel, *the shadow boxers*, "Let yourself go...piss and piss and piss"...yet he was the greatest rewriter of them all. What appears to be unbridled spontaneity was often worked and reworked, with enormous labor. And speaking of labor, in one of his recordings, he compared the birth of a baby with the birth of a poem.

And speaking of babies, oh how he loved them! I shall never forget, the combination of gaiety and gentleness in his voice as he said, "I was crazy about babies, the contempt all babies have for adults. They don't give a damn what goes on and they let go with everything they have and sometimes it's not too attractive. I was saying to myself with every baby I saw, 'Okay, baby—carry on, because I'm going to write you down.' " And so he arrived at the *White Mule*. "I'd heard a lot about Flossie's babyhood from her family and I thought it was a good true picture of a baby. Why not write about Floss's babyhood, combining all the material I had learned about her with all that I had learned about babies." Later, in the sequel *In The Money*, there is a wonderful monologue of a baby frightened and "touched by the night"—surely an epiphany of all our lost childhoods. One reviewer said, "The baby steals the show."

As a baby doctor in Rutherford and near-by towns, he was known to each mother as a personal friend and often his prescriptions said—this or that is what Floss uses...no need to pay money to a drugstore. They loved him, swore by him, often could not pay him. Some of them typed his manuscripts and learned that each page must mirror his version exactly.

White Mule, as a title, was, as many of his titles were, the nearest he came to symbolism. "The devil was in me. What should I call the book? Then it came to me, *White Mule*. Floss, I knew was a mule and she was white. There was another meaning. At that time, during the Depression, we were drinking White Mule. Floss was like a shot of whisky to me, her disposition cantankerous like all women, riding her man for his own good whether he liked it or not."

He was fascinated by titles and talked to me a lot about them. *Sour Grapes* was a snub to the world who ignored his poetry ...because sour grapes are as beautiful as ripe ones. *First Act* had a double meaning...he said he meant to put the emphasis on *Act*. *Make Light of It*, he said, should emphasize the word *Light*...a glimpse into deeper meanings. *The Knife of the Times* is an apt title for the book of the poor during the Depression.

And speaking of titles. While I was working with him, he showed me a Ms called *Your Grandmother, my Sons*. Both Floss and I questioned the title...somehow it suggested *his* grandmother rather than the boys'. I'm not sure how the title got changed to *Yes, Mrs. Williams*. Young Dr. Williams said it was a form of politeness he used toward all women.

An interesting side of him was his querulous, even angry, reactions to any possible change any of his typists might make in the form of lines on a page...the spacing and punctuation (when there was punctuation) had to be exactly as he wrote it. He came as near to irritation with me when I presumed too much. He had allowed me to make excerpts from the manuscript *Your Grandmother, my Sons* for the first issue of *The Literary Review*, a little magazine published by Fairleigh Dickinson University. I called the vignettes, "From Notes About My Mother." I was so enchanted with the idea, I suggested to him that we make a little book of vignettes which seemed to me to suit perfectly the wanderings of his mother. He wrote me a frantic letter:

> Whatever you do with the notes on my mother I handed you last week, keep the originals intact—including my title for them: *Your Grandmother, My Sons*. Make copies of them, push them around as you please, we may adopt your version in the final draft but I don't want to lose the first alignment of any part of it, including the canceled versions which I included with the others... I didn't quite go along with you about a "small book.''...I decided at the time to think that over. We'll have to go slow, giving me time to study the matter.

Another letter came to me, with an impatient, "Send me back Lena—in the two parts. She has to be dressed for a party." I had taken the piece, a very short story, to *Vogue* where I worked. The feature editor said the story did not even fill a page and could the poet add more. Which he did. But before the editor had time to decide about publication, Bill sent the hurry call to get Lena back. He went on to say in his letter:

> Editors are queer fry, they remind me of the angler (fish) with a little flag fastened before their heads (by their bosses) which they have to follow. But they're often nice. But I do want Lena back,

especially the first part which is a unique copy, as quickly as possible. No matter who has it, take it away and send it to me quickly if you can do so without too much putting yourself out.

The letter was signed "sincerely" instead of the usual "affectionately."

He liked being asked to be judge of a Creative Writing Contest held at the college. But typically, he gave first place to a story called "The Party"...about a bunch of kids drinking up all the beer in the house when their parents were away. It was plotless but not formless. All colloquial conversation, with a last line when the mother came home, "It's all gone, boys. My goodness you people drank a whole case. A whole case."

Naturally the judges picked a story with plot as the winner, so the story Bill picked was only a runner-up. Bill must have liked the dialogue and the repetition at the end. He often used the trick of echoes, himself,

> "I am lonely, lonely
> I was born to be lonely, . . ."
> (Danse Russe)

and the joyous motion in "The Dance":

> In Breughel's great picture, The Kermess,
> the dancers go round, they go round and
> around . . .

Floss was a dominant figure in our meetings during that long hot summer. She trusted me with the key to her secretary where first editions were kept, so that when she and Bill went on a trip I could view each book by myself. She was, as always, a woman of straight talk. When Bill said, dramatically, "Nobody would publish me," she answered, "Everybody was publishing you...all the little magazines." "But not *Poetry*," he said. "Not what *you* sent...but I sent them six and they published them all."

He has said that three determined women determined his fate: his mother, his grandmother and his wife. His relationship with Floss was so close that they almost spoke in unison when a point was made. Once there was a disagreement and he lashed out at her. She said, "Bill, you shouldn't talk to me like that." And he answered in the most gentle voice in the world, "Darling, you're right."

JOHN G. DOLLAR

WILLIAM CARLOS WILLIAMS
AND THE POLYTOPIC CLUB

So complete has been the identification of Dr. Williams with avant-garde movements in poetry and art on the one side, and with the raw vigor of lower middle class and immigrant New Jerseyites on the other, that his own upper middle-class background has often been neglected. We are accustomed to seeing programs that show Williams against the smokestacks and factories of industrial New Jersey, and we are even told in one of the newest books on Williams that he comes from the industrial town of Rutherford.

With this impression of the poet, one comes to Rutherford and is surprised to find that not only does the town have no industry, but it doesn't even have any taverns. In fact, it is an old-fashioned town, with tall elms and maples and oaks. The yards bloom with the flowers that Dr. Williams loved, and the houses are set in clusters of azaleas, rhododendrons, and forsythia. The town itself has many large, turn-of-the-century homes, with large porches, little second-story balconies, unused and perhaps unusable, and little wooden turrets, which modestly imitate from afar aristocratic splendor. And on one of the most spacious streets in town, across from the Gothic Presbyterian Church, at 9 Ridge Road, lived Dr. Williams and his wife.

The town at its inception had hoped to be a kind of Tuxedo Park, a home for millionaires. It even had a castle in its center. But even though it has never lived up to such pretensions, it did have old and prosperous families, some even going back to colonial days and beyond, to the Dutch settlement of the Hudson. Inevitably, the town attracted intellectual and cultural societies, the most distinguished of these early clubs being the Fortnightly Club. Mr. and Mrs. Paul Herman, the parents of Flossie Williams, belonged to this club, and in Chapter 18 of the *Build-Up* Dr. Williams described a typical meeting of the club, at which the best people in town, the men in tuxedos and the ladies in evening gowns, gathered for an evening of music, art, and fun at the home of the mayor.

In 1916 ten Rutherford couples, including Dr. and Mrs. Williams, as well as Mr. and Mrs. Edgar Williams, started a new club, modeled on the Fortnightly, but more irreverent. The meetings were to be held once a month from October to May at the homes of various members. The president would be chosen irrespective of sex, though the first and only lady president was not elected until 1940 when Naarni Stetler was chosen president and given a rolling pin as a gavel. The programs would range over any topic of· human interest. At the meeting the men would appear in tuxedos and the women in evening gowns. Only once was there an attempt to change the dress standards. In 1921 Mr. Stetler wrote an article on the "Why Not's of a Dress Suit." "Mr. Stetler's ideas were not kindly received by the feminine members of the club and after considerable discussion pro and con no formal action was taken and the dress suit remains with us."¹

At the first regular meeting of the club "papers had been prepared setting forth both sides of a political situation. Mr. Quinton then read an able and interesting paper in support of Mr. Hughes, followed by an equally convincing paper in support of President Wilson. After a friendly discussion of the facts as stated, dainty refreshments were served by the hostess and a pleasant social hour concluded the successful first meeting of our club." At the second meeting "Dr. Williams read a comprehensive and entertaining paper on Modern Poetry." But the Minutes do not elaborate on the details of this paper.

During the next three years the club held meetings on Irish drama, epileptics, government ownership, G. B. Shaw, tiger hunting in China, mahjong, Dante, the high cost of living, James Whitcomb Riley, Franz Liszt, and *Kora in Hell*, the speaker being usually some expert from outside the club. At every meeting musical selections were played, and music became especially important after 1924, when Mrs. Madeleine Spence, an expert pianist with a repertory from Bach to nonsense, joined the club. Every meeting ended in a social hour when "dainty refreshments" were served.

One of the first problems facing the club was a name. Suggestions came from all the members: The Lunarites, The Klever Klub, The Rutherford Research Society, St. Paul (all things to all men), and The Assorted Nuts. But as none of the names suggested

1. All quotations in this paper are taken from the Minutes of the Polytopic Club. All materials from the Minutes relevant to Dr. Williams are to be found both in the Rutherford Public Library and The Fairleigh Dickinson University Library, Rutherford.

seemed appropriate, a committee was formed to recommend a name. The committee, in fact, came up with two names: The Polytopic Club and R.A.N. (The Rutherford Assorted Nuts). Two months later the unanimous choice of a name was The Polytopic Club.

Though the club was basically serious, it always had a flavor of the Rutherford Assorted Nuts about it, especially at Christmas time when a Christmas party was usually held. In 1922 "the Christmas meeting of the Polytopic was held at the home of Dr. and Mrs. Williams on Saturday night. . . . Elizabeth and Lee then presided as host and hostess, and did themselves proud in entertaining the children. The costumes were fearlessly and wonderfully made and worn, and each one excelled the other. Prizes were awarded to Louise and Edmund as Huckleberry Finn and Little Boy Blue. Second childhood reigned supreme: Games of all sorts were played and enjoyed, and the children had lollipops with their games. The tree was lighted for the good little children, and they found cornucopias with candy in them. They had ice cream and cake, and coffee and nuts, and there seemed no lack anywhere. Every child received a present," which was something clever and cheap from the Five and Ten, "and the whole affair was a great success. The Heckmans deserve a vote of thanks, for a wonderful time was had by all. The Williams deserve some credit, for it was in their house that the children played." In 1924 "Edgar [Williams] Santa Claus then gave out the presents and each little girl and boy skipped up and received just what he had asked for." Again the presents were cheap and clever. The next year Edgar composed a giant crossword puzzle "gorgeously illuminated." But "the marvel of the whole thing really dawned upon the crowd as the puzzle neared completion," for "all the names of the club members were incorporated in the overlaps." It was a great success. We thank Bill and Florence for the many hours devoted to that piece of work. With our presents (costly and rare)" again from the Five and Ten, "which Santa Claus graciously left under the Williams' tree there was much merriment."

The most elaborate of the Christmas festivities occurred in 1930, when a group of Polytopicers calling themselves The Tyro Theatre Group put on three plays for the club's amusement, complete with a playbill announcing William Carlos Williams, Producer, and Andrew Spence, Manager. According to the Minutes "now it seemed that the committee was mentally wearied and bodily fatigued by the Christmas rush and decided to call a doctor—our own Dr. Williams, in fact; he being a writer also, prescribed plays, and so the stage was set in one end of the Donaldson living room and the curtain opened on Bill and Flossie" entering from different sides of the stage, Bill's face completely covered with shaving cream and Flossie's face hidden under a mud pack. Suddenly they faced each other and found they were both hidden in masks. They acted out "a very natural little sketch from the life of a husband and wife, entitled 'Intimate Strangers' (A GroTesQue in onE SittIng)—it might have been a sketch from any married couples' lives except that the arguments were somewhat more literary. This was followed by Hulda [Mrs. Edgar Williams] as the Dowager returning from the Opera, dressed in the elegant attire of 1890. . . . Next on the program came a play entitled 'Les Americans or What Have You (A Parisian Cafe Klotch),' satirizing the American traveler in Paris. The scene opened on Edgar and Drew representing a head waiter and chasseur in a Parisian Cafe Klotch called 'Le Pere Tranquil,' as was manifest by a huge poster and huge menu-cards decorated for the occasion by our able architect and artist. These two are plotting how to get the most money out of gullible Americans that patronize their shop. As they are scheming, in come Flossie and Madeleine—two hard-boiled American women who are 'doing Paris.' When asked their order they demand 'Deux Ombs (one boiled and the other stewed)' and some mineral water, much to the chagrin of the headwaiter who is looking for big money. His desire is fulfilled, however, when in come Earl and Russel Robinson and the two Louises, trying their best to look like multi-millionaires; and Earl, in his inimitable French orders everything the waiter suggests from Oysters to Champagne with much emphasis on the 'Sham Pain.' Flossie and Madeleine immediately size up the two men as 'possibilities' and ask the waiter if these are their 'Ombs' (Hommes). The curtain falls with the waiter nodding 'yes, Madame, but they are not quite ready yet—a little patience, Madame!' "

The exuberance of spirits created by this program carried over into the February meeting when a whole group of puppet plays were put on for the entertainment of the club. Edgar Williams had constructed a puppet theatre complete with a special backdrop for each play. "During the business meeting we had been gazing upon a very professional-looking, miniature stage, so we were not surprised when programs were distributed disclosing the fact that the entertainment was to be a puppet show. 'Polytopic Puppets' was the official title but 'Seeing Ourselves as Others See Us' is a little more descriptive of the performance: and there followed a sketch from the lives of each and every couple in the club. Yes, we were all there—clothed characteristically and performing as the committee would have us! The care and precision with which every detail of scenery, stage settings and costumes had been worked out, merits the highest praise; and the committee and their husbands deserve to go down in the records as providing one of the best entertainments ever enjoyed by the Polytopic Club. . . . It is a great temptation to repeat in detail every sketch as produced—they were all so good—but time and space compel me to recall only the ones of such astonishing significance as Grace and Raymond Silvers setting out to clean Hell; and Florence Donaldson finding a similarity in the Bible-reading to some of Bill Williams' modern literature!"

For this program Dr. Williams wrote his own little playlet called

THE DOCTOR'S DILEMMA

(The curtain goes up on a dark stage, with sounds of snoring. There are three wall telephones, one of which is starting ringing. Light increases gradually, showing a double bed, with two occupants. The wife answers.)

She   Hello! He's not in, hasn't been in for some time, and I do not expect him. . . . (a pause) Well, is he dying?

He   (hissing) Creosote! Creosote!

She   Well, the regular treatment for that is a creosote tablet with a half a glass of water. Repeat occasionally if not dead and apply hot towels to the face and feet. (Hangs up)

       (second telephone rings—she answers it) No, he won't be in this week, but I expect him next Tuesday evening. What is it? He swallowed a five dollar gold piece?! In these times! Well a half a creosote——

He   (jumping out of bed, tearing off the covers and leaping to the phone) Wait a minute. I'll handle this case. (Takes the phone) Was it a good five? You have not called anyone else, have you? I'll be right down there with a can opener and a stomach pump! (Hangs up) I'll take this case on "spec" and for once be sure to get the fee right out of the patient! (exits hastily)

She   (third telephone having rung) No, he just left on an important surgical case, where a large amount of money is involved. He may never come back, but a half a creosote tablet in a glass of water generally proves effective in such cases. What's your address?

CURTAIN

For the finale of the program Madeleine banged out a piece called "The Two Room Blues" in which the women of the club lamented that the men were always going off to themselves and leaving the women "neglected in the dining room." Each verse ended with a chorus:

> Get asked and join the Polytopic
> Parlor TOPICS, POLYFLOPICS
> You must have five a year to pay your dues
> You must have brains to prove you're not coo coos
> Some go to business, others chase the muse
> Polyglotic Polywogs.

The minutes are strewn with poetry like this, all of it showing a strong, rollicking, old-fashioned beat.

For the Christmas celebration of 1933 Dr. Williams was himself the entertainment. "The business meeting was then declared adjourned and the punch bowl was soon emptied. . . . The speaker thought the members needed to see a new face and hear some new things as he feared they might be getting in a rut, so in a moment by the aid of an attachable moustache he transformed himself and a strong resemblance to Herr Hitler was seen. By a series of questions and answers the club was enlightened along various lines and but for the fact that part of the speech was lost or froze up on the way to the meeting, all might have been very wise people before the evening was over. As it was, some interesting facts were learned about the eyes of men and animals. As an interlude Dr. Williams read parts of 'Pig and Pepper' from *Alice in Wonderland* and closed his informative program by reading an article on Child Psychology from the *American Mercury*."

For the next Christmas celebration, "Dr. Williams explained that he had arranged a trio, with Florence at the piano, himself playing obligatos for the violin, composed by Madeleine. He added as an afterthought that his 'brother was singing the solos.' The interesting family group rendered 'God Rest Ye Merry, Gentlemen,' and 'The Holly and the Ivy.' They started rather timidly but gained assurance as they proceeded." Later in the program, a poem by Harriet Bush, entitled "A Christmas Raving" was read. In this poem Mrs. Bush told of a vision in which all the Polytopic members came to her and demanded what they wanted for Christmas. Each member was given appropriate gifts, but only gifts beginning with the first letter of his name. Dr. Williams was given a whole set of *w's*:

> · "Wistfully," whined Willie Williams,
> "I have wished for worlds of things—
> Whistles, wine, and watermelon,

What I worstly want is wings—
For although you may not know it
Wings would be a wondrous help to
Any rising poet."
So I gave them to him gladly, tho' I
          really could not see,
Just how wings would be an aid to
Such a realist as he."

In January 1933 Dr. Williams was in charge of an Ancestors Meeting. The Committee had handed out a brochure at the previous meeting, complete with escutcheon, stating that every member of the club was to give at least a five minute talk on his ancestors. The Minutes do not indicate anything about the meeting itself. "But after the tooting was over, Dr. Williams called for food and food forth came. Hurrah for the Polytopicus!"

Usually unrestrained merriment was reserved for Christmas, but on other rare occasions meetings were devoted to sheer delight. Often Halloween went by without any notice. But the Halloween party in 1936 gives the following picture of Dr. Williams: "The program opened with a short sketch of the history of Halloween, followed by the sepulcral reading of the witches' scene from *Macbeth*. This was accompanied by a shadow pantomine so realistic that we still feel no enthusiasm for restaurant soup. Then our host gave us the tale of a small town boy who arrived in the big city and finally made good in the show business—one Will Shakespeare. Like Steve Brody or Jack Dempsey he capitalized on his name by opening a corner tavern and dispensing good cheer with his poetry. With her usual vivacity and flawless technique Mrs. Spence then played us the Overture from *Othello*—on the phonograph. Dr. Williams thinly disguised as Othello brutally murdered Mrs. Desdemona Silvers and the party took an intermission while the corpse was being dragged out. . . . The refreshments were consumed with a gnashing of teeth quite in keeping with the blood-thirsty evening."

And just one last note about the doctor at play. In 1937 Dr. Williams was made chairman of a special committee to suggest ways of spending the club's funds. The Minutes indicate that the president "appointed Bill Williams, Madeleine Spence, Ethyl Tamblyn, and finally evidently realizing such a committee would only talk co-ops he added Gertrude Irvine. No name was given to this committee by the president but the rest of the club was heard to mutter among themselves something about the 'dregs of society.' The committee was actually formed to recommend to the club ways that it might spend its accumulated funds." Instead of reporting two or, at the most, three suggestions, Williams wrote a three page, single-spaced report with over twenty suggestions. The committee had actually made so many suggestions, he wrote, because "it was felt in the first place that the committee did not represent the full mature opinion of our membership. On the contrary it was stated that the committee was composed, as aptly stated by one of us, of the dregs of the club so that it would more become us to humbly submit our inadequate opinions and await further instructions before proceeding. While awaiting the club's pleasure a proposal was made that we invest the entire treasury at a safe margin in some standard stock as against the expected rise of the market in April. . . ." The committee then made a number of sensible suggestions:

1. That the club subscribe to a pair of balcony seats at the opera to be used serially by the club members.
2. that we go as a club to see Ed Wynn in *Horray for What?*
3. or to Madison Square Garden for a hockey match with supper before or after.
4. that we buy sweepstake tickets for individual members of the club, the club as a whole to retain a 50% communal interest in each ticket or part thereof, should anyone by a miraculous chance win anything.

But mixed in with the sensible suggestions were a number of others calculated to set the company in a roar:

1. that the club buy a ceremonial robe for the president consisting of a full Sioux Indian regalia to be worn at the first meeting of the year.
2. that the club present a liberal bonus to that couple presenting the club with its first female progeny provided the name Poly Topic be chosen for it or if a boy the initials P.T.
3. [and finally in desperation] that we put the money in an iron pot and bury it somewhere.

Williams put every aspect of his personality into his writings except his humor, and that he kept for his friends and family alone.

Though the activities of the club were mostly serious, much of what was recorded about Williams had to do with fun and jollity. The reason for this is that secretaries record what is humorous in great detail and pass over what is serious with vague generalities. Dr. Williams' talks, for example, on modern poetry or on Mrs. Sanger and birth control are mentioned simply as occurring. There are no details given. But his serious interest in the local scene is apparent throughout the minutes. One of the earliest talks he gave to the club was "on the work being done by the Bergen County Mosquito Commission. Dr. Williams was most interesting, and showed some splendid before-and-after pictures, giving us a very good idea of the surprising amount of work that has been accomplished." When, at a later meeting, the speaker told of Boystown and the greatness of Father Flanagan, "at the conclusion of the talk Dr. Williams called our attention to a home of junior delinquents right in our own county and suggested we get acquainted with it." Dr. Williams, in fact, was almost the only one in the club who kept referring to the local scene. When a lawyer did some outstanding work in a jury-fixing trial in Passaic, Dr. Williams asked the club to acknowledge his work. "A motion was made and carried that the secretary in collaboration with Dr. Williams write Mr. Carpenter a letter of congratulations and appreciation."

But the most colorful account of Dr. Williams' interest in the local scene had to do with the East Rutherford Day Nursery: "The Secretary here asked each member of the club to give ten cents to the East Rutherford Day Nursery. Dr. Williams moved that the club give five dollars to this cause. It being brought to the attention of the members that Dr. Williams preferred spending $5.00 of the club's money to ten cents of his own, this motion was lost. Dr. Williams at once challenged the club members, and said that he would give fifty cents if anyone else would. After much discussion Mr. Wagner moved that each member give ten cents, and the club give ten cents per member in addition. This motion was carried. There being twenty-one members the sum would total $4.20. Mr. Higbee here arose and said that though not a member of this club it would afford him great pleasure to contribute eighty cents, thus bringing the amount up to five dollars. This offer was unanimously accepted. It is to be hoped that hostesses in the future will emulate the example set by Mrs. Quinton, and invite to our meetings people who are as good scouts as Mr. Higbee. Several members called Dr. Williams' bluff, with the result that this secretary collected ($7.00) seven dollars for this charity."

The last important reference to Williams occurred in the Minutes in 1951. A Mr. Anspaugh had given a slide lecture on his trip down the Colorado River in the Grand Canyon. The secretary did not feel that she could do justice to this talk and asked Dr. Williams to write that part of the minutes. He gave her a four page essay, which was read at the next meeting, put into the minutes, and promptly forgotten by everyone. Here is the essay:

NAVAHO COUNTRY

The River Rat according to Mr. Anspaugh, who showed us his stereoscopic pictures of the Grand Canyon last March, is a special order of the human species. There are not many of them, a hundred or so who have gone through the hazardous initiation, more than two hundred who are known to have failed, several at the cost of their lives. We are speaking of the whole trip, the complete passage from Arizona Point to Lake Mead. The San Juan River Canyon is easier and parts of the Colorado Gorge itself, which taken in three stages can be negotiated without too much danger, but the River Rat at his best, considers the whole trip the real test.

You can see it's a mystical ordeal as well as a physical one. It's serious, it's useless. That's the spirit of the Navaho himself, that's what gives all humanity its dignity. That's what we live for. It is the antithesis of the dope peddler, the political thief, the coward walking up to his waist in a muck of money.

The River is the antagonist, a godlike quality that brings out all the qualities of the Rat, the devotee; the man or woman who submits himself to the guide, gets into the boat and starts downstream. The loyalty of the tribe starting out in search of its winter pasturage, the dependence one upon the other like the Indian, comes to life again in these creatures who, fed up with the world we live in, go there to be scoured clean for a few weeks, twenty-nine days of ablutions at the bottom of the grandiose canyon where the river has been eating out a bed for five or ten million years. The water is itself 60% sand to grind away not only the sandstone of the region itself but in the same way to rinse, scour the spirits of the River Rat until it comes at the end clean again.

The cat's paw, the thorny ocotillo showing tall canes lined with flowers but no leaves, a few ferns red as the sand itself, or a girl or young man standing among the rocks represented all the foliage of the place. The rest of the 6,000 foot deep canyon was rock eroded in every imaginable and unimaginable shape, arches and caverns out of which sometimes ran narrow, crystal clear streams to the river itself. Far above, known to everyone was the desert on all sides beyond a narrow ledge where the bleached skeleton still lies—minus its head stolen by one of six known souvenir hunters. Higher still an abandoned Indian granary. So that at the bottom of this enormous and savage gorge inhabited by the living there, the Colorado itself, a man feels cloistered, alone, drawn close to those about him for comfort. He cannot get out and live to cross the fiery desert. He cannot go back, upstream. His only hope, and it is a real one, is to go ahead, under guidance to the next landing. Rock surrounds him on all sides, barren rock. The experience is a spiritual one.

Add to this the heat reaching at times 120 degrees or more, though Mr. Anspaugh thought little of it since all one need do was to dip one's shirt in the stream and put it on wet to feel refreshed. But the water being more than half sand, the fresher bath, even though the water might be no more than six inches deep, was a delight when a small stream from the sideshoot to the great canyon was discovered.

There everybody, ladies and all, stretched out in the water. Or trout might be caught and cooked over an open fire. It was a pleasure too to drink fresh water without waiting for the sand to sediment out of it when it was drunk from the open river.

It was never just riding downstream, there were rapids often so dangerous that even the guides didn't dare take the boats through them. Here the boats had to be "lined" as they call it, portaged in short, upstream over the boulders at great cost in sweat and muscle. It would take a whole day at times to get the boats past some particular obstacle before they could be put into the water again.

The really marvelous pictures, when you think of the difficulties under which they were taken, showed all this. The individual members of the party were caught at their tasks or standing at the edge of some cliff. The rapids looking like muddy lace, all the colors of the rocks, the young women going up the rocks of the natural bridge—were all revealed to us. But first we had to put on the special spectacles of polarized lucite or cellophane or whatever it was that made it possible to get the stereoscopic effect which we needed to make the pictures live. Sometimes the special glasses in a paper frame would slip off the nose. At such times if we looked at the screen all we could see would be a jumbled mess as the simultaneous images of the dissimilar pictures, one for the left eye and one for the right, appeared unfused on the screen.

Finally, after the party, looking a bit disheveled and worn, had been burned black by the desert sun, their eyes looking strained from the constant wind and sand encountered from day to day, and no doubt having rested none too well on their air mattresses on the bare rock—the little closely knit band came to the last barrier, a rapids full of explosion waves (the rocks under them) had to be passed by the boats. Loaded.

No chance here to go along the shores, there were none. Just rock walls. Life preservers were adjusted, food was stored. Everyone got in his place and as they shoved off Mr. Anspaugh had his camera in hand poised to take the pictures. It would have been easier in the San Juan canyon. That one is just as picturesque and safer. There if you are thrown into the water all you have to do is to hold your breath when submerged and when your head comes above the surface, take a deep breath waiting for the next submersion—knowing that within a comparatively short time you will be washed up by the stream into shallow water where all you'll have to do is stand up and walk ashore.

But here, as with camera in hand, you faced the explosion waves, three of them one after the other, you weren't so sure of what would follow. And if the boat went under here—it wouldn't be the first fatality that had occurred in this area.

But they went through and lived to tell us the tale.

In the early days many of the club members were sceptical of Dr. Williams' poetical ability. In fact, Flossie told him not to read his poetry any more at the club meetings because some of the members were laughing at the wrong places. But by 1926, when he won the Dial Award for Poetry, the club was beginning to be in admiration of their poet-doctor. His many subsequent honors are recorded with pride, and he is often asked to read from his works.

However, the only work of his described in any detail in the Minutes was *The First President*, which he read to the club in 1938, Madeleine playing appropriate eighteenth century music between the acts.

Williams, on his side, loved the club and became so involved with it that he is mentioned in the Minutes at least four times as often as any other member. But Williams did not use the club members either individually or as a group in his writings. These were his friends, not material for literature. He has only two references that I know of to the club. The first occurs in *I Wanted to Write a Poem*, where, speaking about *Kora in Hell*, he states "when it was all done, I thought of the Prologue, which is really an Epilogue. I felt I had to give some indication of myself to the people I knew; sound off, tell the world—especially my intimate friends—what I thought about them." Many of these "intimate friends" were obviously members of the Polytopic. At the March, 1921, Polytopic meeting, which occurred a few months after the publication of *Kora in Hell*, this new book created a little incident. "The chairman of the entertainment committee was disappointed in his speaker at the last moment, so Dr. Williams gave us an informal talk on 'What is Art and Why is Poetry?' He showed himself to be an exponent of the theory that art is due to the spontaneous combustion and committed to paper for the sole satisfaction of the combustee. He dethroned the poet from the seat of the prophet and preacher and placed him rather in that of the mental photographer. The doctor then illustrated his point with several of his own 'Improvisations,' gracefully suppressing the poetic plates which suffered from over-exposure. General discussion followed but the hostess avoided fatalities by diverting attention to real ice cream and very festive cake and all the trimmings. Finally we all went to bed to see if 'Kora' could counteract coffee. Reports of sleeplessness are now in order." Obviously, Williams was "sounding off" to his "intimate friends" at the Polytopic meeting, and they were sounding off right back.

The second reference to the Polytopic is in *Yes, Mrs. Williams*, where he refers to a meeting that occurred in 1937. "Living in the suburbs as we did, our gang, during the past twenty or thirty years, to relieve the occasional monotony of our lives, formed a group which we called the Polytopic Club. At one time I was elected president of the entertainment committee. I developed the curious idea to have a reading of poems from the masters, but the feature of this reading, this dramatic reading, was to be that it would be in the original language in every case. We had some unexploited talent in the club, as will be seen, my mother among them, more or less as a hanger-on. She loved to listen, but seldom took part in the programs. . . . The Superintendent of schools read from *The Odyssey*, from the original Greek. My brother, who knew his *vero toscano* and could deliver it with distinction, gave a passage from Dante's *Inferno*. . . . We had readings from Shakespeare, from Lope de Vega, from Faust and Bobby Burns from a Scotsman among the club members. Then, the meeting at our house, it came my mother's turn to do her bit. She was almost blind with cataracts, but when I called on her, the room anticipating what was to take place, was intently listening. We could have heard ourselves breathe. Taking her time she delivered, in French, a speech from Corneille ending in the famous curse, 'Rome enfin que je hais!' which left us speechless."[2]

Dr. Williams has been pictured as a lonely man in Rutherford, one whose soul was apart from the suburban scene. The Rutherfordians he talks with are described as dull and without any art in them. In his conversations with them, we are told, "He was there, he was part of it, but quiet, withdrawn."[3] And his poetry reinforces this picture of loneliness in any number of places; for example, in Dance Russe:

> If when my wife is sleeping
> and the baby and Kathleen
> are sleeping
> and the sun is a flame-white disc
> in silken mists
> above shining trees,—
> if I in my north room
> dance naked, grotesquely
> before my mirror
> waving my shirt round my head
> and singing softly to myself:
> "I am lonely, lonely,
> I was born to be lonely,
> I am best so!"

Undoubtedly, Williams was often alienated from the town and its mentality. But the Minutes show him not as a lonely genius withdrawn in a corner, but as a person supremely at home in the Rutherford setting and loving every minute of it. He is usually in the center of activities. When the club members rendezvous before setting off in their cars for a weekend on Long Island, they gather at his house. And during the weekend of swimming, clambakes,

---

2. William Carlos Williams, *Yes, Mrs. Williams* (New York: McDowell, Obelensky), pp. 17-18.
3. Reed Whittemore, *William Carlos Williams: Poet From Jersey* (Boston: Houghton Mifflin Company, 1975), p. 72.

and informal games, the men played quoits, "Mr. Wood and Dr. Williams being the best." At the meetings themselves he often introduces the speaker, and the secretary comments on his "jovial humor, characteristic of the successful physician after a hard case." On another occasion he is referred to as "our gory capitalist, who . . . controls the instruments of production as an obstetrician." He mingles in easy camaraderie with "our gang."

But all things must come to an end. In 1955, at the age of seventy-two, Dr. Williams and his wife resigned from the club and were given honorary membership "in consideration of their long association in and with the Polytopic Club." Today, the club still goes on. The men still wear tuxedos, and "dainty refreshments" are still being served. But there has been lost a little of the fun of the original Rutherford Assorted Nuts. We miss our fellow club member, Dr. Williams.

The Tyro TheAtre Group

presents

3 Plays aNd 2 InterLudeS

*(See Below)

William Carlos Williams, Producer

Andrew Spence, Manager

1.

INTIMATE STRANGERS
(A GroTesQue in onE SittIng)

his WIFE - - - - ‘ * - - - - - - FlosSie
HER HusbaNd - - - - - - - - - ‘ BiLL

2.

INTERLUDE
(The ReturN from tHe Opera – cosTumes of 1870.
WaTch THIS!)

The DowAger - - ‘ - *- - - - - HULDa
Her MaId - - - - - - - - ‘ - - tOPSY

3.

LES AMERICANS or What HAVE YOU?
(A ParIsIan Cafe KLotcH)

HeadWaiter - - ‘ - - - - - - - - EDgar
Older Woman : . . . . FLOssie
Younger Woman - - - - - - - - Madeline
Waiter, Chasseur, etc. - - - - - - DreW
Will - - - - - - - - - - Russel
BILL - - - - - - - - SIR Henry IrvIng
2nd. Older Woman - - - - - - LouIse R.
2nd. Younger Woman - - - - - - Louise W.

*Choose your NeaRest eXit now. IN case of fire walk to it. do noT RuN. Do not tRy to OverTake your NeighBor. Heppy New Year!

The Management.

ANCESTORS MEETING

BY THE GHOSTS OF YOUR FOREBEARS YOU
ARE ORDERED TO BRING WITH YOU TO
THE NEXT MEETING OF THE POLYTOPIC
CLUB, JANUARY 28.TH 1939 A FIVE
MINUTE PAPER OR SPEECH RELATING TO
YOUR ANCESTORS ~ SOMETHING AMUS-
ING, INTERESTING, TRUE ~ WHO THEY
WERE, WHAT THEY DID, AND WHAT IF
ANYTHING THEY SAID. ~ ~ ~ ~ ~

(SIGNED) THE COMMITTEE

ROBERTA CHESTER

ON THINKING ABOUT AN INTERVIEW WITH
WILLIAM CARLOS WILLIAMS ON THE SUBJECT OF
THE AESTHETIC PHILOSOPHY IN THE POETRY OF
WALLACE STEVENS

Years ago, when I lived in Passaic, New Jersey, a town across the river from Rutherford and William Carlos Williams, I must have passed him coming and going countless times. My sisters Alice and Wendy were born at the Passaic General, the "contagious Hospital," several blocks from our home on Passaic Avenue, and my friends Judy and Jane Engelhardt lived just a few blocks from his house on Ridge Road. For six months, I took lessons from a piano teacher on the Rutherford side of the bridge—a teacher who should have been chased out of town for making passes at little girls. I made it to the drawbridge just before it closed to traffic—running the two miles home in record time—and have long assumed that run-for-life might have been one of the reasons why jogging has never seemed like fun.

But except for him, Rutherford always appeared quiet and well-behaved compared to Passaic which was both more ethnic and industrial and did more than its share to pollute the Passaic River that Williams celebrated in *Paterson*. But years before my discovery of the poem, and during the days when the river was not so polluted that my best friend Gail Schaffran's little brother couldn't sit on a rock and catch a dozen catfish, this river was never far away from all of our lives.

Those were the days when I discovered theater—when I could buy a standing room ticket for $1.75—and Rutherford was the first town the intercity bus stopped at on my way to New York. After going around the rotary in the center of town, the bus would make a stop at the station which was just a few blocks down the hill from his home. It is even possible that we rode that bus together even though ". . . New York was far out of my perspective. . . ." he wrote in the author's note to *Paterson*. I hesitate to dwell on that possibility for fear of regretting my own belated poetic development and the turns my life would have taken if I had once sat next to the man whose passion for poetry might have inspired me to get on with it in earnest. As it was, I just narrowly missed the bus ride that killed Lenore Lerner, another friend from Rutherford who had been—like all the young people in Rutherford—one of Williams' pediatric patients.

But even before those weekly trips to New York, my father used to take us every Saturday morning to a corner store in Rutherford which we called "the secret store." We were each given fifty cents to spend on the gift of our choice, no easy task considering the fact that the walls of that place were lined from floor to ceiling with toys and games of every description. The man who owned the store had a bald head, as I recall, and whenever I saw him he was reading on a high stool behind a counter filled with what I really wanted—a shiny, dark blue Parker pen. Outside the store there was a tall ornate clock that never once, during all those visits, told the right time.

Years later, the little town of East Rutherford where my father stopped each morning for a cup of coffee was in the news briefly when it was discovered that the incidence of leukemia, the disease my father died of, was startlingly high. Dr. Williams would have had a great deal of information to contribute to that investigation which seemed to me, in Maine, to be over rather quickly.

So Rutherford had long since taken root in the memories of my childhood when I called William Carlos Williams late in 1959 to see if he would speak to me about Wallace Stevens, the subject of my senior tutorial project. After nearly flunking analytical geometry and breaking a dozen beakers in the chemistry lab, I'd given up my dream of being a doctor to be a poet.* I was almost eighteen when I discovered Williams and Stevens in the library of Chatham College, slipped a poem under Dr. Eldedge's office door, and wrote a long letter to my father to the effect that I was not going to join the long list of family doctors. It never occurred to me that I could have done both, probably because I couldn't have. All I knew then was that even though I knew little about poetry, I had a neighbor who could help me decipher Stevens' late poems and I was presumptuous and ignorant enough to ask.

So it was with some trepidation that I approached the big Victorian house that took command over the fork in the road. It

---

*That took a lot of courage since one of the first words I heard was "eccentric" and it was used to describe the few poets in the family whom, I was told very early on, I was not to emulate.

was on the corner in an area which had become commercial and it seemed like the last bastion of a grander, more sedate time. My friend Rita Bloomfield's father had a pharmacy across the street and I probably stopped there both before and after the meeting with Williams. There was lot of snow—I remember that—and I crawled up to what I thought must have been the front door, since they hadn't shovelled out yet. The office door was clear, but he had asked me to come the other way. It was snow that was deep enough to make you feel as if you were drowning in it, if you were four years old like Williams was when he stepped off the porch as he described the incident to his biographer.

·   ·   ·   ·   ·

The woman who greeted me and ushered me into the large sitting room on my right was Flossie. The room was dark, although there were windows at either end, and the colors were mostly brown and gray. I sat in an overstuffed victorian sofa facing the fireplace, and it was only a minute or so before Flossie brought in some cookies—big, lemon cookies that were homemade and very good. I must have been alone for a bit because I remember getting up to read the Christmas cards on the mantle and I distinctly remember seeing one from T. S. Eliot.

The man who appeared in the doorway was old and rather frail looking, thin and with a small build, but very friendly. I don't know what I expected to hear, but I had come with a pad and pen and was ready to take copious notes. I came away from that interview with two rather interesting bits of information, and the kind one can easily remember. "The key to Stevens' poetry," Williams said rather emphatically, "was his wife. She was a bitch." And then he took a coin out of his pocket. "Most people don't know this," he said, "but this is her likeness on the dime."

Since he'd already told me the key to Stevens' poetry, I am sure I would not have dared ask him for more information. I can't remember the rest of the interview, but it wasn't about Stevens because I didn't take a single note. I did ask him, however, if I could send him some of my own poems because I did. That was years before I realized that there are "no ideas but in things" and the poems I sent were full of ideas but short on things. It would be years before I would or could go back to that world which was so full of the same details and mine that rich vein to discover the universal.

What I did get from him was a postcard with only two words, and again, a message I could commit to memory. What I wanted to hear was "your poems are wonderful" and "you have a great talent." All I read was "keep writing" and that was the real message regardless of what those poems were really like. It took me sixteen years to understand that advice and really take it to heart. Years later, I discovered in the *Autobiography* WCW's visit to Arlo Bates [p. 54] and learned that he'd received the same advice.

In that time the Passaic River earned the reputation as the "deadest" river in the United States, the price of theater tickets jumped 2000 percent, and my mother, who always had an exasperating passion for cleaning, threw away a postcard I would have liked to save all the rest of my days.

ROY MIKI

DRIVING AND WRITING*

" 'Write going. Look to steer': Improvisational
Form in William Carlos Williams' *Kora in Hell:
Improvisations* (1920)"

I

The car must have revolutionized the daily life of a small-town
doctor who had to make the rounds, so much faster than a horse
or a bicycle, and so incomparably more efficient than feet. Here as
well was a completely new kind of machine—a self-moving *thing—*
that demanded in its own particularity a careful attention to
details to make use of it, a vehicle that might, especially if its
operator were a writer with the kind of mind Williams possessed,
change the very way he could think about the art of writing. In
the chapter "First Years of Practice" from his *Autobiography*, a
book that reconstructs his life as a writer, Williams singles out the
event of purchasing his first car:

> I walked to my calls or rode a bicycle. Then I hired a little mare,
> Astrid, for a few months. I made seven hundred fifty dollars my
> first year. Then late in 1911, I got my first Ford! A beauty with
> brass rods in front holding up the windshield, acetylene lamps,
> but no starter! Sometimes of a winter's day I'd go out, crank the
> car for twenty minutes, until I got it going, then, in a dripping
> sweat, leave the engine running, go in, take a quick bath, change
> my clothes then sally forth on my calls. Once the thing kicked
> back and the handle of the crank hit me above the left eye. It
> might have been worse. The trick was to use the left hand in
> cranking, so that when the kickback came the handle would jerk
> out of the fingers instead of striking the wrist and breaking it. I
> had used the left hand, got it over the eye instead.[1]

*This essay is a shortened version of a chapter from *The Prepoetics of William Carlos
Williams: Kora in Hell* forthcoming from UMI Research Press.
1. *The Autobiography of William Carlos Williams* (New York: New Directions, 1967),
p. 127; hereafter abbreviated *A*. The quotation in the title of this essay ("Write going.

"The trick was"—and we notice immediately the kind of mind that works against any difficulty by treating it as a specific difficulty, in this sense cutting its way through an impasse, not by consulting a manual, but by finding a solution, any solution, with the material at hand. In other words, it simply improvises:

> 1. to compose, or simultaneously compose and perform, sing, etc., on the spur of the moment and without any preparation; extemporize. 2. to make, provide, or do with the tools and materials at hand, usually to fill an unforeseen and immediate need: as, he *improvised* a bed of leaves. [*Webster's New World Dictionary*] [2]

The two definitions strike to the heart of what happens in *Kora in Hell: Improvisations* (1920), the first of a series of major books—*The Great American Novel* (1923), *Spring and All* (1923), "The Descent of Winter" (1928), and *A Novelette and Other Prose* (1921-1931) would follow its lead in the 1920s—through which Williams developed a method of writing based upon improvisational form. Thinking back to the composition of *Kora* in *I Wanted to Write a Poem* (1958) he calls it a "unique book, not like any other I have written." [3] Although we are unfortunately not offered any further explanation, the "book" may well have remained so unusual in his mind because, as he says, he "had no book in mind" [*IW*, 27] when he began writing it:

> For a year I used to come home and no matter how late it was before I went to bed I would write *something*. And I kept writing, writing, even if it were only a few words. . . . [*IW*, 27]

What eventually became the text *Kora in Hell: Improvisations*, published by The Four Seas Company in Boston in 1920, was in effect the amazing product of a process that began from scratch, from nothing. And Williams points to the somewhat "unique" way *Kora* came together:

> The book was composed backward. The Improvisations . . . came first; then the Interpretations which appear below the dividing line. Next I arrived at a title and found the Stuart Davis drawing. [*IW*, 29]

Look to steer.") comes from *A Novelette and Other Prose*, in *Imaginations*, ed. Webster Schott (New York: New Directions, 1970), p. 278; hereafter abbreviated *AN*.

2. Mike Weaver in *William Carlos Williams: The American Background* (London: Cambridge University Press, 1971), suggests that Marsden Hartley, a friend of Williams, "could just as well have provided the subtitle to *Kora in Hell: Improvisations* through Kandinsky" [p. 42]. Kandinsky in *Concerning the Spiritual in Art* mentions "improvisation" as a method. Parts of this book, as Weaver points out, appeared in Alfred Stieglitz' *Camera Work* (April 1912) directly through Hartley's influence, Hartley having met Kandinsky in Germany in 1912-13.

3. *I Wanted to Write a Poem: The Autobiography of the Works of a Poet*, reported and ed. Edith Heal (Boston: Beacon Press, 1958), p. 26; hereafter abbreviated *IW*.

> Finally, when it was all done, I thought of the Prologue which is
> really an Epilogue. [*IW*, 30]

In the process of writing *Kora*, backwardly, as it turned out,
Williams came to discover how to improvise, which is to say, he
learned how to compose and perform (or think and write) simultaneously, this act carried out on the sharp, risky *spur* of the
moment inside the writing. In his *Autobiography* where he re-situ-
ates *Kora* in its wartime environment, he implies that the text
began out of a burning need to find a way, a compositional way,
of moving through the immediacy of a literary dead-end brought
on by the war:

> Damn it, the freshness, the newness of a springtime which I had
> sensed among the others, a reawakening of letters, all that delight
> which in making a world to match the supremacies of the past
> could mean was being blotted out by the war. [*A*, 158]

It was at this specific time that he sat down to

> write something every day, without missing one day, for a year.
> I'd write nothing planned but take up a pencil, put the paper   ·
> before me, and write anything that came into my head. [*A*, 158]

The writing ("anything that came into my head") issued from a
personal breakdown of belief—his "self was being slaughtered"
within what he envisioned as the "calculated viciousness of a
money-grubbing society" [*A*, 158]—but the improvisational
method uncovered by sticking to the material at hand, the day-by-
day writing itself, allowed the writer-Williams to drive himself
through the crisis, the text of *Kora* the final result of this movement.

In "Seventy Years Deep," an essay written in 1954, Williams
reminisces about his long life as a doctor and writer in Rutherford,
New Jersey, and describes vividly those countless times bits and
pieces of phrases broke into his mind as he drove, most likely
because he drove. "When the phrasing of a passage suddenly hits
me," he says, "knowing how quickly such things are lost, I find
myself at the side of the road frantically searching in my medical
bag for a prescription blank."[4] And he explains further the
urgency that lay behind his need to write while driving:

---

4. "Seventy Years Deep," *Holiday*, 16, No. 5 (Nov. 1954), 78. "By the Road to the
Contagious Hospital," the opening poem of *Spring and All*, was originally written on
prescription blanks, probably in the car.

    William Eric Williams, Williams' son, provides a lovely first-hand account of his
father's attachment to cars in "Cars," a brief essay published in the *William Carlos
Williams Newsletter*, 3, No. 2 (Fall 1977), 1-5. Here he provides some anecdotes concerning what he calls "the classic man-auto duel" [1].

I burned internally with something I had just heard or that had occurred to my mind; it is evanescent, either you put it down at once—or it is gone. I would look out of my car for a place to park. People must have wondered at me—maybe a boy on a bicycle would be pedaling by—but the urge was on me and I had to get it off my chest.[5]

The memory of these intense moments should alone remind us that the doctor-Williams spent a great deal of time on the road, driving "unwitnessed to work," as Louis Zukofsky comments, "no one but himself to drive the car through the suburbs."[6] The short and well-known poem, "The Young Housewife"—"I pass solitary in my car"—was first published as early as 1916 in *Others*,[7] only a few years after Williams got his first Ford, and only a year before the opening set of improvisations for what would become *Kora* was published in *The Little Review* (October 1917).[8]

Right from the beginning of his writing life, then, Williams could hardly have resisted the perception of an original connection between the car as a technological object and a (new) writing technique—improvisational form—that he aligned so closely with modernist writing. The car as a self-moving thing, an *auto-mobile*, was a natural embodiment of the modernist concern with the experience of movement. As any beginning driver quickly discovers, this vehicle offers a sense of movement wholly particular to itself. Get into it, and the first thing that becomes apparent is the separation of an out from an in, perhaps no momentous event, but the subtle cleavage that occurs makes available a consciousness of things otherwise unavailable. The mind finds itself inside an outside, and when the driving begins, the driver enters the play of a doubleness: not only an inside experienced as an outside, but now as well an outside experienced as an inside. The driver in transit passes through a field of many surfaces, his eyes shifting and turning with photographic rapidity, things appearing and disappearing. What the driver finds himself in is process, that flow of events in which no given perspective is an end but simply a point in an activity experienced in its temporality. Thus Williams *thinks* driving in "A Novelette," a series of improvisations written much

5. "Seventy Years Deep," 78. Williams also comments on the curious literary fate of these fragments. "It amazes me when I realize that these same prescription blanks with my scribbled notes are now reposing in the Library of the University of Buffalo, and at Harvard and Yale" [78].
6. Louis Zukofsky, *Prepositions: The Collected Critical Essays of Louis Zukofsky* (New York: Horizon Press, 1968), p. 143.
7. "The Young Housewife" was published in a group of sixteen poems in *Others*, 3, No. 4 (Dec. 1916), 15-31.
8. "Improvisations," *The Little Review*, 4, No. 6 (Oct. 1917), 19.

later than *Kora*, but in which he uses the "same method as in the *Improvisations*" [*IW*, 49] :

> And nothing—opens the door, inserts the key, presses the starting pedal, adjusts the throttle and the choker and backs out, down-hill. Sees the barberry gouts. Seize the steering wheel and turn it sharply to the left, the lilac twigs—that have lost prestige through the loss of plumage—scrape the left front fender sharply. [*AN*, 278]

While driving, at least while we are conscious of being in the act of it, there are no fixed laws. The only constant is the fact of change. The dying lilacs scrape the fender, sharply, as a particular does when it strikes the eyes.

In other words, driving involves its own kind of risk because it places the mind of the driver in a vulnerable situation. Inside the spatial dimension of an environment on the move, things neces-sarily are experienced as an invasion of mind, the eyes inevitably being struck, in a way *stung* by particulars that appear in view and as quickly disappear. The driver who is capable of maintaining himself in the doubleness of this perceptual process must pay attention to what Williams in his "Prologue" to *Kora* calls "the thing itself without forethought or afterthought."[9] The effect of this experience of otherness is similar to the effect of the epidemic in "A Novelette," the stress of which, we are told there, "pares off the inanity by force of speed and a sharpness, a closeness of obser-vation, of attention comes through" [*AN*, 273] .

It is precisely this kind of immediacy that the poet/driver of "The Right of Way" in *Spring and All* enacts when he resigns him-self to the particulars appearing on the road. The poem itself begins within the negative state of emptiness that results from this subtle shift into the spatial moment of the drive:

> In passing with my mind
> on nothing in the world[10]

Here the mind of the poet/driver becomes itself a "nothing," a vacant cavity that projects, as a moving film projects images on the screen, the cinematic quality of things in time that strike the eyes. Driving is the event of this process: "I saw," so the poem proceeds, as the poet passes through a field of shifting appearances, "an elderly man who / smiled . . . a woman in blue / who was laughing and leaning forward. . . ."

---

9. *Kora in Hell: Improvisations*, in *Imaginations* (ed. Webster Schott), p. 8; hereafter abbreviated *K*.
10. *Spring and All*, in *Imaginations*, pp. 119-120; hereafter abbreviated *SA*.

```
Why bother where I went?
for I went spinning on the

four wheels of my car
along the wet road until
```

And of course everything, even the humorous laughter of the poet, hangs suspended in the gap following the prepositional hinge: "until" the mind is invaded again by something other, *this time*:

```
I saw a girl with one leg
over the rail of a balcony
```

On the ·road, things become non-transparent surfaces that make this closeness of attention ("one leg / over the rail") a necessity. "The Right of Way," then, is a poem that extends a methodological assumption: that driving, considered in both literal and figurative terms, actualizes a mode of consciousness in which the poet has access to the experience of a constantly moving world. Had he not allowed himself to pass with his mind "on nothing," he would have removed his nameless self from the event of experience. His mind on "something"—or as it were, something on his mind—he would not have noticed anything. The play on the "right of way" he enjoys "by // virtue of the law" strongly hints that his method of seeing runs contrary to established forms of perception. And his method of speaking as well, for he adopts the frozen language of traffic signs that police our movement through a territorialized space and makes it operative again in his poem, more specifically, with his words. We are told elsewhere in *Spring and All* that "The pure products of America / go crazy" [*SA*, 131] because there is no way, no method in America to lift the world of its immediate desires into a revelation of itself:

```
No one
to witness
and adjust, no one to drive the car [SA, 133]
```

The word-play in *no one* echoes Williams' desire throughout *Spring and All* for a cleansed consciousness, not only of things, but of words as well, words themselves as particulars. Here again the push is for "the thing itself without forethought or afterthought but with great intensity of perception."

II

In the midst of composing *Spring and All* Williams pays homage to *Kora*, recalling how its method of composition, which at the time seemed like a make-shift solution to what was potentially a devastating personal crisis in his writing life, in fact shaped the subsequent form and direction of his work:

> The *Improvisations*—coming at a time when I was trying to remain firm at great cost—I had recourse to the expedient of letting life go completely in order to live in the world of my choice.
>   I let the imagination have its own way to see if it could save itself. Something very definite came of it. I found myself alleviated but most important I began there and then to revalue experience, to understand what I was at—
>   The virtue of the improvisations is their placement in a world of new values— [*SA*, 116]

The whole of *Spring and All* with its careful attention to the shining surfaces of things—in Zukofsky's words, the "full sight of the immediate"[11]—indicates that Williams' "world of new values" is a result of letting himself go with the movement of experience, witnessing and adjusting as he goes. In short, he affirms the act of improvising his way through a field of things:

> I ascend
>
> through
> a canopy of leaves
>
> and at the same time
> I descend
>
> for I do nothing
> unusual—
>
> I ride in my car [*SA*, 143]

The poet who drives through the world in *Spring and All* is also driving through a world of words. Williams says that "the form of poetry is related to the movements of the imagination revealed in words" [*SA*, 133] : *in* words, which is to say, in *words*, those very things that constitute the spatial moment of writing. This principle he learned back in *Kora*, hence its "virtue" as the one book by Williams in which we can literally see him figuring out how to drive within the density of words that appear and disappear on the writing road. It was back in *Kora* that Williams first discovered that the necessity to keep adjusting to changing avenues of awareness while driving a car relates to the necessity in writing as an act—

> If one should catch me in this state!—wings would go at a bargain. Ah but to hold the world in the hand then—Here's a brutal jumble. And if you move the stones, see the ants scurry. [*K*, 36]

---

11. Louis Zukofsky, *Prepositions*, p. 141.

—to hold onto the words at hand. "Write going. Look to steer." And what emerges out of this state, an improvisational state of consciousness, is a language experience, the effect of which becomes immediately audible in the slippery speech of a fool's voice in *Kora*. Writing can now return to the elemental power of words as they invade the mind of the writer and come ringing into his ears, as they literally do in "Improvisation XXIII.1":

> Baaaa! Ba-ha-ha-ha-ha-ha-ha-ha! *Bebe esa purga*. It is the goats of Santo Domingo talking. *Bebe esa purga!* Bebeesapurga! And the answer is: *Yo no lo quiero beber!* Yonoloquierobeber! [*K*, 75]

The particles of sound here enter from an outside, from the distance of an otherness that embodies the nature of a foreignness. But as they configure (or cohere), goats begin to talk, and the listening writer, wrapt by the liquid quality of these particles of sound, is tempted to lose himself in a sea of laughter. Or the reverse, repeat a phrase over and over, and soon it will willy-nilly disintegrate into particles of sound, even further, into the confusion of undifferentiated sound, all the syllables merging into one stream, precisely how they are first heard as sound. And yet, short and cryptic as this improvisation is, its richly textured language, so characteristic of all the writing in *Kora*, implies that the process is "double-edged" [*K*, 80]. Caught on the edge of words, that point at which they break apart into sound at the complete expense of sense, the writer is tempted to lose himself completely. But at this end there is finally no virtue in getting drunk simply for the sake of getting lost in a sea of sound. That end leads to the death of speech and is, to that extent, suicidal. "The sea is not our home," as Williams in *Paterson* will later tell us.[12] The pull is strong and real enough; language has that appeal. Moreover, a writer who has never experienced its siren-like force will never become conscious of its largeness, or, in terms of this improvisation, of its primacy when heard in those unexpected moments its sounds overtake his mind. But it is right here, as well, that the writer has to resist that finality, must resist it, and pull himself back, toward that edge where sound ceases to be mere sound and becomes morpheme. Sounds thus *become* words, and words a configuration of sounds.

On the other side of this edge is another edge with a different kind of pull, equally strong, that absolves one from taking what the writer in *Kora* considers the necessary risk of allowing words to have their own way. The bitingly humorous—and hysterical—miniature drama within the language drama of the improvisation

---

12. *Paterson* (New York: New Directions, 1963), p. 235; hereafter abbreviated *P*.

implies that all too often writers do turn their backs on the otherness of language. They thereby lose that edge where words are
caught in the gap between sense and sound, and instead retreat
into a wholly self-possessed use of words, a use that denies their
objectivity. Words no longer enter from outside but are consumed,
drunk up like a purgative, and so manipulated, taken as nothing
more than a medicine to cure the mind of its disorders—or to
adopt a term the doctor in Williams plays with in *Kora* of its
dis-eases. This too is a dead-end, because what is lost is precisely
the foreignness of words when they invade the mind and cleave its
narrow orders. For the writer in *Kora*, this flowing in of language—
"the words themselves," as Williams says much later in his *Autobiography*, "beyond the mere thought expressed" [*A*, 380]—
demands that the writer resist the mind's tendency to use words
to its own willful advantage alone, merely as tools for ordering
its thought. No wonder the defiant voice in the miniature drama
refuses to drink the purgative forced upon him by a willful authority ("*Bebe esa purga*"). The dis-ease brought upon a writer who
acknowledges the otherness of words—to return to our initial
response to the improvisation—is a necessary edge. It is here that
they are "the words themselves," not tools a writer is given to
further, or ex-press, his predetermined view of the world. Words
are never, in this sense, simply given; for a writer they appear to
him as things appear to a driver as he experiences the world as a
movement through a field of particulars, his mind on "nothing"
but the words heard. This process, in *Kora*, is that tense edge, a
threshho!d—or what we might call a "transitional" space—that ties
the imagination of the writer to an actual world. This is the same
world that strikes the passing mind of the poet in "The Right of
Way," one that exists by virtue of an incessant process within
which forms appear and disappear, live and die, as quickly as the
blink of the eyes.

    What matters, then, or what is at stake in *Kora*, concerns a
mode of consciousness that would enable a writer to adjust to the
traffic of "the words themselves" in writing. In "Improvisation
XXV.2," again the writer resists getting lost, but his attention now
turns to sight rather than sound. In flight as well as in submersion
(in *Kora* ascent and descent are constantly doubling back on one
another) there is the equal danger of a loss of that tension between
appearance and disappearance which constitutes the field ōf
experience. The writer of *Kora* attempts to remain within the
contrariety, within what Williams in "The Desert Music" comes to
call the protective "film"[13] where the skin of any live thing

13. *Pictures from Brueghel and Other Poems: Collected Poems 1950-1962* (New York:
New Directions, 1962), p. 120; hereafter abbreviated *PB*.

meets the skin of the world. It is the tension itself that resonates the music of existence:

                    The music
        guards it, a mucus, a film that surrounds it,
        a benumbing ink that stains the
        sea of our minds—to hold us off—shed
        of a shape close as it can get to no shape,
        a music! a protecting music   [*PB*, 120]

The tension is that "stain" that makes a thing as a creature of nature both a form and a figure, both an I and a You, both an "earthling" and a "deathling," like Jacob Louslinger in "Improvisation I.2" [*K*, 31] whose decaying body grows flowers. And it is this tension that the writer in *Kora* wants, for it is here also that desire as a force comes into its own:

> A man can shoot his spirit up out of a wooden house, that is, through the roof—the roof's slate—but how far? It is of final importance to know that. To say the world turns under my feet and that I watch it passing with a smile is neither the truth nor my desire. But I would wish to stand—you've seen the kingfisher do it—where the largest town might be taken in my two hands, as high let us say as a man's head—some one man not too far above the clouds. What would I do then? Oh I'd hold my sleeve over the sun awhile to make church bells ring. [*K*, 79]

The interpretation juxtaposed against this improvisation reveals (as so many of the interpretations do) the methodological shift of consciousness implied in the desire *to stand* at that point in the mind where the world may be "taken in my two hands." The shift, needless to say, is not into stasis, a fixed view of the world. It is not a journey with a definable beginning, middle, and end, but an effect—the estranged writer of *Kora* re-enters the play of the world from the other side, from the "back side" [*K*, 80] of perception, there where the world appears, not as a completed perception, but as the event of it, a creative act:

> *It is obvious that if in flying an airplane one reached such an altitude that all sense of direction and every intelligible perception of the world were lost there would be nothing left to do but to come down to that point at which eyes regained their power.* [*K*, 79]

It is the edge of the indeterminate the writer in *Kora* seeks, that edge of perception where improvisational form constitutes itself. In this way, the form of *Kora* becomes a major part of its content.

III

Perhaps extending Williams' lead, Robert Creeley in an interview comes to talk about the act of writing in relation to driving a car. "A man who can't drive at all," he says,

> is obviously embarrassed to go down a road that's opening before him. The most articulate driver is he who can follow that road with precisely the right response to each condition there before him. I would feel those might be in some way equivalent contexts.[14]

Like driving, writing is an indeterminate movement through a language field in which words are constantly appearing and disappearing as the writer *goes*. The road is opening before him. Or as Creeley explains in another interview in *Contexts of Poetry*, this time discussing "open form" writing (Olson's "composition by field"), ". . . there can be no prior determination of the form except that which is recognized as the writing occurs."[15] Creeley's account of the writing process is sharp and pointed, so clearly articulate, and yet it is significant that we can recognize in *Kora* the beginning of this sense of writing that would by mid-century, when *Kora* was finally being read as an early modernist text by such writers as Creeley, come into its own. By then, even Williams was talking about the poem as a "field of action" [*SE*, 280].[16] In the early years of the century, however, these terms were not available to Williams. There was the pressing sense that a new century demanded new forms of writing, but how that demand was to be met still lay dormant waiting to be discovered. For Williams, *Kora* begins the move in that direction and the instance of "the car" acted as one signpost along what must have seemed the crooked way. In "Improvisation IV.2" [*K*, 36-37], the single occasion in which an actual car ride occurs in the textual space of *Kora*, the awakening mind of the writer acts on the tie between driving and the improvisational basis of writing. And significantly enough, the writing in this improvisation, like so much of the writing in *Kora*, works negatively, that is, works through the recognition of the terms in which writing fails as writing, again an indication that the text of *Kora* was a self-justifying activity and an exploration.

---

14. Robert Creeley, *Contexts of Poetry: Interviews 1961-1971*, ed. Donald Allen (Bolinas, California: Four Seasons Foundation, 1973), p. 116.
15. Robert Creeley, *Contexts of Poetry*, p. 26.
16. The strong articulation of the same compositional method in Charles Olson's "Projective Verse" essay (*Human Universe and Other Essays*, pp. 51-61) must have instantaneously struck home for Williams. Olson's sense of "composition by field" so clearly extended his own sense of improvisational form. Williams acknowledged the essay by quoting it at length in his *Autobiography* [*A*, 329-332].

"How smoothly the car runs," so the improvisation begins, and so we are drawn inside the mind of the writer/driver, on the road in late summer or early fall, contemplating seasonal cycles as he drives past "these rows of celery." Then the thought immediately occurs that "they bitter the air," and the writer, without hesitating, quite smoothly gives in to the obvious temptation to read a generalized meaning into the scene. The air is a sign of an end to one season and the premonition of another—"winter's authentic foretaste." In the abstraction of this gem of homely wisdom, however, the "rows of celery" disappear and are replaced by a frame of reference: the cycle of the seasons. The writer then predictably falls into a desire to rest in the *age old* wisdom based upon the lawful orderliness of nature outside the complexity of town life. The landscape of the farms invites him into an apparent timelessness—or a sense of change understood in the image of the seasons as predetermined phases of one universal law:

> How smoothly the car runs. And these rows of celery, how they bitter the air—winter's authentic foretaste. Here among these farms how the year has aged, yet here's last year and the year before and all years. One might rest here time without end, watch out his stretch and see no other bending than spring to autumn, winter to summer and earth turning into leaves and leaves into earth and—

As the writing progresses, we notice that the syntax, as if to imitate the writer's thoughts, bends and coils inward upon itself, so that the language of the improvisation lulls the writer into a state of balance, the tension between the seasons eased, time itself disappearing into the "caress" of images—

> how restful these long beet rows—the caress of the low clouds— the river lapping at the reeds.

The strained lyricism of the passage now subsumes the particulars, which in turn become nothing more than emotional effects, the scene so infused with the subjectivity of the writer that he reads himself into his own projections. No wonder he loses track of direction, even forgets where he is going. At this point, the undercurrent of humour running like a thread through this whole "miniature" drama becomes more explicit, but it is too late for the writer. This drive collapses inward upon itself as we finally reach some vague destination only to find out that the house is empty. The writing journey has been to no avail. There is no one at the other end to receive the message. The words have failed to cross over:

> It's all dark here. Scratch a hurried note. Slip it over the sill. Well, some other time.

The pun on "some other time" exposes the earlier "time without end" as an illusion. That earlier phrase is a fixed thought of a transcendence that is an escape from the town into the narrowness of an anthropomorphic view of the "country." The images in the improvisation are those *"friendly images"* which the writer *"has invented out of his mind and which are inviting him to rest and to disport himself according to hidden reasons"* [*K*, 33]. A phrase like "winter's authentic foretaste" becomes a use of language governed by an intention to impose meaning onto things, the words themselves made to parrot the writer's purely private order that is disguised as a general law. The one spawns the other. This kind of writing leads to a closed order that reveals the writer's inability to drive through the opacity of words that do not conform to patterns of predetermination.

So let's begin again, as the next paragraph in the same improvisation does, and with exactly the same opening line: "How smoothly the car runs."

But this "other" time, we find ourselves inside a darker, much more dense landscape:

> This must be the road. Queer how a road juts in. How the dark catches among those trees! How the light clings to the canal! Yes, there's one table taken, we'll not be alone. This place has possibilities.

The images of dark and light come from an outside, strike the eyes of the writer as they cast patterns, also jut in like unforeseen roads, and as things themselves do in a world that *has possibilities* because it exists in time. This drive, instead of drawing the writer up into a peaceful state of transcendence, pulls him into an equivocal space that declares its unpredictability and at the same time forces him to recognize his own privacy as a privacy:

> Will you bring *her* here? Perhaps—and when we meet on the stair, shall we speak, say it is some acquaintance—or pass silent?

Thus his own voice splinters off from an unnamed, secret intrigue and quickly turns sideways into a language play. In this sense, his privacy is undermined by his inability to maintain a consistent point of view:

> Well, a jest's a jest but how poor this tea is. Think of a life in this place, here in these hills by these truck farms. Whose life? Why there, back of you.

The sentences simply drift into view, one surface after another, and so an incoherent speech emerges, one drawn into an ambiguous "place" that carries in its wake the push of desire:

> If a woman laughs a little loudly one always thinks that way of her.

The words here begin to twist inside a doubletalk that will not resolve itself into a discursive completion. The words themselves tease us playfully without permitting us to make them referential. Laughter takes the place of wisdom in the second half of the improvisation. The secret *rendezvous* never materializes; this "place" in which "poor tea" is served is not a place to live in, dependent as it is upon a nostalgia for an order now emptied of a former vitality. That meaning, in this time, has been reduced to a merely decorative function. And yet the substance of desire is as alive as ever: "But how she bedizens the country-side." The dead-end of meaning is the other side of a release into the absence of meaning, a rich and fertile vacancy that throws the mind back into the immediacy of its emptiness—the experience of the poet in "The Right of Way"—or as Williams says elsewhere in *Spring and All*, "the drift of [its] nonentity" [*SA*, 134]:

> Quite an old world glamour. If it were not for—but one cannot have everything. What poor tea it was. How cold it's grown.

There is no possibility for life outside the realm of possibility, and writing that attempts to fabricate "an old world glamour"—to use some words from "The Desert Music," "out of whole cloth" [*PB*, 116]—is simply another cage to stuff the world into preconceived orders that survive by denying the conditional nature of desire. Writing that is actual moves outward, and away from closures, as the heart does in release. The reawakening of desire this writing journey makes possible points to the future of another present:

> Cheering, a light is that way among the trees. That heavy laugh! How it will rattle these branches in six weeks' time.

This improvisation resists, perhaps even defies outrightly, our critical understanding, but the point of the writing is certainly clear enough. The opaque language of it pushes for a condition of writing that will permit the writer to engage the complexity of language as a complexity. "It is chuckleheaded to desire a way through every difficulty" [*K*, 17], Williams says in his "Prologue." Improvisational form allowed Williams to drive within the field of the crisis that initially led to *Kora*, and by so doing, became the method that helped him drive the car out of hell, out of the heart's dark confusions into the light of wholly new possibilities. "Write going. Look to steer." The necessity to improvise in the midst of a bankruptcy of meaning explains how the history of the text *Kora* assumed its own inherent authenticity. How else, except backwardly, could *Kora* have come together? This is exactly what the writer does when he adjusts his attention to what lies before him in the context the writing itself determines as it goes, the text of this writing an extension of the process.

IV

Years before *Kora* Williams had written a letter to Harriet Monroe, the editor of *Poetry* magazine, outlining his intuitive sense of the basis for a new poetic, and what he foretells there later became the primary issue of *Kora*. First explaining that *Poetry* should be the kind of magazine that does not dogmatically enforce a view of what poetry *ought* to be, instead should be "a forum wherein competent poets might speak freely, uncensored by any standard of rules," he then goes on to argue the contemporary need for this openness (c. 1913):

> . . . most current verse is dead from the point of view of art (I enclose some doggerel showing one of the reasons why). Now life is above all things else at any moment subversive of life as it was the moment before—always new, irregular. Verse to be alive must have infused into it something of the same order, some tincture of disestablishment, something in the nature of an impalpable revolution, an ethereal reversal, let me say. I am speaking of modern verse.
>
> *Poetry* I saw accepting verse of this kind: that is, verse with perhaps nothing else in it but life—this alone, regardless of possible imperfections, for no new thing comes through perfect.[17]

Williams could quite easily be accounting for the value of *Kora in Hell*, its astonishing life. Although this text still lay in the future, Williams in 1913 already sensed the need for a specific kind of poetics. The one he wants would match up to the subversive process of life in which no living form is exempt from the fact of change—and this fact includes poetic form. "Modern verse," so Williams says, must have something of this same quality, some "tincture of disestablishment," some "impalpable revolution," some "ethereal reversal." In this barrage of terms through which Williams strains for a clarity he does not yet possess—he acknowledges this lack to Harriet Monroe, if not in so many words—it is possible to hear him struggling to define the very kind of writing that characterizes the texture of *Kora*, especially the subversive effect of the "brokenness of his composition" [*K*, 16]. Improvisational form embodies a life process that always moves in the

---

17. *The Selected Letters of William Carlos Williams*, ed. John C. Thirlwall (New York: McDowell, Obolensky, 1957), pp. 23-24.

present—"always new, irregular." And like life, it is also a self-generating process determined by time, the actual time that binds the compositional space of the text.

In the twenties, with *Kora* now behind him, Williams came to praise the Cubist artist Juan Gris for this very actuality in his art. Gris also confirmed the reality of his medium, both the spatial opacity of the canvas and the temporal nature of the artistic process in which the artist creates an art-object that is not referential to some preconceived "reality" outside in a generalized distance, but is immediate to the particularity of the artist's engagement with the materials at hand. Gris also recognized the contextual nature of his art and worked from that compositional basis. Williams understood him only too well; his own writing from *Kora* on began on the same plane of activity, *the words themselves* the medium he entered by writing. But more, in *Spring and All* Williams singles out one Gris painting in particular, *The Open Window*, as an exemplification of the importance of design in Gris' work:

> Things with which he is familiar, simple things—at the same time to detach them from ordinary experience to the imagination. . . .
>   Here is a shutter, a bunch of grapes, a sheet of music, a picture of sea and mountains (particularly fine) which the onlooker is not for a moment permitted to witness as an "illusion." One thing laps over on the other, the cloud laps over on the shutter, the bunch of grapes is part of the handle of the guitar, the mountain and the sea are obviously not "the mountain and sea," but a picture of the mountain and the sea. All drawn with admirable simplicity and excellent design—all a unity—[*SA*, 110-111]

Williams emphasizes the opacity of the images in Gris' painting ("One thing laps over on the other"), and by *Spring and All* he could talk about the value of the Cubist's fascination with surfaces as an attempt to disclose the medium of art as a live spatio-temporal field of activity. The design of Gris' painting (non-representational as it is) *is* the very composition that reveals the objectivity of those "simple things" detached from "ordinary experience to the imagination." The design, one opaque object juxtaposed against another opaque object, is a function of the imaginative field of the art-object, and this fact alone constitutes the "unity" of the painting. Like Williams, Gris had learned to paint by going. In "On the Possibilities of Painting," an essay that Williams most likely read, Gris says:

> Until the work is completed, he [the artist] must remain ignorant of its appearance as a whole. To copy a preconceived appearance is like copying the appearance of a model.

> From this it is clear that the subject does not materialize in the appearance of the picture, but that the subject, in materializing, gives the picture its appearance.[18]

The distinction Gris draws between methods of composition has its direct application to the kind of writing that characterizes the text of *Kora*. Writing as an act forces the writer to remain inside the writing as it goes, which is why he will be "ignorant" of any such prior completion as a whole text, since the text as such comes into form only through the composing, its appearance conditioned by what happens in the writing. And not the reverse, which would be the case were the writer not to enter the writing, instead controlling it according to some "preconceived appearance" that takes precedence over the act of composition. Williams, we recall, had no book in mind, no narrative or discursive frame of reference in mind to determine the structure of the individual improvisations. He had no preconceived "subject" in mind, no teleological end in sight, nothing but the writing itself. The writing determined the possibility of the text. There was that risk involved. The time of *Kora* is the time of the composing process. The final "book" that came of this process is thus itself an appearance, the appearance of the text, its separate elements, like the particulars that make up Gris' Cubist painting, opaque surfaces that lap over one another without coalescing into a rational unity. They remain surfaces that play against one another to create the field of the text.

As early as 1914 Pound discussed the nature of "vorticism" in terms of the experienced "surfaces" of Henri Gaudier-Brzeska's sculptures. Mike Weaver tells us that

> Williams noted in the second *Blast* a manifesto by Henri Gaudier-Brzeska in which the sculptor spoke of deriving his emotions solely from the arrangement of surfaces; in sculptural terms this meant the planes and lines by which the surfaces were defined.[19]

The design of *Kora* is an arrangement of surfaces; the basic material of Williams' text, in writing terms, is made up of the words themselves that are first experienced as opaque planes of force. Or as Williams says in his "Vortex," a statement never published, but perhaps a direct response to Gaudier-Brzeska:

> . . . in using words instead of stone I accept "plane" to be the affirmation of existence, the meeting of substances, whether it

---

18. Juan Gris, "On the Possibilities of Painting," in Daniel-Henry Kahnweiler, *Juan Gris: His Life and Work*, trans. Douglas Cooper (New York: Harry N. Abrams, 1968), p. 200. Mike Weaver [p. 41] argues that Williams read this essay when it was published in 1924 in *the transatlantic review*.
19. Weaver, p. 37.

be stone meeting air or a sound of a certain quality against one
of another or against silence.[20]

In *Kora*, therefore, the words themselves, in their opacity, constitute one surface ("plane") of the text. The improvisations that
arise from their interplay, another surface. Two improvisations,
one against the other, another surface. A set of three improvisations, all of them playing back and forth, another surface. Or one
set of improvisations, one against another, or others, still another
surface. Then add some equally dense "interpretations," and
another surface appears. And these "interpretations," one against
another, or against a single improvisation, or a group of them,
more surfaces. Such a process of generating surfaces is potentially
endless, of course, because the variabilities are endless. Davis'
drawing, then, is another surface, as is the "Prologue." And even
the term, *Improvisations*, the subtitle to the text, is yet another
surface, likewise the title, *Kora in Hell*, and the cover with the
stylized drawing of the ovum impregnated by a single sperm,
which "completed the design" [*A*, 158], as Williams says in his
Autobiography. To state it simply, the text *Kora*, "in materializing," came into the form of an appearance. There is consequently
no attempt on Williams' part, as a writer, to merge all the elements
according to a coherent pattern, no single determining "thematic"
intention external to the text around which, or through which, all
the parts are ordered hierarchically. Rather, by allowing all the
surfaces of the text to assert their particularity, Williams allows
them to meet in an interchange that is an "affirmation of existence." *Kora*, then, is itself a live thing—a space, medium—or a
place where all of its separate elements come together to create a
"field of action," one that constitutes it as the text of an actual
composition. Williams in his "Prologue" so aptly writes:

> . . . one does not attempt by the ingenuity of the joiner to blend
> the tones of the oboe with the violin. On the contrary the per-
> fections of the two instruments are emphasized by the joiner; no
> means is neglected to give to each the full color of its perfections.
> It is only the music of the instruments which is joined and that
> not by the woodworker but by the composer, by virtue of the
> imagination. [*K*, 19]

---

20. Quoted by Weaver, p. 37. This piece has recently been published in *A Recognizable Image: William Carlos Williams on Art and Artists*, ed. Bram Dijkstra (New York: New Directions, 1978), pp. 57-59.

RICHARD C. ZBORNIK

ON STEALING PATERSON I AND OTHER POEMS
FOR WILLIAM CARLOS WILLIAMS

An Afternoon With Dr. Williams

My earliest memory of William Carlos Williams' poetry was discovering *Paterson* IV in the fall of 1951. I found the book at Kidd's book store in Cincinnati and realized this was poetry unlike any other contemporary verse I had been reading. I bought the book and it became a treatise to me.

I was attending Cincinnati Medical School, not sure about being a doctor or a writer, and along came Williams saying maybe I could do both. Not only that, but the poetry was alive—the things you heard in the streets—and humane.

I felt no compatability with the "learned" poets—the T. S. Eliots and Allen Tates. Here was a man who said it didn't have to be that way, and a doctor as well.

In the winter of '52, knowing about his generosity in responding to strangers, I decided to write to him. I can still remember the day his letter arrived. It was a trophy I wanted to hide, to keep for myself. "From Dr. William C. Williams—9 Ridge Rd. Rutherford, N.J.—a major American poet." In the morning while we were shaving, I confided in a fellow med student (now an obstetrician) and showed him the letter. "What a lousy typist," he said with a chuckle. I should have known better.

The letter was a spur to keep on writing. To "hell with my cautious friend," a woman journalist who was always dissecting my poems on the basis of her admiration for Eliot. In my letter I had praised Williams for his poetry and I'm sure he was pleased. For me at the time his letter was the perfect antidote—the right prescription.

In the summer of 1953 I was in New York and decided to visit Williams. I didn't call but just knocked on the door at 9 Ridge Rd.; Williams answered. Introducing myself, I was cordially invited to spend the rest of the afternoon with him and Flossie.

We sat in the front room and talked. He hadn't remembered our brief correspondence the year before and wanted to know about my literary affiliations. I told him I was in medical school and he seemed disappointed that I was not in literature.

The talk was varied. I brought up the Atom bomb; he was very concerned about its future use and whether or not man could handle this lethal weapon. I told him how much I loved his poem "The Red Wheelbarrow." Yet as the conversation progressed I began to feel we were not connecting. He didn't seem to be as sharp as I thought he would be, but then I knew nothing of his strokes and illnesses. Also I was a very young 23 and Williams was almost 70. He had plenty of poetry and living under his belt and I had little. Undoubtedly, I was expecting a more animated and idealistic afternoon. At one point Flossie provided refreshments, but did very little of the talking all afternoon.

Then, rather suddenly it seemed, our visit was over and I was at the door bidding farewell. When I got to the sidewalk I took a long last look at the house on 9 Ridge Road, glad that I had come, then wheeled and hustled into New York.

About a year later I was in the old Cincinnati Public Library, that grand arcade with marvelous tiers of books, when suddenly Williams appeared again, this time in the form of *Paterson* Book I. After buying *Paterson* IV I was able to pick up Books II and III in short order but never Book I. I felt I needed that book more than anyone else in Cincinnati and in some peculiar way that it also needed me. I made my strike and later wrote a poem.

The Master Speaks

March 10, 1952

Dear Dick:

You know and I know, being professionals or on the way to it, that the profession of writing is an art. When you have learned it it becomes or may become easy to you—though you may lose it in the course of time—while you possess it it consists of technical proficiency. That's why you have to be careful when the uninitiated praise you. You have to be careful not to [be] taken in by your own performances.

I may be a good writer but many professionals or at least a good many, do not think so. It looks, sometimes, as if I'm merely putting down haphazardly what I feel in something called "free verse".

That isn't so. I write as I do, rightly or wrongly, because I think my way of writing has taken the contours of a way of thought which is essential to the modern world which I know, eminently here.

I say these things to point out to you that I have to be guarded when I accept your good words. What the hell do you know? You aren't an expert.

And yet I'm for you. And I'm proud that, through some obscure instinct you've discovered or at least perceived in my writings something that has given you confidence in your world— and mine.

What I want to believe is that it's in the technical structure of the verse that that effect lies. It lies, if I may presume to trust you that far, in a new measure or a new way of measuring the poetic line. A measure, taking off from that, to a total measure of everything that as sentient creates we do with ourselves. This is dangerous ground. It can lead to much sloppy thinking.

But if we cling to our categories such thinking can be rewarding.

Best luck to you in your thinking. Your letter is very appealing to me. Whatever you become if you continue to show an intelligent appreciation of the serious matter of the poem at its best you will have much to enrich your life. It is not a static thing but contains many hints toward a right understand of what is about you. To hell with your cautious friend.

Sincerely yours

William Carlos Williams

9 Ridge Road, Rutherford, N.J.

The Disciple Writes

ON STEALING *PATERSON* I FROM THE CINCINNATI PUBLIC LIBRARY

It was Summer 1954
and I, I in the stacks once more

Looking, searching for (God
   knows what?)
         love perhaps

My eyes were fingering their way along
the slim jim sheafs of poetry
                    jewels to me.

And suddenly it shone

          Paterson I

                    precious rare stone.
(limited to 1000 copies and sold out everywhere)

To have it—To have it
     compulsion seized me

I slipped it inside my shirt

I wanted to run

I walked

Out of the stacks

Passed the desk

Thru the revolving door
                    and out
To the safe noisy street

          a warm rain was
          kissing my face
          I slipped around the
                    corner
          And then into space.

BOOK BUYING

I almost
          bought the "Farmer's Daughters"
                    by Wm. Carlos Williams

but that is part of his world.

                   instead

I bought
            "The Old Prague Jewish Cemetary"
                      because
            it is part of my world.

I shall continue
                   to gather an alphabet of symbols

                      until
They mount into a language
                      all my own.

THE CHICKENS' UPON WHOM SO
MUCH DEPENDS OR VICE VERSA

He
      told me he'd left Monsanto and now
      works for a chicken factory in Calif.
Oh
      he wasn't the usual chicken plucker mind you
      but rather a mechanical engineer
                         doing automation
      moving chickens & eggs and providing the
                         "saleable bird"
      his new Co. had even found a way to
      convert chicken shit into energy and
            I told him that was a marvelous invention
            since there was so much of it
                               around.
As
      I played it straight he kept dishing
      out and even got to like me after
      asking all those questions about
            his energy conservation plan

      His wife had just moved out—they'd bought
      a 1913 house and were fixing it up.
            They had each other, the chickens, a small
      town in California & nothing very much.

MY SON JOHN

He told me today   (he's 24)
That he knows what I mean   and more
                          about Carlos Williams
          the simple statement   a pure and
                                    honest rendering
(after getting that 12 lb treatise from the
prof at KSU   (everything from Darwin
to Jesus Christ knows what)

          a regular Einstein no less

Anyway   we talked about
the cat stepping into the flower pot
the plums in the ice box
the white chickens.
The Williams of '23
like some men who raise an athlete
a doctor or what

          this was a subtle achievement
                          a key
      a nice coming together for

John & me

[I sent a copy of "On Stealing *Paterson* I and Other Poems for
William Carlos Williams" to Theodora Graham. She responded
with a poem of her own, which I include as a "Coda" to these
verbal peregrinations.]

CONCESSION

I wanted to write a poem
for you, Bill Williams—
some minor blue howl
to leap from
the white page
and wrench you from
Denise Levertov and old memories
of Marcia Nardi.

Bold and frank, to be more than
a black woman
with a broken nose
or dumpy pregnant scientist
with dirty finger nails.
More than a teasing nurse
or Italian peasant,
pushing fiercely for her eighth brat
and you.

To break across your vision
a violent female image,
piercing to your marrow,
denuding that essential
trembling
bride.
Will this, dead lover, do?

THE POET I

Williams with sons William Eric [L] and Paul [R] around 1930.

EZRA POUND

*THE TEMPERS**

Mr. Williams' poems are distinguished by the vigour of their emotional coloring. He makes a bold effort to express himself directly and convinces one that the emotions expressed are veritably his own; wherever he shows traces of reading, it would seem to be a snare against which he struggles, rather than a support to lean upon. It is this that gives one hopes for his future work, and it is his directness coupled with the effect of colour—and the peculiarly vivid and rich range of colour in which his emotions seem to present themselves, "gold against blue" to his vision—that produces the individual quality of his verse. His metres also are bold, heavily accented, and built up as part of himself.

The moon of *The Tempers* varies from that of the splendid "Postlude" (which appeared in these pages some weeks since—in a group of poems headed "The Newer School"); with its

> Let there be gold of tarnished masonry
> Temples soothed by the sun to ruin
> That sleep utterly.
> Give me hand for the dances,
> Ripples at Philac, in and out,
> And lips, my Lesbian,
> Wall flowers that once were flame.

to the macabre humour of *Hic Jacet*, which I quote entire.

> The coroner's merry little children
>   Have such twinkling brown eyes,
> Their father is not of gay men
>   And their mother jocular in nowise,
> Yet the coroner's merry little children
>   Laugh so easily.

---

*Pound arranged for Elkins Mathews to publish Williams' second volume of verse, *The Tempers*. "To whet the appetities" of readers, he included 7 poems from the book along with a note in *The Poetry Review* in October. He wrote the following review of it for *The New Freewoman*, 1, 12 (1 Dec. 1913) 227.

> They laugh because they prosper.
>   Fruit for them is upon all branches.
> Lo! how they jibe at loss, for
>   Kind heaven fills their little paunches!
> It's the coroner's merry, merry children
>   Who laugh so easily.

At times he seems in danger of drifting into imaginative reason, but the vigour of his illogicalness is nearly always present to save him; and he is for the most part content to present his image, or the bare speech of his protagonist, without border or comment, as he does in the *Crude Lament*:

> The men that went a-hunting
> Are asleep in the snowdrifts.
>   You have kept the fire burning.
> Crooked fingers that pull
> Fuel from among the wet leaves,

or in the more or less unintelligible rune of *The Ordeal*, where someone is evidently praying to the fire-spirit to save a companion from witchcraft or some other magic.

One is disappointed that Mr. Williams has not given a larger volume, and one hopes for more to come.

DENISE LEVERTOV

THE IDEAS IN THE THINGS

There are many more 'ideas' in William Carlos Williams' 'things' than he is commonly credited with even today; and this is true not only of Paterson and the post-Patersonian, clearly meditative poems in triadic lines, but also of a great deal of his earlier work. Because he did write numerous poems that are exercises in the notation of speech or in the taking of verbal Polaroid snapshots, it is assumed that many other short or medium-length poems of his are likewise essays in the non-metaphorical, the wholly objective. And because he said, 'Let the metaphysical take care of itself, the arts have nothing to do with it,' it is forgotten that he immediately followed those words with these: 'They will concern themselves with it if they please.' It is not noticed that he himself frequently *did* so please. Williams, for much of his life, did take on, it is true, the task of providing for himself and others a context of objective, anti-metaphysical, aesthetic intent in order to free poetry from the entanglement of that sentimental intellectualism which only recognizes the incorporal term of an analogy and scorns its literal, sensuous term. This view denies the equipoise of thing and idea, acknowledging only a utilitarian role for the literal (as if it were brought into existence expressly, and merely, to articulate the all-important abstract term), rather than perceiving concrete images as the very *incarnation* of thought. This view insults the imagination, for the imagination does not reject its own sensory origins but illuminates them, and connects them with intellectual and intuitive experience. Williams, working against that insult to imagination, needed to assert and re-establish a confidence in the actuality and value of observable phenomena and a recognition of the necessity of sensory data to the life and health of poetry. But by so doing he incurred much misunderstanding from his admirers (not to speak of his detractors) and, I suspect, endured a good deal of (mainly unacknowledged) inner conflict; for he was frequently obliged to betray his stated principles in favour of the irresistible impulsion towards metaphor which is at the heart of *poeisis*.

I find it interesting to sort out, in the *Collected Early Poems*, those poems which are indeed snapshots, descriptive vignettes, notations of idiom and emphasis (as are some of the very late shorter poems also), from those which have unobtrusively the resonance of metaphor and symbol.

The mystery and richness of *further significance* which such poems of his possess is akin to what R. H. Blyth delineated for us in his commentaries on Japanese haiku. The allusive nature of the Zen art, possible only in a culture alert to the ubiquity of correspondences and familiar with an elaborate symbology, has of course no exact parallel in 20th century America; yet Blyth could have been evoking the art of W. C. W. when he quoted this haiku by Kyoroku,

'Even to the saucepan
where potatoes are boiling—
a moonlit night.'

and commented, 'It is only when we realize that the moon is in the saucepan with the potatoes that we know the grandeur of the moon in the highest heaven. It is only when we see a part that we know the whole.'

Readers who come to Williams' pre-*Paterson*ian or pre-*Desert Music* poems with the expectation of simple depictive Imagism of a classic, ascetically single-visioned objectivity (which was not in fact the stated aim of the objectivists, incidentally) miss these resonances, that sense of discovering, in a vivid part, the adumbration of an unnamed but intensely intuited whole; they forego the experience of becoming aware precisely through the physical *presentness* of what is *de*noted, of the other presentness—invisible but palpable—of what is *con*noted. They come to the poems solely for the Things, but inherent in the Things are the Ideas.

I'd like to present two examples, and a running commentary on what I believe is to be found beneath their surfaces:

'The Farmer,' the third poem from *Spring and All* (a series detached, in CEP, from its prose context), is not a depiction of a farmer which compares him to an artist, but vice versa. Read thus, as a portrait of the artist, each of its images has a double meaning. The literal *is there*, vivid in every detail. But climate, landscape, everything, takes on *along with* (not instead of) its denotative significance a symbolic one. The poet is a *farmer*, one who tends the land of language and imagination and its creatures, who makes things grow, poem-things, story-things, not out of nowhere but out of the ground on which he walks. At present the rain is falling, the climate is cold and wet, as was the critical climate of the time for Williams the poet; he is exposed to that wet and cold, and his fields—the fields of his art—are apparently empty. But he's trudging around *in* that climate and *in* the fields of language, calmly, hands in his pockets, intent on imagining the future poems; and the rain prepares the soil and the seeds. 'On all sides / the world rolls coldly away'—he's left quite alone with his imagination. The orchard trees are black witn the rain—but it is spring (the preceding prose has announced, 'Meanwhile, SPRING, which has been approaching for several pages, is at last here'—and the poem states that it is March). Soon those trees (the deeprooted anatomy of what grows from his terrain) will be white with blossom: there are implied poems in this superficially unpromising landscape; and the very isolation in which the poet is left by the world gives him 'room for thought.' His dirt road (his own road among his fields) is sluiced (and thus deepened) by the rain that will help the seeds to sprout. He's not a small, lost figure in nature, this artist farmer—he 'looms' as he moves along past the scratchy brushwood that, trimmed and dried, will make good tinder. The poet is *composing* as he goes—just as a farmer, pacing his fields on a Sunday at the end of winter, composes in his mind's eye a picture of spring growth and summer harvest. He is an *antagonist*—to what? To the hostility of the environment, which, however, contains the elements that will nourish his crops. And in what sense? In the sense of the struggle, *to* compose, not to *im*pose order but to *com*pose the passive elements into a harvest, to grow not tares but wheat.

A poem I'm very fond of and which, besides being full of implication and resonances, has many of the qualities of a short story, (indeed, as well as being *set* in Russia, it has a flavour or tone quite Chekhovian), is 'A Morning Imagination of Russia,' a part of *The Descent of Winter*. Webster Schott's selection from Williams' prose and poetry, *Imaginations*, restored the full context of that series, as well as of 'Spring and All'; and Schott, unlike some of Williams' critics, doesn't treat him as wholly lacking in thought. Nevertheless, intent upon an enthusiastic, but careless, reading of this poem, which sees it as speaking figuratively of Williams' own situation *vis-a-vis* American poetry, he misses the clear drama of its narrative. He quite unjustifiably claims that it depicts *Williams himself on an imaginary visit* to Russia after the revolution, whereas (however much he may be a projection of the poet's sensibility) it seems to me quite clear that the protagonist is not intended as a persona in the sense of a mere mask for the self, but is a more fully projected fictive personage, a member of the intelligentsia who is casting his lot with the masses. The time is very early in the revolution. Nothing has yet settled down. No new repressive bureaucracy has yet replaced the old oppression—the whole atmosphere is like that of a convalescent's first walk in pale sunshine after a time when bitter storms in the world outside paralleled his inner storm of fever and life-and-death struggle.

> The earth and the sky were very close
> When the sun rose it rose in his heart,

it begins. The dawn is, equally, an actual one and the dawn of an era. And he feels one with it.

> It bathed the red cold world of
> the dawn so that the chill was his own.

The red is the red of sunrise *and* of revolution.

> The mists were sleep and sleep began
> to fade from his eyes . . .

The mists are both morning mists and the mists of the past, or prerevolutionary sleep. His consciousness is changing.

> below him in the
> garden a few flowers were lying forward
> on the intense green grass where
> in the opalescent shadows oak leaves
> were pressed hard down upon it in patches
> by the night rain . . .

The beauty of flowers and grass, opalescent shadows, patches of rain-soaked dead oak leaves, is vividly evoked. It can all be read with validity as pure, precise description. But it too has a doubleness; the whole scene has been through a night of storm, the flowers are bowed forward by it, the grass is more vividly green than it would have been without it, but parts of the grass are hidden and half-smothered by the fallen brown leaves. All this is the counterpart of his own experience and of events in the historical moment. The flowers and common grass of his own life, after the storm, are more vivid and yet almost broken—and some of his life is gone, is fallen, like the leaves, gone with the lives and the ways of living fallen in war and revolution.

> . . . There were no cities
> between him and his desires,
> his hatreds and his loves were without walls
> without rooms, without elevators
> without files, delays of veiled murderers
> muffled thieves, the tailings of

> tedious, dead pavements, the walls
> against desire save only for him who can pay
> high, there were no cities—he was
> without money—
>
>   Cities had faded richly
> into foreign countries, stolen from Russia—
> the richness of her cities.—

Here, deep in rural Russia, deep into the attempt to construct a new society, he is not impeded by the complexities of urban, Westernized Russia. His nature—with its desires, hatreds, loves—is out in the open; and the 'city' here clearly stands for more than an architectural and demographic agglomeration, but for the money values of capitalism. He has no money—but here and now he doesn't need it. All the desirable contents of Russia's cities have been stolen away, gone West with the emigrés.

> Scattered wealth was close to his heart
> he felt it uncertainly beating at
> that moment in his wrists, scattered
> wealth—but there was not much at hand.

The 'scattered wealth' he feels (scattered like money and jewels dropped by fleeing thieves) is his own and Russia's—it has not been, and cannot be, wholly robbed, absconded with. He feels that, feels it close. But also he feels a tickling wave of nostalgia:

> Cities are full of light, fine clothes
> delicacies for the table, variety,
> novelty—fashion: all spent for *this*.
> Never to be like that again:
> the frame that was. It tickled his
> imagination. But it passed in a rising calm.

He feels a nostalgia for all which (for now, anyway—and perhaps forever) must be given up for the sake of the new thing yet to be defined. The old context, the frame, gone. But now '*this*': the 'few flowers,' the vividness he will know.

But it passes (that wave of nostalgia) in a *rising* calm—not the sinking calm of resignation, but a lift of the spirits.

> Tan dar a dei; Tan dar a dei!
> He was singing. Two miserable peasants
> very lazy and foolish
> seemed to have walked out from his own
> feet and were walking away with wooden rakes
> under the six nearly bare poplars, up the hill.
> There go my feet.

Singing with lifted spirits, (singing, one notices—and there is an irony in this—that medieval refrain we associate with spring, love

and courtesy, ancient forests, knights errant and troubadours) he
feels as much one with the peasants he watches from his window
as he had with the chill red dawn. He sees them as lazy and foolish,
as well as miserable, just as he might have done from the viewpoint
of prerevolutionary class privilege: he does not idealize them; but
the difference is that now he identifies with them, lazy and
foolish as they are, and with their task—to rake away rubbish,
perhaps dead leaves—to which they must go *up hill.* 'There go my
feet.'

> He stood still in the window forgetting
> to shave—
> The very old past was refound
> redirected. It had wandered into himself
> The world was himself, these were
> his own eyes that were seeing, his own mind
> that was straining to comprehend, his own
> hands that would be touching other hands
> They were his own!
> His own, feeble, uncertain . . .

In this new world—around him and within him—he finds ancient
roots, not the immediate past which has been razed but the *'very
old past,'* taking new directions. Identified with what is happening
historically, he feels himself a microcosm; the proposition invites
reversal—it is not only that he is intimately and intensely involved
but that, just as his mind strains to comprehend, so the mind of
the peasants, the mind of all Russia collectively, strains to see, to
comprehend. His hands, reaching out to touch others, are feeble
and uncertain, though; and so are the hands of the multitude.

>   . . . He would go
> out to pick herbs, he graduate of
> the old university. He would go out
> and ask that old woman, in the little
> village by the lake, to show him wild
> ginger. He himself would not know the plant.

He will go humbly, as pupil of the old peasant, the ancient root
wisdom—not as teacher of others.

> A horse was stepping up the dirt road
> under his window

—a live thing moving on unpaved earth: not merely a descriptive
detail but a metaphor.

> He decided not to shave. Like those two [the two peasants]
> that he knew now, as he had never
> known them formerly. A city, fashion
> had been between—

Nothing between now.

> He would go to the Soviet unshaven. This
> was the day—and listen. Listen. That
> was all he did, listen to them, weigh
> for them. He was turning into
> a pair of scales, the scales in the
> zodiac.

This is evidently the day of the regular meeting of the local Soviet, which he is attending not for the first time, as one can gather from the syntax,—but it is also the day of a new access of consciousness and resolve, a *first* day in some sense. He puts his university education at the service of the community. Perhaps he weighs physical supplies—grain, fertilizer, medicines—bringing specific professional skills into play: that's not specified. But there's more to weighing than that. He not only feels, with a mixture of humility and amusement, that he becomes his function, becomes a pair of scales, but that they are the zodiacal scales, charged with moral, mythic, psychological symbolism.

> But closer, he was himself
> the scales . . .

That is, not only did his work of weighing transform him into a function, but he was anyway, intrinsically, an evaluator, he realizes.

> The local soviet. They could
> weigh . . .

That is, in his new sense of identification with his fellows, others too are intrinsically, as humans, evaluators.

> . . . If it was not too late.

That is, if too much damage had not already been done, too much for the revolution to have a future after all, too much for that human ability to measure for themselves, to evaluate justly, to manifest itself among the many.

> . . . He felt
> uncertain on many days. But all were uncertain
> together and he must weigh for them out
> of himself.

His 'weighing' is a service he performs as an intellectual, contributing his ability to listen closely, which has been trained by education; but his judgements must be made out of a commitment, a centre in himself, and not merely abstractly, which would be perfunctory. It is 'out of himself,' his very substance, he must act.

> He took a small pair of scissors
> from the shelf and clipped his nails
> carefully. He himself served the fire.

He reasserts his education, maintains his standards of hygiene and decent appearance. But to attend to the fire in his hearth himself— this is new for him. To use his hands, with their clean, clipped nails. And that fire: it is literal, and it is the fire of life, hope, revolution. Now he soliloquizes:

> We have cut out the cancer but
> who knows! perhaps the patient will die

He reiterates his own realistic uncertainty. Then he proceeds to define the 'patient,' which is not solely Russia, a country in the throes of total reorganization:

> The patient is anybody, anything
> worthless that I desire, my hands
> to have it—
> . . . anybody, anything

lines which I would gloss thus: . . . anybody, anything, *albeit considered* 'worthless,' that I desire, my hands *desiring* to have it— that's to say, the 'patient' is the sum of things that, though the world think them tawdry, assigning them no value, Williams consistently saw as having the glitter of life, cats' eyes in the dark. Beautiful Thing. 'Melon flowers that open / about the edge of refuse' / . . . 'the small / yellow cinquefoil in the / parched places.' Or those starlings in the wind's teeth. And, too, the 'patient' whose survival is in question is desire itself, the desire to touch that aliveness with bare hands,

> —instead of the feeling [he goes on]
> that there is a piece of glazed paper
> between me and the paper—invisible
> but tough running through the legal
> processes of possession—

That glazed top sheet, a transparent obstacle to touch, covers the surface even of the documents that proclaim possession of what is desired; and thus cancels out the *experience* of possession.

> —a city that
> we could possess—

that is, *my hands desire to have a city that we could possess.* (The syntax is clearer here if instead of dashes before the word 'instead' and after the word 'possession' we enclose those lines in parentheses.) A city, then, that—unlike the cities that have 'faded richly / into foreign countries' and were only to be enjoyed by those who 'can pay high'—would embody an accessible life.

It's in art, it's in
the French school.

What we lacked was
everything. It is the middle of
everything. Not to have.

Here both 'it's' refer back to the 'patient' in the aforementioned
sense of that embodiment of the quality of immediacy which, in
the prose passage immediately preceding 'A Morning Imagination
of Russia' in the *Descent of Winter* sequence, and dated only one
day before it, Williams had said was the very goal of poetry:
'poetry should strive for nothing else, this vividness alone, *per se*,
for itself'—and further, 'The vividness *which is* poetry.' So, '*It's*
in art, in the French school,'—here he draws on his own educated
knowledge and experience, on all that makes him different from
those two 'miserable, lazy, and foolish' peasants—and also '*It* is
the middle of everything'—*it* is not *only* in art but in all kinds of
things, common experience, and here he reasserts his sense of
brotherhood. But 'What we lacked was everything . . . *Not to
have*,' was what, till now, we experienced. I am reminded here of
Wallace Stevens' lines

'That's what misery is,
Nothing to have at heart':

Both the intellectual, because of his sense of that invisible wall
of glazed paper between him and life, and the oppressed and
ignorant people, have hitherto been cut off from the 'everything'
in the middle of which are found the sparks of vivid beauty;
instead they have experienced only *not having*, absence.

We have little now but
we have that. [The 'it,' the sparks, the poetry.]
We are convalescents. Very
feeble. Our hands shake. We need a
transfusion. No one will give it to us,
they are afraid of infection. I do not
blame them. We have paid heavily. But we
have gotten—touch. The eyes and the ears
down on it. Close.

The whole people is convalescent from the convulsions of revolution. The transfusion they need is not forthcoming—seen historically, such a 'transfusion' would have meant international support
for their experiment, instead of an economic and psychological
blockade. But other nations, other governments, were scared. The
protagonist, like a true Chekhovian character, says he can't blame
them; he sees what scares them, and why—he is not doctrinaire.
And he recognizes that a great price has been paid, and will

perhaps be further exacted. But what has been gained is precisely what he has desired: touch itself. Williams the doctor knew how the touch of hands could diagnose, cure, bring to birth; his fictive Russian knows the imagination as an intimate form of touch— without which all is dull, hopeless, ashen. What he celebrates— here, at the end of the poem, returning to its opening, when earth and sky are close, known, touched with the imagination—is the sun rising in his heart.

The prose which immediately follows the poem and is dated four days later, begins with the words, 'Russia is every country, here he must live. . . .' And a few pages further on Williams breaks off from diverse topics to return to the protagonist of the poem, in these sentences, 'He feels the richness, but a distressing feeling of loss is close upon it. He knows he must co-ordinate the villages for effectiveness in a flood, a famine.' I see two ways of reading that, and they are complimentary, not conflicting. If, as I've been doing, one reads the poem without disregard for its narrative reality, the truth of its fiction, and thus the universality of the poem's Russia—'every country; here he must live'—then the richness that 'he,' the protagonist, feels is the richness of new beginnings, the reassertion of the 'very old' past, and also the democratic 'everything' of human experience; while the 'dis-tressing feeling of loss' that comes close upon it concerns the equally real subtleties, nuances, desirable complexities, that 'scattered wealth' he earlier felt 'beating at his wrists,' which as yet we have not figured out how to attain in any social system without sacrifice of justice and mercy. But one can also read 'A Morning Imagination of Russia' somewhat as Webster Schott chose to do, that is, as a parable of Williams' poetic struggle in the twenties (it was written in 1927). According to the first reading, the hero's recognition of the need to 'co-ordinate the villages for effectiveness in a flood, a famine,' reminds one of Chekhov's letters in the early 1890s when he was an unpaid local medical inspector during the cholera epidemic. If one looks beyond the Russian scene (set just a few years before the writing of *The Descent of Winter*) to an analogy in Williams' own struggles to establish a new sense of poetry and the imagination in the American 20s, we may see in those words about co-ordinating the villages an almost Poundian missionary spirit, for then one takes the 'villages' to be outposts of intelligent poetry, and the flood or famine as aspects of the hostile or uncomprehending world of readers, critics, other poets, the public at large. Webster Schott, reintroducing *The Descent of Winter* in 1970, saw it as *entirely* a struggle 'to verbalize a theory of contemporary poetry' and 'to realize a clear conception of himself as an artist.' That is partially true; but when Williams wrote the words 'We have paid heavily. But we / have gotten–touch' he was not speaking in a vacuum, as if from an airtight aesthetic island in which the political images with which, in *A Morning Imagination*, he had chosen to work, had no meaning *except* as metaphor, as figurative ways to speak about literature. Those images work as Chekhovian narrative description; they work as implications of political ideas; *and* they work as analogies for the poet's need to act in society, humbly and with an understanding that in trying to serve the commonweal he will serve also his own need for intimate experience of the living mystery. Ideas without Things are vaporous, mere irritants of the detached and insensate intellect; but Things abound, and are choc-a-bloc with the Ideas that dance and stumble, groan or sing, calling and beckoning to one another, throughout the decades of his poetry.

CID CORMAN

SPRING & ALL

The year before I was born—to connect with him—*Spring & All* was published (1923)—dedicated to his painter friend Charles Demuth.

The name of the press was Contact and the opening words bring us back even yet to our tradition—to ourselves—which is either poetry or (and?) nothing:

> If anything of moment results—so much the better. And so much the more likely will it be that no one will want to see it.

Ironically he remains "right": for few readers have yet turned to the poems in this book—amongst them some of his best and most famous pieces—and felt them—as Shakespeare's songs must also be felt—within the living context provided.

He continues:

> There is a constant barrier between the reader and his consciousness of immediate contact with the world. If there is an ocean it is here. Or rather, the whole world is between: Yesterday, tomorrow, Europe, Asia, Africa,—all things removed and impossible, the tower of the church at Seville, the Parthenon . . .

The scholars and critics have yet to realize—beyond momentary polemics—that Bill is our continuance—is our poet—beyond any limitations put upon him. He is regarded as a fool by some—when he is—in blatant fact—our purest intelligence:

> What do they mean when they say: "I do not like your poems; you have no faith whatever. . . . The poems . . . are heartless, cruel, they make fun of humanity. . . . Have you no tolerance for human frailty? Rhyme you may perhaps take away but rhythm! . . . Is this what you call poetry? . . . Poetry . . . used to go hand in hand with life, . . . interpreted our deepest promptings . . . inspired . . . led us forward to new discoveries, new depths of tolerance, new heights of exaltation! . . .
>
> they mean that when I have suffered (provided I have not done so as yet) I too shall run for cover; I too shall seek refuge in fantasy. And mind you, I do not say that I will not. To decorate my age. . . .

This is not the blind poet quite. This is a man trained as a scientist but never losing the infantgiven power of seeing through the body—and that seeing being his spiritual reach.

> The reader knows himself as he was twenty years ago and he has also in mind a vision of what he would be, some day. Oh, some day! But the thing he never knows and never dares to know is what he is at the exact moment that he is. And this moment is the only thing in which I am at all interested . . .

> And if when I pompously announce that I am addressed—To the imagination—you believe that I thus divorce myself from life and so defeat my own end, I reply: To refine, to clarify, to intensify that eternal moment in which we alone live there is but a single force—the imagination. This is its book. I myself ((Walt Whitmanically)) invite you to read and to see. . . .

He immediately and deliberately and with the rhetoric of a deeper concern breaks open all chapter and "order" conventions—to speak with us—imagination to imagination:

> I speak for the integrity of the soul and the greatness of life's inanity; the formality of its boredom; the orthodoxy of its stupidity. . . .

Virtually every poet—at least in the USA—worth mentioning has picked up—mostly indirectly—from these fresh tracks—this trailblazing in this century.

The Desert Music is adumbrated here—as if he had to return to this in order to move once again into the open of his depths.

Pound had said MAKE IT NEW. But Bill declares everything so: "THE WORLD IS NEW."

> By the road to the contagious hospital
> under the surge of the blue
> mottled clouds driven from the
> northeast—a cold wind. Beyond, the
> waste of broad, muddy fields
> brown with dried weeds, standing and fallen
>
> patches of standing water
> the scattering of tall trees
>
> All along the road the reddish
> purplish, forked, upstanding, twiggy
> stuff of bushes and small trees
> with dead, brown leaves under them
> leafless vines—
>
> Lifeless in appearance, sluggish
> dazed spring approaches—

They enter the new world naked,
cold, uncertain of all
save that they enter. All about them
the cold, familiar wind—

Now the grass, tomorrow
the stiff curl of wildcarrot leaf
One by one objects are defined—
It quickens: clarity, outline of leaf

But now the stark dignity of
entrance—Still, the profound change
has come upon them: rooted they
grip down and begin to awaken

I don't know whether Bill wrote the poems in this book first and then added the prose afterwards or vice versa or however. I know—however—that the poems AS THEY OCCUR fall with startling immediacy and with absolute persuasion of being in the right place at the right moment. And if he literally did write them in the order in which they stand—it is only the more remarkable. To have brought them off!

He does so many things in this poem that were NEW to that day and that even now will—no doubt—bother academicians and their camp. (These things he did with teasing deliberation—light-hearted contempt for "the rules.") He—as anyone can feel if anyone will read the words aloud—prose and poetry—is discovering where he is at by being—word for word—there—PRESENT (and beautifully accounted for).

And the language itself invites us to participate in it—doesn't put us off with prettinesses—projects and perceives—long before Charles Olson unwound.

We can hear and feel already in this piece the repetitions that work more resonantly yet in later Oppen. We catch the open language found in Creeley and Levertov—Enslin and myself. There is the tensile strength within the shift of weight from line to line—careful but not worryingly so—that modulates into Zukofsky and Duncan.

The breakdown of ordinary syntax and stanzas—pushing the nouns to hold their gambit positions—fearless of saying what he thinks of what he sees and saying what he has found to say with clarity eluding the trite.

The "save" is not the language of a Polish mother—nor are the opening words—and yet this is the language of a live community: the poem OPENS and its very "stark dignity" grips down and awakens us. Or no God can help us.

As he says: "The rock has split, the egg has hatched, the prismatically plumed bird of life ((later rediscovered near Juarez)) has escaped from its cage. . . ."

> The imagination, freed from the handcuffs of "art," takes the lead! Her feet are bare and not too delicate. In fact those who come behind her have much to think of. . . .

Reminds me of an artist friend of mine viewing with me Rembrandt's *Bathsheba Bathing* in the Louvre and remarking that he could smell her feet! These are the contacts.

WCW—and in this book above all— has been grossly over-looked as our salient root poet. As he says: "meanings have been lost through laziness or changes in the form of existence which have left words empty."

If his critical charity sometimes exceeds his judgment—the poetry he brings to life offers us all the evidence we need of where we are and can find ground: "The word must be put down for itself, not as a symbol of nature but a part, cognisant of the whole—aware—civilised."

When he writes the following poem he is decades in advance of Zukofsky's memorial to him in *Some Time*:

No that is not it
nothing that I have done
nothing
I have done

is made up of
nothing
and the diphthong

ae

together with
the first person
singular
indicative

of the auxiliary
verb
to have

everything
I have done
is the same

if to do

is capable
of an
infinity of
combinations

involving the
moral
physical
and religious

codes

for everything
and nothing
are synonymous
when

energy *in vacuo*
has the power
of confusion

which only to
have done nothing
can make
perfect

As his footnote to this Bill adds: "The inevitable flux of the seeing eye toward measuring itself by the world it inhabits can only result in himself crushing humiliation unless the individual rise to some approximate co-extension with the universe."

"When we name it"—he asserts—"life exists." And he affirms it in poetry and as poetry when he writes:

so much depends
upon

a red wheel
barrow

glazed with rain
water

beside the white
chickens

It is painful—no doubt— for two or more generations of teachers/professors to have to deal with this poem. I was given it and told as an undergraduate—allowed no context for it—that it was/is a hoax. That was already 20 years after its advent. And it took me another 5 years OUT OF SCHOOL—to find it again— for myself. And Bill is no fool—who lays out the poem so decisively—to make us sound every word and syllable—so that each word assume/resume its life—which is ours. If the imagination occur.

It is the imagination on which reality ((our pet)) rides—It is the imagination—It is a cleavage through everything by a force that does not exist in the mass and therefore can never be discovered by its anatomization.

Poetry does not tamper with the world but moves it—It affirms reality most powerfully and therefore, since reality needs no personal support but exists free from human action . . . it creates a new object, a play, a dance which is not a mirror up to nature but—

As birds' wings beat the solid air without which none could fly so words freed by the imagination affirm reality by their flight.

And he sees too that the issue of poetry is not in likening it to music—but within the act of language itself—

as if the earth under our feet
were
an excrement of some sky

and we degraded prisoners
destined
to hunger until we eat filth

while the imagination strains
after deer
going by fields of goldenrod in

the stifling heat of September
Somehow
it seems to destroy us

It is only in isolate flecks that
something
is given off

No one
to witness
and adjust, no one to drive the car

You can find here ground that Bronk and Creeley mined. And Olson.

I'm sorry: you are going to have to read the book yourself. That's what it's here for. You.

MARJORIE PERLOFF

"TO GIVE A DESIGN": WILLIAMS AND THE
VISUALIZATION OF POETRY

William Carlos Williams, aged 73, in conversation with Edith
Heal about his characteristic verse forms:

> Free verse wasn't verse at all to me. All art is orderly.... From the
> beginning I knew that the American language must shape the
> pattern; later I rejected the word language and spoke of the
> American idiom—this was a better word than language, less aca-
> demic, more identified with speech. As I went through the poems
> I noticed many brief poems, always arranged in couplet or qua-
> train form. I noticed also that I was peculiarly fascinated by
> another pattern: the dividing of the little paragraphs in lines of
> three. I remembered writing several poems as quatrains at first,
> then in the normal process of concentrating the poem, getting rid
> of redundancies in the line—and in the attempt to make it go
> faster—the quatrain changed into a three line stanza, or a five
> line stanza became a quatrain, as in:

The Nightingales

Original version	*Revised version*
My shoes as I lean	My shoes as I lean
unlacing them	unlacing them
stand out upon	stand out upon
flat worsted flowers	flat worsted flowers.
under my feet.	
Nimbly the shadows	Nimbly the shadows
of my fingers play	of my fingers play
unlacing	unlacing
over shoes and flowers.	over shoes and flowers.

> See how much better it conforms to the page, how much better
> it looks?[1]

---

1. *I Wanted to Write a Poem: The Autobiography of the Works of a Poet,* reported and
edited by Edith Heal (Boston: Beacon Press, 1958), pp. 66-67. Subsequently cited as
IWWP.

Like most of Williams' attempts to account for his own prosodic inventions, to theorize about verse, this one is confusing and
contradictory. "Free verse isn't verse to me"—over and over again,
Williams made this declaration,[2] and yet the fact is that "The
Nightingales" is written in "free verse," there being no measurable
recurrence of phonic elements—the stress count ranges from 1
("unlácing") to 3 ("flát wórsted flówers"); the syllable count
from 3 to 6—no definable pattern of word repetition or even of
syntactic parallelism. Again, Williams' repeated insistence that his
poetry is written in "the American idiom"—"the language as
spoken"[3]—belies what is actually on the page, for what conceiv-
able voice speaks this way?

> My shoes as I lean unlacing them stand out upon flat worsted
> flowers under my feet. Nimbly the shadows of my fingers play
> unlacing over shoes and flowers.

From the "as" clause, awkwardly embedded between subject and
verb, to the gratuitous repetition of "unlacing" and especially that
final curious locution "unlacing over" where we would expect a
direct object, this surely is *not* the natural American idiom.
Nor does Williams' reference to tempo make much sense: the
elimination of a single short line, "under my feet," from a nine-
line poem cannot make it appreciably "go faster"; indeed, when
we listen to the second version read aloud, we may well distinguish

---

2. As early as 1913, Williams declared: "I do not believe in *vers libre*, this contradiction
in terms. Either the motion continues or it does not continue, either there is rhythm or
no rhythm. *Vers libre* is prose." See Mike Weaver, *William Carlos Williams: The American Background* (Cambridge, England: Cambridge University Press, 1971), p. 82. Weaver
produces the whole unpublished essay "Speech Rhythm," submitted to *Poetry* but returned by Harriet Monroe as being incomprehensible: see pp. 82-83. For other important
versions of this argument, see *The Selected Letters of William Carlos Williams*, ed. John
C. Thirwall (New York: McDowell, Obolensky, 1957), p. 129; "Studiously Unprepared:
Notes for Various Talks and Readings: May 1940 to April 1941," ed. Paul Mariani, in
Sulfur, (1982): 12-13; Walter Sutton, "A Visit with William Carlos Williams" (1961), in
Interviews with William Carlos Williams, ed. Linda Wagner (New York: New Directions,
1976), pp. 38-39; and William Carlos Williams, "Free Verse," in *Princeton Encyclopedia
of Poetry and Poetics*, ed. Alex Preminger (Princeton: Princeton University Press, 1974),
pp. 288-290. Ironically, it is customary to treat Williams as one of *the* inventors of
free verse: see Charles O. Hartman, *Free Verse, An Essay on Prosody* (Princeton: University Press, 1980), pp. 93-106, and passim.
3. IWWP, p. 75. See also, "Note: The American Language and the New Poetry, so
called," enclosed with a letter to H.L. Mencken, 17 December 1934, cited by Weaver,
p. 81; Williams, "Interview with Mike Wallace" (1957), in Wagner, *Interviews*, p. 74;
Williams, "Some Hints Toward the Enjoyment of Modern Verse" (1952), in *Quarterly Review of Literature* (1953); rpt. in *Contemporary Poetry, A Retrospective from
the Quarterly Review of Literature*, ed. Theodore Weiss and Renée Weiss (Princeton:
Princeton University Press, 1974), p. 125.
    As is the case with free verse, most commentators take Williams at his word.
Thus David Perkins writes: "the lines are arranged to enact the movement of the
voice speaking: they reinforce the natural rhythm by linear notion," *A History of
Modern Poetry from the 1890s to Pound, Eliot and Yeats* (Cambridge, Mass.: Harvard
University Press, 1976), p. 316.

the absence of meter and rhyme, the brevity of the line-units, the preponderance of monosyllables, and so on, but the overall sound structure remains almost the same.

What, then, is the difference that so excites Williams: The *look*, of course. ("See how much better it conforms to the page, how much better it looks?"). The verse of "The Nightingales" is not, Williams would have it, "free" because its look on the page is that of two symmetrical units; indeed, in the revised version, we see two quatrains, almost square in shape. This symmetrical form provides stability against which the words of the little poem push and jostle, just as in, say, an Elizabethan sonnet, the actual rhythm is played off against the chosen metrical base and rhyme scheme. The visual shape also directs our attention to particular words and the relationships between them. "My shoes," for example, does not get a line to itself because it is not, in fact, the subject of the poem; rather, the emphasis is on what happens when something— "unlacing"—is done to them as the poet "leans" in their direction. "Lean" and "unlacing" share the letters *l* and *n*: the act "stands out" visually as well as semantically in juxtaposition to the longer line "flat worsted flowers," with its repetition of *fl* and *t* and the chiasmus of *wo—ow*. In the second stanza, expectation is again raised and deferred. "Nimbly the shadows" must wait for the second line and in turn the third and fourth before we understand what it is that is happening. "Unlacing" gets a line all to itself because it is the key word, and the unlacing now takes on a different meaning as the play of shadows takes precedence over the act. Indeed, the "shoes" previously "stand[ing] out upon/ flat worsted flowers" now become equated with them. In the imaginative metamorphosis of the poem, the shadows of the poet's fingers have become birds—the nightingales of the title—flying through space. Accordingly, the second reference to "flowers," which corresponds visually to the first, no longer means the same thing. The look of the poem on the page thus creates a play of sameness and difference, identity and change.

I do not mean to imply that sound plays no part in this pattern or that the poem is to be perceived instantaneously as a "spatial form."[4] Clearly, the words must be perceived in time as our eye moves from line to line; just as clearly, the visual arrangement foregrounds certain sounds—for example, the voiced spirant endings in shoe*s*, a*s*, flower*s*, finger*s*, shoe*s*, flower*s* (7 of the 25 words or almost one-third); or the three nasals in a vertical row at

4. See Cary Nelson, "Suffused-Encircling Shapes of Mind: Inhabited Space in Williams," *Journal of Modern Literature*, 1, no. 4 (May 1971): 549-564.

line endings in the first quatrain: lea*n*, the*m*, upo*n*. All the same, these are, in Hugh Kenner's words, "stanzas you can't quite *hear*,"[5] in that sentence rhythm (one declarative sentence per stanza) overrides all line endings and that there is no marked rhythm to oppose its forward push. Rather, "The Nightingales" is written in what Kenner calls "stanzas to see": indeed, they could not have existed prior to the invention of the typewriter, an invention that made it possible for the poet to compose directly for the printed page with no intermediary process of transposition.

Stanzas to see—it is interesting that Williams himself never quite understood the workings of his own prosody. Thus when, in an interview of 1950, John W. Gerber asked the poet what it is that makes "This Is Just To Say" a poem, Williams replied, "In the first place, it's metrically absolutely regular.... So, dogmatically speaking, it has to be a poem because it goes that way, don't you see!"[6] But the poem actually goes like this:

> I have eaten
> the plums
> that were in
> the icebox
>
> and which
> you were probably
> saving
> for breakfast
>
> Forgive me
> they were delicious
> so sweet
> and so cold[7]

The stanzas exhibit no regularity of stress or of syllable count; indeed, except for lines 2 and 5 (each an iamb) and lines 8 and 9 (each an amphibrach), no two lines have the same metrical form. What then can Williams mean when he says, "It's metrically absolutely regular"? Again, he mistakes sight for sound: on the page, the three little quatrains look alike; they have roughly the same physical shape. It is typography rather than any kind of phonemic recurrence that provides directions for the speaking voice (or for

---

5. *A Homemade World, The American Modernist Writers* (New York: Alfred A. Knopf, 1975), p. 58.

6. John W. Gerber and Emily W. Wallace, "An Interview with William Carlos Williams" (1950), in Wagner, *Interviews*, p. 17. Subsequently cited as INTS.

7. My notation is a simplified version of the standard Trager-Smith scansion using 4 stresses: primary (╱), secondary (╲), tertiary (╲), and weak ( ). A strong pause is indicated by the standard caesura (‖), a lesser pause, (╱). The poem appears in *The Collected Earlier Poems of William Carlos Williams* (Norfolk, Conn.: New Directions, 1951), p. 354. Subsequently cited as CEP.

the eye that reads the lines silently) and that teases out the poem's meanings.

Williams did not hit upon this visual mode without a good bit of struggle, although in his later years, he wanted his readers to think otherwise. By 1950, he was telling the following story about his poetic beginnings:

> My first poem was born like a bolt out of the blue. It came unsolicited and broke a spell of disillusion and suicidal despondency. Here it is:
>
>> A black, black cloud
>> flew over the sun
>> driven by fierce flying
>> rain.
>
> The joy I felt, the mysterious, soul-satisfying joy that swept over me at that moment was only mitigated by the critical comment which immediately followed it: How could the clouds be driven by the rain? Stupid.
> But the joy remained. From that moment I was a poet.[8]

The spell of "disillusion and suicidal despondency" to which Williams refers was evidently brought on by an episode of heart strain that ended his adolescent dreams of becoming a track star. He was eighteen at the time. Appreciative biographers and critics have repeatedly cited Williams' little story as an instance of the poet's early premonition of his future poetic power.[9] I hope, therefore, that I shall not be thought too irreverent if I suggest that, like so much of the self-invention that characterizes the *Autobiography*,[10]

---

8. *The Autobiography of William Carlos Williams* (New York: Random House, 1951), p. 47; subsequently cited as AUTO. Cf. the slightly different versions Williams gives in IWWP, p. 4, and INTS, p. 8.

9. In *William Carlos Williams: A New World Naked* (New York: McGraw Hill, 1981), pp. 30-31, Paul Mariani, commenting on the cardiac episode, writes:

> Williams was shattered. He had fondly hoped that he would at least shine as a track star, and now he went into a black depression. It was ironically, this touching bottom, this first descent into his private hell, that turned out to yield an unlooked-for gift: the gift of the poem. It was, as far as he could remember, the first poem he had ever written, a short, spontaneous thing, a single sentence containing a symbol of his own despondency. But writing it brought with it a sense of relief, of delight, as though he had done something truly extraordinary.

And Mariani quotes the four lines of the poem.

Similarly, Rod Townley, commenting on the awkwardness of Williams' early verse and exclamatory rhetoric, writes: "But these are all half-measures; none of the poems resulting from them has the clean quiet shock value of the enjambment that concludes the first poem Williams wrote: 'driven by fierce flying/ rain'." See *The Early Poetry of William Carlos Williams* (Ithaca: Cornell University Press, 1975), p. 63. Townley does not ask himself the question: how would the poet who used those "half-measures" as late as 1913, have devised the "clean quiet shock value of...enjambment" as early as 1900?

10. See, on this point, Herbert Leibowitz, "You Can't Bear Innocence: *The Autobiography of William Carlos Williams*," *American Poetry Review*, 10, no. 2 (March/April 1981): 35-47.

this charming account may well be acrocryphal. It provides
a myth of origins for what was in fact a confusing trial-and-
error process; I say "myth" because, judging from the poems
Williams was to publish a full decade later in *Poems* (1909) and
The Tempers (1913), it is doubtful that he would have known
of a convention according to which the four short lines in question could possibly qualify as a "poem," and therefore equally
doubtful that the young Williams would have preserved them as
such.[11] Indeed, his wholly distinctive visual prosody came into
being only gradually as he put first conventional metrics and
then Imagist free verse behind him and began to place poetry
in the context of the visual arts, as those arts were practiced by
his great French contemporaries. How this process took place
and how the resulting visualization of the "poetic page" has
changed our concept of the lyric—this is my subject.

II

Surely few first volumes give as little indication of a poet's
future direction as does *Poems* (1909), published when Williams
was twenty-six. Of its twenty-six (is the number a coincidence?)
poems, fourteen are sonnets, all but three Petrarchan. Here is a
representative octave:

> Sweet Lady, sure it seems a thousand years
> Since last you honored me with gentle speech.
> Yet, when, forsaking fantasy, I reach
> With memory's index o'er the stretching tiers
>
> Of minutes wasted, counting, (as who fears
> Strict-chiding reason, lest it should impeach
> All utterance, must) a mighty, gaping breach
> 'Twixt truth and seeming verity appears.[12]

Williams was to recall five decades later that the early poems were
much "preoccupied with the studied elegance of Keats" (IWWP,
p. 8), but the fact is that the sonnets, quatrains, ballad stanzas,
heroic couplets, and hexameters of *Poems* are not appreciably different from hundreds of other lyrics published in this period: for
example, Madison Cawein's "The Yellow Puccoon" or Percy
MacKaye's "In the Bohemian Redwoods," both of which appeared
side by side with seven of Williams' poems in the special American

---

11. According to Emily M. Wallace, Williams' bibliographer (see note 13) and the editor
of the Williams Correspondence now in progress, the original manuscript of this poem
has not yet been found.
12. *Poems* (Rutherford, N.J.: Reid Howell, 1909), p. 14.

Poetry number of *The Poetry Review* (October 1912).[13] It is as if
the poet had not yet been born; indeed, Williams did not reprint a
single poem from his first volume.

Williams' second book, *The Tempers* (1913), replaces the
Poetic Diction and mechanical verse forms of the genteel poets of
the 1900s with the Ezra Pound of *Personae* (1909) and *Ripostes*
(1912), the latter dedicated to Williams. The results are curious.
Here is the first stanza of "Postlude," a poem H.D. called "a Niké,
supreme among your poems," and Pound, "splendid":[14]

> Now that I have cooled to you
> Let there be gold of tarnished masonry,
> Temples soothed by the sun to ruin
> That sleep utterly.
> Give me hand for the dances,
> Ripples at Philae, in and out,
> And lips, my Lesbian,
> Wall flowers that once were flame.   (CEP, p. 16)

Williams' earliest free verse is distinguished by its slow phrasal
rhythm, its end-stopping and frequent mid-line pauses ("And lips,
my Lesbian"), its conjunction of syntactic and line units, its alliteration, assonance, and open vowel sounds. All these are features found in Pound's early free verse, for example:

Williams:	Let there be gold of tarnished masonry
Pound:	Let us build here an exquisite friendship
Williams:	Temples soothed by the sun to ruin
Pound:	Gods of the wingèd shoe
Williams:	Ripples at Philae, in and out
Pound:	Algae reach up and out, beneath
Williams:	And lips, my Lesbian
Pound:	My City, my beloved....[15]

13. See *The Poetry Review*, I, x (October 1912): 479-81. Williams' poems in this volume
are a selection from *The Tempers*, introduced by Ezra Pound, but the poems included in
this selection are still very close to those in *Poems* (1909). For a list of these poems and
for all subsequent bibliographical information on book and magazine publication, see
Emily Mitchell Wallace's indispensable *A Bibliography of William Carlos Williams* (Middletown, Connecticut: Wesleyan University Press, 1968).
14. H.D.'s comment is made in a letter of 14 August 1916 which Williams reprints in
the Preface to *Kora in Hell: Improvisations* (1920); rpt. in *Imaginations*, ed. Webster
Schott (New York: New Directions, 1970), p. 13. Subsequently cited as IMAG. H.D.'s
letter then goes on to object to the "flippancies" and "hey-ding-ding touch of a slightly
later poem, "March," and Williams responds with some asperity, IMAG, p. 13.
    For Pound's comment, see his review of *The Tempers* in *New Freewoman*, I, no.
11 (December 1913); rpt. in *William Carlos Williams: The Critical Heritage*, ed. Charles
Doyle (London: Routledge & Kegan Paul, 1980), p. 53, and in this volume, pp. 139-140.
Subsequently cited as Doyle. At Pound's request, "Postlude" was published in the June
1913 number of *Poetry* by Harriet Monroe; see Mariani, *A New World Naked*, p. 105.
15. The lines come respectively from "Und Drang," "The Return," "Sub Mare," and
"N.Y.": see *Collected Early Poems of Ezra Pound* (New York: New Directions, 1976),
pp. 173, 198, 194, and 185.

For Pound, the line as unit, composed "in the sequence of the musical phrase, not in the sequence of the metronome," was to remain the basic building block of poetry; his are, moreover, lines to be *heard* as well as seen, their rhythm being highly pronounced and frequently repeated with delicate variations in successive lines:

> Ear, ear for the sea-surge;
>   rattle of old men's voices.
> And then the phantom Rome,
>   marble narrow for seats....   (Canto VII)[16]

Williams' free verse is of a different order. Having begun with Poundian line units:

> O crimson salamander,
> Because of love's whim
>   sacred!   (CEP, p. 23)

he soon shifts to a syntax that purposely goes *against* the line, blocking its integrity. The single line heard as musical phrase is replaced by the set of lines as "suspension system,"[17] whose guiding principle is the syntactic opening or *cut* that decomposes sentences and recombines words into new structures.

In *The Egoist* of 15 August 1914, for example, Williams published nine poems, only three of which ("My townspeople, beyond in the great world" later titled "Gulls," "In Harbour'" and "The Revelation") he later chose to reprint. Most of the rejected poems are again written in imitation of Pound: for example, "Rendezvous," which begins:

> My song! It is time!
> Wilder! Bolder! Spread the arms!
> Have done with finger pointing.[18]

Others bring to mind the Imagist lyrics of Richard Aldington or John Gould Fletcher:

> Slowly rising, slowly strengthening moon,
> Pardon us our fear in pride:
> Pardon us our troubled quietnesses!

But the final poem in the selection, "The Revelation," which Williams was to reprint in *Collected Poems 1921-1931,* contains what are probably the first intimations of Williams' own prosody:

---

16. *The Cantos of Ezra Pound* (New York: New Directions, 1971), p. 24.
17. The phrase is Hugh Kenner's: see *A Homemade World*, p. 59.
18. *The Egoist*, 16, no. 1 (1914): 307-308.

> I awoke happy, the house
> Was strange, voices
> Were across a gap
> Through which a girl
> Came and paused,
> Reaching out to me
> With never a word.

Here the last four lines follow the free verse conventions of the period. In line 4, the subject noun ("girl") is separated from its predicate, but the compound verb "Came and paused" is preceded by a natural speech pause so that this particular cut seems quite normal. Lines 6 and 7 each contain a complete syntactic unit: participial phrase and prepositional phrase respectively.

The cuts in the first two lines are quite different. The separation of subject noun ("the house") from copula, where the syntax allows for no pause, and the suspension of the noun in a short line that already contains one independent clause, creates a tone of hesitation:

> I awóke háppy, **//** the house ➡

Does "house" look ahead to the next line so that the sentence can be completed or back toward the alliterating word "happy"? The same ambiguity occurs in the case of "voices"/ "Were" in the next line. Williams wants, of course, to convey the confusion one feels at the moment of awakening from a particularly absorbing dream; indeed, in the revised version (CEP, p. 39), he removed the last line and added a dash:

> Reaching out to me—

which underscores the sense of tentativeness, of equivocation.

The rest of the poem, both in the *Egoist* and *Sour Grapes* versions, is unremarkable:

> Then I remembered
> What I had dreamed....

and so on. But the prosodic "revelation" of Williams' poem by that title is that when lineation goes *against* rather than *with* the syntax—a phenomenon for the eye rather than the ear—a semantic shift takes place. To put it another way, the linear pull can remove words from their natural habitat in the sentence and create new configurations:

> Was strange, voices
> Were...

becomes

> Was [strange, voices]...

By 1916, a vintage year in which Williams published twenty-two poems in *Others* and six in *Poetry*, he had mastered this cutting technique. It is interesting, in this connection, to compare Williams' own poems of 1916 to the free-verse poems included in the July issue of *Others*, which Williams edited. The issue opens with Marianne Moore's "Critics and Connoisseurs," a poem designed, like those of Williams, to be seen rather than heard, its intricate symmetrical stanzas created by complex typographical and syllable-counting rules. The volume ends with Pound's Fenollosa's poem "To-Em-Mei's 'The Unmoving Cloud'," in which almost every line is a subject-verb-object unit, complete in itself, rhythmic units recurring with delicate variation:

> I stóp in my roóm towaŗd the Eást, quíet, quíet,
> I pát my nêw cásk of wíne.
> My friends are estránged, or fár distant....[19]

Pound and Moore have obviously devised ways of structuring the poem that Williams admires, but their ways are not his, any more than is Wallace Stevens', whose "The Worms at Heaven's Gate," written in blank verse, is included in Williams' selection for *Others*. Rather, we must look at the free verse of such poets as Skipwith Cannell, Alfred Kreymborg, Maxwell Bodenheim, Helen Hoyt, Mina Loy, and Conrad Aiken, free verse that superficially does look like Williams' own and which the audience of 1916 would not have distinguished from his. Consider the following examples:

(1) Helen Hoyt, "Damask"

> White blossoms,
> Frail tracery,
> Born of whiteness
> In a white world,
> You are more shadowy than frost flowers
> Growing in your smooth atmosphere,
> Vivid for a moment,
> Then palely
> Dimmed again:
> White lost in white.   (*Others*, p. 10)

(2) Conrad Aiken, "Illusions"

> Green fingers lifting a pebble,
> green fingers uncurling,
> the slant and splash of a waterdrop
> between eternities;
> earth slipping from old roots,
> and the stealth of white petals in the sun
> all day long;

---

19. *Others*, 3 (1916-1917): 31. Marianne Moore's poem appears on pages 4-5.

    brown chimney pots
    descending against a cloud
    in silence;
    between walls
    the dry whir of a sparrow's wings...
    am I these, or more?   (*Others*, p. 16)

(3) Williams, "Love Song":

    the stain of love
    is upon the world!
    Yellow, yellow, yellow
    it eats into the leaves,
    smears with saffron
    the horned branches that lean
    heavily
    against a smooth purple sky!
    There is no light
    only a honey-thick stain
    that drips from leaf to leaf
    and limb to limb
    spoiling the colors
    of the whole world—

    you far off there under
    the wine-red selvage of the west![20]

All three poems are written in short free-verse lines, the stress count ranging between 2 and 4; in all three, there is much trochaic or spondaic rhythm ("White blóssoms"; "gréen fíngers"; "sméars with sáffron"), but not enough to establish a clear-cut metrical figure. But where Hoyt and Aiken consistently use end-stopped lines and simple repetition of syntactic and rhythmic units, Williams avoids the repeat, cuts in odd places, and positions his words on the page so as to create an effect of what might be called studied clumsiness. Aiken, for example, relies heavily on the noun phrase—

    Gréen fíngers lífting a pébble
    gréen fíngers uncúrling . . .

    eárth slípping from óld róots . . .
    whíte pétals in the sún . . .
    brówn chímney póts— . . .

---

20. Hoyt's "Damask" appears in *Others*, p. 10; Aiken's "Illusions" on p. 16. The first version of Williams' "Love Song" adds three lines at the beginning ("What have I to say to you/ When we shall meet?/ Yet—") and fifteen more lines after "spoiling the colors/ Of the whole world"); it does not have the final couplet. See *Poetry*, 9 (November 1916) 81-82; and *CEP*, p. 173-174. The second version first appeared in *Al-Que Quiere* (1917); see *CEP*, p. 174.

Hoyt, on participial modifiers:

> Born of whiteness
>
> Growing in your smooth atmosphere
> Dimmed again....

The result, in both cases, is a certain laxity as phrase is piled upon phrase with little variety or tension.

Williams' three and four-stress lines are quite different. For one thing, he opens with an isolated line—a single, straightforward sentence, five of its six words monosyllables, its rhythm choppy and abrupt:

> I lie here thinking of you: —

Then another simple sentence, but this time draped over two lines:

> the stain of love
> is upon the world!

The first line here needs the second to complete it and even then we are left in a quandary. For unlike Hoyt's "white blossoms" (the damask) or Aiken's "green fingers" (tree branches), Williams' "stain of love" is less a metaphor than a surrealistic image of eroticism, the poet's semen becoming a mysterious flood that covers all, eating into the leaves and finally "spoiling the colors/ of the whole world." In this context, the repetition "Yellow, yellow, yellow!" is not a descriptive tag like Hoyt's "White blossoms ...Born of whiteness/ In a white world" or Aiken's "green fingers," but an exclamatory particle, the verbalization of the poet's frustated desire.

Williams' strategy is to isolate words rather than to blend them in symmetrical rhythmic phrases: no two lines have the same stress pattern, and yet key words are carefully linked by alliteration—"smears with saffron," "horned heavily," "smooth sky"— and assonance—"eats," "leaves," "smears," "lean"—as well as by what we might call, on the analogy to eye rhyme, "eye assonance" as in "world!"/ "yellow" and "lean"/ "heavily". The word "heavily" gets a line all to itself in what is one of Williams' nicest effects in the poem:

> the horned branches that lean
> heavily
> against a smooth purple sky!

Thus isolated, "heavily" gets heavy stress, as if to suggest the weight of phallic power pressing against the "smooth purple sky." But "heavily," placed precisely at the mid-point of the stanza (the seventh of fourteen lines) refers, not only to the horned branches

but to the "stain of love...upon the world" above it on the page
as well as to the "honey-thick stain/ that drips from leaf to leaf"
a few lines below. "Love Song" thus becomes a design around a
center, and yet the center is displaced as the narrative suddenly
breaks off and gives way to the final exclamation:

> yóu fár óff thêre'únder
> the wíne-rêd sélvage of the wést!

Conrad Aiken, not surprisingly, was not keen on such asym-
metries. Reviewing *Al Que Quiere* (1917) he remarks: "Beauty of
sound [Williams] denies himself, beauty of prosodic arrangement
too: the cadences are prose cadences, the line-lengths are more or
less arbitrary, and only seldom, in a short-winded manner, are they
effective."[21] These charges were echoed by other critics over the
years: as late as 1950, Hayden Carruth complained that Williams'
lines "are not run over, in the Elizabethan sense; nor are they rove
over, in the Hopkinsian sense; they are hung over, like a Dali
watch." The distinction is not incorrect, but for Carruth, the
"hung over" quality of the lines must be a fault: "If this is done
for typographical effect, as it sometimes appears, it is inexcusable,
for it interferes with our reading."[22] A remarkable misunderstanding, implying, as it does, that typography is *detachable* from the
poem, that lineation is just a nuisance, "interfer[ing] with our
reading" of the poem for its substance.

But of course the typography *is* in many ways the poem's
substance. Take a poem like "The Young Housewife," a short
lyric often praised for what James Breslin has called its "tough
colloquial flatness," its "matter-of-fact" verse,[23] but which, more
precisely, uses that flatness for playful purposes:

> At ten A.M. the young housewife
> moves about in negligee behind
> the wooden walls of her husband's house.
> I pass solitary in my car.
>
> Then again she comes to the curb
> to call the ice-man, fish-man, and stands
> shy, uncorseted, tucking in
> stray ends of hair, and I compare her
> to a fallen leaf.

21. "Mr. Williams and His Caviar of Excessive Individualism," *Skepticisms: Notes on Contemporary Poetry* (New York, 1919); rpt. in Doyle, p. 58.
22. Review of *Paterson, Book Three,* in *Nation* (8 April 1950); rpt. in Doyle, p. 221.
23. *William Carlos Williams, An American Artist* (New York: Oxford University Press, 1970), p. 52.

> The noiseless wheels of my car
> rush with a crackling sound over
> dried leaves as I bow and pass smiling.   (CEP, p. 136)[24]

Here the three stanzas are parody stanzas, the first, a neat-looking quatrain that has neither rhyme nor meter but slyly designates the young housewife by the same rhythmic group we find in "At ten A.M.":

> At ten A. M.   the young housewife

The second line, with its odd construction "in negligee" on the model of "in furs" or "in silks," is cut after the word "behind," a word that thus gets construed as a noun (her "in negligee behind") rather than as a preposition. The same sexual innuendo occurs in line 7:

> shy, uncorseted, tucking in

where the separation of the verb from its object ("stray ends of hair") makes us expect a reference to what one usually tucks into a corset. The next line produces even greater surprise:

> stray ends of *hair*, and I compare her

To what, we wonder?

> to a fallen leaf.

An absurd comparison, since surely the young housewife—she is constantly doing things, moving about, calling the ice-man or fishman, tucking in stray ends of hair—is the very opposite of a fallen leaf. Or is she? Never mind the parody period after "leaf": the tercet now brings it all out into the open:

> The noiseless wheels of my car
> rush with a crackling sound over
> dried leaves as I bow and pass smiling.

In his erotic fantasy, the poet wants to make this attractive housewife a "fallen leaf" to the "noiseless wheels of his car," to "rush with a crackling sound over/ her dried leaves." But it is, after all, only a daydream; normal life must continue and so "I bow and pass smiling." The tercet has lines of 7, 8, and 9 syllables (3, 4, and 5 stresses) respectively; the diagonal created by its line endings thus presents an image of one-step-at-a-time accretion, as if to say that, fantasize all we like, we must get on with it. Typography, in a case like this, is destiny.

---

24. "The Young Housewife" first appeared in the December 1916 issue of *Others*.

III

How did the poet of *The Tempers* (1913)—

> Lady of dusk-wood fastnesses
> Thou art my Lady—   (CEP, p. 17)

become, within three or four short years, the poet of "Love Song" and "The Young Housewife"? The Imagist movement clearly made a difference, but then, as we have seen, *The Tempers* is the book that pays the greatest homage to Pound; by 1917 when *Al Que Quiere* was published, Pound's imprint was no longer decisive; neither, for that matter, was that of H.D. or of Conrad Aiken or Carl Sandburg. Rather, the poems of the late teens represent Williams' first attempt to create verbal-visual counterparts to the paintings and drawings exhibited by the Photo-Secession (*291*) Gallery and reproduced in the pages of Alfred Stieglitz's *Camera Work* and later in *291* in the years preceding the entrance of the United States into the Great War. Williams' relationship to the visual artists of his time has been studied frequently, most notably by Bram Djikstra and Dikran Tashjian,[25] and I do not wish to rehearse the story of his reaction to the Armory Show and of his acquaintance with Stieglitz and the Arensberg Circle (Duchamp, Picabia, Man Ray, and others) again here. What I do want to suggest is that when we speak of the Cubist or Dada element in Williams' poetry, we must look, not only at the imagery and semantic patterning of the poems, as most critics, including myself, have done,[26] but also at the actual look of the poem on the page, the distribution of black letters in white space. The *mise en question* of the representability of the sign, raised by Picasso and Picabia as early as 1912-13, is not prominent in Williams' work before *Kora in Hell* (1920); but the visualization of the stanza, and the line cut comparable to the visual cut in Cubist or

---

25. Bram Djikstra, *The Hieroglyphics of a New Speech: Cubism, Stieglitz, and the Early Poetry of William Carlos Williams* (Princeton: Princeton University Press, 1969); Dikran Tashjian, *Skyscraper Primitives: Dada and the American Avant-Garde*, 1910-1925 (Middletown, Connecticut: Wesleyan University Press, 1975). See also, Bram Djikstra (ed.), *A Recognizable Image: William Carlos Williams on Art and Artists* (New York: New Directions, 1978); and, for an account of Williams' relationship with American artists in the twenties and thirties, Dikran Tashjian, *William Carlos Williams and the American Scene* (Berkeley and Los Angeles: University of California Press, 1978).
26. See my *The Poetics of Indeteminacy: Rimbaud to Cage* (Princeton: Princeton University Press, 1981), Chapter Four; Ruth Grogan, "The Influence of Painting on William Carlos Williams" (1969), in *William Carlos Williams, A Critical Anthology,* ed.Charles Tomlinson (Baltimore: Penguin Books, 1972), pp. 265-298; Henry Sayre, "Ready-Mades and Other Measures: The Poetics of Marcel Duchamp and William Carlos Williams, *Journal of Modern Literature,* 8 (1980): 3-22. An excellent essay that does relate Williams' verse form to Cubist art is James E. Breslin's "William Carlos Williams and Charles Demuth: Cross-Fertilization in the Arts," *Journal of Modern Literature,* 6, no. 2 (April 1977): 248-63.

Dada collage—these begin to appear, as I noted earlier, in poems like "The Revelation" (1914); and *Al Que Quiere* is, among other things, an homage to the typewriter.

Picabia's "object-portraits" of 1915, a number of which were reproduced in *291*, present an interesting analogy to Williams' verse. These pen-and-ink drawings of isolated technological objects, many endowed with legends that identify them as particular personalities, look, at first glance, like the mail-order catalogue illustrations and newspaper ads on which they were, in fact, based.[27] Gabrielle Buffet-Picabia recalls:

> They drew inspiration from rudimentary, mechanical or geometric forms, and were executed with the dryness of blueprints. The colors are sober and few; Picabia sometimes added to his paintings strange substances, wood which created relief, gold and silver powders, and particularly poetic quotations which are integrated in the composition and indicate the title of the work.... The whole develops in an imaginary realm, where the relations between words and forms have no objective, representational intent, but recreate among themselves their own intrinsic relations.[28]

Consider *Ici C'est Ici Stieglitz/ Foi et Amour* (Figure 1), a drawing Williams surely knew since it appeared on the cover of *291* in 1915. The top and bottom of what seems to be Stieglitz's own folding camera are rendered realistically, as they might be in an illustrated catalogue. But what is inside this frame has a nice ambiguity. In one sense, Picabia gives us a drawing of magnified camera parts: the bellows, shutter, hinge, flashbulb. But the distortion of scale is such that we also seem to be looking at what is seen *by* the camera: a staircase on the left, a walking-stick and street lamp on the right. Or again, as in all of Picabia's drawings of the period, most obviously in the picture of a spark-plug called *Portrait D'Une Jeune Fille Américaine Dans L'État De Nudité*, the "portrait" of Stieglitz has erotic overtones, reenforced by the words *FOI ET AMOUR* of the title and especially by the word *IDÉALE*, placed over the hole which is also the lens.

In Picabia's drawings, as in a Picasso collage, the verbal is thus incorporated as a commentary on the visual: indeed, the picture must be "read" as well as seen. A similar attempt to fuse word and image is found in Gertrude Stein's verbal portraits, two of which—"Matisse" and "Picasso"—appeared in the special August 1912 issue of *Camera Work*, and a third, "Portrait of Mabel

27. See William S. Rubin, *Dada, Surrealism, and their Heritage* (New York: The Museum of Modern Art, 1968), p. 27.
28. "Some Memories of Pre-Dada: Picabia and Duchamp" (1949), in *The Dada Painters and Poets: An Anthology*, ed. Robert Motherwell (New York: George Wittenborn, Inc., 1951), p. 261.

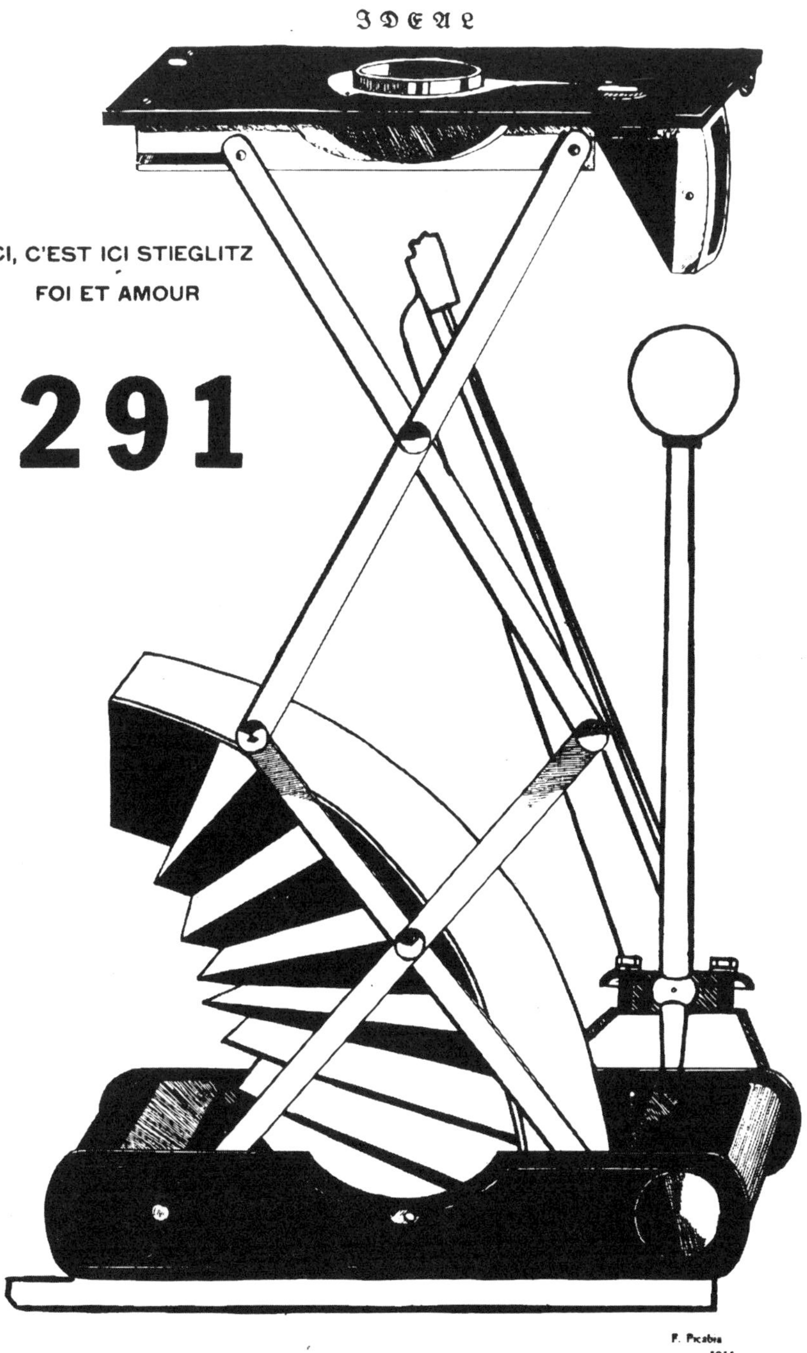
IDEAL
ICI, C'EST ICI STIEGLITZ
FOI ET AMOUR
291
F. Picabia
1915
New York

Dodge at the Villa Curonia," in the June 1913 issue. The latter also has a piece by Mabel Dodge herself called "Speculations," in which she observes that "In a large studio in Paris, hung with paintings by Renoir, Matisse and Picasso, Gertrude Stein is doing with words what Picasso is doing with paint." And again, "In Gertrude Stein's writing every word lives."[29]

Every word lives: Williams, who was to follow Stein in what he called her "unlink[ing]" of words "form their former relationships in the sentence,"[30] surely learned from an artist like Picabia that, if the visual work can also have a verbal dimension, why not the other way around? And so he began to experiment with the visual placement of words in lines: here is "Good Night," first published in *Others* in December 1916:

> In brilliant gas light
> I turn the kitchen spigot
> and watch the water plash
> into the clean white sink.
> On the grooved drain-board
> to one side is
> a glass filled with parsley—
> crisped green.
>   Waiting
> for the water to freshen—
> I glance at the spotless floor—:
> a pair of rubber sandals
> lie side by side
> under the wall-table
> all is in order for the night....   (CEP, p. 145)

Here it is lineation rather than the pattern of stresses that guides the reader's eye so that objects stand out, one by one, as in a series of film shots: first the gas light, then the spigot, then the plash of water, and finally the sink itself. The eye moves slowly so as to take in each monosyllable (all but 4 of the 19 words in the first lines, all but 12 of the 67 words in the whole verse paragraph): *in, gas, light, turn, the, and, watch....* The sixth line, "to one side is," is what Hayden Carruth calls "hung over": it asks the question, what is it that is located "to one side"? The next line tells us: "A glass filled with parsley—." But what does the parsley look like? Again a new line:

> Crísped gréen.

29. *Camera Work*, Special Number: June 1913, pp. 6-8. See *Poetics of Indeterminancy*, Chapter Three.
30. "The Work of Gertrude Stein" (1931), in *Selected Essays of William Carlos Williams* (New York: New Directions, 1954), p. 116. Subsequently cited as SE.

Next there is a wait as the water runs from the tap, and so "Waiting" gets a line to itself and a prominent line at that because it is moved over toward the jagged right margin of the poem. Notice that the poem would *sound* exactly the same if "waiting" were alligned with "crisped" and "for" at the left margin; the effect, in other words, is entirely visual. And again, the ensuing lines are characterized by suspension: a "pair of rubber sandals" (line 12) do what? They "lie side by side" (line 13). But where?

> Únder the wáll-táble

As in Picabia's *Ici C'est Ici Stieglitz*, ordinary objects are granted a curious sexual power.

If we look at the sound repetitions in Williams' poem, we immediately note the alliteration of *t*'s and *w*'s and the assonance of *i*'s. But again, the visualization of these phonemes creates a stronger "echo structure" than does their sound. The first letter in the poem, for example, appears ten times in the 19 words of the first sentence: *in–brilliant-light-I-kitchen-spigot-into-white-sink*. The first line-ending, "light," gets a nice response from "spigot" in the slightly longer second line; it further chimes with "spotless" (line 11) and with the final word of the stanza, "night." From "light" to "night"—one would think that Williams had written a sonnet or Spenserian stanza. "A design in the poem," as he tells Walter Sutton, "and a design in the picture should make them more or less the same thing" (INTS, p. 53). Thus designed, "Good Night" provides us, quite literally with the pleasure of the text. Each line waits for its fulfillment from the next, with "Waiting," coming, as it does, after "crisped green," exerting the central pull. Like "Love Song," "Good Night" is a poem about desire, its "hung over" words reaching for the other even as the poet daydreams about the young girls he saw at the opera:

> full of smells and
> the resulting sounds of
> cloth rubbing on cloth and
> little slippers on carpet—

IV

I have been suggesting that *Al Que Quiere* is Williams' first significant tribute to the printed page as poetic unit; its poems embody the recognition, not shared by many of Williams' contemporaries, that a poem is "a small machine made of words" (SE, p. 256), a verbal text to be *seen* at least as much as to be heard. Steiglitz's photographs, *The Aeroplane* and *The Dirigible*, had appeared in *Camera Work* as early as 1911, and Picabia's machine drawings as well as Duchamp's readymades surely helped to bring the lesson home: the typographical lay-out of the page was not a sideline, some sort of secondary support structure, but a central fact of poetic discourse. Once this basic premise is understood, Williams' later prosodies become much easier to comprehend. Let me comment briefly on three developments in William's poetry.

1

From *Spring and All* (1923) through the thirties, the main thrust is to condense and to refine the principles of cut, displacement, and formal design adumbrated in the poems of the previous decade. Thus the long and slightly shaggy stanza of "Good Night" or of "Love Song" gives way to much smaller, disjunctive units— to very short lines, often no more than three syllables long, arranged in couplets ("At the Ball Game"), or tercets ("To Elsie"), or quatrains ("Death of the Barber").[31] This drive toward minimalism culminates in such poems of the mid-thirties as "Between Walls":

> the back wings
> of the
>
> hospital where
> nothing
>
> will grow lie
> cinders
>
> in which shine
> the broken
>
> pieces of a green
> bottle   (CEP, p. 343)

If we insert two small function words, "the" in the title and "of" at the beginning of the first line, and place a comma after "grow," we have here a perfectly normal sentence:

> Between the walls of the back wings of the hospital where nothing
> will grow, lie cinders in which shine the broken pieces of a green
> bottle.

An independent clause, its subject and verb inverted, embedded in multiple prepositional modifiers. Williams drapes this sentence across ten lines so that each and every word is taken out of its proper syntactic slot and hence defamiliarized:

> of the . . .
> will grow lie . . .
> in which shine . . .

---

31. See *Poetics of Indeterminacy*, Chapter Three, passim.

and so on. But there is something further. The visual pattern—five symmetrical couplets in which the long line is regularly followed by a short one, contradicts the aural one. Compare, for example, the first and third couplets:

| the back wings | will grow lie |
| of the | cinders |

On the page, these are matching couplets, each having a syllable count of 3-2. The first two lines, moreover, each have three mono-syllables almost identical in size. But when the words of the poem are spoken, "of the" (line 2) receives no stress at all whereas line 5 is scanned as follows-

will grow lie

The result is that the first visual stanza has the stress pattern 2-0, the second, 3-1. What looks symmetrical is in fact disparate and other. The poem means, Williams tells Babette Deutsch, "that in a waste of cinders loveliness, in the form of color, stands up alive."[32] But, as so often, the poem Williams wrote is much bet-ter than the portentous meaning he ascribes to it. For what we ad-mire in "Between Walls" is surely less the idea that beauty can be found even among the trash, than the way this small observa-tion is turned into a "field of action" in which line plays against syntax, visual against aural form, creating what Charles Olson was to call an energy-discharge, or projectile. Words are "unlink[ed] from their former relationships in the sentence" and recombined so that the poem becomes a kind of hymn to linguistic possibility.

2

The poems of Williams' last decade are written almost exclu-sively in what has been called the triadic stanza or three-step line:

The smell of the heat is boxwood
  when rousing us
    a movement of the air....[33]

Discussion of this triad has been confused by Williams' own claim that he is now using a unit called the "variable foot," which he de-fines as a foot "that has been expanded so that more syllables, words, or phrases can be admitted into its confines."[34] As such, the variable foot is, of course, a contradiction in terms, rather like

---

32. Letter of May 25, 1948: see *Selected Letters of William Carlos Williams*, p. 265. Subsequently cited as SL.
33. "To Daphne and Virginia," in *Pictures from Breughel and Other Poems* (New York: New Directions, 1962), p. 75. Subsequently cited as PB.
34. "Free Verse," *Princeton Encyclopedia of Poetry and Poetics*, p. 289. Cf. John C. Thirwall, "Ten Years of a New Rhythm," PB, pp. 183-184.

an elastic inch.[35] It has been argued, most recently by Charles O.
Hartman, that the three-line units of the triad are isochronous.
Here Hartman is following Williams himself, who explained his
"new measure" to Richard Eberhart with the following example:

> (count):—not that I ever count when writing but, at best, the lines
> must be capable of being counted, that is to say, *mea-*
> *sured*—(believe it or not).—At that I may, half conscious-
> ly, even count the measure under my breath as I write.—
> (approximate example)
>
>   (1) The smell of the heat is boxwood
>   (2) when rousing us
>   (3) a movement of the air
>   (4) stirs our thoughts
>   (5) that had no life in them
>   (6) to a life, a life in which
> (or)
>   (1) Mother of God! Our Lady!
>   (2) the heart
>   (3) is an unruly master:
>   (4) Forgive us our sins
>   (5) as we
>   (6) forgive
>   (7) those who have sinned against
>
> Count a single beat to each numeral. You may not agree
> with my ear, but that is the way I count the line. Over the whole
> poem it gives a pattern to the meter that can be felt as a new
> measure.[36]

Hartman comments: "The prosody works for two reasons. First it
builds on the convention of line division, essential to and
recognized in all verse. Second, Williams became sufficiently well-
known so that through letters and essays he could establish single-
handedly the convention that all lines take the same time—though
only for his poems."[37]

Here Hartman bases his argument on the linguist Kenneth
Pike's theorem that "the time-lapse between any two primary
stresses tends to be the same irrespective of the number of syllables and the junctures between them" (p. 42). But the problem is
that, in the example from "For Eleanor and Bill Monahan" that
Williams gives Eberhart, the line "Mother of God! Our Lady!"
has three primary stresses, whereas the next line, "the heart," has
only one. If I insist on making these two lines isochronous, I have
to make a wholly unnatural speech pause after "the heart":

---

35. See Alan Stephens, "Dr. Williams and Tradition," *Poetry*, 101 (February 1963): 361;
A. Kingsley Weatherhead, "William Carlos Williams: Prose, Form, and Measure," ELH,
33 (1966): 118-131.
36. Williams, letter to Richard Eberhart, May 23, 1954, in SL, pp. 326-327.
37. *Free Verse*, p. 35, and cf. p. 69.

Mother of Gód! Oúr Lády!
    the héart - - - -
            is an unrúly máster....

The argument for isochrony thus seems to me to be no more satisfactory than an argument for a measure made up of "feet" that are somehow "variable." In the interview with Walter Sutton, Williams makes a more helpful comment about the triad. When Sutton asks him whether he thinks of feet in terms of stresses, Williams replies: "Not, as stresses, but as spaces in between the various spaces of the verse" (INTS, p. 39). This is, it seems to me, the point. Take the following passage from Book II of "Of Asphodel, That Greeny Flower":

> So to know, what I have to know
>   about my own death
>   if it be real
> I have to take it apart.
>   What does your generation think
>   Of Cézanne?
> I asked a young artist.
>   The abstractions of Hindu painting,
>   he replied,
> is all at the moment which interests me.
>   He liked my poem
>   about the parts
> of a broken bottle,
>   lying green in the cinders
>   of a hospital courtyard.
> There was also, to his mind,
>   the one on gay wallpaper
>   which he had heard about
> but not read.
>   I was grateful to him
>   for his interest.   (PB, pp. 162-163)

The line units here are related neither by stress count nor by isochrony: there is, for example, no way to equalize "What does your generation think" and the next line, "of Cézanne?". But on the page, the three-step line creates an attractive shape; it gives Williams a definite frame within which to lay out his sentences, a successor to such visual stanzas as the quatrains of "The Nightingales" and "This Is Just To Say."

My own sense, however, is that this particular frame does not have the complexity and tension of Williams' earlier visual forms; on the contrary, the three-step grid is an externally imposed geometric form, a kind of cookie cutter. For what happens is this. The locutions of prose ("There was also, to his mind, the one on gay wallpaper which he had heard about but not read") are forced into the triadic mold without sufficient attention to the relation between positioning and line-cut on the one hand and the structure of meanings on the other. Compare, for example, Williams' little poem "Between Walls," which I discussed earlier, to the reference to that poem in lines 11-15 above, and the difference will become clear. Syntactic units now break predictably enough at the point of natural juncture:

> about the parts
> of a broken bottle,
> lying green in the cinders
> of a hospital courtyard.

In the case of "Between Walls," a change of word placement or the elimination of a single word would destroy the poet's mobile, the machine made of words which is the poem. In the case of "Asphodel," we read on pleasantly enough, but the sequence of words about the broken bottle or about the gay wallpaper has no inevitability, no sense of interacting force-field.

Such comparisons help us to understand that visual prosody is, after all, just as difficult as any other. In the wake of Williams, we have now lived through three decades of American poems that claim our attention by the sheer irregularity of pattern: words spread all over the page, words capitalized and in small letters and italics, lines that step up or down or go sideways. But just as a poem written in traditional meter—say, a Shakespeare sonnet—depends for its effectiveness on the relation of the phonemic to the semantic, so the visualization of the poem, the anchoring of its lines on the printed page, demands more than a typographical frame.

3

The premise that the poetic unit is no longer the metrical stanza or even the individual line but rather the printed page itself stands behind what is surely one of Williams' central contributions to American poetics: namely, the alternation and juxtaposition of "verse" to "prose." Williams began to experiment with the prose-verse page as early as *Spring and All* (1923) and *The Descent of Winter* (1928): in these works, lyrics are inserted into expository and narrative prose passages of some length. In *Paterson*, the opposite happens: the basic frame is the long free-verse stanza, and that frame is "cut," even as the line is cut in the earlier poems, by prose passages—documentary accounts of the history of Paterson, letters from friends like Allen Ginsberg, Edward Dahlberg and Marcia Nardi, case reports about patients, fictional narrative, and so on.

Critical speculation on the relation of prose to verse in *Paterson* has not been very helpful, the tendency being to assume that prose and verse must represent some sort of clear-cut dichotomy: for example, the dichotomy between the world of hard facts or "things" (prose) and the world of their imaginative transformation (verse).[38] Williams' own comments, however, stress fusion rather than difference. Thus he writes to Parker Tyler on October 3, 1948:

> All the prose [in *Paterson*] including the tail which would have liked to have wagged the dog, has primarily the purpose of giving a metrical meaning to or of emphasizing a metrical continuity between all word use. It is *not* an antipoetic device.... It *is* that prose and verse are both *writing*, both a matter of words and an interrelation between words for the purpose of exposition, or other better defined purpose of *the art*.... I want to say that prose and verse are to me the same thing, that verse (as in Chaucer's tales) belongs *with* prose.... Poetry does not *have* to be kept away from prose as Mr. Eliot might insist....

And in the same year, to Horace Gregory:

> The truth is that there's an identity between prose and verse, not an antithesis. It all rests on the same base, the same measure... the long letter [at the end of *Paterson*, Book One] is definitely germane to the rest of the text.[39]

In what sense can there be "an identity between prose and verse"; in what sense does their juxtaposition emphasize "a metrical continuity between all word use"? What Williams means, I think, is that once the *page* rather than the foot or line or stanza becomes the unit of measure, the typographic composition of that page can consist of prose as easily as of verse, provided that there is some juxtaposition of the two so as to create visual interest, provided that, in Hugh Kenner's words, "art lifts the saying out of the zone of things said."[40] Poetry, in this larger sense that would include both "verse" and "prose," is a form of writing, of *écriture*, that calls attention to words as words rather than as referents to a particular reality.

Take, for example, the passage in Book One, Part III in which the poet meditates on the fragmentation of self:

> Let it rot, at my center.
>   Whose center?
>   I stand and surpass
>   youth's leanness.

38. See, for example, Walter Peterson, *An Approach to Paterson* (New Haven: Yale University Press, 1967), passim.
39. Cited by James Laughlin in "William Carlos Williams and the Making of Paterson: A Memoir," *Yale Review*, 71 (Spring 1982): 193-94.
40. *A Homemade World*, p. 60.

> My surface is myself.
>   Under which
> to witness, youth is
>   buried. Roots?
>
> Everybody has roots.[41]

Abrupt quatrains full of word repetition give way to open tercets, in which Williams lashes out at the university, a place ruled by "clerks/ got out of hand forgetting for the most part/ to whom they are beholden." The passage concludes with the single line:

> Something else, something else the same.   (P, p. 44)

What is that "something else" which is the same as the *trahison des clercs*? We now read the following prose passage, printed in reduced type:

> He was more concerned, much more concerned, with detaching the label from a discarded mayonnaise jar, the glass jar in which some patient had brought a specimen for examination, than to examine and treat the twenty and more infants taking their turn from the outer office, their mothers tormented and jabbering. He'd stand in the alcove pretending to wash, the jar at the bottom of the sink well out of sight and, as the rod of water came down, work with his fingernail in the splash at the edge of the colored label striving to loose the tightly glued paper. It must have been varnished over, he argued, to have it stick that way. One corner of it he'd got loose in spite of all and would get the rest presently: talking pleasantly the while and with great skill to the anxious parent.

And this in turn gives way to four long free-verse lines, lines distinguished from normal prose only by the jagged right margin:

> Will you give me a baby? asked the young colored woman
> in a small voice standing naked by the bed. Refused
> she shrank within herself. She too refused. It makes me
> too nervous, she said, and pulled the covers round her.;

The three visual units—lyric (quatrains and tercets), prose narrative, and free-verse block—are thematically related: they all center on the nature of "divorce," of alienation from others and from one's work, of the search for and loss of "roots." But the change in prosody signals a change in tone: if the lyric poet of the first part speaks to us directly, ruminating on the universal nature of pain—"Youth is/ buried. Roots?"—the subject of the prose passage is that same poet carefully distanced by an urbane voice that uses the language of the lab report or case study, recording the poet-doctor's compulsive-neurotic behavior, his bizarre concentration on the label of the mayonnaise jar as an

---

41. *Paterson* (New York: New Directions, 1963), pp. 32-33.

escape from all human contact. The intrustion of the free-verse passage:

Will you give me a baby? asked the young colored woman

provides a third perspective: the personal account, evidently given by the doctor to whom the question is addressed, gives us a sense of what it is that the man obsessed with the mayonnaise jar (who is, of course, the same poet-doctor) is afraid of: the confrontation with another, "the young colored woman" whose demands he cannot satisfy.

Each of the three passages in question might have been in "verse" or "prose": it is not their metrical (or non-metrical) status or even their lineation (or non-lineation) that matters, but the very fact of transition from an A to a B and C, the shift in typographical format signalling a change in perspective, in tone, in mood. Thus the personal pathos of the lyric ("we go on living, we permit ourselves/ to continue") gives way to the macabre humor of the mayonnaise-jar story, and in turn to the intimacy of the free-verse passage with its embedded speech.

Such consistent shifting of ground, such change in perspective propels the reader forward through the poem. Try to imagine *Paterson* without such prose-verse alternation, try to imagine all the prose anecdotes and letters and documentary catalogues absorbed into the larger free-verse fabric or viceversa, and the point will become apparent. The difference between Williams' "verse" and his "prose" is thus *not*, as he rightly says, meter; it is the manipulation of tone implicit in the visual presentation of a small stanza versus a prose paragraph with justified left and right margins, and so on. The page is to be seen, its contrasting juxtaposed elements recalling the bits of newspaper or photographs pasted into Cubist or Dada collage.

4

James Laughlin has recently suggested that the influence of modern painting, regularly cited with respect to such earlier works as *Kora in Hell*, "extended to the composition of *Paterson*": "In the revolutionary works of those French painters he saw ways to revolutionize the very nature of writing in English."[42] Certainly,

---

42. Cf. Eleonor Berry, "Williams' Development Of A New Prosodic Form—*Not* The 'Variable Foot,' But The Sight-Stanza," *William Carlos Williams Review*, 7, no. 2 (Fall 1981): 28. Berry writes: "The sense of regularity, sometimes, indeed, monotony, that is induced by Williams' triadic-line verse would seem to be due to the fact that the intervals between the prominent syllables of successive intonantional units in spoken English tend to be perceived as equal." As I have argued above, I question the isochrony of the three

the collage-structure of *Paterson* would not have been possible without the Cubist or Dada model. Indeed, I would posit that when Williams exchanged this particular visual paradigm for the simple numerical grid of the geometer, as he was to do in the step-triads of his last decade, he denied himself the possibility of the *play* that makes poems of his middle years like "Between Walls" and "The Gay Wallpaper" so remarkable. The prosodic trick was to de-center, or, as Williams put it in "The Attic Which Is Desire":

Here

from the street
by
   * * *
   * S *
   * O *
   * D *
   * A *
   * * *

ringed with
running lights

the darkened
pane

exactly
down the center

is
transfixed   (CEP, p. 353)

---

parts of the Williams triad, but I do agree with Berry that this form is "essentially anti-thetical to the sight stanza [e.g., the quatrain or tercet used in the earlier poetry] in its operation."

    For an interesting counter-argument, in which the variable foot is related to the rhythm of Theocritus' idylls, which Williams was reading closely in the early fifties, see Emily Mitchell Wallace, "A Musing in the Highlands and Valleys: The Poetry of Gratwick Farm," *William Carlos Williams Review*, 8, no. 1 (Spring 1982): 27-30.

DIANA COLLECOTT SURMAN

TOWARDS THE CRYSTAL:
ART AND SCIENCE IN WILLIAMS' POETIC

1.   *To make a start . . .*

In Paris in 1925, two Cubist painters, Amédée Ozenfant and Charles-Edouard Jeanneret (better known as the architect Le Corbusier) published a book on modern painting, in which they discerned "a tendency towards the crystal."[1] This treatise issued from a crisis in Cubist aesthetics, occasioned by the almost simultaneous appearance in different artistic centres of the western world of anarchistic individuals such as Tristan Tzara and Marcel Duchamp, who aimed to bring the experimentalism, spontaneity and "lawlessness" of Picasso's art into the public sphere by a programmatic mystification known as Dada. Ozenfant and Jeanneret reacted against these chaotic tendencies by developing Purism, which insisted on the more rigorous style of synthetic Cubism, stressed the laws of structure and composition, and envisaged a new culture based on technology and "planning." "The crystal, in nature, is one of the phenomena that touch us most" they argued in *La Peinture moderne*, "because it clearly exemplifies to us this movement towards geometrical organization." The sculptor Henri Gaudier-Brzeska expressed a similar tendency when he wrote in 1914:

> . . . we have crystallized the sphere into a cube, we have made a combination of all the possible-shaped masses.[2]

Edward Fry has described the aesthetic attitude of Ozenfant and Jeanneret as a "Calvinistic Cubism" since it replaced the resonant organicism of an artist like Cézanne, with an intellectual exercise which deliberately reflected the mechanistic aspects of

---

1. Ozenfant and Jeanneret, *La Peinture moderne* (1925); translation from Edward F. Fry ed., *Cubism* (London: Thames and Hudson, 1966) p. 170.
2. "Vortex Gaudier-Brzeska," *Blast* (1914); repr. in Ezra Pound, *Gaudier-Brzeska: a memoir* (Hessel, E. Yorks: The Marvell Press, 1960; orig. publ. 1916), p. 31; (New York: New Directions), p. 24.

modern civilization.[3] In general, the Purists' canvasses lacked the humour of a painting based on somatic perceptions ; as their preference for *nature morte* suggests, they substituted for the tension of felt space and time in the paintings of Braque, Picasso and Juan Gris, the dead ambiguities of technical drawing. However the Purists included among their number Fernand Léger, who showed his humanism by a delight in the body and in natural forms which links him with Williams. He also sensed the liveliness which light and movement brought even to manufactured objects. In "The Machine Aesthetic," he writes of "the charm of colour" which manufacturers had learned to exploit commercially and discusses the accidental conjunction of beauty and utility in the motor car:

> You may perhaps miss the fancifulness, but the geometrical austerity which could put you off is compensated by the light playing on the white metal. . . .[4]

"Each machine object" Léger continues, "has two material qualities: a constant surface . . . which absorbs light . . . another surface which reflects light and takes the role of unlimited imagination." The Purists are relevant to our theme, because they shared with William Carlos Williams a fascination with the role of the "unlimited imagination" in art and life, and its analogies with playful light. The "true cubists," wrote Ozenfant and Jeanneret, show their tendency "towards the crystal" by seeking:

> . . . a state of clarification, condensation, firmness, intensity, synthesis; they will end up by achieving real virtuosity in the play of forms and colours. . . .[5]

In 1929 Kenneth Rexroth saw the consonance of interest between the American poet and these European painters, when he made the following remark about Williams' articles in the expatriate magazine *Blues*:

> I certainly prefer any essay of Wms to the masterpiece of (Yvor) Winters in the forthcoming *Caravan*. But neither of them has done for modern poetry what Gleizes or Ozenfant have done for plastic (art).[6]

From the 1920s onwards, Williams persistently expressed his intuitions of a new poetic in crystalline images. "Poetry has to do with the crystallization of the imagination" he wrote in *Spring and All [I, 140].* The crystal embodied the idea of "peculiar

3. Fry, p. 171.
4. Léger, "The Machine Aesthetic, The Manufactured Object, The Artisan and the Artist," *Bulletin de l'éffort moderne* (1924); repr. in *Léger and Purist Paris* (London: The Tate Gallery, 1970), pp. 87-92, p. 88.
5. Fry, p. 170.
6. "San Francisco Letter," *Blues* 7 (Fall 1929) pp. 42-43.
*Page references given parenthetically in the text are to the following editions of Williams' works, here accompanied by the abbreviations used.
†CEP   *The Collected Earlier Poems of William Carlos Williams.* London: MacGibbon and Kee, 1967.

perfection" which Williams introduced in the Prologue to *Kora in Hell*: it illustrated both the Emersonian sense that "the universe is represented in every one of its particles," and Williams' own delight in multiplicity. Whereas, as the end of *The Waste Land* implies, T. S. Eliot saw madness in the fragmentary quality of contemporary consciousness, Williams appears to have shared the Transcendentalists' belief that by devoting themselves (in Tony Tanner's words) "to ensnaring the crystalline fragments of momentary experience," they could achieve wholeness.[7] In Emerson we read: "A leaf, a drop, a crystal, a moment of time, is related to the whole, and partakes of the perfection of the whole. Each particle is a microcosm, and faithfully renders the likeness of the whole." "(A)ll things enter into the singleness of the moment" Williams writes in *A Novelette*, "and the moment partakes of the diversity of all things. . ." [*I*, 282].

The crystal also concentrates the poet's wonder at the diversity of the natural world; in *Paterson* Book One it is found in local images. "Colored crystals the secret of those rocks" [*P*, 17] tells us that the Park's pre-history is present in its geology, and after hearing the roar of time in the Falls, we catch our breath at the fate of Sam Patch: "a body found next spring / frozen in an ice-cake" [*P*, 31]. Sometimes the crystal merely means to Williams the sparkling clarity of water, ice or air: "the radiant nothing / of crystalline / spring" [*CEP*, 286] or "This crystal sphere / upon whose edge I drive" [*CLP*, 54]. When, in the 1960s, the firm Steuben Glass invited a number of contemporary writers to submit an unpublished poem from which their artists might derive designs, they sensibly stipulated "that the poems not concern crystal or glass."[8] From Williams they received "The Birdsong" whose

†*CLP*   *The Collected Later Poems of William Carlos Williams*, London: MacGibbon and Kee, 1965.
EK   *The Embodiment of Knowledge*, ed. Ron Loewinsohn. New York: New Directions, 1974.
I   *Imaginations*, ed. Webster Schott. N.Y.: New Directions, 1970, 6th printing.
IAG   *In the American Grain*. Norfolk, Conn.: New Directions, 1956.
†*IWWP* *I Wanted to Write a Poem*, ed. Edith Heal. London: Jonathan Cape, 1967.
P   *Paterson*. New York: New Directions, 1963.
PB   *Pictures from Brueghel and Other Poems*. Norfolk, Conn.: New Directions, 1962.
SE   *The Selected Essays of William Carlos Williams*. New York: Random House, 1954.
SL   *The Selected Letters of William Carlos Williams*. New York: McDowell Obolensky, 1957.
RI   *A Recognizable Image: William Carlos Williams on Art and Artists*, ed. Bram Dijkstra. New York: New Directions, 1978.

† indicates English editions (numeration may differ in American editions).
7. Tanner, *The Reign of Wonder* (Cambridge, England: Cambridge University Press, 1965), pp. 36-37.
8. *Poetry in Crystal by Steuben Glass* (1963); see Emily Mitchell Wallace, *A Bibliography of William Carlos Williams* (Middleton, Conn.: Wesleyan University Press, 1968), p. 159.

fluid line breaks over particulars like its own image of the brook,
recalling the music of Messiaen:

Disturb the balance, broken bird
the distress of the song
cuts through an ample silence
sweeping the trees.

It is the trouble
of the brook that makes it loud,
the current broke to give
out a burbling

breaks the arched stillness,
ripples the tall grass
gone to heady seed, bows the heads
of goldenrod

that bear a vulgar happiness,
the bay-berry,
briars—
breaks also your happiness for me.

[*CLP*, 73]

The earlier poems of *Spring and All* are less exquisite than
this: like anaclastic glasses which refract the broken rays of light,
they relate in style to the structure of the crystal, rather than in
idea to the lucidity of glass. "Words are indivisible crystals" we
read in *The Great American Novel* [*I*, 160] and Williams takes up
this toughness in "An Essay on Virginia": "Not only is it necessary to prove the crystal" he writes, "but the crystal must prove
permanent by fracture" [*I*, 322]. This conjures with the crystal's
infinity, since "in nature" (to echo Ozenfant and Jeanneret) a
shattered crystal reveals its resistance by multiplicity: it recreates
itself a thousand times. In the same essay, Williams ransacks the
history of Virginia for American expressions of the same idea,
snatching at "Indian arrowheads of quartz" and an "Indian war
club; a cylindrical rod of stone encrusted with natural garnets"
[*I*, 324]. Like the "Brazilian brilliants—that shine of themselves,
uncut as they are" of "The Poem as a Field of Action" [*SE*, 285]
or the costly and "curious artifices" that are listed among Monte-
zuma's gifts to Cortez in "The Destruction of Tenochtitlan" [*IAG*,
28-31], these are seen as instances of a cultural potential that has
been obscured. Climactically, Williams hits on:

. . . some heirloom like the cut-glass jelly stand that Jefferson
brought from Paris for his daughter, a branching tree of crystal
hung with glass baskets that would be filled with jelly—on occas-
sion. This is the essence of all essays [*I*, 324].

2. *The new arts*

This witty apparition, the "branching tree of crystal," exemplifies Williams' poetic ideal of translucence and complexity. "Brought from Paris" it is presented as an inspiration for American art. In *A Novelette*, with which "An Essay on Virginia" was published in Toulon in 1932, Williams glancingly acknowledged "that diversity of the mind which is excellence, like a tree" as "French—it is surrealism" [*I*, 281]. This book is full of his admiration for the French, and his envy for their "invention" of Surrealism. Later, Williams confessed that it "showed the influence of Dadaism" adding: "I didn't originate Dadaism but I had it in my soul to write it" [*IWWP*, 60]. While he was writing *A Novelette* Williams was also translating *The Last Nights of Paris* by Philippe Soupault: Williams had met and liked Soupault on his visit to France in 1927, when the French writer was "all wound up in Dadaism," and he was attracted by the amusing and "contradictory" quality of his work [*IWWP*, 59]. Ezra Pound had earlier recognized a tolerance of contradiction in the Cubists, whose work implied for him the many-sidedness of complex ideas:

> When I find people ridiculing the new arts . . . when they laugh
> at our talking about the "ice-block quality" in Picasso, I think
> it is only because they do not know what thought is like. . . .[9]

This recognition depended on Pound's whole-hearted promotion of Vorticism; he added: "The vorticist is expressing his complex consciousness."

For Williams, the "ice-block quality" of the new arts, their recognition of complexity, accorded with his own intense visual apprehension of the actual world. We read of Williams' *persona* in *A Voyage to Pagany*:

> The world existed in his eyes, recognized itself ecstatically there
> . . . everywhere he saw reality, split, creviced, multiplied. The
> brilliant hardness of the world, clear, full of color and outline,
> depth, shadow, reaffirming light, filled him with security and
> contentment. . . .[10]

Elsewhere in the same novel, Williams identifies his vision of Paris with "Braque": "It linked completely with the modern spirit. It was France, cold, grey, dextrous, multiform, and yet gracious. . . ."[11] It appears that, just as Pound was grateful to the Vorticists for a recovery of brightness—echoing Yeats' claim that Berkeley, in revealing the limitations of Newtonian optics, had

---

. Pound, "Vorticism," *Fortnightly Review* (1914); repr. in Harriet Zinnes ed., *Ezra
Pound and the Visual Arts* (New York: New Directions, 1980), pp. 199-209, p. 204.
0. Williams, *A Voyage to Pagany* (New York: Macaulay, 1928), p. 119.
1. Ibid., p. 57.

"brought back to us the world that only exists because it shines and sounds"—so Williams gained from the Cubists the new and ecstatic recognition of reality which he expressed in his references to the crystal. In the Prologue to *Kora in Hell*, dated 1 September 1918, Williams records one of his earliest contacts with Cubism in New York, soon after the Armory Show had introduced the painters he mentions to the American public:

> Once when I was taking lunch with Walter Arensberg at a small place on 63rd Street I asked him if he could state what the more modern painters were about, those roughly classed at that time as "cubists": Gleizes, Man Ray, Demuth, Duchamp—all of whom were then in the city. He replied by saying that the only way man differed from every other creature was in his ability to improvise novelty and, since the pictorial artist was under discussion, anything in paint that is truly new, truly a fresh creation, is good art. Thus, according to Duchamp, who was Arensberg's champion at the time, a stained-glass window that had fallen out and lay more or less together on the ground was of far greater interest than the thing conventionally composed *in situ* [*SE*, 5].

This delight in novelty, even at the risk of chaos and decreation, demonstrates Williams' inclination towards Dada and Surrealism, rather than towards the stricter aesthetic of the Purists and Vorticists with which Pound must be aligned.

Their variance was already apparent in the way each related to Imagism. As a poet, Williams has been characterized as a "spontaneous" Imagist;[12] as a critic, it is spontaneity rather than orthodoxy that he most respected. "The attention has been held too rigid on the one plane" he argued in his Prologue, "instead of following a more flexible, jagged resort" [*SE*, 11]. Although freedom from traditional poetic norms was essential to the London Imagists, they followed Pound's insistence on concentration, single-mindedness, and condensed their poetic into a three-point programme. The remoteness of New York from London allowed the American poets associated with *Others* to keep their distance from the group around the *Egoist*. By the 'twenties, this distance was paradoxically asserting itself in an approach to Paris that had been made possible by the presence of war-exiles like Duchamp and Gleizes in the States, well before the exodus of American poets to France. But the distance can earlier be observed in the difference between the rhetoric of London Imagism and the idiom of the "Others."

Hardness, clarity and the immediacy of concrete particulars were the desiderata of the Imagists, and the words "crystal" and "crystalline" were consequently part of their critical vocabulary

---

12. See K. L. Goodwin, *The Influence of Ezra Pound* (London: Oxford University Press 1966), p. 1.

Ultimately, both the ideal and the terms in which it was expressed, derived from France: from such works as Gautier's *Emaux et Camées*, and from the criticism of de Gourmont and also Baudelaire, who described the writing of Poe as "carefully wrought, precise and transparent as a crystal jewel." Hence the typical hyperbole of May Sinclair:

> Sharpness, precision, purity, the cold clearness of crystal, the hardness of crystal, hardness obtained by concentration, by sheer pressure of spiritual intensity—you will find all these qualities in the later work of Jean de Bosschère.[13]

The stress on *concentration, pressure, intensity* is distinctive to the Imagists in England (who of course counted a high proportion of expatriate Americans among their number). H.D., for instance, whose early work is quintessentially Imagist, recalled that she grew tired of hearing these poems referred to as "crystalline"; yet she realised that was merely the current way of registering their quality of intensity:

> . . . For what is crystal or any gem but the concentrated essence of the rough matrix, or the energy either of over-intense heat or over-intense cold that projects it?[14]

This invites a comparison with Williams' praise, in 1925, of Marianne Moore. He calls her poetry "a true modern crystallization," in which each word stands "crystal clear" [*SE*, 129, 128]. Yet these metaphors are presented in a context that emphasises the eccentric rather than the concentrated, multiplicity rather than intensity, fragmentation rather than completeness. For him, the modernism of Marianne Moore expressed not a new formalism but "a break through all preconception of poetic form . . . a flaw, a crack in the bowl" [*SE*, 121]. When, in 1931, Williams reviewed Pound's *A Draft of XXX Cantos*, he praised the "faceted quality" of his friend's verse, but made an implicit distinction between it and that of Marianne Moore: "It is not by any means a synthesis, but a shot through all material—a true and somewhat old-fashioned analysis of his world" [*SE*, 110]. When Williams indicated a political analogy for this method—"It is still a Lenin striking through the mass, whipping it about, that engages his attention. That is the force Pound believes in" [*SE*, 111]—he was registering his own discomfort with the totalitarian tendencies that had earlier been evident in Vorticism. Pound's close association with the visual

13. Sinclair, Introduction to de Bosschère, *The Closed Door/Portes Fermées*, trans. F. S. Flint (London and New York: John Lane, 1917), p. 6.
14. H.D. "Notes on Recent Writing" (c. 1955), unpublished ts. cited by Rachel Blau DuPlessis, "An essay on H.D. and the muse of the woman writer." *Montemora* 6 (1979), pp. 146-147.

artists Henri Gaudier-Brzeska and Percy Wyndham Lewis led him
to assert an austere, masculine aesthetic, in which formal values
were dominant. Pound defined Vorticism as an "intensive art"
which had to do with the "organisation of forms";[15] from Gaudier's sculpture, he transposed to poetry the geometric notion of
"planes in relation." Such definitions do not leave the crystalline
ideal of Imagism far behind.

Herbert Read's distinction between "tough-minded" and
"tender-minded" Cubists proves useful here.[16] If Pound and his
associates represent the "tough" in Modernist aesthetics, then
Williams and his represent the "tender." This tenderness of Williams is evident in his own "Vortex," written in response to the
"Vortex Gaudier-Brzeska" published in *Blast*. In it he took up
Gaudier's key phrase "planes in relation" and affirmed, in a
manner reminiscent of Whitman: "I will not stop at planes but
go on to content" [*RI*, 58] ; a deleted parenthesis explained:

> (I amplify "planes" to include sounds, smells, colors, touch
> used as planes in the geometric sense, *i.e.*, without limits except
> as intersected by other planes.) [*RI*, 57]

Here "in the geometric sense" allows Williams to adopt and
refine the scientific rhetoric of the Vorticists (as he was later to do
in his essay on Marianne Moore) while actually shifting the attention from the purely formal to the sensual or accidental. Like
Fernand Léger, who humanized the Purist aesthetic, Williams
attempts to humanize Vorticism. In doing so, he exposes an expressive theory of art and a romanticism that must have seemed naive
to his London friends: "I will express my emotions in the appearances : surfaces, sounds, smells, touch of the place in which I
happen to be" [*RI*, 58]. To distinguish the origins of a larger
divergence between the poet of "contact" and the expatriate
Pound,[17] one might compare the tendency towards abstraction
in the following:

> The eye *likes* certain plainnesses, certain complexities, certain
> arrangements, certain varieties, certain incitements, certain reliefs
> and suspensions.
>   It likes these things irrespective of whether or not they form a
> replica of known objects.[18]

---

15. Pound, pp. 206, 208.
16. See Read, *Art Now: an introduction to the theory of modern painting* (London:
Faber and Faber, 1933; rev. edn. 1936), pp. 109-111; the terms, of course, are William
James'.
17. Bram Dijkstra points out that Williams' notes on the ts. of his own "Vortex" prob-
ably represent the first appearance of the term 'contact' " in his work [*RI*, 57; note 1].
Williams was to discuss the difference between his own position and Pound's in "A
Tentative Statement," *The Little Review* XII, 2 (May 1929), pp. 95-98.
18. Pound, Note on Coburn's Vortographs, *Pavannes and Divisions* (1918); repr. in
Zinnes, *Ezra Pound and the Visual Arts*, pp. 154-157, p. 157.

This issue of the place of "known objects" in the modernist aesthetic is not only crucial to an understanding of Dr. Williams' position, but enables us to distinguish it from T. S. Eliot's as well as Ezra Pound's. In his "Reflections on Contemporary Poetry" of 1917, Eliot remarked:

> One of the many ways by which contemporary verse has tried to escape the rhetorical, the abstract, the moralizing, to recover . . . the accent of direct speech, is to concentrate its attention upon trivial or accidental or commonplace objects.[19]

Eliot is of course resuming the strategies adopted by both Imagists and Georgians in their reaction against what they considered to be the bad habits of nineteenth-century poets. This did not meet with Eliot's complete approval: he found the English "preoccupied with trivialities," and criticized the Russian novelists for their dissolution of emotion in sensational detail. His own formula for a correction of equilibrium was subsequently presented as the "objective correlative": a development of symbolist strategy in which, as he puts it in "Reflections on Contemporary Poetry," "The feeling and the material symbol present exactly their proper proportions."[20] The fine early poems in which Eliot achieves this end, though usually described as "Imagiste" are thus in an essential respect "Symboliste": in the "Preludes" and "Morning at the Window," each "material symbol" is an efficient purveyor of the mood which generates the whole poem. This is also the mode of those poems of Williams which concentrate most successfully on a single emotion: "An Elegy for D. H. Lawrence" [*CEP*, 361] or "There are no perfect waves—" from "The Descent of Winter" [*CEP*, 298]. The poem most often used to illustrate Eliot's supposed Imagism, "Rhapsody on a Windy Night" is pervasively *fin-de-siècle* in tone: its celebrated "twisted branch upon the beach" and "broken spring in a factory yard" get their full complement of meaning when they are recognized as vehicles of the depression which creates a "heap of broken images" in *The Waste Land*.

It is, however, in the rhythms of Eliot's poetry that we find an essential identity with predecessors such as Mallarmé and Baudelaire. Roland Barthes has pointed out that the "admirable rhetoric" of these French poets depends upon a use of stress which allows the line (conceived as a unit of meaning which is often extended through enjambement) to operate through a

19. Eliot, "Reflections on Contemporary Poetry I," *The Egoist*, IV, 8 (Sep. 1917) pp. 118-119.
20. Ibid., compare "Hamlet" (1919); repr. in Frank Kermode ed., *Selected Prose of T. S. Eliot* (London: Faber and Faber, 1975), pp. 45-49.

particular word, and thus "tie up all its metaphysical threads in a single knot."[21] In the same way, Eliot's interest in "the point of intersection" has an analogue in his poetic method. Early and late, lines like the following are characteristic of his verse:

> Like a patient *etherized* upon a table
>
> And along the *trampled* edges of the street
>
> April is the *cruellest* month . . .
>
> But a lifetime *burning* in every moment
>
> The silent *withering* of autumn flowers

This technique imparts an "overall" quality to Eliot's verse, which it shares with the best English prose. It is almost never present in the work of Williams or Ezra Pound, although W. H. Auden has it, and so (occasionally) does Wallace Stevens. Barthes describes its counterpart in Baudelaire as an "adjectival *skin*," which he compares with the "luster" or "sheen" on a Dutch still-life, and although Eliot's effects are usually less radiant than those of *Les Fleurs du Mal*, this is a feature which lays a patina of meaning over every detail in its ambience.

Williams' *Improvisations* show the tenuous influence of this symbolistic mode: he refers there to "talk with the patina of whim upon it" [*SE*, 14]. But in his more mature verse, Williams' particularity is of a quite different kind from Eliot's, and more essentially imagistic. He takes his cue from the other poet's comment on "trivial or accidental or commonplace objects" but concentrates on their objective quality almost to the exclusion of "meaning" and emotion. Williams' comments on Alfred Kreymborg reveal a mutuality of interest:

> Kreymborg's idea of poetry is a transforming music that has much to do with tawdry things. . . [*SE*, 20].
> . . . It consists in the skillful use of small words, the artistic effect depending on the musical design and not on the values noted and connoted by the words themselves [*SL*, 33].

Williams' idea of a "transforming music" involves not a single verbal point of intersection but a pattern of interstices. Hence his verse is refractive or translucent, but rarely lustrous; he says with sympathy of Marianne Moore: "The interstices for the light and not the interstitial web of the thought concerned her. . . . Thus the material is as the handling: the thought, the word, the rhythm—all in the style" [*SE*, 128]. His own method was not to use particular words or objects to convey symbolic meaning, but to find new meanings through the manipulation of a particularity inherent in

21. Barthes, "Alain Robbe-Grillet," *Evergreen Review* XI, 5 (Summer 1958) pp. 113-126, p. 118.

his linguistic and perceptual materials. He tentatively described Joyce's style as "truth through the breakup of beautiful words," and maintained that it was "forced upon him . . . by the facts" [*SE*, 75, 77].

As a consequence of his very different intent, Williams' poetry has an appearance of carelessness in comparison with Eliot's careful constructions. A poem like "Della Primavera Trasportata Al Morale" diffracts itself through indiscriminate particulars so that the end result is less like "meaning" than "musical design." An ice-cream price-list, hospital notices, things seen in the street, are treated like the bits of wood, crystals and found objects of which Alvin Langdon Coburn, with Pound's encouragement and collaboration, made his Vortographs: placed in a triangle of mirrors, they created the first truly abstract photographs. By Coburn's account, the mirrors "acted as a prism splitting the image formed by the lens into segments."[22] Pound respected Coburn as an inventor; but the photographer's inventions did not share the formal insistence of the Vorticist paintings of Wyndham Lewis. Rather, they have in common with the works of the American Cubist Realists who were closest to Williams (Sheeler, Demuth and Stuart Davis), a respect for the concrete object which remains recognizable even as it is transposed to abstract form. In Pound's praise of Coburn, we glimpse the artist as "a Lenin striking through the mass": "the vortographer," writes Pound, is distinct from the photographer in that he "combines his forms *at will*. He selects just what actuality he wishes, he excludes the rest."[23] Compare Williams' statement of his own "Vortex": "I will not value one part of my life more than another" [*RI*, 58]; in his responsive Whitmanism, Williams denies the aggressive Vorticism that his statement might superficially appear to support. His own experiments in what J. M. Brinnin has called "polyhedral" poetry[24] express both his response to "known objects" and his interest in the Cubist aesthetic of intersecting planes. "St. Francis Einstein of the Daffodils" [*CEP*, 379], for instance, combines "sounds, smells, colors, touch" etc. with scraps of quotation reminiscent of the newsprint in a cubist *collage*, in a relaxed manner that is not wilful but nevertheless expressive of the poet's emotions: appropriately, its themes are relativity and America, conjunctions both of the known and the unknown, the concrete experience and the abstract idea. More telling perhaps, in this

22. *Alvin Langdon Coburn, Photographer: an autobiography* (London: Faber and Faber, 1966), p. 102. Coburn first exhibited crystal Vortographs at the London Camera Club in 1917, when Pound contributed to the catalogue (see note 18 above).
23. Pound, ibid., p. 156.
24. John Malcolm Brinnin, *William Carlos Williams* (Minneapolis: University of Minnesota Press, 1963), p. 36.

context, is Williams' celebration of the Cubist painter Juan Gris in the prose of *Spring and All*. A picture like "Still Life in Front of an Open Window" exemplifies for Williams "the modern trend"; in it Gris uses "the forms common to experience" [*I*, 107]:

> Things with which he is familiar, simple things—at the same time to detach them from ordinary experience to the imagination [*I*, 110].

This is the context in which Williams writes of poetry as a "crystallization of the imagination," a context in which the familiar and the accidental have their place, and ordinary experience is the starting-point for art. His own version of modernism was less austere than that of the Imagists and more relaxed than that of the Vorticists. They lacked the gaiety that attracted him to the French Dadaists and was present in his own *Kora in Hell* and *Spring and All*: "Call it, this house of ours, the crystal itself of laughter, thus peaked and faceted" he wrote in the *Improvisations* [*I*, 72], and in "Two Pendants: for the Ears" he reflects, in his rapid passage through particulars, on his need as a poet

> (To make the language
> record it, facet to facet
> not bored out—
>   with an auger [*CLP*, 228].

3.   *From mathematics to particulars*—

"A course on mathematics would not be wasted on a poet, or a reader of poetry," wrote Williams in 1925, "if he remember no more from it than the geometric principle of the intersection of loci: from all angles lines converging and crossing establish points." This is from his 1925 essay on Marianne Moore; he continues: "He might carry it further and say in his imagination that apprehension perforates at places, through to understanding—as white is at the intersection of blue and green and yellow and red. It is this white light that is the background of all good work" [*SE*, 122]. The geometric analogy allows Williams to identify the factual precision of this work that he admires (he goes on to speak of the way in which each concept in Marianne Moore's writing has "edge-to-edge contact with the things which surround it"), while the analogy with the physics of light allows him to celebrate poetry as "the white of a clarity beyond the facts" [*SE*, 127, 124]. Thus, in this double image of *intersection* and *diffraction*, Williams was able to make a highly transcendentalist connection between the particular and the general, the concrete and the abstract, the prosaic and the poetic.

At the same time, he enriched the significance of "crystal-line" as a critical term for readers who did not share his scientific background. In the 'twenties, Williams' thinking on poetics went through a "phase-transition" comparable to those noticed by present-day physicists. The "tendency towards the crystal" in the fragmentary prose and poetry of *Spring and All* (for instance) coincided with a breakthrough in the development of the modern science of crystallography. The discovery of X-rays in 1912 had made possible the study of the three-dimensional structure of crystals. In order to plot crystalline structure, diffracted light obtained from X-rays was passed through crystals. This gave first a two-dimensional grid or *net-plane*, then a three-dimensional diagram of the crystal's inner space: this gave not merely the points of the net-plane, but a deeper structure of intersections known as the *space-lattice*. The true geometrical form of the crystal is determined by perpendiculars to the faces drawn from any point within.[25] Other poets besides Williams were excited by such scientific discoveries; Ian Bell has shown that for Pound this interest went a good deal further than his contemporary nicknane X-Ray.[26] We have noticed that Eliot's use of the mathematical term "point of intersection" bears comparison with Williams' concern with "interstices"—if only to show that the latter indicates a new way of thinking, while the former belongs to an older sense of structure. The new way of thinking was that of Einsteinian physics and the Special Theory of Relativity, which continued to engage Williams' poetic imagination to the end of his life. John Berger has argued that for Einstein, as for Hegel and Marx "Understanding became a question of considering all that was *interjacent*"; the Cubists too, he points out, "were concerned with what was *interjacent*."[27] Just so, the essential factor in crystalline structure is not the crystal's outward shape, but the geometrical relationships between its faces. It is in incorporating this sense of relativity into his poetic that Williams is most modern. And at precisely this point, we find him at his most relaxed and playful: at the beginning of *Spring and All*, he invites his readers to imagine the New World "in all its prismatic colorings" [*I*, 90] ; likewise he is stimulated by Marianne Moore's title "In the Days of Prismatic Color" [*SE*, 128]. Yet it is not a question of a return to the past: we are being invited here to "enter a new world" [*I*, 134], the world of a new

25. See R. W. James, *X-ray Crystallography* (London: Methuen, 1953), ch. 1: "Crystal Form and the Space-Lattice."
26. Bell, *Critic as Scientist: the modernist poetics of Ezra Pound* (London: Methuen, 1981).
27. Berger, *The Success and Failure of Picasso* (Harmondsworth, Middx.: Penguin Books, 1965), pp. 67, 69.

science and a new poetic, where (Williams hopes) it will be possible to reconcile precise observation with visionary revelation; he continues:

> Poetry has taken many disguises which by cross reading or intense penetration it is possible to go through to the core. Through intersection of loci their multiplicity may become revelatory [*SE*, 126].

Williams' fascination with the *faceted* qualities of a work of art reflected a felt need for forms both harmonious and complex. He appears to have agreed with Kenneth Rexroth that: "Any aesthetic object is a fake universe and is good insofar as it produces the illusion of that richness of potential pattern which is a function of universe (sic)."[28] The poet of *Spring and All* was, nevertheless, suspicious of "illusion": his aesthetic difficulty consisted in an impulse to include within the poem as much as possible of the pattern and variety of the material world. Yet from first to last he was also convinced that "Only the imagination is real!" [*PB*, 179]. The disparate quality of *Kora in Hell* resulted in part from its writer's struggle to reconcile these extremes. The *Improvisations* contain many hints at the solution Williams eventually found in Objectivism, for it is an important theme of this work that the imagination manifests itself in its ability to disclose "*Each thing . . . secure in its own perfections*" [*I*, 65]. Here Williams introduces the image of the dance to indicate the "potential pattern" of particularity: "*the imaginative qualities of the actual things being perceived accompany their gross vision in a slow dance*" [*I*, 67]. The vein of Platonism that shows in these remarks is also present in "The Desert Music"; but even in his later work, Williams does not posit an ultimate micro-/macro-cosmic harmony after the fashion of Sir John Davies' Elizabethan poem, "The Orchestra." His tone is essentially inductive: he hesitates to extrapolate from present instances to an absolute *Gestalt*; hence "the dance" is habitually related to current perceptual experience. In one of the Improvisations, Williams recalls that "poets of old" set down their intuitions of "hidden" harmony in rhyme and metre, to show its provenance from another realm of existence: "*Nowadays*" he comments, "*the elements of that language are set down as heard and the imagination of the listener and of the poet are left free to mingle in the dance*" [*I*, 59].

The aesthetics glimpsed in *Kora in Hell* are curiously accordant with the Bergsonian theories of T. E. Hulme, who believed in an "other world" of the imagination, which revealed itself only

---

28. Rexroth, *Blues*, pp. 42-43.

through particularity, and man's *consciousness* of particularity.
As a student of biology, Hulme had witnessed, under the microscope, "Things revealed, not created, but there before, and *also*
seen to be in an order."[29] Since he was killed in 1917 Hulme
never experienced, as did Williams, the refined discoveries of
twentieth century physics; he retained the apocalyptic vision of
Victorian science, and his philosophy depended on a vivid apprehension of physical entropy: at one extreme, Hulme saw the
chaos of gross particulars (which he nicknamed "cinders") and at
the other, the "organization of cinders" in an orderly freedom,
which he too expressed in an image of the dance, but which he
knew to be "liable to revert to chaos at any moment." Williams'
poetry also operates between these poles: the tapestry of *Paterson*
Book Five, bears lovely images of harmony and cohesion ("All
together, working together— / all the birds together." [*P*, 270])
yet its threads threaten to snap in places under the strain of what
Hulme called "cindery reality." It is both one of the finest examples of an attained equilibrium in Williams' poetry, and an illustration of Hulme's tenet that: "The unity of Nature is an extremely
artificial and fragile bridge, a garden net." Williams is more opti-
mistic than Hulme about the power of art to substantiate the
fragility of nature's net:

The purpose of an orchestra
                is to organize those sounds
                        and hold them
to an assembled order   .
            in spite of the
                    "wrong note." . . .

[*PB*, 80-81]

Although Hulme was both theoretical and doctrinaire, while
Williams was neither, he resembled the American poet insofar as
his aesthetics were ultimately based on scientific pragmatism. He
too repudiated illusion in art, maintaining that:

All experience tends to do away with all sentimental escapes to
the infinite, but at the same time to provide many deliberated,
observed, manufactured, artificial, spectacular, poised for seeing
continuities and patterns.[30]

It is of such perceptions that *Paterson* is composed, and it is also
thus that (as far as the "assembled order" permits) the poem
resolves itself for the reader. The poet engages the reader in his
own effort at observation, composition, indicating ". . . a mass of

29. Hulme, "Cinders" in Herbert Read ed., *Speculations* (London: Routledge and Kegan
Paul, 1924), p. 226; subsequent quotations are from pp. 227, 224.
30. Ibid., p. 232.

detail / to interrelate on a new ground, difficultly" [*P*, 30]. The presence of the man Paterson in the poem is a strategy to identify this project as one of the perceiving consciousness. However, the fictive doubling of "Mr. Paterson" and Paterson the personified place in Book One complicates this at the outset:

> Who are these people (how complex
> the mathematic) among whom I see myself
> in the regularly ordered plateglass of
> his thoughts, glimmering before shoes and bicycles?
>
> [*P*, 18]

The context of the "plateglass" metaphor subverts the meanings of "regularly ordered" and hints at more complicated reflections ("among whom I see myself"). We are reminded of Atget's photographs of Parisian shop-fronts, where Realism meets Surrealism in the way the plateglass both displays what is behind it and reflects what is before it. Emerson's notion of the poet as "a mirror carried through the street, ready to render an image of every created thing" was echoed in Williams' initial question as a twentieth-century American poet: "How shall I be a mirror to this modernity?" ["The Wanderer," *CEP*, 3]. He now finds an answer that goes beyond realism, and with the French surrealists who were his contemporaries makes the text an interface between what is inside and what is outside the mind—between the perceiver and the perceived. In the quoted lines from *Paterson* the notion of *reflection* is present in both its meanings: behind the physical meaning of reflected light is the mental meaning of dealing with the data of sensation. Thus, too, the text works both ways.

Williams resolved this issue with less difficulty in his prose—and did so by invoking the crystal. In "Science and Philosophy" he wrote:

> People, that's all there is in the world—and animals and plants and Pasteur's crystals—with whom we do not think. It is nothing but a cheated existence to think, think, think. And to do, do, do is still worse: but to know is everything and includes both knowing and thinking, for it is a clarity, objects come up clear. People seem crystals. They are crystals when we do and know what we do [*EK*, 26].

Williams' insistence on a knowledge that is "poetic" as well as scientific, that is not reductive and "regularly ordered" but amply conscious of its own complexities, is constant from *Kora in Hell* to *Paterson*. In *The Embodiment of Knowledge* he reaffirms the centrality of consciousness to the process of knowing; aware of Heisenberg's hypothesis, he argues that knowledge can never be purely objective and that it is in the individual that object and subject meet:

> There is a unity, of course, and the final term of all investigation;
> it is the individual himself. Anyone must have as his fundamental
> determination a complete association of all the activities of his
> life and their implications. It is the various implications which
> constitute the sciences, arts, philosophies and so forth. But the
> unity they seek is behind them not before. Before them exists
> only an infinite fracture, an even smaller division until—as in
> chemistry the constitution of an electron, or in astronomy ever
> farther and larger objects (to reverse the process) puts objective
> investigations beyond the question. By further investigation, that
> is to say, unity is not by any means achieved, but multiformity
> [*EK*, 73].

The Preface to *Paterson* Book One starts with the despairing conclusion that "we know nothing, pure / and simple, beyond our
own complexities" [*P*, 11-12].

Williams' approach to the world about him is consequently
made with humility; this humility unexpectedly entails a sense of
self that is rigorously excluded from much recent scientific thinking, as it is popularly presented to us. Consider the following:

> The whole . . . of our world—radiant energy and protean matter,
> crystals and cells, stars and atoms—all built of modules, whose
> identity and simplicity belie the unmatched diversity of the
> works of man and nature. The world is atomic, which is to say
> modular; our knowledge is modular as well. All can be counted
> and listed; our very analysis implies atoms of knowing, as the
> material itself is atomic. The prodigality of the world is only
> a prodigality of combination, a richness beyond human grasp
> contained in the interacting multiplicity of a few modules, but
> modules which nature has made in very hosts. . . .[31]

Williams shares this writer's awareness of the modular character of
material existence and is also aware of the modular character of
our grosser ways of knowing it. Yet he rejects the categorizing
arrogance which asserts that "all can be counted and listed" and
uses dismissive expressions like "only a prodigality"; believing
such knowledge to be ignorance, Williams maintains that "Science
is a deceit" [*EK*, 26]. *Paterson* Books One to Four do in fact
trace the trajectory described in this scientific account of the
universe, as they range from "The multiple seed, packed tight with
detail" to "Uranium, the complex atom" [*P*, 12, 209], but they
do so in an attitude of imaginative wonder.

Similarly, the development of his poetic entails the evolu-
tion of a method whereby the poet does not merely name and

---

31. Philip Morrison, "The Modularity of Knowing" in Gyorgy Kepes ed., *Module, Symmetry, Proportion* (London: Studio Vista, 1966), p. 1.

enumerate the surface structure of the world about us, but imitates its deep structure in his or her own creativity. In *Spring & All* Williams wrote:

> Nature is the hint to composition . . . because it possesses the quality of independent existence, of reality which we feel in ourselves [*I*, 121].

He went on to distinguish between poetry and prose in the following way:

> There is no form to prose but that which depends on clarity. If prose is nòt accurately adjusted to the exposition of facts it does not exist—Its form is that alone. . . .
>   Poetry is something quite different. Poetry has to do with the crystallization of the imagination--the perfection of new forms as additions to nature—[*I*, 140].

This passage anticipates the language of the essay on Marianne Moore in making a comparatively crude distinction between poetry and prose—a distinction similar to the one between poetry and science that we have noticed in *The Embodiment of Knowledge*. The "broken prose" of *Spring & All* belies or eludes the distinction, resembling the "canvas of broken parts" which Williams wanted the modern poem to be.[32] Williams' rebellion against his outdated scientific education and against traditional form in the arts caused him to smash out with these blunt definitions, to prefer with the Cubists the "stained-glass window that had fallen out and lay more or less together on the ground" to the "regularly ordered plateglass" of Mr. Paterson's thought. Yet the difference between these two conditions is overcome in Williams' definition of poetry as "the crystallization of the imagination." This metaphor synthesises brokenness and perfection, transcending the contradiction between them.

The crystal, then, exemplifies the tension between simplicity and complexity which Williams observed both in the world and in himself. The various areas of knowledge to which he had access— his writing, his practice as a physician, his attention to the natural world through gardening and merely moving about in it—all contributed to an understanding of periodicity, that presence of pattern in nature which is fundamental to life, as Alfred North Whitehead emphasised in 1925 in his *Enquiry Concerning the Principles of the Natural Knowledge*. In a poem like "Every Day," Williams places this "objective" knowledge in a thoroughly

---

32. Williams, "The Broken Vase," unpublished ms. cited by Bram Dijkstra, *Cubism, Stieglitz, and the Early Poetry of William Carlos Williams* (Princeton, New Jersey: Princeton University Press, 1969), p. 76.

subjective context. This accords with Heisenberg's Uncertainty Principle, which concludes from the Quantum Theory that:

> Natural Science does not simply describe and explain nature; it is part of the interplay between nature and ourselves; it describes nature as exposed to our method of questioning.[33]

In Williams' poem everyday living is shown to be a thoroughly relative condition. It follows a movement of thought from poetic structure ("a consideration of the dithyrambic / poem") to the structure of plants; yet this occurs within, accompanies, the movement of the poet's body as he goes through the garden to his car. In the very movement of the verse then, observation is known to be relative to point of view; time as well as space makes what is seen "Every day" differ from day to day, as plants grow in season:

> Coarse grass mars the fine lawn
> as I look about right and left
> tic toc—
> And right and left the leaves
> upon the yearling peach grow along
> the slender stem
>
> No rose is sure. Each is one rose
> and this, unlike another,

                                                                    [*CLP*, 147]

Here again, reflection is present in both its meanings. Moreover the poem not only takes note of nature's symmetry, imitating it in the repetition of "right and left," it also admits asymmetry ("No rose is sure . . ."); thus, both in structure and content, the poem creates "new forms as additions to nature—."

We may compare this poem, with its relaxed "everyday" manner, and the more intense but equally distinctive early poem "The rose is obsolete . . ." from *Spring & All*, with the assertive position taken by the biologist D'Arcy Wentworth Thompson in his study *Growth and Form*:

> Cell and tissue, shell and bone, leaf and flower, are so many portions of matter, and it is in obedience to the laws of physics that their particles have been moved, moulded and conformed. They are no exception to the rule that God always geometrises.[34]

Thompson's outlook was informed by a line of philosophy reaching back to Plato and Pythagoras, which was restored to aesthetics by the Purists' realization of the uses of geometry for taming multiplicity. The Platonists' belief that all matter could be

---

33. Heisenberg, *Physics and Philosophy* (1959); cited by Berger, p. 68.
34. Thompson, *Growth and Form* (1915); cited by Alan Mackay, "Mandala Thinking," *Image* VII, 1 (Spring 1968), pp. 28-32, p. 32.

reduced to fundamental particles represented by the five regular solids (the tetrahedron, cube, octahedron, dodecahedron and icosahedron) has a modern corollary in Cézanne's reduction of the formal elements of painting to "the sphere, the cylinder and the cube." The sixteenth-century chemist William Davidson tried to bridge the gap between the Platonic mystery and the actual structure of crystals, but could not do so: his book contains both mandala-type drawings, and realistic pictures of crystalline form.[35] The discovery of X-ray diffraction made it possible to realize the speculative mathematics of repeating patterns; but scientists and inventors have continued to be inspired by the Platonic solids: Linus Pauling believed, as did the Greek philosopher, that the icosahedron is the key to the liquid element; the crystallographer J. D. Bernal showed its relevance to the architecture of viruses, and Buckminster Fuller used it as the fundamental module of his geodesic domes. All these developments have taken place in Williams' era.

Williams shared this sense of form, but his interest in the crystal expresses both his Platonic desire for a pristine simplicity, and his engagement with the actual variety of life. The latter both fascinated and disturbed him: "Why then all this . . . multiplicity we push between ourselves and our desires?" he exclaims in "Jacatacqua" [*IAG*, 178]. Williams' recognition of multiplicity as a feature of the relative world especially evident in the complexity of modern civilisation, entailed an intuition that multiplicity might itself hold a clue to artistic form. "The Simplicity of Disorder" contains a passage entitled "Fierce Singleness," in which Williams throws together all the difficulties of day-to-day existence: his marriage, his profession, his writing; these things, he says, "have made up an actuality of which I am assembling the parts" [*I*, 294]. But his method of assembly does not resemble the calm procedure of the geometer or that of the Purist painter who painstakingly collected bottles, spare parts, and what Jeanneret habitually refers to in the titles of his pictures as *nombreux objets*. Williams speaks of the immense difficulty of composing his life, and finally decides that it is to be resolved "not . . . by quietness, but by a greater fracture" [*I*, 294]. He maintains in "An Essay on Virginia" that "the crystal must prove permanent by fracture"; here he suggests that the finite particularity, the very "brokenness" of his own world, can constitute a breakthrough to infinity:

> Try as I will the thing comes only when I have one stocking on,
> the telephone is ringing, my mind is full of difficulties and you

---

35. Mackay, p. 32.

have asked me a question. In a flash it comes and is gone. Words on a par with trees. . . .
 It is a thing so penetrant, so powerful, so inclusive of all good that I cannot believe the difficulty real. . . . It is entirely new. . . [*I*, 294].

This passage from "The Simplicity of Disorder," with its anticipation of "The Desert Music," has a contemporary counterpart in the vision with which the refractory verse of "Della Primavera Trasportata Al Morale" culminates:

The forms
of the emotions are crystalline,
geometric-faceted. So we recognise
only in the white heat of
understanding, when a flame
runs through the gap made
by learning, the shapes of things—
the ovoid sun, the pointed trees

[*CEP*, 64]

HUGH WITEMEYER AND E. P. WALKIEWICZ

DESERT MUSIC: CARLOS WILLIAMS IN THE GREAT SOUTHWEST

Recalling his first visit to Santa Fe in 1947, Williams wrote: "I spent no more than a night there, if I spent that much time, but the impression I had of the place was overwhelming. It took me all the way back to the beginnings of our country, to the times of Coronado and the Pueblo Indians and I was deeply moved."[1] The landscape and history of the Great Southwest entered fully into Williams's imagination of America only after World War II. Between 1947 and 1955, he made three trips through the region and wrote a number of poems—including "The Desert Music"—about his experiences there. The striking scenery and the distinctive mixture of Indian, Spanish, and Anglo cultures in the Southwest appealed strongly to Williams's sense of the local. And his own lineage helped him to feel an affinity with the place and its people. "Of course he was partly Spanish ('Carlos,' his mother)," observed Winfield Townley Scott in a Santa Fe interview, "and he felt a kinship with this country and the background of this country, and he was very excited about it."[2]

Williams paid a flying visit to the Southwest when he was a young man, but he found precious little opportunity to look about him on that occasion. In December of 1907, he travelled by train from New York via Laredo, Texas, to San Luis Potosí in Old Mexico. En route, he acted as personal physician to a dying Mexican businessman named Gonzalez, who was going home to live out his last days in familiar surroundings. Williams spent just three hours in San Luis Potosí before catching a train

1. Letter from William Carlos Williams to Winfield Townley Scott, 15 November 1954, John Hay Library, Brown University; quoted in Donald D. Eulert, "Winfield Townley Scott: Conversations on Poets and the Art of Poetry," Diss. New Mexico 1969, p. 245, and in Scott Donaldson, *Poet in America: Winfield Townley Scott* (Austin and London: Univ. of Texas Press, 1972), p. 279. The Brown University Library has generously permitted us to quote from the papers of W.T. Scott houses there. Quotations from previously unpublished letters by William Carlos Williams are copyright 1983 by William Eric Williams and Paul Williams.
2. Eulert, p. 58. Eulert's conversations with Scott took place in Santa Fe between April 2, 1966, and January 14, 1967.

back to New York. What he saw of Texas and Mexico on this trip, he saw mainly from the window and rear door of the express.[3] And he did not venture west again until 1947, his sixty-fourth year. It is therefore not surprising that the map of America in Williams's *In the American Grain* [1925] extends westward only to Texas, where Sam Houston defeats Santa Ana at the battle of San Jacinto. Farther than that, the chronicler had not himself gone.

Williams's imaginative annexation of other Southwestern territories had to wait until he was invited to spend part of a summer at a writers' workshop sponsored by the University of Utah in Salt Lake City. The workshop lasted from July 7 to July 18, 1947 [Mariani, p. 546]. Then Williams, his wife, and his sister-in-law motored into southwestern Colorado and northern New Mexico. "The two features of most importance to us, aside from the Conference itself and the common scenes along the roads," he reported upon returning to Rutherford, "were a very brief visit to the cliff dweller ruins at Mesa Verde and our trip with Bob McAlmon to Taos."[4]

In Colorado, the Williams party "drove the 'Million-Dollar Highway,' a name given it because of the gold quartz with which it had been inadvertently paved. That day we saw too the miraculous relics of the cliff-dwellers at Mesa Verde—far more extensive than I had imagined" [*Autobiography*, p. 312]. The tourists put up at a hotel in Cortez, the town nearest the Anasazi ruins. There Williams began "The Testament of Perpetual Change," a poem written in response to the diversity of cultures he had recently encountered.

On Monday, July 21, the Williams party arrived in Taos, where they took rooms at La Fonda Hotel. They visited Taos Pueblo, Kit Carson's house, and the splendid adobe church at Ranchos de Taos. They also called upon Frieda Lawrence, who since 1932 had made her permanent home near Taos on the mountainside ranch given her by Mabel Dodge Luhan in the early 1920s. The next day, Williams was joined by his old friend, Robert McAlmon, who came up from El Paso, Texas [Mariani, p. 548]. McAlmon had lived there since the early 1940s, working for a

---

3. See *The Autobiography of William Carlos Williams* (New York: New Directions Publishing Corporation, 1967), pp. 72-75, and Paul Mariani, *William Carlos Williams: A New World Naked* (New York: McGraw-Hill Book Company, 1981), pp. 61-62; hereafter cited in the text and notes of this essay as *Autobiography* and Mariani, respectively.
4. *The Selected Letters of William Carlos Williams*, ed. John C. Thirlwall (New York: McDowell, Obolensky, 1957), p. 261.

surgical-supply house owned by his brothers, and battling tuberculosis.[5]

After a meal in Taos, the writers drove down through the Rio Grande gorge to Santa Fe. There they parted company, Williams and his party heading toward Oklahoma and the east. Somewhere in northern New Mexico they passed a Navajo woman walking beside the road, and just outside of Tulsa they saw a Cherokee woman hitchhiking. Williams later wrote poems about each of these female figures: "Navajo" and "Graph."

Sherman Paul argues that Williams's poetry was "not significantly informed" by the 1947 trip.[6] Certainly it inspired nothing comparable to "The Desert Music," the major work which grew out of the poet's 1950 visit to El Paso and Juarez. Yet Williams did write four poems as a result of his first journey through the Southwest. They record some of his immediate impressions of the local landscape, they interpret the ethnic contrasts of the region in terms of the culture-myths which Williams had generated in *In the American Grain*, and they anticipate some of the most prominent themes of "The Desert Music."

In both subject and technique, "The Testament of Perpetual Change" is a poem of ironic juxtapositions and contrasts. One contrast is between the cultural situation of the contemporary Pueblo Indian and that of his Anasazi ancestor. Whereas the Anasazi was centered in the magnificent adobe cliff-dwellings at Mesa Verde (fig. 1), his twentieth-century descendant is lured away from the land (the "Radiance Rose...among the unprotected desert foliage") by the meretricious commercialism of Anglo-Saxon civilization ("a bottle of cheap perfume" in the window of a Walgreen's drugstore). This contrast is actually an extension of the one that dominates *In the American Grain*. The heart of that book is the dramatic confrontation between the indigenous Indian spirit, conceived as living in constructive harmony with the generative powers of nature; and the invading Puritan spirit, conceived as life-denying, walled-off, and exploitative. In "The Testament of Perpetual Change," that confrontation is re-enacted as "Walgreen carries Culture to the West."[7]

5. See Robert E. Knoll, *Robert McAlmon: Expatriate Publisher and Writer* (Lincoln: Univ. of Nebraska Studies, 1959), p. 19, and William Carlos Williams, "Letters to Norman Macleod," *Pembroke Magazine*, No. 6 (1975), 159.
6. Sherman Paul, *The Music of Survival: A Biography of a Poem by William Carlos Williams* (Urbana: Univ. of Illinois Press, 1968), p. 16.
7. *The Collected Later Poems of William Carlos Williams* (New York: New Directions Publishing Corporation, 1967), p. 103; hereafter cited in the text and notes of this essay as *CLP*.

The battle against an alien spirit has a literary as well as an ethnic front in the poem. For Williams's impressions of Colorado alternate with the opening lines of Robert Bridges's *The Testament of Beauty*, creating a tense montage of poetic styles. Whereas Williams writes in a contemporary, colloquial idiom, Bridges employs an archaic, highly literary language that seeks to revive and preserve the diction and sensibility of seventeenth-century England. Indeed, the Puritan spirit itself may have peeked out at Williams from the allegorical imagery and homiletic tone of Bridges's lines:

> Mortal Prudence, handmaid of divine Providence,
> hath inscrutable reckoning with Fate and Fortune:
> We sail a changeful sea through halcyon days and storm,
> and when the ship laboureth, our stedfast purpose
> trembles like as the compass in a binnacle.
> Our stability is but balance, and wisdom lies
> in masterful administration of the unforeseen.[8]

Though he respected Bridges's experiments with archaic diction and quantitative meter, Williams could not accept them as models for the distinctively American poetry of which he was in search. Thus his title emphasizes not the timeless "beauty" which Bridges seeks to enshrine, but the "perpetual change" which demands new styles for new historical conditions. In effect, Bridges's lines skillfully epitomize the British cultural hegemony against which, during the conference in Utah, Williams had just reaffirmed his enduring rebellion [Mariani, pp. 546-47]. The American poet, so to speak, sides with the American Indian in his attempt to live on and with the land.

The Indian mode of life, Williams believed, stays in vital contact with the earth which sustains it. When he describes the Aztecs in the third chapter of *In the American Grain*, for example, Williams speaks in Lawrentian terms of

> the tribe's deep feeling for a reality that stems back into the permanence of remote origins.... It was the earthward thrust of their logic; blood and earth; the realization of their primal and continuous identity with the ground itself, where everything is fixed in darkness.

Often Williams celebrates this chthonic "identity with the ground" in sexual and floral figures of speech; he habitually conceives of "the New World as a woman" who must be husbanded in order to

---

8. Williams identified the source of these lines in a note that appeared with "The Testament of Perpetual Change" when it was first published in the *Partisan Review*, 15 (October 1948), 1101. He committed a slight error when he transcribed "the compass' (line 5) as "a compass."

flower and grow fruitful. Thus Williams's Daniel Boone understands the spirit in which the Indian has married the land.

> There must be a new wedding. But he saw and only he saw the prototype of it all, the native savage.... If the land were to be possessed it must be as the Indian possessed it. Boone saw the truth of the Red Man...as a natural expression of the place, the Indian himself as 'right,' the flower of his world.[9]

Carrying this cultural/sexual myth with him to the Southwest, Williams naturally applied it to his descriptions of two Indian women whom he saw along the roadside. In "Navajo," a woman observed in New Mexico embodies many of the poet's preconceptions about the Indian spirit:

> stalking
> the grey brush
> paralleling
> the highway...
> —head mobbled
> red, red
> to the ground—
> sweeping the
> ground—
> the blood walking
> erect, the
> desert animating
> the blood to walk
> erect by choice
> through
> the pale green
> of the starveling
> sage

The eyes of this regal figure ("mobbled," "sweeping") are "cast down" to symbolize not humility but a proud blood-contact with the land which sustains her. She gazes on the ground also "to escape" the narrator of the poem, the Anglo tourist who is invading her world. Although Europeans have named the nearby Sangre de Cristo mountains after the blood of their god, the blood-link between the land and its earliest inhabitants antedates the mythology of Spanish Catholicism:

9. William Carlos Williams, *In the American Grain* (New York: New Directions Publishing Corporation, 1956), pp. 33-34, 220, 137-38; hereafter cited in the text of this essay as *IAG*. Williams's interest in the pre-Columbian civilizations of Mexico was lifelong. In 1959, he published translations of "Three Nahuatl Poems" in *The Muse in Mexico: A Mid-Century Miscellany*, ed. Thomas Mabry Cranfill (Austin: Univ. of Texas Press, 1959), pp. 90-91; rpt. *Pictures from Brueghel and Other Poems* (New York: New Directions Publishing Corporation, 1962), pp. 59-60, and *Technicians of the Sacred: A Range of Poetries from Africa, America, Asia, & Oceania*, ed. Jerome Rothenberg (Garden City, N.Y.: Doubleday and Co., 1968), pp. 222-23. See also Steven Weiland, "William Carlos Williams and the Aztecs," *Arizona Quarterly*, 35 (1979), 42-48.

```
Red woman,
    (Keep Christ out
    of this—and
    his mountains:
    Sangre de Cristo
    red rocks that make
    the water run
    blood-red)
squaw in red
red woman
```

[CLP, pp. 101-02]

The primary tints of the scene affirm the Indian's "primal and continuous identity with the ground itself."

The same identity is briefly limned in "Graph," a companion-poem to "Navajo."[10] Here Williams characteristically associates the fertility of the earth with the fertility of a woman's womb:

```
There was another, too
a half-breed Cherokee
tried to thumb a ride
out of Tulsa, standing there
with a bunch of wildflowers
in her left hand
pressed close
just below the belly
```

[CLP, p. 102]

In an earlier draft, the flowers were "held carelessly" and the poem was entitled "Pick-Up," implying perhaps a seductive intention on the part of the hitchhiker.[11] Nevertheless, the floral imagery recalls Williams's earlier description of the Indian as "the flower of his world." Both the Cherokee and the Navajo women ultimately represent Williams's beloved archetype of the life-giving earth-mother. The same muse heartens the speaker of "The Desert Music" in the persons of a young Indian woman carrying a baby in the Juarez marketplace and an old stripper in a nearby bar.

"The Desert Music" is a product of Williams's second visit to the Southwest, in November of 1950. McAlmon had extended an invitation to Mrs. Williams early in the year, when he learned that she and Williams were contemplating a visit to her sister in

10. "Navajo," "The Graph," and "A Woman in Front of a Bank" were originally published together in the *Yale Poetry Review*, No. 8 (1948), 4-5. In manuscript, all three portraits belonged to a series entitled "Some Women—5 Poems"; see Steven L. Meyers and Neil Baldwin, *The Manuscripts and Letters of William Carlos Williams in the Poetry Collection of the Lockwood Memorial Library, State University of New York at Buffalo: A Descriptive Catalogue* (Boston: G. K. Hall and Co., 1978), pp. 32, 52.
11. The manuscript of "Pick-Up" is cited with the permission of the Poetry/Rare Book Collection of the University Libraries, State University of New York at Buffalo.

Los Angeles. "I hope you and bill [*sic*] do get to L. A. to see
Charlotte and then stop off over here for a few days. With Juarez
I can show you and [*sic*] good time and know you will find it,
the curios, jewelry, handicraft work, and types intereeting [*sic*]."
The invitation was renewed in September: "Think we can make
things interesting for you, as Juarez has its points, and good food
and good nightclubs and bars. One of my sisters-in-law wants to
give a party for you two and invite what local talent or brains there
are about."[12]
  Williams accepted the invitation in a spirit of excitement.
"Damned nice of your sister to want to give us a meal or a ban-
quet or whatever it is. Accepted with pleasure. Do we need our
passports to go over the line? If so we'll have to get some as we
haven't any to hand...So here we are on the brink of another
adventure if you'll consent to call it that. If I hadn't of been a
writer, it would never have happened. I feel all upset inside
even over such a mild program, can't stand excitement the way
I uster. But it'll be fun."[13]
  The "adventure" included a series of lecture/readings at
universities up and down the West Coast. "I've been on a swing
around the country lecturing at Washington U., Reed College,
U. of Oregon and U.C.L.A.," Williams reported to Norman
Macleod three days after returning from the circuit.[14] From
Los Angeles, Williams and his wife took the *Sunset Limited*
across southern Arizona and New Mexico to El Paso, arriving
in the afternoon of Sunday, November 19. "At dawn I saw the
sign Tucson on a station platform," he recalled, "and the same
day at three, after crossing the desert miles near the Mexican
border, left the beautiful train...to meet Bob McAlmon coming
grinning up the platform at El Paso. . ." [*Autobiography*, p. 388;
Mariani, pp. 625-27]. McAlmon had met Williams under similar
circumstances before—in Paris, during January of 1924 [Mariani,
p. 219]. On both occasions, the artist in residence acted as Williams's guide into a foreign world.
  For Spanish-speaking Texas and Mexico were only slightly
less foreign to Williams than France had been. He had passed
through both territories in 1907, but he had been too preoccupied

12. Letters from Robert McAlmon to William Carlos Williams, 27 January and 17 September 1950, Beinecke Rare Book and Manuscript Library, Yale University. The Beinecke
Library has generously permitted us to quote from many letters in its American Literature Collection.
13. Letter from William Carlos Williams to Robert McAlmon, 4 [?] October 1950,
Beinecke Rare Book and Manuscript Library, Yale University.
14. Williams, "Letters to Norman Macleod," p. 160. On Macleod's own literary activities in the Southwest, see Knoll, p. 17, and E. P. Walkiewicz and Hugh Witemeyer,
"Ezra Pound's Contributions to New Mexican Periodicals and His Relationship with
Senator Bronson Cutting," *Paideuma*, 9 (Winter 1980), 442-48.

then with another's health and with his own role as healer to attend closely to his surroundings. Now he was older, closer to the condition of the waning Sr. Gonzalez than to that of the waxing Dr. Williams, and much more interested in the roots of his own middle name. The highlight of his brief stay along the border in 1950 was the promised excursion across the Rio Grande to Ciudad Juarez, in the company of McAlmon, his two brothers, and their wives. "Juarez, across the bridge," Williams jotted in his journal. "Three cents the trip. *Sur le pont d'Avignon*—is all I could think of. The sparrows at night in the park—Bob and his brothers, George and Alec and their wives—tequilla at five cents a glass, a quail dinner and the Mexicans, the poor Indians..." [*Autobiography*, pp. 388-89]. To cross the bridge was to enter a world where prices are low, where poverty is widespread, yet where life is fecund and paradoxically rich.

The contrasts between the United States and Mexico struck Williams so forcibly that the bridge over the Rio Grande began almost at once to assume symbolic dimensions in his imagination. The transformation manifested itself first in a picture-postcard which he mailed from the El Paso train station, just before he departed on the afternoon of Wednesday, November 22. Addressed to the ailing McAlmon, the card shows on one side the "International Bridge Connecting El Paso, Texas, and Juarez, Old Mexico." On the other side, Williams wrote: "This bridge symbolizes some not soon to be forgotten hour. Stick it out, keed, things may change even for the better" [figs. 2 and 3].[15] Already the bridge signifies for Williams transition of several sorts: from one land and people to another, from the past to the present and thence to the future, from hard times to better times. The seed of "The Desert Music" had been planted, though its full flowering required another six months.

Of his transition by train from El Paso to New Orleans, Williams recorded some impressions which he later transcribed into his *Autobiography*. He observed the agriculture and industry of the Permian Basin area as well as its geological configuration and native vegetation (the *cholla* is a variety of cactus). "Next day the desert, across from the cotton fields, the railroad track dividing them. Copper, the smoke of the smelter stretching out across the desert miles—the endless waste of rubble—nightfall on the desert and the train gradually ascending in slow curves a thousand feet in a few miles. *Cholla, Okeechoya*. The moon coming up"

---

15. Beinecke Rare Book and Manuscript Library, Yale University; slightly misquoted by Mariani, p. 627.

[*Autobiography*, p. 389]. Williams and his wife reached Rutherford on November 26, 1950 [Mariani, p. 627].

"The Desert Music" was written during the following May for presentation at the Harvard University Phi Beta Kappa commencement ceremony on June 18, 1951 [Mariani, pp. 631-632]. Several months after his return from the Southwest—late in March, to be precise—Williams had suffered the first of the cerebral strokes that plagued his later years. The writing of the poem was therefore inextricably bound up with his recovery, and it was a slow, arduous process for a poet accustomed to working rapidly. "It has taken me a month or more to write it, transcribe it, have it typed, correct it and polish it," he told Norman Macleod on June 11.[16]

Nevertheless, the poem was completed and delivered on schedule. Williams later recalled the occasion with a mixture of pride and glee.

> Just before I had my cerebral accident, I had received an invitation to read a poem at Phi Beta Kappa exercises at Harvard. I had no poem to read them so I wrote one. I had just returned from a trip to the West and the picture of the desert country around El Paso was fresh in my mind. I'd crossed the desert and *seen* the desert. It is always important to me to be familiar with what I am writing about. I was honored by the invitation to read at Harvard (but was perhaps not so honored after I had read). The students were tickled to death but some of the gentlemen sitting on the platform disapproved. After all, it is a pretty shocking poem, speaking as it does of the whores of Juarez.[17]

To the stricken poet, the memory of the desert and the whores had been as healing as a vision of Helicon and the Muses.

Sherman Paul has written eloquently about the autobiographical aspect of "The Desert Music," showing how Williams poignantly affirms his survival as an artist by creating in the poem a symbolic pattern of psychic descent and ascent, or death and rebirth.[18] In retrospect, Williams saw his trip across the Arizona desert as a quest through an inner wasteland of personal crisis. His initial description of the desert emphasizes its potential fertility, and defines its sound as a "music of survival"; but that music is as yet only "half/heard" by the speaker:

> Leaving California to return east, the fertile desert
> (were it to get water)
> surrounded us, a music of survival, subdued, distant, half
> heard; we were engulfed

---

16. Williams, "Letters to Norman Macleod," p. 162.
17. William Carlos Williams, *I Wanted to Write a Poem: The Autobiography of the Works of a Poet*, ed. Edith Heal (New York: New Directions Publishing Corporation, 1978), p. 88.
18. Paul, pp. 22-23, 67-68, 102. See also Mariani, pp. 632-36.

by it as in the early evening, seeing the wind lift
                    and drive the sand, we
passed Yuma. All night long, heading for El Paso to
                    meet our friend,
we slept fitfully.

Sounds, sights, and sleep are all fitful at this stage of the speaker's transit through the "jagged desert."[19]

Juarez slaps the poet awake and jolts his senses into focus by dint of its sheer otherness. The place is at once exotic and alien, liberating and threatening. Williams is struck first by the vivid colors of the public market, a roofed, two-story structure lined with booths which are rented by the individual vendors:

The Old Market's a good place to begin:
                    *   *   *   *   *
                    What color! Isn't it
wonderful!

          —paper flowers (*para los santos*)
baked red-clay utensils, daubed
with blue, silverware,
dried peppers, onions, print goods, children's
clothing . the place deserted all but
for a few Indians squatted in the
booths, unnoticing (don't you think it)
as though they slept there

          There's a second tier. Do you
want to go up?

In addition to the vivid array of goods, Williams is aware of the Indians who are selling them. The Indians seem dormant and "unnoticing," but Williams is convinced that they, like the woman in "Navajo," are intensely alert to the Anglo tourists invading their environment. The apparent somnolence of the Indians masks the creative energy which has produced their "wonderful" wares, an energy not yet fully shared by the poet who "slept fitfully" on the train.

No less picturesque and no less unsettling are the crowded environs of the Old Market, with their street stalls, their accessible shops, and their thronging customers. Here the static lassitude of the Old Market gives way to a kinetic flow of ceaseless commercial activity. One is reminded that Juarez is no torpid border town but a bustling business center. (Today, it is a prosperous community of 425,000 people, the fifth largest city in Mexico.)

---

19. William Carlos Williams, "The Desert Music," in *Pictures from Brueghel and Other Poems*, p. 110. Subsequent quotations of "The Desert Music" come from this edition.

> —returned to the street,
> the pressure moves from booth to booth along
> the curb. Opposite, no less insistent
> the better stores are wide open. Come in
> and look around. You don't have to buy: hats,
> riding boots, blankets .
>
> Look at the way,
> slung from her neck with a shawl, that young
> Indian woman carries her baby!
>
> —a stream of Spanish,
> as she brushes by, intense, wide-
> eyed in eager talk with her boy husband
>
> —three half-grown girls, one of them eating a
> pomegranate. Laughing.

The speaker is attracted by the human spectacle of the Mexican market district, but also vaguely disturbed by the multitudinous demands which the unfamiliar environment makes upon his attention. His stress reveals itself in such nouns and adjectives as "pressure," "insistent," "intense," and "eager." It appears also in such imperative verbs as "Come in/ and look around" and "Look at the way." The torrent of new impressions threatens to engulf the speaker; at one point, the solicitations of the street beggars become so intolerable that he enters a bar to take refuge from the "obscene fingers" upon his "naked/ wrist."

For the otherness of Juarez consists not only of its picturesque charms but also of its potential menace. Williams feels the mild paranoia inevitably experienced by any tourist who carries a standard set of middle-class, Puritan-American prejudices into a Mexican environment. He is warned not to drink in the side streets, and told the story of "H.," who was "terribly/ beaten up in one of those joints." He learns that the mayor was recently convicted of extorting "$3000 a week from/ the whorehouses of the city." He fears that he will contract typhoid fever from eating the lettuce in a restaurant salad. He recalls that most of the inhabitants of the city are not Spaniards but "Indians who chase the white bastards/ through the streets on their Independence Day/ and try to kill them," thus re-enacting the ancient conflict between native inhabitants and European invaders. His experience of Mexico makes the poet intensely aware of the stark extremes of beauty and danger, life and death. Like the Aztecs of *In the American Grain*, the people of Juarez are in touch with a "mysterious secret of existence whose cruel beauty" at once threatens life and renews it [*IAG*, p. 34].

In this context, the women of Juarez stand out in bold relief. As during his earlier trip through New Mexico and Oklahoma, Williams's eye is drawn to female figures who seem to incarnate the mythical attributes of archetypal womanhood. In the description of the market district already quoted, for example, he encounters types of Demeter and Koré in quick succession: the woman with a baby and the girl with a pomegranate. Fleetingly but unmistakably, they symbolize the cyclical mysteries of birth, death, and rebirth. Later in the poem, the speaker is fascinated by an old stripper in a bar. Though not an Indian, she, too, embodies woman's fertile contact with the earth and its life-powers.

"Look at her.... Look at those breasts," exclaims the tourist, echoing the imperatives of the marketplace scene. From her breasts, his attention moves to "her hips" and "her belly." She

> is heavy on her feet.
> That's good. She
> bends forward leaning
> on the table of the
> balding man sitting
> upright, alone, so that
> everything hangs for-
> ward.

The earth draws the female organs of the stripper toward it, as the gravitational force of enjambment draws the reader's eye toward the bottom of the page. Her solid grounding leads Williams finally to associate the stripper with a Greek myth of vulnerable womanhood in contact with the earth: "Andromeda of those rocks." He discovers "the virgin" in "an old whore," and experiences her archetypal womanhood as another aspect of the threatening but life-renewing otherness of Juarez. In the bar scene, the poet's surrogate is the "balding man sitting/ upright, alone"—the phallic figure with whom the ageless, sleazy muse nearly comes into contact as she leans across the table.

The most important surrogate for the speaker of "The Desert Music" is not the man in the bar, however, but a Mexican Indian derelict, asleep on the bridge between Juarez and El Paso. Williams first encountered him on the way back to McAlmon's at the end of the eventful day in Mexico. The figure was "huddled into a lump against the ironwork of the bridge at night—safe perhaps from both sides, incredibly compressed into a shapeless obstruction—asleep" [*Autobiography*, p. 389]. This unhoused lump entered the poet's imagination, lodged in his journal and *Autobiography*, and eventually found a permanent home in the opening and closing lines of "The Desert Music."

The derelict incorporates all of the transitions that the bridge had come to symbolize in Williams's mind. The sleeper is "interjurisdictional," midway between two countries and their laws, between life and death, between the human and the non-human:

Is it alive?

neither a head,

legs nor arms!

It isn't a sack of rags someone
has abandoned here   torpid against
the flange of the supporting girder   ?

an inhuman shapelessness,
knees hugged tight up into the belly

Egg-shaped!

What a place to sleep!
on the International Boundary. Where else,
interjurisdictional, not to be disturbed?

The gender of the figure is indeterminate ("A woman. Or a very shriveled old man"), and the very time of day is transitional ("unrecognizable/ in the semi-dark").

Sherman Paul rightly argues that this denizen of the borderland is an aspect of Williams himself, an *alter ego* representing the precarious condition to which he had been reduced by his stroke.[20] The Indian's ambiguous sleep, which may signify either death or recuperation, is related to the fitful sleep of the poet on the train. The shape on the bridge, in effect, is Carlos.

As Williams confronts Carlos, the half-heard music of survival, which began in the Arizona desert and continued in the streets and bars of Juarez, becomes fully audible to him at last. Images of the arts begin to mingle with images of gestation. First, the foetal position of Carlos promises a rebirth. Then, by a curious transposition of vowels and consonants in the second syllable, the "music" in the poet's head becomes "mucus," a protective placenta out of which the poem is delivered:

a child in the womb prepared to imitate life,
warding its life against
a birth of awful promise. The music
guards it, a mucus, a film that surrounds it,
    *   *   *   *   *
a music! a protecting music   .

I *am* a poet!-I
am. I am. I am a poet, I reaffirmed, ashamed

Now the music volleys through as in
a lonely moment I hear it. Now it is all
about me. The dance! The verb detaches itself
seeking to become articulate

---

20. Paul, p. 82. See also Audrey T. Rogers, "William Carlos Williams's 'New World': Images of the Dance," *Arizona Quarterly*, 35 (1979), 17-19.

Williams' poetic imagination turns androgynous, as it bears a child and dances to an earthy music—functions which earlier in the poem belonged to the women of Juarez. He rouses himself from sleep, and partners himself in a fling of the spirit: "NOT, prostrate, to copy nature/ but a dance! to dance/ two and two with him—/ sequestered there asleep,/ right end up!" The memory of his visit to Mexico reunites the woman and the man, the Indian and the white bastard, the artist and the tourist: "So this is William/ Carlos Williams, the poet."

In addition to his own personal kind of desert music, Williams was interested both in the work of other artists who lived in the Southwest and in the periodicals which published and reviewed that work. Between 1944 and 1960, Williams sent at least nine items—either poems or short essays—to editors in Arizona, Colorado, New Mexico, and Utah.[21] In a little magazine named *Suck-Egg Mule*, one of the young New Mexican writers, Judson Crews of Taos, expressed his appreciation of Williams's support: "The university quarterlies, generally, are committed to academicism. This is why the little magazine is still important and still necessary and why Williams has been its constant friend and champion."[22]

Crews recalls that Williams contributed not only poems but also hard cash.

> When Jay Waite of Arroyo Hondo [a village just north of Taos] begin publishing *Gale* magazine in about 1948 (maybe 1949), he sent letters to a few established poets, requesting manuscripts. I believe Williams was the only one ever to respond. When Jay Waite sent him a copy of *Gale* he was delighted with it because of its lack of pretentions. He singled out a poem of mine for comment, and wrote a cheque for $15 "for the poet" he wrote impulsively. Then he crossed that out and said, "No—for the magazine." Which was proper. It financed an entire extra issue of the magazine.

21. See Emily Mitchell Wallace, *A Bibliography of William Carlos Williams* (Middletown, Connecticut: Wesleyan University Press, 1968), pp. 208-240. The items are: "The Province," *Rocky Mountain Review* (Murray, Utah), VIII, 2 (Winter 1944), 23; "Thinking Back toward Christmas: A Statement for the Virgin," *Experiment* (Salt Lake City, Utah), I, 1 (April 1944), 11; "The Horse," *Arizona Quarterly* (Tucson), II, 1 (Spring 1946), 4; "Song, from Paterson III, " *Gale* (Arroyo Hondo, New Mexico), I, 2 (May 1949), 15; "Poem," *Gale*, II, 1 (February 1950), 4; "Patrocinio Barela," *El Crepusculo de la Libertad* (Taos, New Mexico), VIII, 31 (August 4, 1955), 9; "To Flossie," *Colorado Review* (Fort Collins), I, 1 (Winter 1956-57), 39; "The Greenhouse in the Garden," *Arizona Quarterly*, XIII, 1 (Spring 1957), 89; "To Be Recited to Flossie on Her Birthday," *Inscape* (Albuquerque, New Mexico), No. 6 (Winter 1960-61), 1. The last of these items was originally published as a broadsheet on April 18, 1959 (Wallace, p. 255). Robert Creeley subsequently arranged for the poem to be reprinted in *Inscape* and to be included in *CLP* (letter from Robert Creeley to Hugh Witemeyer, 25 September 1981).
22. Judson Crews [review of *The Autobiography of William Carlos Williams*], *Suck-Egg Mule*, No. 5 (1951-52), [20].

Later Williams sent Crews enough money to pay for ten subscriptions to *The Naked Ear*, a little magazine that Crews had just founded. The extra subscriptions were for Robert McAlmon, Ezra Pound, Louis Zukofsky, Winfield Townley Scott, and Alfred Kreymborg, among others.[23]

When Crews and two friends of his prepared a book on the sculpture of Patrocinio Barela (1908-1964), a remarkable Taos woodcarver, they "sent a copy to Williams and asked him to review it." Williams sent back "not a review, but an article on Barela."[24] In this brief article, Williams again makes use of the culture-myths which informed his perception of the Southwest. Although Barela's subjects are mostly drawn from Christianity and Spanish folklore, his carvings seemed to Williams to incorporate other local influences.

> His pieces remind me of Navajo sandpainting in their simplicity and primitive fervor—though they are definitely not associated with the old culture. The ritual is more Christian, influenced by the alien race, but the gentleness is not forced, it springs from under the earth from which the corn itself grows and the Indian understands it.[25]

In other words, Barela's sculpture unites the indigenous, vitalistic Indian spirit ("the old culture") with the invading Spanish-Catholic spirit ("the alien race"). The ancient ethnic and religious conflict is harmonized by the mediation of art (figs. 4 and 5). Barela's touch resembles the Catholic touch of Père Sebastian Rasles in the eleventh chapter of *In the American Grain*. Because he came "with gentleness," Rasles "could approach the Indians" as the Puritans could not [*IAG*, p. 129].

In June of 1955, Williams paid his third and last visit to the Southwest. He arrived in Santa Fe on Saturday, June 4, having just completed a reading tour of California; and he departed for the east on Tuesday, June 7.[26] He stayed at La Posada inn as a guest of his friend, Winfield Townley Scott. Scott and Williams had known each other by correspondence since the early 1940s, when Williams contributed poetry to Scott's "New Verse" column in the *Providence Sunday Journal*. They had first met in March 1950, at the inaugural National Book Awards ceremony in New York.[27]

3. Letter from Judson Crews to Hugh Witemeyer, 28 August 1981.
4. Letter from Judson Crews to Hugh Witemeyer, 7 August 1981.
5. Williams, "Patrocinio Barela," p. 9. The essay was reprinted in *Poetry Taos* (Ranos de Taos, New Mexico), No. 1 (1957), [9]. It is also quoted in the introduction Mildred Crews, Wendell Anderson, and Judson Crews, *Patrocinio Barela* [2nd ed.] aos, N.M.: Taos Recordings and Publications, 1962), p. 10.
5. Donaldson, p. 279. Williams's dated hotel bill is among Scott's papers at the John ay Library, Brown University. Mariani (p. 688) errs in saying that Williams had returned to Rutherford by June 5.
. Eulert, p. 54, and Donaldson, pp. 165-166, 226.

When Scott moved to Santa Fe in the spring of 1954, Williams enthusiastically recalled the impression which the place had made upon him seven years before.

> It is wonderful for me to think of you hanging out your sign (for the postman) in Santa Fe. I think you will be very happy there if for no other reason than you have come from New England and are so much a part of New England that your present environment cannot be other than a perpetual shock to you. I spent no more than a night there, if I spent that much time, but the impression I had of the place was overwhelming. It took me all the way back to the beginnings of our country, to the times of Coronado and the Pueblo Indians and I was deeply moved. I envy you this experience, make the most of it, I don't know of a city in the country that I would rather visit, write me sometime when you have the chance telling me how you find the place. Is it still what I imagine it?[28]

In a letter of 15 April 1955, Scott answered this request for a description.

> Santa Fe is a small city—yet really a city. An excellent hotel, some good restaurants & shops. Everything is a little walk away; but it IS a city. Manageable. And around it the UNmanageable landscape: the Sangre de Cristo Mountains just east of us, the highest peaks (10,000 feet) now snow-covered still as they have been for months—fifty miles out our west windows, the Jemez Mountains, and under them at night, all night long, the chain of lights at Los Alamos.[29]

Scott's account stirred Williams's imagination. "That country has always fascinated me," he wrote back, "with its dream of savage well being, Coronado and his Spaniards."[30] The "dream of savage well being" probably refers to the legend of the seven golden cities of Cibola, which lured Coronado's expedition of 1540-42 north from Mexico to explore the territory that later became Arizona and New Mexico.

Williams seemed frail and exhausted when he fulfilled his desire to revisit Santa Fe in June of 1955. Scott "took things easy with him; picnicked & drove around; only once had half a dozen people in to meet him...WCW tires easily."[31] When he and Scott

---

28. See n. 1 above.
29. Letter from Winfield Townley Scott to William Carlos Williams, 15 April 1955, Beinecke Rare Book and Manuscript Library, Yale University.
30. Letter from William Carlos Williams to Winfield Townley Scott, 20 April 1955, John Hay Library, Brown University; quoted by Mariani, p. 840.
31. Letter from Winfield Townley Scott to Charles and Deborah Philbrick, 25 June 1955, John Hay Library, Brown University. The group which met Williams included Santa Fe writers Lucile Adler and Tom Mayer. Witter Bynner was not present, although Williams had initiated a correspondence with him in 1949 (letter from William Carlos Williams to Robert McAlmon, 13 March 1949, Beinecke Rare Book and Manuscript Library, Yale University).

went out to the juncture of Camino del Monte Sol with the Old Santa Fe Trail, Williams perceived in the vista to the southwest a touch of the sublime. "The other afternoon I stood in front of the Folk Art Museum at the south edge of town with William Carlos Williams," Scott recalled. "We gazed out across the piñon-pocked foothills flounced with green cottonwoods and 'accented' by poplars in the seemingly arrested sunlight. He said, 'It looks like eternity.'"[32] Whereas Scott speaks of the landscape in metaphors drawn from fashion design, the ailing Williams borrows a simile from Christian eschatology.

On Sunday, June 5, Scott organized a picnic excursion to Chimayo and Truchas, two old, Spanish-speaking villages in the hills northeast of Santa Fe. Again, Williams was deeply moved by the prospect.

> On the Sunday [we] drove up to Chimayo, where we picknicked ...and then up the mountains to Truchas. Both these are ancient, little, Spanish towns—Bill, of course, is partly Spanish. Coming down from Truchas you are driving high in the air with the Rio Grande, sandy badlands, terracotta buttes & mesas, vast blue mountains beyond—all spread out. "This is it," said Bill. "O.K., baby," said Floss. They were both enraptured by the city and the landscape ("It looks like a preview of eternity," said Bill) and want to come back—really want to.... He said coming down from Truchas, "I don't know how I could use all this, but I have a notion I shall."[33]

Scott's report did not sentimentalize Williams's response; for in the bread-and-butter letter which he wrote after returning to Rutherford, Williams thanked his host "for taking such good care of us in Santa Fe and for seeing to it that the whole countryside was made ours."[34]

Although Williams was unable to return to the Southwest, his subsequent correspondence with Scott reflects his continuing interest in the region and its culture. In December of 1955, he requested information about Indian kachina dolls.[35] In September of 1957, he commented upon the premiere season of the Santa Fe Opera: "We have been made conscious of Santa Fe by news of

32. Winfield Townley Scott, "A Calendar of Santa Fe," *New World Writing*, No. 12 (1957); rpt. in Scott, *Exiles and Fabrications* (Garden City, N.Y.: Doubleday and Co., 1961), p. 210.
33. Letter from Winfield Townley Scott to Ben and Betty Bagdikian, 20 June 1955; quoted by Donaldson, pp. 279-80. Written shortly after the event, this letter probably contains a more accurate version of Williams's remark about eternity than does Scott's "A Calendar of Santa Fe."
34. Letter from William Carlos Williams to Winfield Townley Scott, 10 June 1955, John Hay Library, Brown University.
35. Letters from William Carlos Williams to Winfield Townley Scott, 16 and 24 December 1955, John Hay Library, Brown University. The letter of 16 December is reproduced by Eulert, p. 246.

your opera, it must have been brilliantly successful in that unusual setting. You must have been among its spectators. The whole region is to be congratulated."[36] In 1959, he inquired whether the opera might be interested in producing a work by Theodore Harris based upon "an old script of mine on the theme of Geo. Washington."[37] Santa Fe, Williams assured Scott, would always be among "the places on the earth that I have knowen [*sic*] and loved."[38]

Williams never carried out his intention to "use" in new writings the impressions of his final visit to New Mexico. But the effect of the landscape upon him is recorded in a poem which grew out of his first visit to the state in 1947. In "New Mexico," Williams explains how the life of the desert can calm a troubled mind by diminishing its anger and increasing its love:

> Anger can be transformed
> to a kitten—as love
> may become a mountain in
> the disturbed mind, the
> mind that prances like
> a horse or nibbles, starts
> and stares in the parched
> sage of the triple
> world—of stone, stone
> layered and beaten under
> the confessed brilliance
> of this desert noon.[39]

The "triple/world" of rock, mountain, and brilliant sky puts urgent human passions into perspective, and steadies the skittish Pegasus. Desert music, as Williams learned, has charms to soothe a savage breast.

If Williams was a poet of the local, he was never a poet of only one locale. The imagination of Carlos Williams could take root in Ciudad Juarez as well as Jersey City, in El Paso as well as Paterson. His Spanish heritage made him especially attentive to the landscape, history, and culture of the Great Southwest.

---

36. Letter from William Carlos Williams to Winfield Townley Scott, 21 September 1957, John Hay Library, Brown University.

37. Letter from William Carlos Williams to Winfield Townley Scott, March 1959, John Hay Library, Brown University.

38. Letter from William Carlos Williams to Winfield Townley Scott, 12 February 1956, John Hay Library, Brown University.

39. *CLP*, p. 169; first published in *The Golden Goose* (Columbus, Ohio), No. 1 (Summer 1948), 5. The authors are grateful to the following people for their generous assistance in the preparation of this essay: Lucile Adler, George Arms, Robert Bertholf, Robert Creeley, Judson Crews, Barbara Filipac, Tom Mayer, T. M. Pearce, E. W. Tedlock, Emily Wallace, Marta Weigle, and David Witt.

Embodied in the ethnic and religious contrasts of the region, he found several of his most deeply cherished culture-myths of America. The Southwest inspired Williams to create poetry at a time when he feared that his powers of imagination were dying. As he explained to Winfield Townley Scott, an environment which provides "a perpetual shock" may be as salutary as an environment which provides a perpetual comfort.

Figure 1: Cliff Palace, Mesa Verde National Park.

Figure 2: Cliff Palace Ruin. Constructed A.D. 1200-1300. Had 220 rooms and 23 kivas when fully constructed and being lived in. Abandoned about A.D. 1300, probably as a result of a long drought. Photo courtesy of Mesa Verde National Park and the United States Department of Interior, National Park Service.

Figure 3: Postcard from WCW to Robert McAlmon, 22 November 1950. Photo courtesy The Beinecke Rare Book and Manuscript Library, Yale University.

Figure 4: Patrocinio Barela, *Man Who Stands on His Own*. Photo courtesy The Harwood Foundation of the University of New Mexico, Taos, N.M.

Figure 5:   Patrocinio Barela, *A Woman Whose Baby Is Dead*. Photo courtesy The Harwood Foundation of the University of New Mexico, Taos, N.M.

NORMAN M. FINKELSTEIN

BEAUTY, TRUTH AND THE WANDERER

William Carlos Williams' *The Wanderer: A Rococo Study* was
first published in *The Egoist* in 1914 and later was used as the
concluding poem in *Al Que Quiere!*, Williams' third volume, in
1917. The poet was thirty years old when he wrote the piece, and
critics generally regard it as a transitional work, in which Williams
finally casts off the influence of Keats both in form and theme,
possibly through the mediation of Whitman, whom Williams also
read carefully early in his career.[1] As a poem of initiation, *The
Wanderer* supposedly marks Williams' entrance into the modern
world, and more specifically, signals his developing objectivist
aesthetic in his confrontation with the tawdry landscape and the
teeming social milieu of urban New York and New Jersey. The
brutal hag who serves as the poet's guide (patterned in part on
Williams' English grandmother, Emily Dickenson Wellcome) is,
in this interpretation, a muse of reality, no idealized Romantic
beauty but the whored virgin, "ominous, old, painted." The journey she forces the young man to take, culminating in his baptism
in the "filthy Passaic," confirms him as a modern poet, for in his
wandering he has learned to be the "mirror to this modernity"
that he wished to become in the beginning of the poem. And although the poem still makes use of some shopworn locutions and
the Romantic structure of the journey into experience, its diction
is more direct than most of Williams' earlier work, and like good
vers libre, it is composed in the sequence of the musical phrase.
Keatsian Romanticism in particular seems to be purged in *The*

---

1. *The Wanderer: A Rococo Study, The Collected Earlier Poems of William Carlos
Williams* (New York: New Directions, 1951), pp. 3-12; cited in the text as CEP. The
view of the poem summarized here may be found, for instance, in Paul Mariani, *William Carlos Williams: A New World Naked* (New York: McGraw-Hill, 1981), pp. 113-
115; Rod Townley, *The Early Poetry of William Carlos Williams* (Ithaca: Cornell
Univ. Press, 1975), pp. 36-37, 75-76; and James Breslin, *William Carlos Williams: An
American Artist* (New York: Oxford Univ. Press, 1970), pp. 19-24.

Wanderer; as Williams himself puts it, "I quit Keats just at that moment he himself did—with Hyperion's scream."[2]

Keats is a symbolist; he seeks to body forth his vision of reality in an interior world, in which acts of consciousness become aestheticized figures, phantasmagoric tropes. Like all poets of Romantic interiority, he must find the proper mediation between notions of poetry as an isolated repository of transcendental beauty and of poetry as congruent to historical truth. Williams is an objectivist; for him, reality is sufficient within itself, and the poetic imagination is that force which allows consciousness to apprehend reality most distinctly. The objectivist seeks to heighten the immediate contact between consciousness and the exterior world, for it is in that contact that beauty and truth coincide. Surely then it is inevitable that Williams should break from Keats' influence in such a poem as *The Wanderer*, even as Modernism itself should come into being as the antithesis of some of the most significant Romantic principles. I would argue, however, that what appears to be a break from Keats in *The Wanderer* is actually Williams' strongest affirmation of Keatsian Romanticism at its most advanced stage of development. Despite the subsequent transformations of form and content we see in Williams' career, he remains true to Keats' most important philosophical and aesthetic conceptions. *The Wanderer* then may be regarded as a gauge in the historical movement from Romanticism to Modernism and from a predominately symbolist to objectivist mode of poetic discourse in Anglo-American verse.

Recent scholarship has tended to stress the differences in these two conceptions of poetry, once they have been defined, and these distinctions must be recognized and acknowledged.[3] But an artistic mode of expression is historically determined, and the origins of Romantic and Modernist ideologies have a great deal in common. Both movements may be regarded as means by which art attempts to achieve a privileged position for itself against the more empirical, positivistic systems of thought fostered by the bourgeois world outlook. As Keats says, arguing for the primacy of the imagination, "I am certain of nothing but of the holiness of the Heart's affections and the truth of Imagination—What the imagination seizes as Beauty must be truth."[4]

---

2. *The Autobiography of William Carlos Williams* (New York: New Directions, 1951), p. 61.
3. Cf. Marjorie Perloff, *The Poetics of Indeterminacy* (Princeton: Princeton Univ. Press, 1981), pp. 109-154 & *passim*; Charles Altieri, *Enlarging the Temple* (Lewisburg: Bucknell Univ. Press, 1979), pp. 29-49; and "The Objectivist Tradition," *Chicago Review* 30, 3 (Winter 1979), 5-22; and J. Hillis Miller, *Poets of Reality* (Cambridge: Harvard Univ. Press, 1965), pp. 284-359 and *passim*.
4. *The Letters of John Keats*, ed. Hyder Edward Rollins (Cambridge: Harvard Univ. Press, 1958), Vol. I, p. 184.

Williams too speaks in these terms in *Spring and All* [1923], at a point at which his Keatsian influence has ostensibly been submerged and his objectivist stance is taking form. Speaking of the artist, he declares that "Taught by the largeness of his imagination to feel every form which he sees moving within himself, he must prove the truth of this by expression."[5]

The emphasis on the imagination as the determinant of beauty and truth in both of these instances is particularly revealing. This mental power, whether it makes of the poem a symbolic interior world or a field of exterior objects, is always the medium through which the poet's notion of perfection takes form. Thus Keats, in the presence of the Grecian Urn and its sublime tautology, can say "that is all/ Ye know on earth, and all ye need to know."[6] The interior refuge of art, for which the Urn is a symbol, can only be regarded as a Utopian trope; its sufficiency within the poem dialectically posits its antithesis, the poem that has yet to be completed in the future. The same is true, strangely enough, for the Urn's Modernist counterpart: Williams' red wheelbarrow. What is it that depends on the red wheelbarrow, which Williams can only describe as "so much"? It is, in a sense, the poems that will follow it, for like the Urn, the sufficiency of the wheelbarrow within the poem cannot survive without the implied futurity that the present figure calls into being. It is because of this phenomenon that readers have perceived both figures as "timeless," despite the fact that the Urn is commonly regarded as a symbol, carrying meaning above and beyond its mere being, and the wheelbarrow is seen as an object, the meaning of which resides purely in its immediacy as a thing. The imagination functions in both instances by creating an appropriate form for the perception of beauty and truth. This perception is, of course, historically determined—but historical vicissitude leads the poet to this same point regardless of the aesthetic theory that seems (in retrospect) to support his work. As Williams puts it, "To refine, to clarify, to intensify that eternal moment in which we alone live there is but a single force—the imagination" [I, p. 89]. Keats, whose work can "tease us out of thought/ As doth eternity" would agree. For the nineteenth and twentieth centuries in England and America saw the gradual intensification of social relationships which caused all poets to create an ongoing, interrelated series of aesthetic strategies, all in the service of a self-perpetuating Utopian ideal.

5. *Imaginations* (New York: New Directions, 1970), p. 105. Cited in the text as I.
6. *The Poems of John Keats*, ed. Jack Stillinger (Cambridge: Harvard Univ. Press, 1978), p. 373. Cited in the text as Keats.

If Williams, despite his objectivism, maintains Keats' conception of the relationship of beauty and truth, and if *The Wanderer* is the poem in which this is confirmed, then it follows that this poem should bear explicit Keatsian overtones. On the surface, this is not the case: it would seem that Whitman's *Crossing Brooklyn Ferry,* with its gulls, crowds, faces and mighty vision of transport is the more significant precursor poem. But for all the Whitmanian accouterments of *The Wanderer's* early sections, there is none of the surgingly confident assertiveness that marks Whitman's transcendental masterpiece. The young ferry traveller of Williams' poem is full of self-doubts, and feels profoundly alienated in the environment that offers Whitman such exhiliration. No, the psychological state of Williams' wanderer is closer to that of the poet in *The Fall of Hyperion*, Keats' last great poem. The two Hyperion fragments are the most important influences on Williams' poem, as the oblique remark from *The Autobiography* reveals, and it is the second version, with its questing poet-narrator, that so subtly yet pervasively informs Williams' own quest. *The Wanderer* and the two Hyperions are all concerned with the poet's struggle to accept historical truth, necessity, the brutal immediacy of reality, seemingly at odds with his remote, aestheticized, "Romantic" notion of beauty. These are poems of discovery and self-consciousness; they are meant to determine the personal and social responsibilities of the poetic identity, and further, to uncover the proper subject matter for the newly awakened poetic consciousness.

The narrators of *The Wanderer* and *The Fall of Hyperion* begin their poems in much the same frames of mind. Both seek to determine whether their belief in themselves as poets is honestly founded, against the strong possiblity that their visions are finally untranslatable, never to be successfully articulated in the welter of mere experience. To be assured of one's poetic identity is a necessity, for as Keats asserts:

> For Poesy alone can tell her dreams,
> With the fine spell of words alone can save
> Imagination from the sable charm
> And dumb enchantment. Who alive can say
> "Thou art no poet; may'st not tell thy dreams"?
> Since every man whose soul is not a clod
> Hath visions, and would speak, if he had lov'd
> And been well nurtured in his mother tongue.
> Whether the dream now purposed to rehearse
> Be poet's or fanatic's will be known
> When this warm scribe my hand is in the grave [Keats, p. 478].

Williams, already anticipating his encounter with his fallen muse, likewise ponders his poetic identity:

> But one day, crossing the ferry
> With the great towers of Manhattan before me,
> Out at the prow with the sea wind blowing,
> I had been wearying many questions
> Which she had put on to try me:
> How shall I be a mirror to this modernity [CEP, p. 3]?

And although Keats relates poetry to dreams and Williams to modernity, both poets are in what the former calls "the Chamber of Maiden-Thought," where

> we become intoxicated with the light and the atmosphere, we see nothing but pleasant wonders, and think of delaying there for ever in delight: However among the effects this breathing is father of is that tremendous one of sharpening one's vision into the heart and nature of Man—of convincing ones nerves that the World is full of Misery and Heartbreak, Pain, Sickness and oppression—whereby This Chamber of Maiden Thought becomes gradually darken'd and at the same time on all sides of it many doors are set open—but all dark—all leading to dark passages—We see not the ballance of good and evil.[7]

Because the young poet experiences this gradual darkening, he must test his intuitive belief in the beauty of his vision against what seems to be the true nature of the world, its "Misery and Heartbreak." But to do so, the poet needs a guide.

In *The Fall of Hyperion*, Keats' teacher is Moneta, towards whose temple he struggles in his dream-vision. In the first *Hyperion* she appears as Mnemosyne, memory, the mother of the muses, retainer of the poetic tradition and keeper of the great past. She is responsible for Apollo's awakening to his role of poet-god, but as Moneta, in the second poem, her role is much more severe. As Walter Jackson Bate points out, her name suggests "admonisher," a role she shares with the old woman in Williams' poem.[8] Her colloquy with the poet, once he has ascended to her temple, reveals both his failings and his responsibilities. As regards his numbing efforts to reach her, she informs him that

> "None can usurp this height," . . .
> "But those to whom the miseries of the world
> Are misery, and will not let them rest.
> All else who find a haven in the world
> Where they may thoughtless sleep away their days,
> If by a chance into this fane they come,
> Rot on the pavement where thou rotteds't half"
>
> [Keats, pp. 481-482].

---

7. Keats, *Letters,* I, p. 281.
8. *John Keats* (Cambridge: Harvard Univ. Press, 1963), p. 596.

Despite his apparent acceptance of bleak reality, he is still accused
of being merely a dreamer, a useless thing that "venoms all his
days." Furthermore, if he clings to a merely aestheticized, ideal
version of reality, he cannot be a poet:

> ..."If it please,
> Majestic shadow, tell me: sure not all
> Those melodies sung into the world's ear
> Are useless: sure the poet is a sage;
> A humanist, physician to all men.
> That I am none I feel, as vultures feel
> They are no birds when eagles are abroad.
> What am I then? Thou spakest of my tribe:
> What tribe?"...
>
> . . . .
>
> ..."Art thou not of the dreamer tribe?
> The poet and the dreamer are distinct,
> Diverse, sheer opposites, antipodes.
> The one pours out a balm upon the world,
> The other vexes it" [Keats, pp. 482-83].

This soothsay, as Williams would put it, is the culminating
statement in Keats' struggle to articulate the relationship between
ideal beauty and historical truth. The genuine poet cannot be a
dreamer; he must accept the world on its own terms, for only
then will the work that he creates prove to be a "balm," and
himself be "a sage; / A humanist, physician to all men." Poetry,
therefore, cannot be a dream in the sense of an escape or refuge;
regardless of its position in consciousness vis-a-vis interiority and
exteriority, it is always *realistic*; it is beautiful only inasmuch as it
is shaped by real events.[9] Thus Moneta is a muse of reality because
she compels the poet to know the world. That is the source of his
art regardless of its subsequent direction, and that is the most advanced version of Keatsian Romanticism, the conception that

---

9. There is a dawning awareness of this relationship even in the opening lines of *Endymion*, despite the terms of aesthetic interiority in which it is cast:

> A thing of beauty is a joy for ever:
> Its loveliness increases; it will never
> Pass into nothingness; but still will keep
> A bower quiet for us, and a sleep
> Full of sweet dreams, and health, and quiet breathing.
> Therefore, on every morrow, are we wreathing
> A flowery band to bind us to the earth,
> Spite of despondence, of the inhuman dearth
> Of noble natures, of the gloomy days,
> Of all the unhealthy and o'er-darkened ways
> Made for our searching: yes, in spite of all,
> Some shape of beauty moves away the pall
> From our dark spirits [Keats, p. 103].

Williams affirms in *The Wanderer*. This too is the insight that causes Apollo's shriek in the first Hyperion poem, which Williams mistakenly credits to Hyperion himself, whom Apollo is to supplant as god of the sun. Experiencing revelation at the hands of Mnemsoyne, Apollo cries:

> Knowledge enormous makes a God of me.
> Names, deeds, gray legends, dire events, rebellions,
> Majesties, sovran voices, agonies,
> Creations and destroyings, all at once
> Pour into the wide hollows of my brain,
> And deify me... [Keats, pp. 355-56].

Apollo is suddenly granted worldly knowledge, and becomes a god—that is, a poet.

The sublime lessons of the two Hyperion fragments are expressed in a lower register, a more mundane setting in *The Wanderer*, but they maintain their severe, revelatory powers. Williams' grandmother muse is Keats' Moneta, bereft of her regal veils and aged a hundred years. But she maintains her imperious command of the poet, and leads him in such ways as Keats had only begun to imagine. What marks a significant difference between the earlier and later poems is the manner in which Williams is taught about the world's misery. In *The Fall of Hyperion*, the poet talks to Moneta in her temple; later, he is made to see the story of the Titans which Keats excerpted from the first version of the work. But *The Wanderer*'s speaker, led by the old woman, is forced to experience personally the most spiritually and materially impoverished aspects of the modern scene. For example, the young man's first actual sight of his guide is coupled with a closeup of the urban poor:

> And instantly down the mists of my eyes
> There came crowds walking—men as visions
> With expressionless, animate faces;
> Empty men with shell-thin bodies
> Jostling close above the gutter,
> Hasting—nowhere [CEP, p. 5]!

An admonishing interchange between muse and poet follows immediately:

> Silent, her voice entered at my eyes
> And my astonished thought followed her easily:
> "Well, do their eyes shine, do their clothes fit?
> These live I tell you! Old men with red cheeks,
> Young men in gay suits! See them!
> Dogged, quivering, impassive—
> Well—are these the ones you envied?"
> At which I answered her, "Marvelous old queen,

> Grant me power to catch something of this day's
> Air and sun into your service!
> That these toilers after peace and after pleasure
> May turn to you, worshippers at all hours!"
> But she sniffed upon the words warily— [CEP, p. 5].

The old woman is wary of the young man's desire to be a poet
for such as these, and as if to give him a stronger lesson in misery,
she moves him from Broadway to Paterson, scene of the mill
strike of 1913. His meeting there with the proletariat simultaneously horrifies and exhilirates him. Williams is unflinching
in his description of the breadline:

> "Faces all knotted up like burls on oaks,
> Grasping, fox-snouted, thick-lipped,
> Sagging breasts and protruding stomachs,
> Rasping voices, filthy habits with the hands [CEP, p. 7].

But he is also capable of close understanding and sympathy:

> "Why since I have failed them can it be anything
>   but their own brood?
> Can it be anything but brutality?
> On that at least they're united! That at least
> Is their bean soup, their calm bread and a few
>   luxuries [CEP, p. 7]!

These excerpts show us the swiftly changing mind-set of the
young poet. Although his muse has stripped him of his previous,
idealized view of poetry's place in the world, he still feels incapable
of giving himself up entirely to the world's truth, its grim reality.
The people he sees are united, if only by their misery: the poet's
greater self-consciousness keeps him from complete identification
with the masses. [10] His terrible longing for purpose and fulfillment, spurred by his vision of beauty but stifled by his knowledge
of truth, creates a Keatsian dilemma that in turn generates a Keatsian solution. Like Keats in the Hyperion poems, Williams' articulation of his dilemma is itself the answer for which he searches.
The poet comes into his own at the moment he recognizes his
poem to be the vessel of historical truth, which in turn vindicates
his ideal of beauty. Thus Keats accepts Moneta's admonition that
the poet and the dreamer are diverse, and thus Williams declares,
at the climax of his encounter with the strikers:

> "Ugly, venomous, gigantic!
> Tossing me as a great father his helpless,

---

10. This dilemma troubles the objectivists for over fifty years, reaching its culmination
in George Oppen's masterpiece *Of Being Numerous*.

Infant till it shriek with ecstasy
And its eyes roll and its tongue hangs out!—

"I am at peace again, old queen, I listen clearer now."

Williams' ecstasy and subsequent peace is that of the modern sublime, anticipated by Keats nearly a hundred years before. Argu-
ably, the rest of *The Wanderer* is an extended confirmation of this
moment, culminating at last with the poet's baptism.

The scene at the river presents the final transformation of the
youth at the hands of his muse. It seems that in bringing him to
the Passaic, the old woman completes a pact with the river, for
she has longed for "The old friend of my revels" and the river has
wished for a "young soul." Hence the doubling of the poet's
being: his innocent self is lost to nature (its place of origin); his
self-consciousness is confirmed in human experience:

Muddy, then black and shrunken
Till I felt the utter depth of its rottenness
The vile breadth of its degradation
And dropped down knowing this was me now [CEP, p. 11].

As regards Williams' loss of his doppelgänger, it should be recalled
that Moneta tells her poet that in his struggle to reach her, "thou
rotted'st half." Keats too undergoes the loss of the old self when
he enters into his new knowledge. Likewise, the scene of Williams'
ritual, once it has taken place, becomes another temple, wherein
the memory of the poet's marriage to the world is enshrined. As
the old queen tells the river in some of the poem's last lines:

Here shall be a bird's paradise,
They sing to you remembering my voice:
Here the most secluded spaces
For miles around, hallowed by a stench
To be our joint solitude and temple;
In memory of this clear marriage
And the child I have brought you in the late years [CEP, p. 12].

This essay is concerned with Williams as the inheritor of a
particular strain of Romanticism, but in conclusion, it would be
disingenuous of me not to state at least some of the implications
of this study that extend beyond the limits of individual poets'
canons. As time goes on, Williams looms larger and larger in the
Modernist tradition. Indeed, with his centennial now upon us, it
can be claimed that more than Eliot, Pound or Stevens, Williams
is central to our understanding of at least one wing of "Post-
Modern" poetry, that wing most concerned with objectivism,
indeterminacy, open form, projective verse, etc. But if Williams
remains as much a Keatsian as I have argued, then it seems to me

that our task of re-evaluation and revision is bound to continue. Keats' poetry of interiority may be traced on through early Tennyson, the Pre-Raphaelite and Aesthetic schools, to such latter-day ironists as Stevens and even Ashbery. That he should also exert such power over Williams is not contradictory, but indicates that adherents to the ideology of Post-Modernism have been too quick to dismiss Romanticism as no longer valid to the contemporary experience—and this despite such poets as Robert Duncan, a self-proclaimed heir to both Modernism and Romanticism. And one has only to remark Williams' life-long devotion to the sensuality of verse (one interpretation of his dictum "No ideas but in things"), and compare it to Keats' extraordinary and pervasive sympathy to a poetry of natural objects, to discover that "objectivism" is not, after all, such a recent phenomenon.

What is at stake here then, against changing fashions and partisan judgements, is the notion of a poetic tradition, and what that tradition always emobdies. As Jack Spicer, one of Williams' boldest heirs, says:

> In my last letter I spoke of the tradition. The fools that read these letters will think by this we mean what tradition seems to have meant lately—an historical patchwork (whether made up of Elizabethan quotations, guide books of the poet's home town, or obscure bits of magic published by Pantheon) which is used to cover up the nakedness of the bare word. Tradition means much more than that. It means generations of different poets in different countries patiently telling the same story, writing the same poem, gaining and losing something with each transformation— but, of course, never really losing anything.[11]

Poets are compelled by changing circumstances—literary, political, economic, philosophical—to tell that story in drastically different ways. But the matter of the story never alters. It is, one could say, a Utopian invariant, a constant discovery of beauty as "a state in which reality takes a part" [I, p. 117]. *The Wanderer* is the record of one such discovery.

---

11. *The Collected Books of Jack Spicer*, ed. Robin Blaser (Santa Barbara: Black Sparrow Press, 1975), p. 15.

THE POET II

Drawing of Passaic Falls by Earl Horton preserved at the State Library of New Jersey.

ROBERT G. BASIL

IMAGINATION AND DESPAIR IN WILLIAMS

That the critic who introduced William Carlos Williams to what New Directions Press expected to be his largest audience could write a sentence like, "When you have read *Paterson* you know for the rest of your life what it is like to be a waterfall,"[1] is evidence that the Rutherford's poet aesthetic was either too revolutionary or elusive for even a respected academic to grasp. One should not cackle at Randall Jarrell, however, for when he wrote his essay the work of Williams was hardly comparable to any other major contemporary poet's and indeed violated the sense most literary theorists had of writing from an Eliot-inspired principle of literary "tradition." We are fortunately richer today. The critic can not only perceive Williams' work in toto and with the aid of increasingly empathetic readers; but the messages, techniques and even "philosophies" of Williams have found various shapes in poets such as Robert Creeley, Charles Olson, Jack Spicer and Denise Levertov. In 1949 though, Jarrell's natural like for what Williams was doing kept collapsing under the non-existence of explicit IDEAS to back him up. So he had to remain outside, I think, and somewhat afraid of what he was hearing. Williams after all turned no readers into trees, nor was he trying to. And, certainly, one does not *know anything* for "the rest of one's life" after reading a Williams poem.

Jarrell's lack of vision into Williams work—an understandable lack, given his era and intellectual location, and a forgivable lack in any era given the oeuvre's immense and radical slipperiness— results primarily from not understanding Williams' singular use and understanding of the concept of *Imagination.*

---

1. Randall Jarrell, "Introduction," *Selected Poems of William Carlos Williams* by William Carlos Williams (New York: New Directions, 1969), pp. xi-xii.
 Other Williams volumes cited in this paper are: *Paterson* (New York: New Directions, 1963), *Pictures from Brueghel and Other Poems* (New York: New Directions, 1967), *Imaginations* (New York: New Directions, 1971). Page numbers following cited quotations refer to these editions.

The *Oxford English Dictionary* defines "imagination" (from the Latin "imaginatio") five ways: "the action of . . . forming a mental concept of what is not actually present to the senses"; "the mental consideration of actions or events not yet in existence"; "that faculty of mind by which are formed images or concepts of external objects not present to the sense, and of their relations (to each other or to the subject) . . ."; "the power the mind has of forming concepts beyond those derived from external objects (the 'productive imagination')"; and, "the mind, or department of mind, when engaged in imagining; hence, the operation of the mind generally; thinking; thought; opinion." It is with some irony, of course, that the *OED* is brought into this—for Williams' use of this word, and most of the others he put down, leap clear of lexical meanings. In another sense, it is clear that the dictionary doesn't assist us here, for Williams' use of the word was essentially "positive"—it was more than a faculty which invented what was not present to the senses or not yet in existence. It was more the opposite. But before we turn to Williams, a brief look at the history of the word's use might be helpful.

"Imagination . . . was a late substitute for 'phantasia' (a simple transliteration of the Gr[eek] from which fancy is derived . . . and they long appeared as synonyms designating the image-receiving or image-forming faculty or process."[2] The classical concept of imagination did not at all give it a high place in the creation of Art. Plato regarded the image as illusory—the Platonic "idea" having absolutely no correlate to the senses. Longinus, whose work Williams declared was the "sole precedent . . . for the broken style of my prologue [to *Kora In Hell*]," in contrast, "recognized the imagination as the source of sublimity when— 'moved by enthusiasm and passion you seem to see the things whereof you speak and place them before the eyes of your hearers.' "[3] Still, the imagination did not amount to much more than mental engineering. A famous example is the winged horse in which two things clear to the sight were combined to create something not found in physical nature.

However, some classical writers, the Roman historian Sallust for example, ascribed a divine element to the mind which created Art:

> The Universe itself can be called a myth, since bodies and material objects are apparent in it, while souls and minds are concealed. Furthermore, to wish to teach all men the truth about the

---

2. A. S. P. Woodhouse, "Imagination," *Princeton Encyclopedia of Poetics*, p. 370.
3. *Ibid.*, p. 371.

gods causes the foolish to despise, because they cannot learn,
and the good to be slothful, whereas (by having the artist) conceal the truth by myths prevents the former from despising
(art) and compels the latter to study it.[4]

Sallust is describing a concern Williams also had: how can one
convey the "souls" in "material objects"—that is, the "radiant
gist" within the "pageless actual"—without desecrating either the
souls or the physical objects? This subversive fear that words will
mislead—or in any case, that words are but dark windows through
which one is directed to something transcending them, and all
together distinct from the word, has stayed with man in every age
since.

In the Renaissance, thinkers modeled their works after
classical theories and thus relegated to the "imitation of nature"
the process and result of Art. Even Shakespeare, who exuberantly
burst through the Aristotilian unities, is suspicious of imputing to
the imagination qualities worthy of the artist. As Theseus says,

> The poet's eye, in a fine frenzy rolling,
> Doth glance from heaven to earth, from earth to heaven;
> And as imagination bodies forth
> The forms of things unknown, the poet's pen
> Turns them to shapes and gives to airy nothing
> A local habitation and a name.
> Such tricks hath strong imagination.
> > —*A Midsummer Night's Dream*
> > V, i, 1. 12-18

William Blake was the first to accept Imagination as a faculty
or force which indeed could body forth "the forms of things
unknown." Isaiah, in "The Marriage of Heaven and Hell," says
that his "senses discovered the infinite in every thing. . . . All poets
believe (a firm perswasion that a thing is so, make(s) it so) . . . & in
ages of imagination this firm perswasion removed mountains; but
many are not capable of a firm perswasion of any thing."[5] Blake's
concept held that "to the man of imagination, nature is imagination itself." To be sure, ultimate reality is spiritual, and that
"imagination is spiritual perception" is "the first principle" of
knowledge. And this knowledge, once discovered, could put the
poet in contact with the supersensible worlds as often as he
wanted. This idea, however, was relatively uninfluential in his
time, and the Romantic stance instead was defined chiefly by
Samuel Taylor Coleridge.

---

4. Sallust, "Diis Mundo," as quoted in Rudolf Steiner's *Christianity and Occult Mysteries
of Antiquity*, trans. E. A. Frommer, Gabrielle Hess, and Peter Kandler (Steinerbooks,
1977), pp. 105-106.
5. William Blake, *The Complete Poems*, Alicia Ostriker, ed. (New York: Penguin Books,
1979), p. 186.

The author of "Kubla Khan" distinguished "imagination" from "fancy" in a way that made it the predominant faculty of the mind behind Art. In the *Biographia Literaria*, the most philosophical of the romantics attacked the prevailing concept, as put forth by the empiricists, Locke and Hume, that the mind was a "tabula rasa" which came to "reason" only through memory and experience. Such an idea made the function of imagination suspect, so that most writers of the 17th and 18th Centuries employed the word to stand for no more than a kind of vivid, linking memory. John Dryden, in his preface to "Annus Mirabilis," wrote that "the faculty of imagination . . . is some lively and apt description, dressed in such colours of speech, that it sets before your eyes the absent object, as perfectly, and more delightfully than nature." Samuel Johnson, in the next century, defined "imagination," in his *Dictionary of the English Language*, as: "Fancy; the power of forming ideal pictures; the power of representing things absent to one's self or others." Coleridge, however, believed imagination to be more than a passive organizer and refiner of memory and experience; it was instead an organic operation which allowed one's mind to pierce the surface of the physical world. He wrote, "The noblest gift of Imagination is the power of discerning the *Cause* in the *Effect* [,] a power which when employed on the works of the Creator elevates and by the variety of its pleasures almost monopolizes the soul. We see our God everywhere—the Universe in the most literal sense is his written language."[6]

J. Hillis Miller, in his book on modern poets,[7] asserts that the aesthetic force behind such writers as Eliot, Thomas and Stevens—and behind Williams most perfectly—does not at all accord with Coleridge's view of "imagination." The common error of equating such poets as Williams—and one can include the entire Objectivist and Surrealist movements as well, I think—with the romantic stance, is that the particularity of the human soul postulated in Coleridge's writings, if it exists at all in these moderns' works, exists in a drastically different way. The Romantics' view of the imagination posited two bifurcations: that of the subject and object, and of Man and God. A poet such as Wordsworth, for example, sought God in nature; his poetry is an attempt to reach a supersensible world in which he (the subject) and the spirit within whatever part of nature he was contemplating (the object) could merge. That "the glory and the freshness of a dream" which

---

6. Samuel Taylor Coleridge, *The Collected Works, Volume I*, K. Koburn, ed. (London: Routledge & Kegan Paul, 1971), pp. 338-339.
7. J. Hillis Miller, *Poets of Reality* (Cambridge: Harvard University Press, 1965), pp. 285-359.

resulted from this merger could only be temporary, was the source of the poet's "romantic agony."[8]

Miller convincingly shows that, since there is neither a voice of a distinct "self" nor any search for God in Williams' work, the doctor from New Jersey was not at all a descendent of the Romantic impulse.

> In Williams' mature work, if something exists at all, it dwells in the only realm there is, a space both subjective and objective, a region of co-presence in which anywhere is everywhere, and all times are one.[9]

The poet is therefore no prisoner of consciousness who, through the transformation enacted in the poem, can come to "know" the spirit of a thing-itself. The poet, being anonymous, has nothing outside of a self to know.

Though Miller has located Williams' work in a new aesthetic in which the relationship between the subject and object is erased, one can see by the vague terminology which one is perhaps forced to use in such an epistomological discussion—the phrase "region of co-presence in which anywhere is everywhere," for example, except as it would obliterate the conventional delineations of matter from matter, and matter from spirit, etc., is absolutely non-descriptive—that the process both towards and of this union, and the loci of the new field of perception this union implies— which may or may not be the same as the field of the new poem— goes undiscussed. I daresay only speculation is possible—at least in the terms we now have to find out about such things.

However, though Miller's criticism is the best I have read concerning the role of identity in Williams' work, he doesn't define a problematical strain which, most potently in *Paterson*, challenges the success with which the poet has erased the bounds of his consciousness. Miller senses this lack, I would bet, as is evidenced by how he quoted the entire twelfth stanza in Book II, Part 2—with the exception of the words, "he dreams." And it is

---

8. This agony is typified in such poems as "Dejection: An Ode" and Wordsworth's "Intimations: Ode on Immortality" in which the poet can only find consolation in the recall of the blessed indivisibility between himself and the God in nature which supposedly existed in early childhood. "There was a time," Wordsworth writes,

> when meadow, grove and stream,
> The earth, and every common sight,
> To me did seem
> Appareled in celestial light,
> The glory and the freshness of a dream.

Even the poem cannot re-enact this vision. In this sense, the poem's imagination is a kind of bemoaning response to consciousness in general, as well as a divine ability to discern, in rare moments, "cause from effect."

9. Miller, p. 288.

crucial that the optimism of this passage is so subverted. That Mr. Paterson has to "dream" to extinguish the "I"—just as both Mrs. and Doc Thurber have to in order to flee their own brutalized cause-effect world in *A Dream of Love*—becomes the cloudiest point of Williams' idea of Imagination.

* * * * * *

In the early poetry, Williams saw that to unbind one's consciousness, one had to release the words one used from their conventional meanings—one had to make them "new," separate from ossified definition. To be sure, one *can* in fact make the bounded meaning disappear from words. Repeat "garage door" two hundred times, for example, and you can't open it to let the lexical definition out. The phrase "garage door" loses its phraseness, loses the associations which have been tagged onto it, and becomes sounds and syllables—and the song of *these* is revivified. Poem VIII in *Spring and All* [p. 109] begins,

> The sunlight in a
> yellow plaque upon the
> varnished floor
>
> is full of a song
> inflated to
> fifty pounds pressure
>
> at the faucet of
> June that rings
> the triangle of the air

and goes on to incorporate the following "typo":

> And so it comes
> to motor cars—
> which is the son
>
> leaving off the g . . .

Williams no doubt disrupts the conventional senses of these words through their odd apposition. Because neither the "sunlight" nor the "song," in our "normal" way of knowing what we see, be "inflated to / fifty pounds pressure / at the faucet of / June," the first twelve lines, which do form a logical linguistic unit, are impossible to swallow as a single image. Instead, the sunlight illuminates *each word*, so to speak, one by one—as nouns, verbs, etc., made naked by the absence of narrative context, and as song, Williams surely choosing "inflated to / fifty," for example, to chime with the "f's" of "floor / is full" in the preceding lines—those being set up by "f's" unvoiced "twin" beginning the word "varnished."

However, just as Williams means to sing, he would as well explode these words—foreground them, so to speak—deploying them in such a way that the deployment itself becomes the center of the poem. This insistence upon the essential meaninglessness of words—as vehicles for something inorganic to them—has, of course, been the philosophical spine of the structuralist and deconstruction movements. It has been convincingly posed (by Roland Barthes, Claude Levi-Strauss and Jacques Derrida, for example) that the link between the linguistic signifier and signified is an arbitrary one; that our language, instead of budding from a ground of transcendent meaning, is much less, merely a system of differences. "Rose" by any other name would still signify a rose as long as the other name could not be confused with the names for "pen" or "car" or "defibulator" or any one of a million other things one is not aiming at.

"Rose," however, remains Williams' favorite *word* as well as *meaning*—a flower which dies each year, forced back into the ground as seed; just as Kora must, to please Pluto, annually return to Hell; and a flower both universal—in its design, determined by DNA—and local, feeding from the minerals in the earth about its roots and, in Williams' case, photosynthesizing Rutherford's carbon dioxide. Williams, though in accord with the idea that words can and for the most part do control our thought, resists the vision of an anarchy of values which one finds in Derrida—by believing: words, once the foreign framework of meaning which has been imposed upon them is subverted, can be informed by an organic sense when re-composed in a local "measure"; and also, possibly as a corollary, that these words made new become pregnant with myth—both local (the falls and "Beautiful Thing" in *Paterson*, for example), and as the autochthonous revival of archetypical motifs.[10]

* * * * * * *

Perhaps the most revolutionary aspect of Williams' conception of the imagination is that it is less an internal cerebral function than one aimed externally at the universe, i.e., an *organ of perception*. The classical "imaginatio" described the part of one's

---

10. Jerome Mazzaro, *William Carlos Williams: The Later Poems* (Ithaca: Cornell University Press, 1973). Mazzaro's book cites in great detail a number of recurring Jungian archetypes in Williams' work: "the wise old man," the unicorn, and most persistently, the myth of Kora. Williams' obsession with women is discussed in terms of the Jungian "anima."

mind which put together pictures to either model a sublime thought or, in Plato's less enthusiastic opinion, to paint errant illusions. Johnson's mid-eighteenth century belief in imagination properly doing no more than mirroring the common and recurrent aspects of sublunary nature echoes Plato. Williams', in contrast, more than put together pictures and re-presented forgotten facts and truths; the imagination, in his mind, plugged into both the worlds of sensible and supersensible reality in all its transience.

The first appearance of the word "imagination" in a major book by Williams is found in the "Prologue" to *Kora In Hell*— [p. 7];[11] and it is noteworthy that the major themes of his work all show up here.

> If a man cheat (my mother) she will remember that man with a violence that I have seldom seen equaled, but so far as that could have an influence on her judgment of the next man or woman, she might be living in Eden. And indeed she is, an impoverished, ravished Eden but one indestructible as the imagination itself. Whatever is before her is sufficient to itself and so to be valued.

On the next page he continues:

> (She sees) the thing itself without forethought or afterthought but with great intensity of perception. . . . She is a creature of great imagination. . . . She is a despoiled, molted castaway but by this power she still breaks life between her fingers.

The first of the themes of which Williams will never let go during his long career is that of the imagination being located, through the necessity of living *now* and *in America*, in a shambled paradise—"a ravished Eden"—in fact, in a kind of Hell. And the poet—like Orpheus, like Kora—must live there and, like Asphodel, bloom. While Williams is not bemoaning the relative paucity of immediately apparent delight in his local materials, as compared to those of Shakespeare's day, for example, he is in agreement with Gertrude Stein's claim that today one no longer lives in a world "drunk with nouns," where the names of things are not polluted with lateral and increasingly deadening associations. Likewise, the land and the spiritual opportunities of the poet's community are debased; he lives in "a country whose flowers are without perfume and whose girls lack modesty," and where, "in accordance with the local custom," the "spectacle of . . . ripe flesh" "will be left to wither without ever achieving its full enjoyment" [*Imaginations*, p. 54]. A second theme concerns imagination's power to "break life between (the) fingers" and to "see"

---

11. The 1918 Prologue.

something outside of linear time, with neither forethought nor afterthought. This idea becomes, in Williams' later work, the ability to perceive one's entire past, along with the eternal potential of such cyclical archetypical myths as Kora's descent into Hell, spontaneously. In *Paterson V*, for example, Allen Ginsberg's trip to the Arctic is essentially a re-enacement—a *permutation*—of the principle of beauty making such a "splash" that the "riot squad" is to be called out; and this principle, eternally true, is vivified by Art, as in the Cloister tapestry, in which, "The Unicorn / the white one-horned beast / thrashes about / . . . / calling / for its own murder." And because the poet can see the common spiritual motive behind such disparate entities as a Ginsberg and a unicorn, he can relate them to each other with utter disregard for linear time, physical difference and causal narrative.

Two more extracts from *Kora* show well enough how Williams placed the "imagination" as man's foremost perceptual—as opposed to cerebral—organ, and also that Williams hesitates both in describing this primary organ's anatomy and its (if it has any) limits—in favor of demonstrating how this faculty can be employed in writing. In the italicized "explanation" of XV, 3 [*Imaginations*, p. 59], Williams posits a "hidden language" "which shifts and reveals its meaning as clouds shift and turn in the sky" and is composed of the mingling of the "talking in our day's-affairs" with "what we see in the streets" as well as our "imaginations." "This is the language to which few ears are tuned so that it is said by poets that few men are ever in their full senses." The troubling aspect of this idea is brought into relief in his assertion, echoing Sallust, that "the old poets would translate this hidden language into a kind of replica of the speech of the world with certain distinctions of rhyme and meter to show that it was not really that speech. Nowadays the elements of that language are set down as heard and the imagination of the listener and of the poet are left free to mingle in the dance" [*Imaginations*, p. 59]. Williams never explicitly describes the composition of this "hidden language." Does it employ *our* spoken language? Or must poets enact a complete translation from it to ours? And can the words we speak every day be rid of the stain of sense so much that they can be filled with the supersensible qualities of the imagination and spirit?

In XVIII, 3 (italicized portion), Williams obliquely addresses this problem of transferring "actual" things' spiritual nature into the corrupt medium of one's regular language.

> The wish would be to see not floating visions of unknown purport but the imaginative qualities of actual things being perceived accompany (the eye's) gross vision in a slow dance, interpreting

as they go. But inasmuch as this will not always be the case one
must dance nonetheless as he can [*Imaginations*, p. 67].

This movement between the successful perception of the spirit
inside of "actual things" and this being "not always . . . the case,"
is found in the design of many Williams' poems. The tension of
this movement is often called "despair" in Williams' later work.

In poem IX in "Spring and All" [*Imaginations*, p. 113],
perhaps Williams' most "foregrounded" poem, this movement of
despair is vividly enacted. He begins by asking the widest question:
"What about all this writing?" He "answers,"

> O "Kiki"
> O Miss Margaret Jarvis
> The backhandspring
>
> I: clean
>   clean
>   clean: yes . . . New-York
>
> Wrigley's, appendicitis, John Marin:
> skyscraper soup—
>
> Either that or a bullet!

Though each line insists on its own distinctness from the others
in this "sentence," compelling the reader to read very slowly,
there is an important unity in the passage that renders it more
than random squeaking and gibbering. Each word is a burst of
local language, gathered as one would the signals up and down a
radio dial.[12] In the prose passage immediately following the
poem, Williams explains the seemingly chaotic rush of words
answering the poem's first line: "The only means (the poet) has
to give value to life is to recognize it with the imagination and
name it." And to name something without assigning old biases
or glosses is to let the words speak for themselves—"clean," as
he insists, "straight to the mark." Near the end of the poem, Williams addresses the word "clean" directly:

---

12. The radio has been employed, in fact, as a wonderfully suggestive metaphor for this
dynamic, fleeting center of consciousness, by Jean Cocteau in his film *Orpheus*, for
example, and, most notably, by Jack Spicer throughout his work. This poet-as-radio idea
describes the artist as a passive instrument—with a particular design, in a local place—
which gives language to "martians," the term by which Spicer represents the sensible
and supersensible object world. What is put in the poem is not, of course, martian
language, just as our radios don't project pure radio waves. After all we are in contact
with radio waves all the time—with or without a radio. But when the radio is turned
on, we perceive a truly united spirit: the electrical energy of the radio waves and the
design of the radio are effaced as separate entities and become one in the literal song.
Similarly, the perfect "thereness" of Williams' "red wheelbarrow"—there in its *muteness*
before recognized by Williams—asserts its unconditional existence in a local dialect as
breathed by the poet.

> Clean is he alone
> after whom stream
> the broken pieces of the city—
> flying apart at his approaches

Paradoxically, it is the "broken pieces" which are given full value in their remove from narrative or imagistic sense. This aesthetic finds mammoth—indeed, *epic*—shape in *Paterson*, where the poet has completely erased any division between his consciousness and the objects of his locale. The hundreds of voices and artifacts speak in a democratic collage, the poet not at all their master, but one and the same with each utterance. Indeed, just as there is no fixed "I" in the poem, identities are not assigned to the authors of the fragments. (It is in this sense that the compiling of an "annotated" *Paterson* would be ridiculous.) For in the poem, by perceiving Paterson and its "objects" in a supersensible way, the poet has *changed* them—in part by spiritually uniting with them, and also by lifting the New Jersey town into the realm of imagination, a realm in which authors don't exist, so much as correspondences. And in Poem IX, these "pieces," "flying apart," are the reason for the writing, which, like most of Williams' writing, enacts the poet's *approach* to them—to the chairs, the hospital and the woman in the bed. This movement is to a union with his native agency and landscape which requires—or carries with it—a sexual energy which in fact accelerates through the poem. "I watched / you . . ." transforms into "I was your nightgown / I watched!" Indeed, in this watching of the woman sobbing, beating her pillow, tearing her hair, etc., *the poet is being her for a time.*

This union breaks, however; and the subject-object split is defined again, perhaps more starkly than before. So in the poet's afterglow, he admits, "I merely caress you curiously"; and in the last stanza, he moves "fifteen years" away from her, his only knowledge of her not at all supersensibly elicited through direct imaginative contact; it isn't even first-hand. He can only guess that she "still go(es) about the city," because a vague "they" say so.

The unclenching of the love embrace appears often in Williams' work, perhaps most strikingly in the final verse passage of Book II, section II of *Paterson*. The poet is addressing an unidentified "you"—which is perhaps "love," "the radiant gist," some heuristic deity, or the imagination—in which he says, "I forget / myself perpetually," and also in which, "I find my . . / despair!" This reaction—despair—in that it follows the lines, "But you / never wither—but blossom / all about me," can appear paradoxical, for contemplating something that blossoms is conventionally depicted as being at least a solace, if not a kind of activity leading to spiritual cleansing or redemption. To Williams, however, this type of satisfaction cannot come—for merely gazing upon a beautiful object is not in itself a poetic experience, in that there is still defined the subject-object schism. Nothing changes within the spirit of the poet when he is a voyeur; he must be the object of delight as well. (Jerome Mazzaro points out that this theme appears often in Williams, "Danse Russe," for example, depicting the author as both observer and participant in the naked dance, in which "the mirror becomes . . . an image of his poetic field and the means of somatic observation."[13])

"You are the eternal bride," Williams writes in the second stanza of this section. But as the "lover . . . / appraises every feature of his bride's / comeliness," he experiences "terror" at, one presumes, the approaching consumation of their marriage—terror at the singleness and transience of promised delight, and in knowing that his bride's virginity is irretrievable after their union. They will "fall," by means of the same shared imagination which let them know transcendence, into defiled, magnified separateness—into "despair."

Yet the imagination whose "features amaze and delight," will emerge just as powerfully elsewhere—"a simple miracle that knows / the branching sea, to which the oak / is coral, the coral oak." (While it is no doubt tenuous to assert an equation between the word "coral" and Kora by orthographic inspection alone, the fact that coral is a luminous plant buried, in a sense, by the ocean—just as Kora is seasonally empitted in Hell—is suggestive. Likewise, the choice of the "oak" to match "coral" is especially felicitous—"oak" being a mirror image of Kora in both spelling and sense.) It is the discontinuous nature of the imagination's periodic resurrection which prompts the poet to ask, "Why should I move from this place / where I was born? knowing / how futile would be the search / for you in the multiplicity / of your debacle." To be sure, "debacle" ("a breaking up of ice in a river [and] . . . a sudden deluge or violent rush of water which breaks down opposing barriers and carries before it blocks of stone and other debris"—*OED*) is the perfect word to describe the withering of the ecstatic ego-dissolving marriage bed, as it resonates with the motif of the Passaic River, which contains Mrs. Cummings' and Sam Patch's bodies, "both silent, uncommunicative," and which acts throughout as a soporific to—if not death of—consciousness. And though there is no map to guide the poet to another epiphany, Williams is convinced that through the "despair" of imagination's "composition and decomposition," knowledge is achieved.

---

13. Mazzaro, p. 24.

* * * * * * *

At this point, it might be well to set down that Williams' poetry can be divided, not too artificially, into two types: both involve the poet's ego successfully dissolving in the presence of another thing, whose "essence," in part due to the poet's tough concentration upon it, also dissolves, thereby creating a new center of perception infinitely more powerful than either of the two which formed it. This expanded "super-perception" is derived both from the conventional idea of empathy—knowing what it's like to be in another's shoes, etc.—and (much more crucially) from the freedom this union affords: freedom from the illusion that one's spirit is impenetrable, and from the Kantian theorem (which dominated Romantic poetics) that said that one cannot know the thing-itself. The first kind of poem records the loci of this "super-perception" to which a new, temporary center of con-sciousness gives rise. These poems, I daresay, make up the bulk of Williams' oeuvre. The second type, touched upon earlier in the discussion of *Paterson*, attempts to describe the "radiant gist" and the "union" itself. Before we continue our look at Williams' examination of the process of this union—which he takes, finally, to be unsuccessful—a glance at one brilliant and short late poem, "The Woodthrush" [*Pictures from Brueghel*, p. 16], can serve as an example of what I mean by the first type of Williams poem, in which the perception of this union is the poem.

"The Woodthrush" has no point-of-view in the conventional sense. Although the poet is speaking, there is a super-individual nature to the perception in the poem which combines the poet, the woodthrush and perhaps even the undefined spirit of "tragic winter." This sense of unified perception is accomplished in part through a syntactical design which perfectly obscures the cases of the nouns. Many nouns are both subject and object. The lines,

> he looks at me silent without
> moving
>
> his dappled breast reflecting
> tragic winter
> thoughts my love my own

can be read several ways on the literal level alone. Is it the bird or the "me" which is "silent" "without moving"—or is the bird not "silent" but still looking "without moving"—or, if the bird in fact is not "moving," is he not moving in general or not moving "his dappled breast"? Or is the "silent" "me" not "moving his dappled breast"? Or is his "dappled breast" the subject of the verb "reflecting," which puts "tragic winter"–or perhaps "tragic winter thoughts"–into the accusative case? And so forth. Instead of a progression from subject to verb to object, rendering a discrete linguistic unit, each word resonates both in sense and syntax with many other words, permuting the number of possible literal readings–to employ an expression from Mathematics–factorially.[14] This vibration between the various readings is not a result of ambivalence or ambiguity on Williams' part. What is established is a higher level of perception all together–one not from a single point-of-view, but one including the incursions of several.

"The Woodthrush" is not perfectly self-referential, of course–Godel has shown us that no "system" is–and the last two lines, "tragic winter / thoughts my love my own," point almost serenely *outside* the "things" in the first seven lines. Are these the ideas which are in things–after Williams' familiar exhortation? And are these ideas–which the woodthrush and poet discover together–impossible to put into words relating to the five senses? One difficulty comes from the ironic vagueness of "no ideas but in things." This statement can turn many ways; that there exist no ideas–period–that do not correlate to a thing presumably available to the senses; or that, though there may be ideas without sensory correlates, only those ideas which *do* have correlates to local things are fit for the poem; or, expanding in the direction of theosophical thinkers, perhaps this statement equates to "no things but in ideas," which suggests a supersensible world of ideas and perhaps even higher beings whose forms sometimes have prongs dipping into the sense and therefore language world. And if the last of these suggestions is the one best fitting Williams' poetry–and I believe it is–how much of the idea in the thing can be enacted? Or more particularly, can Williams write poetry which actually describes the world of the "radiant gist" which powers the superperception found in "The Woodthrush," or, coming as close as an object fashioned by man can come, merely, in the end, just point to "the hidden language" evoked in *Kora*?

Williams answers this question for himself, of whether this realm from which the imagination springs can be illuminated in

---

14. If there are n objects to be put in an order, there are "n ways" to place the first one, "(n-1) ways" to place the second one, and so forth. The total number of arrangements possible is given by the expression:

$$n(n-1)(n-2) \ldots (n-n+1) = n! \quad (\text{"n factorial"}).$$

A conservative counting of the literal meanings of "The Woodthrush"–absolutely ignoring a word's possible multiple meanings, based only on a word's multiple cases–employing a variation of the above formula, is 1,152.

the poem, in *Paterson* III—negatively. For not only does the poet know "how futile would be the search" for the Imagination "in the multiplicity of (its) debacle"—so elusive is its source—he also recognizes that he will "never / separate that stain of sense, / an offense / to love . . ." "from the inert mass. Never. / Never that radiance / quartered apart, / unapproached by symbols" [*Paterson*, p. 108]. The inert mass—language—no matter how relieved it is from "lateral associations" and unlocal, untimely convention, resolves into symbols.

"Let the words / fall anyway at all—" he writes in *Paterson* [p. 142],

> that they may
> hit love aslant. It will be a rare
> visitation. They want to rescue too much,
> the flood has done its work.

This "rare visitation" of "love" implies that it is the "love" that will descend to the world of sense—in which "inert" words are found—not that the poet can hope to ascend to the realm where love is continuous, *as a poet*, i.e. with his words. Close thereafter [*Paterson*, p. 145], in Book III's final verse sequence, Williams writes that the "language cascades into the invisible," the falls of the filthy Passaic its only "visible part." Yet to "comb out the language" and to find "my meaning and lay it, white / beside the sliding water" is nonetheless the poet's task. And as far as it goes, "this rhetoric is real." Perhaps the chemical image suggested by "inert" can be expanded a little to point to a resolution of the paradox of words being both essentially stained *and* vehicles for recording the loci of super-perception. Though his words cannot escape their status as sense symbols, the poet can escape his status as a mere material being. Through the imagination, he becomes, vis-a-vis the various realms of sensible and supersensible perception, as lithium is, vis-a-vis most of the rest of the periodic table— *multi-valent*. The poem, stains arranged as only an unstained one can arrange them, is Williams' proof.

CHRISTOPHER COLLINS

THE MOVING EYE IN WILLIAMS' EARLIER POETRY

There are two kinds of writing which critics must sharply differentiate, Pound declared in 1934. One kind are "books that are intended and that serve as REPOSE, dope, opiates, mental beds." The other kind are:

> Books a man reads to develop his capacities: in order to know more and perceive more, and more quickly, than he did before he read them.[1]

Being instruments which serve the reader's active cognitive purposes, these latter are to be distinguished from passively enjoyed conveniences: "You don't sleep on a hammer or lawn-mower, you don't drive nails with a mattress."[2]

The writings of William Carlos Williams are certainly instruments for action. But what kind of instruments and what kind of action? They do indeed seem intended to help us "know and perceive more," but they only rarely operate like hammers or lawn-mowers. Their penetration into the world of phenomena is gentler but no less insistent.

Williams was always quite clear about our need for such instruments. Some of his most emphatic statements he wrote in the prose sections of *Spring and All* (1923). Between the myriad sensory stimuli of the here-and-now, and our full attention to any of these, lies the barrier of memory, abstraction, and irrelevant fantasy—

> Yesterday, tomorrow, Europe, Asia, Africa,—all things removed and impossible, the tower of the church at Seville, the Parthenon.[3]

Such thoughts are the "vaporous fringe which distracts the attention from its agonized approaches to the moment." And what resource do we have with which to dissipate this "vaporous fringe"?

1. Ezra Pound, *ABC of Reading* (New Directions, 1960), p. 88.
2. *Ibid.*, p. 88.
3. WCW, "Prose from *Spring and All*," in *William Carlos Williams: A Collection of Critical Essays*, ed. J. Hillis Miller (Prentice-Hall, 1966), p. 15. [Henceforth: Miller].

> To refine, to clarify, to intensify the eternal moment in which
> we alone live there is but a single force—the imagination.[4]

Note that in uttering this sacred, traditional term, he did not mean the same thing that Coleridge or Mallarmé or Stevens variously meant by the word. The imagination which he here opposes to the "beautiful illusion" is our ability 1) to perceive direct images of our world and 2) to employ verbal means, as writer or reader, to simulate such perception. The imagination is a faculty which requires its proper facilitating instrument. As that instrument, the poetic text can serve to train the perceiver in discovering the world. But if it "fails to release the senses," to engage the "sympathies, the intelligence [of the reader] in its selective world, [it] fails at the elucidation" of that world.[5] Imagination, as Williams uses the term, is therefore a skill which subsumes both the perception and the visualization of images and which fashions art as its instrument:

> In the composition, the artist does exactly what every eye must
> do with life, fix the particular with the universality of his own
> personality. . . .[6]

If we might make a theoretical deduction from Williams' own poetic practice, we may add that it fixes this particular in the *present tense*, relegating the past tense to the poetics of memory, e.g., narration and Wordsworthian meditation.

Being "anterior to technique,"[7] this ability to perceive and visualize is the foundation upon which all literary art is built. When that foundation begins to rot, it must be renewed. At various points in his long writing career Williams took upon himself a number of "making-it-new" projects: the examination of local cultural meanings, the sensitization to American speech, and the fashioning of a new metric. His one, ongoing, perennial project, however, was to uncover, clean, and display the *prima materia* of poetry—the particulars of experience, the *things*.

"Williams is the master of the glimpse," wrote Kenneth Burke in 1922:

> The process [of composition] is simply this: There is the eye, and
> there is the thing upon which the eye alights; while the relation-
> ship existing between the two is a poem.[8]

These "minute fixations" mark the "shortest route between object and subject."[9] Though this route is short and, during a reading

---

4. *Ibid.*, p. 16.
5. *Ibid.*, p. 17.
6. *Ibid.*, p. 17.
7. *Ibid.*, p. 17.
8. Kenneth Burke, "Heaven's First Law," *The Dial*, LXXII, (1922), in Miller, pp. 47-4?
9. *Ibid.*, p. 49.

can seem invisible, it nevertheless possesses the extension of language. A different but perhaps more useful analogy for the function of the typical Williams text was that formulated by Wallace Stevens in 1957:

> Williams is a writer to whom writing is the grinding of a glass, the polishing of a lens by means of which he hopes to be able to see clearly.[10]

His own statements of purpose together with these insights of his contemporaries lead us to assume that for Williams the poetic text was the verbal record of a direct sensory encounter, or encounters, with a world beyond language and that the art he aspired to was one of sharpened perceptual, predominantly visual, acuity.

Such conclusions, however, are only preparatory to our real activity: that of actually viewing his world—*our* world—through the optics of his poetry. After the poet's death in 1963, his old friend Kenneth Burke stressed once again the function of visual imagery as a means by which the knower and the known coexist in phenomenological interpenetration:

> Typically in his poems the eye (like a laying on of hands), by disguised rituals that are improvised constantly anew, inordinates us into the human nature of things.[11]

These are somewhat cryptic expressions, worthy of the Smaragdine Tables or Burke's own rhetorical treatises on rhetoric. What are these disguised rituals which the eye performs in order to disalienate the reader from this world of things? They could not be the named referents of his texts, the objects and persons observed behaving in customary fashion. There is nothing disguised about them; what they do are *revealed* rituals. Nor can they be the techniques of the poet's art, that is, if we understand techniques in the usual sense of verbal forms and figures. These disguised rituals of the eye, to which Burke alludes, may well be disguised for the very same reason that our eyes are unseen in the act of seeing. These transparent mechanisms permit us to perceive the world in all its thingy opacity. Not only do we not see our eyeballs when we see the world, but we are happily unaware of the various intricate operations which they perform to enable us to maneuver successfully in visual space. But a poet who wished to reproduce sensory phenomena as they are perceived, a poet with more than

---

10. Wallace Stevens, "Rubbings of Reality," from *Opus Postumous* (Knopf, 1957), in Miller, p. 65.
11. Kenneth Burke, "William Carlos Williams, 1883-1963," *New York Review of Books*, I, 2, (1963), in Miller, p. 56.

a passing interest in human physiology,[12] might well attempt to capture in his verbal medium some of the dynamics of visual perception.

The artistry of this poet, as I hope to demonstrate, lay not only in his portrayal of objects but in his simulation, in language, of the processes (the "disguised rituals") by which these objects are perceived. In this sense, the subject and the object are not linked by any route, however short. They are co-extensive, the subject and his or her manner of perceiving the object being revealed precisely *in the revelation of the object.* I think this is what Williams had in mind when he wrote in *Spring and All*:

> The inevitable flux of the seeing eye toward measuring itself by the world it inhabits can only result in crushing humiliation unless the individual raise himself to some approximate co-exten-sion with the universe. This is possible by aid of the imagination. Only through the agency of this force can a man feel himself moved largely with sympathetic pulses at work—[13]

Yet the passionate tone of this quote implies more. The ultimate purpose of this poet's visual precision is not accuracy either for art's or its own sake, but the establishment of a sympathetic bond between the knower and the known, a sustained moment of "I-Thou" intimacy, which assuages the loneliness of a con-sciousness confronted daily by the "burthen of the mystery, / . . . the heavy and the weary weight / Of all this unintelligible world." His close mimesis of the perceptual act was, in its way, a conjuring of what Wordsworth called "A motion and a spirit, that impels / All thinking things, all objects of all thought, / And rolls through all things."[14] It was, as Burke said, a constantly improvised set of optical rituals which "inordinates us into the human nature of things."

What I propose to examine is the relation between these "rituals" (which I take to be types of eye movement) and the structure of some of Williams' earlier texts. In so doing I am well aware that I am running counter to one of the cherished traditions of Anglo-American criticism, the scrupulous avoidance of psycho-logical borrowings. Ever since I. A. Richards incurred the wrath of the New Humanist and then the New Critical establishment, "psychologism" has been a most dread imputation. The serious use of psychological terms in a critical context has been condemned

---

12. It is interesting to note that at the medical school of the University of Pennsylvania Williams' special interest was neurology. In his *Autobiography* [p. 52] he says he almost specialized in it.
13. WCW, "Prose from *Spring and All*," in Miller, pp. 16-17 [as emended by the editor]
14. Wordsworth, "Tintern Abbey," ll. 38-40, 100-102.

as jargonizing. R. P. Blackmur's 1948 dictum that "psychology turns aesthetics into the mechanics of perception"[15] was a typical warning to would-be cross-disciplinarians and an encouragement to staunch literary territorialists. I trust time has softened some of these prejudices.

In the pages which follow I will be appropriating several technical terms from cognitive psychology, specifically from the psychology of visual perception. They may ring barbaric to some ears. This cannot be helped. Although the sciences and the humanities are methodologically different, whenever their areas of concern overlap, formulations drawn from one discipline may generate further insights in another. I have no desire to see psychology turn aesthetics into the mechanics of perception. My concern here is rather in tracing the ways Dr. Williams used the mechanics of perception to turn psychology into aesthetics.

Saccadic Movement on the Pictorial Plane

Our visual field is an oval lying on its side, outlined by our brows, cheekbones, and nose. In order to see objects outside these limits we must shift this illuminated oval by moving our head. Yet even inside this oval field not everything seems clear. In fact, all but a tiny area is blurred. That tiny area, only about the size of our thumbnail held at arm's length, happens to be the segment of the visual field which each lens of the eye projects on a *fovea* (the part of each retina which is packed with light-receptor cells). When we want to inspect any of the contents of our oval visual field, we must use our eye muscles to rotate our eyes in such a way that these different details of our visual field can be projected onto the foveas. In other words, by moving our eyes we in effect shift our *foveal field*. As soon as we shift it from some particular item, that item passes back into the large, more or less blurry surrounding area, called the *peripheral field*.

It takes a little effort for most of us to visualize this normal visual process. One way might be to imagine we are using a flashlight in a dark room. Though we can never illuminate the entire room at once and can only cast the narrow beam radially, now here, now there, we can still succeed in getting a sense of the contours and contents of the room because our memory, apparently, forms one composite schema out of all these separate projections.

15. R. P. Blackmur, "A Burden for Critics," *The Lion and the Honeycomb*, in *Issues in Contemporary Literary Criticism*, ed. Gregory T. Polletta (Little, Brown, 1973), pp. 66-57. See also Blackmur's *Language as Gesture*, pp. 353-354, where he shows little sympathy with WCW's poetics.

Though this is very much the way the eye orients us in visual space, this analogy is still not sufficiently exact. The shifting movements of the eye, called *saccades*, are sudden, unidirectional jerks. With our flashlight we could pan about the room as slowly and as meanderingly as we liked, but when we shift our foveal field in a saccade, our movement is so swift and bullet-like that we cannot slow down or veer from our trajectory for an interesting item—or even see it! We see only when the saccade-driven foveal field comes momentarily to rest in an optical *fixation*. But since most objects in our environment are larger than the foveal field (remember: the thumbnail held at arm's length), we must perform a whole series of saccades and fixations before we can form that composite which we recognize as the image.

Saccadic movement, then, is the eyes' technique for exploring visual space, searching for items, and perceiving shapes and relationships. It is the movement we use when we look at paintings and when we read a line of print. With the help of memory it can produce a complex spatial image all parts of which are understood to be simultaneously present. Nevertheless, from an operational point of view saccadic vision is no less sequential than language. It constitutes, in fact, a sort of pre-linguistic syntax. Conversely, spoken language with its rapid shifts of attention from lexeme to lexeme bears a striking resemblance to saccadic shifts and fixations. Not surprisingly, the verbal cues to image-formation which we find in literary texts imitate quite closely these rapid series of eye movements.

Some of the finest examples of verbalized saccades are to be found in Williams' classic short texts. "The Red Wheelbarrow,"[16] to begin with a familiar example, contains three major visual elements. If we construct this scene as we might actually perceive it at a distance, say, of 20 or 30 feet, we will probably have to make several short saccades in order to form each element. The verbal format, however, simplifies this process somewhat by naming these three elements—the red wheelbarrow, its rain-glazed surface, the white chickens—thereby treating them each as a separate fixation or cluster of fixations (a unitization which, by the way, is counterpointed by the fragmentation effect of the line-breaks). However one imagines the complexity of saccadic movements implied by this text, this taut little illuminated scene requires that the "mind's eye" perform a minimum of three fixations, linked by two saccades. A red wheelbarrow is of course

---

16. WCW, *The Collected Earlier Poems of William Carlos Williams* (New Directions, 1938), p. 277 [Henceforth: *CEP*].

the first image formed. (Note that even so simple an image as this is not automatically flashed in its entirety on the mind's inner "viewing screen": no matter how quickly it is imaged, it is pieced together in a simulation of actual optical saccades.) This is followed by a saccadic shift from the contours of the colored figure (which had indicated that it was a wheelbarrow and not some other object) to a detail of its surface texture which indicates that it is "glazed with rain water." Then a distinct saccade occurs with the word "beside" which draws our gaze laterally toward the "white chickens."

Several points emerge from this optical analysis: 1) saccadic shifts may fixate details within portrayed objects (nouns); 2) they may spatially relate separate objects (nouns); 3) the principal indicators of saccades are prepositions; and 4) nouns of indeterminate number induce an indeterminate, i.e. optional, number of saccades and fixations (how many white chickens are there beside this red wheelbarrow?).

Let us turn now to another short imagist text, "Nantucket."[17]

Flowers through the window lavender and yellow	1. indeterminate number of saccades and fixations
changed by white curtains— Smell of cleanliness—	2. additional flowers partially occluded by diaphanous curtain (non-visual percept)
Sunshine of late afternoon— On the glass tray	3. luminance visible on surfaces 4. sharp fixation, the prep. anticipating saccade to . . .
a glass pitcher, the tumbler turned down, by which	5. the pitcher, then 6. the tumbler (also on the tray?), prep. "by" anticipating saccade to . . .
a key is lying—And the immaculate white bed	7. the key dash + "and" (paratactic saccade-indicators) anticipating saccade to 8. the bed

"The Red Wheelbarrow" and "Nantucket" exemplify Williams' urge to rival in words the painter's and photographer's art of selecting and minutely fixating percepts on a two-dimensional pictorial plane. Three others are "To a Solitary Disciple," "Young Sycamore," and "Young Woman at a Window."[18] These all have a

---

17. *Ibid.*, p. 348.
18. *Ibid.*, pp. 167, 332, 369.

quality of stillness about them, not only because the objects and persons portrayed are motionless, but also because the imaginary viewer is fixed in space, thus stabilizing the visual field.[19]

Yet even in the most motionless portrait or still life we can say there is swift movement—in the eye of the beholder. When we view the painted surface, these saccades are overt muscular responses;[20] when we visualize from a written text, they are simulated by the imagination. Accordingly, saccadic movement is the compositional key to Williams' even more obvious experiments in ekphrasis, e.g., such early texts as "Winter Quiet," "Spring Strains," "Conquest," and "The Pot of Flowers,"[21] as well as the later *Pictures from Brueghel.*

Visual perception absolutely requires ocular movement. Because, apparently, we cannot fixate for very long without our vision blurring, our focus "drifts" and must be refreshed by continual saccadic corrections. Visual perception, together with its homologue, visual imagination, implies active search and discovery. There is nothing static about the process. In the later text, "Raindrops on a Briar,"[22] Williams explains that at one time he, a writer, was "hipped on / painting," but never considered the effects of painting to be "static." On the contrary, "the stillness of / the objects—the flowers, the gloves" was precisely what freed them from "a necessity merely to move / in space" the way animated humans move about. They presented to him, he says, "a more pregnant motion: a / series of varying leaves / clinging still, let us say, to / the cat-briar after last night's / storm. . . ." This effect of pattern-with-variation induces eye movement by leading the eye through a series of fixations not unlike the replicated contours of cubist painting.

Depth Imagery and Vergence

If the only movement our eyes were capable of were saccadic movement, ours would be a flat world at a fixed distance, a

19. For a useful study of WCW's debt to the visual arts, see Bram Dijkstra, *The Hieroglyphics of a New Speech: Cubism, Stieglitz, and the Early Poetry of William Carlos Williams* (Princeton, 1969).

20. Some psychologists have reported "incipient motor reactions" in response to reading texts, as though subjects were enacting the situations they were imagining—producing a sort of interpretive dance of muscle contractions. See F.J. McGuigan, "Imagery and Thinking: Covert Functioning of the Motor System," in *Consciousness and Self-Regulation: Advances in Research and Theory*, vol. II, eds. Schwartz and Shapiro (Plenum, 1978), pp. 37-100.

21. *CEP*, pp. 141, 159, 172, 242. While there occur references to depth in these texts, it is more often than not the depth of perspectivist illusion. Our gaze is never allowed to drift far from the flat pictorial surface.

22. WCW, *The Collected Later Poems of William Carlos Williams*, revised (New Directions, 1963), p. 99 [Henceforth: *CLP*].

picture-on-the-wall world. Depth perception is largely the result of our having one visual field maintaned simultaneously by two sense organs lying some two-and-one-half inches apart. To avoid double vision, which would be the logical outcome of having two sources of visual information, our eye muscles pivot our eyeballs in such a way that the image of an object projected on the retina of one eye corresponds as closely as possible to that of the other eye. Saccadic movement is called "conjugate" because both eyes rotate in the same direction like a pair of yoked horses. The movement we are considering now is one of opposite rotation: the closer the object, the greater degree of convergence; the further away we focus our gaze, the more our visual axes *di*verge until, viewing a distant hill or cloud, they are virtually parallel. Psychologists have called this particular movement *vergence*. Whenever the angle of vergence is imprecise for a given object, that object becomes blurred. If I focus on my extended hand, the wall across the room is blurred; if I then focus at that wall beyond my hand, it is my hand that seems blurry.

This adjustment for depth is part of our standard everyday repertoire of perceptual skills. Combined—almost invariably—with saccades, vergence allows us to zoom in on objects at various distances from the eye—in effect, to break the pictorial plane and enter a three-dimensional perceptual environment. An analogy might help clarify the collaborative function of saccades and vergence. Suppose I am peering through a small hand telescope at the tiled roof of a red barn two hundred feet away. Should I decide to explore the hillside above and beyond it, I must perform two operations: I must shift my angle of vision and readjust my scope for depth. In this rough analogy the telescopic field represents my foveal field; the shift of angle, the saccade to the new fixation point; and the adjustment, the vergence.

The early poems of Williams provide several striking examples of vergence, texts which can be read as presenting one or several visual fields at different degrees of depth and demanding that the reader imagine not only the images but the processes of perception as well. In "Tree and Sky"[23] the eye moves first in a saccade from the upper branches of a tree to its base. We do not have to imagine our vantage point as near the base, but, if we do, this shift of focus from branches to base will require the simulation of a (con)vergence of our eyes and a blurring of the upper portion of the tree. After this, the view is shifted back upwards, this time past the branches, which would now blur as the eyes diverge in order to

---

23. *CEP*, p. 102.

focus on the "shufflings / of the distant / cloud-rifts." Finally, they approach parallel as they contemplate the "unmoving / blue." "The Tulip Bed"[24] reverses this direction and, beginning with the "May sun" and "bluegauze clouds," takes us through a set of progressively closer details: leafy trees, suburban street corners, houses, front lawns, and finally a fenced-in tulip bed. So, from the distant "May sun—whom / all things imitate—" our eyes are gradually directed to a patch of small close-at-hand imitators, "yellow, white and red."

In the first half of "Spring and All"[25] the fixations take the form of a rapid darting in three depth projections: vertical, frontal, and lateral. As usual, the prepositions govern the principal shifts in fixation. The one exception to this is the first preposition, "*By* the road. . .", which merely establishes the vantage point of this invisible observer, this Emersonian "transparent eyeball." The first real saccadic preposition tells us that if we cast our gaze upward from the road (probably moving our head and with it our visual field), we will see that we are "*under* the surge of blue / mottled clouds. . . ." Then we are directed to look "*beyond* [the road]" and to perform a series of fixations[26] which allow us to generalize that over there is a "waste of broad, muddy fields" within which one can discern, again serially, "dried weeds, standing and fallen" and [further in the distance?] "patches of standing water / the scattering of tall trees." Then we are asked to look "All *along* the road . . ." from a relatively distant point where we see "bushes and small trees" to a closer and lower point where we see more minute details: "dead, brown leaves *under* them" and "leafless vines" [italics added]. The final half of the poem is a set of generalizations based presumably on these serial fixations, plus several single tachistoscopic images of plant growth.

Among these examples of vergence taken from the first half of "Spring and All" there are series or clusters of fixations but no instances of the "zooming in" effect. To be zoomed in on an object must be totally perceived in a single fixation, i.e., it must fit wholly within the foveal field (present a visual angle of less

---

24. *Ibid.*, p. 221.
25. *Ibid.*, p. 241.
26. One of the modern pioneers in the study of visual perception was J. J. Gibson. Here is how he explains the function of serial fixations: "At the stimulus level we have a succession of overlapping images. At the level of experience we have a panoramic world, all parts of which are concurrent. In ordinary visual perception there is no sense of either the *sequence* of fixations or the *time-lapse* between them." These successive images are not absolutely discrete. "They overlap and, to that extent, are transpositions of the just-preceding images. Instead of saying that the visual world is based on a succession of images, therefore, it is possible to say that it is based on a continuous but changing image." *The Perception of the Visual World* (Houghton-Mifflin, 1950), pp. 158-159.

than 2°). If it appears larger than that, it must be perceived in a series of fixations. A text ordinarily indicates serial fixation in two ways: *contextually*, by conveying an image which appears to be too large and/or too near the implied viewer to be perceived adequately in a single fixation (e.g., the waste of broad, muddy fields and the road), and *grammatically*, by simply using the plural form of nouns (e.g., the patches of standing water).

For some final examples of vergence, plus serial fixation and zooming in, let us turn to the tiny text "Between Walls."[27] The title, which begins the one-sentence poem, initiates by its preposition a set of crisscrossing saccades over a yard of cinders.

the back wings of the	too large and plural, therefore serial fixations crisscrossing between vertical planes
hospital where nothing	
will grow lie cinders	too large and plural, therefore serial fixations over horizontal plane. the angle of the viewer to this plane will necessitate several vergence adjustments
in which shine the broken	"in which" indicates a narrowing of the saccadic area and anticipates the fixing of the object of interest at a particular distance in depth
pieces of a green bottle	a zooming in on this object

This visual analysis assumes that the viewer is far enough away from the broken bottle to view it in a single foveal fixation.

Williams relied upon vergence (in combination with saccadic movement) to organize some rather more complex visual arrays. "View of a Lake" and "Blueflags"[28] deserve mention as two exceptionally rich explorations of three-dimensional visual space.

The Moving Image

Modernist poetry developed with close connections to the visual arts. At first this meant an emulation, à la Gautier, of the artifact. Poems were to be hard as carved alabaster, small and perfect as classical medallions, powerfully still as Japanese prints.

27. *CEP*, p. 343.
28. *Ibid.*, pp. 96, 225.

Somewhat later, however, inspired by the attempts of Cubists and
Futurists to deal with the problems of time and motion in visual
perception, poets began to introduce into their verbal medium
similar kinetic effects. In his *Autobiography* Williams recalls—
somewhat enigmatically perhaps—Duchamp's "Nude Descending a
Staircase" at the "Armory Show" in 1913: "I laughed out loud
when first I saw it, happily, with relief."[29]

In 1934, looking back on his break with the early Imagists,
Pound cited this as an important aesthetic issue:

> The defeat of earlier imagist propaganda was not in misstatement
> but in incomplete statement. The diluters took the handiest and
> easiest meaning, and thought only of the STATIONARY image.
> If you can't think of imagism or phanopoeia as including the
> moving image, you will have to make a really needless division of
> fixed image and praxis or action.[30]

A year later Williams defined a poet as "a man / whose words
will bite / their way home—being actual / having the form / of
motion."[31] And in 1944 he likened the poem to a machine: "As
in all machines its movement is intrinsic, undulant, a physical
more than a literary character."[32] It *moves*—and has the form of
movement—because language moves.

To conceptualize poetry as a time-art was one thing—to solve
satisfactorily the stylistic problems posed by narrative and dramatic action was quite another thing. Not many of Williams'
contemporaries were content with the solutions exemplified by
the work of Frost and Jeffers. For such systematic workers as
Pound and Williams it was the simple image that had first to be
set in motion before the art of sustained narration could be
resuscitated. (Though the overall structure of both *The Cantos*
and *Paterson* is hardly narrative, both works contain numerous
narrative episodes.)

Moving images may be usefully divided into two classes:
gestural, in which parts of an otherwise stationary object are in
motion, and *translocal*, in which the entire object is observed in
the act of moving through a stationary environment. A cat, for
example, may be observed licking its paws and preening itself,
then suddenly racing across the lawn after a butterfly. For the
human perceiver these are not just two degrees of motility—they
induce two significantly different eye movements which the

---

29. WCW, *The Autobiography of William Carlos Williams* (Random House, 1951), p. 134.
30. Pound, *ABC of Reading*, p. 52.
31. *CEP*, p. 68.
32. WCW, "Author's Introduction to *The Wedge*, in *Selected Essays of William Carlos
Williams* (New Directions, 1969), p. 256 [Henceforth: *SE*].

poet, if he or she is at all concerned with reproducing perceptual events, must manage carefully.

In simple terms gestural motion transforms the still life or portrait into the "moving picture" and does so without having to shift the visual field. In other words, the reader as imaginary viewer establishes a fixed positionpoint and from that point observes an otherwise immobile figure performing an action. This form of motion is ordinarily detected by serial fixations which, like the separate frames of a film, display a progressive displacement of the parts of the object. An old woman reaches into a bag, takes out a series of plums, and munches them; a big, young, bareheaded woman in an apron toes the sidewalk and takes a nail out of her shoe; a little girl bounces a ball, stops, runs her fingers through her hair, pulls up a stocking, lets her arms drop, waits. . . .[33]

What I have called translocal motion induces a totally different eye movement which psychologists have termed *pursuit*. In contrast to saccadic movement, which is jagged, rapid, and often clustered in series, pursuit is smooth, considerably slower, and fixed upon one moving "quarry" at a time. It is the movement we use to fixate and track a free-moving object, like a bird in flight. The stable background (the peripheral field) is thus made to stream past in a fluid blur, while what is actually moving appears fixed relative to the eye. To keep the object comfortably in foveal focus, the head is often turned in conjunction with the eyes, thus causing the entire visual field to shift.

Pursuit is a most difficult eye movement to simulate in the medium of poetry. It is not easy, nor is it terribly interesting perhaps to describe blur, yet peripheral blur is a necessary accompaniment to this specific eye movement. Williams' inventiveness seems to have been provoked by the difficulty of this problem. "Spring Strains,"[34] an early experiment which seems mostly concerned with the painterly fields of force generated by the massive shapes and colors of the scene, nevertheless contains those uncontainable, magical beings:

> two blue-grey birds chasing
> a third struggle in circles, angles,
> swift convergings to a point that bursts
> instantly!

And again:

> On a tissue-thin monotone of blue-grey buds
> two blue-grey birds, chasing a third

33. *CEP*, pp. 99, 101; *CLP*, p. 120.
34. *CEP*, p. 159.

at full cry! Now they are
flung outward and up—disappearing suddenly!

Note how their acceleration is described in terms of the observer's inability to maintain them in a visual field. But though a proper peripheral blur is provided (the "tissue-thin monotone"), this is not true ocular pursuit, for no single observer could pursue three birds simultaneously. Perhaps because of the difficulty of the task, the poet asks us to imagine the trajectories in terms of geometric after-images.

It is quite difficult in poetry to convey an image in continuous realistic motion without making careful reference to an environment. It is the old problem of presenting a figure without a ground.[35] The effect produced is one of hovering and looming, an uncanny effect used with such great success by Pound in "The Return" and Yeats in "The Magi." In two perhaps equally notable texts Williams dealt with the problem by alternating between pursuit and saccadic manoeuvres, i.e., between a mobile tracking of the moving figure and a static correlation of its trajectory to its environment. The simplest example to cite is "Poem."[36] The syntax of the text suggests that the motion of the cat is continuous, yet our simulated gaze is diverted from this cinematic action twice by prepositionally specified saccades which momentarily freeze the action as in a still photograph: "over / the top of / the jamcloset" and "into the pit of / the empty / flowerpot." A more complex example is "The Yachts."[37] For a poem on a yacht race one would suppose pursuit would be the appropriate eye movement and that any distraction from this continuous tracking mechanism would be disruptive. The seascape, however, does not lie back in this poem and conveniently furnish the yachts with a peripheral blur. It first becomes a personified antagonist, then a nightmarish entanglement of all those lives that are neither free nor feckless nor naturally to be desired. The poet continually diverts our attention from the fluid motion of the boats to the contorted sea over which they pass. The technical difficulty of verbally conveying this particular eye movement thus aids rather than hinders the thematic development of this poem.

One last example of the moving image—"The Well Disciplined Bargeman":

The shadow does not move. It is the water moves,
running out. A monolith of sand on a passing barge,
riding the swift water, makes that its fellow.

35. See my article "Figure, Ground, and Open Field," *New York Quarterly*, 10 (Winter, 1971).
36. *CEP*, p. 340.
37. *Ibid.*, p. 106.

> Standing upon the load the well disciplined bargeman
> rakes it carefully, smooth on top with nicely squared
> edges to conform to the barge outlines—ritually: sand.
>
> All about him the silver water, fish-swift, races
> under the Presence. Whatever there is else is moving.
> The restless gulls, unlike companionable pigeons,
>
> taking their cue from the ruffled water, dip and circle
> avidly into the gale. Only the bargeman raking
> upon his barge remains, like the shadow, sleeping[38]

This poem plays with some of the paradoxes of perceived motion. The shadow of the barge does not move . . . why? Because, while we fixate the shadow in pursuit eye movement, the retinal displacement of this image is 0° and it is only the peripheral water that does the moving. In addition, the contours of the shadow do not change (it exhibits no "gestural" motion).[39] When we shift our gaze to the "monolith of sand" which accompanies its own moving shadow, we see that it, too, is motionless upon its peripheral ground of swift water. In the second stanza our eyes converge on the small figure atop the sand and seem to associate our visual field with his: from the shore our pursuit eye movements have immobilized the squared-off pile of sand. From his point of view also the pile is motionless but, in his case, because he is travelling at the same rate and direction as his immediate environment. Poised as he is, he needs discipline to ignore the dizzying trajectories of creatures above and below him and to attend to this unmoored piece of land as though it were *terra firma*. One is reminded of Melville's Nantucket whaler who can sleep peacefully in his bunk at night while leviathans plunge beneath his pillow. It is a precarious sort of cosmos they both maintain.

The Moving Observer

If I stroll along with my gaze unfocused, I may with a little effort become aware that my world behaves oddly. When I turn my head to the right the contents of my visual field shift to the left. When I raise my head, the horizon plunges and, when I lower it, the horizon rises over it. And, as I move myself through space, stationary objects loom toward me, twisting their contours as I pass.[40]

---

38. *CLP*, p. 98 [The only visual analysis of a poem *not* appearing in *CEP*].
39. Cf. Whitman's "Crossing Brooklyn Ferry" for a similar treatment of this paradoxical movement.
40. Cf. Ted Hughes', "The Wodwo." See also Jacqueline Tyrwhitt, "The Moving Eye," in Carpenter and McLuhan's *Explorations in Communication* (Beacon Press, 1960), pp. 90-95.

Fortunately, we have a mechanism which corrects all the jiggles, wobbles, jumps, and contortions which would otherwise destabilize our visual field when we move. It is called the vestibulo-ocular mechanism, a link-up between the semi-circular canals of our inner ear, which keep us balanced, and our eye muscles. If, as I walk, I fixate my foveal field on an object, my eyes begin automatically to make rotational adjustments for even the slightest jog of my head. Without such adjustments, the slightest movement on our part would dizzy and disorient us.[41]

Yet the deformations in our visual field produced by locomotion do give us valuable information. For one thing, the changes in our orientation toward an object, tell us more about it. We rotate a small artifact in our hands or we walk around a large sculpture. The inevitable distortions in angle of vision, experienced as we move about in space, also tell us about the relative distance of objects. Simply put, the phenomenon of *motion parallax* occurs as nearer objects seem to flow past us faster than more distant ones. Locomotion allows us to take a series of "fixes" on a visual array: an object which, for example, seems to move past us to the left when we move to the right is judged closer to us than the object which seems to move with us to the right. Thus at night the moon always seems to travel with us as we walk or drive, while all stationary sublunar objects "move" past us at a rate determined by our speed and their distance from us. Another obvious clue to relative depth is *occlusion*: an object which seems to pass in front of another object is deemed closer. Motion parallax and occlusion are the principal ways we judge the relative distances of hills and trees when travelling in the country and are absolutely necessary sources of information for steering a vehicle in traffic.

A century and a half ago Emerson commented upon the interesting effects produced by even "a small alteration in our local position."

> We are strongly affected by seeing the shore from a moving ship, [or] from a balloom. . . . The least change in our point of view gives the whole world a pictorial air. The man who seldom rides needs only to get into a coach and traverse his own town, to turn the street into a puppet-show.[42]

41. The recognized authority on the vestibulo-ocular system, Geoffrey Melville Jones, gives some examples: "Imagine . . . the 'engineering' accomplishment of a system which allows one to 'keep one's eye on the ball' when running and weaving at top speed in a football game, or to hold the eye on successive 'stepping stones' during an exhilarating run down a mountain path." "The Vestibular System for Eye Movement Control," in *Eye Movements and Psychological Processes*, ed. Richard A. Monty and John W. Senders (Lawrence Erlbaum Associates, 1976), p. 3.
42. *Selections From Ralph Waldo Emerson*, ed. Stephen E. Whicher (Houghton Mifflin, 1957), p. 43.

His fellow townspeople suddenly lose their stable reality (become "unrealized," he says). And how strange a familiar countryside seems when viewed from a "railroad car." Invert your entire world, he cheerfully recommends, by looking at it through your legs "and how agreeable is the picture. . .!" Imagine how he would have responded to a ride on a roller-coaster, a mechanism purposely designed to frustrate the vestibulo-ocular system.

Such altered states of vision are brief, however. As has been proven by many experiments, notably those using prism-equipped goggles, our visual system adjusts to even the most thoroughgoing distortions and delivers us back within a day to our old quotidian world.[43] Emerson, who showed that he understood this by specifying *the man who seldom rides* as the observer most likely to achieve this momentary liberation, knew that art, specifically poetry, was the surest means of seeing the world anew. On this point Williams was to agree with Emerson, specifically on the need to focus more closely on the neglected aspects of our everyday experience, to defamiliarize, and thereby reveal, the American landscape. As I have been suggesting, this required above all the retraining of the sense of sight in particular procedures. Among these were the curious transformations and visual adjustments which occur as the observer relinquishes the privileged fixed vantage point and ventures forth *into* visual space.[44]

One sort of moving observer, as Emerson noted, is the rider in or driver of a vehicle. The motorist—like the coach-rider, only more so—can indeed turn persons into enigmatic puppets. Williams' "The Right of Way"[45] exemplifies the fugacity of these wayside apparitions which, as Emerson said, are "wholly detached from all relation to the observer, and seen as apparent, not substantial beings."[46] This is the apparitional experience preserved by Pound in "In a Station of the Metro."[47]

"The Source"[48] is a quite ambitious study of the ocular exploration of space. It is divided into two sections: the first details a single visual field, indicating saccadic and vergent eye movements; the second recounts the changing views which appear as the implied observer walks *into that visual field*. The process

43. See I. Kohler, *The Formation and Transformation of the Perceptual World*, trans. H. Fiss (International Universities Press, 1964).
44. See my *The Uses of Observation: Correspondential Vision in the Writings of Emerson, Thoreau, and Whitman* (Mouton, 1970).
45. *CEP*, p. 258.
46. Whicher, p. 43.
47. Cf. also Dickinson's "Because I Could Not Stop for Death" and Robert Bly's "Driving Toward the Lac Qui Parle River" in *Silence in the Snowy Fields.*
48. *CEP*, p. 346. First published in *The Dial*, Nov. 1928, in three sections, this poem makes an intriguing contrast with Frost's "Directive."

calls to mind the story of the ancient Chinese master who, having just unveiled his painted landscape before the Emperor and his court, calmly strolled away into it and vanished up a tiny brush-work path of pine trees.

Section I is a very careful composition of a visual field. One imagines the observer in a fixed position, perhaps looking out his bedroom window. The excitement he seems to be feeling as he discovers this landscape in morning light suggests that he arrived at this farm house or cottage only the night before. The "inner eye" of the reader is instructed to visualize first a "slope of . . . heavy woods" which vanish in a "wall of mist" which lies below a peak over which "last night the moon—" (the text stops abruptly: this is morning now and memory has no place in this immediate series of perceptions). The eye movements which had been moving upward (saccadically) and away (vergently) are now set in reverse. We now begin at the margin of a pasture marked by "silhouettes of scrub / and balsams" and then, focusing nearer, fixate on "three maples / . . . distinctly pressed / beside a red barn" the shingles of which are "cancelled" (occluded?) by an elm. This tree appears to occupy the foreground of this visual field, for it is close enough to reveal its lichened bark and "wisps of twigs" which "droop with sharp leaves."

Section II begins with one of Williams' casually abrupt transitions:

Beyond which lies
the profound detail of the woods
restless, distressed

soft underfoot
the low ferns

Suddenly we have been told to shift our gaze from the "fitfully" moving branches of the nearby elm back outward toward the woods and there to zoom in on an overwhelmingly replicated pattern of minute activity, an effect he had already produced in the crowd scene of "At the Ball Game."[49] Then with equal sud-denness we are asked to imagine the soft ferns underfoot; which is to say we are asked to enter through the pictorial plane into the depth dimension we have heretofore traversed only through ocular adjustments. The fact that this series of images could be viewed only by a walker, not some disembodied sensorium, should prompt us to simulate the appropriate sort of visual procedures, viz. fixations briefly stabilized by the vestibulo-ocular system and objects continually occluding one another and being displaced by

---
49. *CEP*, p. 284.

motion parallax.[50] What we receive are separate, precariously sustained glimpses of roots, fungi, hoof print, and cow dung amid shifting lines of trees, alder bushes, and, with increasing excitement, finally the source itself:

> An edge of bubbles stirs
> swiftness is moulded
> speed grows
>
> the profuse body advances
> over the stones unchanged

And suddenly—without punctuation—the poem ends with this vision of changeless change.

The often anthologized, but problematical, "Flowers by the Sea" is, I believe, one of the best examples of what Burke meant when he spoke of Williams' disguised rituals of the eye.

> When over the flowery, sharp pasture's
> edge, unseen, the salt ocean
>
> lifts its form—chicory and daisies
> tied, released, seem hardly flowers alone
>
> but color and the movement—or the shape
> perhaps—of restlessness, whereas
>
> the sea is circled and sways
> peacefully upon its plantlike stem[51]

This one-sentence poem with its branching clauses seems to represent a process: when A happens, then B changes, which then affects A. It is a sort of feed-back loop. This text has been variously interpreted as dreamlike, surrealistic, and ekphrastic,[52] but in the case of Williams we would do well to ask first whether a simpler, phenomenologically realistic interpretation is possible.

In the first stage of this process we visualize a "flowery, sharp pasture's / edge"—a clearly focused line in the middle distance. The ocean is as yet "unseen" but anticipated both syntactically ("When over . . .") and perhaps olfactorily (by its salt smell). In the third line the dependent clause attains its resolution

---

50. This statement seems to be asking a lot of the reader. Lest there be any misunderstanding, I do *not* mean by this or any similar analyses that the reader is to go adventuring among literary masterpieces armed with a glossary of visual mechanics. These terms are useful only as they draw the reader's attention to the actual physical responses he or she has been making to the visual world since early childhood and suggest ways of applying these responses to the operations of the literary imagination.
51. *CEP*, p. 87.
52. For example: "it is hard to forego the impression that Williams' observations are taken from one of that painter's [John Marin's] watercolors rather than from a landscape personally seen." Dijkstra, *Hieroglyphics of a New Language*, p. 184.

with the predicate "lifts its form." But how does the ocean *do* this? By inundating the flowers? Daisies and chicory have no business growing in tidal salt marshes. Anyway, they are edging a *pasture*. The simplest explanation (the key to the poem, I would argue) is that the "consciousness of the poem" is a moving observer walking toward the flowers at the edge of the pasture, a headland overlooking the ocean. The ocean "lifts its form" because it is gradually coming into view in the process of motion parallax.

In the second stage of the process, the flowers, first "tied," then "released," lose their identity as particular flowers and become "color and the movement—or the shape / perhaps—of restlessness." What otherwise might seem some rather arbitrary metamorphoses become quite clear if we apply a visual analysis to this passage. If we interpret "tied" as visually fixated and "released" as put out of focus by vergence, then the loss of definition which these flowers undergo is perfectly understandable. As the observer adjusts his eyes to the more distant form of the ocean by vergence, the nearby flowers, already in his peripheral field, appear in an unfocused "double exposure." In short, they are reduced to a blurry lower foreground of white, yellow, blue, and green motion.

The final stage in this optical transformation is the synthesis of both images, the rounded horizon of the sea, with its distant details of swells and troughs, appearing to rest like a broad flower upon the "stem" of the wavy unfocused foreground. The eye thus composes an optical metaphor, the flowers becoming sea-like, the sea flower-like—an interesting anticipation of one of the central motifs of *Asphodel*.

When he spoke of enlarging his definition of phanopoeia to include moving imagery, Pound evidently had in mind narrated action in which the reader is asked to visualize the movements of a dramatis persona. In such situations we tend to keep our aesthetic distance and let the actors play out their roles on the other side of the proscenium arch. But texts like "The Source" or "Flowers by the Sea"—"Morning"[53] is another good example— actually make the reader the central human actor. It is the reader who does the moving within this word-created environment, this place which is both made and found each time the text is read. The process which such a poetic text represents we might conveniently call "topopoeia" and define it as the art of constructing an image large enough to enclose its own imager.

---

53. *CEP*, p. 393.

Some Conclusions

As a means of arriving at a general interpretation of Williams' work, the approach I have taken here has certain limitations. It excludes from consideration questions of the voice, that other element of immediacy which Williams incorporated into his poetry and increasingly relied on as the shaping principle of his later work. Apparently by the late 1930s he was ready to attribute some degree of concreteness to the word itself—a phonetic thingness—and to the poem as a verbal object. Abstractions, historical references, even literary allusions began appearing more and more in his poetry. He had, it seems, taken to heart the criticisms of fellow poets like Babette Deutsch who in a review of *Collected Poems 1921-1931* (published in 1934) had written:

> People, accustomed to the passionate imagery of Yeats, to Eliot's suggestive music, to the panoplied mysticism of Hart Crane or the rich allusiveness of Pound, to name four of the more influential poets of our time, will find themselves at a loss before this stark and unashamed simplicity of statement. For this man the object seen, the clear line, the pure color, is enough.
>
> . . .
>
> The reliance on the eye, the singling out of the brief moment, however intense, is a limitation upon his work. . . . The narrowness of attention which makes for concentration also may make for a certain meagerness. . . .[54]

In the period before and during World War II Williams seems to have gone through an artistic self-reevaluation. What he had been calling his "localism" had always been based, after all, on voice as well as eye. He had always known how to localize the speaker in the moment of improvised utterance, just as he had known how to localize the observer in visual space. However, despite the changes which occurred in his style as he struggled to extend the range and length of his poems, the eye never lost its precision, never lost its special function in particularizing the real, the "local." The texts I have chosen to demonstrate his close concern for the perceptual dynamics of sight come from the *Collected Earlier Poems*, which covers the 24-year span 1914-1938. (All analyzed texts except "The Well Disciplined Bargeman" come

---

54. Babette Deutsch, "Williams, the Innocent Eye and the Thing-In-Itself," *New York Herald Tribune Books* (April 1, 1934), p. 16, in *William Carlos Williams: The Critical Heritage*, ed. Charles Doyle (Routledge and Kegan Paul, 1980), pp. 130-131. Such criticism must have hurt. We know that his friend Stevens' preface with its reference to the "anti-poetic" rankled in him long afterwards. See also *The Selected Letters of William Carlos Williams*, ed. John C. Thirlwall (McDowell, Oblensky, 1957), pp. 147 and 264.

from that edition.) These are, as it were, études of the optical imagination. Yet Williams never lost or renounced his ability to direct the reader's eye toward what lay before it in the common light of day. At his stylistic crossroads in 1939, he reaffirmed what he had first declared in the early 20s:

> If I succeed in keeping myself objective enough, sensual enough, I can produce the factors, the concretions of materials by which others shall understand and so be led to use—that they may the better see, touch, taste, enjoy—their own world *differing as it may* from mine.
>
>   . . .
>
> That—all my life I have striven to emphasize it—is what is meant by the universality of the local. From me where I stand to them where they stand in their here and now—where I cannot be—I do in spite of that arrive! through their work which complements my own, each sensually local.[55]

The key question we must ask in choosing a critical approach to these earlier poems is, *What do these texts signify*? I find it hard to disagree with Hillis Miller's conclusion that "Williams has no fear of the referential power of words."[56] He had himself asserted in *Paterson III* that "The province of the poem is the world."[57] He never said his words were there to signify other words and other texts, though sometimes indeed they did and were obviously fashioned to do so. Despite the presence of inter-textuality in his work, his later work especially, there is another form of signification here which, though it begins in language, culminates in the non-verbal visual image. His words, therefore, signify not only further signifiers and so forth *ad infinitum*, but also and, I would argue, more insistently they *signify the images they evoke*. Once they have delineated a "portrayed world," as the phenomenologists call it, their visual, though not necessarily their semantic, work is done. I make this distinction based on the findings, now widely accepted, that our minds regularly process and store information bimodally, as images and as language.[58] A verbal stimulus, a Williams poem for example, will initiate two simultaneous processes, one which remains verbal and ushers the text into the resonating chamber of language, the other which translates the text into a visual code, drawn from a mute archive

---

55. WCW, "Against the Weather: A Study of the Artist," *Twice a Year*, 1939, in *SE*, pp. 197-198.
56. Miller, pp. 10-11.
57. WCW, *Paterson*, Book III, section i (New Directions, 1963), p. 99.
58. See Allan Paivio, *Imagery and Verbal Processes* (Holt, Rinehart and Winston, 1971).

of stored imagery, where it comes to rest as a unique artifact of the imagination. I would agree that poetry is referential generally and ultimately to a world beyond language and mental imagery but that it refers particularly and immediately to information stored in these two codes. In the case of Williams' earlier poetry I would submit that the visual code tends to dominate and that in the texts we have examined in this essay our more or less common store of mental imagery is instructed to form itself into particular visualizations following the same perceptual processes by which we perceive and imagine visual arrays.

For these reasons I am suggesting that for these texts a strictly language-based interpretation, e.g., a semiotic or deconstructionist analysis, is deficient. Nor is a strictly literary approach useful either—an approach which elucidates these texts in terms of the traditional forms and genres of Western poetry. Neither what we have come to understand as linguistic competence nor literary competence provide a sufficient set of norms.[59] The basic repertoire of reader-responses which I have appealed to in this article may be termed *cognitive competence* which I would venture to define in general terms as an implicit understanding of the operations of perception, memory, and space- and time-awareness. In this article, I have, of course, dealt only with perceptual and space-awareness aspects.

This competence we all possess, but, as with every skill, we are usually unaware of it until something breaks down or dysfunctions. While our cognitive processes are in healthy operation, we go about our daily rounds gobbling experience—sights, sounds, tastes, plans, recollections, and so forth—but, because we so seldom reflect on our modes of consciousness, we seldom savor what we consume. Williams' message was that so much depends upon our ability to *enjoy* the simple fare which sustains our waking life. What he most prized in the art of poetry was its power to

> revive the senses and force them to re-see, re-hear, re-taste, re-smell and generally revalue all that it was believed had been seen, heard, smelled and generally valued. By this means poetry has always in the past put a finger on reality.[60]

For him, to "imagine" meant simply to "re-see." Simply and literally to re-*see*. To understand how the human imagination

---

59. See Jonathan Culler, *Structuralist Poetics: Structuralism, Linguistics, and the Study of Literature* (Cornell, 1975), chap. 7.
60. WCW, "The Tortuous Straightness of Chas. Henri Ford," Introduction to *The Garden of Disorder and Other Poems*, by Charles Henri Ford (New Directions, 1939), in *SE*, p. 235.

works, it would follow that one must understand how human seeing works. To arrive at such an understanding, one must be prepared to oversee oneself in the various acts of seeing. One might also learn from science: when they are used as field guides and as owner's manuals, studies in the psychology of visual perception can be extremely helpful to the reader of poetry.[61]

The work which Williams undertook he knew was difficult. Early in his career he acknowledged that

> the thing that stands eternally in the way of really good writing is always one: the virtual impossibility of lifting to the imagination those things which lie under the direct scrutiny of the senses, close to the nose.[62]

If the difficulties of seeing and re-seeing test the poet's skill, they also test the reader's. Toward the very end he acknowledged with a poet's pride and a wise man's resignation:

> It is difficult
> to get the news from poems
>   yet men die miserably every day
>   for lack
> of what is found there.[63]

† † † † † † †

What follows is a partial list of psychological texts consulted in the preparation of this article. The books starred are those I found most helpful.

Buswell, Guy Thomas, *How People Look at Pictures: A Study of the Psychology of Perception in Art* (University of Chicago, 1935).

Cotton, John W. and Klatzky, Roberta, eds., *Semantic Factors in Cognition* (Lawrence Erlbaum, 1978).

*Gibson, J.J., *The Perception of the Visual World* (Houghton-Mifflin, 1950).

Gibson, J.J., *The Senses Considered as Perceptual Systems* (Houghton-Mifflin, 1966).

61. See brief bibliography below.
62. WCW, Prologue to *Kora in Hell*, in *SE*, p. 11.
63. WCW, "Asphodel, That Greeny Flower," *Pictures from Brueghel and Other Poems* (New Directions, 1962), pp. 161-162.

*Haber, Ralph Norman and Hershenson, Maurice, *The Psychology of Visual Perception*, 2nd ed. (Holt, Rinehart, and Winston, 1980).

*Horowitz, Mardi Jon, *Image Formation and Cognition* (Appleton-Century-Croft, 1970).

*Kosslyn, Stephen Michael, *Image and Mind* (Harvard, 1980).

*Monty, Richard A. and Senders, John W., eds., *Eye Movements and Psychological Processes* (Lawrence Erlbaum, 1976).

Neisser, Ulric, *Cognitive Psychology* (Appleton-Century-Croft, 1967).

*Paivio, Allan, *Imagery and Verbal Processes* (Holt, Rinehart, and Winston, 1971).

Reynolds, Allan G. and Flagg, Paul W., *Cognitive Psychology* (Winthrop, 1977).

Segal, Sydney Joelson, ed., *Imagery: Current Cognitive Approaches* (Academic Press, 1971).

JONATHAN MAYHEW

WILLIAM CARLOS WILLIAMS
AND THE FREE VERSE LINE

> I do not pretend to follow all
> of his volts, jerks, sulks, balks,
> outblurts and jump-overs; but
> for all his roughness there
> remains with me the convic-
> tion that there is nothing
> meaningless in his book, not
> a line.
> —Ezra Pound, 1918

Free verse evades prosody in a number of ways. The model of form which seems most suited to more traditional verse, based as it is on the interplay between an abstract, normative pattern and expressive variations, cannot explain verse which lacks any fixed metrical constant. The major alternative to this unworkable distinction between meter and rhythm, the grammar and the rhetoric of prosody, is to abandon prosody altogether, to say that the appearance of the poem on the page or its patterns of syntax takes the place of sound and rhythm. Such a displacement of attention usually begins with a suggestive analogy, drawn from nature, science, or the other arts, which is then applied to the poem on too literal a level. One aspect of the poem is taken for another and the study of the movement of sound through time, which could reveal the nature of one of the most significant developments in modern poetry, gives way to secondary concerns.

   The work of William Carlos Williams has suffered from the inadequacy of contemporary prosody in exactly this way. Williams himself used analogies to the poem's structure in his attempts to come to a formulation of his prosody, and critics have used Williams' own statements as a starting point. But Williams is more concerned, in his own prosody, with reconciling two somewhat contradictory notions of what form ideally should be. The nineteenth century concept of "organic form" still governs him: he demands that the intrinsic qualities of his world come into the poem without distortion. But the artist, without destroying the intrinsic shape of things, must at the same time assert an order of his own through his art, organize his materials actively and creatively. Williams called "the imitation of the senseless / unarrangement of wild things" "the stupidest rime of all" [*CEP*, p. 330]. The terms which Williams uses for the structure of the poem do not go far in explaining how his own poems work, but an examination of these poems themselves in the light of other kinds of "free verse" makes Williams' solution to the problem of form at once clearer and more arresting. Williams breaks apart the "unit of sense" of earlier free verse and makes the line a unit of performance. By making the line "arbitrary" in this sense he destroys the distinction between the grammatical and the rhetorical functions of rhythmic language, between the rhythm implicit in the words of the poem and the rhythm the poet himself imposes from "outside." Williams controls the movement of verse with the line itself, making "intrinsic" rhythms more precise without destroying them.

One result of Williams' experiments with the line is that the poem takes on a distinctive appearance on the page. A prevalent misinterpretation of his practice, one that inevitably diverts attention from prosody as such, is to take his line as an exclusively visual device. Williams representation of the world finds parallels in Cubist painting. But Williams' typography is in no way "painterly." The danger in seeing "the visionary in the visual,"[1] to take a phrase from John Hollander, is the false opposition created between sight and sound, space and time. The eye comes to replace the ear and Williams' techniques become exclusively visual:

> This is as visual a poem in every sense as one could find, a sound-less picture of a soundless world, its form shaped rather than incanted, its surface like that of so much modern poetry, now reflecting, now revealing its depths and, as the conscious wind of attention blows over it, now displaying the wavy texture of its surface. Put together from fragments of assertion, it has virtually no rhetorical sound.[2]

Hollander's metaphor of surface and depth converts "Spring and All," a powerfully rhythmic poem, into a kind of painting, all representation and no rhetoric. Karl Shapiro gives a similar version of Williams' techniques, confusing the image which Williams represents in the poem with the appearance of the poem on the page:

---

1. John Hollander, "The Poem in the Eye," *Shenendoah*, Vol. 23, No. 3, Spring 1972, 32.
2. Ibid.

> The poet's emotions, ideas, and sensations are selected and
> tranquilized in the eye; then distributed on paper as ideographs,
> and finally arranged, as an artist arranges the elements in a
> picture.[3]

Such a statement robs the poem of its vital dimension in time. If
Williams uses the space of the poem on the page as an indication
of how it is to be read aloud, then the emphasis which critics place
on the visual is a form of synechdoche taken literally: part of the
poem's prosody is taken for the whole, or the effect of Williams'
experiments, the look of his poems on the page, is taken for the
cause.

At the root of the confusion as to Williams' techniques is a
slighting of rhetoric and of the temporal aspect of language
associated with it. T. E. Hulme, a founder of the Imagist movement, distrusts the temporality of language, which cannot represent the simultaneity of pure perception: "Thought is prior to
language and consists in the simultaneous presentation to the mind
of two different images. Language is only a more or less feeble
way of doing this."[4] The element of language which most distorts
perception is rhythm:

> The new verse resembles sculpture rather than music; it appeals to
> the eye rather than the ear. It has to mould images, a kind of
> spiritual clay, into definite shapes. . . . It builds up a plastic image
> which it hands over to the reader, whereas the old art endeav-
> oured to influence him physically by the hypnotic effect of
> rhythm.[5]

Rhythm is rhetorical; it attempts to influence the reader. Hulme
is calling for a poetry of pure, disinterested contemplation. Williams' poems, on the other hand, are never pure representations;
they take the form of impassioned statements of something
which must be said. However Imagist they might seem they rarely
present a static picture: they are usually studies in movement, or
in the movement of perception. Since the ear follows this movement as the poem is read, it makes no sense to speak of the eye as
a replacement for the ear. Williams himself protested vehemently
when it was suggested that he wrote for the eye rather than the
ear, or that he was confused in his methods:

> Damn the bastards for saying that you can't mix auditory and
> visual standards in poetry. Who the hell ever invented these two
> categories but themselves? . . .

3. Karl Shapiro, "Study of 'Philomena Andronico,' " in *William Carlos Williams: A Collection of Critical Essays*, ed. J. Hillis Miller (Englewood Cliffs, N.J.: Prentice-Hall,
1966), p. 152.
4. Quoted in Herbert Read, *The True Voice of Feeling* (London: Faber and Faber,
1958), p. 109.
5. Ibid., p. 107.

> What they, the formulators of that particular question, do not
> know, is that an auditory quality, a NEW auditory quality, under-
> lies and determines the visual quality which they object to
> [*Selected Letters*, pp. 176-177. Hereafter abbreviated, *SL*].

The "auditory quality" determines how the poem will appear
on the page because the written poem is a score, a set of indications for performance. Williams came to this idea early; in 1916 he
complained to Harriet Monroe, who had rearranged the lines of
one of his poems in *Poetry*:

> As long as the poem in question is read aloud as intended, it
> makes no difference how it is written, but it will be physically
> impossible for anyone to guess how I intended it to be read the
> way you have rearranged matters [*SL*, p. 39].

A different arrangement will not ruin the poem's appearance, but
obscure the poet's metrical intentions. Charles Olson in "Projective Verse"[6] emphasizes the rigidity, precision, and convention-
ality of the printed page as score, but in Williams' poetry the page
is at once less rigid and more selective in its indications: it is an
assertion of an ideal order rather than a mechanical transcription.
Most aspects of performance virtually take care of themselves. At
the same time, line and stanza breaks have no precise meaning; a
reader could pause longer at the end of some lines than at others
and still remain faithful to the text. The text as score becomes
truly crucial when it indicates the divergence of two systems of
organization, syntactical and metrical, which each has its own
spatial representation. Punctuation indicates breaks in syntax;
the structure of lines and stanzas indicate other pauses, added by
the poet for rhythmical effect. The printed page can juxtapose
these two systems without confusion, distinguishing between
types of pauses and giving a clear idea of the poet's metrical intentions. It is only in this sense that Williams' prosody is "visual."
The printed page is most essential when the poet indicates a performance that is most removed from the ordinary cadences of
prose, when the metrical and the syntactical organization of the
poem are the most differentiated.

    Of course, the use of space to distinguish between syntactical
and metrical patterns also underlies more traditional verse. A line
of blank verse, for instance, does not necessarily correspond to a
unit of sense: line breaks mark off metrical units while punctuation takes care of other stops. The essential difference between
Williams' enjambment and that of earlier poets is that Williams'

---

6. Charles Olson, "Projective Verse," in *The Poetics of the New American Poetry*, ed.
Donald Allen and Warren Tallman (New York: Grove Press, 1973), p. 154.

cannot be predicted from the interior structure of the line. The line breaks in metrical verse reinforce units which are already inherent in the language of the poem. Even if there are irregularities it is obvious where the lines begin and end, so that the choice of where to break the line is still not given. A similar predictability marks the free verse of the nineteenth century. The line is a unit of sense and no enjambment is even allowed. Édouard Dujardin, a French poet close to the origins of *vers libre* in France, explains how the line is determined on the one hand by "l'unité de pensée," the unity of thought, and on the other by "l'ignorance du nombre des syllabes." A line can have any number of syllables but must end with an "arrêt du sens," a break in the sense. Dujardin's explanation of enjambment is curious: he claims that it results from a movement from "la pensée poétique" toward "la pensée prose."[7] What Dujardin himself does, though, is to identify the line with the phrase, the basic unit of prose, replace a metrical unit of a given number of syllables with a semantic unit. The division into lines remains a device which reinforces implicit divisions in the poem:

> Twenty-eight young men bathe by the shore, twenty-eight young
> men and all so friendly; twenty-eight years of womanly life and
> all so lonesome.

Anyone familiar with the techniques of *Leaves of Grass* could divide this paragraph into its three original lines. The line break in nineteenth-century free verse is even less significant than it was in metrical verse; it is not yet an independent variable with a force of its own.

Williams begins writing free verse in lines more or less determined by the unit of sense. Like the Imagists, he uses the short phrase rather than the long cadence of Whitman:

> The little sparrows
> hop ingenuously
> about the pavement
> quarreling
> with sharp voices
> over those things
> which interest them [*CEP*, p. 124].

But even in very early poems he separates the definite article from the noun and the preposition from its object. In *Al Que Quiere*, published in 1917, such jarring enjambments are rare, but they become more frequent in *Sour Grapes*, 1921, and almost the rule in the poems of *Spring and All*, 1923. Few other poets of this

---

7. Édouard Dujardin, *Mallarmé par un des Siens* (Paris: Édition Messein, 1936), pp. 114-117.

period break their lines with such apparent arbitrariness, and none with such deliberate prosodic intention. The line is no longer a mere typographical convention, but an independent variable with a force of its own. Williams can distinguish between two apparently identical texts on the basis of the line-structure alone:

> The sparrows
> by the iron fence-post
> hardly seen
>
> for the dry leaves
> that half
> cover them— [*CEP*, p. 458]
>
> .   .   .
>
> The sparrows by the iron fence post—
> hardly seen for the dry leaves
> that half cover them— [*CLP*, p. 55]

The identity of the line, of course, is not totally arbitrary like the margins of prose. Instead, it can be determined by a number of different factors simultaneously. The lines of a given poem can be roughly equivalent in length, having the same number of accents or filling up the same amount of time. Some lines may coincide with units of sense. The break between two lines may be significant in itself, foregrounding the words on either side of the pause and creating a meaningful break in sense. Finally, the system of lines as a whole controls the poem's movement; individual lines and line-breaks cannot be considered in isolation. Since no one aspect of prosody is fixed, none can be considered the metrical base, there can be no grammar of prosody. Accents, syllables, durations, syntax—all are expressive and none merely a normative base.

Williams, like the Romantics, seeks to avoid a dualism which makes all expression relative to convention. He would object to the idea that rhythm can only be meaningful within the context established by a fixed, normative pattern: "In verse we cannot have expressive variation unless a clear metrical pattern already exists."[8] A danger in organicist theory, however, is that, instead of taking the poem as a whole, it often takes part of the poem and acts as if it were the whole; it substitutes synecdoche for dualism. When the line is associated with the unit of sense, prosody becomes the study of syntax and rhetoric. The free verse of Whitman often suffers from this approach. Since rhythm follows the patterns

---

8. Harvey Gross, *The Structure of Verse: Modern Essays in Prosody* (New York: Fawcett, 1966), p. 182.

created by syntactic parallelism, there is no longer any sense of language being ordered by abstract patterns which bear no relation to what is being said; syntax and rhythm, both organized in the same way, do not come into conflict. The result is that many critics begin to speak of syntax as a replacement for rhythm, just as others speak of verse for the eye rather than the ear. Dujardin, championing "poetic thought," fixes the line as a unit of prose sense. Terms like "rhythm of thought" suggest that the sound of the words ceases to function as such in the poem. As with "visual prosody," the prosody of syntax silences the poem.

Williams avoids this danger by reintroducing, in his line, the division between syntax and rhythm. Syntax becomes only one factor of organization among others; the line is determined by other factors as well. One result of Williams' lineation is that it allows for a dualistic system of analysis. Charles O. Hartman in his recent study of free verse reintroduces the "counterpoint" of more traditional prosody, claiming that the lineation of free verse is equivalent, in its function, to the meter of regular verse.[9] The essential difference, of course, is that lineation is itself dependent on a variety of factors; considered as a metrical constant, it is itself variable. This is perhaps one explanation of Williams' name for his new measure, the "variable foot," a term which puts into one the notions of fixity and flux. Paul Fussell points out "the vagueness about the fundamental psychology of base and varia-tion" in Williams' term.[10] But it is not that Williams is confused about "base and variation" but that he deliberately subverts the distinction. Williams' notion of a relative meter, like Pound's "absolute rhythm," destroys any neat division between the grammar and the rhetoric of prosody.

Of course, the idea of the variable foot has done little to illuminate Williams' poems. His most significant innovations in prosody, furthermore, occur long before Williams coins the term, in the fifties. Critics have paid too much attention to the later, on the whole less interesting poems while neglecting the prosody of the early Williams, with his "Imagist" or "visual" concerns. The same essential technique can be found in poems of different phases of Williams' career. "Flowers by the Sea," first published in 1930, and "Iris," a poem of the nineteen-fifties, both illustrate Williams' use of the line as a unit independent of both meter and syntax. This basic technique can be seen with greater ease in a

---

9. Charles O. Hartman, "Counterpoint," in *Free Verse: An Essay on Prosody* (Princeton, N.J.: Princeton University Press, 1980), pp. 61-80.
10. Paul Fussell, *Poetic Meter and Poetic Form* (New York: Random House, 1965), p. 105.

simpler poem in which Williams establishes a pattern of syntactical
parallelism and then throws his lines out of kilter with this pattern:

> flowing edge to edge
> their clear edges meeting—
> the winds of this northern March—
> blow the bark from the trees
> the soil from the field
> the hair from the heads of
> girls, the shirts from the backs
> of the men, roofs from the
> houses, the cross from the
> church, clouds from the sky
> the fur from the faces of
> wild animals, crusts
> from scabby eyes, scales from
> the mind and husbands from wives ["The Winds," *CEP*, p. 349]

Lines correspond in number to the parallel phrases, but with "the
hair from the heads of / girls" the strict identity is broken. "Girls,"
a word which looks forward to the climactic phrase in the series—
"husbands from wives"—is thereby given rhetorical emphasis.

In "Flowers by the Sea" Williams uses the line-break in
similar ways, and for similar rhetorical effects. The poem consists
of a single sentence which describes the juxtaposition and mutual
influence of two opposing elements. More than a painting in
words, as it might first appear, it is a study in the movement of
perception, a movement in which the rhythm of the words themselves plays an important part.

> When over the flowery, sharp pasture's
> edge, unseen, the salt ocean
>
> lifts its form—chicory and daisies
> tied, released, seem hardly flowers alone
>
> but color and the movement—or the shape
> perhaps—of restlessness, whereas
>
> the sea is circled and sways
> peacefully upon its plantlike stem [*CEP*, p. 87]

This poem can be divided into "units of sense" equal in number
to the stanzas and lines of Williams' original. A poet in the tradition of earlier free verse might have transcribed it like this:

> When over the flowery, sharp pasture's/edge,
> unseen, the salt ocean//lifts its form—
>
> chicory and daisies/tied, released,
> seem hardly flowers alone//

but color and the movement—
or the shape/perhaps—of restlessness,

whereas//the sea is circled
and sways/peacefully upon its plantlike stem

Williams' line and stanza divisions, marked here by single and double slashes, only coincide with those of this version in one place, at the half-way point of the poem. Williams breaks apart each phrase, putting its end on one line and its beginning on another. One effect is to create meaningful breaks in sense, a sharp edge between the first and second lines and a lifting motion between the first and second stanzas. But more significant is the effect of the system as a whole. The dual organization of the poem is complicated by a system of sound relations which underscores the eight part division. When both line endings and phrases are considered, a pattern of assonance emerges: *unseen . . . form . . . released/seem . . . alone; shape . . . restlessness . . . sways . . . stem.* *Alone* and *stem*, ending the two halves of the poem, pick up echoes from *form* and *restlessness* respectively, words which end units of sense but which are imbedded within lines. *Unseen* and *released* are exactly parallel to each other in the first two stanzas, and this parallel is emphasized by a rhythmic pattern: *edge, unseen . . . (lifts its form) . . . tied, released. Unseen* also echoes *seem,* in that both words begin phrases. In the second half *shape* and *sways* end the first lines of their respective stanzas; the assonance is marked off by line breaks. It is hard to know when to stop the analysis: since the poem is organized in more than one way, there can be no clearcut division between significant and insignificant details. Some elements are thrown into relief by the line division, whereas others receive less emphasis. Williams' overlapping systems of organization give him control over the movement of the poem, a control which would be lacking in the relatively flat version organized solely by units of sense.

It is clear that Williams distorts natural speech rhythms in his verse; his emphasis on the "American Idiom" should not mislead us. As noted above, the "score" of the poem is most necessary when the performance demanded is most contrary to "natural expectations." Critics who assume that a natural reading is intended must resort to the visual as an explanation; they ignore the indications on the printed page while appreciating their appearance. A remark made by Marjorie Perloff in her study of Frank O'Hara is especially revealing in this respect:

> "Playing the typewriter" rather than writing in longhand inevitably leads the poet to emphasize visual prosody. For example O'Hara used long lines frequently, evidently because he liked their

appearance on the page—their ability to convey sensuality and strength. When spoken, however, these lines tend to break down into groups of twos and threes, as in the following example:

Now the violets are all gone,//the rhinocereses,//the cymbals

What is heard does not, then, reflect what is seen. O'Hara was not, for that matter, a particularly good reader of his own poetry. Like Williams, he wrote primarily for the eye rather than the ear....[11]

The passive constructions in this passage—"when spoken," "what is heard," "what is seen,"—beg the whole question of performance. "Visual prosody" in this sense implies a lack of correspondence between the written and the spoken poem. Perloff flattens the effect of O'Hara's poem, in which short units of sense are grouped together in longer lines. The commas where she has marked pauses receive little emphasis in comparison to the line-breaks:

Now the violets are all gone, the rhinocereses, the cymbals
a grisly pale has settled over the stockyard where the fur flies
and the sound
                is that of a bulldozer in heat stuck in the mud[12]

The longer line found in the poetry of O'Hara brings up an important point, that breaks between lines not only interrupt units of sense, but also create their own units. If line-breaks are to receive emphasis, syntactical pauses within lines must be robbed of some of their force. Combining Williams' original line-division with the natural divisions between units of sense produces this version:

When over the flowery, sharp pasture's/
edge,
unseen, the salt ocean//
lifts its form—
chicory and daisies/
tied, released,
seem hardly flowers alone//

but color and the movement—
or the shape/
perhaps—of restlessness,
whereas//
the sea is circled
and sways/
peacefully upon its plantlike stem

---

11. Marjorie Perloff, *Frank O'Hara: Poet Among Painters* (Austin and London: University of Texas Press, 1979), pp. 116-117.
12. Frank O'Hara, *The Collected Poems of Frank O'Hara*, ed. Donald Allen (New York: Alfred A. Knopf, 1971), p. 346.

A pattern of alternating long and short lines recurs in each half
of the poem, but the positions of sense-breaks and line-breaks
are reversed. The two halves look the same but sound quite different. In the first half of the poem Williams ends the line just
before the phrase itself is finished. The next line ends one phrase
and begins another with a rush. The effect is one of an impatient
heightening of tension, as in the closing lines of "To Elsie":

> No one
> to witness
> and adjust, no one to drive the car [*CEP*, p. 272]

The previous stanzas of this poem consist of a short line between
two longer ones, so that one would expect

> No one to witness
> and adjust
> no one to drive the car

But Williams syncopates this pattern, creating a sort of anti-pause
between *adjust* and *no one*. This effect is especially pronounced in
the beginning of "Flowers by the Sea," in the lines "edge, unseen,
the salt ocean//lifts its form—chicory and daisies." The break
between *daisies* and *tied* is less abrupt, so that the last line of the
first half of the poem is less tense. The second stanza ends in
equilibrium, with a coincidence of prosodical and syntactical
pauses. The poem moves from the tension created by the abrupt
juxtaposition of flowers and ocean to a temporary state of balance,
as the two very different things begin to exchange their qualities.

This exchange becomes complete in the second half of the
poem, as the process of perception reaches its resolution. The
effect of enjambment here is the mirror-opposite of that in the
first half: a new phrase begins near the end of each line and ends
leisurely in the next. The first line creates a state of tension
which the second relieves. Williams uses this type of line arrangement to end many of his poems: ". . . rooted, they/grip down and
begin to awaken," [*CEP*, p. 242] ". . . the pot/gay with rough
moss" [*CEP*, p. 242] ". . . And the/immaculate white bed" [*CEP*,
p. 348]. This movement is very pronounced in the last two lines
of "Flowers by the Sea":

> . . . whereas
>
> the sea is circled and sways
> peacefully upon its plantlike stem

The first half ends with a negation, a statement that the flowers
are more than they appear, "hardly flowers alone." The second
half fills in the blank created by this negation, first making

tentative movements toward defining the qualities of the flowers, and then speaking of the ocean in more definite terms. The last stanza answers the phrase which begins with "chicory and daisies" and ends with "restlessness." The more definite verbs contrast with the tentativeness of *seems* and *perhaps*. As the flowers seem to take on the qualities of the sea the sea itself becomes a flower which "sways / peacefully upon its *plantlike* stem." The disturbing element of the beginning of the poem, which reveals the restlessness of a seemingly tranquil field of flowers, becomes itself a peaceful flower. The last line of the poem falls smoothly into alternating stressed and unstressed syllables, with harmonious alliterations. The nervous, chaotic rhythm of the first lines of the poem, with their juxtapositions of stressed syllables and their tense line breaks, moves toward a tranquil equilibrium at the end of the poem.

Williams continues to use similar techniques in his poems throughout his career. A briefer analysis of "Iris," a short poem which he wrote toward the end of his life, will show the essential similarity of the later to the earlier prosody. "Iris," like "Flowers by the Sea," is a study of perception:

> a burst of iris so that
> come down for
> breakfast
>
> we searched through the
> rooms for
> that
>
> sweetest odor and at
> first could not
> find its
>
> source then a blue as
> of the sea
> struck
>
> startling us from among
> those trumpeting
> petals [*PB*, p. 30]

The units of sense would look like this:

> a burst of iris so that/
> come down for/breakfast//
>
> we searched through the/rooms
> for/that//sweetest odor

and at/first
could not/find its//source

then a blue
as/of the sea/struck//

startling us from among/
those trumpeting/petals

The first and the last stanzas present the basic pattern: a long line followed by two shorter ones. In the second stanza the word which should echo *breakfast, odor*, is cut off. The break has an effect similar to that between the first two lines of "Flowers by the Sea." *Source* is detached from the third stanza in exactly the same way, but the fourth is complete in itself: the reader of the poem has a chance to catch up and complete the phrase within the same stanza. The fifth and final stanza repeats the structure of the first. The first two units of sense both have four major stresses; the second two have three stresses each. The final unit of sense, which coincides with the final stanza, has four once again. As the search for the flowers is recounted, the phrases run ahead of their stanzas and become shorter; the movement is fast and anxious. With the burst of blue the flowers are found and the original pattern is restored: *struck* ends the fourth stanza and the poem moves back into a state of equilibrium.

Despite the necessary arbitrariness of Williams' lines, then, they result in greater control and more precise movement. A more detailed analysis of Williams' individual poems would discover even more signs of his careful craftsmanship. Williams' solution to the problem of intrinsic form is paradoxical: he makes a kind of system from what is apparently the most external aspect of form, the way in which the poem is to be performed. At the same time he avoids any other metrical constant. Thus all of the traditional resources of verse are set free for expressive purposes; no one element is made the grammatical base of prosody. Frank O'Hara, in some lecture-notes, speaks of a quality of verse which he calls "design," "the exterior aspect as opposed to the interior structure we call form."[13] "Design," of course, is a spatial word, as are "exterior" and "interior"; O'Hara discusses the appearance of the poem on the page in various poets. But design means much more than typography; it is an attitude toward poetry which enables the poet to escape from the twin dangers of "formal smothering" and "emotional spilling over." A traditional form might

---

13. Frank O'Hara, "Design etc.," in *Standing Still and Walking in New York*, ed. Donald Allen (Bolinas: Grey Fox Press, 1975), pp. 33-36.

take the poem right away from the poet and run off into the distance with the speed of half-thoughts, turgid emotions, second-hand insights, and all the rest, including a pat ending.

Free verse, on the other hand, invites the opposite danger:

The other monster . . . is the poet's passion for poetry and his own ideas; this too will tend to run away with the poem and after it has happened a few times, the poet feels that his emotions are more important than any poem, that indeed they, not words, *are* the poem.

Williams' poems contain his own solution to the apparent dilemma between form and emotion. He shifts attention to the outside of form, freeing the inside without losing control. In the end, the very distinction between exterior and interior form, like that between the grammar and the rhetoric of poetry, cannot be sustained. Williams makes a seemingly arbitrary factor, the division of verse into lines, into the very essence of his technique. In a performance of "Flowers by the Sea" or "Iris" the distinction between the intrinsic rhythms of the words and the form which is arbitrarily imposed upon them disappears. By introducing the factor of performance into prosody itself, Williams creates a form which is at once sensitive to the intrinsic shape of the materials at hand and to the demands of the artist in remaking his world.

ANNE JANOWITZ

PATERSON: AN AMERICAN CONTRAPTION

From the time William Carlos Williams first sparred with Ezra Pound on the University of Pennsylvania campus, parrying bread against caviar,[1] a mythological Dr. Williams has been developing: objective and resilient, commonsensical yet sentimental. A jack of all trades, the Doc embodies an American *bricoleur* sensibility, as proficient at writing a poem as delivering a baby. In the process of "delineating" an American poetic measure, Williams also delineated a modern poet-character, compounding a measure of Whitman[2] and an even greater part of a thoroughly American, though not usually *poetic* type, the indigenous "tinker," or inventer. If T.S. Eliot's model for poet resembles an anonymous white-coated laboratory researcher mixing emotions to find new objective correlatives, Williams' own working model can more often be found puttering around in a garage: adding and adjusting bits of machinery to make a new poem-invention. Poems, Williams said, are "mechanical objects,"[3] his metaphor culled from the other side of the romantic fence, where the image of the poem flourishes as a developing plant whose tender gardener is the poet. No, for Williams the poet cuts a figure more like that of Henry Ford, musing "that the big money [is] in economical quality production, quick turnover, cheap interchangeable easily replaced standardized parts,"[4] and though money is not the poet's goal, progress and efficiency are. Williams saw the invention of a poem as something which "the hopeful artist [might] manufacture of the materials of his art."[5] Williams returned again and again to a

1. Quoted by Harvey Breit, *The Writer Observed* (New World Publishing, 1956), p. 100. "When I was at the University of Pennsylvania, around 1905, I used to argue with Pound. I'd say 'bread' and he'd say 'caviar.' It was a sort of simplification of our positions."
2. Miller, James E., Jr., *The American Quest for a Supreme Fiction* (Chicago: University of Chicago Press, 1979), pp. 126-162.
3. Williams, W.C., *Interviews with William Carlos Williams:* "Speaking Straight Ahead," ed. Linda Wagner (New York: New Directions, 1976), p. 73.
4. Dos Passos, John, *The Big Money* (New York: Modern Library, 1973), p. 50.
5. Williams, W.C., *Interviews*, p. 77.

mechanical, manufacturing image for the "creation" of a poem. The poem must be something which "will be an organization of materials on a better basis than it had been before."[6] Williams is explicit about the poem's place within a family of inventions; just as an "automobile or kitchen stove is an organization of materials . . . poems are mechanical objects made out of words to express a certain thing."[7]

This view of the poem as an invention created by the poet-inventor fits securely within an already vital American folk myth of indigenous inventiveness. As early as 1743 Benjamin Franklin called for the American Philosophical Society to bring material wit into alliance with philosophical investigations. He suggested that the society contrive ". . . new mechanical inventions for saving labour . . . and all philosophical experiments that let light into the nature of things."[8] From Walter Hunt, inventor of the safety-pin, and Elias Howe, inventor of the sewing machine, through Bell and Edison,[9] the history of American thinking is caught up in an interest in the vitality of materials themselves. So many contraptions had been assembled by the early part of the nineteenth century that a new Patent Law had to be written in 1836. Whereas previously one had simply to pay a fee to register a patent, now one had to prove that "an invention was new, useful and workable," not merely fanciful.[10] The ability to produce such inventions shaped an heroic type in popular culture. Self-reliant, imaginative and adaptive, the inventor was capable of grappling with even the most unusual circumstances, viz. Mark Twain's Connecticut Yankee, whose home-grown inventiveness stands him in good stead in King Arthur's court: "I could make anything a body wanted—anything in the world; it didn't make a difference what; and if there wasn't any quick new-fangled way to make a thing, I could invent one."[11]

By describing the poem as an assembly of parts, Williams puts the poet in the company of those inventors, enamored with technology, who populate the nineteenth and early twentieth century landscape. In his role as tinker poet, Williams envisions his task as one of finding words to use "as objects out of which you manufacture a little mechanism you call a poem which has

6. *Ibid.*, p. 77.
7. *Ibid.*, p. 73.
8. Quoted by Edmund Fuller in *Tinkers and Genius* (New York: Hastings House Publishers, 1955), p. 89.
9. Norman, Bruce, *The Inventing of America* (New York: Taplinger Publishing Co., 1976), *passim.*
10. National Geographic Society, *Those Inventive Americans*, (N.G.S., 1971), p. 78.
11. Twain, Mark (Samuel Clemens), *A Connecticut Yankee in King Arthur's Court* (New York: Dodd, Mead, 1960), p. 5.

to deliver the goods."[12] Rather than exhibiting an aesthetic monument to intuition, the poet inventor must present an object whose aim is to be as useful as the radio, Model T, or at the very least, R.M. Gardiner's "Combined Grocer's Package, Grater, Slicer, and Louse and Fly Trap," or A. Jackson, Jr.'s "Eye Protector for Chickens" (chicken-sized spectacles designed to keep fowl from pecking out one another's eyes).

Williams' choice of a metaphor emphasizing inventive assembly was neither unprepared for nor isolated within his own community of poets and artists. His friend Robert McAlmon had written a series of essays in *The Ace* promoting the productivity and validity of an American educational system oriented towards functionality and engineering. Mike Weaver has noticed the connection between McAlmon's essays and John Dewey's essays in *The New Republic*, which voiced similar attitudes and placed a great deal of importance on what Williams would later aphoristically sum up as "No Ideas but in Things."[13] In one of his essays, Dewey says with respect to bridge-building what Williams says of poetic particularity:

> Now detail means things in concrete existence. We are familiar only with things which specifically enter into our lives and which we steadily deal with. All concepts, theories, general ideas are thin meager and ineffectual in the degree in which they are not reflective expressions of acts and events already embodied, achieved, in experience.[14]

The American poet ought to be an inventor, like the tinker who puts radios and saluting devices together out of concrete parts. The raw material of both invention and poem is detail, and it is through the arrangement of details that both UNIVAC and *Paterson* are meaningful assemblages.

The idea that within the details and within the materials one may locate a full repository of meaning is part of a curious American version of Romanticism, a sensibility which attempts to rescue spiritual values from the most banal and material objects of everyday life. The inventor who takes the available materials and turns them into a gramophone must have a special kind of faith in the materials themselves. This is the spirit of Orville Wright's report of the first flight at Kitty Hawk:

> I look with amazement upon our audacity in attempting flights.
> . . . Yet faith in our calculations, and confidence in our system

---

12. Williams, W.C., *Interviews*, p. 69.
13. Williams, W.C., *Paterson* (New York: New Directions, 1963), p. 9.
14. Dewey, John, "Education and Engineering," *The New Republic*, September 20, 1922, in *Education Today* (New York: Putnam and Co., 1940), p. 151.

> of control . . . had convinced us that with a little practice [the
> machine] could be flown.
>
> This flight lasted only twelve seconds but it was nevertheless
> the first in the history of the world in which a machine carrying
> a man had raised itself by its own power into the air in full
> flight. . . .[15]

The notion that some immanent truth can be extracted from
material objects is a hallmark of the tinker variety of American
heroism. An early and rather touching example can be found in
Walden, where the $8.74 worth of food that Thoreau eats over an
eight-month period is both exhaustively accounted for and cited as
exemplary; for so Thoreau learns that a man may use as "simple
a diet as the animals and yet retain health and strength."[16]
Throughout *Walden* we find that the "higher laws" Thoreau
learns are located through close attention to the material details
around him, be they "mechanical" or "organic." There is no
tremendous gap between appearance and ineffable reality: the
transcendent is immanent in and born from the objects in Thoreau's world.

Emerson, in his essay, "The Poet," makes a more particular
case for the hidden spirit of material things, which the poet, by
reattaching "things to nature and the whole" is able to extract
by his labors. In an even more explicit alliance of spirit and
machine, Emerson writes, "Machinery and Transcendentalism
agree well. Stage Coach and Rail Road are bursting the old legis-
lation like green withes."[17]

Whitman's 1871 "Song of the Exposition" gives a strong
voice to the idea of a latent spirit of invention. In his poem the
Muse is sighted "Bluff'd not a bit by drain-pipe, gasometers,
artificial fertilizers / . . . She's here, installed amid the kitchen
ware." To off-set the charge that American inventiveness exists
only for financial gain, Whitman declaims, "Think not our chant,
our show, merely for products gross or lucre / —it is for thee, the
soul in thee, electric, spiritual!" [lines 55-58, 236].[18]

An early twentieth century example of this same Romantic
desire to locate spiritual values in material objects appears in *The
Great Gatsby*, where Jay Gatsby's closet of shirts in a myriad of
colors represents to him the elusive spirit of success, while it also
rescues Daisy's tears from some inarticulate deep reservoir of

---

15. Norman, p. 208.
16. Thoreau, Henry David, *Walden* (New York: Clarkson Potter, Inc.), p. 194.
17. Emerson, Ralph Waldo, cited in John F. Kasson, *Civilizing the Machine* (New York: Penguin, 1977), pp. 117-118.
18. Whitman, Walt, *Leaves of Grass*, ed. Blodgett and Bradley (New York: New York University Press, 1965), pp. 195-205.

feeling: " 'They're such beautiful shirts,' she sobbed, her voice muffled in the thick folds. 'It makes me sad because I've never seen such—such beautiful shirts before.' "[19]

While these American Romantics were able to endow the machine with the spirit of the garden, Williams' use of the theme of invention is particularly his own, and distinctively Modernist. Unlike Emerson, Williams is less interested in discovering a latent spirit animating materials than in utilizing the solidity of the objects themselves. He begins from the premise that the word-objects which he uses to combine and jimmy together and arrange are themselves only, and evidence of nothing more than their thingness, their "quidditas." Rather than being repositories for feelings, deep truth, etc., things have their lives as they appear and as they combine. In *Paterson III*, Williams writes,

> Let us read

> and digest: the surface
> glistens, only the surface.
> Dig in—and you have

> a nothing, surrounded by
> a surface, [*P*, p. 123]

In 1947 Williams said, "A work of art is all surface, believe it or not. We think it is depth, but it is not."[20] Williams reunderstands an American obsession with the meanings of *things*, but unattached to a tradition of "depth," he is free to make a poetry of surface "dissonance" and "contaminant[s]." Things do not reveal a hidden spirit for Williams, as they did for his Romantic ancestors and cousins, but they do behave and make meanings through assemblages and alliances as the poet works to discover how

> to find one phrase that will
> lie married beside another for delight   ? [*P*, p. 140]

These assemblages will run like new-fangled, idiosyncratic American machines.

In the third Book of *Paterson*, the poem which advances most clearly Williams' ideas of the poem as invention, he draws a precise image for the uselessness of "digging" to find meaning. In the third section of *Paterson III*, under the sub-title "SUB-STRATUM," Williams places a "tabular account of the specimens found" [*P*, p. 139] in the Artesian well at Passaic Rolling Mill, Paterson. What follows is an account of depth readings at various

---

19. Fitzgerald, F. Scott, *The Great Gatsby* (New York: Penguin, 1975), p. 99.
20. Williams, W.C., cited in Mariani, *William Carlos Williams: A New World Naked* (New York: McGraw-Hill, 1982), p. 716.

feet, starting at 65 feet below ground level, and proceeding by
assorted increments to 2100 feet below ground level. What is
striking about the list of readings is the absence of variation among
them. At 400 feet, the specimens are filled with red shaly sandstone, and twenty-six readings later they are shaly sandstone again.
All that digging reveals little or nothing new, and Williams juxtaposes this piece of Paterson documentation against the idea of a
poetic assembly of phrases "married for delight." Williams wrests
the idea of marriage from a purely organic context and makes it
function as a method of construction. Later, in *Paterson IV*,
Williams will expand this notion and allow not only useful assembly but also that which appears inharmonious, dissonant, to
operate as the productive counter-method to excavation:

> Dissonance
> (if you are interested)
> leads to discovery [*P*, p. 176]

Throughout his work, though most extensively articulated in
Paterson, Williams proposes or searches for an alternative to the
idea of immanent revelation by focusing instead on dissonance,
assembly, and invention as methods of meaning production. He
describes the difference between his own and Hart Crane's work
in a manner which makes explicit the difference between depth
and surface poetry: "I suppose the thing was that [Crane] was
searching for something inside, while I was all for a sharp use of
materials."[21] The poet inventor is not burrowing into his soul to
make poems, but operating on fixed and visible materials.

Williams' choice of the inventor's method was not simply a
matter of making a metaphor out of the technique of poetic
assembly. It implied also a way of actually producing a poem; a
way of working in which the poet might take

> .   a mass of detail
> to interrelate on a new ground, difficultly;
> an assonance, a homologue
>   triple piled
> pulling the disparate together to clarify
> and compress [*P*, p. 20]

This method implied also a different notion of what constitutes "success" and "completion" in a poem. The Wright Brothers'
airplane could be considered successful the moment it worked, yet
it was liable to an enormous number of additions, deletions,
adjustments, etc. The plane that flew at Kitty Hawk is the basis of

---

21. Williams, W.C., cited in Conarroe, *Paterson: Language and Landscape* (University of
Pennsylvania, 1970), p. 23.

the supersonic Concorde, but was not considered incomplete because it was not a space age transport. When dealing with inventions, in other words, completion can never be assumed. If the Sony Walkman is complete, how can we describe the Walkman II? Similarly, Edison's phonograph was successful when it worked, but could be improved upon and added to, viz. the Dolby stereo systems of today. The poem-invention also can be considered successful and whole without being finished in the sense of rigidly closed. The poem-invention can have a measure of integrity at any stage at which it works, without precluding the possibility of supplementary ornamentation, increased efficiency or added functions. Of course, the poem is read across time, and so additions must *work* with parts that come earlier. Williams took this "inventerly" approach to his own writing and also to his reading of other poems: "In considering a poem, I don't care whether it's finished or not; if it's put down with a good relation to the parts, it becomes a poem."[22]

Paterson was originally conceived as a four-part poem, but that plan was supplemented by the addition of *Paterson V*, in 1958. The completion of a poem thus becomes a relative matter: if the relation between parts is good, and if it delivers the goods, then it is successful. The *Paterson* invention is designed for everyday life: "It wouldn't do to have a grand a soul-satisfying conclusion, because I didn't see any in the subject."[23] An invention works smoothly or it breaks down; it is useful or it isn't; it succeeds or it doesn't; but it rarely *concludes*, the way a novel or a film does.

In *Paterson*, Williams works out the possibilities of his inventor's model of the poem as a contraption. A periodically updated, assembled poem, *Paterson* was the result of a tinkering process begun as early as 1926, and continuing up to Williams' death.[24] The entire year before the first printing of *Paterson I* (1946), Williams tampered and puttered with the galleys. In a letter to Rexroth, he describes this process: "I slashed, right and left, reedited bits here and there, pulled things together as best I was able. . . ."[25] The technique Williams used allowed for easy redistributions and rearrangements: "cheap easily interchangeable parts." A romantic or narrative poem, on the other hand, conceived of as an organism, may atrophy if limbs are severed, and

22. Williams, *Interviews*, p. 53.
23. Sankey, Benjamin, *Companion to Paterson* (Berkeley: Univ. of California Press, 1971), p. 211.
24. Laughlin, James, "William Carlos Williams and the Making of *Paterson*," *The Yale Review*, 71 (1981), p. 188.
25. Williams, W.C., cited in Mariani, p. 509.

certainly would not admit to a form constructed rather than immanently developed.

As a contraption worked on over three decades, *Paterson* necessarily is something of a map of the poet's development as man and poet, somewhat disparate in the topics it picks up and leaves off again, and somewhat rambling, sometimes inconsistent. At the same time, however, such discrepancies, disparities, and developments are inevitable in an encyclopedic genre of poetry where, as Robert Lowell said of *Paterson*, "the best readers, as well as the simple readers, are likely to find *everything*."[26] The structure of the poem is embracing, and this inclusiveness is articulated by the end of *Paterson IV* as the triumph of the "dissonant," but such a structure of inclusivity must be won through the course of the poem. Williams had some difficulty maintaining his commitment to a method of assembling materials which posits no revelation of a latent truth or principle. Against his desire to show things in their discrete, articulate form, Williams must contend with the weight of the Romantic inventerly tradition, positing ineffability beneath particularity. The organic image of the Passaic Falls and River, emitting an inarticulate roar, stands in opposition to the mechanical materials of invention. Williams, however, was anxious to circumvent the lure of the Falls, and much of the process of *Paterson* is a struggle against the claims of Romanticism. Against the pull of a subtending One, Williams appeals to the "one" of the particular; the particular one which can combine and be multiplied to make meaning. In his essay on Marianne Moore, Williams wrote that good modern work displays a "multiplication of impulses that by their several flights, crossing at eccentric angles, *might* enlighten."[27] As the tabular account reveals that at 2100 feet below surface one finds only more shaly sandstone, so Williams argues against the idea of poetry revealing knowledge. Poetry *makes* knowledge.

The "Preface" to *Paterson* can be read as an anti-Romantic manifesto. Williams opens the poem by figuring the traditional poem-plant as festering and unproductive:

> (The multiple seed,
> packed tight with detail, soured,
> is lost in the flux and the mind,
> distracted, floats off in the same
> scum) [P, p. 4]

26. Lowell, Robert, review in *The Nation*, 19 June 1948, in Charles Doyle, ed., *W. C. Williams: The Critical Heritage* (Boston: Routledge & Kegan Paul, 1975), p. 185.
27. Williams, W.C., "Marianne Moore," in *Imaginations* (New York: New Directions, 1970), p. 312.

Against organicism, Williams counterposes organization and inductive reasoning, making a "start, / out of particulars . . . / rolling / up the sum" [*P*, p. 3]. The list which stands in apposition to the opening of the "Preface," begins out of nowhere, following an unanchored colon: ": a local pride; spring, summer, fall and the sea; . . ." [*P*, p. 2]. It quickly heaps up pieces so that there may be "by multiplication a reduction to one." The "one" is the efficient contraption, composed of discrete bits working together, not a transcendent One which subtends materiality. The poet's task is to make an order out of pieces—an order made through an art challenging European models by "rolling up" bits, instead of excavating into depths, as its method of making poetic meaning. Gathering the materials to meet that challenge takes up the greater part of the poem. His "means," he says, are "defective" [*P*, p. 3]. By the end of *Paterson IV*, however, the idea of the defective will be transformed into the triumphant poetic of the "dissonant": like Madame Curie's radium, the unexpected dissonance will become the site for the production of meaning. In the "Preface" to *Paterson I*, however, all Williams can be sure of is that latent, undisclosed and hidden meanings are much the same as *no* meanings at all:

> knowledge,
> undispersed, its own undoing [*P*, p. 4].

In one of the first sustained reviews of *Paterson I*, Randall Jarrell wrote, "The subject of *Paterson* is: How can you tell the truth about things?"[28] The first book of *Paterson* counterposes two ways of "telling the truth": the intuitive way of the pre-articulate roar of the Falls, and the clumsy but necessary speech of human society and everyday life. It is not that Williams chooses one above the other, but rather that he wants to mediate between "the roar of the river," chaotic but full, and the weak, but potentially communicative voice of contemporary language. Analogous to the deep force we have described in the Romantic unfinished poem, the pre-articulate river in *Paterson* shares with Romanticism a notion of latency, but significantly, Williams is not prepared to make it a metaphysic. The Romantic depth in Williams' terms is more like Tennyson's brute nature: not benign, but dangerous.

The Falls is "A Wonder!" Without a human language, it is capable of beckoning to those who intuit its force and its violence. *Paterson I* houses characters who rush headlong into the water's "violent torrent" and then disappear. Mrs. Sarah Cummings

---

28. Jarrell, Randall, review in *Partisan Review*, 13 (1946), in Doyle, p. 175.

apparently chose the water above her husband, while Sam Patch, daredevil, is an accomplice of the Falls until he attempts to turn its power into discrete words. When he turns to speechifying, Patch loses touch with the water. Patch's failure to make the flowing pre-articulate roar of the Falls concrete is captured in a section Williams quotes directly from Charles Pitman Longwell's *A Little Story of Old Paterson* (1901):[29]

> But instead of descending with a plummet-like fall his body
> wavered in the air— Speech had failed him. He was confused.
> The word had been drained of its meaning [*P*, p. 17].

While the Falls devour, they also illuminate the principle of original undifferentiated potential which is also an erotic principle:

> We sit and talk,
> quietly, with long lapses of silence
> and I am aware of the stream
> that has no language, coursing
> beneath the quiet heaven of
> your eyes
>
>   which has no speech [*P*, p. 24]

The "stream / that has no language" is both welcoming and erotic, but it is also dangerous, viz. the deaths of Patch and Mrs. Cummings. Williams' problem is to find a way to translate the "coursing" force of the water into the discrete language of the poem-invention.

As *Paterson I* opens, the inhabitants of the town are also languageless, "incommunicado," but their lack of speech reflects a damming up, not a release. Their autism is a loss, an emptiness in sharp contrast to the fullness of the falling waters: "They do not know the words / or have not / the courage to use them" [*P*, p. 11]. Though their minds are as tempest tossed as the Falls,

> They may look at the torrent in
>   their minds
> and it is foreign to them [*P*, p. 12].

The poet must intervene among these dammed up people and "comb out" a "common language" [*P*, p. 7]. To bridge the distance between those whose language has "failed" and a theoretical or abstract poetic, Williams mandates, "Say it! No ideas but in things" [*P*, p. 9]. In this way Williams prepares to translate the flowing, prearticulate world into the terms of specific forms and objects, not in the terms of unspoken, vague longings. The river stands beside life in the city in much the same way that life stands

---

29. Weaver, Mike, *William Carlos Williams: The American Background* (Cambridge: Cambridge University Press, 1971), p. 118.

beside poetry: prior, unmediated, flowing. Williams wants to transform that essence into the discrete, combinatory pieces that make up the poem-invention: pieces of prose and verse, letters, historical documents. The principle of assemblage and juxtaposition disrupts the "disease of thinking in essences"[30] by building instead of excavating.

When the poet makes his invention the center of his concern, however, he may have to pay a price, and Williams acknowledges this risk in the letters from "Cress" strewn through the text of *Paterson*. The danger incurred by focusing on perfection of the work and not the life is mentioned in the first prose passage interwoven with *Paterson I*'s verse passages. "It was," "Cress" complains, "the human situation and not the literary one that motivated my phone call and visit" [*P*, p. 7], introducing a theme that will reoccur many times in the whole of *Paterson*. As the river challenges the poet by its inarticulate roar, so Cress challenges him by her intransigent feelings.

Speech, like Sam Patch's and like that of the Reverend Cummings, is an instrument of divorce and separation, and yet it is the only tool with which one can invent the American poem. The artist may be liable to the kind of criticism "Cress" makes, yet his kind of work is necessary if divorce is to be mended. As the second part of *Paterson I* opens, divorce is named as "the sign of knowledge in our time" [*P*, p. 18]. Divorce embraces a variety of forms: connubial, imaginative, political, economic—and yet, paradoxically, as a sign of knowledge, the discrete, divorced words *are* the ways that knowledge is conveyed. Language originates in differentiation, alienation, and divorce—the fall from the Tower of Babel—but must be made the instrument for the functional poem-invention. Williams experiments with a poetic language which will inself be undifferentiated, undivorced; a language which will mime the flow of the river itself. He does this in a section filled with words whose sounds blend into one another, shifting meanings as "divorce" is temporarily overcome through sliding sounds: " . . . The how (the howl) . . . my disposal (proposal) . . . our ears (arrears)" [*P*, p. 18]. This experiment is rather limited, however, and the words each emerge individual and intact. This trial at an "organic" language is jettisoned again through the image of

> a bud forever green,
> tight-curled, upon the pavement, perfect
> in juice and substance but divorced, divorced
> from its fellows, fallen low— [*P*, p. 18]

---

30. Roland Barthes, quoted in Gerald Graff, "Textual Leftism," *Partisan Review*, 4 1982), p. 568.

Though nostalgically drawn to the organic metaphor, Williams turns elsewhere to find the structural principle for his poem-invention. While the "roar / of eternal sleep" [*P*, p. 18] lulls, "Two halfgrown girls" [*P*, p. 18] make an image for the paradox Williams explores: they are cut from a piece, like the ribbons which bind their hair; but they are also individual and "disparate among the pouring / waters of their hair" [*P*, p. 19]. In order to make a poem-invention, the poet must uproot things from their origins, name and articulate what is visibly in front of him. Thus, though he inevitably loses the immediacy of the unspoken experience, the *meaning* of the experience can be recorded. While so many Romantic poems hover at the edges of articulation, stepping off into the ineffable, the Williams poem will embody a poetic of *what is*: "No ideas but in the facts" [*P*, p. 28].

The image of the river continues to pull at the poet's imagination. The river swallows people and their languages, returning only ice-caked or mud-racked bodies, "silent, uncommunicative" [*P*, p. 21]. The river, unfathomable as the African wife upon whose photograph Williams meditates, is a mystery at once "a source, a scourge" [*P*, p. 21]. The oscillation between the flowing and the discrete is played out again here, for as much as the river can preclude communication, the pre-articulate offers direct contact with the speechless imagination, like the flower which

> crouching
> among the ferny rocks, laughs at the names
> by which they think to trap it. Escapes!
> Never by running but by lying still— [*P*, p. 22]

or like the "stream that has no language" linking lover to lover. It is this pre-articulate organic pull that opens the third part of *Paterson I*:

> How strange you are, you idiot!
> So you think because the rose
> is red that you shall have the mastery?
> The rose is green and will bloom,
> overtopping you, green, livid
> green when you shall no more speak, or
> taste, or even be [*P*, p. 30].

Life recovers itself infinitely, while the same has not been proved for poetic machinery. Yet only through that poetic concatenation of pieces can such "overtopping" principles of life be imaged concretely. Without the poetic communication offered through assembled images, the truth of the source/scourge lies

```
                    shut from
   the world—and unknown to the world,
   cloaks itself in mystery—  [P, p. 39]
```

There may very well be, within the romantic river, a depth harboring the principle of "Earth, the chatterer, father of all / speech ..." [*P*, p. 39], but such a principle is ultimately unproductive if left untranslated for the human ear into a concrete image. Williams replaces the familiar notion of an Earth Mother with that of a Father to emphasize the unproductiveness of the uncommunicative speech of the falls. It is the Mother who brings new beings into the world, translating passion productively, while the father of speech, though he harbors a latent principle, cannot make it concrete. More important than a principle is what is actually produced: what can be said and assembled and constructed out of language on the surface of the world. The poem-invention should be the articulate form of the chaotic falls. In a 1929 essay, "The Simplicity of Disorder," Williams had used an image analogous to this concern: "Writing should be like that . . . the storm grown vocal."[31]

The opening to Book II of *Paterson* approaches the external world "concretely" [*P*, p. 43], and what appears most concretely to Paterson's ear is the variety of the American voice. In a 1948 essay, "The Poem as a Field of Action," Williams made explicit his notion of the importance of speech to the new poetic: "Where else can what we are seeking arise from but speech? From speech, . . . from what we *hear* in America."[32] Paterson, doctor and poet, strolls through the park on Sunday and witnesses the multiformity of life through its voices. Williams himself desired artistic and aesthetic multiformity, and he associated such a delight in the many faceted with the future of the American poem-invention; "It is as though for the moment we should be profuse, we Americans; we need to build up a mass, a conglomerate maybe, containing few gems but bits of them . . . that shine of themselves, uncut as they are."[33] These "brilliants" populate the Park scene and though they do not generate light, they do emit

```
                         Voices!
   multiple and inarticulate      voices
   chattering loudly to the sun, to
   the clouds. Voices!
   assaulting the air gaily from all sides [P, p. 54].
```

31. Williams, W.C. "The Simplicity of Disorder," in *Selected Essays* (New York: New Directions, 1954), p. 95.
32. Williams, W.C. "The Poem as a Field of Action," in *Selected Essays*, pp. 289-290.
33. *Ibid.*, p. 285.

Williams pulls together snatches of conversations from among the picnickers and assembles them into a collage of local sounds:

> Come on! Wassa ma'? You got
> broken leg? . . .
> Look a' me, Grandma! Everybody too damn
> lazy [P, p. 57].

The voices of the park people blend with Paterson's own, generating the imaginative poem machine:

> So during the early afternoon, from place
> to place he moves,
> his voice mingling with other voices
> —the voice in his voice [P, p. 56].

It is in combination with other bits of gadgetry that the raw material, the multiple and inarticulate voices, become productive and useful, their voices becoming part of the one entity of his voice.

Early in Book II, Williams, with a parodic glance at Pound's "Usura" canto, inserts a section on "invention," playing with its meanings as classical rhetorical term, as imaginative expression, and as modern mechanism. This section culminates in a sequence of lines which hark back nostalgically to a mythical moment when articulation and ineffability could be combined:

> without invention the line
> will never again take on its ancient
> divisions when the word, a supple word,
> lived in it, crumbled now to chalk [P, p. 50].

The poet wishes to recover, through invention, an elastic "supple" word, a word capable of overcoming the divorce which is "the sign of knowledge" in his times. A hawk soaring beyond the park's parameters renders an image of just such elasticity:

> —and the imagination soars, as a voice
> beckons, a thundrous voice, endless
> —as sleep: the voice
> that has ineluctably called them—
> that unmoving roar! [P, p. 55].

But in the image we hear the tone of the dangerous voice of the river, beckoning in order to silence, through sleep. Invention must proceed differently—by multiplication. To countervail the undifferentiated voice of an "unmoving roar," human voices must be heard—"defective" though those voices may be. His fundamental sympathy with these raw sounds is markedly different in tone from Eliot's attitude towards his "young man carbuncular."[34]

---

34. Eliot, T.S. *Collected Poems* (New York: Harcourt, Brace, & World, 1963), p. 62.

The poet inventor advances not through the nostalgia for the pre-articulate, but by embracing the various world around him: "an elucidation by multiplicity" [*P*, p. 61].

When the second part of *Paterson II* begins, it is with a heavy pun: "Blocked," the poet writes, "(Make a song out of that: concretely)" [*P*, p. 62]. Williams wonders here whether the effort towards poetic concretion will make the poem invention thick and heavy. Will a commitment to the particular in all its multiform materiality forbid access to the truth and meaning promised by the ineffable river? The crisis of *Paterson II*, a series of blockages experienced by "Cress," by Paterson, by the very body of America, deepens in the third section, relieved only by the invocation of memory and by Williams' introduction of his newest invention: the triadic foot of the variable American measure.

The third part of *Paterson II* is the most frightening and exhilarating moment in the poem so far, for here the poet pits the intensity of the river's roar against the necessity to

> Be reconciled, poet, with your world, it is
> the only truth! [*P*, p. 84]

As the section begins, Williams meditates on the transformation of the blockages and defeats into new and unexpected productions:

> No defeat is made up entirely of defeat—since
> the world it opens is always a place
>   formerly
>   unsuspected [*P*, p. 78].

Amidst the solid concretion of "things" ranges memory, which can produce and invent, modifying "things" themselves until

>   no whiteness (lost) is so white as the memory
> of whiteness   . [*P*, p. 78]

Paterson approaches the river again as the park begins to empty at the end of the long day. A dialogue then ensues between the poet's voice and that of a woman who argues for the "inventorly" action above the "organic" roar: "Stones invent nothing, only a man invents" [*P*, p. 82]. The woman's voice holds out a productive call to the poet:

> Invent (if you can) discover or
> nothing is clear— [*P*, p. 84]

Robert Lowell reviewed *Paterson II* by saying that it is about failure: the failure of marriage within a more general failure of the masculine and feminine principles to connect.[35] And so it may be,

---

35. Lowell, *The Nation*, in Doyle, pp. 188-189.

partially, but it is also about the possibility of failure generating
the new in a significant manner, as "a world unsuspected / beckons
to new places" [*P*, p. 78]. Noteworthy also is that it is in the
midst of a section about failure that Williams first unveiled what
was to him his most important technical invention: the triadic
variable foot.

The structure of the foot has been most aptly described by
Williams himself, who points out that the variable triadic line has
as its most salient feature its *relative* quality. He links the concept to Einstein's theories and to non-Euclidean geometries: "A
relative order is operative elsewhere in our lives. . . . Are we so
stupid that we can't see that the same things apply to the construction of modern verse. . . ?"[36] The relative character of the
variable foot makes it supple, something to be *worked* with,
veering far from the rigidity of patterns like the iambic pentameter: "We have today to do with the poetic, as always, but a *relatively* stable foot, not a rigid one."[37] The variable foot is an
invention which fuses the impulse of romantic organicism with the
functionalism of machinery. This impulse is organic in that its
suppleness allows an unmediated individuality of timbre, voice
and imaginative thrust in any particular poetic passage, yet it is
machine-like in its clear delineation of a (relatively) equalized
length of time alloted to each foot. "If the foot itself is variable
it allows order in so-called free verse. Thus the verse becomes not
free at all but just simply variable, as all things in life properly
are."[38] Unlike iambic pentameter, however, where boundaries
are rigidly maintained for each line, the variable foot is like the
invention which can be added to, extended or shortened to
accommodate the needs of a particular line.

Williams closes the third book of *Paterson* with a succinct
statement of his poetic goal:

> I must
> find my meaning and lay it, white,
> beside the sliding water: myself—
> comb out the language—or succumb [*P*, p. 145]

In the course of *Paterson III*, a meditation on the local library, the
swell of language in books mounts ever higher until it is indis-
tinguishable from the river's roar: language is the "visible part" of
the Falls. The poet must choose between succumbing, diving into
the roar, or combing out the language, giving it particular discrete and concrete meanings. The poet must "find a place / apart

---

36. Williams, W.C. "On Measure," *Selected Essays*, p. 337.
37. *Ibid.*, p. 340.
38. Laughlin, p. 192.

from " the roar where he can manage and then *use* language: he must escape from being "its slave, / its sleeper, bewildered." By so doing, Paterson/poet may be able to name and so capture the Beautiful Thing who haunts the pages of *Paterson III*, but who is alive and immediate, a counterpoint to the musty books which

> mount and complicate them-
> selves, lead to further texts and those
> to synopses, digests and emendations [*P*, p. 130].

The library is filled with the smell of "stagnation and death"; it is there ironically, amidst all that codified speech, that one is exhorted to "SILENCE." The Beautiful Thing to whom the poet addresses *Paterson III* eludes the library's volumes, for "the province of the poem is the world," and Beautiful Thing is utterly of the world. What kind of construction, then, can the poet assemble to distinguish his work from the "texts and further texts" which litter the library? One way is through multiformity and what Williams referred to as "profusion": "We seek profusion, the Mass—heterogeneous—ill-assorted—quite breathless—grasping at all kinds of things."[39] The "new constructions" Williams wants to build will be created through assembly: "Not at *this* time an analysis so much as an accumulation."[40]

The task for the poet, to invent a song "to make death tolerable," relies for its realization, not on a single purposeful archaeology, but on a "defiance of authority," visualized on the page as an assortment of surprises and fragments and bits, like Sappho's poems, "unwrapped, fragment by fragment, from / outer mummy cases of papier mâché inside / Egyptian sarcophagi" [*P*, p. 119].

The act of writing a poem transforms clutter into assembled organization, though the clutter may be gathered from a variety of sources. But the poem is not a junkyard of pieces, and Williams avoids the completely random in his juxtapositions of debris. Only one page of *Paterson* mimes DADAistic conventions of mislinea-ations, non-sequitors, and arbitrary juxtapositions. That page con-trasts with the more inventive juxtapositions which constitute the body of the text of *Paterson*. In fact, though Williams had a strong connection personally to New York DADA through Man Ray and others, he did not see his interleaving of poetry and prose as an "anti-art" manner.[41] He had earlier produced similar effects in *Spring and All*, of which he said:

39. Williams, W.C. "The Poem as a Field of Action," *Selected Essays*, p. 284.
40. *Ibid.*, p. 285.
41. Tashjian, Dickran. *William Carlos Williams and the American Scene* (New York and Berkeley: Whitney Museum of Art and University of California Press, 1978), p. 60.

> As a poet I was using a means of getting an effect. It's all one
> to me—the anti-poetic is not something to enhance the poetic—
> it's all one piece.[42]

These letters, prose passages from historical texts, remembered
conversations, lists, anecdotes, etc. are assembled into a working
machine. Like other inventions, it is capable of being added to,
enlarged, expanded in form and content:

> I was aware that it wasn't a finished form, yet I knew it was not
> formless. I had to invent my form, if form it was. I was writing
> in a modern occidental world.[43]

For the most part, the assemblage technique of *Paterson* is a
generating, productive combination of *perspectives*. The kinship
between the form of *Paterson* and Cubism lies in the way in
which, for example, the juxtaposition of historical documentation
and contemporary observation force the reader into shifting
perspectives on the same phenomenon. The materiality of the
Falls oscillates between nineteenth and twentieth century views,
between "historical" and "imaginative" ones. What is finally
generated is less a sense of the "true" falls than multiple ways of
"seeing" them. This technique is similar to Cubist painting, for
example Braque's "Pitcher and Violin," which superimposes a
variety of perspectives one atop the other.

It is just such a rattling of perspectives as an overall structure
that allows the reader to find a multiplicity of meanings in *Paterson*. One early reviewer wrote:

> Through *Paterson* one may walk or fly or stagger a dozen times—
> one proceeds in a different way at each reading of the poem—and
> emerges each time with a different set of meanings, a different
> sense of the fusion of the parts, and a different feeling of exhalta-
> tion and exasperation.[44]

With a myriad of juxtapositions grouping themselves into ever
larger configurations throughout the poem, the multiformity that
Williams aspired to was constantly regenerated. For example, the
juxtaposition of the fierce and real letters of "Cress" against the
imaginary stroll of the giant Paterson creates a new arena of meaning where neither the imaginary nor the real take precedence, but
both vibrate and electrify. There is nothing more or less real, more
or less "true" to choose, and so without befores, behinds, aboves
and belows, the surface of the poem creates an *excess* of meanings
rather than revealing an *essential* meaning.

---

42. Williams, W. C. *I Wanted to Write a Poem* (New York: New Directions, 1977), p. 52.
43. *Ibid.*, p. 74.
44. Honig, Edwin, review in *Poetry*, 1947, in Doyle, p. 180.

In the process of *Paterson*, the romantic search for a hidden or latent truth is replaced by a surface radiation of meanings, expressed most clearly in the image of Marie Curie's discovery of radium, "the stain of sense," and "the radiant gist that / resists the final crystallization" [*P*, p. 109], which is hinted at in Book Three of *Paterson*, but developed most fully in *Paterson IV*. The image of radium works well as a vehicle for what Williams wants to express because the "luminous stain" is an image of a vibrating excess. There ought to have been nothing left at the bottom of Madame Curie's retort, and instead there appeared a luminous contaminant. The residuum cannot be accounted for methodologically. Its appearance is an unexpected supplement, and signals a break-through. Radioactivity and luminosity are not buried essences, but surface excesses.

It is here that the poem-invention begins to differentiate itself from a practical invention or machine, precisely by its excess. And its excessiveness is a function of poetry's "self-delighting"[45] mode of functioning. While it may be pleasurable to fly an airplane, that pleasure is really only a by-product of the plane's major purpose, which is to transport. Most inventions are produced for a purpose: air travel, the transmission of sound (telephone), popcorn. We might say that inventions in general are "transitive," while the particular character of the poem-invention is that it is "intransitive." The poem-invention simply produces itself, and in this self-generating process it produces an *excess* of itself. I do not mean to suggest that the poem "invents" itself. *Paterson* was clearly written by W. C. Williams; but the goal or purpose of *Paterson* is to be a poem and what the assembly makes is poem-ness. The work may embrace a host of themes and concerns, ranging from ones as general as "how to tell the truth," to ones as specific as Williams' relationship with "Cress." However, the poem's mode is intransitive in that what it produces is not detachable but surfacely *supplemental* to itself. The collage of pieces generate meanings that are neither traceable to a subtending principle nor reducible to essential qualities of the pieces. In *Paterson V*, Williams explained it this way:

> In poetry, you're listening to two things . . . you're listening to the sense, the common sense of what it says. But it says more. That is the difficulty [*P*, p. 225].

---

45. Yeats, W.B. "Prayer for My Daughter," *Collected Poems* (New York: Macmillan, 1956), p. 214.

The intransitively productive machine—the poem-invention—while it radiates and generates, is also subject to and suffers breakdowns. As opposed to a conventional machine, however, the poem-invention can still be productive even when *en panne*: thus is it mechanically superior to the popcorn machine. For example, the "blockages" in Book II, the frequent doubts and misgivings which litter the text of *Paterson* are the mechanical breakdowns which generate new meanings and themes. Williams' central metaphor for this breakdown and generation is that of radium and uranium:

> Uranium, the complex atom, breaking
> down, a city in itself, that complex
> atom, always breaking down
> to lead [*P*, p. 178].

In that breakdown, that "dissonance in the valence" of uranium, something new is engendered. When the parts don't work properly, a discovery can be made, "a new world unsuspected."

> Dissonance
> (if you are interested)
> leads to discovery [*P*, p. 176]

As the stain turns luminous, the contaminant wrenches askew ". . . order, perfect and controlled / on which empires, alas, are built" [*P*, p. 179]. The contaminant which produces "knowledge" is not revealed or pulled out from some great depth, but emitted, like a pulse. Luminosity from a stain, discovery through dissonance, a new awakening through descent—these are all modes of redemption which mend a failed language machine and achieve concretion in *Paterson IV*'s radium metaphor.

In the final section of *Paterson IV*, the voice of the poet struggles once again against the organic ocean, protesting that "the sea is not our home" over and over in an incantatory charm against the great roar where the river meets the ocean. Like Odysseus exhorting his men against the voices of the sirens, Williams calls,

> I say to you, Put wax rather in your
> ears against the hungry sea
>   it is not our home!
>
>   draws us in to drown, of losses
> and regrets   . [*P*, p. 201]

In this struggle against the claims of the pre-articulate oceanic roar, the poet puts himself fully on the side of invention, drawing on the strength of the woman interlocutor who had admonished him earlier, "stones invent nothing, only a man invents." The "Blast," the "eternal close" that follows Paterson walking "inland, followed by the dog" [*P*, p. 203], is an understated vision of the poet reconciled to his world: a world in which he stands close to the water and, though part of him longs for its inchoate roar, he turns to produce the inventorly poem through discrete words.

Unexpectedly, *Paterson V*. Just at the moment when the poet had reconciled himself to the world, the world itself reemerges as Art. The prose passages which intercept the poet's argument with himself are now populated, in the early pages of *Paterson V*, by the poetic values that have been the ground of the poem. The letter-writers have become fully poets. And as poets, they are representatives of a poetic enjoining,

> Not prophecy! NOT prophecy!
>   but the thing itself! [*P*, p. 208]

"Cress" is replaced by "Josie," who understands the right relation of work and life: "How lovely to read your memories of the place; a place is made of memories as well as the world around it" [*P*, p. 210]. Allen Ginsberg, whose own poem, *Howl*, is juxtaposed to Williams', in an "optional feature" of the *Paterson* machine, writes to Williams, "In any case Beauty is where I hang my hat. And reality. And America" [*P*, p. 213]. Williams' voice is incorporated in *Howl* as the introduction, and Ginsberg's is a collage-element in *Paterson*. The world and art are interconnected.

As the poet turns to reality in order to write, from reality there issues a new contaminant, death. The dissonance between death and the imagination generates an escape hatch for the poet. Through a rent, a "hole in the bottom of the bag," death is displaced by

>   the imagination
> which cannot be fathomed.
> It is through this hole
> we escape [*P*, p. 212].

The imagination, allied to memory, now triumphs *in* reality, not as a threat against it:

> Pollock's blobs of paint squeezed out
> with design!
> pure from the tube. Nothing else
> is real [*P*, p. 213].

As the poet watches the reality of approaching death,

> —the aging body
>   with the deformed great-toe nail
> makes itself known [*P*, p. 232]

that reality itself is transfigured by the imagination clambering up out of the hole and making its transformations on the assemblages of the invention. The Romantic idea of the deep principle is translated into the image of a hole: an escape route rather than a limit. When Williams was asked how *Paterson* would end, he said that the only way to close the poem would be to "go on repeating it."[46] In his absence the poem repeats and replicates itself, constantly shifting its juxtapositions and collage effects; the *Paterson* machine keeps working.

---

46. Williams, *Interviews*, p. 73.

MARILYN KALLET

"CONVERSATION AS DESIGN" IN
"ASPHODEL, THAT GREENY FLOWER"*

One way in whcih Williams manages to make his extended poem "Asphodel, That Greeny Flower" sound simple and direct is by creating a tone of intimacy. The speaker in the poem, the aging poet Williams, talks directly to his wife as if he were speaking to himself. He appeals to his wife's understanding and generosity:

> I call on you
> as I do on myself the same
> to forgive . . . [PB, p. 175]†

It is remarkable that Williams can sustain an atmosphere of intimacy throughout a thirty page poem, one that includes references to other works of art from Homer to Rimbaud. This modern confessional poem has epic qualities; it is inclusive of cultural figures and historical notes in the way that Pound's *Cantos* are inclusive, or in the way that Joyce's *Ulysses* manages to include a world in its story. "Asphodel" covers the epic space of the seas, but "seen" through the bones and body of the aging bard, Williams; covers a deep vertical space or "stem" in its mythic journey

*Copyright © 1955 by William Carlos Williams.
†The following abbreviations of book titles are used in the essay. All works are by William Carlos Williams.

A   *The Autobiography of William Carlos Williams* (New York: New Directions, 1967).
CEP   *The Collected Earlier Poems* (New York: New Directions, 1966).
I   *Imaginations* (New York: New Directions, 1971).
IWWP   *I Wanted to Write a Poem* (Boston: Beacon Press, 1958).
P   *Paterson* (New York: New Directions, 1963).
PB   *Pictures from Brueghel* (New York: New Directions, 1962).
SE   *The Selected Essays of William Carlos Williams* (New York: New Directions, 1954).
UTA   Humanities Research Center, University of Texas at Austin holdings of Williams' manuscripts.
YALC   Yale American Library Collection of Williams' manuscripts. Yale University, New Haven, Connecticut.

All previously unpublished writings by William Carlos Williams copyright © 1978 by the Estate of Florence H. Williams.

to the depths of memory. Chaos, the sea, has been ruled for the moment by the measure of the poet's love, and "the sea . . . sways / peacefully upon its plantlike stem" [*CEP*, p. 87]. "Asphodel" tells a story of renewed love in old age. But within the poet's account of his relearning to love, his song includes an interweaving of various thematic strands or leitmotifs. The narrative is more circular than linear, moving from an address to Flossie, out to an examination of self in the world, and of the world's history, back to Flossie again. The poem becomes a symphony, a world with its complexities, yet "Asphodel" is primarily a personal lyric because of its tone. Intimacy provides a unity of effect: the poem is a gift for Flossie: "I bring you / a last flower" [*PB*, p. 178].

Epic poets in the heroic age of Greece were credited with "qualities of memory and vision" that enabled them to "rescue the past from oblivion, restoring it to life and moving their hearers to pity and fear."[1] Williams wants to rescue his past with Flossie, to restore their love, and move her to pity and love. Through the story of their love's renewal "every man / who wants to die at peace in his bed" will learn of the imagination's powers [*PB*, p. 162]. The song is launched with an inverted phrase that calls to mind the opening line of *The Aeneid*. Yet instead of "arms and the man" Williams sings "to you" "of asphodel," the "greeny," ghostly flower of memory. He turns the impulse for war into a journey to love; he wills this new beginning with a mythical flower, made delicate and personal in his song.

The effect of embracing a modern epic within the lyric, personal voice is to make the world personal for the reader, to create the "human universe" that Charles Olson spoke of in his essay by that name.[2] The poet or reader who is intimate with his or her feelings, whose response to the world begins at the skin, feels a connection to others and to the world. He or she cannot treat the world as refuse. Williams refers to the threat of the atom bomb within his love poem—the bomb is there as a warning against the impersonal. Like Anais Nin, for whom Williams felt an affinity,[3] Williams speaks with the conviction that the personal voice, the particular voice, is responsible for the world:

> To make a start,
> out of particulars
> and make them general . . . [*P*, p. 11]

---

1. "Epic. Theory," *Princeton Encyclopedia of Poetry and Poetics*, 1974 Edition, p. 242.
2. "Human Universe," *Human Universe and Other Essays* (New York: Grove Press, 1967), pp. 3-23.
3. Williams, "Men . . . Have No Tenderness," *New Directions* 7, ed. James Laughlin (Norfolk: New Directions, 1942), pp. 429-436.

Williams involves the reader through direct address: "I come, my sweet / to sing to you" [*PB*, p. 153]. Here the poet sings to his wife, but establishes a connection with the reader as well, makes the reader into a friend. Baudelaire also implicates the reader by means of direct address: "Tu le connais, lecteur . . . / – Hypocrite lecteur,–Mon semblable,–mon frère!"[4] But Williams' tone is one of tenderness, not derision. Williams and his wife are "semblables," equals, because they have lived long together, and Williams will create his readers into equals by sharing his experience with them. The poet and his readers are "innocent of heart" in this collaboration, this attempt to oppose the creations of the imagination against death's destroying powers. Williams cannot afford to be a hypocrite in "Asphodel," for the poem is a death song, a song of resoluteness and affirmation in the face of death. His song is a test and a proof of having existed; he sings as a tribal warrior would sing:

> Let us see, is this real
> Let us see, is this real
> This life I am living.[5]

The poems in *Journey to Love* test the existence and sustaining power of love:

> . . . I love you
> or I do not live
> at all   ["The Ivy Crown," *PB*, p. 124]

Williams relies on the strength of personal pronouns throughout the poem. While he addresses his wife Flossie as "you," he never uses her name in the poem. The poem is particular, special, "to you / and you alone," but not exclusive; the poet involves the reader in his strategy of intimacy. Williams repeats himself, with a purpose:

> There is something
>   something urgent
> I have to say to you
>   and you alone   [*PB*, p. 154]

The repetition of "to you" creates the effect of establishing a direct line to the wife, but also to the feminine element within the poet's self. The poet knows that there is a creative, and merciful feminine principle within his voice:

> I do not come to you
>   save that I confess

---

4. Charles Baudelaire, *Oeuvres complètes* (Paris: Editions Gallimard, 1961), p. 6.
5. *In the Trail of the Wind American Indian Ritual Poems and Ritual Orations*, ed. John Bierhorst (New York: Farrar, Straus and Giroux, 1971), p. 131.

                    to being
                    half man and half
          woman   ["For Eleanor and Bill Monahan," *PB*, p. 84].

Often the "you" in "Asphodel" is used as the object of a preposition, to bring the poet nearer to his wife, or to the feminine:

          It is a curious odor,
                    a moral odor,
                              that brings me
          near to you   [*PB*, p. 155].

Through prepositions used with pronouns the poet can approach
his wife with the gift of the poem and with his way of seeing.
Twice, he says, "I come, my sweet / to sing to you" [*PB*, pp. 153,
161].

      The poet continues to involve his wife and the reader through
the use of a question to the listener, again, directed familiarly to
"you":

          We danced,
                    in our minds,
          and read a book together.
                    You remember? [*PB*, pp. 157-158]

"Asphodel" is composed of three Books and a "Coda." In Book I
alone the poet uses the pronoun "you" twenty-three times. The
result of the repetition is to assert the poet's need for intimacy
with his wife, to reaffirm their connection.

      Williams relies on the pronoun "we" to emphasize what he
and his wife, or he and his listeners have shared. The wife is asked
to will an acknowledgement of shared experience:

          We lived long together
                    a life filled,
                              if you will,
          with flowers. . . [*PB*, p. 153].

Bill and Flossie lived in Rutherford, not far from the ocean;
metaphorically they were born as a couple by exploring the
common landscape of their experience:

          for we were born by the sea,
                    knew its rose hedges
                              to the very water's brink [*PB*, p. 156].

The couple will live on together in memory, signified by the wedding scene at the end of the poem. "Asphodel" covers distance,
the distance to the "water's very brink," the time of aging
together, and the inner time of shared memories.

      Possessive pronouns add to the bond that the poet is estab-
lishing. His seeing and his feeling touch the eyes of his beloved:

What do I remember
  that was shaped
    as this thing is shaped?
while our eyes fill
  with tears [*PB*, p. 153].

"Our eyes" refers not only to that which the poet and his wife share in their seeing, but to the seeing that the poet gives the reader.

The extensive use of pronouns to bind the lyric structure as well as the desire to create a shared language remind us of Paul Eluard's love poetry. Through the use of pronouns, Eluard too made the world habitable, a shared place, illuminated by song:

The lamp is filled with our eyes
We inhabit our valley
Our walls our flowers our sun
Our colors and our light

The capital of the sun
Is in our image
And in the shelter of our walls
Our door is a human door.[6]   ["By a Kiss"]

Williams knew early in his career that he wanted to break down barriers between poet and reader: "Whenever I say, 'I' I mean also, 'you.' And so, together, as one, we shall begin," Williams writes in 1923 [*I*, p. 89]. The poet's attitude of collaborating with the reader creates a different kind of reader from the merely objective critic—Williams seeks a reader who is willing to experience the immediacy and truth of feeling in his language. J. Hillis Miller takes an extreme position on the relationship of Williams and the critic: "To accept the embrace Williams offers means the impossibility of 'criticizing' his work, if criticism means viewing with the cold eye of analysis and judgment. The critic must resign himself to the poet's world and accept whatever he finds there."[7] Williams would have disagreed; there is no reason why the reader cannot examine Williams' work with a critical eye, since Williams himself worked so hard on design. Williams hoped that readers after him would understand subtleties in his work that he himself could not as yet describe. But there is more to a critical reading of the poem than analysis; to be a partner with the poet in the language of the poem, the reader has to allow his or her imagination to play over the grid of words, to "suspend

---

6. Paul Eluard, *Last Love Poems*, trans. Marilyn Kallet (Baton Rouge: Louisiana State University Press, 1980), pp. 2-3.
7. J. Hillis Miller, *Poets of Reality Six Twentieth Century Writers* (Cambridge, Mass.: The Belknap Press of Harvard University, 1966), p. 291.

disbelief" for a time. Williams would have wanted his work to stand up under the "cold eye" of critical judgment, as long as the critics had done him the justice of understanding his design.

In "The Simplicity of Disorder" (1921-1931), Williams had begun to meditate upon a poem with "conversation as design," conversation between husband and wife. The poet speaks to himself as he imagines the design:

> By this singleness do you, my dear, become actually my wife.
>   By design do you become bright, purely what you are (and visible), not to bear me a message–but as a wife you carry me the freshness of all women. There is no necessity for witty fingers. The solidity of the pure lends itself by pure design in which you are accomplished.
>   That would be a writing.
>   What's that?
>   In which conversation was actual to the extent that it would be pure design.
>   How?
>   Till death do us part   [SE, p. 98].

In "Asphodel," love for Flossie is transposed into the "pure design" of the triadic line and the variable foot, her presence becomes actual through the song. The fact that the poem may be conceived of objectively, as a design, does not detract from its effect as a statement of emotion. In a late interview, Williams spoke of his goal in writing "Asphodel": "My main aim is to break up the usual metric pattern. In order to get away from the conventional thing, dividing it by breath, by inflection. I wanted to get away from everything that is English."[8] He believed, in fact, that the form of his poem would itself generate a response: "When you are emotionally stirred, you don't speak with the emotions. ... We want a familiar pattern, a 'home' pattern to bring the conviction out in the listener."[9] In "Asphodel" the poet's measure syncopates natural speech rhythms with the ebb and flow of imaginative seas, with the "inner voice,"[10] the voice of memory. The triadic line and variable foot punctuate the poem with a regular beat that does not distort the pace and flow of the American idiom; the reader feels at home in Williams' language.

That Williams did not get away from "everything English" is obvious in his use of Spenserian phrases of song. But the measure,

---

8. Wagner, Linda W., ed., *Interviews with William Carlos Williams "Speaking Straight Ahead"* (New York: New Directions, 1976), p. 68.
9. Williams, "Talk about Poetry," March 28, 1954. On tape at the Rutherford Free Public Library. Listed in Emily Mitchell Wallace's *Bibliography of William Carlos Williams* (Middletown, Conn.: Wesleyan University Press, 1968), as item F7, p. 261.
10. *Insights II Denise Levertov: In Her Own Province* (New York: New Directions, 1978), p. 33.

the cuts that give the poem character, the swiftness of pace that propels it along are Williams' "local" pattern that assimilates British prosody for its own uses (for the poem's love of pageantry). Williams assimilates Spenser to enrich the American poem, the way Spenser had assimilated words and rhythms from Italian and other European languages to enrich the English language. The naturalness of American speech patterns dominates "Asphodel's" song. "Asphodel" is a dialogue with the past and with the future of poetry.

On one rough draft copy of "Asphodel," found in the Yale Collection, Williams wrote "a dialogue" at the top of the poem, in pencil and in brackets.[11] Perhaps he was referring to his earlier thought of a "conversation as design." Perhaps he thought of the poem as creating a sense of closeness and connecting voices, "a reciprocal language," as Paul Eluard put it, where poet and reader could share a common language of love. The poem would include the syntax and cadences of conversation to make its lines direct. As we can see, the final version does not include Flossie's part of the conversation. The poet's speaking is Flossie's speaking; her listening is all the participating she gets to do, at least in the poem. Perhaps the poet meant the poem to be something of a dialogue with himself, a meditation on love and wholeness in the manner of Stevens' "The World as Meditation," or "The Final Soliloquy of the Interior Paramour."[12] In any case, he erased the reference to "a dialogue" in the final version.

Book II of the poem is both more somber and more wide-reaching than the first book. "Approaching death," perhaps "the death of love" as well, the poet meditates on his place in history, on the treacheries and discoveries in history and in modern times. The modern poem is a dance, reflecting universal concerns through the modern measure. But "the bomb puts an end / to all that" [*PB*, p. 165]. The use of fewer personal pronouns in this section, the reliance on "I" rather than "you" or "we" throughout most of this book, corresponds to the devastating thought of the bomb, created by those who cannot imagine the existence of others. In this Book the poet surveys his losses, and the world's losses through war's destruction of art. The Book ends with the poet's greatest sense of loss, the loss of his capacity to create shared words: "I regret most— / that there has come an end / to them." Book II is a canto concerned with fragmentation and endings; though it contains memories of "pinnacles" of personal history, the Book is also a deliberate facing of death [*PB*, p. 169].

---

11. Unpublished worksheets for "Asphodel," YALC.
12. Wallace Stevens, *Poems* (New York: Random House, 1959), pp. 163, 157.

Book III begins with a renewed appeal to the other, the "you" of the poem: "What power has love but forgiveness?" [*PB*, p. 169]. Having been shown the shattering effects of the bomb, of lovelessness, Flossie is called upon to heal the poet's sense of a fragmented world through her love. The wife is like the imagination itself—she can restore his spirits:

> You have forgiven me
> > making me new again.
> > > So that here
> > in the place ,
> > > dedicated in the imagination
> > > > to memory
> > of the dead
> > > I bring you
> > > > a last flower [*PB*, pp. 177-178].

Having given the gift of understanding, the wife receives the gift of the poem, which is the best that Williams can give, a poem ruled by love.

Yet in this section Williams voyages outside of Flossie's domestic realm. Entering the depths of subways and caves, the poet makes contact not only with the image of his father and the fathers of art, but with the image of the "Venus" in prehistoric caves. His love carries him back to the eternal feminine principle, to Demeter or Kore, to the "Big buttocked" figures of the Great Mother. By "sympathetic magic," by contact with "his father's beard," the poet seems to move effortlessly in an archaic landscape. His "draftsmanship" permits him to imagine a world beyond the personal, to "build a picture of all men." Then humbly he returns home, to thoughts of Flossie "compassionately pouring at the roots" of her plants. Not Rhea or Demeter, goddesses of vegetation and grain, but Flossie is *actually* with him, "moved by kindness" to warm and care for him [*PB*, pp. 174-175].

The "Coda" [*PB*, p. 178] at the end of the poem sings of light, the mind's light, celebrated through the image of a wedding. The mind is at peace with itself; the marriage of art and life has taken place through the poem's evocation of memories. Williams watches the light of his lines rhythmically stroke the page, as Mrs. Ramsay in *To the Lighthouse* watched the lighthouse beams bend across the marriage bed and stroke the floor. Like Mrs. Ramsay, the poet experiences a growing tenderness or generous pity towards others as towards himself in the steady light of his seeing. In *To the Lighthouse*, Mrs. Ramsay's contemplative mind meets with itself in a wedding: "There rose, and she looked with her needles suspended, there curled up off the floor of the mind, rose from the lake of one's being, a mist, a bride to meet her lover."[13] Williams, like this fictional Mrs. Ramsay, also "celebrates the light" of wholeness of mind, as much as he celebrates his love for Flossie.

Light or love, or the imagination, is wedded to speech in the pageantry of the poem; light triumphs:

> The light
>> for all time shall outspeed
>>> the thunder crack [*PB*, p. 181].

Light is made personal at the end of the poem, for the poet's memory shines on the details of his wedding to Flossie. He returns to the particular, to the image of Flossie:

> At the altar
>> so intent was I
> before my vows,
>> so moved by your presence
>>> a girl so pale
> and ready to faint
>> that I pitied
>>> and wanted to protect you [*PB*, p. 181].

Light, the imagination, takes on an odor, becomes sensual:

> It is late
> but an odor
>> as from our wedding
>>> has revived for me [*PB*, p. 182]

Flossie's marriage to Williams, a "sweet-scented flower," [*PB*, p. 182] did blossom and enable the poet to create, to add light to the world with his creations; "the palm goes / always to the light" [*PB*, p. 180]. Through the imagination the marriage of the poet and his wife has been transposed into the light or "pure design" of the poem. Now, Williams turns the imagination back to the immediate world again, offers the poem as a sensual reality to the reader.

Williams keeps the vocabulary of the poem simple. Monosyllabic words often prevail; ordinary words bear the gifts, *are* the gifts of songs, flowers:

> I come, my sweet,
>> to sing to you.
> We lived long together
>> a life filled,
>>> if you will,
> with flowers [*PB*, p. 153].

---

13. Virginia Woolf, *To the Lighthouse* (New York: Harcourt, Brace & World, 1955 edition), p. 98.

Williams avoids affectations of speech in his poetry. In Book III he speaks out against affectation:

> It is ridiculous
> what airs we put on
> to seem profound
> while our hearts
> gasp dying
> for want of love [*PB*, p. 170].

Poetry is speech, natural speech, for Williams. He sings of love in the American idiom. Poetry is an act of communication, of reaching out towards a listener, as the poet reaches out for understanding in "Asphodel." "Hear me out," he asks, simply [*PB*, p. 156].

The poet's use of a "general simple" vocabulary "makes certain words leap out in contrast."[14] In the first line of "Asphodel, That Greeny Flower" [*PB*, p. 153], the word "asphodel" is curious, because it gives the reader a specific name of a flower. Though the flower itself may be common enough to find, the name has an uncommon sound to it. The long "o" sound chimes later in the poem in assonance with "forebodingly," to create a gloomy effect. (One thinks of Poe's description of how he composed "The Raven." Entranced by the beauty of melancholy subjects, Poe thought that the word "nevermore" seemed promising as a beginning, with its long "o," its melancholy sound effect.)[15] Yet "asphodel" also has a "del" sound (or dell within it); the word unfolds through a landscape evocative both of sorrow and of the fields of a pastoral landscape. The word "greeny" in the first line stands out; it picks up the tone from "asphodel" to a lighter, happier sound, and reinforces the suggestion of a pastoral world. Though the word "greeny" is simple, it is a made-up word. The reader has to ponder its meaning. "Greeny" suggests a fertile, rolling place, suggests the sea; "asphodel," a white flower that Williams remembers from his childhood and from the underworld of Homer's *Odyssey*, comes from a personal, and a deep, universal place. Thus "asphodel" and "greeny" link suggestions of life and death together in the first line; the poem has to it the quality of a living imagination moving among ghosts. The reader who is familiar with Williams' work will remember his line from "A Celebration": "Time is a green orchid" [*CEP*, p. 190]. Both green and flowering have for Williams associations with time.

14. Peter Meinke, "William Carlos Williams Traditional Rebel" in *Profile of William Carlos Williams*, ed. Jerome Mazzaro (Columbus, Ohio: Charles E. Merrill Publishing Co., 1971), p. 110.
15. Edgar Allan Poe, "First Principles," in *Literary Criticism of Edgar Allan Poe*, ed. Robert L. Hough (Lincoln: University of Nebraska Press, 1965), pp. 20-32.

The most unusual word in the poem is "guerdon." The
poet is speaking about love and says:

> There is a hierarchy
>> which can be attained,
>>> I think,
> in its service.
>> Its guerdon
>>> is a fairy flower;
> a cat of twenty lives [*PB*, p. 157].

The word "guerdon" is a hybrid, between Middle English, Old
French, Middle Latin sources ("guerdon," "guerredon," "modified
by Latin" "donum," gift,); and the Old High German "widarlon"
from "widar," "against," and "Ion," "reward."[16] It is interesting
to find the Old High German meaning of "to ward against" mixed
in with the meanings of reward and recompense. This meaning of
"warding against"embedded in the modern meaning of reward
may suggest that the gift or recompense has a quality to it of
warding off evil. In "The Desert Music" the formless, embryonic
life-in-death image of the beggar does this "warding off" of
endings; the accompanying imaginative music in the poet's lines
is called "a protecting music" [*PB*, p. 120]. In "Asphodel," the
image of the flower protects against meaninglessness; throughout
his poetry Williams uses the flower as a "shield" against darkness,
the way Aeneas uses the golden bough in *The Aeneid*. The flower
image is Williams' way of travelling through dangerous realms, for
him the flower is a comfort and a protection. The image of the
flower has become for Williams his own emblem for his craft, his
way of depicting an escape from death through the imagination.

In "The Yellow Flower," Williams refers to the common
mustard flower as a curing flower, a "sacred flower" [*PB*, p. 89].
Just as Michelangelo used marble, made it "bloom" as a way of
exerting an immortal power, so the poet sees

> through the eyes
>> and through the lips
> and tongue the power
>> to free myself
>>> and speak of it, as
> Michelangelo through his hands
>> had the same, if greater,
>>> power.

The poet has no marble, only

>> the tortured body of my flower
> which is not a mustard flower at all
>> but some unrecognized
>>> and unearthly flower [*PB*, p. 91]

16. "Guerdon," *Webster's Third International Dictionary*, 1971. See also, "guerdon,"
College Edition Webster's New World Dictionary of the American Language, 1962.

The flower image for Williams provides "a hole / in the bottom of the bag," through which "we escape" death [*P*, p. 247].

The "fairy flower," or "guerdon," also suggests the precious flower of immortality sought by Gilgamesh and Enkidu in Sumerian mythology. Gilgamesh lost the flower in a deep lake after a long quest.[17] For Williams, who also knows that he will lose, that death is inevitable, the flower represents art's power:

> If no one came to try it
> the world
> would be the loser [*PB*, p. 157].

Williams uses simple statements in "Asphodel" to attain a striking effect of directness and immediacy. His commands, or appeals, add a tone of urgency to the poem. "Hear me out. / Do not turn away," Williams insists, always speaking in his own voice [*PB*, pp. 156-157].

These lines remind us of an earlier poem, where Williams depicts a woman as coy, attempting to keep her lover with her for a while longer. In "Two Pendants: for the Ears," Williams says his thoughts are

> like
> the distant smile of a woman who
> will say:
> —only to keep you a moment
> longer. Oh I know I'm a stinker—
> but
> only to keep you, it's only
> to keep you   . a few moments
>
> Let me have a cigarette [*CLP*, p. 218].

In his old age, Williams cannot afford to be coy in his plea for love and for time. ("I love you / or I do not live / at all.")

Time threatens Williams with death, as it threatens the world with its "flower," the bomb [*PB*, p. 165]. Williams conveys a sense of immediacy as he speaks of

> . . . something
> something urgent
> I have to say to you

But even speech must wait, as the poet appreciates his wife's approach:

> but it must wait
> while I drink in
> the joy of your approach,
> perhaps for the last time [*PB*, p. 154].

---

17. Norma Lorre Goodrich, ed., *Ancient Myths* (New York: Mentor Books, 1960), p. 23.

Williams plays on our feelings here, letting his wife and the reader know that we should not deny the poet his last statement; we should appreciate his "approach" and what he will say.

Despite the directness and sense of resolve in Williams' tone, there is an undercurrent of precariousness and vulnerability. When the poet asks his wife not to turn away, he is reminding us of Book V of *The Aeneid*, where Aeneas appeals to Dido in the underworld: "Don't move away! Oh, let me see you a little longer! / To fly from me, when this is the last word fate allows us!"[18] There is an echo of sorrow, of tragedy in Williams' lines, evoked through the reference to the ancient story of ill-fated lovers who, even in hell, had limited time.

Almost all of the lines of Williams' personal epic are made of sentences whose syntax is regular and straightforward. The sentences are syncopated by the triadic line. There are narrative passages, which read like ordinary speech:

When I was a boy
        I kept a book
                to which, from time
to time,
        I added pressed flowers
                until, after a time,
I had a good collection [*PB*, p. 155].

There are no distortions of speech or sentence structure in these lines. Instead, Williams uses the "cadences discoverable in prose" but imposes the regular beat and shape of the triadic line. The result is to spin out the story, to place emphasis in this passage on "time" and to effect the simple, "hopping" cadence of a boy playing towards his destiny.

Sometimes the poet will slow down or even drag out the pace of his verse, to indicate that he is stalling for time in his words. Speech is his only weapon against his annihilation:

And so
        with fear in my heart
                I drag it out
and keep on talking
        for I dare not stop.
                Listen while I talk on
against time [*PB*, p. 154].

As the poet "talks on against time" we feel the pressure of time bearing down on him. Williams repeats the word "time" six times on pages 154-155; the repetition shows us the poet's

---

18. C. Day Lewis, trans. *The Aeneid of Virgil* (New York: Doubleday Anchor, 1953), p. 143.

concerns. The writing in "Asphodel" is not hurried, does not have the nervous rhythm of Williams' early poems. The writing is paced, measured, through the variable foot and the three-ply line. The longer line length holds off terror, holds off death for a time. The measure works as a strategy for the poet to keep his beat regular. Memory holds off the pressure of time, for

> Memory is a kind
> of accomplishment,
> a sort of renewal
> even [*PB*, p. 73]

Song puts off time, too, for the music of love makes us forget the "sorry facts" of mortality: "Of love, abiding love / it will be telling" in the poet's song [*PB*, p. 153].

The form of "Asphodel," the triadic line, is the same as that of "The Descent" [*PB*, pp. 73-74]; most of the poems in *Journey to Love* and *The Desert Music* that use this form have in them something of the theme of descent into memory. The triadic line forms a picture on the page—the lines seem to cascade downward on the page in waves, in falls. The picture presented on the page by the lines shows the reader that descent is inevitable; the movement is "downward to darkness, on extended wings," even in the most beautiful lines.[19]

But the line gives the poet time and a steady voice to speak against the fall into death, as a person has time to create beauty in the measure of his or her life. The regularity of the three-ply line has its advantages, for the lines are ordered and inevitable, too. Every fourth line will begin again at the margin of the page. Williams sought out a sense of formal predictability in his late poems; it was the lack of "inevitability" in Olson's lines that led Williams to have some qualms over Olson's verse.[20] The reader knows what to expect in terms of "Asphodel's" formal progression, and this leads to a certain calm for poet and reader. Williams' admiration for *The Iliad* permeates "Asphodel"; his measure was his way of establishing a "sea-change," a sea-beat, to match the roll of the ancient music [*IWWP*, p. 83]. As another aging poet reflected, "There was an ease of mind that was like being alone in a boat at sea."[21]

But the poem does not merely roll and flow. When the poet speaks of the imagination's resistance against death, we can feel the tension of creation against destruction in the lines, the poet's defiance:

---

19. See *Paterson*, Book Two, p. 96, for Williams' first use of the triadic line in 1946.
20. Williams, "Letter to Cid Corman" dated 5/16/53. The Humanities Research Center, The University of Texas at Austin. Cited as UTA.
21. Stevens, *Poems*, p. 161.

```
Only the imagination is real!
        I have declared it
                time without end.
If a man die
        it is because death
                has first
possessed his imagination [PB, p. 179].
```

The poet sets his words in the lines against the weather of death, much as he admired the starling's "manoeuvre" against the wind:

```
I saw the two starlings
coming in toward the wires.
But at the last,
just before alighting, they

turned in the air together
and landed backwards!
That s what got me—to
face into the wind's teeth [CLP, p. 88].
```

A tone and theme of simplicity permeates, penetrates the poems in *Pictures from Brueghel*. Williams liked the words "penetrate," "penetrant." As he stated in "The Descent of Winter" (1923), "such must be the future; penetrant and simple—minus the scaffolding of the academic, which is a 'lie' in that it is inessential to the purpose as to the design" [*I*, p. 259]. Particulars must suffice. At the end of "Asphodel," Williams sings

```
but an odor
        as from our wedding
                has revived for me
and begun again to penetrate
        into all crevices
                of my world [PB, p. 182].
```

The particular, the tangible thing seen or remembered, has the power to extend itself into the crevices of one's feeling and understanding, to create a world. The particular, the memory of a flower seen in boyhood, can transport the poet to the depths of the sea, to a sense of universality, or can show him the glint of light on the waves, the beauty of surfaces and order, of pageantry.

The simplicity in *Pictures from Brueghel* is the wise simplicity of an old man, one who is handing on what he knows to others, penetrating the future.

In the poem, "Paul," Williams teaches his grandson how to fish:

```
when you shall arrive
as deep
as you will need go
```

                    to catch the blackfish
                    the hook
                    has been featly baited

                    by the art you have
                    and
                    you do catch them [*PB*, pp. 22-23]

Implicitly, unobtrusively, Williams is talking about style in this poem, rejoicing in his own style. Go deep, he advises his grandson, invent a strategy, a craft, to hook the fish or the reader. Translate that "glistening body," that sensual reality into a language as bare and clean as the art of cutting can make the object. Enjoy the poem, share and reveal in your own style of cutting, in the way you make your line breaks, "however you / divide / and share."

The "scrupulous bareness"[22] of Williams' early poems becomes all the more stringent in the late poems. The discipline of careful word choice, "chastity" of speech, served the poet well in the poems composed in the triadic line as well as in the short poems. The triadic lines are like wires, humming.

All of the poems in *The Desert Music* and *Journey to Love* that are written in the triadic line seem to be part of one composition. The lines of the poems resemble chords, and remind one of the way music might be scored. The poems written in the new measure are part of the "fugal music" of Williams' personal epic, his journey through memory to renewal.

Poems from *Pictures from Brueghel*, written in short, terse lines, in triadic stanzas often, form a continuity with the other poems as well. For all the poems in the book have the bareness of language mentioned earlier, and all have common themes: simplicity, memory, renewal through art and love. The last books mark a turning point in Williams' writing, for in "Shadows" the poet says that "Memory / is liver than sight" [*PB*, p. 150]. But Williams has been trained to see clearly all his life, and even what he sees in memory has a tangible clarity to it, like the image of Flossie at the altar.

The theme of simplicity is mentioned explicitly in several poems in the last books. In "The Host," where Williams describes nuns and a cleric in a restaurant, Williams says of what he sees and imagines, "It was a simple story" [*PB*, p. 94]. In the poem, "The Mental Hospital Garden," Williams talks of Saint Francis, and says,

                    All mankind
                            grew to be his debtors,
                    a simple story [*PB*, p. 97].

---

22. J. Hillis Miller, *Poets of Reality*, p. 344.

The "simple story" is that "Love is in season." A mood of love, a season for a common language of love, permeates the one continuous "simple story" found in the late poems. Perhaps Williams found the Christian virtues of chastity, poverty, humility, inspiring to his late aesthetics. His talk of nuns and of Saint Francis, of "Deep Religious Faith," would lend support to this assumption [*PB*, p. 95]. But it would be inaccurate to press this point too far.

For in "The King!" Williams refers to the facts about "the King's whore," Nell Gwynn, as "a simple statement." In this poem Williams delights in elaborating on the "simple statement"; through his fantasies Williams adds to this story. "The King's body was served" [*PB*, p. 133].

There is no mention of simplicity in "The Sparrow," but the poem is a statement about Williams' poetic style and mastery. Late in life the poet identifies his craft almost completely with his image of the sparrow:

> This sparrow
>   who comes to sit at my window
>   is a poetic truth
> more than a natural one [*PB*, p. 129] ;

The sparrow is somewhat comic,

>   Nothing even remotely
> subtle
>   about his lovemaking.

But his technique is sharp:

>   The way he swipes his bill
>   across a plank
> to clean it,
>   is decisive [*PB*, p. 131].

Williams might be describing his own technique of cleaning up and shaping his lines. At the end the sparrow is no more than a "dried wafer," but the bird is more eloquent than ever in this state; he is

> an effigy of a sparrow
>   a dried wafer only,
>   left to say
> and it says it
>   without offense,
>   beautifully;
> This was I,
>   a sparrow.
>   I did my best;
> farewell [*PB*, p. 132].

Williams dedicates this poem to his father, who disapproved of his poetry. The poem is Williams' justification of his work, his answer to his dream of his father saying, "severely, 'You know all that poetry you're writing. Well it's no good' " [*A*, p. 14].

All of these parts of "a simple story" form a prelude to "Asphodel." Yet there is no mention of the word "simple" in that poem. In two rough draft versions of "Asphodel," Williams refers to Asphodel as "a simple flower,"[23] but deletes the comment in the final version. Perhaps Williams saw that comment as a note of explanation to himself that was unnecessary for the reader. Or he might have realized that asphodel, found in Homer's Hades, could not be as simple as all that.

The theme of simplicity is not mentioned in "Asphodel," because the poem demonstrates simplicity through the nature of its language without any need of self-conscious references. The words used are the theme, the thing itself. "—Say it, no ideas but in things—" [*P*, p. 14].

In particulars, in single images, Williams sees the general, or universal. There are a "thousand topics / in an apple blossom," a generosity waiting to be explored in any single image; there are many women in Flossie, perhaps "a field made up of women / all silver-white" [*PB*, p. 160]. (Though Williams thought he saw "endless wealth" in the arms of Flossie, we cannot help but remember that he still needed to play that "silver-white" field.)

Williams' imagery in "Asphodel" belongs to the magic world of the imagination where one image can be transformed into another, into its opposite, even; metamorphosis does not frighten the imagination at play. The sea, the universal, becomes a garden, the ordered image, and then the image breaks open again, to release the sea as Williams sings,

> The whole world
>   became my garden!
> But the sea
>   which no one tends
>   is also a garden
> when the sun strikes it
>   and the waves
>   are wakened [*PB*, p. 156].

The sea, "that profound depth" casts up its treasures, its particulars:

> . . . there are the starfish
>   stiffened by the sun
> and other sea wrack
>   and weeds [*PB*, p. 156].

---

23. Unpublished worksheets, YALC.

In an earlier poem, "Flowers by the Sea," Williams had shown the imagination's power to create new, mythical forms with its "esemplastic"[24] waves. The imagination for Williams has the power to unbind, to loose the general from the particular, and then to bring back the flow into an image of order:

> When over the flowery, sharp pasture's
> edge, unseen, the salt ocean
>
> lifts its form—chicory and daisies
> tied, released, seem hardly flowers alone
>
> but color and the movement—or the shape
> perhaps—of restlessness, whereas
>
> the sea is circled and sways
> peacefully upon its plantlike stem [*CEP*, p. 87].

Williams' imagination creates equivalents throughout "Asphodel," bringing diverse images into a unity through love:

> Are facts not flowers
>   and flowers facts
> or poems flowers
>   or all works of the imagination,
>   interchangeable?
> Which proves
>   that love
>   rules them all [*PB*, p. 178].

Not only images but the energy behind the images is one: "Light, the imagination / and love, / . . . maintain / all of a piece / their dominance" [*PB*, p. 180].

Williams' delight in contradictions, his embracing of transformations, reminds us of the tribal imagination as it describes its existence in "Magic Words (after Nalungiaq)," an Eskimo song:

> In the very earliest time,
> when both people and animals lived on earth,
> a person could become an animal if he wanted to
> and an animal could become a human being . . .
> All spoke the same language.
> That was the time when words were like magic.
> The human mind had mysterious powers.
> A word spoken by chance
> might have strange consequences.
> It would suddenly come alive
> and what people wanted to happen could happen—
> all you had to do was say it.[25]

---

24. Samuel Taylor Coleridge, *Coleridge: Poetry and Prose* (New York: Bantam Books, 1965), p. 173.
25. *Shaking the Pumpkin: Traditional Poetry of the Indian North Americas*, ed. Jerome Rothenberg (New York: Doubleday and Co., 1972), p. 45.

The form of "Asphodel," the triadic stanza in which three lines form one unit, gives us a picture through structure of how the one can contain many experiences, and the many be embraced as one. Often, the fourth line or the opening line of a new triadic unit breaks the order just established, or provides a counterpoint. With the lines, "But the sea," unity surges into multiplicity again, proliferates itself:

      A thousand topics
            in an apple blossom.
                  The generous earth itself
      gave us lief.
            The whole world
                  became my garden!
      But the sea
            which no one tends . . . [PB, pp. 155-156].

Williams admired Dante's use of the terza rima form, his emphasis on structure. According to Williams, every fourth line of Dante's verse "contains a dissonance . . . Throughout the *Commedia*, this fourth unrhymed factor, unobserved, is the entrance of Pan to the Trinity which restores it to the candid embrace of love. . ." [SE, p. 207]. Williams' fourth line, "But the sea," may be seen as an example of how Williams includes a dissonance into his ordered world, how he floods the garden with the chaotic depths of his love. In the fourth line, "But" is the loophole, the unfinished or broken off place like that left by the Hopi basketweaver who has to guard against a finished work. For if the design is finished, the weaver or the poet is finished. And "Death / is not the end of it," the spirits must be allowed to enter. "Asphodel" ends with crevices, permeated with the odor of newly awakened love.

ROD TOWNLEY

BIDDING FOR FAME AT 50: WILLIAMS'
COLLECTED POEMS 1921 - 1931

At a high-toned cocktail party, one martini sipper turns to
another and says, "I can never get it straight. Was William Carlos
Williams the doctor or the insurance man?"

This exchange was immortalized a couple of years ago in a
New Yorker cartoon by Koren and so tickled Williams' son that
he taped it up on his wall. Indeed it is a wonderful comment on
the way our society gradually assimilates its poets, without, of
course, actually experiencing their work. Fame, it would seem,
has caught up with William Carlos Williams at last.

There's also something oddly appropriate about the pairing
of Dr. Williams and insurance executive Wallace Stevens, poets
who chose, bravely, to remain in America working full-time in
mainstream professions while all the literary glamour boys were
sailing off to Europe to live the life of *artistes*.

When Williams' first *Collected Poems* was published in 1934,
gathering work from 1921 through 1931, it was a fellow stay-at-
home, Wallace Stevens, who wrote the preface. Williams might
have had Ezra Pound send something from Europe, perhaps, if it
was the imprimatur of a famous name that he wanted. Certainly,
Stevens' name did not convey anything to the general public, although his one book, *Harmonium*, had received some critical
attention when it appeared eleven years earlier. Further, in important ways Williams and Stevens spoke different aesthetic
languages. The "metropolitan softness of tone" that Williams detected in Stevens [*Selected Letters*, p. 233] and especially the
predilection for symbolism were at odds with the spikey realism
of Williams.

Perhaps it was simply that Stevens was available and Pound
was not—although Pound was named an "advisor" to the publishing project that included this volume. Then, too, Pound had
become the official champion of T.S. Eliot, Williams' opposite
and nemesis. Indeed, for Williams, the decade 1921 to 1931 was a

time of difficult rebuilding after the "atomic blast," as he called it, of Eliot's success. But not too much ought to be made of the choice of Stevens over Pound as an introducer. Both poets remained dear and difficult friends to Williams, and in fact brief comments by Pound, Marianne Moore and René Taupin are quoted on the dust jacket of the 1934 collection.

The matter comes up at all only because Williams hated the preface Stevens wrote. He hated particularly the term "anti-poetic" used by Stevens to describe an essential quality of Williams' verse. The 1934 volume was, after all, Williams' first and (for all he knew then) perhaps only collected poems; it was an important benchmark, even though he later seemed to play down its significance, calling it merely "a lovely gesture from my own gang"[*I Wanted to Write a Poem*, p. 52]. He was now over fifty and had been struggling for decades to win critical recognition of the validity of his poetic voice; and here comes Stevens calling his work "anti-poetic."

Stevens himself was never really part of any literary "gang," although he and Williams had known each other since the *Others* magazine days during WWI, and Williams had quoted and discussed a letter from Stevens in the introduction to *Kora in Hell* (1920). The "gang," in this instance, was a group of writers known as Objectivists who had formed The Objectivist Press with a view to publishing one another's works. Besides Williams, there were George Oppen, Louis Zukofsky, Charles Reznikoff and Carl Rakosi—impressive names now, but then unknown. Williams' *Collected Poems 1921-1931* was the first book produced by this collective, but no one knew much about marketing or distributing and only a few of the 500 copies printed were sold.

One more commercial failure, in other words, to add to the dozen unsuccessful books of prose and poetry that Williams had already published. The disappointment must have been all the keener because this 134-page, well-printed volume contained a decade's work and it bid for attention in a way that the quirky earlier books did not. (Several of them had not even been published in this country.)

The book included—mercifully without the prose interludes—the best poems from *Spring and All* and "The Descent of Winter," as well as the wonderfully spirited "Primavera" poems of 1928. "Primavera" and "Descent" had had only magazine publication before. The decision to bring them together in a volume, along with *Spring and All* and other poems of the period, should have been cause for celebration. "The Red Wheelbarrow," "This Is

Just to Say," "Young Sycamore," "The Sea Elephant," "To Elsie," poems that now seem to us quintessential Williams, were for the first time easily available in the United States for two dollars flat.

That the book did not sell was bad enough; that it contained an irksomely "wrong" preface added to the pain. After all, if someone as intelligent as Stevens didn't get what Williams was up to, what could be expected from the public at large?

Actually, the misunderstanding may have been partly Williams'. If he had substituted his favorite word, "contact," for the objectionable term, "anti-poetic," he might even have approved of the preface. Whether Stevens' meaning would have been distorted by such a change is another question. It would have been— but not by much.

There were subtler misunderstandings as well, based on temperament. Because the two poets were obsessed with the relationship between reality and imagination, one might assume that they shared the same views. But in fact they possessed different types of imagination and thus saw different realities. Both found materials for poetry in the chaos of external life, but Stevens approached this disorder with the care (even fastidiousness) of a connoisseur, whereas Williams rushed at it with the impulsiveness of a lover:

> I must tell you
> this young tree...

It is not surprising, then, that in his preface Stevens called Williams sentimental.

In a letter written sixteen years earlier, Stevens criticized Williams' 1917 collection, *Al Que Quiere!*, for its lack of stylistic unity. "Given a fixed point of view, realistic, imagistic or what you will, everything adjusts itself to that point of view." And he confided, "Personally, I have a distaste for miscellany."

For "miscellany" one could read "disorder," a condition for which Williams had a *decided* taste, even while he wrestled with form. Williams had once tried a book with *Harmonium*-like unity of form and tone; it was his first volume, *Poems* (1909), and it died stillborn for lack of air. He simply did not have the Olympian temperament. He was too impulsive.

Stevens, on the other hand, for all his brilliant exoticism, always maintained a seemly decorum in his verse, a conventional, even granitic, exterior, avoiding the messiness of overt experimentalism. His books are monuments, building from parapet to parapet; Williams' books tend to have a more hodge-podge appearance.

Williams blamed the disorder of his works on his own instability. All his life he flirted with the idea of madness, in part as an antidote to his structured bourgeois life. But also, there was for him something about reality itself that was dark and "mad"—as impervious to civilized thought as the jagged spikes of green glass behind the hospital. He was in love with this glinting reality the way a suicide is in love with drowning or a drunkard is in love with gin (both similes recur in his writings). He dove into the daily chaos and came up clutching dripping poems.

Stevens, was astute enough to see this, but it was not in his temperament to follow Williams' lead. An "Earthy Anecdote" by Stevens is not as earthy as an anecdote that Williams would tell. His blackbirds are thirteen propositions in a philosophical demonstration, not the querulously real sparrows of Williams' "Pastoral." Nor does Stevens' wonderful "firecat" inhabit the same world as the cat in Williams' cellar that

> climbed over
> the top of
>
> the jamcloset
> first the right
> forefoot
>
> carefully
> then the hind...

One must not make the mistake of saying that Williams' cat is real while Stevens' is imaginary; both spring from the imagination straight into literary history, but they spring from different kinds of imagination. Williams, more formally innovative, makes his cat walk a precarious verbal line down the page, coming into existence in the process. Stevens' firecat bristles with symbolism at the center of a metaphysical concept.

Stevens' preface is wonderfully right in pointing out Williams' romanticism, his emotionality, and the conflicting attractions of "the ivory tower" and "the public dump"; but except for a suggestive phrase about "the ambiguity of bareness," he is almost silent about form. In his own poems, of course, Stevens often invoked a "blessed rage for order" and a "rage against chaos" (whatever "rage" might mean to so controlled a sensibility). Williams, however, wrote about the possibilities that chaos offers for new fecundities and more natural forms.

> From disorder (a chaos)
> order grows
> —grows fruitful.

Admittedly, Williams' 1934 collection (being a miscellany) exhibits a variety of poetic structures, some so loose as to recall the worst abuses of imagism. But Williams was now allying himself with a movement called Objectivism and had become obsessed with discovering—inherent in the materials—new forms through which those materials might be expressed. As he wrote later in his *Autobiography* [p. 265]:

> The poem being an object (like a symphony or a cubist painting) it must be the purpose of the poet to make of his words a new form: to invent, that is, an object consonant with his day. This was what we wished to imply by Objectivism, an antidote, in a sense, to the bare image haphazardly presented in loose verse.

The effort to create significant structures appropriate to the historical moment was not always rewarded with success in *Collected Poems*. But it's important to realize what Williams was trying for. Stevens does note that a poem like "Young Sycamore" leaps up in one's imagination like a serpent, but he doesn't add that the poem accomplishes this feat by following the twists and reachings of the tree itself. It is an achievement that borders on the revolutionary (even as it takes us back to George Herbert's "Easter Wings" in the seventeenth century). It goes way beyond conventional imagism.

A dozen such achievements, scattered throughout the book, are what make the appearance of *Collected Poems 1921-1931* an event of importance in our literary history. To alert minds in 1934, the book showed that new forms could be found that would not "deform" the language—or distort the reality that the poem was written to capture and transmute.

THE PROSE WRITER

Portrait of Floss by unknown artist done in 1928.

EZRA POUND

DR WILLIAMS' POSITION*

There is an anecdote told me by his mother, who wished me to understand his character, as follows: The young Williams Carlos, aged let us say about seven, arose in the morning, dressed and put on his shoes. Both shoes buttoned on the left side. He regarded this untoward phenomenon for a few minutes and then carefully removed the shoes, placed shoe *a* that had been on his left foot, on his right foot, and shoe *b*, that had been on the right foot, on his left foot; both sets of buttons again appeared on the left side of the shoes.

This stumped him. With the shoes so buttoned he went to school, but . . . and here is the significant part of the story, he spent the day in careful consideration of the matter.

It happens that this type of sensibility, persisting through forty years, is of extreme, and almost unique, value in a land teeming. swarming, pullulating with clever people all capable of competent and almost instantaneous extroversion; during the last twenty of these years it has distinguished Dr Williams from [the] floral and unconscious mind of the populace and from the snappy go-getters who'der seen wot wuz rong in er moment.

It has prevented our author from grabbing ready made conclusions, and from taking too much for granted.

There are perhaps, or perhaps have been milieux where the reflective and examining habits would not have conferred, unsupported, a distinction. But *chez nous*, for as long as I can remember, if an article appeared in Munsey's or McClure's, expressing a noble passion (civic or other) one cd. bank (supposing one were exercising editorial or quasi-editorial functions) on seeing the same article served up again in some fifty lyric expressions within, let us say, three or four months.

Reprinted from *The Dial*, Nov. 1928; typographical errors and misspellings have been silently corrected and editorial conventions have been made consistent; e.g. french in the original has been changed to French. —C.F.T.

Our national mind hath about it something "marvelous porous"; an idea or notion dropped into N. Y. harbour emerges in Santa Fe or Galveston, watered, diluted, but still the same idea or notion, pale but not wholly denatured; and the time of transit is very considerably lower, than any "record" hitherto known. We have the defects of our qualities, and that very alertness which makes the single American diverting or enlivening in an European assembly often undermines his literary capacity.

For fifteen or eighteen years I have cited Williams as sole known American-dwelling author who cd. be counted on to oppose some sort of barrier to such penetration; the sole catalectic in whose presence some sort of modification wd. take place.

Williams has written: "All I do is to try to understand something in its natural colours and shapes." There cd. be no better effort underlying any literary process, or used as preparative for literary process; but it appears, it wd. seem, almost incomprehensible to men dwelling west of the Atlantic: I don't mean that it appears so in theory, America will swallow anything in theory, all abstract statements are perfectly welcome, given a sufficiently plausible turn. But the concrete example of this literary process, whether by Williams or by that still more unreceived and uncomprehended native hickory Mr Joseph Gould, seems an unrelated and inexplicable incident to our populace and to our "*monde*—or whatever it is—*littéraire*." We have, of course, distinctly American authors, Mr Frost for example, but there is an infinite gulf between Mr Frost on New England customs, and Mr Gould on race prejudice; Mr Frost having simply taken on, without any apparent self-questioning a definite type and set of ideas and sensibilities, known and established in his ancestral demesne. That is to say he is "typical New England." Gould is no less New England, but parts of his writing cd. have proceeded equally well from a Russian, a German, or an exceptional Frenchman—the difference between regionalism, or regionalist art and art that has its roots in a given locality.

Carlos Williams has been determined to stand or sit as an American. Freud wd. probably say "because his father was English" (in fact half English, half Danish). His mother, as ethnologists have before noted, was a mixture of French and Spanish; of late years (the last four or five) Dr Williams has laid claim to a somewhat remote Hebrew connexion, possibly a rabbi in Saragossa, at the time of the siege. He claims American birth, but I strongly suspect that he emerged on ship-board just off Bedloe's Island and that his dark and serious eyes gazed up in their first sober contemplation at the Statue and its brazen and monstrous nightshirt.

At any rate he has not in his ancestral endocrines the arid curse of our nation. None of his immediate forbears burnt witches in Salem, or attended assemblies for producing prohibitions. His father was in the rum trade; the rich ichors of the Indies, Hollands, Jamaicas, Goldwasser, Curaçoas provided the infant William with material sustenance. Spanish was not a strange tongue, and the trade profited by discrimination, by dissociations performed with the palate. All of which belongs to an American yesterday, and is as gone as *les caves de Mouquin*.

From this secure ingle William Carlos was able to look out on his circumjacence and see it as something interesting *but exterior*; as he cd. not by any possibility resemble any member of the Concord School he was able to observe national phenomena without necessity for constant vigilance over himself, there was no instinctive fear that if he forgot himself he might be like some really unpleasant Ralph Waldo; neither is he, apparently, filled with any vivid desire to murder the indescribable dastards who betray the work of the national founders, who spread the fish-hooks of bureaucracy in our once, perhaps, pleasant bypaths.

One might accuse him of being, blessedly, the observant foreigner, perceiving American vegetation and landscape quite directly, as something put there for him to look at; and this comtemplative habit extends, also blessedly, to the fauna.

When Mr Wanamaker's picture gallery burned in the dead of winter I was able to observe the destruction of faked Van Dykes etc, *comme spectacle*, the muffler'd lads of the village tearing down gold frames in the light of the conflagration, the onyx-topped tables against the blackness were still more "tableau," and one cd. think detachedly of the French Revolution. Mr Wanamaker was nothing to me, he paid his employees badly, and I knew the actual spectacle was all I shd. ever get out of him. I cannot, on the other hand, observe the national "mansion" befouled by Volsteads and Bryans, without anger; I cannot see liberties that have lasted for a century thrown away for nothing, frontiers tied up by imbecile formulae, a bureaucracy and system exceeding "anything known in Russia under the Czars" without indignation. And this comparison to Russia is not mine, but comes from a Czarist official who had been stationed in Washington.

And by just this susceptibility on my part Williams, as author, has the no small advantage. If he wants to "do" anything about what he sees, this desire for action does not rise until he has meditated in full and at leisure. Where I see scoundrels and vandals, he sees a spectacle or an ineluctable process of nature.

Where I want to kill at once, he ruminates, and if this rumination leads to anger it is an almost inarticulate anger, that may but lend colour to style, but which stays almost wholly in the realm of his art. I mean it is a qualificative, contemplative, does not drive him to some ultra-artistic or non-artistic activity.

Even recently where one of his characters clearly expresses a dissatisfaction with the American milieu, it is an odium against a condition of mind, not against overt acts or institutions.

2

The lack of celerity in his process, the unfamiliarity with facile or with established solutions wd. account for the irritation his earlier prose, as I remember it, caused to sophisticated Britons. "How any man could go on talking about such things!" and so on. But the results of this sobriety of unhurried contemplation, when apparent in such a book as *In the American Grain*, equally account for the immediate appreciation of Williams by the small number of French critics whose culture is sufficiently wide to permit them to read any modern tongue save their own.

Here, at last, was an American treated with a seriousness and by a process comprehensible to an European.

One might say that Williams has but one fixed idea, as an author; i.e., he starts where an European wd. start if an European were about to write of America: sic: America is a subject of interest, one must inspect it, analyse it, and treat it as subject. There are plenty of people who think they "ought" to write "about" America. This is an wholly different kettle of fish. There are also numerous people who think that the given subject has an inherent interest simply because it is American and that this gives it ipso facto a dignity or value above all other possible subjects; Williams may even think he has, or may once have thought he had this angle of attack, but he hasn't.

After a number of years, and apropos of a given incident he has (first quarterly number of *transition*) given a perfectly clear verbal manifestation of his critical attitude. It is that of his most worthy European contemporaries, and of all good critics. It is also symptomatic of New York that his analysis of the so-called criticisms of Antheil's New York concert shd. appear in Paris, a year after the event, in an amateur periodical.

The main point of his article being that no single one of the critics had made the least attempt at analysis, or had in any way tried to tell the reader what the music consisted of, what were its modes or procedures. And that this was, of course, what the critics were, or would in any civilized country have been, there for. This article is perhaps Williams' most important piece of critical writing, or at any rate his most apposite piece; failing a wide distribution of the magazine in which it appeared, it shd. be reprinted in some more widely distributable journal.

As to the illusion of "progress," it wd. seem that this illusion *chez nous* is limited to the greater prevalence of erotic adventure, whether developed in quality or merely increased in quantity I have no present means of deciding; as to any corresponding "progress" or catching-up in affairs of the intellect, the illusion wd. seem to rise from the fact that in our literary milieux certain things are now known that were not known in 1912; but this wd. not constitute a change of relation; i.e., wd. not prove that America is not still fifteen years or twenty years or more "behind the times." That is to say we must breed a non-Mabie, non-Howells type of author. And of the possible types Williams and Gould perhaps serve as our best examples—as distinct from the porous types.

I mean, not by this sentence, but by the whole trend of this article: when a creative act occurs in America "no one" seems aware of what is occurring. In music we have *chefs d'orchestre*, not composers, and we have something very like it in letters, though the distinction is less obvious.

Following this metaphor, it is undeniable that part of my time, for example, has been put into orchestral directing. Very little of Dr Williams' energy has been so deflected. If he did some Rimbaud forty years late it was nevertheless composition, and I don't think he knew it was Rimbaud until after he finished his operation.

Orchestral directing is "all right" *mais c'est pas la même chose*. We are still so generally obsessed by monism and mono-theistical backwash, and ideas of orthodoxy that we (and the benighted Britons) can hardly observe a dissociation of ideas without thinking a censure is somehow therein implied.

We are not, of course we are not, free from the errors of post-reformation Europe. The triviality of philosophical writers through the last few centuries is extraordinary, in the extent that is, that they have not profited by modes of thought quite common to biological students; in the extent that they rely on wholly unfounded assumptions, for no more apparent reason than that these assumptions are currently and commonly made. Reputed philosophers will proceed (for volumes at a time) as if the only alternative for monism were dualism; among distinguished literati, *si licet*, taking personal examples: Mr Joyce will argue for hours as if one's attack on Christianity were an attack on the Roman church *in favour of* Luther or Calvin or some other half-baked ignoramus and the "protestant" conventicle. Mr Eliot will reply, even in print, to Mr Babbitt as if some form of Xtianity or mono-theism were the sole alternative to irreligion; and as if monism or monotheism were anything more than an hypothesis agreeable to certain types of very lazy mind too weak to bear an uncertainty or to remain in "uncertainty."

And, again, for such reasons William Williams, and may we say, his Mediterranean equipment, has an importance in relation to his temporal intellectual circumjacence.

Very well, he does not "conclude"; his work has been "often formless," "incoherent," opaque, obscure, obfuscated, confused, truncated, etc.

I am not going to say: "form" is a non-literary component shoved onto literature by Aristotle or by some non-literatus who told Aristotle about it. Major form is not a non-literary com-ponent. But it can do us no harm to stop an hour or so and con-sider the number of very important chunks of world-literature in which form, major form, is remarkable mainly for absence.

There is a corking plot to *The Iliad*, but it is not told us in the poem, or at least not in the parts of the poem known to history as *The Iliad*. It wd. be hard to find a worse justification of the theories of dramatic construction than the *Prometheus* of Aeschylus. It will take a brighter lad than the author of these presents to demonstrate the element of form in Montaigne or in Rabelais; Lope has it, but it is not the "Aristotelian" beginning, middle and end, it is the quite reprehensible; BEGINNING WHOOP and any sort of a trail off. *Bouvard and Pécuchet* wasn't even finished by its author. And of all these Lope is the only one we cd. sacrifice without inestimable loss and impoverishment.

The component of these great works and *the* indispensable component is texture; which Dr Williams indubitably has in the best, and in increasingly frequent, passages of his writing.

3

In current American fiction that has often quite a good deal of merit, and which has apparently been concocted with effort and goodish intentions, the failure to attain first-rateness seems to be mainly of two sorts: The post-Zolas or post-realists deal with subject matter, human types etc, so simple that one is more entertained by Fabre's insects or Hudson's birds and wild animals and the habits or the reactions of "an ant" or "a chaffinch" emerge in a more satisfactory purity or at least in some modus that at least seems to present a more firm and sustaining pabulum to reflection.

Secondly: there are the perfumed writers. They aim, one believes, at olde lavender; but the ultimate aroma lacks freshness. "Stale meringue," "last week's custard" and other metaphorical expressions leap to mind when one attempts to give an impression of their quality. One "ought" perhaps to make a closer analysis and give the receipt for the *fadeur*; though like all mediocre dilutations it is harder to analyse than the clearer and fresher substance. When I was fourteen people used to read novels of the same sort, let us say *The House of a Thousand Candles* etc of which one may remember a title, but never remembers anything else, and of which the author's name has, at the end of five or ten years, escaped one.

It is perfectly natural that people wholly surrounded by roughnecks, whether in mid-nineteenth century or in The Hesperian present, should want to indicate the desirability of sweetness and refinement, but . . . these things belong to a different order of existence, different that is from pity, terror, $\tau\grave{o}$ $\kappa\alpha\lambda\acute{o}\nu$, and those things with which art, plastic or that of the writer is concerned.

Now in reading Williams, let us say this last book *A Voyage to Pagany* or almost anything else he has written, one may often feel: he is wrong. I don't mean wrong in idea, but: that is the wrong way to write it. He oughtn't to have said that. But there is a residue of effect. The work is always distinct from the writing that one finds merely hopeless and in strict sense irremediable.

There is a difference in kind between it and the mass of current writing, about which there is; just nothing to be done, and which no series of retouches, or cuttings away wd. clarify, or leave hard.

Art very possibly *ought* to be the supreme achievement, the "accomplished"; but there is the other satisfactory effect, that of a man hurling himself at an indomitable chaos, and yanking and hauling as much of it as possible into some sort of order (or beauty), aware of it both as chaos and as potential.

Form is, indeed, very tiresome when in reading [a] current novel, we observe the thinning residue of pages, 50, 30, and realize that there is now only time (space) for the hero to die a violent death, no other solution being feasible in that number of pages.

To come at it another way: There are books that are clever enough, good enough, well enough done to fool the people who don't know, or to divert one in hours of fatigue. There are other books—and they may be often less clever, and may often show less accomplishment—which, despite their ineptitudes, and lack of accomplishment, or "form," and finish, contain something for the best minds of the time, a time, any time. If Pagany is not Williams' best book, if even on some counts, being his first long work, it is his worst, it indubitably contains pages and passages that are worth any one's while, and that provide mental cud for any ruminant tooth.

4

And finally, to comply with those requirements for critics which Dr Williams has outlined in his censure of Mr Antheil's critics: The particular book that is occasion for this general discussion of Williams, *A Voyage to Pagany*, has not very much to do with the "art of novel writing," which Dr Williams has fairly clearly abjured. Its plot-device is the primitive one of "a journey," frankly avowed. Entire pages cd. have found place in a simple autobiography of travel.

In the genealogy of writing it stems from *Ulysses*, or rather we wd. say better: Williams' *The Great American Novel*, 80 pages, Three Mountains Press 1923 was Williams' first and strongest derivation from *Ulysses*, an "inner monologue," stronger and more gnarled, or stronger *because* more gnarled at least as I see it, than the *Pagany*.

The other offspring from *Ulysses*, the only other I have seen possessing any value is John Rodker's *Adolphe*, 1920. The two books are greatly different. *The Great American Novel* is simply the application of Joycean method to the American circumjacence. The *Adolphe*, professedly taking its schema from Benjamin Constant, brings the Joycean methodic inventions into a form; slighter than *Ulysses*, as a rondeau is slighter than a canzone, but indubitably a "development," a definite step in general progress of writing, having as have at least two other novels by Rodker, its definite shaped construction. And yet, if one read it often enough the element of form emerges in *The Great American Novel*, not probably governing the whole, but in the shaping of at least some of the chapters, notably Chapter VII, the one beginning "Nuevo Mundo."

As to subject or problem, the *Pagany* relates to the Jamesian problem of U. S. A. vs. Europe, the international relation etc; the particular equation of the Vienna milieu has had recent treatment "from the other end on" in Joseph Bard's *Shipwreck in Europe*, more sprightly and probably less deeply concerned with the salvation of the protagonist; I think the continental author mentions as a general and known post-war quantity: the American or Americans who comes or come to Vienna to find out why they can't enjoy life, even after getting a great deal of money.

In the American Grain remains, I imagine Dr Williams' book having the greater interest for the European reader. In the loose-ish structure of the *Pagany* I don't quite make out what, unless it be simple vagary of the printer, has caused the omission of *The Venus* (July *Dial*), pages obviously written to occur somewhere in the longer work, though they do form a whole in themselves, and pose quite clearly the general question, or at least one phase of the question posed in the *Pagany*.

In all the books cited, the best pages of Williams—at least for the present reviewer—are those where he has made the least effort to fit anything into either story, book, or (*In the American Grain*) into an essay. I wd. almost move from that isolated instance to the generalization that plot, major form, or outline shd. be left to authors who feel some inner need for the same; even let us say a very strong, unusual, unescapable need for these things; and to books where the said form, plot, etc, springs naturally from the matter treated. When put on, *ab exteriore*, they probably lead only to dulness, confusion or remplissage or the "falling between two stools." I don't mean that Williams "falls"; he certainly has never loaded on enough shapings to bother one. As to his two dialectical ladies? Of course he may know ladies who argue like that. There may be ladies who so argue, aided by Bacchus. In any case the effect of one human on another is such that Williams may elicit such dialectic from ladies who in presence of a more dialectic or voluble male wd. be themselves notably less so. No one else now writing wd. have given us [the] sharp clarity of the medical chapters.

As to the general value of Carlos Williams' poetry I have nothing to retract from the affirmation of its value that I made ten years ago, nor do I see any particular need of repeating that estimate; I shd. have to say the same things, and it wd. be with but a pretence or camouflage of novelty.

When an author preserves, by any means whatsoever, his integrality, I take it we ought to be thankful. We retain a liberty to speculate as to how he might have done better, what paths wd. conduce to, say progress in his next opus, etc. to ask whether for example Williams wd. have done better to read W. H. Hudson than to have been interested in Joyce. At least there is place for reflection as to whether the method of Hudson's *A Traveller in Little Things* wd. serve for an author so concerned with his own insides as is Williams; or whether Williams himself isn't at his best—retaining interest in the uncommunicable or the hidden roots of the consciousness of people he meets, but yet confining his statement to presentation of their objective manifests.

No one but a fanatic impressionist or a fanatic subjectivist or introversialist will try to answer such a question save in relation to a given specific work.

RON LOEWINSOHN

THE SOURNESS OF SOUR GRAPES: *WILLIAMS AND THE RELIGION OF ART*

The last laugh is supposed to be the longest and the sweetest. When he titled his fourth collection of poems *Sour Grapes* Williams was courting ridicule.

> This brought the psychiatrists about my head, if not the Freudian analysts.
> "*Sour Grapes*! Do you know what that means?" they said. . . .
> "It means you are frustrated. That you are bitter and disappointed. . . ."
> I got it from all quarters: "*Sour Grapes*, yes, that's regret. *Sour grapes*—that's what you are and that's what you amount to."
> But all I meant was that sour grapes are just the same shape as sweet ones:
> Ha, ha, ha, ha![1]

This last laugh may sound pretty weak to us, but in fact Williams is perfectly serious. In *I Wanted to Write a Poem* he goes into the same issue in a little more detail.

> Everyone knows the meaning of sour grapes, but it had a special meaning for me. I've always thought of a poet as *not* a successful man except in his own mind, which is devoted to something entirely different than what the world thinks of as success. The poet puts his soul in his work and if he writes a good poem he *is* successful. When I decided on the title I was . . . [thumbing] . . . my nose at the world. All the poems are poems of disappointment, sorrow. I felt rejected by the world. But secretly I had my own idea. Sour grapes are just as beautiful as any other grapes. The shape, round, perfect, beautiful. I knew it—*my* sour grape—to be just as typical of beauty as *any* grape, sweet or sour.[2]

---

1. W. C. Williams, *Autobiography* (New York: Random House, 1951), pp. 157-158. Hereafter cited in the text as *A*, followed by the page number.
2. W. C. Williams, *I Wanted to Write a Poem* (Boston: Beacon Press, 1958), pp. 32-33. Cf. also his later poem "Perfection," *Collected Later Poems*, p. 40.

The period that produced the poems in this collection (1917-1921) was a deeply frustrating one for Williams. To the Bohemians of the Village he remained essentially an outsider.

> "You don't really let yourself go, [they told him]. . . . The young Frenchmen, yes, . . . But you, you are an American. . . . You live in the suburbs, you even *like* it. . . . And you pretend to be a poet, a POET! Ha, ha, ha, ha! A poet! You!" [*A*, 157]

He was shocked by the decadence of their parties—a young French girl lying on a divan being caressed by half a dozen men, the great bed hanging by chains from the ceiling in Margaret Anderson's and Jane Heap's apartment. "After a drink or two . . . [I] wandered wearily home, as was my wont" [*A*, 141]. "I bumped through these periods like a yokel" [*A*, 137]. His own gang, the writers connected with the magazine *Others*, was falling apart under a variety of strains. He had arranged with Alfred Kreymborg to put on a double bill at the Bramhall Theater—one short play by each of them. Kreymborg betrayed him and put on a play of his own with one by Edna St. Vincent Millay [*A*, 140]. (*Sour Grapes* would be dedicated to Kreymborg.) By 1919 *Others* had collapsed. The previous year Williams' father had died after a long, painful and debilitating struggle with cancer.

The poet gives his mood in even darker colors in statements written during this period.

> I go in one house and out of another practicing my illicit trade of seeing, hearing, touching, tasting, weighing . . . I have no other profession. I do not always get on well in this town. I am more likely to turn out a bankrupt any day. I will move away then.[3]

By 1919 he could complain, "Old as I have become . . . I'll dance still on a proper occasion when I have grown so ankylosed that only a grimace is left me."[4] He was thirty-five years old, in the middle of the way of his life's journey, and felt the lack of—everything, even a dark wood in which to find himself. "There is nothing to stand on. I receive nothing for my work. There is always nothing, nothing—everywhere."[5] He envisions himself as a twentieth century Job sitting on his ash-heap of a suburb.

> Perhaps I am a sullen suburbanite, cowardly and alone. . . . Perhaps it is a preposterous longing for the wealth of the world. I sit a blinded fool, with withered hands stretched out into the nothingness around me. . . . Perhaps what I call my singing is a stench born of these sores. I deny that that makes any difference.

---

3. "Three Professional Studies," *The Little Review*, vol. V, nos. 10-11 (Feb.-Mar., 1919), p. 38.
4. "Gloria," *Others*, vol. V, no. 6 (July, 1919), p. 3.
5. "Three Professional Studies," p. 37.

AT LEAST I AM THAT . . . Perhaps it is all a vain regret . . . AT
LEAST IT IS THAT. At least I exist in that.[6]

This slough of despond is almost certainly exaggerated,
though the overriding tone of both of the books to come out of
this period—*Kora in Hell* and *Sour Grapes*—is frustration, as we
might guess from their title. But this Job, histrionically self-pitying
as he is, doesn't curse the day of his birth. On the contrary, he
sings louder for every tatter in his mortal dress, his sores giving
birth to a stench that is a singing. From this frustration he actually
derives an affirmation of himself: "AT LEAST I AM THAT . . . At
least I exist in that."

This self-affirmation is one of the benefits of the religion of
art Williams practices, sustaining himself on his own hunger. His
writing is all he has, and he clings to it as his only salvation, his
only way to survive the loss of youth or love, "the loss of everything[,] and it is not a poem, one poem, it is not a folk melange.
It is art."[7] These religious overtones are suggested by the vocabulary of his later comments on his title *Sour Grapes*: the poet's
mind is "*devoted* to something entirely different than what the
world thinks of as success. The poet puts his *soul* in his work. . . ."

He was initiated into this religion around 1903, when he was
about twenty. This baptism or confirmation (which seems to be
the experience at the center of his early long poem, "The Wanderer") took the form of

> a sudden resignation to existence, a despair—if you wish to call
> it that, but a despair which made everything a unit and at the
> same time a part of myself. I suppose it might be called a sort of
> nameless religious experience. I resigned, I gave up. I decided
> there was nothing else in life for me but to work. . . . It seems so
> much more important to me that I *am*. Where shall one go? What
> shall one do? Things have no names for me and places have no
> significance. As a reward for this anonymity I feel as much a part
> of things as trees and stones. Heaven seems frankly impossible. I
> am damned as I succeed. I have no particular hope save to repair,
> to rescue, to complete.[8]

He is *damned* even as he succeeds (this letter was responding to
Marianne Moore's enthusiastic review of his *Collected Poems:
1921-1931*), and since heaven seems frankly impossible he resigns

---

6. "Belly Music," *Others*, vol. V, no. 6 (July, 1919), p. 26. The capitalization is Williams'.
Cf. Eliot on Baudelaire (*Selected Essays*, New York, 1964, p. 380): "So far as we are
human, what we do must be either evil or good; so far as we do evil or good, we are
human; and it is better, in a paradoxical way, to do evil than to do nothing: at least, we
exist." For Eliot it's action that affirms existence; for Williams it's writing.
7. *Ibid*.
8. W. C. Williams, *Selected Letters* (New York: McDowell Obolensky, 1957), p. 147.

himself to existence. But this resignation or despair is the first
stage of a secular mysticism that unites his environment and him
with it.

We can easily see how this sort of mysticism might lead to—
or be derived from—the Epicurean aestheticism of Pater, Wilde
and early Yeats, not to mention Williams' classmate at Penn, Ezra
Pound, who in those days worshipped Yeats' poems and imitated
Wilde's manner. Since heaven and all values deriving from heaven
are impossible, one could reason, as Pater did, that it isn't "the
fruit of experience, but experience itself" that is the end or goal
or life. Since the world for each individual is

> dwarfed into the narrow chamber of the individual mind . . .
> ringed round for each one of us by that thick wall of personality
> through which no real voice has ever pierced on its way to us, or
> from us to what we can only conjecture to be without . . . each
> mind keeping as a solitary prisoner to its own dream of a world

—it follows that "success in life" consists of "burn[ing] always
with this hard, gemlike flame" of aesthetic appreciation for the
"counted number of pulses [that] is given to us of a variegated,
dramatic life," a life of "constant and eager observation."[9] "Such
a manner of life," Pater speculated,

> might even come to be seen as a kind of religion—an inward,
> visionary, mystic piety or religion, by virtue of its effort to live
> days "lovely and pleasant" in themselves, here and now, and with
> an all-sufficiency of well-being in the immediate sense of the
> object contemplated, independent of any faith or hope that
> might be entertained as to their ulterior tendency. In this way,
> the new aesthetic culture might be realizable as a new form of the
> contemplative life, founding its claim on the intrinsic "blessed-
> ness" of "vision"—the vision of perfect men and things.[10]

We may feel a little uncomfortable associating Williams with
the high aesthetic line of Pater and Wilde:[11] Williams insists on a
democratic inclusiveness and a Whitmanesque grotesqueness. He
doesn't have any of the aesthetes' elegance or *slink*; his common
American language comes out of the mouths of Polish mothers
[*A*, 311]. The scruffy details of *Sour Grapes*—the "green ice of
the gutters,"[12] the lice of the poor and the fleas of a dead cat, a

9. Walter Pater, "Conclusion," *Studies in the History of the Renaissance*, (1873) (New
York, 1919). *Cit.* Richard Ellman and Charles Feidelson (eds.), *The Modern Tradition*
(New York: Oxford University Press, 1965), p. 182f.
10. Walter Pater, *Marius the Epicurean* (1885) (New York, 1921). *Cit.* Ellman and
Feidelson, pp. 184-185.
11. See W. S. Gilbert, "Bunthorne's Song," from *Patience*. *Cit.* G. B. Kauvar and G. C.
Sorenson (eds.), *The Victorian Mind* (New York: Capricorn Books, 1969), p. 372: "If
you're anxious for to shine in the high aesthetic line as a man of culture rare, / You must
get up all the germs of the transcendental terms, and plant them everywhere."
12. W. C. Williams, *Sour Grapes* (Boston: The Four Seas Co., 1921), p. 39. Hereafter
cited in the text as *SG*, followed by the page number. All of the poems from this volume

dishmop [*SG*, 52, 53, 65]—seem particularly foreign to the candle-lit drawing rooms of *L'art pour l'art.* In his *Autobiography* Williams goes to some lengths to dissociate himself from Pound's aestheticist poses, recounting how exasperating it was to listen to Pound reading his own poems aloud. "His voice would trail off in the final lines . . . until they were inaudible—from his intensity" [*A*, 56]. He could never tolerate, Williams says, the " 'side' that went with all [Pound's] posturings as a poet" [*A*, 58]. In London Pound took him to hear Yeats read.

> It was a studio atmosphere, very hushed. . . . Yeats, in a darkened room, was reading by candlelight to a small, a very small gathering of his protégés, maybe five or six young men and women. . . . It was not my dish [*A*, 114].

When H.D. wrote him in 1916 that "real beauty is a rare and sacred thing," he told her, "There is nothing sacred about literature, it is damned from one end to the other."[13]

But we've got to take Williams' rejections of this religion of art with some caution. Many of his poems actually practice the heightened sensory receptivity Pater preached, and throughout his career he explicitly characterizes art as a salvation. In *Paterson V* art is the hole at the bottom of the bag of death.

> So through art alone, male and female, a field of
> flowers, a tapestry, spring flowers unequaled
> in loveliness.

> Through this hole
> at the bottom of the cavern
> of death, the imagination
> escapes intact.[14]

Earlier, at the time of *Sour Grapes*, he could be even more explicit and more thorough.

> I should like to make St. Francis of Assisi the patron saint of the United States, because he loved the animals. The birds came to him not for wheat but to hear him preach. . . .
> The columns of the trees in his forests were a lesson to him; he looked up between them and mingled with the animals as an equal. . . .

---

which are discussed in this essay are reprinted in *Collected Earlier Poems*. To the best of my knowledge no previous articles have appeared devoted exclusively to *Sour Grapes*. However, many of the book-length studies of Williams' work contain chapters or substantial sections devoted to this collection, which they discuss in varying degrees of detail. These would include studies by Linda W. Wagner (1964), Alan Ostrom (1966), James Guimond (1968), Thomas Whitaker (1968), James Breslin (1970), and Rod Townley (1975).

13. W. C. Williams, *Kora in Hell* (Boston: The Four Seas Co., 1920). Reprinted in *Imaginations*, ed. by Webster Schott, (New York: New Directions, 1970), p. 13.

14. W. C. Williams, *Paterson* (New York: New Directions, 1963, fourth printing), p. 247. Hereafter cited in the text as *P*, followed by the page number.

> If men are to meet and love and understand each other it must be as equals. . . .
>
> And in proportion as a man has bestirred himself to become awake to his own locality he will perceive more and more of what is disclosed and find himself in a position to make the necessary translations. The disclosures will then and only then come to him as reality, as joy, as release. For these men communicate with each other and strive to invent new devices. But he who does not know his own world, in whatever confused form it may be, must either stupidly fail to learn from foreign work or stupidly swallow it without knowing how to judge of its essential value. *Descending each his own branch man and man reach finally a common trunk of understanding.*
>
> The only possible way that St. Francis could be on equal footing with the animals was through the word of God which he preached with fervent breath of understanding. *Here was a common stem where all were one* and from which every paired characteristic branched. *It is the main body of art to which we must return again and again.* . . .
>
> Those who would meet the best in Europe with invention of their own must go down into *the trunk of art, which is their word of God,* where conversation can take place.[15]

Art for Pater is religion for solipsists or Leibnitzian monads, each dwarfed in the narrow chamber of his own consciousness, sealed off from other subjectivities and even the world around him by the thick wall of his own personality. His religious practice— "success in life"—doesn't consist of action (What can a "solitary prisoner [in] its own dream of a world" do?), but of "constant and eager observation." When he speculates about more than one such prisoner or dreamer Pater imagines an "aesthetic culture . . . realizable as a new form of the contemplative life," a culture of dreaming prisoners, solitary, incommunicado.

These are the counsels of despair, and Pater's "Conclusion" is the point of departure for Williams, who doesn't imagine a prison-house or monastery of solitary observers, but an organic forest in which creatures of different species interact as equals and communicate in a common language. Here that common language is the preaching of St. Francis, "the [tree] trunk of art, which is their word of God, where conversation can take place." Later it would be the roar of the Great Falls of the Passaic River— "What common language to unravel from that rafter of a rock's lip?" [*P*, 15]. For Williams art is only one member of a trinity.

---

15. "Comment," *Contact*, no. 2 (Jan., 1921) n.p. Reprinted in Williams' *Selected Essays* (New York: Random House, 1954), pp. 27-29 [my emphasis]. Hereafter cited in the text as *SE*, followed by the page number.

> . . . why not live and write? . . . I want to write . . . it is the holy
> ghost of that trinity: The Senses, Action, Composition. I am
> damned only when I cannot write.[16]

(It should be pointed out that Yeats and Pound also developed socially engaged versions of the religion of art. Yeats, who'd
had the religion of his youth taken from him by Huxley and
Tyndal, made himself a new one, "almost an infallible church of
poetic tradition, [out] of a fardel of stories, and of personages
and of emotions, inseparable from their first expression." But the
goal of this religion was a culture unified in its art—"a world where
I could discover this tradition perpetually, and not in pictures and
in poems only, but in tiles round the chimney-piece and in the
hangings that kept out the draft."[17] By 1919 Pound too had tired
of the reveries of the inward gaze, and was more than impatient
with poets who neglected the relation of the state to the individual. In *Mauberley* he paints the aesthete-artist as a kind of Elpenor
who falls from the grape arbor of self-indulgence. His own ideal is
Odysseus, man of action and social responsibility.[18])

Williams would expand and refine his senses, but only the
better to *perceive*, to assimilate fully into himself the particulars
of his environment. And not just the finer, more rarified particulars (Pater's "some form . . . perfect in hand or face; some tone on
the hills or the sea"), but all of them, including the ugly, the painful and the apparently empty. Williams wants this mystical union
with Rutherford, New Jersey—not because any one place is intrinsically better than any other ("Things have no names for me and
places no significance")—but so that he might truly recognize and
appreciate the value of things and people foreign to that place.
Ultimately, Williams' *local* environment is himself, his own body
and subjectivity, and Williams' art is a religion of *contact*, of
intersubjective communication, between countries and between
individuals. Knowing each man his own world, each descends his
own branch, reaching finally a common trunk of understanding.

Art serves, not to save men from boredom in their isolated
prisons, but to unite them in a common language while acknowledging their integrity and distinctness. "It is a common language
we are seeking . . . we all meanwhile retaining our devotional
character of Wolf, Sheep and Bear" [*SE*, 29]. If the poet creates

---

16. "Three Professional Studies," p. 39.
17. W. B. Yeats, "The Trembling of the Veil," (1920); reprinted in *Autobiography* (New
York: Collier Books, 1969; third printing), p. 77.
18. Ezra Pound, "Hugh Selwyn Mauberley," *Personae* (New York: New Directions,
1926), p. 185ff.

himself, makes himself real in his art ("AT LEAST I AM THAT
. . . At least I exist in that"), he also creates his local environment,
his time and his people.

> If we are to love or to know France, or any France, or any
> country it will be through the mature expression of . . . men
> in whom France has physically realized herself for better or
> worse. . . . There alone France exists in a mode capable of serving
> for international exchange [*SE*, 27].

Later on he would make the same point again: "Until your artists
have conceived you in your unique and supreme form . . . you
have not in fact existed."[19]

Art *is* a religion for Williams, but a religion whose service,
devotion and worship are directed only at man and nothing whatever beyond him. He agreed with Whitman in this, who had
affirmed in his 1855 Preface that "There is nothing in the known
universe more divine than men and women." To say that "Heaven
seems frankly impossible" may sound like sour grapes. But then to
celebrate the human and the actual particulars of the local environment as the measure of the divine is to *eat* those sour grapes, to
nourish himself on his own frustration.

† † † † † † †

So far we've been trying to reconstruct Williams' conception
of art as a democratic, egalitarian, secular religion. What would the
practice of such a religion look like? What sorts of poems would it
generate? Maybe more important for us, what shape would these
poems make when "composed" into a book?

In his previous book, *Al Que Quiere* (1917), this religion had
produced poems written in a language that's almost anything *but*
democratic or egalitarian, even though its vocabulary often makes
gestures in those directions. Williams translates his title as "To
Him Who Wants It,"[20] and while that sounds democratic enough,
we can also hear in the phrase an undertone of haughty disdain:
"To whomever wants it, and if nobody at all wants it, that's OK
too." The book's dust jacket spells this out.

---

19. "An Approach to the Poem," *English Institute Essays* (New York: Columbia University Press, 1947), p. 60.
20. He gives the same translation at least twice, in *I Wanted to Write a Poem* (p. 19) and
again in the *Autobiography* (p. 157), where he reveals some hesitancy: "*Al Que Quiere,*
which means, unless I am much mistaken, *To Him Who Wants It.*" In fact, he is mistaken. The phrase lacks a direct object, and should read *Al Que Lo Quiere.* As it stands
the title translates as: To him who wants, or To him who likes. He had thought of sub-
titling the book, "The Pleasures of Democracy." [*Selected Letters*, p. 40].

> This book is a collection of poems by William Carlos Williams.
> You, gentle reader, will probably not like it, because it is brutally
> powerful and scornfully crude. Fortunately, neither the author
> nor the publisher care much whether you like it or not. The
> author has done his work, and if you *do* read the book you will
> agree that he doesn't give a damn for your opinion.[21]

In *Al Que Quiere* the speaker of most of the poems is a kind
of Whitmanesque orator-evangelist—more prophetic than messi-
anic, self-consciously "earthy," posturing and self-aggrandizing.

> My townspeople, beyond in the great world,
> are many with whom it were far more
> profitable for me to live than here with you [*AQ*, 18].

He does a good deal of finger-wagging at these townspeople—

> Oh, I know you have your own hymns, I have heard them—
> and because I knew they invoked some great protector
> I could not be angry with you, no matter
> how much they outraged true music— [*AQ*, 19]

> I begin with a design for a hearse.
> For Christ's sake   not black—
> nor white either—   and not polished!
> Let it be weathered—   like a farm wagon— [*AQ*, 26][22]

—but often he isn't really talking to them. Poems like "Tract" are
ostensibly addressed to his townspeople, but in these poems the
speaker is obviously more concerned with his *readers*, whom he
seems to imagine sitting behind him on the dais as he holds forth.
These readers form an audience far more sophisticated than his
townspeople. These readers share his values and appreciate his wit
and his fervor. In "The Wanderer," the final poem in *Al Que
Quiere*, this prophet plunges into the filthy Passaic, symbolically
partaking of his townspeople's condition—their on-going, every
day, day-after-day, days-in-a-row condition. But in that poem he
still addresses them from afar.

> I shouted over the country below me:
> "Waken! my people, to the boughs green
> With ripening fruit within you!" [*AQ*, 82]

The distance between this speaker and his people is not horizontal,
a distance between equals, but vertical, the prophet looking down
upon his people, whom he is willing to try to elevate to his own
level. This is not St. Francis, but a combination of Isaiah and Walt
Whitman.

---

21. Reprinted in Emily Mitchell Wallace, *A Bibliography of W. C. Williams* (Middletown,
Conn.: Wesleyan University Press, 1968), p. 11. Further quotations from *Al Que Quiere*
will be cited hereafter in the text as *AQ*, followed by the page number.
22. These line breaks differ markedly from those in the version of the poem which
appears in *Collected Earlier Poems*.

Al Que Quiere was published in 1917, though its final poem had first appeared in 1914.[23] The "sudden resignation to existence" on which it is based occurred in 1903, when Williams was about twenty. This plunge into despair that's also a plunge into the painful and ugly reality of his neighbors' lives—their quiet desperation—is, in "The Wanderer," a poetic gesture. A sincere one, even though its uniqueness insists on its status as a *synechdoche*, the part that stands for the whole, the momentary plunge symbolizing the commitment of a whole life to this living stream. To fulfill that commitment took the rest of Williams' life, and *Sour Grapes* is one half of his response to the first seven years or so of the living out of that commitment.[24]

Kreymborg—just before he betrayed Williams at the Bramhall Theater—had actually lost the manuscript of another Williams play, a "playlet in verse" called "The Old Apple Tree."

> Then, and this is important, I wrote my first small playlet in verse called *The Old Apple Tree.* . . . The blossoms were her daughters called upon by the bees, their suitors. . . . at one time the old tree-mother offered one of the callers a cup of tea, that is, the sap of the tree itself.
> "It's bitter," said the man.
> "Have some more," said she [*A*, 139-140].

Williams suggests that he didn't call the grapes of his title sour because he couldn't achieve them, like the fox in Aesop's fable, but because he *had* achieved them, found them sour or bitter, and accepted them as such, as he accepted and celebrated the "perfections" of his autumnal landscape in *Kora in Hell.*[25] The sour grapes of this book, then, are the poems themselves, and the experiences from which they were distilled. In "The Wanderer" he had drunk deeply of the bitter sap of his own and his townspeople's lives; now he was having some more, sustaining himself on his own failures and disappointments. (He does much the same thing in his later poem "Lines on Receiving the Dial's Award," in which he drinks from an empty bottle a toast to a Pyrrhic

---

23. The poem first appeared, in a version slightly different from the one in *Collected Earlier Poems*, in *The Egoist*, vol. I, no. 6 (Mar. 16, 1914), pp. 109-111.
24. The other half is *Kora in Hell*, which was written, evidently, over a stretch of one year between 1917 and 1918, that is, simultaneously with the poems in *Sour Grapes*. At least one poem in *Sour Grapes* ("To A Friend," p. 46) appears in a prose version in *Kora* (see *Imaginations*, p. 61).
25. The phrase "Autumnal landscape" is Sherman Paul's, from his excellent essay on *Kora*, "A Sketchbook of the Artist in his Thirty-Fourth Year," collected in Melvin Friedman and John Vickery (eds.), *The Shaken Realist* (Baton Rouge: Louisiana State University Press, 1970), pp. 21-44. See also my essay, "Fools Have Big Wombs: W. C. Williams' *Kora in Hell*," *Essays in Literature*, vol. 4, no. 2 (Fall, 1977), pp. 221-238.

victory–the money from the award went to pay off a legal judgment against him.[26])

As opposed to the chest-thumping Whitman of *Al Que Quiere*, the self that speaks throughout most of *Sour Grapes* is less strident, quieter, in the later poems almost non-existent, having effaced himself so completely from the reader's view. It's almost as if the speaker of *Sour Grapes* had read and taken to heart John Gould Fletcher's review of *Al Que Quiere*.

> Is it . . . possible for a poet to be always himself? Must he not, to some extent, share not only the feelings of many people in the past, but also the feelings of men and women of his day? Certain words of . . . Andre Gide come to mind in this connexion: "A great man has only one care: to become as human as possible: let us say, rather, to become banal; and admirable fact, it is thus that he becomes most individual."
>
> In these words there is a lesson for Dr. Williams.[27]

In many of these poems, especially in the first part of the book, the speaker is one kind of "nobody," a failure who complains of the flat trajectory of his literary career, of his advancing middle age, of the tawdry "successes" of his love life. But in some of the book's better poems, especially in the second half or so, the speaker is "banal" in just the sense Gide intends: a "nobody" who becomes an *everybody* in part by his refusal to arrogate to himself the kind of soap-box selfhood he'd embraced on the dust jacket of *Al Que Quiere*. (According to the title page of *Sour Grapes*, the poems are in fact written by nobody: nobody's name appears as author.)[28] This progressive loss of ego doesn't proceed consistently: some of the poems in the first half of the book are outstanding and anonymous in this way (notably, "To Waken an Old Lady"), while a few poems in the latter part still "crow" or intrude. The description of the fire truck in the book's last poem as "tense" is an often-discussed example of authorial intrusion, actually a pathetic fallacy. But the general tendency toward a self that is anonymous or banal is unmistakable.

Sour Grapes was more "composed," he told Kenneth Burke in 1921, than any of his previous books. "The fact of its appearance," he went on, "is due more to the pressure of . . . having a lot of stuff lying around, than to anything else" [*SL*, 53]. But

---

26. *Collected Earlier Poems*, p. 350. See also Williams' *Autobiography*, pp. 241-243, for the story of the lawsuit.
27. John Gould Fletcher, "Two American Poets," *The Egoist*, vol. 4, (April, 1818), p. 60.
28. See Appendix, following notes, for a reproduction of the title page. See also the *Autobiography*, p. 108, for an account of how Williams decided on his literary signature. Given this concern, it's difficult to imagine that the omission of his name here could be accidental.

some very good poems of the period were *left* lying around,
excluded from *Sour Grapes*: "Le Médecin Malgré Lui," "For Any
Girl's Locket," "A Coronal," "To Marc Antony in Heaven," "St.
Francis Einstein of the Daffodils," and "Portrait of a Lady." The
optimism and healthy self-irony of these poems would have
warmed up these wintry pages, and moderated their picture of
sterility, frustration and loss.

The poems of *Sour Grapes* and the order into which Williams
composed them function to constitute an autumnal or wintry
landscape and also their own author, who proceeds through this
landscape toward the goal of a self-effacement that's actually a
self-assertion, a movement away from the egotistical sublime
toward a genuine negative capability. The book moves from a
singer who complains of being out of phase with the awakening
world of nature ["The Late Singer," *SG*, 11] to a fire truck whose
"unheeded" song is recorded in the poem rather than complained
about ["The Great Figure," *SG*, 78]. The movement is not from
winter to spring, but from conditions that are complained about
to conditions that are accepted, tasted, assimilated. This acceptance is part of the praxis of this secular, egalitarian, horizontal
religion of art, in which all things exist on the same level of value.
Since the transcendent values of heaven are "frankly impossible,"
it isn't things or experiences that are sacralized—broken bottles,
dishmops, flowers—but the experience of accepting them as they
are, a perception that grasps them thoroughly into the self and the
self thoroughly into them. In this religion it's the act of eating
them that transmutes the ordinary bread and wine into flesh and
blood. "The world is made to eat, not leave," he would say in a
few more years, "that the spirit be full, not empty."[29]

The composition—the order into which Williams arranged
these poems—serves to constitute their author by first presenting
us with poems that call our attention to their speaker and his
complaints. ("I have had my dream—like others— / and it has
come to nothing" [*SG*, 43.]) This self is established so firmly
that even the three poems in the early portion of the book that
concern other people ["To Waken an Old Lady," "Time the Hangman," and "To a Friend"] don't distract our attention from him.
This frustrated mood of self-involvement and self-pity continues
through the two short poems "Memory of April" and "Epitaph"
[*SG*, 54, 55], exercises in disappointment and nostalgia. At this
point this mood is broken by the four outstanding flower poems

---

29. W. C. Williams, *In the American Grain*, (1925) (New York: New Directions, 1956;
fifth printing), p. 205.

that follow—"Daisy," "Primrose," "Queen-Ann's-Lace" and "Great Mullen"—which focus our attention, not on the speaker and his condition, but on acts of observation in which the perceiving subject merges with the object. These four poems form the brief "summer" of this book's year, and in this generative season the poet discovers his own creative powers by losing himself in meticulous observations that are in fact transformations.

> One turns the thing over
> in his hand and looks
> at it from the rear: brownedged,
> green and pointed scales
> armor his yellow
> But turn and turn,
>
> the crisp petals remain
> brief, translucent, greenfastened,
> barely touching at the edges:
> blades of limpid seashell [*SG*, 56]

The three poems that follow pick up the earlier tone of bitterness and lament. "I am greeted by / the happy shrieks of my children / and my heart sinks. / I am crushed" [*SG*, 60].

"To a Friend Concerning Several Ladies" [*SG*, 63] is the book's fulcrum or pivot, the point at which this speaker chooses himself and his condition, chooses himself in the face of the tempting "great world beyond" which, in his previous book, he thought a "more profitable" place to live. Here, instead of the bright lights and glamor of New York he chooses the marshes outside of Rutherford, a place of darkness and ignominy, but also of generative life, where

> the crickets run
> on the sunny dike's top and
> make burrows there, the water
> reflects the reeds and the reeds
> move on their stalks and rattle drily.

The last thirteen poems differ from the earlier poems in the book not only in mood, but more importantly, in tone and in voice, the speaker's attitude toward himself. "The Widow's Lament in Springtime" [*SG*, 73] doesn't present Williams' mother as a stand-in for himself, but himself as subsumed into the figure of the widow, who doesn't "lament" so much as long to be subsumed herself into the same generative marsh Williams has also chosen.

> Today my son told me
> that in the meadows,
> at the edge of the heavy woods
> in the distance, he saw

trees of white flowers.
I feel that I would like
to go there
and fall into those flowers
and sink into the marsh near them.

The four poems that follow, the last four in the book, complete the process of constituting for us an author who is anonymous by first giving him to us and then taking him away. First "Light Hearted William" and "Portrait of the Author," which focus our attention on the poet in two opposed moods and modes of creation (and self-creation), and then "The Lonely Street" and "The Great Figure," which focus on the things seen, the "I" reduced to a point of view.

At the same time that the order of these poems enacts this process of self-making (and un-making), it creates a landscape whose essential, fundamental season is winter, a blankness which spring and summer only decorate, temporarily and thinly, like a veneer. Underneath those grasses, flowers and birds, January maintains its grip on the ground and on the poet's insides. "Winter is long in this climate / and spring—a matter of a few days / only" [*SG*, 12]. When spring does arrive it's as often as not blighted, its reawakening and abundance mocking the deadness and poverty of the poet's mood. "Too much of sumac buds . . . I had no rest against that springtime" [*SG*, 21]. Even though the first two poems in *Sour Grapes* are set in spring, it isn't until we're two-thirds of the way through the book that we encounter a set of truly celebratory poems—the four flower poems we've already noted. Winter is long in this book, and spring a matter of a few poems only. These four positive, energetic pieces are immediately followed by poems of complaint and poems set indoors, where the only nightingales are the shadows of the poet's fingers as he unlaces his shoes on the flowers of his bedroom carpet. But it's precisely that kind of envisioning that allows this poet to live in this climate, finding his sustenance in these sour grapes.

† † † † † †

Five of the poems in the early part of the book ["March," "A Celebration," "A Goodnight," "Overture to a Dance of Locomotives," and "Romance Moderne"] are substantially longer than the other poems in the volume. They are also noisier and, unlike the better poems, built up out of conventional "effects." They are ambitious in just the wrong sense of his "My Townspeople" poems—they play to a gallery of poets.

The weakest of these is "Overture to a Dance of Locomotives" [*SG*, 24]. An affectation of the grand manner, it attempts
to mythologize Grand Central Station with nothing but generalizations, flaccid epithets and preciosity.

> Men with picked voices chant the names
> of cities in a huge gallery; promises
> that pull through descending stairways
> to a deep rumbling.

The image of the engines straining against their brakes to pull out
of the station is almost euphuistic. "Poised horizontal / on
glittering parallels the dingy cylinders / packed with a warm glow—
inviting entry— / pull against the hour." This language is as
orotund as Grand Central , but nowhere does Williams indicate
any awareness of this ironic parallel. The poem only parodies
itself: "Important not to take / the wrong train!"

"A Celebration" [*SG*, 18] and "March" [*SG*, 12] sound
more like the Williams of *Al Que Quiere* than anything else in this
book. They are aggressive, self-consciously literary, over-written
(longer than they need to be),and postured. But they are the most
interesting and the best of this group of five longer poems. Both
are concerned with poetry as a flower that struggles for survival
in a cold, inhospitable climate. "A Celebration" establishes winter
as the ground condition of the poet's world: "A middle-northern
March, now as always." In such an environment the orchids (for
Williams a symbol of violent sexual passion) survive only in a
hot-house, cut off from local particulars, tamed by deracination
and made into a "tiresome pastime."[30] Williams is more interested
in the bare oleanders standing leaflessly in the cold outside the
orchid-house, their dark branches revealing "the very reason for
their being." Looking at them, he doesn't imagine some prettier,
leafier condition for them, but perceives the dark ground of their
being, their essential tree-ness.[31]

> It is this darkness reveals that which darkness alone
> loosens and sets spinning on waxen wings—
> not the touch of a finger-tip, not the motion
> of a sigh.

---

30. Cf. "Asphodel, That Greeny Flower," *Pictures From Brueghel*, p. 153f: "The sexual
orchid that bloomed then . . ." (p. 158). Cf. also Williams' discussion of the American
Puritans in *In the American Grain* (p. 63): "The Pilgrims were seed of Tudor England's
lusty blossoming. The flamboyant force of that zenith, spent, became in them hard and
little. Among such as they its precarious wealth of petals sank safely within bounds to
lie dreaming or floating off while the Restoration throve, a sweltering seclusion of the
hothouse surrounded by winter's cold.
31. Cf. "The Botticellian Trees," *Collected Earlier Poems*, p. 80: "The alphabet of / the
trees / is fading in the / song of the leaves. . . . / The strict simple / principles of / straight
branches / are being modified / by pinched-out / ifs of color."

Bored with "reading" the literary orchids that will "take the prize tomorrow / at the palace," he goes home to build a fire, a different kind of flower that will "at least warm our hands / and stir up the talk."

"March" is the most complex of these longer poems. Originally published in 1916, it actually belongs with the defiant poems of *Al Que Quiere.* The first of its five sections establishes the bitter sterility of early spring in America struggling against the "fierce jaws" of a predatory winter, and implicitly contrasts this condition with some other, unnamed climate. In Part II the other climates are named as Williams apostrophizes March, and relates it in three (somewhat overcontrived) similes to the "stript" and opened pyramids of the Metropolitan Museum, to Fra Angelico painting frescoes at Fiesole (a fresco is painted on plaster that hasn't yet set, as the season, in March, isn't yet fully manifest), and finally to a band of contemporary poets, his grotesque fellows who "have not yet learned / the blessedness of warmth / (or have forgotten it)."[32]

March, in this poem, is both the first month of spring and a procession of artists, from the artists who carved the splendors of Babylon to Williams' contemporaries. The remaining three sections of the poem flesh out the metaphors established in Part II, moving from the religious interior wall-carvings and wall paintings of the sunny past to the windy outdoors of the present, no longer art but "the real thing." In this hostile landscape Williams and his grotesque fellows are both the destructive winds and the flowers they seek.

Part III is all hunting and violence. "Ashur-ban-i-pal, / the archer king . . . with drawn bow–facing lions / . . . his shafts / bristling in their necks!" Part IV seems all gentleness, "a virgin–in a blue aureole / sitting on a three-legged stool, / arms crossed– / . . . intently serious, / and still," listening to an angel announce her own impregnation. The scene is spring, March in northern Italy. "On the ground there are flowers, / the trees are in leaf." But this gentle scene does include some threat and aggression. "The angel's eyes / holding the eyes of Mary / as a snake's holds a bird's."

The artist-winds of the last section are both masculine ("snake-like") and "serious as a virgin." Mary conceives in March and gives birth (to The Word) in the dead of winter. In Williams' climate spring is much like December, and as an artist he seeks as

---

32. These "grotesque fellows" were only sought for in "Sub Terra," the opening poem of his previous book, *Al Que Quiere*: "Where shall I find you, / you my grotesque fellows / that I seek everywhere / to make up my band?"

much to destroy the sterile conventions that promote this coldness ("Fling yourselves upon / their empty roses— / cut savagely!") as to preserve himself ("seeking one flower / in which to warm myself!"). He wants to be both the fertilizing wind and the fertilized virgin, and as he rouses his fellow poets to battle and murder he also urges them to gentleness. "Think of the painted monastery / at Fiesole." Both the violence of Ashur-ban-i-pal and the mildness of Mary endure and create warmth.

"March" is far and away the best of these longer poems— richer, subtler, more complex, more certain in its use of metaphor and in its weaving of analogous and contrasting images. But its own cleverness works against it, giving us a sense of contrivance and also a sense of a man exploiting both nature and art to illustrate a position worked out in advance. The poem is an elaborate demonstration or sermon.

Other poems in *Sour Grapes* are weakened by sentimentality or melodramatic self-pity. "Blizzard" [*SG*, 34] sketches a storm that has become an element in which Williams lives, the way a fish lives in the sea. "Years of anger following / hours that float idly down— / the blizzard / drifts its weight / deeper and deeper for three days / or sixty years." The poem achieves one clear, striking image—"hairy looking trees standing out / in long alleys"— and then dissolves into stock idioms and melodrama. "Over a wide solitude / the man turns and there— / his solitary track stretched out / upon the world."

"Complaint" [*SG*, 37] demonstrates both a gain over the poems in *Al Que Quiere* and a failure to make progress. In his earlier book he had "admired" the houses of his impoverished townspeople as lessons in aesthetics, observing them from the outside and then self-consciously pointing to them as being "of vast import to the nation."[33] Here he enters these houses and finds the damned human anguish of a woman

> on her side in the bed.
> She is sick,
> perhaps vomiting,
> perhaps laboring
> to give birth to
> a tenth child. Joy! Joy!

The repeated "perhaps" weakens the image even while it expands this one house call, suggesting repeated calls to almost identical houses. Only the maladies change; the anguish is constant. Williams' complex response to this pain is clear—both compassionate and ironic, both sympathetic and hard-nosed.

---

33. See "Pastoral," *Al Que Quiere*, p. 14.

> Night is a room
> darkened for lovers,
> through the jalousies the sun
> has sent one gold needle!
> I pick the hair from her eyes.

The stated sentiment of the closing lines—"I watch her misery / with compassion"—is totally unnecessary, intrusive and distracting, calling our attention to a speaker who insists that in spite of his ironies he is really a decent chap.

"The Desolate Field," "The Dark Day" and "Waiting" [*SG*, 30, 44, 60] are all similarly marred by self-pity or sentimentality. Curiously, their statements of feeling don't allow us any greater intimacy. They give us only the outside of the speaker's behavior, and all three poems suggest that Williams himself has not penetrated to the core of his own subjective experience, even though the intimate tone of musing and the often flat and unpoetic surface of these poems suggest that we are being given, not "art," but "the real thing." These stated sentiments aren't evocations or enactments but specifications or behavior that leave us outside, merely observers of actions to which Williams has attached labels. In a four-line poem, "The Gentle Man," [*SG*, 47]

> I feel the caress of my own fingers
> on my neck as I place my collar
> and think pityingly
> of the kind women I have known.

we have to conclude that Williams, like us, is only a spectator who has no authentic experience of the "kind women" he mentions, since they exist only as the object of what he calls his knowledge, labelled as easily as he labels his own thoughts. In this poem he "knows" only his own behavior, a man looking in his mirror.

Other poems are marred by Williams' evident inability to restrain himself from making extraneous authorial comments, as if he'd forgotten Pound's lesson that the natural object is always the adequate symbol.[34] If it weren't for these intrusions, usually pathetic fallacies, these would be outstanding lyrics. "Willow Poem," [*SG*, 31] for instance—

> It is a willow when summer is over,
> a willow by the river
> from which no leaf has fallen nor
> bitten by the sun
> turned orange or crimson.

---

34. Ezra Pound, "A Retrospect," *Pavannes and Divisions* (London, 1918). Reprinted in *Literary Essays* (London: Faber, 1954), p. 9: "I believe that the proper and perfect symbol is the natural object."

> The leaves cling and grow paler,
> swing and grow paler
> over the swirling waters of the river
> as if loath to let go,
> they are so cool, so drunk with
> the swirl of the wind and the river—
> oblivious to winter,
> the last to let go and fall
> into the water and on the ground.

—is built of very little. It repeats and inverts its few words and phrases in slow, sarabande-like rhythms, imitating the meagerness of the season and the movement of the willow. (Willow-over-willow-river; fallen-bitten-crimson; cling and grow paler-swing and grow paler; swirling waters of the river-swirl of the wind and the river; *l*ast to *l*et go and fa*l*l; oblivious to winter-into the water) If the pathetic fallacy of lines nine and ten were omitted the metaphor of a being that gives itself to the *flow* of time and so preserves itself (briefly) against the decay of winter would be strengthened.

The following poem, "Approach of Winter," [*SG*, 32] is weakened in the same way. The leaves of these autumn trees "*refuse* to let go," but when they do they "stream out *bitterly* to one side." In "Winter Trees," [*SG*, 36] nature is again anthropomorphized. These "*wise* trees" have "prepared their buds" and "stand sleeping in the cold," sure of surviving the season. The comparison with Williams himself, in the context of this collection, is obvious and invidious. "The Soughing Wind," [*SG*, 48] a three-line poem, is interrupted and sidetracked, not by a pathetic fallacy, but by a comment or gloss that calls our attention to a speaker who is more intent on easy aphorizing than on perceiving.

> Some leaves hang late, some fall
> before the first frost—so goes
> the tale of winter trees and old bones.

When Williams holds off from these intrusions in *Sour Grapes* he is able to write studies that compare internal human states with the world of nature and the seasons that are among his best poems. The two poems in this book written explicitly for his mother (then in her seventies)—"To Waken an Old Lady" and "The Widow's Lament in Springtime" [*SG*, 35, 73]—show Williams genuinely and immediately involved with the experience of old age, as opposed to his earlier poetic gesture of acceptance, "seeing himself old" in "The Wanderer." These two poems, the first a conceit, the second a dramatic monologue, are among his

finest and most often discussed poems, praised by even so demanding (and hostile) a critic as Yvor Winters.[35]

Sour Grapes is not exclusively concerned with winter, old
age, autumn and impending death. Some of the better poems here
focus on spring, youth, birth and beauty, and in the best of these
we find very little of the sentimental or romantic. The coming
of spring is as ineluctable as the approach of any season. Seen
from its beginning it's as painful and messy as human births. Williams was a physician, and birth for him was more than just a
metaphor. In the best of his spring poems and nature studies he
looks closely and observes accurately, as he must have in his
medical practice. "I am interested in babies because . . . diagnosis
rests almost wholy upon perception of the objective signs,"[36] he
said at about the time he was writing these poems.

"The Birds" [*SG*, 69] begins like a conventional celebration
of spring and dawn. "The world begins again!" Yet it shifts
immediately into qualifications and specifications, sketching
crucial contrasts quickly and concretely, and using its few words
with great economy. The flatness of its language eventually works
a subtle and ironic magic.

> The world begins again!
> Not wholly insufflated
> the blackbirds in the rain
> upon the dead topbranches
> of the living tree,
> stuck fast to the low clouds,
> notate the dawn.
> Their shrill cries sound
> announcing appetite
> and drop among the bending roses
> and the dripping grass.

This world may be new, but its most active creatures—like asphyx-
iated or unbaptized (or newly born?) people—haven't yet had life
breathed into them. They inhabit the topmost (and dead)
branches of a still-living tree, and are themselves the notes (black
dots on lines) they "sing." Those songs—actually shrill cries—
announce, not *love* or *rebirth*, but appetite. This poem is dead set
against the pathetic fallacy. Their cries *fall* from those dead
branches to the living roses and grass. Reading quickly, we might
think that the *birds* have made that drop, but they aren't wholly
alive or awake yet, and stay on their dead heights. It's their *songs*

35. Yvor Winters, "Poetry of Feeling," *Kenyon Review*, I (Winter, 1939), pp. 104-107.
Reprinted in J. Hillis Miller (ed.), *W. C. Williams: A Collection of Critical Essays* (Englewood Cliffs, New Jersey, 1966), pp. 66-69.
36. "Three Professional Studies," *The Little Review*, vol. 10-11, (Feb.-Mar., 1919), p. 39.

("cries") that fall, to "notate" the low but living vegetation. If the birds were wiser, more alive or more awake, they would follow their songs, come down off their high perches to the ground, where they would stand a better chance of satisfying their hunger. The poem has already shown them how, by dropping straight down from its opening generalization and high-falutin vocabulary to the concrete particulars of its close. The magic the poem works is to breathe life into both these birds and their world. At the end of line two we think that "insufflated" must modify "world." As we move on to the next line we think it goes with "blackbirds." Of course it describes both, and the poem's job is to complete that inbreathing.

In most of the poems following "To a Friend Concerning Several Ladies" Williams concentrates on the particular details of commonplace things that make up his world and his life, things that don't even have the glamor of being "vulgar"or "forbidden"— none of the public latrines, dog-lime, naked dances and hag-muses of his previous book. The narrower horizon of these poems helps to indicate the shift in Williams' self-concept as a priest of this religion: from his earlier "prophetic" position above his world, he has dropped down into a more intimate, more democratic orientation to things. And these quotidian things—a dishmop, a pair of slippers, a vase of flowers, the shadows of his fingers, a trip to the marsh at the edge of town—are presented in a language whose surface is as ordinary as the things themselves.

Williams follows the frustration and resignation of "To a Friend Concerning Several Ladies" with the paradoxical satisfaction of "Youth and Beauty" [SG, 65].

> I bought a dishmop—
> having no daughter—
> for they had twisted
> fine ribbons of shining copper
> about white twine
> and made a towsled head
> of it, fastened it
> upon a turned ash stick
> slender at the neck
> straight, tall—
> when tied upright
> on the brass wallbracket
> to be a light for me
> and naked,
> as a girl should seem
> to her father.

A single long sentence of quotidian, domestic fantasizing, a sentence made up of the simplest words, that simultaneously focuses

our attention on the activity of minute observation and on an
extremely dense linguistic texture of rhyme, alliteration and
assonance. (mop-daughter-copper; fine-shining-white twine; about-
towsled; stick-slender-straight; stick-neck; tied-upright-light; brass-
bracket-naked) The apparently simple metaphor (dishmop=daugh-
ter) is constantly reminding us of its two terms, keeping them
distinct even as it joins them. In its last four lines the metaphor
opens out to include two new terms: the dishmop-daughter is a
light, "as a girl should *seem* / to her father," *seeming* to reveal all
and yet at that moment changing into something else. Now a
dishmop, now a daughter, now a light. The poem's satisfaction is
paradoxical. It doesn't provide him with a daughter, but a poem.
Not a vision but an act of envisioning.

The next poem, "The Thinker," [*SG*, 66] similarly focuses
our attention (by its title) on its speaker who *observes* not his
wife, but her slippers, a speaker who lives in his own "secret
mind." He notices that the slippers are "perfect," without a spot
or a stain. Waking up in the morning with a shiver, he envies them
lying together all night under his wife's bed. (He has lain all night
alone in his own.) Throughout the day he continues to observe
them,

> And I talk to them
> in my secret mind
> out of pure happiness.

The poem pointedly maintains the secrecy of that mind, a subjectivity that remains private in the poem as in the marriage. The
focus of the poem is the experience of the man who thinks, but
what he thinks is kept from us, just as it's kept from his wife. We
see him observing, but his experience remains private.

"The Nightingales" [*SG*, 70], also gives us an act of envisioning. The poem begins with a disappointment, the "come-down"
from the exotic birds-of-poetry of its title to—shoes being unlaced
as they stand on a flowered rug. But that disappointment is
replaced by the pleasure of watching the "nimble" shadows of the
speaker's fingers as they "play" over the "flowers." The only
substantial things in the poem are shoes (and the feet in them) and
play—the movement of the shadows that replace (imitate) the
birds of the title, and the movement of the mind that observes and
analogizes, or rather, that simply juxtaposes the word "Nightingales" with the image of the shoes being unlaced, allowing us to
discover for ourselves analogies where we least expect them, to
take part in the play.

Each of these poems *plays* with disappointment. Their titles
lead us in one direction, the texts take us someplace else, which

at first seems to be worse, but only at first. Not "youth and beauty," not a statue by Rodin or a philosopher or intellectual, not nightingales, but three acts of envisioning.

The things he envisions are resolutely *banal*. They aren't symbols or metaphors. They don't stand for anything or refer to anything. They don't undergo any transformation. Even the dish-mop doesn't become a daughter, it remains a dishmop seen in a fanciful way. Earlier in this book he had looked closely at four flowers that are similarly banal, un-poetic—and discovered in each of them something "larger." The daisy becomes a sun, the prim-rose a color that infects and dominates its world, the wild carrot the body of a woman loved, the mullen a proud man. In these later three poems the dishmop, the slippers, the shoes and shadows all remain what they are, valued as such and all the more as "what they are" is discovered in an act of envisioning that's also an act of self-discovery and self-renewal.

Williams doesn't disappear from these poems. He insists on himself as the "I" who perceives and revalues these banal things, but in actualizing them for himself and us that "I" remains a per-sonality-less, ego-less sensibility that keeps its hands off the things it brings to life. The only purpose his presence serves is to remind us that things themselves remain ordinary, flat, "not wholly insuf-flated," until a perceiving "I" interacts with them. And the flat surface of these poems serves to remind us that the poems (objects themselves) also remain dead until we as readers interact with them, discovering their life and coherence, as Williams has done.

Curiously, the very anti-literariness of these three poems marks them as literary. That is, Williams is able to foil our expec-tations precisely because his three titles refer us to concepts or images that are part of a solidly established literary convention or tradition. It's this reference that causes us to have conventional expectations in the first place, and only after these have been provoked by the titles can the poems do their job of simultaneous deflation and enrichment.

"Blueflags," [*SG*, 72] one of the last poems in the book, does even more. It uses standard literary devices in an extremely sophisticated way, while maintaining the "banality" of its surface. Its strategy is almost the precise opposite of juxtaposing a prepos-sessing title and a "disappointing" text. "Blueflags" is just the common name for a common flower. It isn't until the end of the poem that its images and its language begin to resonate for us as something else, and it's at that point that we begin to revalue the commonplace things in it, including the "everyday" quality of the

poem itself, which begins with a common enough event, a little
excursion to the country, to let the kids run off some energy.

> I stopped the car
> to let the children down
> where the streets end
> in the sun
> at the marsh edge
> and the reeds begin
> and there are small houses
> facing the reeds
> and the blue mist
> in the distance
> with grapevine trellises
> with grape clusters
> small as strawberries
> on the vines
> and ditches
> running springwater
> that continue the gutters
> with willows over them.

This single sentence locates the poem at the meeting place
of civilization and nature, the marsh's edge "where the streets
end . . . and the reeds begin." The marsh is a place of darkness,
overhung with willows, while the streets remain in sunshine. These
two worlds remain separate and opposed here, yet bound together
in a single sentence. The poem doesn't state any overt metaphor,
but its preoccupations start to become clear as it backtracks,
repeats part of an earlier line, and then makes its only simile.

> The reeds begin
> like water at a shore
> their pointed petals waving
> dark green and light.

"But," the poem continues, "blueflags are blossoming / in the
reeds. . . ." Across that shore or boundary, within that foreign
element of darkness and unchecked vegetable growth, some
common but lovely and attractive flowers are coming into being,

> which the children pluck
> chattering in the reeds
> high over their heads
> which they part
> with bare arms to appear
> with fists of flowers
> till in the air
> there comes the smell
> of calamus
> from wet, gummy stalks.

The central metaphor here is the crossing of a boundary. The children leave the sunlit world of civilization, enter the dark marsh and bring back some of the natural beauty they find there. The calamus recalls Whitman's "washed root of sweetflag," a symbol of masculine sexual energy, and suggests that the transgression has a sexual component, like Williams' search for Kora in the dark underworld of *Kora in Hell*. As the two worlds of civilization and nature are united in the poem's first long sentence, so the children and the flowers are joined in its long closing sentence. When they reappear the children have taken into themselves aspects of the marsh world and are transformed (re-created)—in that subtle play on the genitive—into plants, "with fists *of* flowers." To fully perceive the beauty of nature, to realize it, we have to participate in it, to enter it. In doing so we imitate nature itself (which always includes us, though we often forget that), "we become nature or discover in ourselves nature's active part" [*A*, 241]. This is just what the speaker has done. "Lost" in his fascination with the details of the landscape, he suddenly perceives his children differently and accurately: they are part of the world of nature.

On yet a deeper level, *blueflag* is the common name for Iris, a flower, but also the messenger of the Greek gods, "who bears their behest from the ends of the earth even to the river Styx, and into the depths of the sea. . . . She resembles Hermes, and therefore carries the herald's staff."[37] The children behave like divine messengers carrying blossoming herald's staves, travelling from one world to another,[38] entering the Styx-like marsh to bring back some flowering bits of beauty. They also behave like the poet, who similarly communicates with the past (of ancient myth) and with the lower world of darkness in realizing—making real—the presentness of the past and the force with which the underworld animates each action of our daily lives.

The children are transformed into flowers and divine messengers while remaining children. At the beginning of the poem they enter the marsh world, but at the end they return to the sunlit streets of civilization. The poem doesn't celebrate a Rousseau-esque or Wordsworthian notion of "natural man," but enacts a shift of consciousness. Williams has witnessed what is immediately before him in detail, but the witnessed transformation remains subtle in the poem, allowing us to discover it for ourselves.

---

37. Oskar Seyffert, *Dictionary of Classical Antiquities* (Cleveland and New York: Meridian Books, 1956), p. 324.
38. Cf. "A Negro Woman," *Pictures from Brueghel*, p. 123: "Carrying a bunch of marigolds / wrapped / in an old newspaper: She carries them upright . . . / What is she / but an ambassador / from another world."

We might usefully compare Williams' mythology, as adumbrated in this poem, with Pound's. *The Cantos* is socially, politically engaged (Alas! we may want to say), but it *assumes* a heaven ("Le paradis n'est pas artificiel") and an order of divinity existing on a level somehow "higher" than that of ordinary, quotidian human reality. ("The 'magic moment' or moment of metamorphosis, bust thru from quotidian into 'divine or permanent world.' Gods, etc."[39]) Pound's religion of art is hierarchical, the world of myths and divinities existing either in hypostasis, somehow "underneath" the everyday, human one, or in some Dantesque realm of unchanging perfection. Williams' religion is horizontal. The world of the marsh (the realm of dark, unchecked natural generation) is different from the world of the town (the area of light, of order and therefore of stasis), but both of these worlds are found on the same map; they exist on the same level, and the poem's ordinariness underscores the continuousness of our commerce between them.

In "The Lonely Street" [*SG*, 77] he does much the same sort of thing he did in "Blueflags." Here the schoolgirls, "in white from head to foot . . . in yellow, floating stuff," walking at ease in the heat of summer, eating cotton candy, are transformed into goddesses. "They hold / pink flames in their right hands . . . like a carnation each holds in her hand." Yet they remain children. It's significant that in both these poems it isn't Williams or the speaker who is transformed, but nameless children. The speaker is only the anonymous witness to these metamorphoses, and instead of announcing himself as a visionary, he quietly allows us to participate in his vision.

The ironies in the title of the book's final poem come through most clearly in the context of its placement in this collection, Williams' fifth book, published at a time when he was, by his own admission, not cutting a very great figure, either in New York or Rutherford. Though he'd been making a lot of noise, nobody had been listening. But out of the unheededness of the fire truck Williams constructs not a lament or a complaint, but an enactment of a great heed, a great attention paid to the figure of the truck by an "I" that's here subsumed into the very thing it sees.

† † † † † †

---

39. Ezra Pound, *Selected Letters* (New York: Harcourt Brace, 1950), p. 210. Pound uses the phrase "Le paradis n'est pas artificiel" several times throughout the Pisan Cantos. See, for instance, Canto LXXVI.

In *Sour Grapes* Williams is much less aggressive, much less a self-appointed public figure than he had been in his previous book. If "The Wanderer" had plunged into the filthy Passaic, the Williams of this book had been immersed for years in the quotidian life of his middle-class community. "The Wanderer" had been a poetic gesture, the enactment of an insight. The subsequent years were reality, during which he drank deeply of the bitter sap of his townspeople's disappointment and frustration, becoming more like them, participating in the actual stream of their lives, no matter how much more sensitive or aware he was than they.

As Williams becomes more "ordinary" in this book, the language of his poems becomes less stridently disjunctive, less fragmentary than it is in *Kora*, even less irregular than it was tending to become in *Al Que Quiere*. With very few exceptions, the poems of *Sour Grapes* are written in an idiom whose surface features wouldn't be recognized as unusual on the streets of Rutherford. Fragmentation, where it occurs in this book, involves whole poems that present themselves as fragments, sometimes not even making up an "image" as we think of in connection with the Imagists, but only an isolated shard of thought or perception, sometimes only a line or two of internal monologue. But consistent with Williams' vision throughout his career, these fragments affirm an underlying continuity. The best of these short poems also avoid the epigrammatic or the aphoristic. They don't have that pretension. "Lines," [*SG*, 51] a two-line poem, is itself a fragment that deals with fragments, yet its business is cohesion.

Leaves are grey green,
the glass broken, bright green.

It unites fallen leaves and broken glass simply because they together constitute virtually all of the poem. They aren't compared, except as *we* compare them in seeing them juxtaposed here. The leaves and the glass form a harmony, not because of any overt statement of relation, but because the rhyme, alliteration and assonance of these lines unite the two images while keeping them distinct.

Williams' voice in this book is much less histrionic than it was in *Al Que Quiere*, more the voice of a man musing to himself, whether the thrust of a given poem is celebration or complaint. With few exceptions, his voice isn't even conversational, but private, meditative, the voice of many of the entries in *Kora*, in which Williams isn't addressing a crowd but only himself. This quietness is complex. It suggests that Williams feels close to his audience. We almost always raise our voices to address a distant person, whether the distance is physical or emotional. In anger we shout, in love we whisper. Yet this quietness coexists in this book with an apparently contradictory isolation: Williams resolutely avoids any identification with a group, out of which he might speak as "we" ("March" is an exception), and speaks only as an "I" who takes his stands against a "them" that sometimes includes artists as well as philistines. Sometimes this "them" includes the world of nature, which he'd previously assumed to be his own domain. There seems to be a vast distance between this "I" and his audience, yet he speaks so softly, as if there were no distance at all.

In his "banality" Williams has *become* his audience, both artists and suburbanites. The best poems of *Sour Grapes* are quietly lyrical: they don't seek to convince but to include the reader, who recognizes the experience the lyric enacts because he has already been there. Like his townspeople, Williams is—on the surface—middle class, suburban, conventional. He is like them because he has drunk of the same bitter sap they have. Below this surface he is intensely private, isolated, different—as they are, both from him and from each other. On a deeper level yet he discovers and affirms those aspects of his privateness and isolation which he shares with them. This book is Williams' attempt to find that common trunk of understanding, the word of God, a common stem where all are united while remaining distinct and equal.

APPENDIX A

SOUR GRAPES

A Book of Poems

BOSTON

THE FOUR SEAS COMPANY

1921

APPENDIX B

All of the poems of *Sour Grapes* are reprinted in the *Collected Earlier Poems* (the book's one prose piece, "The Delicacies," is omitted), though not all in the section titled "Sour Grapes." In addition, that section of the *CEP* contains a number of poems not included in the original edition, and all these poems appear in *CEP* in a different order from that in the first edition. Following is a list of the contents of *Sour Grapes*, in the order in which they appeared in the 1921 edition.

The Late Singer
March
Berket and the Stars
A Celebration
April
A Goodnight
Overture to a Dance of Locomotives
Romance Moderne
The Desolate Field
Willow Poem
Approach of Winter
January
Blizzard
To Waken an Old Lady
Winter Trees
Complaint
The Cold Night
Spring Storm
The Delicacies
Thursday
The Dark Day
Time, the Hangman
To a Friend
The Gentle Man
The Soughing Wind
Spring
Play

Lines
The Poor
Complete Destruction
Memory of April
Epitaph
Daisy
Primrose
Queen-Ann's-Lace
Great Mullen
Waiting
The Hunter
Arrival
To a Friend Concerning Several Ladies
Youth and Beauty
The Thinker
The Disputants
The Tulip Bed
The Birds
The Nightingales
Spouts
Blueflags
The Widow's Lament in Springtime
Light Hearted William
Portrait of the Author
The Lonely Street
The Great Figure

GILBERT SORRENTINO

POLISH MOTHERS AND "THE KNIFE OF THE TIMES"

> The language, the language
> fails them
> They do not know the words
> or have not
> the courage to use them
> —*Paterson One, I*

It is obvious that when Williams remarked that his American language came "from the mouths of Polish mothers" he was not speaking merely of a language whose patterns, inflections, syntax, etc., were those of the imperfect tongue spoken by immigrant women. The comment should be construed to mean that American is made up of linguistic elements that are quite different from those of English—native locutions growing out of "the weather," sketchy and distorted syntax, a "revised" grammar designed for rapid communication, unorthodox verb placement, suffixal prepositions and conjunctions, heavy doses of a constantly changing colloquial, and an expressive slang whose older examples often survive as instances of irony or mockery. A great deal of this language is never written down or "formalized" in any way at all.

Williams' short stories, with the curious exception of "The Knife of the Times," employ this spoken American language. The language of "The Knife of the Times," however, is false, and works to prevent the communication of anything other than the superficial, the removed or twice-removed. In Williams' hands it acts brilliantly to reveal the divorce of its users from the reality of their feelings, to deny these feelings except insofar as they are located on a plane of unreality or stale fantasy.

Many of Williams' strategies of construction are deployed in the story, e.g., a third-person narrator whose voice is neither omniscient or limited, but is that of what can be termed an "absent" first person; a non-functioning past—time is ignored or foreshortened, so that all the action develops in an "eternal" present; a lack of description or characterization; a contempt for "realistic" motivation—the characters *are now*; and great forward momentum, made possible by the eschewal of standard transitional devices. But the language of the story, in its discrete words and those words in varying combinations, is very different from that of Williams' other short fiction, so much so that it may be thought of as foregrounded: it is so relentlessly wooden and artificial that it directs continuous attention to itself. Yet the entity presented has no "style," neither is it a parody of a style—it floats free of a recognizably literary tradition. An examination of the story reveals three distinct modes of language out of which it is composed. But first, let us look briefly at the narrative.

The theme of the story is that of one character's (Ethel's) growing lesbian desire for another character (Maura), over a period of years which has seen them, after a childhood friendship, separated and gone into conventional married lives. Ethel's passion is projected through the mails, with her letters growing progressively and, to Maura, disconcertingly more amorous. Maura hides the letters, and after twenty years (!) they meet at Ethel's insistence, have a brief but decidedly sexual moment together, and go back into their normal lives, with Ethel's invitation to Maura to visit her so that they may finally sleep together controlling the last sentence of the story: "Why not?" That we don't know whether this is Maura's question to herself or Williams' question to his story is a precise example of Williams' use of the ambiguous narrative voice. A simple story, and one that would be expected to attract Williams. But the story is not important to Williams, or, more clearly, Williams is not interested in *what happens* or *what will happen* to his characters. The story is a constant, outside time, inflectionless. This static infinitive is embedded directly in the failed language used to tell the story, and this language reveals a social and emotional malaise at once caused and unrelieved by it. Williams' cavalier treatment of the conventions of the fictive temporal erases any notions we may have that the passage of time is relevant to the overwhelming emptiness that the story generates—nothing that *happened* makes the slightest difference to what *is happening*; and what is happening will make no difference to what *will happen*. Ethel and Maura are frozen in time, buried in a present that is created of a language insufficient to permit them understanding or relief. They are inarticulate, "speech-less," and hence sealed in misunderstanding and confusion.

Ethel and Maura are void of imagination and cannot understand each other or themselves because of their poverty of language. The story is not written in Williams' usual brusque "short-hand" American; rather the language is emblematic of the impotence which has separated these two women from their deepest selves. Their responses to all experience are automatic, superficial, and banal. The entire work is composed of words and phrases distinct from a speech of even the most common denotation or perception, a speech incapable of the delineation of actuality: it is a false language, one that, paradoxically, the intensity of their secret relationship has given birth to, that it has, in fact, made obligatory so that the intensity may be *mistaken*. Williams has constructed this language with exquisite care to show that the impossibility of contact between his heroines is caused by their chosen language's destruction of the imagination. They can be neither lovers nor friends; they cannot confront the fact that they cannot be lovers or friends. The reality of their predicament is unrecognized by them because they have no language with which to plumb it other than one that connotes the spurious: a language of the void. Their words have both invented and stranded their lives.

As I have noted, this work is made of three distinct modes of language, each separate from the other, each at best inadequate, at worst sham. Carnal passions and fears are presented in a rigid and dead etiquette of the verbal. Let us look at these three modes:

a. Automatized language.
b. Polite or refined language.
c. The language of popular romance-fiction.

The first mode is used without thought, and is the language that enables us to get through the usual business of day-to-day living, to convey and receive necessary information; it is a "transitive" language that, as Valéry has it, disappears after its message has been carried. An example from the story: "And both began to bring up families.Ethel especially went in for children. Within a very brief period, comparatively speaking, she had three of them, then four, then five, and finally six."

The second mode is learned, as manners are learned. It is an affected speech, designed to reveal the speaker's sense of the niceties, the sort of language used at funerals, weddings, etc. My mother, contemporaneous with Williams, called this, as did her peers, "refined" language—even the word "refined" was refined. It is a *special* language, brought out on particular occasions, and is dissimilar from the first mode. To use it is an effort of the will, and it is usually intended to gloss over the reality of the situation that calls it forth—it homogenizes what it touches. Essentially a language of concealment, it acts as a figure that concretizes the *social* understanding existent among those who use it. Signatures of this language are often its stilted verbs and verb forms, its penchant for the passive voice, its polite and exhausted idiom, its many inversions of normal sentence structure. It is hard to *say*, and is meant to be, since it is, in essence, counterfeit speech, a "written" language. Example: "But the steamer was met, the sister saluted; the day came to an end and the hour of parting found Ethel still keeping close, close to the object of her lifelong adoration."

The third mode is that of the romance-fiction of "ladies' magazines" or popular novels of romantic love. Not so incidentally, four of Williams' contemporaries were champions of this genre: Faith Baldwin, Fannie Hurst, Kathleen Norris, and Viña Delmar. Their books are primers of the craft, their pages studded with examples of Williams' third mode in its virginal state. This language is notable for its delicate avoidance of the overtly sexual, which is dealt with by the use of a fixed repertory of euphemism and cliché. It is a strictly codified language whose rule of thumb is that the closer it approaches the sexual the more breathlessly asexual it becomes. Example: "She spoke of her longings, to touch the velvet flesh of her darling's breasts, her thighs. She longed to kiss her to sleep, to hold her in her arms." "Longings," "velvet," "darling's," and "sleep" all serve to defuse the carnal, rendering it risqué and "spicy," rather than erotic or pornographic.

None of these modes is sufficient to define the nature of the emotional complex that these women form; on the contrary, they blur and distort it.

Williams uses all three of these modes (and none other) throughout the story. They are his sole materials. The story develops a supreme resonance of the banal when he combines two or more modes in single, or contiguous sentences: "And through it all (a) she kept in constant touch with her girlhood friend (a), dark-eyed Maura (c), by writing long intimate letters (b)." "Franker and franker (b) became her outspoken lusts (c). For which she begged indulgence (b)."

The interested reader may go through the story and make three lists, by mode, of all the phrases and sentences that make it up. He will discover that he has made three small handbooks of habitualized and empty language.

Three things should be noted about these modes. 1. They are each responsible for roughly one-third of the total language of the story—a nice balance. 2. Each is used to specific effect by its placement in the text, i.e., one mode sometimes persists for two or more sentences; one mode is used to separate two units of another mode; each mode is used in turn; one mode is used to throw another into relief; two or more modes are mixed in the same sentence or phrase. 3. Williams' antennae are so finely tuned that his surface is continuous, so that each mode slides into the next in a process of elision. They begin to blur: e.g., "nobody but you can appease my grief" is an example of the third mode because of where it is placed in the text, but it could quite easily be an example of the second mode, and "not a little fear," here used as an example of the second mode, could be an example of the third, and so on. The story is linguistically seamless, despite its separable modes. *All* the language is exhausted and carries with it no clear intentions other than its own impotence.

"The Knife of the Times," then, is atypical Williams. In it he partially solved a problem that he poses in his essay, "The Work of Gertrude Stein," in which he writes: "Observation about us engenders the very opposite of what we seek: triviality, crassness, and intellectual bankruptcy. And yet what we do see can in no way be excluded. Satire and flight are two possibilities. . . . But if one remain in a place and reject satire, what then? To be democratic, local . . . [the] artist must for subtlety ascend to a plane of almost abstract design to keep alive. . . . what actually impinges on the senses must be rendered as it appears, by use of which, only, and under which, untouched, the significance has to be disclosed. It is one of the major problems of the artist."

"The Knife of the Times" fulfills the requirements that Williams set for himself. More importantly, it proved to him that it was possible to write in a debased language without satiric or parodic intent, to write, that is to say, in a language that seemed to have no possibilities for literature. This empty and pathetic story of two human beings caught in a language unfit to assist or relieve them, and unaware of it, is, in a sense, made of the speech of Polish mothers become Americans. It was, for Williams, an act of absolute creative recovery.

KERRY DRISCOLL

THE MYTHOS OF MOTHER OR YES, MRS. WILLIAMS

When William Carlos Williams' memoir of his mother, *Yes, Mrs. Williams*, was first published in 1959 the critical attention it attracted was predominantly negative. Reviewers faulted the book for being formless, sentimental, and banal, and agreed that its primary value was as an autobiographical document rather than literary text. As Williams' friend John C. Thirlwall, commented in *The New York Times Book Review*: "This little book would be nothing more than a faded pastiche of verbena and caracoles did it not throw significant light on the career as poet and physician of son Willie."

Perhaps because of its initial reception, *Yes, Mrs. Williams* is still regarded as a minor addendum to the Williams canon; it is a text often referred to in passing, but never considered at length. This is a serious oversight, because in spite of its obvious flaws, the memoir is a conscious, complex literary work. It is also, I would argue, an invaluable matrix for assessing and interpreting Williams' development as a writer.

Although *Yes, Mrs. Williams* was published only four years before the poet's death, its composition spans most of his active writing career. He began the text in the early 1920s by recording unusual bits of his mother Elena's conversation and continued working on it sporadically over the next thirty years. For this reason, the memoir echoes many of Williams' major poetic concerns, and is closely related to the rest of his oeuvre in style and theme. The format of the text, for example, resembles his early improvisational piece, *Kora in Hell* (1920), which also consists of brief paragraphs followed by an italicized commentary. Interestingly, Williams' mother figures prominently in this text as well, both in the prologue where he establishes her as a model of poetic perception and in several of the improvisations themselves.

Williams' depiction of his mother through the idiosyncracies of her own idiom links the memoir to another early work, *In the American Grain*. In fact, the methodology he describes in the preface to that volume is equally applicable to *Yes, Mrs. Williams*:

> Thus, where I have found noteworthy stuff, bits of writing have been copied into the book for the taste of it. Everywhere I have tried to separate out from the original records some flavor of an actual peculiarity the character denoting shape which the unique force has given. [*IAG*, v].

The fragmentary, highly anecdotal structure of the memoir creates an impression of intimacy and artlessness, as if Elena were speaking directly to the reader. This sense of familiarity and immediacy is ultimately illusory, however, since Williams in his role as editor, arranger, and commentator rigorously controls the image we formulate of his mother. By placing her in a text, the poet converts Elena into a fiction which he can manipulate at will, much in the same way she molded his sensibilities as a child. This implicit reversal of origins, in which the son becomes the creator of his own mother, subverts the historical chain of cause and effect, and places Williams and Elena in a timeless web of mutual influence. Their relationship, like that which exists between man and the city in *Paterson*, is "an interpenetration, both ways" [*P*, 3].

Paradoxically, the memoir is also a veiled self-portrait. In attempting to write his mother's biography, Williams' own life becomes a critical subtext, not only because of the enormous influence she exerted on it but because their personalities and temperaments were so much alike. In many of the italicized interpolations in the memoir, Williams omits all personal pronouns so that it is impossible to determine the source and subject of particular statements. This technique effectively doubles the authorship of these passages and blurs the distinction between mother and son. The conflation of their identities is augmented by the poet's disruption of linear time in the text. He describes Elena as being older and younger than him, stating at one point, "This 'Contemporary' is my mother" [60], as though she were a member of his generation rather than the preceding one. In addition to obscuring the vast difference in their ages, this reference establishes a strong spiritual and ideological bond between mother and son; both are, in Elena's words, "practical workers in the army of fate" [97], united by common ambitions, attitudes, and concerns.

Williams' mother is, in many respects, his grotesque double, the other through and against whom the poet defines himself. As he worked on the memoir throughout the late forties and fifties, Williams was beginning to experience the difficulties of old age; thus, Elena's debilitated condition became, perhaps unconsciously at first, a precursor of his own fate. Within a few years of his mother's death in 1949, Williams suffered a series of increasingly serious strokes which left his right arm paralyzed and his eyes unable to focus. In light of these circumstances, certain anecdotes in the memoir assume an almost prophetic quality. For example, in response to her son's question as to why she no longer plays the piano, Elena shows him her hands and says, "I can't make them go anymore. And this one drops down" [50]. This passage is followed by an equally poignant one in which Elena laments her loss of sight:

> It's because I can't read. I want to see something, but I can't see
> it. That tune is always in my head. I am saying something, but I
> hear it there all the time. It makes me crazy. [50].

Moreover, Elena's dependence on Williams in old age prefigures his own reliance on Flossie after his stroke. The memoir thus reflects the uncanny manner in which the poet "becomes" his mother, re-enacting the slow, inexorable process of her decline. As the following excerpt from the 1960 poem "Tribute to Neruda" reveals, Williams perceived the fundamental similarities between their plights:

> Now that I am all but blind,
> however it came about,
> thought I can see as well
> as anyone—the imagination
>
> has turned inward as happened
> to my mother when she
> became old: dreams took the
> place of sight . . . [*CLP*, 267]

The complex interrelation of mother and son's characters makes *Yes, Mrs. Williams* crucial to a comprehensive understanding of the poet's life and work. It is a private, obsessive text—one which Williams was compelled to write, yet could never satisfactorily bring to fruition. Beneath the memoir's cranky convoluted syntax, repetitions, and apparent inconsistencies, lie important clues which explicate and unify the disparate strands of Williams' poetry from its beginnings in 1909 through *Paterson 5* and *Pictures from Brueghel*.

NEIL BALDWIN

THE STECHER TRILOGY: WILLIAMS AS NOVELIST

I. *White Mule*: an American tapestry

William Carlos Williams was no stranger to the novel form by
the time he completed *White Mule*, the first volume in his "Stecher
trilogy" in 1937. He had been working on the book intermittently
for ten years, and "bits here and there [dated] back thirty years."[1]
The book is dedicated to Richard Johns who, as editor of the
magazine *Pagany*, brought out chapters from summer 1930
through winter 1933. Additional sections of the novel were published in *The Magazine*, from March 1934 through May-June 1935.
    Williams' earlier fiction efforts included *The Great American
Novel* (1923), "a satire on the novel form,"[2] a multifaceted collage; *A Voyage to Pagany* (1928), a thinly-veiled account of
Williams' sorties to Europe and his "first serious novel";[3] and *A
Novelette* (1932), further experiments in improvisation, fragmentation, and stream of consciousness.
    And of course, all during the twenties and thirties, there were
short stories published in periodicals and collected in *The Knife of
the Times* (1932) and *Life Along the Passaic River* (1938), giving
vent to Williams' obsession with "the plight of the poor,"[4]
accounts of a family doctor's visits to the other side of the tracks,
there to glimpse the anarchy of poverty.
    At its most improvised and free-written, Williams' fictional
prose reads like unbroken poetic lines. The language is plastic, the
tongue runs free, coming out of the resolution, say, to write something every day of the year. Williams the journalist, the day-book

---

1. William Carlos Williams, "*White Mule* Vs. Poetry," *The Writer*, Boston, L.8 (August
1937), pp. 243-245.
2. Williams, *Autobiography* (New Directions, paperbook, 1967), p. 237.
3. Williams, *I Wanted to Write a Poem* (New Directions, paperbook, 1978), p. 45. Edited
by Edith Heal.
4. Williams, *ibid.*, p. 63.

writer, makes no attempt to hone his words. The white-heat writer builds that heat into the work itself, letting it be.

However, *White Mule*, labored for a decade and more, departs from the improvisatory fiction which laid the groundwork for it. Williams had already shown that he had the stamina to extend the language. In *White Mule*, the prose is worked, and pared down. Stylistically, it is a landmark book. It was also New Directions' first gesture of endorsement for an author who, up to that time (Williams was 54 years old) had had no ongoing commitment from *any* publisher.

His poems show us Williams the pointillist. His novels and other fiction show us the documentarian, engaged in the endless record of his life with others; the social being against an historic backdrop.

† † † † † †

White Mule, In the Money, and *The Build-up* together present the fictionalized story of Williams' wife, Florence, from her birth in the early 1890s, to her marriage to the young doctor "Charlie Bishop" in 1912 and the birth of their first child soon after. Along that time curve is plotted the financial rise and emotional decline of her father, "given the fictional name Joe Stecher, a Silesian immigrant to New York City in the latter part of the nineteenth century; and his wife, Gurlie, a restless, ambitious, and troubled Norwegian immigrant."[5]

"After all I was a physician and not only that I was a pediatrician and I'd always wanted to write a book about a baby,"[6] Williams told Edith Heal. And indeed, the baby Flossie is *White Mule*'s contact-point, bringing us back into the story over and over, the true center of attention; and in that respect, part of Williams' life-long homage to his wife culminating in the late poem *Asphodel*. "Floss was like a shot of whiskey to me—her disposition cantankerous, like all wives, riding her man for his own good whether he liked it or not."[7] The book and its successors gradually reveal a woman, in part imagined, lifted out of her daily domestic life into something greater—as were all things plucked from the world at large, and placed into Williams' work. Flossie was ennobled by her very inclusion.

---

5. Robert Coles, *William Carlos Williams: The Knack of Survival in America* (Rutgers University Press, 1975), pp. 64-65.
6. Williams, *I Wanted to Write a Poem*, p. 60.
7. Williams, *ibid.*, pp. 60-61.

White Mule is "life on the page without rhetoric."[8] It is a no-nonsense, direct, auspicious beginning to the Stecher series. Williams admitted that the following two volumes did not come up to its level; but he also seemed to know why, as we shall discover.

The same constellation of details characterizing Williams' best poems—when we see and hear phenomena imitated, never copied; the vignettes, aperçus, snatches of pictures, fragments of heard conversation; the juxtaposition of thought upon action without creating any sense of disorientation—give *White Mule* its backbone, its consistency and unity. "Prose can be a laboratory for metrics," Williams wrote Kay Boyle in 1932, "It is lower on the literary scale. But it throws up jewels which may be cleaned and grouped."[9] The clinician who composed poems by lifting up and setting down words, mindful of their inherent properties, also composed a novel in the same manner.

Just as in the poetry, *tension* drives the story forward, from the outset. Joe Stecher's purity of intention, his desire to do a job and do it well, is aligned immediately with the purity we expect in a newborn baby who resembles her father and soon comes to idealize him. Joe will not be corrupted. He is an immigrant, but his sensibility reminds us of the Puritan elders.

On the other hand, Gurlie, his wife, is just as single-minded in her desire for more and more money, which will come to her only through her husband's labors. ". . . because everybody wants to beat the next one, said Joe. That's the American way. Unless you have more than anybody else you have to feel ashamed of yourself."[10]

Like D. H. Lawrence, a writer he much admired, Williams' essential preoccupations can be found in some form in everything he wrote. And they are—again as with Lawrence—repeated and insistent, so that we receive his themes musically, chords sounded over and over: ". . . the United States of America—money. Without money, nothing. Money" [*WM*, 13]. *White Mule* is a recurrent

---

8. Reed Whittemore, *Williams Carlos Williams: Poet from Jersey* (Houghton Mifflin, 1975), p. 231.
9. Williams, *Selected Letters* (McDowell, Obolensky, 1957), p. 130. Edited by John C. Thirlwall.
10. Williams, *White Mule* (New Directions paperbook, 1967), p. 138. Hereafter, all page references to the novel, and to the two succeeding, *In the Money* (New Directions paperbook, 1967), and *The Build-up* (New Directions paperbook, 1968), will be cited in the text.

sounding of themes on one grand theme of America; Williams the vestigial romantic looks at the country he glorifies for its indigenous values, knowing that there is in fact nothing truly indigenous about it. Rather, the country is given meaning by what people like Joe and Gurlie bring to it.

Joe Stecher fights to remain uncorrupted against Gurlie's hunger for money. He also fights against the temptation to organize by joining the labor union, which would mean sacrificing his individuality. And he persists against a backdrop of New York City at the end of the nineteenth century; men at work are driven harder to it by wives and families at home; they are pushed out into a gritty world to find means for providing, under great pressure.

In a well-made Williams poem, each part has a specific functional relationship to each other part. The poem's imaginative syntax is crucial to its understanding. In *White Mule*, each character's thematic role becomes clearer through repetition. Joe emerges as the victim of *usura*; his wife as the raw power behind him—the counterstress in direct opposition; and the baby, Flossie, like a little "flower that is just opening" [167], provides a perfect focus for Williams' observations about a new and fresh world. She is his testimony to the immediate beauty he is compelled to find words for. He saw babies' processes as "not yet affected by calcification,"[11] and Flossie's very nakedness gives *White Mule* an aura of novelty.

In a well-made Williams poem, there is a linear movement; we find narrative even in a dozen lines, the sense of being taken through by someone with an instinctive knowledge of the mind's natural paths. Well-imagined images are synthesized by the strength of sheer presentation and we can *see* movement from A to B to C. *White Mule* possesses many such moments:

> It was an enchanting spectacle to Gurlie, rolling hills, then as the road took a turn they entered a little glen, almost a tunnel of leaves, with a steep embankment to the left made up of small balsams and heavy underbrush while to the right went off sharply a stony bank to a tumbling stream churning itself white over large rocks. A cooling air came up from this small chasm. . . . Then, unexpectedly, the horse turned to the right, leaving the highway, and began to climb a side road all grown with grass down the center. Just two tracks for the wheels either side. They bumped over several large rocks [226].

Williams' impulse, here and many places elsewhere, is to order the world into a succession of coherent perceptions so that

---

11. Williams, "Three Professional Studies," *The Little Review*, V, no. 10-11 (March 1919).

we follow along as the eye moves, fixing objects and people in space. The overall effect is reassuring. The natural world of *White Mule* is a place to seek the security the characters lack within themselves.

Williams is a successor to the "transparent eyeball" in Emerson's prose; the nineteenth-century romantic and his twentieth-century follower possess the same missionary zeal, the same endorsement of the world around them as the only true source for spiritual enrichment. In the cinematic movement of the paragraph below, Williams takes us from the weather outside, into the windows of the Stecher flat; he then alights to focus upon Joe—in action but still—and then one more step down to the baby. Through the eloquence of simple presentation we notice that Joe does not interfere with baby Flossie. We are led to perceive one more *detail* about him to add to the build-up of his character:

> The last Saturday in January, it was snowing hard outside, the driven flakes striking with an almost imperceptible seething sound against the back windows of the flat as the husband and wife sat in the kitchen for Joe to drink his hot coffee before starting downtown. The baby was at his knee holding on precariously and grinning up to him as usual. Its little hands, none too clean, rested on his pants' knees but he didn't disturb them [148].

Two pages later, the falling snow has smothered the city to the extent that it has obligerated "meaningless detail. . . . *The illusion of an imposed order*, the cleanliness—touched Joe and gave him contentment watching the storm" [150. Emphasis mine]. It is a subtle footnote, keying us in to the artifice that makes the work a fiction.

When Gurlie retreats to the country for the summer with her two daughters, "where there's light and air" [189]; and she goes for a walk in the forest, noticing "small points of green which near at hand you had to look close to discern in the distance [taking] on a shape" [179], she prefigures the ambulatory poet of *Paterson*, exploring Garret Mountain Park of a Sunday afternoon. Gurlie in the country endorses what is unspoiled, in direct counterpoint to Gurlie in the city, pushing for status and wealth. She mourns for her native land, and the farms she enjoyed as a child. She exalts the pastoral, past and present.

Neatly positioned in tandem with Gurlie's country days, Joe spends the summer in the city by himself and, in one of *White*

Mule's finest episodes, he goes to a baseball game on the Fourth of July.

The great American pastime is intercut with Joe's preoccupations about the approaching competition for a contract he needs to gain, a lucrative deal to print U.S. Government Money Orders. His thoughts proceed as the game does—and again, we think ahead to the *Paterson* poet in "a world / subject to [his] incursions."[1] [2]

Joe anticipates the bidding war he will soon have to face, a test of manhood. On the playing field, George Wiltze, the Giants' pitcher, in trouble, faces a similar test, pulling "his cap down and [taking] a stand once more" [271]. The pitcher's determination segues into Joe's thoughts about how to counter his *own* antagonists the next day—which will be a work-day for him, even as the Fourth of July is a work-day for these ballplayers.

Joe finds validation for the way he likes to work in Wiltze's pitching technique: repeating the pitch that succeeds for him, when least expected by the opposing batter. Joe also prefers to stick with what he knows best. They are both men eager to be put to the test, eager to show how they can work their way out of tense situations. Joe—like Wiltze—wants to take control and make the opposition's defects work to his advantage: "Got to play safe," Joe thinks, like the Giants Manager McGraw, who "thinks of everything" [272].

As the game progresses and deepens into the final innings, Joe's thoughts turn to hopes for success on the playing fields of business, and he can taste its approach, "something, nearer definition now than ever before in his life" [276]. The game is unresolved, but of course there can be only one winner. Wiltze, tenaciously heroic, remains on the mound, watching his lead dwindle, then suffering as his team falls behind. Running between first and second base in the final inning, Wiltze is hit by a ball and called out—ironically, the last out of the game. The very man whose daring had contributed to advancing the team this far is, ominously, also responsible for its defeat.

Joe walks hesitatingly onto the field and inspects the pitcher's mound. He notices details he had not seen from a distance—the mound's height, the coarseness of the grass which seemed so smooth from afar. The same qualities that drove Wiltze to the top pulled him down; and the situation in which he operated looked one way from the spectator's vantage point and now looks startlingly different. Joe learns more than he had bargained for at the ball game.

---

12. Williams, *Paterson* (New Directions paperbook, 1963), p. 57.

The whole book comes to a pivot on this penultimate chapter. It underscores Williams' commitment to exploring the problematic relationship of a man (and women and children) to the world: how much is imagined and how much is enacted? The ball game, a quintessentially American spectacle, draws out Joe's thoughts on characteristically American concerns, competition the most prominent. The ball park is a theatre which holds glamor from a distance but from close at hand reveals flaws and distortions, much as any struggle appears to change when we decide to become actively engaged instead of remaining disinterested. Joe, on the brink of a major shift in his life, moving toward an inevitably deeper involvement in commerce, is experiencing the dilemma of *what point of view to take. White Mule* is an American tapestry; it is also an intellectual exercise.

II. *In the Money*: transitional problems

Soon after *White Mule* was published, Williams began work on *In the Money* (New Directions, 1940), writing the book over a span of two years from 1938. Chapters appeared in *Partisan Review*, Spring 1939; and *Hika*, May 1940.

He described the book to Edith Heal in 1958: "Floss is still a baby, as mysterious as ever in her own way. It is the story of Flossie's family, specifically the success story of her father and the establishing of his own business in New York as a printer."[13]

The motif of *struggle* in this second volume of the Stecher trilogy is even more apparent: between Joe and Gurlie, to stake out emotional territory within their stormy marriage. On one level, the novelist paints a critical portrait of his mother-in-law, Nannie Herman, a contentious woman who never really came to terms with the young poet's work.[14] But at other times, Williams identifies with the same defiance he ridicules. In Gurlie's dream of going back to Norway someday to "show them" [*ITM*, 24] how wealthy and prestigious she has become, we hear echoes of the author's own oft-stated wishes to stand hard on American ground and thumb his nose at the throngs who retreated to other shores, in search of the imaginative essence he found in his own small town.

Gurlie is aggressive and avaricious. She compares herself incessantly with her neighbors, and constantly casts her eye about

---

3. Williams, *I Wanted to Write a Poem*, p. 67.
4. Paul Mariani, *William Carlos Williams: A New World Naked* (McGraw-Hill, 1981), p. 77.

toward other women, to see who might be wearing a nicer dress, who might be living in a more elegant home. She never lets go of Joe for a moment. He receives a parting gift from his co-workers before striking out to begin his own business, a silver cup engraved "to Joseph Stecher from his faithful employees of Wynnewood, Grossman Co., Inc., June 30th, 1901." Her immediate comment—utilitarian, impatient as always, is "What is it good for?" followed by "I'll bet it didn't cost them much" [53].

She is interested only in things that will add to her (insecure) sense of well-being, and in people who can help her reach an (undetermined) goal. She never has enough of anything, and she lets Joe know it at all times. Her direct desire for more and more money—"all you need is a little money and me to push you" [72]—intensifies in relation to her anxiety about Joe's ability to make it on his own. Yet it becomes clearer in *In the Money* that Joe really does not lean on Gurlie as much as she thinks he does. This disjunction between her own perception of her importance to him, and his actual, expressed need for her—often, he carries on his affairs silently, not even bothering to tell her what happened at work on a given day, then springs surprises on her— informs their marriage and fuels Gurlie's resentment even more: "I'm sick and tired of having everyone praise the wonderful Joe! He's no wonder, I can tell you that. . . . My husband is a lucky man to have found me" [377]. Or so she thinks.

Struggles—and more struggles—of domesticity laid bare, of marriage's maddening rhythms and repetitiveness, of siblings Lottie and Flossie constantly feuding with each other. Joe is frustrated as he finds out just how difficult it is to be a small businessman with large expectations. It must have been equally difficult for a country doctor with two young sons to function at the outset of his career. The conspiracy to stop Joe from succeeding is a design for Williams' assessment of a condition in the world at large, preventing most men from expressing their natural energies, against the grain.

Even when Joe and Gurlie share intimate moments, there is an undercurrent of conflict. The war between the sexes never ends. Lady Macbeth-like, Gurlie comes over and kisses him violently on the mouth. "I know you can beat them," she hisses to Joe. "Nobody can beat you—" [111]. In another incident, Joe's former employer, and current competitor, Mr. Wynnewood, asks him, "Why didn't you come out into the open and tell me you were going to put in a bid on the contract? Then it would have been a fair fight" [204-205]. The war between men and women parallels the war between companies; all of life is a battleground in

In the Money. And we must not forget that Williams was writing the novel against the backdrop of World War II: "The war is the first and only thing in the world today" he declared in his "Author's Introduction (1944)," to *The Wedge.*[15] The ultimate war, as always for Williams, was with his materials, with the very language itself.

† † † † † † †

In the Money moves closer to personal history and documentary and away from the traditional novel feeling of *White Mule*. It is a record of Williams' encounter with his changing times: "Here were the . . . strain and driving growth that were forcing the nation on to no easy fate, the same forces burning in Joe's own breast" [89]. As the Stecher family seeks a home in "Riverdale" (i.e., Rutherford) New Jersey, to get out of the oppressive city and set up a household of their own, Joe is witness to a stream of immigrants coming into America, the beginnings of urban sprawl; and it troubles him. The increasing complexity of his own life mirrors the crowded world he sees on all sides. Thus the novel opens up widely, beyond character study, to portray the extreme growth in American society in the early years of this century; an old-timer reminisces to a younger man as they walk down city streets together, "there have been many changes in myself and the city . . . since [the old days]" [151]—and again, we hear the voice of *Paterson* pushing through, as man and city are identified with each other.

Joe and Gurlie's new home in Riverdale is a compromise meeting-ground, satisfying Joe's need to be near the hustle and bustle of New York, and Gurlie's desire for the status that a place in the country represents. The Stechers put down roots, and the distance between author and subject contracts. The careful reader identifies certain traits in Joe: his commitment to hard work ("one man that pays attention to what he is doing and knows what to do about it" [180]); his love for the locally stimulating ("They never see anything simple. It's all right there—but they don't know it" [181]); his tendency to become silent and withdrawn when an important issue burns in his head or heart; his grudging good nature about his family; his awkward but sincere affection for his children; his tolerance in general for children over adults. Williams did indeed feel a rapport with his father-in-law, "Pa Herman" (the model for Joe); but these characteristics could apply equally well to the poet himself.

15. Williams, in *Collected Later Poems* (New Directions, 1963), p. 3.

† † † † † †

The boat-hand jumped from his position at the winch, grabbed a short rope-end and pulled the panel of planking into place, bridging boat and dock to make a safe footway. A second man who had been standing waiting on the boat in the center of the teamway pushed up the iron extension gates, first on one side then the other with a dull clank, automatically freeing them at the passenger exits beyond the stanchions where they were fastened. The people surged forward [231].

In passages such as this one—where the rhythm of Williams' phrasing follows the rhythm of natural events in their proper order—we are pulled into the craftsmanlike work of a writer in control of his medium, and the work lives up to the sermons within it. Philosophy and enactment are in concert. For vast stretches of *In the Money*, however, Williams is an eloquent advocate in theory for bearing down "on reality," but in practice he lets us down. He lets *himself* down, too: "I hoped it would be a good book but it doesn't come up to *White Mule*."[16] There is too much perceptual shorthand. Focus and distillation seem randomly achieved because he wrote to see what he was thinking—but unlike the work on his poetry, he did not pull back and revise sufficiently. Details work in isolation: "In the bare trees, especially a gracefully branching elm growing there, blackbirds would shake themselves, preen and flutter their tails in the greedy sun" [307]; observed bits of life come along whole and tightly-written. But whereas in *White Mule* the details were threaded together, here, they fade in and out, surrounded all too often with filler-language.

This novel is one hundred pages longer than its predecessor, yet it holds less of the world. There is no sense of restraint. Rather, it is more properly seen as a bridge-work, a transitional period between the achieved artifice of *White Mule* and the achieved autobiography of *The Build-up*'s final sections. *In the Money* is a moody sounding-board, with "needle-points" [297] of detail caught here and there.

III. *The Build-up*: from biography to autobiography

"I had trouble [with *The Build-up*]," Williams recalled. "I found much of what I was writing was too personal. I had to change names, fictionalize situations, so that living persons would

---

16. Williams, *I Wanted to Write a Poem*, p. 67.

be protected. As in the case of the *Autobiography*, I was still in a hurry because I had the respect of any businessman for a contract."[17]

The contract was with Random House. *White Mule* marked the beginning of Williams' relationship with New Directions; *The Build-up* was part of a separate agreement with Random House which included *The Autobiography*, and other prose, in temporary breach with James Laughlin's company.

Most of it was written in the aftermath of a heart attack and a stroke. Williams began the book in March 1946, wrote a chapter, then put the project aside for six years,[18] as if he knew all through the process that—as he told Norman Macleod—"It's going to be a job for me."[19] Williams was even more candid and despairing about his compositional difficulties in an interview with editors of *A.D. Magazine*: "I've got about a hundred pages written—and how it stinks! It's terrible! . . . You see, I just can't write without getting involved in form. There is no meaning of a novel as a novel. It is the way the thing is written, apart from the story."[20]

Aesthetic questions about adherence to the doctrine of what a novel should be aside, *The Build-up* embodies Williams' fears about it; it is the least-worked, most formless of the books in the Stecher trilogy—and signals Williams' cross-over into autobiography. He gives up trying so hard to remake life into art; and finally, simply, tells us what happened, when, and how. When he resolves the conflict of the first two-thirds of the book, he leaves pretenses behind, and delivers the poignant and revealing story of his early relationship with Flossie.

The Build-up turns into a modern love story, a remembrance over forty years composed by a stroke-crippled husband for the wife he values more and more as infirmities increase. *The Autobiography* was begun from a hospital bed while Williams recovered from his heart attack in February 1948.[21] The same premonitions of mortality inform *The Build-up*, the need to leave behind a document of another phase in his past life, to set the record straight.

But until we reach that point, the narrative suffers from lack of pacing. The first two-thirds of the book, the "build-up" to its resolution, is a flood-tide of language. Disproportionate,

17. Williams, *ibid.*, pp. 86-87.
18. Mariani, *op. cit.*, p. 528.
19. Williams, *Selected Letters*, to Norman Macleod, June 11, 1951, p. 301.
20. Williams, *Interviews, Speaking Straight Ahead* (New Directions, 1976), p. 36. Edited by Linda Wagner.
21. Neil Baldwin and Steven L. Meyers, *The Manuscripts and Letters of William Carlos Williams at SUNY/Buffalo* (G. K. Hall, 1978), p. 96.

unmodulated episodes follow one upon the other with no dynamic shifts between them. Everything is of equal importance to everything else, most of the time.

To begin with, Williams experiments with "real time." Flossie, Lottie, Gurlie, and Aunt Olga are riding in a carriage from Hackensack to Riverdale, New Jersey: "And here they were. When they got out of the cab they felt very strange, their legs especially, but everything was strange. They walked around in circles stretching their legs. . . . The street was completely empty. Just nobody there. It felt odd. And there was the cab. They looked at it from the outside now. And the horse. It was a brown horse with black feet and a white nose. . ." [*BU*, 13]

At other points, parenthetical comments are left in, as: "what a difference just a few months, a few weeks you might almost say, were making in her. . ." [16]. The story is riddled with after-thoughts, erratic shifts from stylized reality to documentary narrative. Every so often, as we have seen previously, a perfect paragraph rises up from the surrounding landscape of flat prose like a white flower from the swamp—as if the entire book were a metaphor for Williams' view of a world in which we will hear a clear note only if we are attuned to the day-in-and-day-out hum of experience at all times; a world in which only if we are open to the endless greyness, will we notice a flash of clear color, a *revelation*.

As he moves closer and closer to that inevitable time in the story when he must become a character in his own novel, Williams' narrative problems intensify. Then, abruptly, beginning with Chapter XXII, when we meet "Charlie Bishop . . . an intern without money in a New York hospital," and his brother, "Fred, an architect," the familiar tension returns. We are pulled back in with a vengeance.

Williams' *In the American Grain* (1925) reconceives history. Texts from long-ago times, Columbus' journal, Pere Rasles' letters, are arranged to personalize events and give new form to documentation. We hear the author's voice through the way in which contemporary information is presented. *The Build-up* revives that kind of history: one man's creative offering of the facts.

† † † † † † †

"Her little Dutchie would beat them all and she'd damn well see to it that he did" [47]. Gurlie's never-ending insistence— "We've got money now. We've got to move up in the world" [35] —takes on a sadly ironic twist in this final volume. Joe does indeed reach the top of his profession, but we are told less and less about how he spends his days. He retreats deeper into himself. He falls into an emotional decline as his daughters reach marrying age. His wife spends most of her energy social climbing, determined "to ascend the social anthill" [236] to such an extent that her "blind drive, inarticulate but dominant" [245] causes people to veer away from her. Her legendary contentiousness reaches a fever-pitch, and she reflexively disagrees with everything Joe says. Even during labor with her third child—a son, who dies young in a hunting accident—she cannot resist heaping abuse upon her husband. She settles into a hermetic, gossipy life in Riverdale; Joe accuses her of letting her home "go to hell" [87] while he is out clawing and scrambling for the dollars she needs.

But Williams steps firmly away from tired, domestic scenes in *The Build-up*. The voice of the satyr pushes through, moving toward young love and romance, admiring Lottie and Elvira, young girls in their summer dresses, as they pick berries in the heat of a Vermont summer, then are caught in a sudden rainstorm: "Then it really rained. . . . the two girls were soon soaked to their skins. Their hats drooped, their sheer dresses clung to their breasts and their thighs. . . . 'Damn!' said Lottie, her white hat hanging about her ears, looking down at her own sturdy legs to which the dress was stuck. Out of sheer instinct she pulled it away from where it was stuck to her belly" [181].

He intensifies the erotic atmosphere as Lottie thrills to being touched by a young man she meets in the country—her first love: ". . . she felt something that she had never felt in her life before. It gripped her firmly, without hesitation, live, giving, governing her uncertain steps. It was an arm, his arm about her waist. . . . It was her whole passionate resolve to keep that arm in place, touching her, steadying her through life" [179].

The romantic stage is set for the appearance of the young doctor-poet.

Although "Flossie . . . had her own admirers. Her straight legs, narrow hips, and high forehead were not unobserved" [201], Dr. Charlie Bishop is initially attracted to elder sister Lottie because she was almost always surrounded by other young men, and that sense of competition appeals to him. One of the men is his own brother, Fred, adding to his conviction that the pretty prize must be won. Everyone fears Lottie's enigmatic personality, her

musical brilliance at the piano, her guarded nature. She keeps
the men guessing; Flossie is more direct, lacks mystery.

Lottie is puzzled, though, by the young doctor's experiments
in verse: " 'Why do you write like that?' she would ask him. . . .
'I don't think a poem, to be a poem, should use ugly words, dirty
words, vulgar . . . A poem should be beautiful'. . . . He would
laugh to himself sardonically" [238]. He counters her mystique
with his poems, counterstress to her beauty and musical talent.
He competes with the woman he seems to want to marry. The
very thing Charlie uses as a testimony to the world around him—
his poetry—puts Lottie (and her mother) off. It is an intimation
of the fundamental gap already between them, two very different
ways of looking at life that could never be accommodated into
one marriage.

"Holy and pure, as their natures demanded their thoughts
to be, buoyed aloft on wings of song, nevertheless [Charlie and his
brother Fred] were practical enough to find themselves on the
brink of action" [257]. Architect Fred's star is in the ascendancy;
he wins the Prix de Rome, enabling him to study abroad for a
year. He and his brother know that events are building to the
point where Lottie will have to choose one of them—and one
alone. She does: Fred.

Charlie's reaction is spontaneous and instinctive. The choice
signals for him the end of his relationship with his brother as it
has existed for their whole lives up to that point. Charlie immediately, almost in the same breath of defeat, approaches Flossie,
fully aware that he has never given her much more than a fleeting
glance.

There is enough of her sister in her, the way there is doubt-
lessly something of his brother in him. On a chemical, almost
abstract level, the proposal of marriage to Flossie is something he
ought to do. He tells her, "I don't love anyone, but I want to
marry you" [261]. Charlie is determined to have a relationship
in his own way, to set it up on his terms—with a woman he thinks,
at least in the beginning, wants him, and has always been waiting
for him. Flossie is a woman he can feel superior to. There will be
no competition with an equal as there was with Lottie. Rather,
this woman will be a wife and helpmeet, to support his deepest
drives and suppress her own.

Charlie and Flossie's romance is on *both* sides the romance
of rejection. She is the younger sister of a beautiful, outgoing, and
talented woman; he is the brother of a successful suitor; he is the
poet whose poems remain unknown and unread, the poet without

an audience. Theirs is the love founded on the "passion of despair, as all life is despair" [262].

Williams here is no longer the satyr, he is the Keatsian, seeing himself back through forty years as consumed by the fires of religious love. It sounds more as if he is about to enter a monastery than get married and start a family. Resignation is further compounded by resolution: that he will *get* this woman come hell or high water. He poses the question to her and then steps back to see how she takes it, feeling much more comfortable and resolved from a stance of control, taking the initiative instead of letting someone else step in and do it for him—*a triumph of the will.*

The proposal is safe because the two immediately go their separate ways, she to the country and he to Leipzig for a year. There is no time for any descent into carnality.

In a telling episode while he is abroad, Charlie receives a retouched photograph of his betrothed; and the young man is "infuriated" at "that God-damned photographer. . . . He took the blade of a knife and, by scraping the surface of the photo away, restored the normal, the actual, not beautiful contours of the neckline" [266]. Is this finally what Flossie represents to him, in a way that Lottie never did, or could have—a woman more aligned with his vision of the world, a woman reflecting the *necessarily actual* world, equally alluring by virtue of its unadorned presence?

Lottie enters into a new liaison, with a painter who has already been married several times. Charlie finds himself still captivated. He focuses upon her music to distract himself away from her. It "filled the room" as she played, "making the ornate vases and drapings seem strangely out of place" [284]. A woman artist is better kept as a friend and companion, not as a wife.

The final events of *The Build-up* move outward and upward from the intimate focus upon courtship and marriage. Charlie and Flossie's first son is born; her brother Paul dies of a shotgun wound; Joe goes into his descent; and the heartbreaking events of World War I begin to infect everything.

Joe's depression is intensified by his sense of betrayal as the war effort deepens: ". . . he was not a subject of the Kaiser, he was a United States citizen. He scorned disloyalty to his adopted country. . . . he deeply resented the implication that by favoring Germany he was in any way disloyal to the United States" [324-325]. Joe's quandary is the dilemma of a melting-pot society. Who can count himself wholly American?

Joe reacts with defiance—by giving his wife the mansion on a hillside she has always wanted. Supervising the excavation, he literally *blasts* himself out of his depression, counterpunching with the only power remaining to him. Joe is the true hero of these three books, just as Flossie, by her alignment with her father, spiritually and temperamentally, is the heroine.

Joe has to touch bottom, to be at his "lowest ebb" [333]—to lose daughters to marriage, son to death, wife to avarice, and country to jingoism, before he can experience the most exhilarating freedom of all: "Let her have [the house]" he cries. "She wants it—for all it's worth" [334].

William Carlos Williams understood all too well the necessity to tear down before being able to rebuild, anew: his fight began with the poetic line, as the basis for a new American idiom, requiring the transcendence of all tradition that had come before, so that the poem could be reconstructed in a manner appropriate to the current times. Joe's final gesture is therefore the perfect metaphor with which to conclude the Stecher trilogy. It is a poet's act, a bold decision, to let go of all preconceptions, in "a reversal / of despair,"[22]—recognizing that it is impossible to reside too long in the undefined, indecisive world between the ascent and the descent.

---

22. Williams, *The Descent*, in *Pictures from Breughel* (New Directions paperbook 1962), p. 74.

BRUCE COMENS

WILLIAMS, BOTTICELLI, AND THE RENAISSANCE

Williams' general rejection of Europe is so well known that little critical attention has been paid to more detailed analysis of his response to European art. Yet such an analysis can shed a great deal of light, both on Williams' specific reasons for rejecting European art, and on the development of his own poetics. In particular, the Renaissance, as a major turning-point in the history of art and culture, provided Williams with a focus for his somewhat ambivalent views. Despite a natural respect for the creativity of Renaissance Italy, he disliked much of what he actually saw in Italian art: the Christian elements, the imitation of foreign models, and the tendency toward representation, rather than imitation, of nature. But one artist, Botticelli, proved to be a kindred spirit. Both the Italian's style and the conjunction of images of beauty, love, Spring and sensuality contained in his *Birth of Venus* and *Primavera* made him particularly congenial to Williams.

Williams' most explicit response to Italian art is recorded in his fictionalized account of his own 1924 trip to Europe, *A Voyage to Pagany*. In the central chapters Dev, like Williams a doctor-writer, directly confronts the art of Florence and Rome. Although Dev admires the energy of Renaissance artists—"the crudeness of the material they used, the size, the coarseness even, he ate up with joy"[1]—most of what he sees repels him. The

---

1. William Carlos Williams, *A Voyage to Pagany* (New York: New Directions, 1970), p. 100. Subsequent references are abbreviated *VP* in the text. References to other works by Williams are abbreviated in the text as follows:

SA: *Spring and All* in *Imaginations*, edited by Webster Schott (New York: New Directions, 1970)

WM: *White Mule* (Norfolk, Conn.: New Directions, 1937)

IWWP: *I Wanted to Write a Poem: The Autobiography of the Works of a Poet*, reported and edited by Edith Heal (New York: New Directions, 1978)

Rome: *Rome*, edited with an introduction by Steven Ross Loevy, *Iowa Review*, 9, 3 (Spring 1978), pp. 1-65.

CEP: *Collected Earlier Poems* (New York: New Directions, 1966)

CLP: *Collected Later Poems*, rev. ed. (New York: New Directions, 1963)

PB: *Pictures from Brueghel and Other Poems* (New York: New Directions, 1962) "strange Christian influence" that he feels "with disgust, with despair" [101] gives Renaissance art an other-worldly quality that obscures its actual setting, Italy, and is also responsible for the softness and suffering that Dev perceives and intensely dislikes. And the artists are also guilty of "petty imitations of the Assyrian, the Egyptian and the Greek," which again obscure the world of Italy [101]. Michelangelo's *David* is usually acknowledged to be one of the supreme achievements of Renaissance art, but Dev's response is entirely negative:

> The false crudity of Angelo, the delicate torment drove him wild again. That's Christian, big with mental anguish, the genesis of which is the impossibility of fusing the old power with the new weakness. The pain, the weakening is the charm! Agh! He twisted the Greek; put the anguish of the soul into it. The Christian anguish. [102]

The weakness of Renaissance art, Dev feels, can be countered only by a more pagan, more primitive art that eagerly celebrates life on this world.

The representational tendency of Renaissance art also provoked Williams to dislike the period. This is not mentioned in *A Voyage to Pagany*, but may be inferred from *Spring and All*, which was published the year before Williams' trip to Europe. Speaking there of literature, Williams sees the European tradition of realism, of a mere copying of nature, as having received much support from Shakespeare:

> I suppose Shakespeare's familiar aphorism about holding the mirror up to nature has done more harm in stabilizing the copyist tendency of the arts among us than—
>
> the mistake in it (though we forget that it is not S. speaking but an imaginative character of his) is to have believed that the reflection of nature is nature. It is not. It is only a sham nature, a "lie."
>
> Of course S. is the most conspicuous example desirable of the falseness of this very thing.
>
> He holds no mirror up to nature but with his imagination rivals nature's composition with his own. [*SA*, p. 121]

Williams does not mention the Italian painters, but it should be clear that he would not like their much-celebrated development of perspective and of modelling skills, since these paved the way for the European tradition of realism. Nor, given his attack in *A Voyage to Pagany*, does he seem likely to have thought that they escaped "the copyist tendency."

Renaissance art is thus deprecated both for its lack of innovation—it retained Christianity and adhered to foreign models—and for its formal innovations—it initiated the European tradition of copying nature's appearance rather than imitating its activity. Williams' encounters with Renaissance art did help him to formulate his own objectives: he seeks a pagan art that will celebrate life in this world, but which itself possesses enough life that it can avoid "the copyist tendency." The strong element of paganism that Williams could feel in Italian society also gave him a new perspective on the more repressive aspects of Puritan America. Indeed, his immediate reactions to Italian society and art during the 1924 journey were generally much more positive than *A Voyage to Pagany* would indicate.[2] In his journal of that time, *Rome*, Williams wrote:

> But Rome I love, its abandon to the whole waste of flesh swimming through its idleness   with a rush   that threw stones like a volcano—and they settled about the ruin of their go [sic. God? gods? egos?] building up their life with an intensity of stone—[55]

And of Venice: "The great Venetians—were great thinkers and great artists—" [20]. The journal was apparently intended for *A Voyage to Pagany*, as an example of Dev's writing while in Europe. But Williams seems to have decided that the dangers of American imitation of Renaissance art outweighed the benefits that might be gained from what little would be useful in America, and therefore the fragments of *Rome* never made it into his novel. Moreover, the turbulent and fragmentary nature of *Rome* indicates that Williams was probably uneasy with his own positive response. In any case, Botticelli appears to be the only painter to have escaped Williams' later, considered rejection of the art of the Italian Renaissance.

Venus is an important presence even in *A Voyage to Pagany*, recurring in Dev's meditations and appearing in the flesh in the form of a young German girl who stays at the same pension in Rome. Dev's only conversation with the German Venus occurs in "The Venus," a chapter that was deleted from the novel and published separately as a short story.[3] The description of Fraulein von J. is clearly modelled on Botticelli's *Birth of Venus*:

> In her unstylish long-sleeved German clothes, her rough stockings and heavy walking-shoes, Evans found her, nevertheless, ethereally graceful. But the clear features, the high forehead, the brilliant perfect lips, the well-shaped nose, and best of all the shining mistlike palegold hair unaffectedly drawn back—frightened

---

2. For an account of the trip to Italy, see Paul Mariani, *William Carlos Williams: A New World Naked* (New York: McGraw-Hill, 1981), pp. 225-230.

3. "The Venus" was to be the central chapter of *A Voyage to Pagany*; when his publisher thought the manuscript too long, Williams deleted this chapter because he thought it the best. See *IWWP*, p. 45. The story has since been printed as an appendix to the 1970 New Directions edition of *A Voyage to Pagany*; my references are to that printing.

> him. For himself he did not know where to begin. But she looked
> at him so steadily, for some strange reason, as if she recognized
> him, that he was forced at last to answer her. [*VP*, 259]

Fraulein von J.'s seeming recognition of Dev suggests that the
beauty of Renaissance art, of European art, recognizes in him the
new artist, the maker of a new beauty. Significantly, their conversation takes place outside Rome in a grove that Williams designates
as "pagan"—neutral ground, then, since the place is still in Europe
but remains untainted by Christianity. Their conversation is a
curious mixture of mutual sympathy and incomprehension. Fraulein von J. is intensely curious about America and about Dev's
views on art, but Dev cannot adequately convey his sense of
either. He speaks rather vaguely of America's "primitive air"
[263], claiming that "it is useful to us . . . because it is near
savagery" [265]. But Fraulein von J. is in Rome to become a
nun, and although she acknowledges that "you are brave . . . to
want to find some other way—and one that is American" [267],
the conversation and the story end at the impasse of Christianity:

> Do you believe then that the church is an enemy to your
> belief?
> Yes.
> She looked away.
> Oh come on, said Dev, let's get out of this. [267]

Fraulein von J. perceives the power of America, but cannot dislodge herself from the European tradition. And Christian Europe
remains, paradoxically, Pagany, for it cannot comprehend, much
less adopt, Williams' missionary zeal for the New World and a new
art.

Despite this rejection of the European Venus, Williams continued to draw on Botticelli's paintings. However the *Birth of
Venus* and *Primavera* may have been harmonized with Christianity, neither painting contains any explicitly Christian references,
and Williams does not seem to have perceived any melancholic
weakness in the figure of Venus. Nevertheless, his vision of an
American Venus is far removed from Botticelli's graceful maiden.

When Richard Johns adapted the title of *A Voyage to Pagany*
for his new "little magazine," *Pagany: A Native Quarterly*, he
reversed the application of "Pagany," but accepted Williams'
belief in the need for native expression. His "Announcement" in
the first issue, January-March 1930, explains the implications of
the title:

> *Pagus* is a broad term, meaning any sort of collection of peoples
> from the smallest district or village to the country as an inclusive
> whole. Taking America as the *pagus*, any one of us as the *paganus*,

the inhabitant, and our conceptions, our agreements and disagree-ments, our ideas, ideals, whatever we have to articulate is *pagany*, our expression. [*Pagany*, I, 1, p. 1]

Not surprisingly, Williams enthusiastically supported Johns' magazine, acting as an unofficial co-editor and writing *Pagany*'s brief "Manifesto." Since Johns had covered the importance of place, Williams renewed his attack on the tradition brought over from Europe, this time its scientific aspect:

"The ghosts so confidently laid by Francis Bacon and his followers are again walking in the laboratory as well as beside the man in the street", the scientific age is drawing to a close. Bizarre derivations multiply about us, mystifying and untrue as—an automatic revolver. To what shall the mind turn for that with which to rehabilitate our thought and our lives? To the word, a meaning hardly distinguishable from that of place, in whose great, virtuous and at present little realized potency we hereby manifest our belief. [1]

The final statement of belief is rather vague and formulaic, so that it seems to lack enthusiasm. But this probably indicates only Williams' distrust of general statements; the work itself was statement enough.

Johns responded to Williams' support by actively encouraging him to continue his work in fiction. As a result, Williams renewed work on a novel he had abandoned seven years earlier,[4] and *White Mule* began serialization in the third issue, July-September 1930. The opening paragraph presents an utterly transformed "birth of Venus":

She entered, as Venus from the sea, dripping. The air enclosed her, she felt it all over her, touching, waking her. If Venus did not cry aloud after release from the pressures of that sea-womb, feeling the new and lighter flood springing in her chest, flinging out her arms—this one did. Screwing up her tiny smeared face, she let out three convulsive yells—and lay still. [*WM*, 1]

It should be clear that Williams is not interested in importing and then adapting the European Venus; this is a native birth—the subsequent history of this baby girl in fact draws upon the childhood and family life of Williams' wife. Although the *Birth of Venus* is not actually present in this passage, the painting undoubtedly provides a contrasting background for Williams' insistence on the physicality of life, on its primitive and perhaps ugly, but nevertheless powerful, vitality.

---

4. WCW, Letter to Richard Johns, June 5, 1930, in *A Return to Pagany*, edited by Stephen Halpert with Richard Johns (Boston: Beacon Press, 1969), p. 127. Subsequent references to this book are abbreviated *RP*.

A subsequent passage in this first chapter records the baby's first attempts at articulation:

> La, la, la, la, la, la, la! it said with its tongue—in the black softness of the new pressures—and jerking up its hand, shoved its right thumb into its eye, starting with surprise and pain and yelling and rolling in its new agony. [2]

"La, la, la . . ." might well be a first attempt at song, at a purely native song, uninfluenced by Europe. Indeed, the whole of the first chapter can be taken as a metaphor for the clumsy, painful and occasionally floundering birth of a new, American poetry—a metaphor for the "rather shabby spectacle America still makes from the writers [sic] viewpoint," as Williams wrote to Johns [*RP*, 124]. The chapter is in fact a much more vigorous manifesto than the one Williams wrote for the first *Pagany*. However, such a reading should not dislocate the literal significance of the story, for it is in the literally, locally true that, for Williams, the new writing must be grounded.

Although Botticelli's painting of Venus was thus inappropriate for America, Williams did find Botticelli's works congenial. Because he rarely used foreign languages in his work, the Italian title of his 1931 collection, *Della Primavera Trasportata Al Morale*, stands out as a specific acknowledgement of Botticelli's presence in his thought and art. The last poem in that collection, "The Botticellian Trees," was and remains widely admired.[5] It has not received as much critical attention as might be expected, but it well repays close study.

The Botticellian Trees

The alphabet of
the trees

is fading in the
song of the leaves

the crossing
bars of the thin

letters that spelled
winter

---

5. I should note that there is some confusion as to whether *Della Primavera Trasportata Al Morale* is a collection or a sequence. Although the other poems are obviously relevant to this paper, my justification for treating "The Botticellian Trees" apart from the others is based on Williams' own practice: he allowed the poem to be published alone by Zukofsky in the Objectivist issue of *Poetry* (Feb. 1931), and by Pound in his *Profile: An Anthology Collected in MCMXXXI*. And there is no indication that the poems form a sequence in their final printing in *Collected Earlier Poems*.

and the cold
have been illumined

with
pointed green

by the rain and sun—
The strict simple

principles of
straight branches

are being modified
by pinched-out

ifs of color, devout
conditions

the smiles of love—
. . . . . .

until the stript
sentences

move as a woman's
limbs under cloth

and praise from secrecy
quick with desire

love's ascendancy
in summer—

In summer the song
sings itself

above the muffled words— [*CEP*, 80-81]

Williams had evidently been attracted to Botticelli's trees for some time; a note from the Spring of 1908 records that a "dainty light" Mulberry tree, "not yet in full leaf," reminded him of Botticelli.[6] The poem is not explicit as to which painting the title refers to, but the rich vegetation in *Primavera* makes that painting a likely candidate. And "a woman's / limbs under cloth" could easily have been suggested by the depiction in *Primavera* of Flora and the Three Graces, while "the smiles of love" might refer either to the slight smile of Venus herself or to the more sensuous

---

6. Rod Townley, *The Early Poetry of William Carlos Williams* (Ithaca and London: Cornell University Press, 1975), p. 191.

smile of Flora.[7] Indeed, the poem could be read as a commentary
upon, almost a translation of, Botticelli's *Primavera*. But another
painting probably suggested the poem's starting point. Botticelli's
Bardi Altarpiece (now in the Staatliche Museen, Berlin) portrays
the Madonna enthroned and flanked by St. John the Baptist and
St. John the Evangelist. The most unusual feature of the painting
is the absence of an interior architectural setting; instead, the
figures are placed in a garden, and the background of the painting
is dominated by extraordinarily rich, meticulously rendered
foliage. Williams would probably have liked this change in setting.
But the plants are not merely instances of precise representation,
for each has a symbolic value: on small ribbons that blend into the
foliage are passages from Ecclesiasticus that draw attention to the
allegorical meaning of the picture.[8] It only requires a shift into the
temporal—and Williams was always very aware of the world as
process—to see this picture as the portrayal of a moment just
before the vegetation grows so profuse as to completely obscure
the written texts, when the "strict simple / principles" of allegory
will be overwhelmed by particulars.

Despite a simplicity of expression, "The Botticellian Trees"
presents a complex series of contrasts and comparisons. A mere
tabulation of these, however, would falsify the movement of the
poem, which delicately keeps the reader off balance, suspending
him, much like the *Bardi Altarpiece*, between concrete particulars
and abstraction. Even the first lines are likely to create confusion:

> The alphabet of
> the trees

"Trees" is unexpected, and if we suspect that a comparison is
being made, Williams certainly refuses to make it explicit. The
trees are not like an alphabet, they comprise, or possess, an
alphabet. And if we nevertheless transform Williams' terms into
a comparison, it in any case remains unexplained at this point.
The next line,

> is fading in the

allows us to settle down somewhat. Since "alphabet" is inexplicable, we have most likely seized on "trees," which can indeed
fade. But they fade in the distance or in the dusk: we need an

---

7. I follow L. D. and Helen S. Ettlinger's convincing identification of the figures in
Primavera: to the right is Zephyr, who is chasing Chloris, a nymph of the fields. When
he touches her, she metamorphoses into Flora (third from the right), nymph of flowers
and mistress of Spring. For more detail see their *Botticelli* (New York: Oxford University Press, 1977), p. 124 ff.
8. My information is again drawn from the Ettlingers' *Botticelli*, p. 72.

appropriate noun to confirm this gathering stability. Williams first delays the noun to the next line, and then frustrates our expectations:

song of the leaves

Trees do not fade into song; we are forced back to "alphabet." A rational habit of mind infers the presence of a metaphor: trees fade in leaves as an alphabet fades in song. And we can also infer that the criss-crossing bare branches look like letters of the alphabet. But the poem still refuses equilibrium, for it focusses not on the trees and leaves that provide a concrete ground, but on the alphabet and song. And how do leaves "look" like song? How, in any case, does an alphabet fade in song? Singing can obscure words, but such a reading would wrest "fade" away from its visual meaning, with which we feel comfortable. What we want, then, is the concrete visual world of trees and leaves, for this offers a tantalizing security, just out of reach.

The poem plays on this desire for the concrete in the lines following:

the crossing
bars of the thin

After "crossing" we hope for "branches"; "bars" keeps us off balance, but only slightly—this could still be a description of branches. And surely "thin" refers to branches. But it does not:

letters that spelled

The minor displacement of "bars" increases our disequilibrium, increases our desire for a solid, visual ground, and thus increases the frustrating effect of "letters." Led to expect trees and leaves, we have been thrust back to the alphabet. And then "letters that spelled" makes another promise that the poem does not keep, at least in the way we would expect.[9] For letters surely spell a word, but "spelled," after another crisis at the line-end, shifts from literal to metaphorical meaning:

winter

(and to solidify this shift:)

and the cold

"Winter" returns us from alphabet to trees, and "bars" and "thin" in retrospect suggest the imprisonment and poverty of Winter.

---

9. Note, too, how "letters that spelled" delays the expected verb, thereby increasing the reader's anticipation and suspense. Hugh Kenner has discerned this "principle of syntactic leverage . . . everywhere in Williams' work of the 1920's." *The Pound Era* (Berkeley: University of California Press, 1971), p. 402.

By mentioning Winter here and then continuing with Spring the poem at last achieves a kind of equilibrium:

the crossing
bars of the thin

letters that spelled
winter

and the cold
have been illumined

with
pointed green

by the rain and sun—

We can now identify three pairs of contrasting terms:

$$\frac{\text{song}}{\text{alphabet}} = \frac{\text{leaves}}{\text{trees}} = \frac{\text{Spring}}{\text{Winter}}$$. Winter and Spring provide a general context for both of the other contrasts, but the equilibrium achieved is not a reduction to one pair of terms. The poem is careful *not* to allow us to take Winter and Spring *literally* when applied to trees and leaves, and then *figuratively* when applied to alphabet and song. Instead, the accumulation of unresolvable semantic crises fuses the three contrasts into one:

$$\frac{\text{song—leaves—Spring}}{\text{alphabet—trees—Winter}}$$ —the figurative and the literal, the abstract and the concrete, indissoluble. The poem's continued refusal of rational paraphrase ensures that the sense of equilibrium remains precarious.

Having almost incidentally articulated the visible setting, the poem now elaborates the significance of alphabet and song:

The strict simple

principles of
straight branches

are being modified
by pinched-out

ifs of color, devout
conditions

the smiles of love—

Williams' ability to combine abstraction with precise and striking description, as in "pinched-out / ifs of color," is remarkable. But more interesting here are the associations now given "alphabet" and "song": a simple sentence expressing "strict simple/principles" becomes song when it receives modifying or conditional clauses. This passage implies a definite historical context, for it situates the poem in the early twentieth century, at the moment when the simple principles of Newtonian physics were giving way to the modifications of relativity theory, when mechanistic models of the world were giving way to models based on interacting forces.

That Williams uses Botticelli to celebrate this transition may seem curious, but it is actually highly appropriate, for Williams is in fact situating himself in a new renaissance that in some respects reverses the direction of the Italian Renaissance. Besides its direct (and, to Williams, detrimental) effect on art, the Italian painters' development of perspective closely parallels the development and subsequent dominance of the mechanistic Classical world-view. The Albertian system of perspective, and variations of it, implicitly assume space to be an empty, geometric grid, and consequently assume that it can be objectively comprehended and represented without loss. Indeed, Raphael's *School of Athens*, though painted some hundred years before Descartes' work, can nevertheless be considered the supreme representation, and celebration, of Cartesian man—who exists only because he thinks—contained within the absolute and unchanging space of Classical physics. The Italians' enthusiasm for representation thus foreshadows the rational enterprise of the Classical age. Since it is that rational view of the world that Williams revolts against—and which we can see "The Botticellian Trees" overcoming, or subverting, by means of semantic substitution—it is not surprising that he rejects most of the Italian painters in favor of Botticelli. For, while Williams in *A Voyage to Pagany* disparaged the other artists for their medieval content, Botticelli's medievalism affected not so much his content as his style.

Botticelli's scant use of perspective and modelling made him something of an anachronism in his own day, rejecting the mainstream emphasis on representation in favor of an art that often seems more *trecento* than *quattrocento*. As Frederick Hartt has noted, his style, "anti-atmospheric, anti-optical, anti-scientific almost from the start," "takes on the character of a personal revolt against the weight of Florentine doctrine."[10] Even in the *Calumny of Apelles*, where Botticelli makes such consummate use of Albertian perspective, he seems to be rejecting it. There are in

---

10. Frederick Hartt, *History of Italian Renaissance Art* (New York: Harry N. Abrams, 1974), p. 282.

fact two vanishing points rather than one, and the podium on the far right draws attention to the distortion imposed by Alberti's system, while at the same time projecting forward "from the space of the picture into that where we stand."[11] These distortions, together with the tension created by the figures in the center and the right, force the viewer to come to rest on the figure of Truth, who is the least realistic of the figures, and an obvious quotation from the *Birth of Venus.* The painting at once uses Albertian perspective to dramatize its moral content, and the moral content to dramatize Botticelli's rejection of representation. Truth is not to be found in the prescriptions of realism.

Botticelli's emphasis on line, rather than chiaroscuro effects, leads to a multiplicity that would also have appealed to Williams, since the shift away from "simple principles" is a shift toward multiplicity.[12] And in many of his paintings Botticelli, like Williams in "The Botticellian Trees" and other works, combines multiplicity of detail with a more abstract significance, but never allows us to reduce the painting to a single allegorical meaning. The *Birth of Venus* and especially the *Primavera* do not so much derive from Neoplatonism as they include Neoplatonism as one subject among others, combining the theistic tendencies of Neoplatonism with a pagan sensuality. Love, being associated with truth, beauty, Spring, sensuality and divinity, clearly dominates these two paintings. It does so, however, not as an abstract entity subsuming all else, but as a force that compels attention to detail and unites disparate particulars.

So Williams, instead of subsuming all to an abstract, quasi-divine Principle, raises disparate particulars to a religious status:

> . . . pinched-out
>
> ifs of color, devout
> conditions
>
> the smiles of love—
> . . . . . .

---

11. My information is drawn from Hartt, pp. 295-296, but I should note that he does not make my inference concerning the significance of the painting.
12. Wylie Sypher, following Woelfflin, points out that a linear style, in contrast to a painterly style, "emphasizes . . . each separate detail in an 'isolating' way" in his *Four Stages of Renaissance Style* (Garden City, N.Y.: Doubleday, 1955), p. 19. And on pp. 20-21 he distinguishes between multiplicity and unity: "In the multiple composition . . . individual details maintain their identity and independence. . . ." Although Hartt does not specifically mention multiplicity in connection with Botticelli, he does observe that Botticelli "wove linear compositions with such subtlety and brilliance that the deveoped polyphonic music of the sixteenth century comes to mind as a parallel" [p. 281]. And the Ettingers remark of the design of the *Primavera* that "the elements making up the painting are simply set side by side like pearls on a string" [p. 122].

"Devout conditions" refers to conditional clauses, of course, but also to that which is conditional: in this case, the darling buds of May. And while "the smiles of love" indicates that these buds are manifestations of an invisible force, the phrase, which provides the ground as well as the turning-point of the poem, also has a sexual reference, and thus anchors the poem in the physical process of sexual intercourse and ultimately of birth. The line of ellipses that follows suggests a silence in the face of what is, for Williams, the numinous. The transformative and creative power of love is inexpressible; it can only be experienced.

Despite this necessary secrecy, the presence of love effects a remarkable transformation in the poem:

    until the stript
    sentences

    move as a woman's
    limbs under cloth

    and praise from secrecy
    quick with desire

    love's ascendancy
    in summer—

The eroticism initiated by "the smiles of love" now infuses the poem and unites the two terms that had previously seemed to be in opposition, alphabet and song. One of Williams' few alterations of the poem, changing "strict/sentences" to "stript/sentences," shows him ensuring that alphabet and song now be seen as the two poles of an erotic tension.[13] If "smiles of love" suggests the female, "love's ascendancy" suggests the male: love becomes ascendant *because* of the stript sentences, the woman's limbs. In the service of love, then, alphabet and song now work together, and their unification may be extended to the other apparent opposites in the poem: trees and leaves, and Winter and Spring.

It is a unified but concrete world that Williams is celebrating here, a world that is neither fragmented into discrete categories nor subsumed by an abstraction. And the poem convinces, in Zukofsky's phrase, "not by argument but by the *form* it creates to carry its content."[14] That is, by its activity, in which the reader, if he is to read, must participate. As Williams wrote a few years earlier in *Spring and All,*

---

13. Townley, p. 172. With regard to the sexuality of the poem, it is worth noting that in its appearance in *Poetry* (Feb. 1931), the line "quick with desire" read "with hot ardor."
14. Louis Zukofsky, *A Test of Poetry* (New York: C. Z. Publications, 1980), p. 52.

> I early recognized the futility of acquisitive understanding and at
> the same time rejected religious dogmatism. My whole life has
> been spent (so far) in seeking to place a value upon experience
> and the objects of experience that would satisfy my sense of
> inclusiveness without redundancy–completeness. . . [*SA*, 115-
> 116].

However, just at this point of unification the poem's time frame
becomes vague. Earlier in the poem the present continuous is used
for events contemporaneous with the poem–the process of Spring.
But "until" and the shift to the present indicative indicate that
this final unification may not yet have occurred, so that if Winter
can represent the Classical age, and Spring the present [1931],
Summer remains in the future. The final lines of the poem, then–

> In summer the song
> sings itself
>
> above the muffled words–

constitute a hope or a wish for a future Golden Age. But the
return to "song" and the use of the present tense rather than the
future undermine the rigidity of this temporal scheme, to suggest
that this Summer exists in the present, whenever it can be attained.
The poem still expresses a hope for the future, but throughout the
poem Williams focusses, after all, on process, not the result of a
process. His emphasis in *Spring and All* and throughout his career
on the power of the imagination to transform the world also
indicates that this Summer is an ever-present possibility. And if it
is the silent act of love that unites the disparate elements of the
world, that act is also an act of the imagination, such an act as
this poem manifests. "Summer," then, can always be achieved in
the poem.

Although in his formative years Williams found Botticelli
particularly attractive, Bosch and especially Brueghel seem to have
displaced the Italian in his later concerns. Perhaps once he had
established a firm ground for his own work, once he had successfully rejected the European traditions of rationalism and realism,
Williams no longer felt such affinity for Botticelli's transitional
position, rejecting the beginnings of those traditions. Reacting
to the shock and confusion of World War II, however, Williams
returned to the Venus in an attempt to clarify the relation between
war and art, between Mars and Venus.

Entitled "The Birth of Venus," the poem was first published
in 1948. It turns on the contrast between the "small waves . . .
rippling, crystal clear," from which Venus should be born, and
"Murder/staining the small waves crimson. . ." [*CLP*, 189].

Williams acknowledges that there might be no art without war, but then wonders

                                              why must
        we suffer
ourselves to be so torn to sense our world; Or believe we
        must so
suffer to be born again? [190]

The poem concludes with a wish that another way be found:

        I wish (and so I fail). Notwithstanding, I wish we
            might
learn of an April of small waves—deadly as all slaughter,
        that we
shall die soon enough, to dream of April, not knowing why
        we have been
struck down, heedless of what greater violence. [191]

It is interesting that Williams returns to Botticelli when he seeks to define his position on basic questions concerning his art (and life), but, aside from the attempt to put war in the larger perspective of a common mortality, there is little that is new here. The poem seems a rather too self-conscious attempt to deal with "large" questions, and even Williams' uncertainty is not expressed with conviction. His "I wish (and so I fail)" seems an acknowledgement that, unlike "The Botticellian Trees," this poem's wish lacks the conviction necessary to make it fully effective. The problem perhaps struck too close to home, since so much of Williams' work (and so much of his sense of life) involved, or was born from, strife.

A much more successful poem in Williams' last collection, *Pictures from Brueghel and Other Poems*, also uses the *Birth of Venus*, and expresses concerns quite similar to those of "The Botticellian Trees." Here is "Song":

        beauty is a shell
        from the sea
        where she rules triumphant
        till love has had its way with her

        scallops and
        lion's paws
        sculptured to the
        tune of retreating waves

        undying accents
        repeated till
        the ear and the eye lie
        down together in the same bed [PB, 15]

This is not a critique of the *Birth of Venus*; Botticelli's painting here provides little more than an image for thought. Williams criticizes those so intent on beauty as to become obsessed with an empty formalism. Trying to write undying verse, they engage only in endless repetition.

But the poem's argument—rather, the argument we can abstract from the poem—is more complex than this, and of greater scope: as usual, Williams' esthetic program is also a social program. The eye presents a relatively stable world, where things can be mapped or modelled and then inspected. Such stability invites a movement from particulars to types, and thence to concepts and systems—to rationalism. The aural world, by contrast, is a world of perpetual activity, of sudden and seemingly random particulars, usually over-lapping. Oral cultures are consequently much more aware than we are of the multiplicity of the world, and of the world as process. The endless and empty repetition suggested in the final stanza can be taken as a view of the emptiness of history as long as rationalism dominates society. All we can retrieve from the sea of particulars is an empty shell, formally beautiful but lacking the real significance that can be obtained only by adhering more closely to the processes of life.

The semantic crisis occasioned by the positioning of "lie" enacts the crisis that such emptiness will create: unless beauty is informed by love, and unless form and content are fused by love, art will lie and man will live a lie. Paradoxically, the roles of ear and eye are reversed in poetry. The visual and rationalist culture produces rigidly formalized verse forms, but these are enforced by the ear. It is therefore the eye that, seeing particulars, must infuse the poem with love. Although the fusion of ear and eye that the poem calls for echoes the fusion of alphabet and song that "The Botticellian Trees" celebrates, the two terms are more evenly balanced here—it is difficult to imagine Williams in 1931 attributing beauty to any of the products of rationalism. And "Song," both more relaxed and more assured than the earlier poem, seems to achieve its fusion of ear and eye without effort. In retrospect, the semantic substitution in "The Botticellian Trees" appears to become almost a mechanical device in comparison to the ease with which "Song" moves from the elemental symbols of sea and shell, through the synaesthesia of the second stanza, to the semantic crisis and resolution in the last lines.

Nor is there any ambiguity here concerning the temporal scheme. The urgency of Williams' need to place his own time in a historical framework has abated since "The Botticellian Trees," for "Song," occurring in a timeless present, makes no reference to specific historical events. The rebirth of love, and so of life, is always possible, but is at the same time a constant necessity, for there is an ever-present danger of lapsing into formalism. Williams devalued the historical Renaissance in order to make way for renaissance, for the possibility of continual rebirth afforded by the imagination—by love—and achieved in the poem, the song itself.

THOMAS SCHAUB

WILLIAMS, SORRENTINO, AND THE ART OF THE ACTUAL

> But such a picture as that of Juan Gris . . .
> is important as marking more clearly than
> any I have seen what the modern trend
> is: the attempt is being made to separate
> things of the imagination from life. . . .
> *Spring and All*, 1923

> The reader will see that what I am driving
> at is that these words that he is reading—
> are words.
> *Imaginative Qualities of Actual
> Things*, 1971

In their writing, William Carlos Williams and Gilbert Sorrentino insist upon a relationship between the imagination and reality that denies the habitual conventions of mimesis. Their conviction that art must be "separate" from the world has been taken to be a denial both of the world and of art's social or political importance, for words such as those cited above seem to define an elitist aesthetic indifferent to the reader's life. On this score, readers are less apt to despair of Williams than of Sorrentino, for Williams' espousal of art's separateness may be "tempered" with his declaration of art's origin in "local" materials. As such, Williams has been gradually assimilated as one of the major American writers of the Twentieth Century. By contrast, Gilbert Sorrentino is a contemporary writer just beginning to gain recognition; but as poet, novelist and critic he belongs with Williams as an artist of the actual.[1]

---

1. To date Sorrentino has published eight volumes of poetry, many poems of which are collected in *Selected Poems, 1958-1980*, and six novels: *The Sky Changes* (1966), *Steelwork* (1970), *Imaginative Qualities of Actual Things* (New York: Random House, 1971)—hereafter cited in the text as *IQA*, followed by the page number—*Mulligan Stew* (1979), *Aberration of Starlight* (1980) and *Crystal Vision* (1981). The most recent Sorrentino bibliography has been compiled by Jerome Klinkowitz in *Literary Disruptions*, Second edition (Urbana: University of Illinois Press, 1980).

For both writers, art does have social and political importance, but this importance depends upon art's autonomy. Moreover, this importance is embodied not in a mimetic reflection of
life, but in its own vitality. This distinction—often stated by Williams as the difference between "copying" and "imitating"[2]—is at
the crux of the disagreement between such writers as Williams and
Sorrentino and their critics. Of late this dispute has been restated
in such books as Gerald Graff's *Literature Against Itself*, which
argues the virtues of the realistic representation that modernism
replaced with "the radical 'autonomy' of the imagination."[3]

There are ineradicable differences between the two views,
but the degree of polarization over this issue derives in part from
the writers' comments. In the context of a demand for realism
in which both Williams and Sorrentino have written, their explana-
tory statements have understandably been almost entirely on
behalf of the imagination's prerogatives; yet this emphasis has
been to the neglect of clarifying the relations fundamental to both
writers between an independent imagination and the world.

Their hostility to realism is part of the modernist rejection,
in which the conventions of realism were associated with a point
of view and a civilization which had had its hypocrisies revealed.
When the man with "owl-eyed glasses" in Gatsby's library
exclaims "What thoroughness! What realism!" he is commenting
upon the exactness of an illusion, and he anticipates the revelation
of Gatsby's fakery, his tawdry "gonnegtions" and the Platonic
idealism such "realism" masked (and which redeems him in
Carroway's eyes). This is one of the great insistences of modernism: realism is an illusion. "[T]he mistake," Williams wrote in
1923, "is to have believed that the reflection of nature is nature. It
is not. It is only a sham nature, a 'lie' " [*I*, 121]. In an essay on
Williams' prose, Sorrentino vents his exasperation with the enduring demand for realism: "Are we mad? Fifty years after Joyce and
Lewis, Williams and Ford, we search for 'flesh and blood' characters who 'walk off the page.' Somehow we wish the novel to be a
reflection of the world that the news tells us is true."[4]

---

2. This distinction runs throughout *Spring and All* (Dijon: Contact, 1923) beginning
with the section subtitled "The Traditionalists of Plagiarism." Reprinted in *Imaginations*,
ed. Webster Schott (New York: New Directions, 1970), p. 94. Hereafter cited in the
text as *I*, followed by the page number.
3. (Chicago: The University of Chicago Press, 1979), p. 5. Hereafter cited in the text as
Graff, followed by the page number. See also Daniel Bell, *The Cultural Contradictions
of Capitalism* (New York: Basic Books, Inc., Publishers, 1978); Warner Berthoff, *A Literature Without Qualities* (Berkeley: University of California Press, 1979); and Irving
Howe, *Decline of the New* (New York: Harcourt, Brace and World, 1970).
4. "The Various Isolated: W. C. Williams's Prose," *New American Review*, Number 15
(New York: Simon & Schuster, Inc., 1972), p. 198. Hereafter cited in the text as Various, followed by the page number.

Such vehemence is the familiar accompaniment of modernist declarations of art's autonomy; and the extremity of such statement, especially as it appears in critical comment never intended to be systematic, has elicited an equally familiar reaction, which continues in current writing about contemporary fiction: "[p] roceeding from the valid insight that something has happened to the sense of reality . . . many writers and critics leap to the conclusion that literature must for this reason abandon its pretensions to represent external reality and become either a self-contained reality unto itself or a disintegrated, dispersed process" [Graff, 9]. Faced with such criticism, proponents of the "new" have generally either attacked such critics as reactionaries or have again defended the rights of the imagination. This essay attempts to moderate that difference by focussing upon the relations of imaginative art to the world.

Sorrentino's inheritance from Williams establishes a line between modernist poetics and postmodern prose, joining the most outspoken exponent of the imagination and a contemporary writer who has tried to extend the lessons of Williams' work to his fiction. Both writers celebrate the imagination: what has been less clear is that this imagination, whose products may be "detached" from life, is nonetheless tied to that life. Such art gives us, in Williams' unifying phrase, borrowed by Sorrentino, "the imaginative qualities of actual things."[5]

II

Some of the confusion surrounding the relations of the imagination to "external reality" is the result of modernist rhetoric. For sympathizers, this presents no hurdle. For example, it is enough for proponents of Williams to say that he speaks for the imagination and the ′importance of contact with the local; the relations between them do not arise as a controversial issue. But their compatibility is not inherently obvious, especially to those committed to some form of mimetic art.

Williams' early work contributes to the confusion, for in *Spring and All* an insistence upon the separation of imagination and life competes with a conviction that the imagination "affirms reality most powerfully" [*I*, 149]. Poetry is "new form dealt with as a reality in itself"; "the form of poetry is related to the movements of the imagination revealed in words—or whatever it may

---

5. *Kora in Hell: Improvisations*, reprinted in *Imaginations*, p. 67.

be—the cleavage is complete" [*I*, 133]. This view of poetic form as autonomous is complicated by Williams' equivocal use of the word "realism." At one point in *Spring and All* he tells us that "where everything is being brought into sight the realism of art has bewildered us," but adds: "The only realism in art is of the imagination" [*I*, 111]. This confusion over the word "realism" is compounded some pages later with the view that "works of art . . . must be real, not 'realism' but reality itself" [*I*, 117].

Of course Williams' somewhat cryptic remarks share a consistent rejection of mimetic realism. He shares with his time the determination to set words free.[6] "My invention this time, my dear," speaks the narrator of *The Great American Novel* (1923) "is that literature is a pure matter of words." The first requirement of "serious writing" then is to "let the words be free" [*I*, 168, 172].

Thus isolated, Williams' hostility to mimetic art must be placed in relation with his other lifelong insistence that the work of the imagination allies us with the world and our capacity for experience. In the "Prologue" to *Kora in Hell* (1918), Williams says the imagination releases "that peculiarity which gives an object a character by itself" [*I*, 14]. Implicit in such a view is an "external reality" to which the imagination is agent and servant: the poet "gives his poem over to the flower and its plant themselves, that they may benefit by those cooling winds of the imagination which returned upon them will refresh them at their task of saving the world" [*I*, 19].

Taken literally as part of a systematic poetic, this view appears to conflict with those cited earlier. We may argue that this apparent inconsistency merely reflects Williams' growth in the years prior to *Spring and All* from a concern with Imagism (the "direct treatment of the 'thing' whether subjective or objective") to a more confident perception of the imagination's power to make an entirely new reality, "detached" from life.[7] But in *Spring and All* and in his works of the next forty years the imagination continued to occupy these two seemingly conflicting roles. Of the things in Juan Gris' picture he said they are "still 'real' they are the same things they would be if photographed or painted by Monet . . . but in this painting they are seen to be in some peculiar

---

6. See Hugh Kenner, "Words Set Free," *The Pound Era* (Berkeley: University of California Press, 1971), pp. 121-144. Williams' sense of this freedom is more related to the concretion of paint, of words as things, than to the "Symbolist revolution" Kenner shows lying behind the work of Pound and Eliot.
7. In *Spring and All*, Williams wrote: "It [empty work] is typified by use of the word 'like' or that 'evocation' of the 'image' which served us for a time. Its abuse is apparent" [*I*, 100-101].

way—detached" [*I*, 110]. And thus, in "The Red Wheelbarrow," "the same things exist, but in a different condition when energized by the imagination" [*I*, 138]. So much depends upon poetry, "yet men die miserably every day / for lack / of what is found there."[8] Williams' commonsense understanding of what we mean by "reality" and the "real" is apparent in these remarks, yet there appear to be two related realities: one of art, one not. Moreover, the relation is one of dependence.

Williams uses such words as "real" and "detached" to express the renewing relation of a free imagination to an otherwise humiliating world [*I*, 105]. This antithesis lies at the heart of the tensions which compose Williams' work, and it is one example of the imagination and the pressures of the environment. This is a dance between a Whitmanian determination to rise "to some approximate co-extension with the universe" [*I*, 105] and the world itself: "Thus a poem is tough by no quality it borrows from a logical recital of events nor from the events themselves but solely from that attenuated power which draws perhaps many broken things into a dance giving them thus a full being" [*I*, 16-17].

In the movements of dance, Williams found a fit figure to embody the opposing intentions of his work. It appears early, in the "Prologue" to *Kora in Hell*, and over thirty years later it initiates the meditation upon experience which became "The Desert Music": "the dance begins: to end about a form" [*PB*, 108]. The dance figure defines the poet as orchestrator of the "real," though here reality is not simply the things outside the self, but a composition of that interaction between self and world: "That which is heard from the lips of those to whom we are talking in our day's-affairs mingles with what we see in the streets and everywhere about us as it mingles also with our imagination. By this chemistry is fabricated a language of the day which shifts and reveals its meaning" [*I*, 59]. This same "chemistry" is the method of *Paterson*'s alchemy: "a mass of detail / to interrelate on a new ground, difficultly";[9] and it reappears in "The Orchestra" of *The Desert Music* (1954): "The purpose of an orchestra / is to organize those sounds / and hold them / to an assembled order" [*PB*, 80].

But that purpose, characteristically, retains in its execution the contraries I have been noting, for his "assembled order" stops

---

8. *Pictures from Brueghel* (New York: New Directions, 1962), pp. 161-162. Hereafter cited in the text as *PB*, followed by the page number.
9. *Paterson* (New York: New Directions, 1963), p. 20. Hereafter cited in the text as *P*, followed by the page number.

short of harmony, being simply a reality of "relation": "together, unattuned / seeking a common tone." The "reality" of the poem, too, is that cacaphonous order which emphasizes not the subordination of parts to a melodic whole, but the "relation / of a flute note / to a drum" [*PB*, 80-81]. The poem exists as a compromise, as it were, between its own autonomous rights and those of the material it seeks to order.

Such unresolved tension is a characteristic of Williams' art of the actual. It was a tension of which he was fully aware when he called *Paterson* his "impossible poem." More than any of his critics, Williams knew that his effort to lift "an environment to expression" would never attain the formal order his readers would demand. To have done so would have falsified his project, either reducing it to the illusion of representation, or elevating it to an internal coherence. Instead, the poem enacts the processes composing both the environment and the poet's engagement with it. It was the shifting relations of that engagement Williams sought to express, not anything fixed or conceived. "Virtue," he wrote, "is wholly / in the effort to be virtuous . / This takes connivance, / takes convoluted forms, takes" [*P*, 189]. Williams had to reject the imposition of harmonious order upon the massive detail of the environment even though the fragmented culture desperately required such unity:

> And the amnesic crowd (the scattered),
> called about—strains
> to catch the movement of one voice.

Paterson was to be that "one voice"—"an elucidation by multiplicity" [60-61]. At their most successful, these two intentions create a composition separate from life but composed of life: a democratic dissonance, a multiplicity composed, of voices "unattuned."

Williams' insistence that "literature is a pure matter of words" pervades Sorrentino's work and critical commentary. In an article titled "The Various Isolated: W. C. Williams's Prose," Sorrentino reminds us, "Novels are made of words" [*Various*, 196]. As such, novels are things, not vehicles of ideas: "Ideas should be left to the people who have ideas—philosophers, politicians, teachers. Artists can be extremely dull in terms of what they believe, what they say, and what they do in their lives. Writers don't think. In *Imaginative Qualities* somewhere, I say that writers don't think except in their work. It was Williams who said that "The poet's intelligence is made manifest in his poem."[10]

10. "An Interview With Gilbert Sorrentino," *The Review of Contemporary Fiction*, Spring, 1981, p. 8. Hereafter cited in the text as Interview, followed by the page number.

Moreover, in words which should recall Williams' description of the imagination as a natural force,[11] "[t] he novel is an invention, something that is made; it is not the expression of 'self'; it does not mirror reality" [Various, 196].

Like Williams, Sorrentino has only contempt for "realism." In his review of Hubert Selby's work, Sorrentino's expressed aim is to help move "criticism of Selby off that spot . . . marked 'realism.' " In contrast to realistic writing, Selby's work, he argues, "is as it is by design. . . . He has disappeared into his books, and his books offer an art made out of trash and garbage. He gives us no commentary, no opinions, no ideas. He gives us . . . no *comfort*. He 'is' the specific vulgarity, cruelty, and madness that relates in a vulgar, cruel, and mad tongue, the vulgarity, cruelty, and madness of his closed world."[12] Thus Selby's work is not about vulgarity, but is vulgarity itself. It is real, not realistic.

But Sorrentino's effort to separate Selby's work from the things of life and focus our attention upon the artistic design present in the words relies upon standards of correspondence we associate with realistic representation. Sorrentino praises Selby's transcription of speech for its accurate "differentiation of language patterns." "These are *real* differences, recorded perfectly" he insists. Later in this same essay, Sorrentino again dwells upon the verisimilitude Selby achieves: "To anyone who knows people like Tralala [a character in Selby's *Last Exit to Brooklyn*], their ideas of elegance, and the big-time, the bar [Selby] sends her to in order to hustle registers with a shock that is so acute one forgets how absolutely perfect a spot it is." His characters "are real because their acts are acts which are utterly true to the environment they inhabit" [Selby, 337, 338].

Thus Sorrentino's aesthetic includes a realistic measure. Correspondence with something outside the work lies at the heart of our most common-sense use of the term "realism." When we say something is realistic, we mean it achieves a high degree of likeness to the world represented. But it is to just this "likeness" that Sorrentino and Williams object: "There is not life in the stuff because it tries to be 'like' life" [*I*, 129]. Sorrentino's use of the word "real," like Williams', cuts two ways, for environment (above) refers both to the world of words and the external world with which Selby "dances." To say that his work has its own life is not to say it bears no relation to the "external reality" of

---

11. "and the unique proof of this is the work of the imagination not 'like' anything but transfused with the same forces which transfuse the earth" [*I*, 121].
12. "The Art of Hubert Selby," *The Review of Contemporary Fiction*, Summer 1981, p. 348. Hereafter cited in the text as Selby, followed by the page number.

Brooklyn life Selby and Sorrentino know first-hand; only that Selby's "imitation" is so good that it achieves a reality "detached" from any necessary correspondence with life, "[t]he prose moves the experience directly to you" [Selby, 337].

Neither Williams nor Sorrentino denies "external reality"; but the cleavage they both argue distinguishes two relations art may have to such reality. "The invented character," Sorrentino writes, "can only reveal the actual if he is the creature of the novelist's *invention*, not a signal whom we stupidly think is doing something 'believable' " [Various, 198]. This distinction between signalling and inventing is comparable to the one Williams drew between "copying" and "imitating." In 1951 he wrote to Frank Moore, "To copy nature is a spineless activity; it gives us a sense of our mere existence but hardly more than that. But to imitate nature involves the verb: we then ourselves become nature, and so invent an object which is an extension of the process."[13] Both writers differentiate between an art which seeks to inspire belief, and one which confronts the reader with its own reality.

Of his fourth novel, *Mulligan Stew*, Sorrentino says, "If you want to understand this book, you must be able to walk around inside of it and understand it in the sense that one understands the real world: that is, you're in it and whatever data and phenomena impinge upon you, you understand them insofar as you are able. That's the way the real world works, that's the way people work in relation to it" [Interview, 24]. Like Williams, Sorrentino creates an art of activity that enacts the movement of the imagination in contact with reality. "If [the novel] is any good at all," he writes, "it mirrors the processes of the real" [Various, 196]. For both writers, the products of the imagination are thus separate from life, but share with life an identity of composition and equality of being. In this "they are as actual, as sappy as the leaf of the tree which never moves from one spot" [*I*, 101]. This is the art of the actual.

III

In the engagement this art requires of the reader, it offers a degree of the social concern and acknowledgement of externality the realist reader demands, but which is so often obscured by the rhetoric of "detachment." However, the real differences between such readers and the writers of actuality should not be overlooked.

---

13. *Selected Letters*, ed. John C. Thirlwall (New York: McDowell Oblensky, 1957), p. 297. Hereafter cited in the text as *SL*, followed by the page number.

For those who urge realistic representation, reality is an object, external and knowable: it may be represented. This is the view underlying Graff's reminder that "many people" have thought literature contributes "to man's understanding of how things really are, not merely how they appear to our consciousness" [Graff, 7]. This is a reasonable expectation to have, but censure of a foolish solipsism should not be confused with the intentions governing the act of the imagination. This Graff seems to do: "The concept of an autonomous creative imagination, which fabricates the forms of order, meaning, and value which men no longer thought they could find in external nature, implicitly—if not necessarily intentionally—concedes that artistic meaning is a fiction, without any corresponding object in the extra-artistic world" [Graff, 35].

But this is the reverse of what Williams and Sorrentino mean when they insist upon the separation of words from life. For this separation is a means of dismantling illusion and discovering the origin of meaning in actual things. Thus Sorrentino's *Imaginative Qualities of Actual Things* focuses upon characters whose illusions allow them to avoid the way "things really are." Sheila Henry, for example, "will not allow her imagination to yield up the clear image that death is the reward and life no preparation for it" [*IQA*, 22]. The characters of this book "are at a loss to comprehend the true anguish of the flesh" [*IQA*, 17] because they are buffered from such comprehension by their own sentimentality, which shields them from the relentless candor of their lives. This candor is thrust before the reader by the reminder that "this story is invention only" [*IQA*, 9]. By insisting upon its reality *as an illusion* the book persistently dis-covers its actuality.

The art of the actual is an art of discovery. Indeed, Williams is unique among modernists in refusing the "impositions of 'art' " [*I*, 150], seeking instead to disentangle words and things to find there the basis of ideas:

> Compose. (No ideas
> but in things) Invent!
> Saxifrage is my flower that splits
> the rocks.[14]

Here external reality is origin, for "saxifrage"—which means "rock-breaking"—earns its name in language from its life in the crevices of the rocks it splits. Word follows thing, and in the composition of Williams' poem the words are given their own reality, as they compose the imagination's recognition. Thus the

---

14. *Selected Poems of William Carlos Williams* (New York: New Directions, 1969), pp. 108-109.

order of the words: "but in things) Invent!" followed by the word that is Williams' "flower." This is the "identity" Williams speaks of between the composition of nature and composition of the imagination.

Both Williams and Sorrentino use the word "actual" to distinguish between an art that "reveals" reality and is real and an art which clothes or surrounds the world it represents. Their distinction concerns both an artistic purity and a purification of life. Williams early on saw his activity as one of releasing, of separating words from life; but for him this was not solely the work of an aesthete. On the contrary, the attachments he sought to dislodge not only obscured the medium he wished to use, but life itself: "Nothing / is gained by saying the night breeds / murder—It is the classical mistake," he wrote in *Spring and All* [*I*, 102]. This mistake puts the cart before the horse, as ideas precede things: "the conscious recording of the day's experiences 'freshly and with the appearance of reality' " limits a man and "makes nature an accessory to the particular theory he is following, it blinds him to his world" [*I*, 120].

Similarly, a speaker in *Imaginative Qualities* recalls a friend of his who had visited Mexico, but seen it through his ideas about Lawrence's *The Plumed Serpent*:

> What most struck him was the image, bright in his mind, of these Indians, squatting by the side of the road, impassive, "their eyes like black stone, onyx, sitting there as if waiting for death." In his speech, "death" came out "Death." Another friend, who *was* a Mexican, said that they were waiting for the bus to come along and didn't feel like standing.

The speaker's friend is "outraged" because his sentimental association has been stripped from the reality it had obscured. The speaker then turns to us and cautions: "The reader will see that what I am driving at is that these words that he is reading—are words" [*IQA*, 37]. By directing us to the reality of the words, Sorrentino applies the lesson of his character's deflated symbolism to our tendency to look *through* words to another world.

Thus in both Williams and Sorrentino the imagination's power to liberate is also the power to debunk. *Imaginative Qualities* in particular concerns itself with the exposure of pretension, of self-serving associations and assumptions. The persistence of such "associational or sentimental value" Williams wrote ". . . is due to lack of imagination" [*I*, 14]. Words have the capacity to rigidify the attention; they "adhere to certain objects, and have the effect on the sense of oysters, or barnacles" [*I*, 149]. Words had made the rose "obsolete," and the words themselves had become sentimental; but the imagination may see the rose anew freeing both the flower and the words so that the rose once again "unbruised / penetrates spaces" [*I*, 109].

This is the importance of invention, of making it new in accord with the need for an art of ongoing vitality. In 1913 Williams wrote to Harriet Monroe, "life is above all things else at any moment subversive of life as it was the moment before—always new, irregular" [*SL*, 23-24]. Art must "imitate" that activity, things as they are be-ing. A poet, Williams insisted, is "a man / whose words will / bite / their way / home—being actual / having the form / of motion."[15]

The motion both writers most often enact is the movement of the imagination as it engages reality. *Imaginative Qualities* acts to defy any static reality words might mirror, and instead demonstrates the imagination of the reader to himself—showing him that he cannot for even a page remain outside of the actuality Sorrentino offers him. The apparent intrusiveness of the speakers in the novel—as in the example above—is not on behalf of authorial honesty, but is a dramatic strategy designed to awaken the reader from the narcosis of reading "about" to his own experience of reading.[16] This is not a rejection of meaning, but an affirmation of experience. "The exaltation men feel before a work of art," Williams wrote, "is the feeling of reality they draw from it. It sets them up, places a value upon experience" [*I*, 129]. Such experience depends upon the autonomy of art.

This activity of mind is the composition of Sorrentino's most recent book, *Crystal Vision*.[17] Here Sorrentino is less caustic, treating his figures—in the words of the presiding Magician—"with more kindness" [*CV*, 49]. In one of the book's crystal visions, the character Richie makes up a story about the lovely Isabel's prom night with Big Duck; but his story conflicts with his friends' own imaginations about this neighborhood girl: "I don't like the idea of her getting sick in front of that son of a bitch." So Richie adds this touch: "Berta, by the way, . . . puts her gardenia corsage in her underwear drawer that night. Nice?" His pals are placated: "Fine. Good, Irish Billy says" [*CV*, 116-117]. Such dialogue is not intended to be a copy of any real [historical] exchange of words, but is an example of what Williams called "conversation as

---

15. Ibid., p. 69.
16. Jerome Klinkowitz misunderstands the intentions governing the work of Sorrentino: "Above all Sorrentino is painfully honest about his work." For Klinkowitz, honesty is one of the common qualities of "post-contemporary American fiction." See *Literary Disruptions* (Urbana: University of Illinois Press, 1980), esp. pp. 154-167, on Sorrentino.
17. (San Francisco: North Point Press, 1981). Hereafter cited in the text as *CV*, followed by the page number.

design" where "the conversation was actual to the extent that it would be pure design."[18] The reader is witness here to the act of the imagination by which these speakers endure their living. Their lives, of course, are present only in their words, which are the material of the novel, not that to which they refer. Certainly these characters are "recognizable" because "we have already seen their natural counterparts" [*IQA*, 111]; but they have life only through the designs of speech Sorrentino has invented for them.[19]

The power of such writing—which lives as it were on the edge between the fragile petal and its penetrating strength, between its familiar reference and its internal autonomy—lies in its ability to confront the reader with experience. In such experience we are treated to what Sorrentino calls "a flash of the actual" as we are alert for a time to the processes by which we compose ourselves and "mingle" in the "language of the day."

Implicit in their emphasis upon an art of process is the conviction that "realism" as a convention of representation is related to nostalgia, to a backward-looking conservatism. In his essay on Williams' prose, Sorrentino inveighs against such convention as a collection of "signals" which "assure us that we are here, oh yes, in the world that we understand"—but quickly adds "what we 'understand' are the signals" [Various, 195]. By contrast, Williams' fiction bears no trace of "comment" or "sentiment." Sorrentino asks us "What does *White Mule* mean? Read it. The signals are missing" [Various, 200]. This conviction is part of the modernist contempt for "emotional slither" and "abstract words," but what Sorrentino finds so admirable in Williams' fiction is his having chosen not to move from sentiment to " 'sophisticated' effects," but to a flatness of presentation. The result is the "revelation of what [Williams] calls the 'isolate flecks' in which the whole meaning of a life, or of a cultural milieu, may be contained" [Various, 193].

What Sorrentino elsewhere calls a "merciless flat prose" [Selby, 337] is an aspect of the determination to avoid sentimentality. A style which includes comment, which tells us what we are to think and feel is a species of directness which subordinates language by making it the servant of opinion or idea. Early in his life as a poet Williams was sure that art is "a matter of concrete indirections. . . . To directly denote the content of a piece is, to my mind, to put an obstacle of words in the way of the

---

18. *A Novelette and Other Prose, 1921-31* (Toulon: TO, Publishers, 1932). Reprinted in *Imaginations*, p. 286.
19. See Jeffrey Bartlett's "Gilbert Sorrentino's *Crystal Vision*," *San Francisco Review of Books*, Vol. VI, no. 10, January 1982, p. 11.

picture" [*SL*, 24]. And one narrator of *Imaginative Qualities* thus deflects his readers, "The novelist's task is to tell you why all this happened. That's why I won't tell you. Isolate flecks" [*IQA*, 92]. To provide explicit comment is to destroy the revelatory power of words and open the door to a lurking romanticism that "redeems" any subject; even ostensible portrayals of defeat and loss are transformed "because we insist on imputing to the losers the knowledge of their own heroic pathos" [Various, 204]. Williams' accomplishment in his Stecher trilogy was to show "us that a family can be defeated in its success and still have a reasonably contented life" [Various, 205].

This refusal in their art to comment on issues directly, to moralize or describe a whole society, is considered a fault by some critics, but Williams' indirections always have a social intention. In his review of Sandburg's *Complete Poems*, Williams wrote:

> The poet in himself, tormented by the things which Sandburg evinces . . . digests that powerful incentive and puts it out as imaginative design, a new thing that embodies all their timeless agonies. It may not seem as effective to the active tormented man as the direct outcry . . . but it has far more carrying power.

Art is an agent of change, but need not be so directly. Art must be "remote" so that the "uninformed," in order to understand this art, will have "CHANGED within himself." This strong revolutionary impulse is everywhere in Williams' thinking, but he insists that such motivations must not appear in the making of the work, for they produce only sentiment: "For him to wince in the slightest degree would make him a cad and a liar."[20] Sorrentino's concern with social impact is apparent in his rhetorical question: "What happens to that writer whose imagination composes not the pseudo-reality, but those facets of reality that bring what we do not know—or do not wish to know—about ourselves into the light?" [Various, 198].

To this degree, both Williams and Sorrentino have thought of themselves as presenting things "as they really are." Of the "plight of the poor in a rich country," Williams said, "I wrote it down as I saw it."[21] In discussing the difficulty of writing fiction, Sorrentino says "the words must be composed so that they reveal the absolute reality of their prey, their subject" [Various, 196]. But in their work, getting to that "absolute reality" is as much a process of unveiling as it is of description. In their view, life as it

---

20. "Carl Sandburg's Complete Poems," *Selected Essays* (New York: New Directions, 1954), pp. 276-277.
21. *I Wanted to Write a Poem*, ed. Edith Heal (Boston: Beacon Press, 1958), p. 49.

is understood, as what we habitually think about it, is exactly the shell separating us from our own contact with life. The imagination breaks this shell, and thus the autonomy of art is explicitly tied to an awareness of social and personal oppression: "We do not know how thoroughly we are bound. It must be a new definition, it must cut us off from the rest," Williams declared in *The Great American Novel* [*I*, 170]. The imagination is the agent of this freedom, for its effect is "to liberate the man to act" [*I*, 150].

This is another aspect of the art of the actual: such art is dynamic, composed of action and inviting action. Williams felt his own life had been lived in "a hell of repression" save for intermittent "flashes of inspiration," and wondered "[w]hat would have happened in a world similarly lit by the imagination" [*I*, 116]. For Sorrentino as well the imagination serves this liberation: "It is this unrelieved quality in American life that the best American fiction does, indeed, relieve" [Various, 199].

Because such writing as that created by Williams and Sorrentino departs from those conventions associated with an objective point of view, it has been dismissed by some readers as having nothing to *say* about the social world. Graff, for example, wonders how "literature can be said to 'illuminate' problems of significance unless it can be given credit for judging these problems from an objective—i.e., realistic—point of view" [Graff, 170, n.]. Graff's equivalence of "objective" and "realistic" begs the question of truth, and subordinates a philosophical puzzle to a literary convention. Such critical views derive from a conception of writing as a kind of instruction from the "outside," as it were. But Williams and Sorrentino write from "inside" reality; the world is not "out there" but always present in our relations with it. An art that furthers this contact must itself be real.

Williams' thinking about art severs the habitual connection between objective representation and realistic portrayal. Writing in 1928 about the reaction to the new painting before World War I, he pointed out "[i]t was a mistake to say, as it was said twenty years ago, that the object of modern painting was to escape representation. Not so. (It was to escape triteness, the stupidity of a loose verisimilitude—to trace a scene and thus to confuse paint values with natural objects.) It *is* to represent nature."[22] This "nature" cannot be a fixed world we view from an Archimedean vantage, but one of processes in which we are engaged. Williams' remarkably durable insight was to see the necessity of

<hr>

22. "French Painting," *A Recognizable Image*, ed. Bram Dijkstra (New York: New Directions, 1978), pp. 69-70.

extending the attention to the point of contact; and it is this relation that is actual and that art represents. Williams thus anticipates much of the contemporary perception that self and world are united in a field defined by their relations to each other. Art's autonomy—that it is real, not merely a reflection of reality— furthers this unity, so that the argument that such independence denies an external world misses the mark. For that there exists a reality of some dimension and social complexity is not at issue.

If held to a philosophical rigor, we must admit that we do not know what reality is; but philosophy is not the concern of either Williams or Sorrentino. For them external reality is most immediately experienced through our imagination. Though all of us live in a shared field, indubitably social, this field is neither static nor the same for each of its members. Any mirror would of necessity fail to record the interpenetrating planes of imagination by which we possess our lives, for the imagination, we may say, is transparent. The art of Williams and Sorrentino enacts the imagination itself, as it holds in its prism the isolate flecks, the imaginative qualities of actual things.

THE TESTAMENT

The desk and office, 2nd floor, 9 Ridge Road.

JOSEPH BROGUNIER

AN ANNOTATED BIBLIOGRAPHY OF WORKS ABOUT WILLIAM CARLOS WILLIAMS: 1974-1982

The Williams bibliography is modeled upon the earlier bibliographies in the *Man and Poet* series—those on Zukofsky, Bunting, and Oppen. Like them, it is a chronological annotated bibliography of all the significant criticism and scholarship about the poet and his work. Items are arranged chronologically, with articles in periodicals that are dated by the month (or more specifically) placed with others dated by the corresponding calendric season (so that "May" and "Spring" are in the same group), and then articles within chronological groups alphabetized by author. Items with only the year date are found at the end of the seasonal groups. Included in the bibliography are articles and books on Williams focused on bibliography, biography, scholarship, critical studies, and edited editions and reprints of Williams' own works. Barring an exception noted later, the bibliography does not include reviews, nor does it include materials in publications other than those indexed in standard professional bibliographies like those of the *MLA* and *American Literature*.

There are some variations from earlier *Man and Poet* bibliographies. Paul Mariani's *William Carlos Williams/ The Poet and His Critics* (1975) thoroughly covers critical and scholarly studies of Williams up through 1973; thus, the starting point of this bibliography is 1974. As a base bibliography I used the *MLA International Bibliographies* for 1974-1980 inclusive. That base was supplemented by articles and bibliographical items in the *William Carlos Williams Newsletter* (later *Review*) for Fall 1975-Fall 1982, and, for the years 1981 and 1982, by the bibliographies in *Twentieth Century Literature* and *American Literature*, and also by the book reviews and book listings in the latter. The *Journal of Modern Literature*'s Annual Review Numbers were also of help in compiling references. Though my helpers and I have very likely missed some important works, as my preceding colleague in this series wrote, "this bibliography is as complete as we could make it, at this time."

Regarding the books: Even for the nine-year period of this bibliography there are so many book-length studies of Williams, and substantial part-of-a-book studies, that eight readers reading for a month of Sundays would have been needed to annotate them all; and I had neither eight readers reading nor a month of Sundays. But there were usually available, for any one book, several or even numerous reviews by knowledgeable and often authoritative reviewers. After compiling a list of the available reviews (principally via *WCWN/WCWR*, the *AL* book reviews, and the *Humanities Index*), I selected one that promised to be especially knowledgeable, judicious, and incisive; and the bibliography gives a reference to and annotation of that review. While one hopes the selected review is representative in judgment also, the reader should know that for a few books only one review was available, and for two, quite recent books, there were no reviews.

Previous bibliographies in this series included annotations of dissertations. That proved impossible to do for the Williams bibliography. Dissertations are instead listed, unannotated and in a group, at the end of the year of their completion. The reader thereby may at least see at a glance how much doctoral study Williams was given in any one year, and the nature of the subjects being studied. The lists of dissertations were compiled from the *MLA Bibliographies* 1974-1980, from *Dissertation Abstracts International*, and from *WCWN/WCWR* Spring 1976-Fall 1982.

Michael Fournier has been an indispensable helper in compiling this bibliography. He helped search available bibliographies to supplement those of the *MLA*; and he did the bulk of the labor of locating articles, arranging the copying of them, placing orders with Interlibrary Loan, and bringing to my office sheaf after sheaf after sheaf of Xeroxed articles. For a few of the articles he supplied annotations (identified by his initials); and he also gathered listings of the dissertations. Overall Michael was the most industrious and reliable "go-for" one could wish for, and I'm grateful to him. Carol Curtis and her staff in the Interlibrary Loan office of Fogler Library of the University of Maine were admirably resourceful in locating items the Fogler lacked, and quick in supplying them. John O'Grady helped to compile the list of reviews of books; and Penny Oakes helped organize the index. All of these people contributed to the gathering, growth, and potential usefulness of the bibliography. For any oversights and omissions I, of course, am responsible.

Some final words: This bibliography uses the *MLA Bibliography*'s abbreviations for the titles of both the most and the more widely known periodicals publishing articles on Williams. And, for economy of space, I abbreviate Williams' name to *Ws* and *Ws'* in my own usage (but not in quotations). Lastly, the bibliography is preceded by an index, alphabetized by author and followed by the number of the item.

† † † † † † †

Altieri, Charles. "Culture and Skepticism: A Response to Michael Fischer." 155

Altieri, Charles. "Presence and Reference in a Literary Text . . .". . . 137

Archer, Stanley. "*Glazed* in Williams's 'The Red Wheelbarrow.' " . 61

Baker, William. "Williams' 'The Use of Force.' " 113

Baldwin, Neil. " 'Pulling the Disparate Together' . . ." 66

Baldwin, Neil. "William Carlos Williams Catalog, Lockwood Memorial Library, Poetry Collection." 21

Baldwin, Neil. " 'The world it opens': William Carlos Williams' 'The Descent.' " 85

Baldwin, Neil. "Zukofsky, Williams, and *The Wedge*. . ." 153

Baldwin, Neil and Steven L. Meyers. *The Manuscripts and Letters of William Carlos Williams in the Poetry Collection of the Lockwood Memorial Library*. 122

Bar-Yaacov, Lois. "Driving into the 20th Century . . ." 179

Bernstein, Rosalyn A. "The Beautiful Unbeautiful . . ." 74

Bernstein, Michael André. *The Tale of the Tribe: Ezra Pound and the Modern Verse Epic* 184

Berry, Eleanor. "William Carlos Williams's 'The Semblables.' " . . . 185

Berry, Eleanor. "Williams' Development of a New Prosodic Form . . ". 208

Bollard, Margaret Lloyd. "The Interlace Element in *Paterson*." . . . 22

Bollard, Margaret Lloyd. "The 'Newspaper Landscape' of Williams' *Paterson*." 27

Bollier, E.P. "William Carlos Williams Between Whitman and Poe." 123

1974

1. Doyle, Charles. "Kora and Venus: Process and Object in
    William Carlos Williams," *Perspective*, 17:iii (Winter 1974),
    189-97.

    Ws' use of the Persephone myth in *Kora in Hell* is a complement to his
    use of the Venus myth in other of his works. In Venus he portrays the
    already realized, intrinsically beautiful thing, and in Kora the soiled
    base and "the 'formless ground.' " Similarly, the form of his "Improv-
    isations" (*Kora* and elsewhere) complement his "short-lined, 'hard,
    dry' poems of 'accurate description,' " while the two are alike in being
    anti-literary. *Kora* is also important for showing Ws' attempt to bond
    "the primacy of the 'thing itself' [with] the transcendent value of
    imagination."

2. Graham, D. B. 'A Note on Howells, Williams, and the Matter
    of Sam Patch," *NConL*, 4:ii (March 1974), 10-13.

    Noting that a variety of texts have been identified as possible sources
    of Ws' knowledge of Sam Patch, as well as acknowledging that no
    evidence is available to show Ws knew of or read Howells, Graham
    proposes one possible source to be Howells' early *Their Wedding*

Journey, citing a number of close similarities between the two authors' views of Patch as well as wider themes and interests to be found in Howells' novel and Ws' writing.

Howells' Basil and Isabel March, on their trip from Boston to upstate New York and Canada, carry on a debate about the beauty of the American landscape, in which "Basil speaks for the American view, Isabel for the European, the New *England*" [DBG's italics]. The debate continues when they arrive at the Genesee Falls. Hearing of Patch's fatal leap, Isabel dismisses him contemptuously ;March argues for the literary authenticity of American scenes and American settings, saying, "We shall never have a poetry of our own till we get over this absurd reluctance from facts, till we make the ideal embrace and include the real." Graham cites March's statement as "match[ing] almost perfectly Williams' well-known credo of adherence to local fact," as well as noting that Ws and March identically attribute Patch's death to the failure of his language.

3. Fiero, F. Douglass. "Williams Creates the First Book of *Paterson*," *JML*, 3 (April 1974), 965-86.

    Via a scrutiny of four drafts of the poem in the Yale library, Fiero emphasizes the origins and introductions of specific passages and various themes—especially that of the poet, searching for an adequate language—in *Paterson* I. Includes ancillary material, especially about "some remarkable letters" to Ws from a young "systems engineer," David Lyle, which letters helped Ws "toward the discovery of the poet as the hero of the poem." Fiero concludes that, starting with the 1927 "Paterson," *Paterson* I grew "from a bare collection of images . . . into a world where the poet's imagination is the active central element," unifying multiplicities and tensions.

4. Duffey, Bernard I. "The Experimental Lyric in Modern Poetry: Eliot, Pound, Williams," *JML*, 3 (July 1974), 1085-1103.

    Of the three poets Duffey chooses as exemplifying what he suggests is "the inclusiveness of experimentalism as a lyric mode in recent decades," Ws is given the briefest treatment [pp. 1100-1102]. Duffey first offers a brief survey of lyric forms, from the earliest and recurrent, in song, through the finding of its own "formal schemes," the romantic lyric, with form the option of the author, to the modern experimental lyric, addressing "a discontinuity of feeling from both an identifiable self and from any clearly defined occasion." Duffey finds "Eliot's poetic of discontinuous feeling" underlying the lyricism of *Paterson*, a finding he illustrates by references to the "Clearly, they say. Oh, clearly! Clearly?" Passage of Bk. I, and to the "beautiful thing" manifested as a "pentecostal fire" in Bk. III.

5. Fox, Hugh. "*The Genuine Avante-Garde* [sic] / William Carlos Williams's Credo," *SWR*, 59 (Summer 1974), 285-99.

    This is a pastiche of quotations and a collocation of assertions on Ws' aesthetic (essentially: Ws "sees the *real* function of the imagination as breaking through the alienation of the near at hand and reviving its wonder") via a race through *Kora in Hell, Spring and All, The Great American Novel, The Descent of Winter, A Novelette,* the Stecher trilogy (in three pages), *I Wanted To Write a Poem,* and the five books of *Paterson.* The pace is accelerated by neologisms and a free use of italics and of absolutes: egs., "Then the supreme statement of the avant-garde mystique: 'The compositions that are smoother, consecutive are disjointed. Dis-jointed. They bear no relation to anything in the world or in the mind.' " and "Avant-gardism a la Williams is *actualism* . . . [ellipsis also in original] and perhaps actualism is an underlying characteristic of *all avant-garde writing*" [pp. 290-91]. The essay seems designed to introduce Ws to new readers, but its helter-skelter pace and manner turns the reader against material from Ws that, encountered more temperately and sensibly, would be valued.

6. Paz, Octavio. "Saxifrage: Some Notes on William Carlos Williams," *London Magazine,* New Series 14:ii (June/July 1974), 33-43.

Paz briefly limns Ws' life and career, discusses his esthetics (touching on his influence on both the Objectivists and the Black Mountain group, and comparing Ws' "non-imitative realism" to that of Jorge Guillén and Frances Ponge), characterizes *Paterson,* and intersperses his essay with the insights of a fellow writer and poet. The one poem he specifically discusses is *Paterson,* of which he writes,

> There is a kind of vacuum at the centre of the concept of Williams (not in his short poems) which is the very vacuum of contemporary American culture. The Christianity of *The Waste Land* is a burnt, blackened truth, one which will not, in my opinion, flourish again, but it was a central truth and one which, like the light of a dead star, still *touches* us. I find nothing similar in *Paterson.* The comparison with the *Cantos* is no more favourable to Williams. The United States is an imperial power and if Pound could not be its Virgil he was at least its Milton: his theme is the fall of a great power. The United States conquered the world but lost its soul, its future—that universal future in which Whitman believed. Perhaps because of his very integrity and decency, Williams did not see the imperial side of his country, its demoniacal dimension.

In balance against this measure of *Paterson*'s failure (Paz judges *The Cantos* to be "a poetry incomparably vaster and richer") are the measures made by "the intensity and the perfection of [a poet's] works. Also by his vivacity." By these measures "Williams is the author of the most *vivid* poems in modern North American poetry" [OP's italics]. Whether Ws is "really the most American of the poets of his epoch," Paz writes, "I don't know and I don't care about knowing. On the other hand, I do know that he is the freshest and most limpid."

Paz ends with a description of two visits to Ws at Rutherford late in Ws' life, the first prompted by Paz's reading a "magnificent translation" Ws had made of one of "a poem of mine, *Hymn Among Ruins.*"

The essay is translated by Donald Walsh.

7. Burke, Kenneth. "William Carlos Williams: A Critical Appreciation." In *William Carlos Williams*. Ed. Charles Angoff. Fairleigh Dickinson Univ. Pr., 1974. Pp. 15-19.

> The book publishes the first of the Leverton Lectures of Fairleigh Dickinson University. This first group of lectures, delivered on the Rutherford campus of the University in Nov. 1972, concern "the career and poetical achievements" of Ws.
>
> Taking as text the poem "In passing with my mind" from *Spring and All*, Burke extrapolates that the traffic therein, "seen in multifarious irregularities," is a paradigm of "the copiousness of the poet's imagination," "linked with a sense of fragmentary, dissociated vignettes, welling from within," and expressive of "the ebullience of a poetic method that could find in anything and everything the makings of a poem."

8. Pearson, Norman Holmes. "The People Who Use the William Carlos Williams Collection at Yale." In *William Carlos Williams*. Ed. Charles Angoff. Pp. 31-36.

> Despite the title, this recounts, as an issue of some of the author's contacts with Ws, the start and some incidents in the growth of the Ws Coll. at Yale. It also gives a brief narrative description of its principal holdings as well as of Ws related material in other Yale archives. With quotations from two Ws' letters to Pearson and from an "apparently unpublished" Ws MS titled "Rutherford and Me."

9. Sullivan, A. M. "Dr. William Carlos Williams, Poet and Humanist." In *William Carlos Williams*. Ed. Charles Angoff. Pp. 37-46.

> Nearly half of this is a general, familiar account of Ws' attention to social and economic issues of his time and place: "As a humanist he realized the need for a readjustment of the power of the machine with the human impulse for equity." Four pp. contain excerpts from the author's 1935 radio interviews with Ws, in which the principal subject was the attempt to bring the familiar, immediate place and language into poetry. As Ws said then, "the major activity of any artist in any period must always be to discover in the idiom of the life about him, the life that his own eyes, ears, nose, mouth, fingers are seeing for the first and only time—to discover therein the lasting qualities of all art and to assert them in the terms he knows, the terms of his day of his own life" [p. 45].

10. Wallace, Emily Mitchell. " 'The Forms of the Emotions . . . the Pointed Trees.' " In *William Carlos Williams*. Ed. Charles Angoff. Pp. 20-30.

> A charming and informative testimony of Ws' "love of trees and plants" and of their appearance in his poetry. Includes a facsimile of the holograph of Ws' earliest poem, "Tree," ca. 1893, notes about *The Sylvan Year* (1876) and Ws' enthusiasm for it, and a hypothesis

by EMW about a poem's growth from observation of things, including trees, to the complex of "a new form, a *made* thing."

11. Davis, Robert. "Flowers and the Unicorn in *Paterson*," *Graduate Eng. Papers* (Ariz.), 6:i (1974), 28-33.

The first four books of *Paterson* bring no "resolution to the problems which Paterson confronts" nor success to his quest, writes Davis. But, "by the end of the last book, the poet rests in confidence that the search will never end, though his personal quest has reached a conclusion in his ability to fully recognize himself as an artist participating in a world of art which will always continue. Unlike the first four books, this final book is poetically controlled by a central subject. The seven Unicorn tapestries at The Cloisters in New York dominate the entire final book, and integrate recurrent themes from the first four."

Davis describes the scenes depicted in the seven tapestries (and later summarizes the mythology of the unicorn) and then, noting the profusion of flowers in "the backgrounds of the tapestries," examines the flower images in Books I-IV and shows that "the flowers in Book V echo [sic] those in the other four books."

After identifying three symbolic levels of significance in the tapestries themselves—those of "the mythological hunt for the unicorn," of "the parallel allegory of Christ's Incarnation and Resurrection," and "of the [royal] marriage of Anne of Brittany to Louis XII in 1499"—and noting Ws' characterization of Brueghel as an artist who both witnesses and envisions," Davis writes, "The process which combines witnessing and imagining, and which results in art, is generated by the artist, who becomes both agent and hero of the integrations in Book V. The aging poet Paterson, now sensitive to both sides of seeing and to the possibilities of the inclusion of both in art, focuses on the tapestries"—tapestries in which the unicorn becomes additionally symbolic of the poet. Davis concludes,

> The poet Paterson is also a doctor, and the mythology of the unicorn whose horn absorbs poison is singularly appropriate identification for a poet-doctor seeking to resolve conflicts. The role of the unicorn absorbs the dangers of both an isolated, imaginative life of the mind and the limited, mortal life of the body by resolving them together in the world of art. The resolution is given a brief history in Book V by evoking figures of the past who seem to have achieved the integration of self in the world, through art, an integration which Paterson now recognizes: Durer, Leonardo, Picasso, Beethoven, Bosch, Gris, and others. The listing of these artists is prefaced by the introduction, "the cure began, perhaps. . . ." Through art, "the physician, having spent a long life healing others, now finally heals himself," and just as the unicorn absorbs poison, so Paterson the poet can absorb "the poision Williams finds in native American life," which leads to the conflicts described in the first four *Paterson* books.

12. Hallberg, Robert von. "Olson's Relation to Pound and Williams," *ConL*, 15:i (1974), 15-48.

Hallberg sees the three poets as sharing, especially in their long poems, an "antisymbolist" poetic; turned from the symbolists' goal of a transcendent vision, they serve art's mimetic function. As regards Olson's relation to Ws, Olson finds *Paterson*'s valuable quality to be its presentation of "so much that is not Williams, so much of Paterson, New Jersey," a quality the poem achieves because " 'Bill HAS an emotional system which is capable of extensions & comprehensions the ego-system [Pound in *The Cantos*] is not' " [p. 24]. Yet Olson also finds three problems in *Paterson*: exactly in contrast to Pound's, "Williams's work is ultimately undone by an inability to properly handle time" [p. 24]; his city is "pastoral and outdated"; and it unrealistically excludes the violence of urban life. As for gains, "the most fruitful lesson Olson took from Ws is the idea of a long poem centered on a single city," with its elevation of the local, though the events and people of the city Olson emphasizes in his poem concern "the uncommon political leaders," rather than the "common people" of Ws' focus. Another subject both poets share (Ws in "The Desert Music" especially) are "poems about how to write poems" [p. 37]. As regards poetics Olson shares something of Ws' prosody, with an emphasis on "concrete images of objective reality" rather than on Poundian ideas/"larger units of meaning" [p. 41]. But in diction he is more like Pound, in his interest in philogogy, etymology, and "the accrued senses of words" [p. 44], and basically rejects Ws' pursuit of the " 'words washed clean.' " In conclusion, "Olson was consistently more dubious of his relationship to Ws than of his relationship to Pound. And yet he took much from both poets."

13. Hardie, Jack. "Williams's 'The Well Disciplined Bargeman,' " *Expl* 33 (1974), Item 10.

Surmising that Ws read Cleanth Brooks's *The Well-Wrought Urn* (1947), a study attentive "only to British poems" and without even a mention of Whitman and Pound," Hardie proposes, interestingly and with some credibility, that Ws' "The Well-Disciplined Bargeman" (1948) is "a rejoinder" to Brooks's book. With images in his poem similar to those in Brooks's analysis of "Composed upon Westminster Bridge," Ws apparently directed the poem itself as "a counterattack on [Brooks's] rigid reading" of Wordsworth's "Immortality" ode.

14. Juhasz, Suzanne. *Metaphor and the Poetry of Williams, Pound and Stevens*. Lewisburg: Bucknell UP, 1974.

Review by Jack Hardie, *JML* (1974 Annual Review), 4:5 (1975), 934-35.

Writing his review at the start of the modern surge of inflation, Hardie indites,

The price of this book is an inspired touch; it is life imitating art—monetary inflation the perfect metaphor of this book's matter and manner. The subject matter that might have made an acceptable journal article or two is inflated into five uneven essays and a postscript. The text itself is inflated by clumsy lists and useless appendices. And six items on metaphor cited in the text swell into the hyperbole of a sixty-five-item Bibliography of Works Consulted. If you have fifteen dollars to spend on a book like this, give it instead to some promising, terse young poet. Fight inflation.

Of Ws, Juhasz writes of "Asphodel, That Greeny Flower" and *Paterson*"; and as in her treatment of the other poets, "For each long work, 'patterns of metaphors' are observed and the figures themselves isolated, often in lists. There is also an effort to discuss each poet's ideas about poetry. The thinness of these discussions!" Enough—or too much.

15. Lahm, Craig A. "Additions to *A Bibliography of William Carlos Williams* by Wallace," *Serif*, 11:ii (1974), 40-43.

Lahn lists some 18 items found in the William Carlos Williams collection of the Kent State University Library and recommends them "as emendations" to Emily Mitchell Wallace's bibliography. Six "appeared after the publication of Wallace's book." Lahn codes and describes all items "in accordance with the format of Wallace's book."

16. Mariani, Paul L. "Williams: The Late Phase," *Paintbrush*, 1 (1974), 42-47.

Mariani notes the critical debate about the value of Ws' late works, acknowledges some of its "faults," and identifies some of the matters criticism has overlooked or needs to study, such as "the specific sense of tradition in Williams' late poems, particularly with respect to the artists whom he celebrated (which means understanding *why* he chose to celebrate this canon of artists and not others)" [PLM's italics]. He also briefly sketches some facets of Ws' achievement in the late works: "the way in which Williams' secular imagination counters the pressure of the final closure" (death), the quality of the "late love poems," to be "placed against Yeats's, for example," and which "can profitably be compared to the Chaucer of *Troilus and Cressida*," and the power of his imagination in its attention to "the particulars of the world." As Ws said of Brueghel, Mariani writes of him: "here in the late poems is the mastery, with 'the mind, the resourceful mind,' governing the whole design."

17. Riddel, Joseph N. *The Inverted Bell: Modernism and the Counterpoetics of William Carlos Williams*. Baton Rouge: Louisiana State UP, 1974.
Review by J. Hillis Miller. "Deconstructing the Deconstructers," *Diacritics*, 5:ii (Summer 1975), 24-31.

Miller's lengthy piece is both a review of Riddel's book and an essay on deconstruction. *The Inverted Bell* he describes as "essentially a reading of *Paterson* . . . in five chapters each roughly corresponding to a book of the poem. There is a constant triangulation from Heidegger and Derrida. Detours are made into other work by Williams, into other modern poets, and into other continental writers. The thematic focus can be even more narrowly defined. Riddel's chief topic . . . is the problematic of origins and beginnings in poetry." He notes that Riddell, unlike Kenner in *A Homemade World*, treats Ws as a philosophic poet, thereby raising the question of "Which reading of Williams is the 'right' one?" and that "Riddell tends to assume that

Heidegger, Derrida, Williams, and he himself are each more or less self-consistent, and that all four are saying roughly 'the same thing,' " thereby raising the question, "Is this in fact the case?"

He then proceeds to explore these and a few related questions. One is that Riddel's method of "triangulating" Ws by means of Derrida and Heidegger may falsely assume that the latter two constitute fixed points—or what Miller calls "solid standing ground[—] on the basis of which to assess the primary writer." But, he states, "the other writers' must themselves be fully worked through, what is most problematic about them fully confronted"; and for writers such as Heidegger and Derrida "this might take a lifetime." In addition, in a matter that presents questions about the value of the periodization of literature, Riddel places Ws among "the Post-Moderns in his commitment to 'freeplay,' " only to contradict himself "immediately (or even simultaneously" by attributing to Ws "the nostalgia for origins of the Moderns."

Though Riddel writes as if Derrida and Heidegger were compatible, "Heidegger, on the whole, wins the day." One evidence of his ascendency is that

> There is a continual, somewhat incantatory, repetition, with slight variation, throughout Riddel's book of the same Heideggerian and Williamsian metaphors: "site," "measure," "whored virgin," "mystery at the origin," "original violence," "bringing to light," "regathering," "house of language," "e-mergence," "presence," "original cleaving," "primordial dance," and so on. The implication is that these figures are privileged in the way they are affirmed to be by Heidegger. They are magical formulas which open the way back to the ground of language and poetry. Riddel's basic paradigm, in fact, and perhaps that of Williams as well, is not that of Derrida's "freeplay." It is the paradigm of a "mysterious" source which violently broke apart or was broken apart into opposites—sexual opposites, opposites of nature and culture, reason and feeling, light and dark, form and power, and so on. The business of poetry is to reveal the radiant gist hidden behind the multiplicity. The notion of primordial opposites locked in some polemical or sexual combat is entirely compatible, however, with metaphysics, with what Riddel defines as "Modernism." It is by no means to be identified with Derrida's "differance."

The greatest difficulty of Riddel's book, Miller concludes, emerges from "his failure to recognize consistently the necessary heterogeneity of any text." Ultimately Riddel's approach ignores the integrity and separateness of each writer, obscures the fact that "they can only be juxtaposed in their manifold differences. Riddel's book may in fact have its greatest value in its apparent unintentional demonstration of the irreducible heterogeneity of the languages of poetry, of philosophy, and of criticism." As a corollary to this maxim, Riddel likewise errs in "not fac[ing] explicitly the heterogeneity of Williams. . . . The result is that he contradicts himself, rather than recognizing the contradictions in the texts he discusses." Rather than "Asphodel" being "a backsliding to . . . Modernism" and *Paterson* V "the fullest example of deconstructive Post-Modernism," as Riddel perceives each, "The fact is that with both poems it is not a matter of either/or but of both/and. Both 'Asphodel' and *Paterson Five* are Modernist and Post-Modernist at once, and can be shown to be so."

18. Williams, William Carlos. *The Embodiment of Knowledge*, ed. and introd. Ron Leowinsohn. N.Y.: New Directions, 1974. Review by Paul Mariani, *WCWN*, 1:i (Fall 1975), 9-12.

> In "spare moments" between 1928 and 1930 Ws wrote "a sheaf of pages in no way meant to be a systematic treatise on epistemology," which, along with five much earlier essays, is printed in this book. Mariani identifies various provocations for Ws writing this group of papers, from umbrage because one of his sons was "do[ing] poorly in his French class at Rutherford High despite his having spent a year speaking French in a Swiss school" ("he refused to learn the subject the way the teacher preferred"), through ripostes at Rebecca West "for her parochial attack on Joyce's *Work in Progress*," "at Wyndham Lewis for his recent attack on Pound's intelligence," and "at Eliot for his neoplagiarism of the tradition in *The Waste Land*." Also, Ws dilates on Shakespeare, for him "a figure of the true artist himself . . . [and] a standard against which Williams can measure the best in modernism." His principal subjects are "those two immensities, Science and Philosophy. He keeps coming back and coming back to those two antagonists, going over the same ground from different points of the compass, trying to break through, in the very process of writing, to some central clarity, some grand simplicity which will mean for him integrity, a human value discovered." Mariani concludes by praising Loewinsohn's editing and noting that his introduction is especially good, being "an extended discussion of just what Williams' poetics are about without upstaging Williams himself."

19. 1974 Dissertations

A. Baldwin, Neil E. "The Manuscripts and Letters of William Carlos Williams in the Poetry Collection of the Lockwood Memorial Library, State University of New York at Buffalo: A Descriptive Catalogue" (Part 2) *DAI* 34:5153A-54A (S.U.N.Y., Buffalo).

B. Daniel, Stephen L. "From Letter to Spirit: A Fourfold Hermeneutic and Its Application to Selected American Poems." *DAI* 35:2935A-36A (Emory).

C. Graham, Theodora R. "Woman as Character and Symbol in the Work of William Carlos Williams." *DAI* 35:2267A-68A (Pa.).

D. Meyers, Steven L. "The Manuscripts and Letters of William Carlos Williams in the Poetry Collection of the Lockwood Memorial Library, State University of New York at Buffalo: A Descriptive Catalogue" (Part 1) *DAI* 34:5193A (S.U.N.Y., Buffalo).

E. Rapp, Carl Allen. "William Carlos Williams and Romanticism." The Johns Hopkins University, 1974. *DAI* 38:789A-90A;

F. Simmons, Andrew M. "The Experimental Prose and the Novels of William Carlos Williams." *DAI* 34:7246A-47A (Mo., Columbia).

1975

20. Perloff, Marjorie. " 'Literary Competence' and the Formalist Model," *Centrum*, 3:i (Spring 1975), 34-44.

> Perloff's subject is the Structuralists' attempt "to refute the Formalist doctrine that literary language is intrinsically different from ordinary language." The Structuralist concept of "literary competence," central to this attempt, she defines (via Jonathan Culler) as " 'the ability to convert linguistic sequences into literary structures and meaning' " and as " 'a set of conventions for reading literary texts.' " She also delineates the three conventions claimed by Culler to "govern our interpretation of poetry" (namely, impersonality, coherence, and significance) remarking on their similarity to basic New Critical concepts.
>
> Ws enters into her essay as a practical test; Perloff proposes to determine whether the Structuralists can supply a reading better than those offered "by the Formalists or even by the despised New Critics" of Ws' "This Is Just to Say." She gives an extended account of a New Critical reading of the poem published in 1966, comparing it to Culler's reading and especially to Culler's contention that it "is only a poem because it is set down on the page as a poem, that there is nothing inherent in its language that makes it 'poetic.' " She concludes that Culler's reading has value in its claim for "the importance convention plays in the reading of poems," but that the Formalists maintain a credible position in insisting that literary and ordinary language are different.

21. Baldwin, Neil. "William Carlos Williams Catalog, Lockwood Memorial Library, Poetry Collection," *WCWN*, 1:1 (Fall 1975), 5.

> This is an "outline of the organization and contents" of the catalog of the Ws collection in the Lockwood Memorial Library at SUNY, Buffalo, a catalog reorganized from a 1973 joint diss. by NB and Steven L. Meyers "to include previously restricted" letters and to add "a comprehensive author/title index." The catalog, which categorizes and identifies "more than twenty thousand pieces of paper," contains seven sections: "mss for poems," items of "Creative Prose," "Critical Prose," "Notebooks and Arrangements," "the first four books of *Paterson*," letters to and from Ws, and miscellanea.

22. Bollard, Margaret Lloyd. "The Interlace Element in *Paterson*," *TCL*, 21 (October 1975), 288-304.

> Observing that in a letter to Louis Martz in 1951, "Williams had come to recognize that rather than inventing a new prosody he was rediscovering certain principles of poetic form which had become obscured," Bollard examines Ws' use of interlace, an esthetic structure analogous to weaving (and therefore analogized in *Paterson* (V) by the Unicorn tapestries), and utilized in some Old English and Medieval art. "Williams counterbalances *Paterson*'s linear structure ('a man in

himself is a city, beginning, seeking, achieving and concluding his life') by presenting his themes, insofar as possible, simultaneously, so that they 'alternate like threads in a woven fabric, one theme interrupting another and again another, and yet all remaining constantly present in the author's and the reader's mind.' "

Of the "two kinds of interlace" Bollard finds in *Paterson*, the first she describes "as the interweaving of originally or logically continuous, or of basically homogeneous, material (such as newspaper items or historical excerpts) throughout a section or sections of the poem." An example of this type is "the interweaving of excerpts from Cress's letters throughout the first two books of *Paterson*." Such interlacing, first, maintains a linear progression in Books I and II, second, "creates an acentric simultaneous effect" as the excerpts are juxtaposed with other materials, and third, by means of the juxtapositions "confer new significance upon the letters and also upon the material with which the letter interacts upon the page."

The other, more "dominant type of interlace ... is the continual process of cross-referencing which occurs throughout the poem," an example of which is Ws' use of the Mrs. Cumming's and Sam Patch's drownings. Those drownings, combined with others in *Paterson* and related in the poem to the theme of the lack of an adequate language, prepare for the contrasting "end of *Book IV* [when] a man walks out of the water, indicating that at least a key to a redeeming language has been found through the enactment of the four books of *Paterson*."

Bollard concludes that, in contrast to a common perception of *Paterson*'s structure as "simply one of theme and variation," it is rather constituted as "a 'field of action' in which meanings and themes arise and gradually emerge through the complex interactions of its materials—through the process and enactment of the poem."

Bollard makes use of the *Paterson* MSS at Buffalo and at Yale; facsimiles of the MSS outlines of Books I, II, III, and IV are reproduced in her article.

23. Creeley, Robert. "Preface to the Williams Catalog, Lockwood Memorial Library, Poetry Collection," *WCWN*, 1:1 (Fall 1975), 5-6.

This note attempts to briefly epitomize the value of Ws to three generations of poets, from his own, of Pound and Zukofsky, to the youngest, of Ginsberg and Levertov and Creeley himself. It recalls, from the *Autobiography*, Ws' own domestic account of the start of the Ws collection at SUNY, Buffalo, and its growth to "the most extensive collection of Williams' material that we now have." Sketching a few of the values of this material, Creeley concludes that the greatest is "the intimate revelation possible when one can so witness the issue of such words as he did write by means of an agency as movingly common as man's own two hands. The human dimension becomes so clearly manifest, and all pretension of formula or abstract objectification fall away."

24. Mariani, Paul. "The Eighth Day of Creation: William Carlos Williams' Late Poems," *TCL*, 21 (October 1975), 305-18.

While still at work on *Paterson IV*, writes Mariani, Ws was already thinking, as his MSS show, of lengthening the poem and writing "about the river in a new dimension: the Passaic as archetype, as the River of Heaven." Not pursued at the time, Ws' illnesses in part spurred his return to this perspective, "the dimension of timelessness, the world of the imagination, the apocalyptic moment, what he referred to as the eighth day of creation." Ws had partly explored this road in the past, had undertaken "repeated decreations . . . in order to come at that beauty locked in the imagination." But the late poems have a new quality, "Williams' more relaxed way of saying and with it a more explicit way of seeing the all-pervasive radiating pattern at the core of so much that [he] wrote." "What marks poems like *Asphodel*₁ and *Paterson V* as different from his earlier poetry is that Williams has come out on the other side of the apocalyptic moment. He stands, now, at a remove from the processive nature of the earlier poetry, . . . is removed from the violent flux," has broken through to a philosophical detachment.

Mariani then proceeds to his three main considerations:

> 1) the movement toward the garden of the imagination, where it is always spring; 2) the encounter with the beautiful thing, Kora, the sensuous virgin to whom the artist pays homage ;3) the figure of the artist, both the all-pervasive creator who contains within himself the garden and the virgin and also the willing victim, a figure moving through the tapestry, seeking his own murder and rebirth in the imagination.

Ws' reading, while at Yaddo, the "working papers" of his friend Nicolas Calas' intensive, detailed and scholarly study of Hieronymus Bosch's triptych, the *Garden of Delights*, lured him, at that time, toward "the garden of the imagination." When, a year later Ws wrote an (unpublished) appreciation of the study, he remarked that "Calas had made Bosch's mind work 'as if it were a contemporary mind,' " from which Mariani deduces that Calas enabled Ws to view Bosch as "brother to the surrealists, whose chief importance, Williams had said elsewhere, was that they too had, through the use of free association, liberated the unconscious." In addition,

> what apparently struck the most responsive chord in Williams was that Bosch, in Calas' judgment, had managed to achieve the eighth day of creation, the apocalyptic vision itself, had in fact managed to annihilate time, to be in at the end, to look at the pattern of his whole life as something accomplished, the artist looking in upon his own world and finding himself there.

Another aspect of Ws' responsiveness is to be seen in the likenesses between Bosch's triptych and his own *Asphodel*, of three parts and a coda. Among these likenesses are the fact than, in a Hebraic, right-to-left "reading" of Bosch's painting, "one begins with the artist in hell and moves to a new beginning, with the bridegroom beholding the luminous bride, the sensuous virgin, apprehended on the eighth day as in the primal garden."

As for the fifth book of *Paterson*,

> What Williams was looking for . . . was to see the river at the heart of his poem as the ourobouros, the serpent with its tail in

its mouth, the eternal river, the river of heaven. This meant, of
course, that time itself would have to change, and a new time
meant a relatively new way of measuring, meant a more secure, a
more relaxed way of saying. That was a question, primarily, of
form, and the emphasis on the variable foot which the critics
went after all through the fifties and sixties like hounds after an
elusive hare was in large part a strategy of Williams' own devising.
But it was an absolutely necessary strategy for him, because just
here the real revolution in poetry would have to occur : here with
the river, metaphor for the poetic line itself.

After reviewing Ws near "obsession" with "the river of heaven
. . . in the early fifties," Mariani, opening his second point, goes back
to the MSS to record an important change Ws made "in the collage
for *Book V*." At as late a stage as "the original galleys" he had
included in the poem "a long letter from Cid Corman to himself dealing with the whole question of modern prosody." Ws removed this
letter and replaced it with one he'd recently received from Edward
Dahlberg, a change which enabled him to shift "attention away from
the question of the line . . . and onto the modern representation of
the central icon of *Book V*, the beautiful thing, Kora," "around
whom all of *Paterson V* radiates." Mariani states that "The woman is
of course all-pervasive in Williams' poems. What is different here in the
long late poems is the more explicit use of Kora as the symbol, in fact,
the central icon of the late poems." Mariani proffers some of the
abundance of evidence on this point, including a find in the *Paterson
IV* MSS that Ws had deleted from the published text: "For Williams
[Phyllis] is, explicitly, the very incarnation of Goya's famous Maja
Desnuda."

Mariani's treatment of his third point—the artist who is, in part,
"the willing victim"—is brief. Williams

had given himself up to be murdered, to offer himself not,as
Pound had, to the pale presences of the past, androgenetically,
but for the virgin, Kora. And yet, there was a way out, a hole at
the bottom of the pit for the artist, in the timeless world of the
imagination, the enchanted circle, the jeweled collar encircling
the unicorn's neck. In the final tapestry of the series, the Unicorn
kneels within the fence paling, (pomegranates bespeak fertility
and the presence of Kora), at ease among the flowers here with
him forever on the eighth day of creation, a world evoked for
Williams, from the imagination.

25. Pearson, Norman Holmes. "Introductory Note to Three
Unpublished Letters from William Carlos Williams to Norman
Holmes Pearson," *WCWN*, 1:1 (Fall 1975), 2-4.

When Ws was ill in 1975, Pearson, as he explains in his note, in an
attempt to help Ws keep his hand in, "suggested he write accounts of
the elders," i.e., of the parents of some of those soon-to-be-famous
youths Ws met at the University of Pennsylvania in the years 1902-'05.
The first letter, following Pearson's note, recounts Ws' memories,
during that period, of Ezra Pound's mother. The second concerns
Pound's father and appears in *WCWN* Spring 1976; and the third, on
H.D.'s parents, is in *WCWN* Fall 1976.

26. Rabin, Christine. "Williams' Autobiographeme: The Inscriptional I in Asphodel [sic]," *Modern Poetry Studies*, 6 (Autumn 1975), 157-74.

> "Williams' assertions [about the search for a new measure] are, in retrospect, more metaphorical than theoretical," writes Rabin. Notably, his 1948 "treatise on 'The Poem as a Field of Action' . . . , when contrasted to the yet-to-be-written *Asphodel*, appears more a thematic prospectus for the later poems than a theoretical model for their metrics. However, the segmentations in *Asphodel*—what the poet called his 'variable foot'—do provide a homologue, not to theories in physics and mathematics, nor to a social and economic order, as he implied, but to a desire for an 'inscriptional presence.' Considered as such, the variable foot has a pronominal function." In the light of this proposal Rabin continues:
>
> > The phenomena of the first person pronoun *I* and the segmentations of the variable foot may be considered in terms of their similar functions. I have combined these similar functions under the single rubric of *autobiographeme*—a neologism that refers to the specific grammatical and rhetorical functions of the pronoun *I* in *Asphodel*, and a corresponding function in the use of the variable foot.
>
> Further definitions are necessary:
>
> > *grapheme* (as Jacques Derrida uses this term) denotes a meaningful unit of inscription. "Meaning," a word which refers in English to both signification and intention, is, for Derrida, precisely the desire for presence implied in the phonic chain it is "meant" to represent. The "erotics" of *Asphodel* can, therefore, be regarded as a desire for what is necessarily lost in a written discourse.
>
> Thus provisioned and armed, Rabin mounts another of those linguistic and Derridean operations on the poem that seem constructed to prove the critic knows better than the poet what he is about.

27. Bollard, Margaret Lloyd. "The 'Newspaper Landscape' of Williams' *Paterson*," *ConL*, 16:iii (1975), 317-27.

> To explain the "Newspaper Landscape" of *Paterson*, Bollard first identifies three principles held by Ws about what "the new, modern poem should be." He "insists that a poem should use 'the same materials as newsprint, the same dregs,' " both of the present and past, the personal and the societal; adopting Pound's dictum that "Literature is news that stays news,' " Ws conceives of the poet as "not merely a reporter but the maker of news, the maker of 'a new thing, unlike anything else in nature, a thing advanced and apart from it' "; and, most importantly, the newspaper's "unity in disparity" is the prototype for the poetic structure of *Paterson*. This last feature, Dollard believes, illuminates the poem's "seemingly abrupt or irrational juxtaposition of material" and should help the reader to forgo seeking "rationally and temporally to connect every piece of writing to every other piece [, which would] indeed succeed in destroying the 'poetic pattern of the work.' " Ws' "presentation of heterogenous items in juxtaposition" not only illustrates his own

statements about the need, of both audience and author, to accept the irrational (a fact of existence, Ws writes, usually excluded from "modern compositions," and excluded to their detriment [*Selected Letters*, p. 309]), but also "creates the impression of a 'community in action and interaction' and a world in miniature."

28. Coles, Robert. *William Carlos Williams: The Knack of Survival in America*. New Brunswick: Rutgers UP, 1975.
Review by Gilbert Sorrentino. "America, America," *PR*, 42 (1975), 463-67.

Coles has written here "a clear, intelligent book on Williams' fiction," writes Sorrentino; and he has also filled in a sizable gap in Ws' criticism, burgeoning though it be in the mass. Sorrentino argues that criticism of Ws' work, when it is forthcoming (and he remarks that the Dean of American Letters, Edmund Wilson, was totally silent about Ws' work) is vitiated by "a search for 'meaning,' " and that this flaw particularly shows in criticism of "the fiction, particularly the Stecher trilogy, *White Mule, In the Money,* and *The Build-Up*. Delightfully, it is to this trilogy that Coles addresses the greater portion of his book. Wonderfully free of cant and hot air, Coles's study is a model of intelligent criticism, trusing completely the surface of Williams's work, his words."

Coles, Sorrentino continues, shares his own judgment "that the Stecher trilogy is the best treatment of the immigrant success story in American letters." "It is Williams's triumph that he saw what success in America means, and to Coles's credit that he sees, with fine precision, Williams's painstaking attention to and accretion of details that make us realize finally that for the Stechers success is an alloy mixed of financial security, loss, destruction, and a nameless anomie, a desolation." Moreover, Ws portrays rather than tells this story: "It is the surface that Williams is concerned with, that surface in which he finds the 'isolate flecks' that suddenly reveal the quality of an entire family, an entire community."

To this concentration on the surface is conjoined Ws' refusal to condemn or demean the Stechers for their failure. "Williams has no smeary sentimentalism in his work concerning the 'good' poor and the 'bad' middle class: at the core of his writing there is a nucleus of ice. He is, in his quiet and unsensational prose, utterly ruthless in his vision." It would seem Ws' technique "could easily allow a reader," especially one "reading 'between the lines,' " to miss the thrust of the trilogy, even to read it optimistically. "But Williams does not allow this—all the information is given, everything is on the surface. It is placid, mundane, ordinary—and terrible."

About the trilogy Sorrentino concludes, "It is Williams's understanding that success in America presupposes loss and misery and destruction that makes his work so valuable, not only as a self-enclosed and isolated demonstration of his artistry, but as a diagram to show us exactly why America is as it is—not happy, not really sad, certainly not tragic, but desolate." And of Coles' study: "Robert Coles has written of all this beautifully, in a plain and serviceable prose, and with a wit and energy that are remarkable. He has done a first-rate job with this book, which is, to date, one of the most valuable additions to the growing body of Williams criticism."

29. Doyle, Charles. "Addenda and Amendments to Wallace: *William Carlos Williams*," *PBSA*, 69 (1975), 407-409.

> The items Doyle lists are "two unrecorded articles, one item which is cross referred, and several corrections of fact." The two articles are Ws: "Ezra Pound: His Exile as Another Poet Sees It" (1927) and "An Informal Discussion of Poetic Form" (1941).

30. Eagle, Herbert. "Miroslav Holub and William Carlos Williams," *Germano-Slavica*, 6 (1975), 43-52.

> Eagle writes of the "similarities in rhythmic organization, semantic structure, [and] thematic interests" shown by Ws and the Czech poet Miroslav Holub, who "was born in Plzen in 1923, studied medicine and the history and philosophy of science at Charles University, and has been associated, as a clinical pathologist and immunologist, with hospitals in Prague, with the Institute for Microbiology of the Czechoslovak Academy of Sciences, and with various research institutes abroad." (Eagle quotes Holub's acknowledgement of Ws' idea that a poem is "a machine made of words"; but he does not claim that Ws influenced Holub.)
>
> Eagle finds likenesses in both the poets' statements about poetry (which "exhibit a sense of experimentation," and in which "the term 'the pace of speech' is crucial to an understanding of the rhythm" of their poetry), and in the poetry itself. Referring to de Saussure's concept of the syntagm, a unit of meaning that may be independent of or break across the formal rules of "grammar or syntax," Eagle analyzes Ws' "A Sort of a Song" and Holub's "Big Brother: The Significance of Poetry" to show in both "the semantic effects achieved through syntagmatic segmentation." And, to show both poets' "deeply humanistic concern about man's plight in the twentieth century" and their skill, if not in finding a solution, in "restat[ing] the problem in such a way that the paths of defiance or of reconciliation become clearer," Eagle analyzes Ws' "For G.B.S., Old" and Holub's "Reality," again focusing on syntagmatic segmentation.

31. Johnson, Kenneth. "Eliot as Enemy: William Carlos Williams and *The Waste Land*," in *The Twenties / fiction, poetry, drama*. Ed. Warren French. Deland, Fla.: Everett/Edwards, 1975. Pp. 377-86.

> Johnson argues that, though Ws in the *Autobiography* wrote that the appearance of *The Waste Land* obstructed a nearly-achieved "new art form," Ws mainly rejected the poem because he and Eliot held opposed world views. Though both, in their poems of the 1920s, portrayed an often debased modern culture, Eliot's betray an "obsessive awareness of . . . impurities which he found intolerable," whereas Ws' "gave the impure temporal world a consummate importance and

value." Sources of perceptive strength shown in Ws and denied in the early Eliot are an "allegiance to physical reality," especially to the local, an "awareness of cyclical recurrence," "the love between a man and a woman," the strength and resilience of the lower class, and [quoting Ws] the power of the artist's imagination " 'to lift . . . the material conditions and appearances of his environment to the sphere of the intelligence where they will have new currency' " [p. 385]. The primacy Ws gives to physical reality, in turn, "led to his lifelong experiments in free verse and accentual verse," as, conversely, Eliot's 1920s emphasis upon "an intense, negative emotion" and his freedom to choose among "any of a large number of concrete particulars" to portray it explains his reliance on "traditional rhythmical form" [pp. 382-83].

32. Kenner, Hugh. *A Homemade World: The American Modernist Writers*. N.Y.: Knopf, 1975.
Review by Marjorie Perloff, *WCWN*, 1:i (Fall 1975), 14-15.

Perloff's review is mainly of Kenner's views and analyses of Ws and Stevens. Kenner has something new to say about the critically over-done "The Red Wheelbarrow," skillfully showing that the poem "perfectly embodies Williams' conviction that 'It isn't what [the poet] *says* that counts as a work of art, it's what he makes,' " and claiming that the poem is not for hearing: "They are stanzas to see."

"Kenner's [basic] strategy is to set Williams' achievement in bold relief by contrasting it to that of Wallace Stevens." The central difference, Perloff explains, is that Stevens saw what the poet says as more important than "the way in which he says it"; thus, Stevens wrote "essentially a poetry of ideas . . . , whereas Williams' poems cannot be 'explicated' because they rely, not on semantic density or ambiguity, but on the positioning of words on the page." Perloff observes that this view of Ws' esthetic is clearly more applicable to the short poems Kenner considers than "it would be for *Paterson* or even 'Asphodel,' " but concludes that "he is surely right in seeing that the Williams' aesthetic, as he defines it, has been the driving force behind the poetry of our own time, whereas the Symbolist poetic of Eliot and Stevens was essentially a European import and looks back to France and the nineteenth century."

33. Kern, Robert. "Williams, Brautigan, and the Poetics of Primi-tivism," *ChiR*, 27:1 (1975) 45-57.

Observing that a major dynamic of American literature generally, as well as of modernism, has been the quest for the new, Kern argues that one path taken to achieve it "has been . . . not to run ahead of history, but to go back of it," and that consequently some versions of modernism and post-modernism "can be construed as forms of aesthetic primitivism—as an ignorance, acquired or real, of the history and rules of art, of culture and civilization, of manners, conventions, and established norms, particularly those associated with Europe." After observing that such an aesthetic creates a problematic concep-tion of literary history, because by its light one is faced "not with a smooth tradition, . . . but with a discontinuous stream of disruptions, none of which has a past or a future," Kern moves on to *In the American Grain*, his major Ws text in the article. In that "prose classic," Ws argues that it was "a terror of the New World that held the Puritans back from a full, vital encounter with the American environment." Among other achievements, the book is "an analysis of cultural malaise as well as a prescription of a cure, and a literary manifesto in Williams' campaign as a stay-at home against the expatriates Pound and Eliot." But most importantly, it establishes Ws "as the best expositor of the peculiar coincidence between the demands of the modernist movement in art and the chief requirement of Americanization as a genuine and lasting and *physical* [RK's italics] encounter with the New World. It is also . . . an essential text in the poetics of primitivism," in which "Williams finds, like Whitman before him, that to be an American is an opportunity to be fully modern, and to be modern is not to be in the vanguard of history, but to be permanently at the beginning of history, to be *pre*-historic—to be new, that is, in the sense of 'first' rather than 'latest.' "

Just as Ws castigates the Puritans for withholding themselves from the "American ground" even as they "exploited" it, so does he implicitly decry that American literature which set its course by European standards and "refused to open itself to local conditions and achieve its own identity in its own physical place."

Kern then proposes that "A primitivist poem is a poem built or made on cleared ground (*is* that ground), without the benefit of historical traditions or conventions as guides" and that the primitivist aesthetic, which characterizes "most American poems," "becomes increasingly prominent in the modern and post-modern periods when the characteristic American demand for originality is given additional impetus by the modernist insistence on novelty."

Finally, he offers Ws' "The Red Wheelbarrow" as "perhaps the classic example of a primitivist poem in the modern tradition," exemplifying, in Ws' own poetic development, the aesthetic he arrived at "in the early nineteen twenties," of a "sheer, impersonal attention to objects." The poem is illustrative of an "utterance occasioned solely by the 'event' it describes—someone's perception of 'the absolute condition of present things' " [quoting Melville]. "It is both particular and unlimited, the achievement of a novelty that will not stale."

After discussing Brautigan as an example of the primitivist post-modern, Kern concludes—in a statement implicitly characterizing primitivism wherever and whenever found: "the undeniable insistence in such writing is that poetry is ultimately located in experience itself, an insistence that demotes the text to an occasion of recognition. And what is recognized is that the true ground of poetry lies beyond all texts, in the world outside the institution of literature."

34. Mariani, Paul L. *William Carlos Williams: The Poet and His Critics*. Chicago: American Library Association, 1975.
   Review by Jackson R. Bryer, *WCWN*, 2:ii (Fall 1976), 17-18.

   Bryer begins with a listing of the numerous "available reference works" and annotated bibliographies in American literature, largely to set a context for showing that, while "the ALA series is an admirable idea, . . . certain standards for volumes of this kind must be stated at the outset." He continues,

> For them to achieve maximum value and minimum redundancy, they should go well beyond the annotated checklists and briefer bibliographical essays already available. They should do this by providing more extensive coverage than the essay form allows and by encouraging more evaluation and ranking of critical materials than is possible in checklists. The book-length format must also lead to coherent ordering of the various stages of an author's critical reception as well as of the different sorts of responses which his work has elicited. Lacking these qualities, the ALA series will not substantially augment previous scholarship ;and it will be missing a wonderful opportunity to do so.

By these standards Bryer finds Mariani's book "partially successful." In its first four chapters "there is little if any attempt . . . to organize the responses around any approach, to account for the nature of the responses, or to evaluate their worth except on a basis of their length or authorship," though Bryer notes that the annotations of the *Paterson* criticism are better. The last chapter, by contrast, is a total success, "a gracefully written, beautifully organized, and extremely coherent ordering and evaluation of recent Williams' criticism" that is "particularly enlightening on Mike Weaver's 1971 study and on J. Hillis Miller's *Poets of Reality* (1966)." "Future volumes in the ALA series," Bryer urges, "should use Mariani's last chapter as a model."

35. Peck, Russell A. "Public Dreams and Private Myths : Perspective in Middle English Literature," *PMLA*, 90 (1975), 461-68.

Where is Ws to be found in this article? In a brief contrast of his "The Red Wheelbarrow" (with its emphasis on "strip[ping] words of cultural accretions in an effort to realize the thing depicted on its own terms") to a brief medieval lyric (whose words evoke the culture and convey "an image of social order and hierarchy" that to its poet is beauty).

36. Pisan, Thomas. "*Paterson*: The Discontinuous Universe of the Present," *CentR*, 19:i (1975), 325-37.

Pison writes that "one of the most profound and tenacious ideas of Western man has been the notion of time's linearity," with its attendant concepts of, for example, causality, meaning, and progress. He proposes that "literary modernity may be defined as a protest against" this conception of time, and observes that, esthetically, the modernist writer is confronted with a problem: "How does one convey the sense of a totality in terms that are a-temporal?" Ws he identifies as one of the first American writers to grapple with this issue, and states that the problem was compounded, in *Paterson*, by the fact that both the length of the poem and some of its basic subjects have traditionally been shaped by a linear temporal order. "How [Ws] eluded its dominance is the subject of [Pison's] inquiry."

By-passing "the familiar back-door of 'organic form,' " Ws creates a structure of discontinuity, disorder and immediacy of experience:

> It is the basic *dis*continuity of all immediate and unanalyzed experience that needs to find its expression in the poem ;and this achievement depends upon the presentation of all events in their ultimate singularity, without reference to larger laws or processes, so that in the presence of their present, time may not become a distorting factor. Against the "Minds like beds already made up/ (more stony than a shore)/unwilling or unable," Williams is both willing and able to move "from mathematics to particulars/divided as the dew" (I, preface, p. 13). In division rather than addition, in the negatives of disorder and discontinuity rather than in their positives, Williams effected a new liberation for his poetry from the age-old imperatives of the line.

Ws frees his poem from linear continuities in a variety of ways: by contradicting earlier assertions of its being completed, by creating a "hero-narrator . . . who–like any dog in the park–is loose, unleashed, sniffing out experience" so that "the whole poem is what-ever comes out of the future at Paterson," by flexing the rules of *genre* definition" [TP's italics], by subverting the linearity of language as fixed in the unit of the sentence, and by emphasizing in the poem's substance "the potentiality and virtuality of experience and words."

In sum, "Williams achieves his discontinuous present" by abjuring the use of "parts as contributive to a whole" and "pushes us to an appreciation of 'parts'–as sensitive, valuable, mobile elements which are an end in themselves," writes Pison, who then extends his interpretation to an extremity many would dispute: "In repeating them [parts], or laying them side by side, he is careful that they should not add up to a general pattern or conclusion, that they should never exhibit a stasis that might be attributed to teleological or structural purposefulness."

37. Pope, Myrtle P. "Williams' 'The World Contracted to a Recog-nizable Image,' " *Expl*, 33 (1975), Item 50.

While conceding that William V. Davis [*Expl.*, 32, Oct., 1973, 13] is probably correct in his assumption that the last line of the poem is an error for "I clung to it as a fly," Ms. Pope enters into an argument in defense of the line as it stands: "I clung to it as to a fly."

The picture on the wall, says Pope, is the only object of stability that the patient, upon emerging from his illness ("which the title identifies as a miniature allegory of the world"), is able to recognize. "He wants to believe that he is still alive [and] that the world still exists. He clings to the picture . . . [because it] argues the presence of the stable wall behind it," "because it is able to cling to something solid. He clings to the fly for the same reason. They are able to with-stand the whirling world."

Ms. Pope concludes: "The theme of the poem is the foolishness and dependability of Faith." [M.F.]

38. Simpson, Louis. *Three on the Tower: The Lives and Works of Ezra Pound, T. S. Eliot, and William Carlos Williams.* N.Y.: William Morrow, 1975.
   Review by Joel Canarroe, *WCWN*, 2:i (Spring 1976), 12-14.

   Conarroe notes that this book was intended "for the common reader, assuming, of course, that there is such a thing," but still finds it not very good. Regarding the section on Ws (which he mostly writes of), Conarroe finds it difficult to distinguish Simpson's voice from that of Ws. In the biographical section on Ws, the details of which "are familiar to any student of the poet," Simpson not only draws extensively from the *Autobiography*, the *Letters*, and *Yes, Mrs. Williams* but also uses Ws' "rhythms and phrasings" with only partial attribution and in a manner that blurs their provenance. In addition, "the book . . . was not meticulously edited" and seems riddled with misquotations. Conarroe writes that his "main criticism, however, is not that the material is badly presented but that it is all so familiar." While acknowledging that "Simpson's criticism is more original and more astute than his summary of the life," Conarroe finds nevertheless that "many of his observations . . . have an air of *déja vu*, and others are unpersuasive."

39. Tashjian, Dickran. *Skyscraper Primitives: Dada and the American Avant-Garde, 1910-1925.* Wesleyan UP, 1975.
   Review by Carolyn Phoenix, *JML*, 1975 Annual Review, 5:iv (1977), 573-75.

   Phoenix notes that Tashjian's book fills a gap : no previous work had given "sustained critical attention to Dada as a phenomenon of some importance in American letters." Tashjian's main coverage includes "critical readings of the early William Carlos Williams and of Hart Crane and E. E. Cummings," in addition to more "historical information on the little magazines" influenced by Dada—"especially *The Soil, Contact, Broom,* and *Secession*"—than was earlier available. In a more specific characterization of the book Phoenix writes that Dada

   was characterized in general by a rebellion against all forms of authority, particularly the tyranny of traditional art with its esthetic predisposition for truth and beauty. Tashjian quite rightly points to the diversity of its manifestations, its "dispersal in all directions from an essential matrix of nonsense." He examines American Dada with an eye to certain recurring indices : the tension between art and anti-art, the complex of attitudes engendered by technology and the machine age, the conflict between formalism and esthetic anarchy, and the ambivalent attitudes of American artists toward European Modernism. One critical difficulty in Tashjian's approach, however, is that the notion of Dada which animates the text is rather too protean and its parameters nowhere clearly indicated ; moreover, the author assumes an understanding of the concept of anti-art throughout without indicating its provenance, its dimensions, or its nature. The reader is left to extrapolate the character of Dada from the critical descriptions of its particular manifestations.

   Tashjian does a better job in giving "historical information" and in his close examinations of the literature, though he has a falling off in "drawing implications from them" and in "coveying their significance." As for his study of Ws: Tashjian prolongs "Williams' Dada phase . . . beyond the automatic improvisations of *Kora in Hell*"; but Phoenix argues that Tashjian rather exaggerates Dada's influence on Ws (and on Crane)—especially the negative influence of Ws' reaction against it. She concludes, "The impression remains . . . that [Dada's] broader impact amounted to the appropriation by a significant number of artists of such Dada techniques—like unorthodox typography and assemblage—as were compatible with their own experimentations and their own iconoclastic attitudes toward traditional approaches."

40. Townley, Rod. *The Early Poetry of William Carlos Williams.* Ithaca: Cornell UP, 1975.
Review by James E. Breslin, *WCWN*, 2:i (Spring 1976), 14-17.

Breslin briefly surveys the current state of Ws' criticism and of more popularly-directed publications about him, arguing that scholarship needs to examine Williams' stylistic growth . . . within either of two contexts—the psychological or the historical." The psychological should repay scrutiny, he writes, because that dimension of Ws' development has been examined only superficially; as for the historical, "the whole question of Williams' place in the modern movement needs to be explored—by someone who can entertain Williams' claims of originality with skepticism, without falling into the dreary trap of attributing every idea in Williams to some external 'source.' "

Breslin finds Townley's book, a study of "Williams' development from *Poems* (1909) to *Spring and All* (1923), to be "unpretentious, enthusiastic and useful," written "with a lively intelligence and critical sophistication throughout." Townley has "an alert sense of how a poem *works* [JEB's italics]—rare among literary critics, who often slide away from poems into 'ideas' "; and he has other strengths:

> The value of Townley's study lies not just in his analyses of individual poems; he makes provocative use of a long 1906 poem, "A Tragedy," included in a letter from Williams to his brother, presents a convincing argument that Williams ordered the 1909 *Poems* as a progression from innocence to perfection, shows the role of the early plays in Williams' poetic development, prints (and briefly discusses) a suite of poems called "PASTORALS and SELF-PORTRAITS" (1914?), explores "Williams' creation of private myths through which covertly to express his strong but inhibited sensuality in *The Tempers*, and argues for a complex version of pastoralism to be found in the poems of *Sour Grapes.*

The drawbacks of Townley's study are that he stays clear of the much needed psychological and historical contexts of his subject of Ws' development, that his ideas require fuller development than he gives them, and a tantalizing sense of incompletion. In the chapter on *Spring and All*, for example, "several knotty questions are raised— Williams' distinction between prose and poetry, his conception of the imagination, his sense of poetic structure—and acute observations are often made on these issues, but they are not pushed far enough, so the effect is to have matters touched upon, rather than probed deeply."

41. Wells, Henry W. "William Carlos Williams and Traditions in Chinese Poetry," *Literary Half-Yearly*, 16:i (1975), 3-24.

> Wells proposes that "many impressive features of [Ws'] work may be illuminated by viewing it in relations, positive and negative, to the aesthetic of the East"—not the Japanese nor Hindu, but the Chinese. While acknowledging that Ws wrote nothing about Chinese poetry in his voluminous criticism, Wells finds in the last 40 years of his poetic career "occasional allusions that almost by their variety suggest a closer knowledge of oriental fields than meets the casual eye"; in addition, Ws "cannot possibly have overlooked nor been unaware of the interest and activities of many of his co-poets"—"above all, Ezra Pound"—"in Chinese poetry and thought." On the bases of these suggestive albeit indirect and fragile evidences of Ws' interest in and knowledge of Chinese poetry,* Wells develops correspondences, of forms and subjects, between Chinese poetry and both Ws' short poems (e.g., "The locust tree in flower") and *Paterson*.

> *Be this as it may, Wells does draw attention to an important late instance of Ws' attention to Chinese poetry—the assistance he gave "David Wand in translation[s] of a considerable number of Chinese poems in a volume entitled 'The Cassia Tree,' reissued in *New Directions*, number nineteen, 1966. This contains renderings from Tu Fu, Li Po, Wang Wei and other Chinese masters." While "the collection bears witness to Williams's sincere interest in the Chinese," Wells adds, it "has received surprisingly little notice at the hands of the large number of critics and bibliographers of Williams's work."

42. Whittemore, Reed. *William Carlos Williams: Poet from Jersey*. N.Y.: Houghton Mifflin, 1975.
Review by Jack Hardie, *JML*, 1975 Annual Review, 5:iv (1977), 836-37.

> Hardie is best quoted at large:

>> Whittemore's *William Carlos Williams: Poet from Jersey* pretends to be an exercise in negative capability, Whittemore himself adopting the sensibility and voice of one of Williams' tough guys. Imagine a biography of Shakespeare written in the voice of Falstaff, or Puck. Here is a biography of Williams written as if by the narrator of "Life Along the Passaic River." There's a lot of new information in this big book. Whittemore quotes liberally from scores of unpublished sources and seems to have worked with the full cooperation of Williams' family. There's some misinformation too—some misquotations and many oversimplifications. But one great oversimplification, a direct function of Whittemore's style here, violates the whole piece of work. It has to do with Williams' character and, by extension, with what Williams has made.

> After noting that other reviewers have "assail[ed] Whittemore" for his "tough guy" approach and "disapproved of [his] hit-and-run literary history," Hardie continues,

>> But what's most disturbing about *Poet from Jersey* is Whittemore's Williams, the image of the man that this book urges upon us with style and content both. Whittemore's Williams is sappy.... Whittemore's Williams is the self-indulgent, sentimental tough guy, the professional amateur, the wise fool. Apparently Whittemore doesn't even like much of what Williams has written. Isn't it something, he seems to be asking, that a guy like William Carlos Williams managed to write a few good things? Whittemore reminds

us, in a discussion of *Paterson*, that Yvor Winters once called Williams "a foolish and ignorant man." Whittemore asks, "Was Winters right?" A rhetorical question, which he answers with a hundred innuendoes. This book could set Williams studies back thirty years.

43. 1975 Dissertations

A. Denham, Richard Lane, Jr. "William Carlos Williams' *Paterson*: An American Epic." *DAI* 35:6708A.

B. Giriat, Marie-France. "Contact in the Poetry of William Carlos Williams." Université de Nice, 1975, Supervisor, Jacqueline Saunier-Ollier.

C. Hofstadter, Marc. "The Dance of Love and the Imagination: A Study of the Shorter Poetry and the Poetics of William Carlos Williams." University of Santa Cruz, 1975. *DAI* 37:308A-09A.

D. Jenkins, Samuel L. "The Poetry of William Carlos Williams: Images of the Poet." University of Minnesota, 1975.

E. Kolich, August. "William Carlos Williams' *Paterson*: Vision and Structure." University of Chicago, 1975. Supervisor: James E. Miller.

F. Oliphant, Edward D. "Poetry and Anti-Poetry in the United States and Chile: Robert Lowell, William Carlos Williams; Enrique Lihn, Nicanor Parra." Northern Illinois University, 1975. *DAI* 36:2190A-91A.

G. Procopiow, Norma. "Trends in the Critical Reception of William Carlos Williams' Poetry from 1909 to the Present." The Catholic University of America, 1975. *DAI* 35:7919A.

H. Westler, Max Jay. "The Sexual Orchard: A Study of Masculine and Feminine Relationships in the Early Poetry of William Carlos Williams" *DAI* 35:7927A.

1976

44. Mitchell, Paul. "Tension in Williams' *Pictures from Brueghel*," *McNeese Review*, 22 (1975-76), 26-35.

Quoting from Ws' 1947 lecture, "An Approach to the Poem," Mitchell infers that Ws "looks upon the poet as a skilled craftsman who creates an engine which transports to the reader the meanings and sensations the poet discovers and experiences in his unique world," and that Ws' "emphasis on the mechanics of the poem" is analogous to what Tate wrote of as "tension" in a 1938 essay. Tate wrote, "good poetry is a unity of all the meanings from the furthest extremes of intension and extension," a unity Tate designates by "lopping the prefixes off the logical terms *extension* and *intension*" and further defines as the fullest possible presence of denotation and connotation within the poem. It is "this stress between the denotative and connotative in some of Williams' poems from the Pulitzer Prize winning *Pictures from Brueghel* [that] is the most striking quality of his verse" and that Mitchell attempts to depict. The poems examined are "The Collar," "The Stone Crock," "The Snow Begins," "The Woodthrush," "The Polar Bear," "To a Woodpecker," "Iris," "To Flossie," "Bird," and "The Dance."

45. Oakner, Larry. "Going Down with Williams: A De/Structural Study of *Kora in Hell: Improvisations*," *Throth*, 16:i (1975-76), 27-36.

Oakner proposes a structural unity theory for the disparate beauties and expressions of *Kora in Hell*, a "de/structural" approach "that destroys the static conception of fixed literary" modes and "that allows for the simultaneous existence of many elements or parts, all moving in different directions at the same time." He finds an analogy for such an approach in the physicist Heisenberg's Uncertainty Principle, which states that in the world of elementary particles it is impossible to have exact knowledge of both the position and velocity of a particle at a given moment; determining a knowledge of one requires a sacrifice—at that moment for that particle—of a knowledge of the other. The analogous principle in *Kora in Hell* "is, simply, Williams' imagination, profoundly elastic enough to encompass all the parts, movements, and directions of *Kora*."

As Ws' imagination structures "the elements in *Kora*," so does "the notion of a descent into the underworld of [his] imagination" give a direction to those elements. Oakner identifies two descent myths, the orphic, which traces a pattern of "loss, attempted recovery, and fragmentary restoration" (or, at times, of an "overwhelming and irrecoverable loss"), and the persephonic, symbolizing "the eternal return that is represented by the myth of Persephone or Kora." Both descent myths appear in the book, and both "appear as mythological allusions . . . [and] as poetic theory." In the latter case the orphic as esthetic creation is contrasted to the persephonic as natural rejuvenation.

Oakner next analyzes Ws' prologue to *Kora*, and concludes that "almost everything finds its way into the writing" of the prologue. By its end, "the reader finds himself virtually a friend of Williams; he has listened to his stories, has been disarmed by Williams' charming manner, and is ready, if need be, to follow the poet into hell."

The last section of the article observes that "*Kora* is a literary work" and raises the question of what recognized forms it thus, at least in part, utilizes and relies on to communicate to the reader. Oakner suggests three: that it supplies commentary as some guide to one's reading of the improvisation, that—given Ws' explanation of the book's origins—there may be an autobiographical structure, and that the "natural seasons" contribute, the entire book having a "loose seasonal structure."

Though Oakner reiterates throughout the article the essentiality of Ws' imagination to the book's structure, he doesn't define "imagination" and uses the full term rather totemistically. The reader is left to infer that "Williams' imagination" is analogously defined by the Uncertainty Principle, but then Oakner drops reference to that after his third paragraph. Psychology, even if insubstantial, elbows physics aside.

46. Hafley, James. "On Abstraction in William Carlos Williams' Poetry," *NMAL*, 1 (Winter 1976), Item 3.

Hafley argues that although Ws in his "statements about poetry . . . is generally . . . talking about technique, he is at the same time . . . forever taking for granted . . . the importance of what poems mean." As a result, critics and readers "have emphasized description in his poems . . . at the expense of their valuative weight."

> Valuative? No. Didactic. Williams is, in every poem of his that I know, primarily a didactic poet : one, that is to say, concerned with ethics—with how we ought to behave. Every one of Williams' poems dramatizes a problem of behavior—and offers a directive for proper behavior. I shall go whole hog, not without having studied his poems as carefully as I was able, and say that there isn't a single one, published or unpublished, that isn't about the right and wrong ways of *doing* things. [JH's italics]

Hafley supports his contention by directing attention to the importance, in Ws' last poems, of abstractions, "especially 'love' and 'memory,' " as well as to harbingers of this emphasis in his early poetry, interwoven with its predominately concrete vocabulary.

47. Dalgarno, Emily K. "DeQuincey and Williams' 'The Yachts,' " *AN&Q*, 14 (April 1976), 119-21.

Dalgarno identifies Part III of DeQuincey's *Confessions of an English Opium Eater* as "a possible source" for Ws' poem and as "suggest[ing] that it is also a poem about conflicting states of the creative mind."

48. Davis, Robert Gorham. "A Note on 'The Use of Force' and Freud's 'The Dream of Irma's Injection,' " *WCWN*, 2:i (Spring 1976), 9-10.

Davis recounts his experience, after teaching "The Use of Force" for many years, of reading Freud's account of his dream of an event similar to the one in Ws' story, published at the start of *The Interpretation of Dreams*. Freud analyzes his own dream; and in the analysis his daughter Matilda and one of his young patients, of the same name, prominently figure. Comparison of the Ws story and the psychoanalytic account convincingly shows that Ws had the latter "explicitly in mind when writing 'The Use of Force.' " Indeed, though Ws is "often rather unfriendly in his references to Freud," he seems in this instance to "acknowledge [his] direct indebtedness" to his fellow doctor "by one significant detail": "the girl in 'The Use of Force' is . . . named Mathilda" [sic].

49. Elder, Thomas C. "A Proposed Origin for the Title 'Canthara,' " *WCWN*, 2:i (Spring 1976), 8-9.

> Mr. Elder, of Elder Pharmaceuticals in Hamilton, Indiana, suggests that Ws' possible medical knowledge of "Tincture Cantharides, or tincture of Spanish Flies," was the basis of his choice of title for the poem beginning "The old black man showed me."
>
> In *WCWN*, 2:ii (Fall 1976), 16 Jacqueline Saunier-Ollier contributes a follow-up to the above. She observes that Ws indicates in *I Wanted to Write a Poem* his knowledge of canthara and its aphrodisiac properties, and that "there exists at the Beinecke Library a manuscript in which Williams' mother tells him about Spanish fly . . . and how it turns women into a state of amorous frenzy."

50. Hynan, Patrick. "CBC Broadcast January 7, 1975," *WCWN*, 2:i (Spring 1976), 7.

> The description of a 90-minute Canadian radio broadcast which included a 1950 interview with Ws [conducted by John W. Gerber and Emily M. Wallace and published in *Interviews with William Carlos Williams*, ed. Linda Welshimer Wagner (1976)] and which focused on interviews with others designed to "attempt to understand Williams' poetry as seen through the eyes of other poets."

51. Keller, Dean H. "Kent State University Library Collection," *WCWN*, 2:i (Spring 1976), 8.

> Describes the Ws material in the Special Collections of the library, which includes "first editions of all of the books, except *Poems, 1909* [sic]," "proof copies of *The Autobiography* and *Yes, Mrs. Williams*," letters, and "A typescript of *Paterson: Book I*, which was used by the printer, together with a set of galley proofs and a set of page proofs."

52. Kodolányi, Gyula. "Radio Kossuth Broadcast, February 18, 1975," *WCWN*, 2:i (Spring 1976), 7.

> A note about a short Hungarian Radio braodcast on Ws, in which an introductory essay written by GK and translations of five of Ws' poems were read.

53. Procopiow, Norma. "William Carlos Williams and the Origins of the Confessional Poem," *Ariel*, 7:ii (April 1976), 63-75.

> Robert Lowell is commonly—and erroneously—credited with originating the confessional poem, writes Procopiow, who then cites some of its much earlier practioners (going back to Sappho), and who argues that, in the modern period, "Williams not only originated but structurally developed this mode as used by Robert Lowell and other poets writing today." Defining the confessional mode as one "in which the subject matter is autobiographical or the characters are related in some personal way to the speaker," Procopiow claims that it is a

mode whose "formal necessities [were] articulated by Williams more extensively through the poems themselves than in his brief, scattered comments about them" and that "Lowell acknowledged this formal necessity [as developed by Ws] . . . and emulated Williams."

"From a technical standpoint," the poems show "Williams was attempting to draw upon his immediate environment, in rejection of both the Symboliste mode and of the 'exile' poetry promulgated by Eliot." Moreover, in accord with J. Hillis Miller's argument that Ws broke through "the subject-object dualism generally embodied in Romantic poetry" and that he did so in Objectivist "poems of process which render their subjects in all their ordinary immediacy," Procopiow urges that, though unacknowledged by Miller, there is in the confessional poems the same focus on "inherent immediacy"; "the same poetic process may be found at work in them."

Lowell's knowledge of "Williams' very early poems on his relatives" is established by his comments on Ws in two journal publications in 1961-62, in one of which "Lowell refers to Williams' vital use of the 'stabbing detail,' that brings with it 'the universal that belonged to this detail and nowhere else.' " The earliest of these poems by Ws is "Dedication for a Plot of Ground" (1917). But to illustrate Ws' influence on Lowell, Procopiow analyzes Ws' poems on his father and mother—"Adam" and "Eve" (1936)—and compares them to Lowell's poems on his parents—"Terminal Days at Beverly Farm" and "Sailing from Rapello" from *Life Studies* (1959). In the poems on the fathers, for example, each poet "depicts his father as ill-at-ease in his universe" and as living his life in thoughtless detachment from his environment, each mixes "fact with figurative language," both use a prosody of "no fixed pattern throughout the poem," and both develop sound structures that function in similar manners. The poems on the mothers, while less closely related, do both "employ direct address" in contrast to the "third person narrative" paternal poems. Both sets of poems show "how Williams and Lowell exploited the tensions and trappings of personal experience" and demonstrate that "what Williams attempted" experimentally "in the twenties has become a vogue for contemporary poets."

54. Ranta, Jerrald. "Palindromes, Poems, and Geometric Form," *Visible Language*, 10:ii (Spring 1976), 157-72.

Ranta conveniently provides an abstract of the article:

> Emphasizing the similarities between the form of the palindrome and the forms of certain modern American short poems, I urge the recognition of a unique kind of little-studied, modern, cyclic, poetic form which, lacking an established term, I call "palindromic" form. Widely used by twentieth-century American poets, this kind of form is distinguishable from the better-known, traditional kinds of poetic form, though it sometimes occurs in combination with them. Cedric Hubbell Whitman's discussion of ring composition and hysteron proteron in the *Iliad* reveals the classical origin of this form and suggests that its larger class is geometric form.

In the article, after citing the standard dictionary definitions of palindrome (as, rather strictly, the reversal pattern or mirror imaging of the letters [of the words] of a saying), Ranta emphasizes that it is a strictly visual form and that the three modern poems she examines are only analogous to palindromes—that "their forms in many respects are like the form of the palindrome and that, consequently, they appear to belong to a single formal class of poems."

Ws' "The Locust Tree in Flower" (along with a poem by Cummings and another by Marianne Moore) is the Ws' poem she analyzes to demonstrate the form. A poem of 13 words, five stanzas, and exclusively one-word lines, her analysis is principally in terms of syllabic-count, letter-count, and vowel and consonant patterns. Ws, she concludes, herein uses the form "as a type of the seasonal cycle to celebrate the turning of the year and the coming of spring."

55. Movius, Geoffrey H. "Caviar and Bread: Ezra Pound and William Carlos Williams, 1902-1914," *JML*, 5 (Sept. 1976), 383-406.

> Movius' purpose is "to trace the relationship between Pound and Williams through the early years of this century [1902-1914], in the belief that it is one of the most important in the history of modern American letters." This is a basically factual account of the two poets' personal and poetic lives and of their relationship in that period, drawing especially upon their published letters, and on Ws' *Autobiography* and other prose. In addition to recounting their early relationship at the University of Pennsylvania, Ws' early visit to Europe, and Pound's visit to Rutherford in 1911, the article focuses on the responses of each to the other's currently appearing poetry, Pound's influence on Ws' poetry and Ws' ambivalent response to it as he sought his own voice, and their debate of the issue of bonding oneself to his native country vs working in the intellectual and creative milieu of Europe. Movius concludes, "The Pound Era did not directly shape Williams' work or aims; rather it was almost exactly at the moment of that era's inception that Williams' poetry and intentions began to stand out in contradistinction to his self-exiled friend's. The existence of Ezra Pound was to remain a strong and pressing consideration for Williams throughout his life. [But Ws] clearly understood . . . that his main chance as an artist lay in excelling, like Whitman, as an 'honest reflex.' "

56. Heal, Edith. "Flossie," *WCWN*, 2:ii (Fall 1976), 8-13.

> Edith Heal, the interviewer and author of *I Wanted to Write a Poem*, here reprints conversations with Flossie which were originally intended to be part of a book on the poet's wife and which, by Flossie's choice, did not go beyond these initial conversations. Flossie speaks of their early married life, of her mother's and Ws' mother's disapproval of his poetry, of Ws' early activities with poetry, of the fact that, despite his own claim, he attended not the first Armory Show, but the second, "where he read along with Mina Loy and others," and of other scattered memories of Ws and of their long life together. Edith Heal's questions are about Flossie and her role in Ws' life as a poet; but Flossie's emphasis is upon the poet himself. Interspersed with poems and quotations from Ws' prose.

57. Mariani, Paul. "The Poem as a Field of Action: Guerilla Tactics in *Paterson*," *IowaR*, 7:iv (Fall 1976), 94-117.

Mariani begins with contrasting images of Eliot and Ws in the 1940s. As a bomb warden in London in the early '40s, Eliot's experience of seeing sections of the city destroyed by firebombs was one genesis of *Little Gidding* and its mystical language of "refining fires"; and in his criticism of the mid '40s, Eliot avers that the language and poetic line had been deployed far enough by the moderns, that it was time to build upon, rather than extend, the achieved work, for "a development of language at too great a speed would be a development in the sense of a progressive deterioration." Ws' consciousness, however, was of the dropping of the atomic bomb on Hiroshima, a fact that "came to inform the very core of [his] poetics, to stand as metonym for the vast open fields of poetry which had not even yet been tapped"; and the job of poets, Ws argued in his criticism of the period, was to explore those fields, not cultivate the old plantings.

For thirty years Ws had moved, "by halts, blurts, and many false starts," towards "the form of his long poem *Paterson*." In 1938, he wrote that "The artist . . . is to be understood not as occupying some outlying section of the field of action but the whole field, at a different level howbeit from that possessed by [the] grosser modes" of idealogues, poetic schools, and "special interest groups." "Only in . . . the poem which adequately incorporated in its expanded base the fact of a living, sensuous present-day reality (as opposed to an idealogical or intellectualized reality) might the poet manage to beat time, that all-consuming fire." In addition, Ws had insisted "from the twenties on," in his poetry and his criticism, "on the need for new forms, for what later became the emphasis on the variable foot." Mariani particularly cites the talks Ws gave at the University of Washington in 1948 (later "published in part" as "The Poem as a Field of Action") and Ws' acknowledgement of those poets moving toward the "new measure"–Zukofsky, Roethke, Olson, Creeley, Levertov, Ginsberg, and "countless others." Opposite this foray into the new were "the forces of the 'great tradition' "–notably Eliot and Auden– and others "who had also failed to develop adequate formal means," especially Hart Crane and Wallace Stevens. In contrast to "Stevens' contention that the modern structure of reality resided in the accuracy of the resemblances between things, ideas, facts, and their lexical and metaphoric referents," Ws' tenet was that "the poem was 'made of nothing else' than a new reality superseding the particular occasion out of which it had arisen, and only as that was made manifest by the *form* [PM's italics] of the poem."

Essentially, looking at his dominant contemporaries of the time, Ws found "the critical weakness in the line itself," a weakness so crucial that "many of their basic structures had become grids, cages, entrapping rather than freeing that elusive beauty: Kora, the radiant gist, the goddess herself." The corrective to the entrappment of "the old iambic pentameter" was "to smash the foot, [. . . to] find a new measurement consonant with our own sense of time, and the effect in terms of released energy could be as revolutionary for good as the bomb had been for destruction." As means to that end, poets could find, as he had, "actual evidence of the new work" in the little magazines and anthologies. They could also, Ws urged, study their own idiom, the American language, the dialect phrase, the green shoot stemming from the solid English trunk, study it as *he* had, by listening to the rhythms of the language as it got itself spoken daily in the streets of whatever polis or place one found oneself in. He could urge them especially to listen hard for the pace of the language, its phrasing, its "acceptable pauses and interludes," its breaks, its heaves, its breath, its very life. He could urge them further to attend carefully to speed values in their lines, to try to trace across the page the mere brushing of a meaning rather than to plod on with metrically "correct" lines which could not hold the elusive life necessary to any good poem. He could urge them too to utilize those loose, colloquial phrases that were in the very grain of the spoken language and which gave the line a certain freedom of manner, a sense, as he put it, "of emotional drive and reality." An idiomatic freshness coupled with an intense care for a syntactic structure which, on the other hand, should be packed tight with meaning, even if that were expressed elliptically, with all the leaps and disjunctures of the mind itself, as Joyce for one had done. *There* was a poetics Williams could subscribe to. For it was words and only words that could unlock the mind, new combinations of words, as free as possible of their old associational weights, words new to the consciousness, new in their measure, radiant tracings of the ever-fleeting moment. That was how one began to create a new force-field, a new field of action.

Thus the criticism: a combined call to arms and "a Cassandra-like frustration about being unable to say clearly what it was he was actually seeing." In the poetry, however, "the hesitancies and the false steps and the frequent descents in *Paterson*, for example, are . . . part of a brilliant guerrilla tactic as Williams brings the city into alignment with himself." Mariani traces Ws' comments, to various people between 1936 and 1945, about his intentions, starts, and frustrations with *Paterson*, observing that "by early 1945 [he had] achieved a major form which, with a plentitude of variations, will be repeated throughout the rest of the poem." Mariani focuses on *Paterson* II to analyze that form and to trace its concomitant thematic development: when in the abandoned field on Garrett Mountain, over whose "old furrows" Paterson the poet pacing creates his new measure, there arises " 'a flight of empurpled wings': grasshoppers in flight, the imagination itself aflare," one sees "out of the breakdown of the old forms, then, the emergence of the new, the still-living."

> Truly, then, here in this most unpromising of places, this abandoned field, Paterson has witnessed an annunciation, as these grasshopper/seraphim, these "couriers to the ceremonial of love," announce by the very presence of their activity, a new poetic life, a new inspiration for Paterson.

Yet even in most of *Paterson* II, Mariani concludes, Ws' achievement of the new form is not in the segmenting of lines and spacing of segments, but in the pacing of lines, in the "loose triple measure that seems to hover over the lines" beginning "On this most voluptuous night of the year." In sum, Ws is better as a poet than a critic, even if, regarding the venture and goal he set himself, "his own [critical] attempts are better than any critic's in his own lifetime."

> His own critical comments on the poem as a field of action, its energy released and realized by a new, more flexible measure, are maddeningly scattered all over the earth. And yet, when brought together, their dismembered corpse will yield up a unified sensibility if not an answer. And what we are finally given is the sense

> of a man coming down hard again and again on the work he has already achieved with that deeper mind which never sleeps and which cannot wait for the critical clarification, not even if that clarification should eventually come from the poet himself.

58. Slate, Joseph Evans. "Williams at Austin," *WCWN*, 2:ii (Fall 1976), 14-15.

> A note on the Ws holdings of the Harry Ransom Center of the University of Texas at Austin, which "contains virtually all of Williams' published work," "critical manuscripts, including reviews of Louis Zukofsky's books," much material on "Williams' connections with Julian Beck and Judith Malina of the Living Theater," and an impressive gathering of Ws' correspondence. The Center has "significantly large groups of letters (each more than 30 items) to Cid Corman, Edward Dahlberg, John Herrman, David McDowell, and Marcia Nardi" and "nearly 500 letters to Louis Zukofsky." Slate provides a facsimile of one of the letters to LZ (Dec. 4, 1929), thanking Zukofsky for "your critical survey of my poems" and describing some of Ws' current poetic labors.

59. Wallace, Emily. "Afterword: The House of the Father's Science and the Mother's Art," *WCWN*, 2:ii (Fall 1976), 4-5.

> An "Afterword" to Ws' letter to Norman Holmes Pearson, this gives added information about the background of Hilda's mother and about her "artistic and social gifts," and concludes with examples of Ws' various attitudes towards H.D.'s poetry.

60. Williams, William Eric. "A Son's Remembrance of Florence Herman Williams (April 18, 1890–May 19, 1976)," *WCWN*, 2:ii (Fall 1976), 7.

> Williams quotes his aunt Charlotte's statement, "She was very proper, with a very good mind and a strong will" as the most exact description he has seen of his mother, and writes of her as "a very stable person[:] it was the stability of the home that she created here at 9 Ridge Road that made it possible for her husband to pursue successfully two careers." This note ends with an account of her declining health and the circumstances of her death "in the same room that had been hers for 63 years since her arrival as a young expectant mother, . . . in the same predawn hours and within a few feet of the spot where Dad had died."

61. Archer, Stanley. "*Glazed* in Williams's 'The Red Wheelbarrow,' " *Concerning Poetry*, 9:ii (1976), 27.

> Archer writes that the one metaphor in the poem, *glazed*, extends and explains its generalized first line, "so much depends." It does so because *glazed*, meaning "*shining*, with a suggestion of hardness" [SA's italics] captures the scene at a very transient moment, just after the end of the storm, "when the bright sun has created the

wheelbarrow's shiny surface and [its light] has made the chickens immaculately white," and just before "the wheelbarrow will be dry, its sheen gone." The poem is a mini-portrayal of the theme that "Periods of danger, terror, stress do not last"; "the glaze, like the rainbow, signals a return to normality or restoration."

62. Camacho De Gingerich, Alina I. "Vicente Huidobro y William Carlos Williams," *Revista Iberoamericana*, 42 (1976), 61-70.

63. Neely, James C. "One Man's Dr. Williams: An Appreciation," *YR*, 65 (1976), 314-20.

As a doctor, Neely is able to provide a provocative insight into the medical profession as it affected, and is reflected in, Williams' work. He gives specific regard to Williams' prose, from which he takes examples illustrative of his view of Williams.

Neely recognizes and admires Williams' ability "to compartmentalise and integrate his entire creative impulse," which impulse he directed into his literary *and* medical professions. He recounts his initial feeling that "Williams' poetry lacked profundity," but goes on to say that:

> . . . reading all of him, particularly the prose, gives a whole different window. His profundity becomes a doctor's uniquely profound feeling for what his limited ability, despite all his learning, allows him is even remotely possible with human beings [sic]. . . . His poetry is often irresolute, maddeningly irresolute. But so is life, and what the doctor is called upon to do for it.

Neely notes that much of the subject matter of Williams' early prose is medical, and that "throughout all of his writing Williams' concern is his patient." "As a gynecologist," observes Neely, "Williams's human insights came best to women." Williams said that "men were his inspiration, and women his energy." Neely makes it clear that this ever present energy, while akin to the libido, was not sexual. Its power lay in the qualities of womanhood that Williams found strikingly manifest during the act of childbirth.

In discussing the opening of *White Mule*, he says:

> The scene is all for women. . . . It is a magnificent passage of what it means to think and feel the wonder of woman's work, and the unfathomed distance from it of man. Ironically, it could not have been written by a woman—unless she was [sic] a doctor.

He understands Williams' complete immersion in his profession, and his complete love for his patients. As a doctor, he confirms the "spiritual sense of rejuvenation" that Williams felt after attending a patient in need.

He concludes: "It was medicine that cranked him up, and the poetry that gave him rest. . . . A man only gains his life by giving it away. Isn't that a thing Christ meant to say? Now the contagious hospital is gone, and Dr. Williams is at last an American phenomenon. You will not find either of them ever again—except in a way of writing."   [M.F.]

64. Wagner, Linda Welsheimer, ed. and introd. *Interviews with William Carlos Williams; "Speaking Straight Ahead."* N.Y.: New Directions, 1976.
   Review by Jack Hardie, *WCWN*, 3:i (Spring 1977), 20-23.

   > Hardie writes that "Wagner has tried to give us two books in one"; one is a partial success, the other is stillborn. The partial success is the reprints of three interviews, John Gerber's of 1959, "a 1952 chat with Dorothy Tooker and Tom Ritt (editors of the little magazine *A.D.*) . . . and Walter Sutton's 1961 conversation" with the poet. Hardie is enthusiastic about the range of dramatized voices, the persona, Ws displays in these interviews, and remarks that "Williams is a good talker—and writer—because he is a good performer."
   > These "interviews are followed by a two-part miscellany," the longer of which is titled "Dialogues." "Dialogues" is comprised of excerpts from eight other interviews, arranged topically by Wagner. Hardie writes that nearly all of these excerpts are available elsewhere, some having been printed several times. And Wagner's topical headings are very arbitrary: "A taxonomy for flowers with categories for Spring, Marigolds, Hothouse, and Yellow would make about as much sense." The gnashing fragmentation of this section and the lesser discordance of the overall text, Hardie speculates, arises from Wagner's having in mind a book whose subject would be Writing and the American Idiom: what she has collected here seems raw material "to a grand treatise that never got written, or that never got beyond a few poorly-organized notes, . . . [on] Williams and Writing in the American Idiom, or something." "Williams has been poorly served," he concludes.

65. 1976 Dissertations

A. Baker, Beulah Pearl, "Energy and Event as Motive, Motif and Design in the Poetry of William Carlos Williams." Michigan State University, 1976. *DAI* 37:7747A-48A.

B. Fox, Nona Werner. "Ritual in the Poetry of William Carlos Williams." Michigan State University, 1976. Supervisor: Linda Wagner. *DAI* 36:8058A.

C. Hattersley, Michael Elkins. "Poets of Light: Ezra Pound, William Carlos Williams, and Wallace Stevens." Yale University, 1976. *DAI* 37.4353A.

D. Higman, Sandra Jean. "William Carlos Williams' *Al Que Quiere!* Poems Made of Words." University of Iowa, 1976. Supervisor: Gayatri Spivak. *DAI* 37:7750A.

E. Jenkins, Samuel Lincoln. "The Poetry of William Carlos Williams: Images of the Poet." *DAI* 36:4491A.

F. Roman, Christine M. "Patterns of Recurrence in the Long Poems of William Carlos Williams and T. S. Eliot." University of Minnesota, 1975. *DAI* 37:300A-01A.

G. Sayre, Henry Marshall. "A World Unsuspected: Gertrude Stein, William Carlos Williams and the Rise of American Modernism." University of Washington, 1976. Supervisor: Arthur Oberg. *DAI* 37:2879A.

H. Starr, Margaret Morgan. "The Usual Imaginations of William Carlos Williams: A Study of *Pictures from Breughel. DAI* 37:317A-18A.

I. Tapscott, Stephen James. "American Beauty: Whitman, Williams and Poetic Form." Cornell University, 1976. *DAI* 38:4172A-73A.

J. Ueijo, Clifford Kiyoski. "Romanticism to Modernism: The Force of the Personae-Self Relationship in the Poetry of Wordsworth, Pound, and Williams." State University of New York at Buffalo, 1976. *DAI* 37:5100A-01A.

K. Woodward, Kathleen Middlekauff. "The Poetry of Old Age : The Late Poems of Eliot, Pound, Stevens, and Williams." University of California, San Diego, 1976. Supervisor: Roy Harvey Pearce. *DAI* 37:5821A.

1977

66. Baldwin, Neil. " 'Pulling the Disparate Together': A Note on the Problem of Order in *Paterson*," *WCWN*, 3:i (Spring 1977), 14-15.

Baldwin writes about Ws' tactics and achievement in organizing *Paterson*, "a confessional poem predicated upon the imagination's pursuit of Beauty and the 'beautiful things' of the phenomenal world [and] also a poem about the need for organization." Drawing upon Ws' MSS and material in the Beinecke Library at Yale and the Lockwood Library at SUNY-Buffalo, Baldwin notes that "At one point, Williams considered run[ning] it all together in one tumbling stream" and that he then went on to some commonsensical methods of organizing his diverse materials, at various stages of composition. Aesthetically, Baldwin argues,

> Williams overcame the conflict of imagination's passion against order by integrating his problem, whole, into the poem. He allowed the inner drama pushing the poem forward to be played out on the page. A model for this process is in Book III, where the burning of the Library, and the Beautiful Thing episodes—at first sequential—are intertwined in the poet's mind and fused into a comprehensive image of destruction and redemption.

67. Breslin, James E. "William Carlos Williams and Charles Demuth : Cross-Fertilization in the Arts," *JML*, 6 (April 1977), 248-63.

After briefly tracing the early biographical connections of the two artists, and the interest each had in the other's medium, Breslin (who explains his "discussion is limited to establishing the affinities between these two artists [;] I make no claims about influence") gives the bulk of this essay to defining "their professional concerns" via examining two pairs of related poems and pictures. The first pair is Demuth's "Tuberoses" and Ws' "The Pot of Flowers," a poem that "appeared as II in . . . *Spring and All*, a book dedicated to Demuth, whose work is praised in the prose just following the poem." Ws' poem is not a literal rendering into words of the watercolor; it is "an independent work of art" that "recreate[s] in words many of the effects of Demuth's watercolor." A formal analysis of watercolor and poem shows that "the effect [of form and structure in the poem] is quite similar to Demuth: opposites such as light and dark, motion and stillness, flowers and pot, are juxtaposed in ways that dramatically reveal the unique qualities of each."

Among a "series of poster-portraits [Demuth] began in 1929" and "dedicated to artists whom he knew well and/or admired" is " 'I Saw the Figure 5 in Gold,' a 'homage to William Carlos Williams' inspired by Williams' poem 'The Great Figure.' " In this picture Demuth "tries to recreate in terms of his own medium the effect of the poem at the same time that he seeks to define the character of Williams and his work." In his analysis of this poem and picture, Breslin finds the picture "abstractionist in ways that Williams' poem is not," but also argues that its "cubist realism" (a designation art historians have given to Demuth's "Figure 5") is "quite close in spirit to much of Williams' work, notably *Spring and All*." " 'Reading' [these paired] works of Williams and Demuth," he concludes, "we enter a world of hard, literal objects, yet a world that is detached from the 'real' world—autonomous, self-referential, multi-directional, the world of the imagination."

With black-and-white reproductions of Demuth's two pictures.

68. Heal, Edith. "Further Conversations with Flossie," *WCWN*, 3:i (Spring 1977), 1-7.

A continuation of the conversations with Flossie in the previous issue of *WCWN*. Mrs. Williams continues to place more emphasis on Ws than on herself. She remarks about mistakes in the *Autobiography*, characterizes Ws' mother, speaks of her and Ws' shared interest in literature, and gives a cascade of anecdotes of their encounters and experiences with other writers. A range of other personal and literary sharings, including memories of their two-week stay at Yaddo in order for Ws "to finish *Paterson* IV." Edith Heal notes that these and the excerpts in *WCWN* 2:ii "comprise the complete manuscript of the conversations."

69. Joswick, Thomas J. "Beginning with Loss: The Poetics of William Carlos Williams's *Kora in Hell: Improvisations*," *TSLL*, 19 (Spring 1977), 98-118.

In this abstract, theoretic rendering of the poetics of *Kora in Hell*, Joswick argues that Ws, in his attempt "to break through to a more comprehensive basis" of art that would raise "the work of my age to a level with greatest work of other ages," begins by rejecting "the boundaries prescribed by literary rules" and instead pursues a unity that is defined as "resolving itself in the very occasion of writing into a 'thing' that is emerging and 'growing' out of the plurality that defines the ground of art." Or, stated differently, "The poetics of *Kora* should not be derived from either the realm of immanence or an intentional literary unity. Writing as a polarized plane is instead the only area within which the imagination can restlessly pursue what seems so close at hand." With the imagination set free, "Williams discovers that *Kora*'s formal 'excellence is the shifting of category. It is the disjointing process.' " More specifically, Joswick, though he acknowledges the centrality of "cyclic form" to the book, argues that its cycle "results in neither a restored immediacy nor the perfection of a completed form. The cycle instead bespeaks a poetics of wandering that affirms amid all instability a constancy of desire and pursuit." Joswick concludes that Ws' poetic allegiance is constant to change and, with a supporting quotation from one of Ws' letters to Kay Boyle, that *Kora* embodies "a poetic of wandering and pursuit for a form in which language and the immediate can dance together by virtue of their difference."

70. Peterfreund, Stuart. "Keats's Influence on William Carlos Williams," *WCWN*, 3:i (Spring 1977), 8-13.

This essay asserts that "the ongoing use of Keats by Williams . . . can be seen throughout the poetry, from the time of *The Wanderer*, characterized by Williams himself as '. . . a reconstruction from memory of my early Keatsian *Endymion* imitation that I destroyed, burned in a furnace!' to that of the later poetry." Offering only a few examples (titles of a handful of poems) to substantiate this general claim, Peterfreund focuses on *Paterson* as manifesting "Williams' ongoing need to formulate a revisionist analysis of the [romantic] seer's task." He proposes that "In its theme, part of its narrative structure and even some of its characters ('Beautiful Thing,' for example) *Paterson* incorporates raw materials supplied by *Endymion* while at the same time revising that poem's vision." A number of different kinds of parallels between each book of *Endymion* and its numerical correspondent in *Paterson* are cited.

71. Rhodehamel, John. "The William Carlos Williams Holdings of the Lilly Library," *WCWN*, 3 i (Spring 1977), 24-25.

Mr. Rhodehamel reports that the Ws' holdings in the Lilly Library of Indiana University include first editions of all but three of Ws' books, and letters to "various friends and associates" (the books and the letters both from the library of Louis Untermeyer), letters to Nicolas Calas, and, possibly the most valuable material, "the only known surviving manuscript of . . . *The Great American Novel*," acquired from the collection of William Bird, publisher of the novel. The manuscript is "of 80 typed pages with printer's notes and penciled corrections by Williams"; and it seems to be the copy used to set the book.

72. Simons, John L. "The Lying Cinders: Patterns of Linguistic Unity in W. C. Williams' 'Between Walls,' " *Concerning Poetry*, 10:i (Spring 1977), 63-70.

> "Between Walls," categorized by its author as an imagistic poem and by the critics as "an example of reductive, or . . . minimal art," is, Simon argues, better seen as an example of Ws' poetic powers: "out of the most disparate, the most common and 'insignificant' of everyday materials, . . . a poem is made in order to rescue the world from an even greater sense of fragmentation and loss." That achievement accrues as a result of the patterns Ws builds into the poem. The patterns are determed by syllable counts per line, alliteration and assonance, Ws' artful termination of his lines, by the absence of verbs in the first part of the poem in surprising contrast to the "introduction of three verbs in line five," and most especially by the poem's "movement from darkness to light," an early instance of that "celebration of the light" with which Ws illuminated "Asphodel, That Greeny Flower."

73. Slate, Joseph Evans. "From the Front Page: A Note on Williams' 'The Death of See,' " *WCWN*, 3:i (Spring 1977), 16-18.

> Noting that Ws was invited to a party for Harry and Caresse Crosby, publishers of *The Bridge*, just three days before the Josephine Bigelow-Harry Crosby murder-suicide sensation, Slate notes that Ws' poem was one of several written on that event and on the public's and sensationalistic journalism's reactions to it. Slate proposes a social-criticism interpretation of Ws' poem, arguing especially that the poem shows "Williams' contempt for journalistic misuse of language and his hatred of its power. Against the newspapers' dirt he sets the poet's 'clean' world, and transforms Crosby, the papers' 'dirty' poet, into 'See,' whose world is ideally white and clean."

74. Bernsteen, Rosalyn A. "The Beautiful Unbeautiful: W. C. Williams' Legacy in 'Pictures from Brueghel,' " *ConP*, 2:ii (Autumn 1977), 25-33.

> Bernsteen's introduction suggests she will focus on Ws' poems on Brueghel in the book, but the last half of the article is brief characterizations of its other poems. As for Brueghel, he and Ws share "vibrant concerns for the real, for clarity of vision, and most of all for the beautiful-unbeautiful of the actual world." Bernsteen surveys those poems on Brueghel that portray peasant life, treat "classic or Christian themes," and that are biographical. A typical treatment is
>
>> This earthy enthusiasm is the chief emotion of "Peasant Wedding" and "The Wedding Dance in the Open Air," whose remarkable mixing of movement and sound recreates the joy of these celebrations. In the first poem, the boisterous guests are contrasted with the silent, virginal bride, and the feast is set forth in ample detail from the food served on an "unhinged barn door" to the spoon stuck in the helpers' hatband. In the second poem Williams discusses the ambiguity of the dancers, bound in a circle "disciplined by the artist," but shouting "oya!/ kicking up their heels." The domestic, the ordinary, has been transformed into Art.

75. Fedo, David A. "The William Carlos Williams-Julian Beck Correspondence and the Production of *Many Loves*," *WCWN*, 3:ii (Fall 1977), 12-17.

> Drawing upon the correspondence between Ws and Beck (at the University of Texas at Austin) as well as other sources, Fedo sketches a history of the play that Ws originally wrote for the Little Theater of Rutherford (which did not produce it), that was published in 1942 by New Directions under the title *Trial Horse No. 1*, and that, 10 years after the start of Ws' and Beck's correspondence, was staged in 1959 as *Many Loves* at Beck's Living Theater in New York City. Fedo characterizes the reviews, notes there were 216 performances of the play, as well as a NY revival and foreign tour (both by Beck) in 1961-62, and characterizes the relationship of Ws and Beck as "a very cordial one," except that Ws had to dun Beck at times for payment of his commission. With illus.

76. Green, Jesse D. "Whitman's Voice in 'The Wanderer,' " *WCWN*, 3:ii (Fall 1977), 17-22.

> Observing that, though "The Wanderer" has frequently evoked discussion of Williams' relationship with Walt Whitman," the poem has not been "looked closely at . . . with this relationship in mind," Green finds, especially in passages in "Crossing Brooklyn Ferry" and one of Whitman's "Broadway poems," evidences of Whitman's impress in the poem. What Ws asks at the start—"How shall I be a mirror to this modernity?"—"is Whitman's theme too." As is "Whitman's challenge [also Ws']: to find peace in the brutal maelstrom of the mass, to find the 'animate' in the 'expressionless' faces, to discover . . . the 'new' in what had passed for the 'old, so familiar,' to know the voice as a mere 'seed in the wind' properly accompanied by laughter, bitter as may be."

77. Heinzelman, Kurt. "Staging the Poem: William Carlos Williams' *A Dream of Love*," *ConL*, 18 (Autumn 1977), 491-508.

> Observing that Ws' plays have been largely ignored by the critics, Heinzelman argues they reward scrutiny because they "are good and deserve attention," because of the "radical claims" their author made for "the power of the drama, particularly in respect to its portrayal of the creative process," and because they demonstrate that "Williams shared his contemporaries' interest in the place of poetry in the modern theater." As for *A Dream of Love* itself, Heinzelman looks at Ws' stage directions "as prescriptive of [his] dramatic principles," analyzes Ws' use of his "Perpetuum Mobile: The City" (1935) as a source for the drama, characterizes its subject as "the creative process," in which "the object to be created is, quite simply, love," and goes on to explore Ws' portrayal of "where and how desire becomes directed from its object." As regards Ws adapting poetry (both "Perpetuum Mobile" and the lyric "Love Song") to the drama (a goal which, Heinzelman suggests, some of Ws' contemporaries at times approached mechanically), Ws is successful: the drama "literally

embodies the two poems together." "The drama becomes poetry—it stages the poem—[as] dramatic form realizes itself out of its own resourcefulness."

78. Hofstadter, Marc. "A Different Speech: William Carlos Williams' Later Poetry," *TCL*, 23 (December 1977), 451-66.

Placing *Pictures from Brueghel, and Other Poems* (1962) within the context of the difficult illnesses of Ws' last 12 years, Hofstadter writes that Ws' repeated encounters with death deepened his perspective and made "his vision . . . more complex." Facing death Ws sought renewal, and found it as "the product of two forces: love and the imagination." Hofstadter then proceeds to a thematic and tonal, as well as formal, characterization of the late poetry. In form the poems are more flowing and dynamic than the earlier; even "the poems employing the triadic line . . . incorporate it into a more fluid medium." And there is a corresponding "ease and naturalness in the manner and tone of the poems." In subject they are "more introspective" than the earlier poetry.

79. Marcus, Mordecai. "Dialogue and Allusion in William Carlos Williams' 'Portrait of a Lady,' " *Concerning Poetry*, 10:ii (Fall 1977), 70-71.

Marcus, understanding the poem to be a dialogue between a man and woman, clarifies the misattribution of the Fragonard painting to Watteau as the man's satiric comment on his own mannered speech, and then, while identifying the speaker of each line, interprets the tonalities and character interactions of the speakers.

80. Perloff, Marjorie. "Williams in the Classroom," *WCWN*, 3:ii (Fall 1977), 6-11.

For an undergraduate class in Modern Poetry that studies some of the essential Yeats, Eliot, Pound, Stevens, and Auden, Perloff writes, "Williams presents a special challenge to the instructor, for [compared to these others] he seems peculiarly 'unteachable.' " Writing from experience, she proposes six "axioms" to guide the teaching of Ws. 1. "Go in fear of anthologies"; and make use of *Spring and All* [available in the ND pb. *Imaginations*] – "the text I would most want to use in an undergraduate modern poetry class." 2. Teach *Paterson* only after "the student is familiar with the shorter poems, the early experimental sequences, and . . . *The Farmers' Daughters*" short stories. 3. "*Kora, Spring and All, Al Que Quiere!, and Sour Grapes* must be viewed in the context of the time and place in which they were written." 4. Do not allow Ws' statements on poetics to impede the poetry's speaking for itself. 5. In part following from the previous: "have the class analyze as closely as possible how the poems under consideration actually *work*" [MP's italics] in contrast to what they say. 6. "The more advanced student in a seminar devoted largely to Williams must read the whole corpus," for by doing so "the student will learn that . . . Williams' ontology is remarkably consistent and genuinely revolutionary."

81. Stapleton, Laurence. " 'Neatness of Finish,' " *Marianne Moore Newsletter*, I:ii (Fall 1977), 16.

> Stapleton suggests the phrase "neatness of finish" in M. Moore's "The Octopus" has its origins in Ws' use of "neatness and finish" in *Kora in Hell* (XXI:2), a book M. Moore reviewed in *Contact*.

82. Tashjian, Dickran. "Some New Williams Citations," *WCWN*, 3:ii (Fall 1977), 22-24.

> Tashjian reports on some publications of the 1930s omitted from the Emily Wallace bibliography, though some were "republished in other works cited by Wallace." The first group, concerning Ws' politics, is comprised of a "Letter to the Editor" of *The New Masses* (December 1930), an article on "Social Credit as Anti-Communism" (published in Gorham Munson's *New Democracy* in 1934), and a subsequent exchange between Pound and Ws about the article.
>
> There is also a group of Ws' pieces in the October 1938 issue of *Hika*, a magazine edited by undergraduates at Kenyon College. That issue of *Hika* published two of his sketches, two poems ("The Half-world" and "The Hard Listener") as well as comments about Ws by Ivor Winters and Wallace Stevens, and a review of *The Complete Collected Poems*.

83. Vose, Clement E. "Addendum to the Williams *Bibliography*," *WCWN*, 3:ii (Fall 1977), 25.

> Vose calls attention to an essay omitted from Emily Wallace's bibliography of Ws. A paper titled "The Attack on Credit Monopoly from a Cultural Viewpoint," Ws read it in 1936 "at a conference on 'Power Age Economics' at the . . . University of Virginia." With the copy of the essay in the Wesleyan University Archives is a note about it by Gorham Munson, who spoke at the same conference: Ws "opposes dictatorship by Left or Right—defends individualism, freedom and the artist—advocates in the closing pages Social Credit as the economic solution."

84. Williams, William Eric. "Cars," *WCWN*, 3:ii (Fall 1977), 1-5.

> A biographical account of the successive cars WCW owned, of his aggressive driving behavior, and of workaday as well as longer trips. "I guess," writes Williams, "the classic auto experience of his life was the trip [with his mother] from West Haven, Connecticut, to Rutherford on the September day of the big hurricane in 1937," a trip made hazardous and much lengthened by fallen trees and other obstacles. At the end of the trip, Ws told Floss that his mother, who was "born and raised in the hurricane belt of the West Indies, had remarked at the height of the storm, 'Why, it's almost like a hurricane!' " Williams also describes the family dog, Ws and Flossie bringing back from their auto trips wild trees and shrubs and flowers, placing them in "a protected spot," and making a daily "circuit of the yard, usually early in the morning before leaving for the hospital, as he and mother inspected and planned the plantings." With illus.

85. Baldwin, Neil. " 'The world it opens': William Carlos Williams' 'The Descent,' " *Ordinary* (Rook Soc.), 1 :i (1977), 3-15.

> Baldwin traces Ws' development of the variable foot, referring both to some of Ws' "critical commentary" on it and the MSS drafts and published version of "The Descent" of *Paterson* II. He quotes and examines (in notes dated "March 47") "the first impulse for 'The Descent' "—a tripartite line form conveying the descent theme, and then pursues the development of "The Descent" in respect to both its "successive drafts" and the contexts Ws placed the passage in. Baldwin concludes that, for Ws, "the 'foot' is a measure of time, not stress," and that "the variable foot . . . demonstrates Williams' structuring of his own American idiom."

86. Brown, Emerson, Jr. "William Carlos Williams' 'Full Moon' and the Medieval Dawn Song," *Southern Humanities Review*, 11 (1977), 175-83.

> Brown sees Ws' poem as both within the tradition of, and a variation on, the medieval *alba*. The *alba* (for which Brown cites several medieval examples and also the lovers' scene in *Romeo and Juliet*, III.5) "is a lyric form that equates darkness and night with the joy of sexual passion and the coming of daylight with the tearful disruption of that joy." Moreover, the *alba* itself is a form "that reverses completely the [far older tenet of the] Platonic, Judaeo-Christian, Neoplatonic tradition," in which light is symbolic of good and darkness of evil. These "two rich and widespread traditions lie behind Williams' poem." At the same time, Ws creates his own reversal of the *alba*: "At least in the world of this brief lyric" is portrayed "the sudden awareness that love can flourish in the warm, the radiant, the all fulfilling day."

87. Eckman, Frederick. "Imagism: the Radiant Center." in *Itinerary 3: Criticism*. Ed. Frank Baldanza. Bowling Green, OH: Bowling Green UP, 1977. Pp. 109-19.

88. Heymann, C. David. "The Case of Ezra Pound," *Shantih: Jour. of Internat. Writing & Art* (Brooklyn, N.Y.), 3:iv (1977), 48-52.

> As the title suggests, Heymann writes (basically a narrative) of Pound's radio broadcasts from Italy during WWII, of the anti-Semitism and economic theories he propounded in those broadcasts, and of the reactions and involvements of his friends and associates, especially American, in the FBI's investigation of Pound. Ws' relationship with Pound and early actions in this imbroglio are briefly presented.
>   A note identifies "portions of this text" as also appearing in Heymann's *Ezra Pound : The Last Rower* (1976).

89. Jauss, David. "The Descent, the Dance, and the Wheel/ The Aesthetic Theory of William Carlos Williams' *Kora in Hell*," *Boston Univ. Jr.*, 25 :i (1977), 37-42.

Jauss asserts that much attention has been given to the technique of *Kora in Hell* but little to "the meaning the technique furthers." "The technique, of course, is that of improvisation," defined by Wassily Kandinsky (whom Ws "mentions in his 1918 Prologue to *Kora*") "as 'a largely unconscious, spontaneous expression of inner character, nonmaterial in nature.' " Though an apparently irrational technique, Ws' use of improvisation in *Kora* "serves a rational end." That end is "the central concern of the book, the exploration of the poetic process, and Williams' resultant poetic theory." In addition, though others have written that "Williams' subjects are certainly the Beautiful Things of the ordinary world," it is a mistake to equate Kora with

> the Beautiful Thing ; rather, [Kora] is what makes the thing beautiful. As the improvisations repeatedly suggest, it is the mystical quality in physical things which, when comprehended by the imagination, makes those things perfect. It is true that the purpose of poetry, in Williams' view, is to "rescue Kora and save the world," but *how* this is done is Williams' important contribution to modern poetics, a contribution as ignored as *Kora in Hell* itself. I propose to elucidate the process by which the mystical perfections of things are discovered and translated into poetry as Williams portrays this process through the three principal metaphors of the book: the descent, the dance, and the wheel.

Jauss argues that the "descent" is the book's "most important metaphor . . . , for it functions both structurally and thematically." The descent structurally "is that of the poet's descent into, and return from, the unconscious. The purpose of the descent . . . is to discover and rescue the Beautiful Things of the World." As for the "dance," Ws uses it "to express how the poet, in his descent, attempts to connect the physical thing with its mystical essence." And "the wheel is a metaphor that explains how [this] dance . . . is transformed into a work of art," in addition to being a figure for the book's structural and thematic "cycle of descent and return." Jauss writes, "the descent involves experiences which the poet cannot bring back intact and so must translate into language that will best represent them. In this way, the wheel is a further explanation of how the two contending forces are translated into the still dance that, for Williams, is poetry."

90. Loewinsohn, Ron. " 'Fools Have Big Wombs': William Carlos Williams' *Kora in Hell*," *Essays in Literature* (Western Ill. Univ.), 4 (1977), 221-38.

After a brief survey of the book's reception and critical responses to it, Loewinsohn remarks that he knows of no attempt to chart the structure of this work, which is "a major document of modern literature, a thorough-going critique of the spiritual, emotional and aesthetic sterility of our twentieth-century hell that anticipates Eliot's *Wasteland* [sic] by some three years, and that also offers what Williams takes to be the remedy of that condition." Loewinsohn goes on to provide a map and commentary of the prologue ("about a third of [the book's] text") including Ws' overview "of the difficulties readers might have with his prose-poems and how those difficulties might be overcome." After a listing of the book's themes (time, the dance, "life or birth vs. death or decay, youth vs. age, perfection (variously defined), day vs. night, violence, love, barrenness vs. finery, rising vs. falling, "making the best of it," and inversion (revaluing things, praising what had been deprecated and vice versa)," the mass and remainder of the essay analyzes the book's "three levels of organization—the individual improvisation, the chapter, and the entire cycle." A detailed analysis of the first improvisation is followed by characterizations of others. The ambiguous and sometimes contrapuntal organization of the chapters, as initiated by "the A-B-A formula" that Ws in the prologue said determined their structure, is next examined. "At the last level of organization," Loewinsohn writes, "the book is bound together by thematic connections between chapters" and by the fact that "all these unifying themes, motifs, and concerns are embodied in the figure of Kora herself." He concludes with a contrasting comparison of *Kora in Hell* and the poem that overshadowed it three years later, *The Waste Land.*

91. Mariani, Paul. "Tomlinson's Use of Williams' Triad," *ConL*, 18 (1977), 405-15.

Mariani considers and analyzes the English poet Charles Tomlinson's use of Ws' triadic line, "variously called staggered tercet, three-ply step-down line, or triple-decker which we associate with Williams' late phase." He compares Ws' "Address:" from *Journey to Love* and Tomlinson's "The Picture of J. T. in a Prospect of Stone," from *A Peopled Landscape*, and considers Tomlinson's poetic "Letter to Dr. Williams" and also his correspondence with Ws, which began in December 1957.

92. Sayre, Henry M. "William Carlos Williams and Robert McAlmon: Two Versions of '*Elsie*' " [sic], *NMAL*, 1 (1977), Item 8.

Robert McAlmon, who with Ws edited *Contact* (1920-23), included in "his first collection" of published prose pieces, *A Hasty Bunch*, a short story titled "Elsie." Sayre says the story is "a thinly veiled sketch of the Williams' household." The title character is "the family maid[,] a [14 year old] refugee of the State Orphan's Home." McAlmon's story described Elsie, her attraction towards "Donald Matthews,' probably McAlmon," and her crushed reaction when he "announced over dinner that he has suddenly married," provoking her to "declare that she is 'through with poetry and poets forever. They never do have any sense anyway.' "

Sayre writes that Ws' poem, "To Elsie," "is quite obviously a poetic rendering of the same essential story," and is designed to show that poetry and prose have different capacities: "In the prose section immediately after the poem in *Spring and All*, Williams writes: 'Or better . prose has to do with the fact of an emotion ; poetry has to do with the dynamization of emotion into a different form. . . . Prose : statement of facts concerning emotions, intellectual states, data. . . . Poetry : new form dealt with as a reality in itself.' "

93. Schevill, James. "Notes on the Grotesque: Anderson, Brecht, and Williams," *TCL*, 23 (1977), 229-38.

"Intended for publication in the Sherwood Anderson issue of *TCL*," Schevill's essay argues that "popular concepts of *grotesque* still prevent our understanding the importance of this idea in American society" and are barriers to our seeing that "beauty and terror" may co-exist. After a brief survey of the literature (especially post-World War II) of the grotesque, Schevill posits that the *American grotesque* [his italics] arises from (1) "the evangelical splintering of our country into hundreds of separatist movements with all the puzzles, repressions, and violence that the splintering has produced" and (2) the contradictions inherent in "the goal of individual, materialistic success."

Schevill's references to Ws are brief but expansive. As in Anderson's, so in Ws' stories: "the grotesque is often beautiful because it is openly human and exposed"; and stories like "The Knife of the Times," "The Use of Force," and "Jean Beicke" show "the true development of Anderson's insights into *American grotesque*," demonstrating that "only an unusual compassion can relate ugliness to beauty."

94. Tapscott, Stephen. "Paterson A'Bloom: Williams, Joyce, and the Virtue of 'ABCEDmindedness,' " *ArQ*, 33 (1977), 348-66.

Beginning with observations on likenesses shared by Ws' Paterson as giant with Joyce's H. C. Earwicker, and noting Ws' several statements of appreciation and interpretation of Joyce's writings, Tapscott continues by sketching a number of thematic and symbolic correspondences between *Ulysses* and *Finnegans Wake* on the one hand and *Paterson* on the other. These linkages, rich as they are, are only a preliminary to what Tapscott claims is "the most significant dimension of Joyce's influence in *Paterson*," namely, the example Joyce set of "breaking beyond the boundaries imposed by English academic criticism." That element of "Joyce's influence is apparently like the liberating and paradoxical influence of Whitman on modern writers, in Williams' estimation: the way to write like Joyce is to write unlike Joyce—and also unlike the 'outmoded' cultural models. Through the objective use of words—in Williams' case a purity of words, in Joyce's case a punning confluence of language and myth—both writers came to acknowledge the gigantic implications of a common linguistic pool." More specifically,

> both Joyce and Williams recognize that the effort to move behind language to its essential structures and to the gist that is obscured and diffracted by a modern decay of linguistic communicability requires a visionary sense of composite, almost unbounded, power and mystery. For both writers, the model of such power is both giant and male, and Tim Finnegan and Paterson each has as his counterpart a female figure whose essence is material, sensual, and essentially wordless. Both "dream" works are epithalamia to a marriage of word and sensual fact.

The remainder of Tapscott's article interprets this theme of marriage, principally in *Paterson*, in its thematic, imagistic, and structural/compositional contexts.

95. Wolf, Thomas J. "A. R. Ammons and William Carlos Williams: A Study in Style and Meaning," *ConP*, 2:iii (1977), 1-16.

96. Wyatt, David M. "Completing the Picture: Williams, Berryman, and 'Spatial Form,' " *Colby Library Quarterly*, 13 (1977), 246-62.

> In a brief initial survey of the debate about 'spatial form' vs. temporal art, Wyatt argues that, from the perspective of making a reading, the concept of spatial form is an ideal, which violates experience. "Reading *is*—is everything. We can only possess a poem by 'reading' it; 'insofar' as reading is the only mode of possession open to us, a poem is entirely part of 'the *temporal process*' " [DMW's italics]. Asserting the same condition is true of paintings, regardless of the common view of them as spatial artifacts, Wyatt turns his attention to Ws' "The Hunters in the Snow" [in *Pictures from Brueghel*] and Berryman's "Winter Landscape"—both responses to "Bruegel's [sic] *The Hunters in the Snow*" [reproduced in the article]. Supplying for each poem a formalist and reader's response analysis, Wyatt concludes that Ws' represents "a poetry only marginally aware of its own past. Its reader follows out a sinuous line of advance; he does not proceed through a fully articulated structure of repetition. . . . The poem is not only an 'emblem of intellectual power,' it confers such power upon the reader. He foregoes aspirations to spatial harmony for temporal rhythms." Berryman's poem, by contrast, is static and "sacrifices movement to momentousness."

97. 1977 Dissertations

A. Bollobás, Enikö. "A Descriptive Typology of Twentieth Century American Free Verse," University of Budapest, 1977. Supervisor: Gyula Kodolányi.

B. Fure, Robert Percing. "The Design of Experience: A Study in the Aesthetic of William Carlos Williams." University of California-Berkeley, 1977. *DAI* 39:872A.

C. Loevy, Stephen Ross. "The Secrets We Share: William Carlos Williams' *A Dream of Love*." University of Iowa, 1977. Supervisor: Sherman Paul. *DAI* 38:4168A-69A.

D. Schultz, Leon. "The Doctor Poet of Paterson and the Science of Art." University of Tulsa, 1977. Supervisor: Manly Johnson. *DAI* 38:791A-92A.

E. Sherwood, Sandra Mason. "The New Poetry of William Carlos Williams: Poetic Uses of Music and Dance." University of Illinois at Urbana-Champaign, 1977. *DAI* 38:6125A.

1978

98. Bové, Paul. "The World and Earth of William Carlos Williams: *Paterson* as a 'Long Poem,' " *Genre*, 11 (Winter 1978), 575-96.

> Bové contends there is a fundamental problem in much of the criticism of *Paterson*, in that "it attempts to impose metaphysical readings upon a text—*Paterson*—which subverts metaphysics and metaphysical criticism." This problem he attacks on the lines of *Paterson*'s form as a long poem, of "the nature of the 'object' in Williams' writing," and of an extension of "certain dimensions of Riddel's analysis [in *The Inverted Bell*] toward a more concrete understanding of Williams' project." Bové considers the issue of *Paterson* as a long poem, and of the possibilities of "the *American* long poem" [PB's italics] within the context of Roy Harvey Pearce's characterization and study of the form in *The Continuity of American Poetry*, wherein he finds contradictions inherent both in Pearce's conception of the American long poem and between his conception and his view of particular poems themselves. His context for "sketch[ing] the basic features of the problem of the object" is a critique of J. Hillis Miller's analysis of Ws' poetry in *Poets of Reality*. The fundamental problem presented by Pearce's, Miller's, and other prominent explorations of Ws' poetry is that, "with some important exceptions, criticism has consistently reified Williams' poetry into metaphysical artifacts whose timeless stasis and successful recuperations of a primal world outside the poem have forgotten man's place in history and his relation to language." One "important exception" is Riddel's *The Inverted Bell*; and in the rest of the essay Bové, extending Riddel's analysis "along paths originally suggested by Heidegger," argues for "an appreciation of Williams as an anti-humanistic, anti-anthropocentric, non-technological writer" and for an apprehension of *Paterson* as a poem of "dynamic relationships and processes instead of appearances fixed to one position and moment." Good, but not new.

99. Bonheim, Helmut, and Reinhard Nischik. "William Carlos Williams in Germany," *WCWN*, 4:i (Spring 1978), 14-18.

> Despite its brevity, the authors, of the University of Cologne, give a systematic and apparently quite thorough account of the extent to which Ws was known at different past periods in Germany, and especially (for the last 10 or 15 years) of the various formats in which his work is accessible to Germans and the extent of knowledge of him among different portions of the population. After reviewing various barriers to Ws' reception as a poet and writer in Germany, they review the early years of that reception (which began in 1931), referring to Professor Hans Galinsky's book on the modern American lyric (1968) as "trac[ing it] in great detail." That review aside, they observe that until 1962 "hardly any note at all was taken of the poet from Rutherford." From 1962 on, there is a rather impressive listing of notes about and boostings of Ws,

translations, in anthologies and book length [a trans. of *Paterson* by A. and J. Hollo was published in 1970], critical studies and interpretative material, inclusions in school texts, a few university courses in which Ws is taught, and some recent academic studies. Much of Ws' *oeuvre* has not been translated; "there are only four book-length translations . . . available here at the moment." But attention is being given; for "German [students] learning English as a second language," Ws' "Pastoral" and "The Red Wheelbarrow" were included in an anthology, *The Word Sublime*, in 1962 ; and the following year the compiler issued a teacher's guide that "includes a full reading of the wheelbarrow poem."

100. Crane, Joan St. C. "The William Carlos Williams Collection in the University of Virginia Library," *WCWN*, 4:i (Spring 1978), 22-23.

Ms. Crane, Curator of American Literature Collections at the University of Virginia, begins her report with observations about the excuisite rarity of *Poems,* 1909, and dazzling anecdotes about the avidity with which the book is pursued and the prices two copies fetched in 1977: "the first copy ever to appear at public auction . . . was knocked down for $16,000 at Sothby Parke-Bernet."

She reports that the fine collection at Virginia lacks a copy of *Poems*, 1909, "a source of frustration to the curator of an otherwise almost complete collection of the major printed works." In some recompense, she writes, it does contain a book that must be nearly as eagerly sought, "the dedication copy of *Sour Grapes* (1921) inscribed to Alfred Kreymborg."

The lode of the collection are the books and papers that Ws' friends, Mr. and Mrs. Clayton Hoagland, had owned. "The Hoagland archive contains holograph and typescript poems, . . . 20 carbon typescripts with changes in [Ws'] hand (among these are over 200 pp. each of *Paterson* and autobiographical notes made in 1950)," letters, postcards, notes, photographs and miscellaneous memorabilia. Among the books "The only major titles lacking are *Poems*, 1909, *Last Nights of Paris* (1929) and *Collected Poems 1921-1931* (1934)."

The collection contains miscellaneous other letters and "the contracts with the Four Seas Company" for three of Ws' early books.

101. Donley, Carol C. " 'A little touch of/Einstein in the night—': Williams' Early Exposure to the Theories of Relativity," *WCWN*, 4:i (Spring 1978), 10-13.

The springboard of Donley's examination is Ws' publication of "St. Francis Einstein of the Daffodils" in the summer of 1921. She posits that what Ws knew of relativity in 1919-1922 he garnered from articles in newspapers and the popular press, a spate of which were prompted by the eclipse expedition of 1919 and its confirmation of the light-bending effects predicted by Einstein's theory. She briefly surveys that journalism of 1919 and 1920, and then notes that "Einstein's visit to America in April 1921" (after which the poem was written) prompted a second wave of journalistic as well as learned interest. She specifies just what of Einstein's theory Ws seems to have understood and adapted to the poem, and concludes that "in 1921 he was interested in the new physics but . . . had not created any formal poetic analogs to it. That came later with *Paterson*."

102. Eckardt, Gladys. "The William Carlos Williams Room at the Rutherford Library," *WCWN*, 4 ɨ (Spring 1978), 19-20.

A genial note by Gladys Eckardt of the Rutherford Public Library, who writes of most Rutherford residents' indifference to and ignorance of Ws' poetry during his lifetime (as contrasted to the "Dr. Williams . . . loved by most Rutherfordians as the doctor who delivered and cared for their children"), and goes on to describe the initial homage the Library accorded Ws, "a collection in a special glass display cabinet," and, when the Library was enlarged in 1975, the room of the title. "The room houses memorabilia of the Doctor as well as copies of his books" "and a few of the little magazines which carried his early work. . . . We have no manuscripts or working papers."

103. Hallberg, Robert von. "The Politics of Description: W. C. Williams in the 'Thirties," *ELH*, 45 (Spring 1978), 131-51.

Hallberg's subject is, to echo his title, Ws' poetry of the 1930s, a decade in which he published "only two books of new poems," the more important being *An Early Martyr* (1935). What makes *An Early Martyr* an interesting book," writes Hallberg, "is its concerns with the problematic relationship between two poles of discourse, explanation and description." During the '30s, "in the poetry one sees [Ws] testing ways of writing that go beyond description, and in his criticism articulating complicated rationales for description."

Hallberg begins with analysis of "An Early Martyr" (the first poem of the book and its best example of "the structure and use of explanation") and compares it to "Flowers of the Sea" (the second poem, and primarily one of description). Writing that "the implicit argument of the book is that certain kinds of description are in fact politically useful," Hallberg moves on to a classification, with examples, of the varieties of the book's modes. The polar modes are of poems that "by flat description document a world," as contrasted to "the parabolic or emblematic poem" (e.g., "Proletarian Portrait"). Modes between those poles include those poems "in which not all the details of the description . . . suggest a transcendent significance," poems which "bring together the two modes of discourse" (such as "The Yachts"–"the most consummate poem of the volume"), and those poems "most clearly Williams' own, those that . . . commonly claim that the surfaces of sense experience require very little interpretation, that their 'meaning' is plain."

Hallberg concludes by recording Ws' advocacy (demonstrated in some or most of these poems) of "democratic inclusion." In notes Ws drafted at the end of the '30s "for various readings and talks," he wrote he wanted his "contribution . . . to contemporary verse" to manifest

> an attitude toward the subject matter or the materials of which verse is to be made that is inclusive—not selective : based on the importance of form (Rembrandt, side of beef). . . . Modern poetry is not selective—as poetry in the past has been. It is inclusive and comprehensive by its definition : to raise or enlarge the imagination to new areas of understanding. It says nothing of what shall be admitted. Nothing is excluded. How can it be? Every conceivable thing is material for poetry under the structural definition. . . . My conception of the last two decades of modern American verse has been that of a verse seeking new adjustments to a new world. Perhaps its final fruition or failure depends on the entire social-democratic survival or collapse. Nothing lives in a vacuum.

104. Heal, Edith. "William Carlos Williams' Personal Library at Fairleigh Dickinson University, Rutherford," *WCWN*, 4:i (Spring 1978), 20-21.

This collection is made up of some MSS and little magazines, and of some 600 volumes from Ws' library, all chosen by Flossie and given to the University several months after Ws' death. The books include ancient classics ("well represented"), works by 19th century American poets as well as by Emerson and Melville, and "many European and English writers." There is a Shakespeare and Co. first, limited edition and numbered copy of *Ulysses*, "nearly all the published work of Ford Madox Ford, an indication of his friendship dating back to Paris days," "fourteen books by Ezra Pound," and six volumes of Faulkner, "five of the six with 1930 and 1931 datelines." Among the "original manuscripts" are *The Cure, Many Loves, A Dream of Love, Tituba's Children, The First President, The Desert Music,* and *Pictures from Brueghel.* EH notes that the books are catalogued; she says nothing about annotations or marginal markings.

105. Laughlin, James. "A Visit," *WCWN*, 4:i (Spring 1978), 1-9.

A note by *WCWN*'s editor, Theodora Rapp Graham, identifies this as a story, written by the publisher of New Directions and "Williams major publisher beginning with the publication of *White Mule* in 1937, after a visit to the poet's home in Rutherford a few years before his death."

106. Ramsay, Roger. "Paterson [sic] : The Seminal Seed Imagery," *Concerning Poetry*, 11:i (Spring 1978), 55-57.

Starting with the conjunction of an apparent resurrection from the sea and the seed-ing image at the end of Book IV, Ramsay recalls and pursues some of the fertile imagery of *seed* in *Paterson*, from "the multiple seed" of the preface, which "floats off in the same scum" that reappears near the end of Book IV bearing seeds inland, through the stymied attempts, "at the beginning of the poem," of butterflies and bees to "tongue"and spread pollen seed, into the images of "roots . . . writhing / upon the surface" of rocks in Book II and the "green bud fallen upon the pavement" of Book I, to the germination of all these images at the end of Book IV : "the man (male/poet/bird/bee/butterfly) spits that seed upon a beach." Even beach sand is, as Ramsay points out, "crushed rock"–splintered, ground, worn rock processed into "the receptive sand." Ramsay's article has, admirably, something of the compact density and clean form of his subject.

107. Tracy, Billy T. "The Phryne Figure in *Paterson*," *NConL*, 8:ii (March 1978), 4-5.

Part of Ws' portrayal of modern civilization as a decline from the classical period is found in the debased modern pastoral dialogue of Corydon and Phyllis at the start of Book IV. In addition to the obvious indicators of decline, writes Tracy, Ws intensified his theme "by making the aging and decrepit Corydon a 'modern replica' " of possibly "the most famous and successful courtesan of antiquity— Phryne." Phryne, "a model for both Praxiteles, the sculptor, and Apelles, the painter, despite severe [skin] blemishes," is thus a prototype for Corydon, with skin blotched "like a toad." And the identification is etymologically sealed by the fact that Phryne "is Greek for toad." Moreover, Ws' theme of the "failure of language" has a parallel, Tracy reveals, in "the most dramatic incident of Phryne's career. . . . Accused of profaning the Eleusinian mysteries, Phryne engaged Hypereides, the renowned Athenian orator, to defend her. When it appeared that despite Hypereides' eloquence and her own impassioned pleas the verdict would go against her, she disrobed and was then acquitted by the impressed judges."

108. Westlake, Neda M. "The William Carlos Williams Collection at the University of Pennsylvania," *WCWN*, 4 :i (Spring 1978), 23-24.

Ms. Westlake, of the Rare Book Collection at the University of Pennsylvania, briefly describes an indisputably unique Ws collection. It is made up of his wife's "personal collection of first editions of Dr. Williams' books and pamphlets, nearly all of them inscribed to her with typical Williams pungency and affection." Moreover, the collection not only contains *Poems*, 1909, but copies of its two different printings: "The 'alpha' copy . . ., full of errors . . . [and with] corrections made by Williams' father, mostly adopted in the second issue,"and a copy of "The corrected first edition [also 1909], inscribed to Mrs. Williams in 1931."

In total, "there are some forty titles, first editions and reprints, of books and periodicals, and thirty-eight serial publications about Dr. Williams. There are no manuscripts or correspondence."

The collection also includes "personalia": "the first National Book Award for poetry, 1949 ; Brandeis University Creative Arts

Award for Poetry, 1957; Dr. Williams' membership pin for the American Academy of Arts and Letters to which he was elected in 1958; the Gold Medal of the American Academy of Arts and Letters, 1963; and a self-portrait in oil" done in 1914.

109. Bruns, Gerald L. "De Improvisatione," *IowaR*, 9 iii (Summer 1978), 66-78.

The first four pages of Bruns' article is a kind of prose lyric, an abundant, barrelling, cascade of characterizations, definitions, and specifications—mostly formal, but also historical—of the improvisation. He goes on to distinguish "rhetorical" improvisation (a king of "embellishment and ornamentation" done to or on an existent work) and the Romantic (an "unschooled and autonomous creation, . . . a studied freedom from readable antecedents"). One of his happier insights is that "Improvisation [*sui generis*] is gameless [i.e., ruleless] play"—free of audience, free of formal rules, free of communicative constraints and thus an expression "inscrutable and unanswerable and presuppos[ing] the operations of a solitary singer."

Such anomalies of the improvisation do not discourage interpreters; indeed, "improvisations are always an incitement to interpretation, with mixed and unimpressive results, the more so as interpretation naturally deforms the improvisation into the sort of discourse it most nearly resembles." Bruns' own text to interpret is *Kora in Hell* (the 1920 edition, he indicates, "which seems to contain fewer omissions than subsequent editions" and "is a beautiful book"). The rest of his article is a rendering of a handful or more of the improvisations of that book, beginning with the first sentence—"Fools have big wombs." and the first paragraph.

His interpretative renderings become occasions for demonstrations *in situ* of certain further laws governing the improvisation and especially Ws' variety. One is that "improvisations tend to occur at the level of the discourse, not at the level of the sentence"—not at the level, e.g., of a sentence like "Colorless green seas sleep furiously." Another, manifest in the improvisation beginning "When beldams dig clams their fat hams . . .," is "the characteristically treasured fact, an observation released from its reasons : simply one of those things Williams tends to notice." The main law, "the law peculiar to an improvisation by Williams is not the law of formal violation pure and simple but the law of unpredictability,"the law that "perhaps . . . makes *Kora in Hell* different from the Continental affronteries with which it is still sometimes associated: there is in Williams no active principle of derangement." Moreover, although Ws' apothegm of "the Good Physician"—" 'After thirty years staring at one true phrase he discovered its opposite was true also' "—is a perception of contradition that normally implies skepticism, in the case of Ws he "regards contradiction less as a sign of unreason or mental failure than as a frequent state of affairs. . . . Whereas contradiction is traditionally the occasion of despair or satires against credulity, for Williams it is (1) good fun, and (2) a condition of plentitude or the completeness of things."

Bruns concludes that "an improvisation by Williams is essentially a private utterance, but only in odd and complicated ways." Though it is unrevised, unintended for an audience, and generally undirected,

> the mild irony is that *Kora in Hell: Improvisations* is a book, and one that swells with many bookish devices ; its making required that private writings be mediated by certain editorial or explanatory alternatives to revision :a prologue, ancillary commentaries, intervening "interpretations" and short statements of principle – varieties of self-exegesis that gather the improvisations into a state of legitimacy.

110. Hammond, John G. "Williams' 'To Mark Anthony in Heaven,' " *Expl*, 36:iv (Summer 1978), 27-29.

Hammond identifies an "interplay" or structural bondings between the speaker of the poem, in his "north room," and the "Mark Anthony in Heaven" he addresses. The strongest bonding is that "the poet's gradual and thorough perception of nature is paralleled with Anthony's [presumed] knowledge of Cleopatra: 'inch by inch/ from slanting feet upward/ to the roots of her hair/ and down again.' " The speaker's parallel knowledge is of "light reflected . . . from grass and trees and clouds" (i.e., in turn, from earth to sky) initially, and then, at the end of the poem, from "clouds and trees and grass" (in reverse sequence). This bonding of speaker and Anthony in turn enables Ws "to make the larger statement that 'salvation' lies in all natural beauty. . . . In pursuing Cleopatra, then, Anthony enlarges his existence and spirit by pursuing natural beauty in general," as, Hammond implies, likewise does the speaker, given the fact that "Williams links nature with love."

111. Loevy, Stephen Ross. " 'Introduction' to William Carlos Williams's *Rome*," *IowaR*, 9:iii (Summer 1978), 1-11.

Loevy's introduction is in large part a biographical account of Ws' sabbatical from medical practice "from the summer of 1923 to the summer of 1924," especially of the six months he and Floss spent in Europe. The "sabbatical did produce significant writing–the major work *In the American Grain*, and a manuscript titled *Rome*."
Loevy writes of Ws' literary encounters in Paris and especially of his co-editorship with Robert McAlmon of *Contact* magazine, setting forth in some detail the literary program and rallying standards the two presented in its first three issues. Essentially, their advocacy of an indigenous art was expressed as "an argument [not] between America and Europe," but "between the local and the universal, between experience and ideology, between immediate relations and traditional values."
Ws' response to Rome, on his entry there, was to see it "as a center of dangerous but fertile chaos . . . where one might shed 'staid and tried acceptances and moralities' and emerge changed, refreshed, in repossession of one's self." It was for Ws, Loevy writes, "a source equivalent to the American wilderness in *In the American Grain*, or the 'hell' of *Kora in Hell*." Ws' MSS *Rome* "belongs

together with an extensive list of writings Williams called 'improvisations,' composed between 1917 and the early 1930's." The work

is a collection of improvisational notes composed in Italy and Vienna, *en route* to a second stay in Paris, and then later in the United States just after his return. It records Williams's immediate response to Europe and to himself in Europe, and the sections written back home test the changes wrought upon him. *Rome* constitutes his voyage to pagany, a descent into antiquity and peasantry, obscenity and art, disease and medicine, and into his own deepest conflicts. Like the other improvisations, *Rome* receives its impetus from conflicting insistences; he is hostile to Rome, threatened by it, and yet deeply attracted to it. The manuscript enacts his struggle to contact an alien and yet familiar (because sympathetic) environment. He performs on himself in and after Europe a kind of procedure he had enacted previously in writing *Kora in Hell*—the act of dis-covering what could be found to be meaningful, vital, and extraordinary amid a welter of responses to a challenging environment.

Loevy provides a physical description of the MSS, notes that Ws did not intend it for publication nor expect it to be published, and gives a statement of his editorial principles and practices, including a legend of the conventions and signs he uses to represent the MSS in printed typography. The printed MSS follows the introduction.

112. Mariani, Paul. "*Paterson* 5: The Whore/Virgin and the Wounded One-Horned Beast," *Denver Quarterly*, 13:ii (Summer 1978), 102-30.

This article (whose title except for "*Paterson* 5:" is the same as the title of Chapter Fourteen of Mariani's 1981 biography and study of Ws) is a (presumably earlier) version of most of the text of that chapter (specifically, of pp. 698-717). Both versions cover Ws' life and writings for the years 1956-1958. A quick comparison of article and book texts suggests the main differences are ones of phrasing, paragraphing, and of additions in the book version.

113. Baker, William. "Williams' 'The Use of Force,' " *Expl*, 37 :i (Fall 1978), 7-8.

This is a general psychological interpretation of the story, specifically of the two central characters and of what Baker sees as each's conflict. The girl patient "feels . . . that if evil is not discovered it does not exist," and her conflict is one of trying to hide her sore throat against the doctor's prying. The doctor's conflict is shown in his "adult's anger at himself when he is required to use force to accomplish his aim—even if the aim is noble in itself."

114. Fure, Rob. "The Design of Experience: William Carlos Williams and Juan Gris," *WCWN*, 4:ii (Fall 1978), 10-19.

"Williams' commitment to formal innovations was due significantly to his professed 'alliance' with modern painters," especially the cubists, writes Fure. Their influence on his poetry is apparent, for example, as "an increased awareness of the relations between objects in his visual field" and of "the often linear tensions between them." Of the cubists, "Juan Gris was for a long period [Ws'] favorite painter." Ws' "The Rose" (*Spring and All*), which is a response to Gris' "synthetic cubist painting *Roses*," is quoted and analyzed to show its relation to the painting as well as its emergent aesthetic. Fure then gives attention to Gris' own writings on art, and, quoting from Ws' *Autobiography*, shows that from the period of "the early twenties onward," Ws analagously and repeatedly said, "The poem is an object" and, especially in *Spring and All*, showed "formalist preoccupations begin[ning] to predominate in his aesthetic." In "The Rose" itself, "experience and design exist simultaneously, in that the poem, on the one hand, expresses dynamic, unfolding relationships between Williams' imagination and the subject and, on the other, exists as 'the intimate association of these relationships within the limited space of the poem itself.' " Fure concludes, "the cubists, and particularly Gris, helped [Ws] to discover and to clarify how the artist's relation to his subject matter, his conversation with the world, might achieve the formal integrity and autonomy of art."

115. Hardie, Jack. "Hibiscus and the Spaniard of the Rose: Williams' Dialogue with Wallace Stevens," *WCWN* 4:ii (Fall 1978), 20-24.

> "Williams' dialogue with Wallace Stevens runs for forty years through private letters, manifestoes, critical essays, book reviews, and poems," writes Hardie ; and it "reveal[s] many of the poets' assumptions about the nature and function of their art." Indicating he attempts in this essay only a beginning analysis of that dialgoue, and taking 1916 as his starting point, Hardie initially makes a chronological survey, basically factual and with much quotation, of the poets' exchanges, including "their first public exchange"—Ws' "El Hombre" and "Stevens' ambiguous tribut[ary]" response, "Nuances of a Theme by Williams." There is an informative and entertaining interpretation of Stevens' "Hibiscus on the Sleeping Shores" (1921, and apparently "a response to the argument in *Kora*") and of Ws' "This Florida: 1924" ("a high point of the dialogue with Stevens" and a poem which "explores the emotional aftermath of *Spring and All*'s, like *Harmonium*'s [both published in 1923], having created hardly a stir"). Hardie ends with some similarly oblique samples of the dialogue from the 1930s and 1940s, especially of Stevens' presumed characterization of Ws in "Esthetique du Mal," an implicit "misreading of Williams . . . called by Hugh Kenner 'one of the most extraordinary misunderstandings in literary history.' "

116. Heal, Edith. "The William Carlos Williams Center for the Performing Arts," *WCWN*, 4:ii (Fall 1978), 32.

> An announcement, aptly heralded by Edith Heal as "another memorable story of the phoenix rising from the ashes," of a commitment by Rutherford to handsomely renovate and enlarge the town's

fire-damaged, and only, theater, and to make of it "a centerpiece for the living arts in the name of the poet who lived for and served the arts." With an "elevation" illus. of the proposed center.

117. Michel, Suzy B. "The Identity of William Carlos Williams's 'Solitary Disciple,'" *MLR*, 73 (October 1978), 741-47.

> Ws' "To a Solitary Disciple" has commonly been construed and praised as an Imagist poem, writes Michel, but "the critics who have analyzed [it] and cleverly pointed out its structural success are hesitant about its message." One aspect of "its message," Michel shows, is that Ws wrote the poem as a response to Musset's "Ballade à la Lune." The two poems share some common images, and the hortatory voice of Ws' poem is implicitly directed to his predecessor. And in contrast to Musset, "Williams insists on the necessity of a literal observation. His images in the first five stanzas are bare, concrete, and owe nothing to the abstracted and connotative quality of Musset's poem." A fillip is added to the humor of Ws' poem (albeit unintended by Ws) in Michel's observation that, though Ws appears to have read Musset's poem as rank with vapid Romanticism, it "is really a witty and railing parody of Romantic poetry."

118. Ricciardi, Caterina. "William Carlos Williams in Italy : Critical Studies and Translations," *WCWN*, 4 :ii (Fall 1978), 29-31.

> Ricciardi, of the University of Rome, provides an annotated bibliography of what must be only the major studies and translations of Ws in Italian. Of the studies, all but three are books: an early introductory essay (1955); Glauco Cambon's *The Inclusive Flame* (Rome, 1962 ; and in English by Indiana Univ. Pr., 1963); Lina Garegnani Unali's *Mente e misura: la poesia di W. C. Williams* (Roma, 1970)— the only book length study of Ws exclusively "to have [so far] been published in Italy"; two essays on Ws' "relations to the figurative arts" by Barbara Lanati; and a projected concordance to *Paterson*, "the result of about ten-year research work carried out at the University of Rome by a group of linguists and teachers of American literature under the direction of Biancamaria Tedeschini Lalli."
>
> The translations listed date from 1961 to 1971 and include editions of "a selection [of] early and later poems," *Paterson*, a selection of short stories, *In the American Grain*, and, the latest, *Kora in Hell.*

119. Saunier-Ollier, Jacqueline. "French Interest in William Carlos Williams," *WCWN*, 4 :ii (Fall 1978), 25-29.

> After noting Ws' biographical connections to France (beginning with his being the son of "a half-French mother"), Saunier-Ollier briefly surveys his contacts with "the French *literati*," and some of his translations of their work between 1928 and 1958. What "little attention" Ws' work was given in France "until the 1960's" is recounted: mainly a few translations and The Living Theater's 1961 staging of *Many Loves.* Ws' lack of recognition in this period Saunier-Ollier

attributes to "the tremendous impact of the American 20th century *fiction* [J.S-O.'s italics] on French literature from the late 30's onwards" and to Eliot's and Pound's overpowering dominance among English poets known in France: "Both lived in Europe, were widely translated and represented a tradition of refined, cultured poetry to which the French had been accustomed for three centuries."

That tradition seems to be yielding, if the author's account of the growth of Ws' post-1960 French recognition is indicative. She mentions several book length studies of Ws or of modern American poetry in which he is prominent (notably *William Carlos Williams et le Renouveau du Lyrisme* (1964) by Hélene Dupeyron-Marchessou), the elevation of *Paterson*, in 1972-1973, to "the list of the ten long-renowned works that compose every year the curriculum of the *agregation*, the highly competitive, nation-wide examination which selects the best English majors of the whole country," and to translations of his work, in separate books as well as anthologies, and including "a superb translation of *Paterson*" as yet unpublished. The author herself has translated the *Autobiography* (published by Gallimard, [n.d.]), and written *William Carlos Williams: The Man and the Poet* (Nice, 1978). She concludes with a survey, for 1973 on, of university courses and academic studies of Ws, adding that though "a great gap remains to be filled," "Williams' influence in France has been growing steadily for the last ten years, mainly through the channel of the universities."

120. Tashjian, Dickran. "Translating Surrealism: Williams' 'Midas Touch,' " *WCWN*, 4:ii (Fall 1978), 1-8.

After indicating Ws' probable dubiousness towards translating, and listing the potential gains accessible to him in that art, Tashjian focuses on Ws' relationship, in 1939-1941, with Nicolas Calas, "a young Greek poet and critic." Calas "would draw Williams as close as he would ever get to Surrealism," and, through Ws' translations of some of his poems, provided the road to gains which were "crucial to the making of *Paterson*." Drawing upon letters in the Lilly Library (at Indiana) and the Beinecke Library (at Yale), Tashjian looks at an essay by Ws ("Midas: A Proposal for a Magazine") prompted by Calas' asking Ws "to help form a new Surrealist movement in America," and at Ws translation, from the French, of Calas' "Wrested from Mirrors," which was printed in a "handsome folio" limited edition by a gallery in mid-town Manhattan. Tashjian includes the texts of this poem and of two other published Ws translations of Calas.

121. Tashjian, Dickran. "The Whitney Museum Exhibition: William Carlos Williams and the American Scene, 1920-1940," *WCWN*, 4:ii (Fall 1978), 9.

This is an announcement of the exhibition, scheduled from December 12, 1978, to February 4, 1979. Tashjian writes that "the exhibition will attempt to make an implicit statement about American culture based on the relationship of objects with twentieth-century intellectual thought, political ideas, and social concepts" and that "the juxtaposition of Williams' ideas and poetry with the visual art of his contemporaries will dramatize the American scene . . . as a cultural category situated on the complex interface between American society and the varied groupings of artists who wanted to create a distinctive and authentic American art." With more description. See also Joel Conarroe's review of the exhibit in *WCWN*, 5:i (Spring 1979).

122. Baldwin, Neil and Steven L. Meyers. *The Manuscripts and Letters of William Carlos Williams in the Poetry Collection of the Lockwood Memorial Library, State University of New York at Buffalo: A Descriptive Catalogue.* Foreword by Robert Creeley. (Ref. Pub. in Literature) Boston: G. K. Hall, 1978.

No review available. But see Neil Baldwin's "William Carlos Williams Catalog, Lockwood Memorial Library, Poetry Collection," *WCWN*, 1:i (Fall 1975), 5. Printed with Robert Creeley's "Preface."

123. Bollier, E. P. "Against the American Grain: William Carlos Williams between Whitman and Poe," *Tulane Studies in English*, 23 (1978), 123-42.

Writing about *In the American Grain* as a book widely believed to be Ws' "major achievement in prose," Bollier addresses the question of "why did Williams devote a whole chapter to Edgar Allan Poe and only one sentence to Walt Whitman?" (and also the subsidiary question of why the critics, while recognizing the importance of the book, have ignored this anomaly of a writer commonly identified as of Whitman's lineage). Bollier observes that, like a number of his contemporaries in America in the '20s, Ws was "searching for a usable past." Unlike them, however, he did not look to Whitman for that "usable past"; rather, "Williams in effect rejects the whole American literary tradition." Inasmuch as "the European past was irrelevant [and] the American past now revealed itself a virtual void," the book seems to be "Williams' version of the waste land, and like Eliot, finding only a few fragments to shore against his ruins, he had to content himself with setting his own land in order." It is within this context of emptiness that Poe offered a potential model for a new and viable esthetic .

> The great thing about Poe, then, seems to be that he was a polyglot like Eliot and Pound who knew European literature as well as they, but not only had stayed home rather than run away, but like Williams had a sense of the local. . . . Poe, therefore, could answer the debasers of American taste, at least in his own time, because he knew more and could use "the smart language" better than they ; and having thus cleared the ground, he could give the local its authentic voice, because he understood, and was the first American literary man to understand, what the local at bottom was. . . . It is a plausible conjecture . . . that for Williams Poe's erudition enhanced his appeal. The Poe who

emerges here seems to have been in his time what Williams, I
suggest, thought Eliot should have been in his : the one American
man of letters who was qualified to destroy the enemies of an
indigenous, a "local" American literature with their own weapons, and who had made a beginning at least towards creating
such a literature. Poe's enemies, the debasers of American taste,
were the native American authors of his day—Williams cites his
attacks on Lowell and Bryant and Longfellow, Hawthorne and
Cooper, among other lesser lights. What Poe wanted was an
American literature which could stand comparison with the best
Europe had produced, and he had the courage to say that
America had not so far produced a single such work, only feeble
imitations (pp. 220, 226). That Poe ultimately, and perhaps
inevitably failed, did not lessen his usefulness to Williams. On
the contrary, Poe had identified the enemy, and his failure to
destroy him helped explain why no American literature yet
existed. Poe's precedent justified Williams' own attack on the
contemporary American poetasters, even though forced to use
different weapons.

In addition, Ws sees in Poe (in Poe's prose and criticism, that is, not
his poetry, which Ws dismisses summarily) not simply an advocate of
the right values, "but the necessity for a new method." "Williams
praised Poe's method," Bollier writes, "because it was by his method
that he made plausible his inventions, gave life to his 'original
material—the often fantastic material he flew 'to the ends of the
earth for' (p. 228)—and it was his method, the more arbitrary it
was, the more it proved his own potency, his own sense of the
local." Bollier concludes,

Considering his known ambitions to be *the* American poet, the
poet who would succeed where both Whitman and Poe had not,
Williams must have been struck by the possibility that an American poet, one wedded like Whitman to the particulars of the
American scene, who could invent a method like Poe's to "confirm his thought" (p. 230) and thus prove that the local was not
simply an American locality, but "*must* be where he *was*"—such
a poet surely would place American literature finally and at last
on solid ground. A poet with a method which did not "copy"
either worn-out methods or the "gross natural array," but which
transformed the raw stuff of experience into an "original" art,
furthermore, would have no peer.

124. Brown, John. "Larbaud et la jeune poésie américaine." In
Valery Larbaud et la littérature de son temps. Paris: Klinck-
sieck, 1978. Pp. 30-39.

125. Fender, Stephen. "Ezra Pound and the Words off the Page ;
Historical Allusions in Some American Long Poems," *YES*,
8 (1978), 95-108.

Fender's article is based on his "work on an edition of American
poetry which included three poems by Whitman, Hart Crane's *The
Bridge*, four of the *Jefferson* Cantos, and Book IV of Williams's
Paterson"; and his examples and conclusions are grounded in these
texts only. Basically, he argues that the historical allusions in Whitman's and Crane's poetry are "much more public than [those in]
Pound's and Williams's." And, as regards the latter two, though

"Williams shared many of Pound's ideas about the misuse of credit for private interests, and he particularly hated the rapid process of industrialization," in the use of historical texts his "sources are even more *recherehés* than Pound's." Fender identifies "two works of local history" that Ws uses in *Paterson* IV, the very hard to obtain *A History of the City of Paterson and the County of Passaic* (1910) by William Nelson, and Charles Pitman Longwell's *A Little Story of Old Paterson* [n.d.], of which one copy survives.

The bulk of Fender's article is a study of the *Jefferson* Cantos.

126. Heal, Edith. "Words about William Carlos Williams." In *The Old Century and the New: Essays in Honor of Charles Angoff*. Ed. Alfred Rosa. Rutherford: Fairleigh Dickinson UP, 1978. Pp. 124-34.

The title expresses two different meanings: 1) Edith Heal's "Words about Williams"—a brief, general commentary with copious quotations from Ws that is mainly an appreciate, celebrative piece on Ws' love of words, and 2) the aura—perhaps a halo?—of words around Ws, the writer. Ms. Heal touches on some of the early works: *The Great American Novel* (a book in which Ws' "love of words and [his] love of the act of writing is apparent in every line"), *Sour Grapes*, and *Spring and All*; and she quotes some of Ws' comments on these works from his *I Wanted to Write a Poem*, which Ms. Heal edited.

An editor's note identifies this piece as "adapted from *The Columbia University Forum*, Spring 1967, Volume X, Number 1."

127. Hurry, David. "William Carlos Williams' *Paterson* and Freud's *Interpretation of Dreams*," *L&P*, 28 (1978), 170-77.

Ws wrote "in 1948 that he accepted Freud's *Interpretation of Dreams* 'holus bolus' "; and his notes on *Paterson* show he saw a potential use for "Freud's ideas on the structure of dreams and the role of the dreamer." Hurry first briefly outlines Ws' goals as a poet following his statement on the weakness of Imagism. These goals included the desire "to 'get rid of the lyrical interference of the individual as ego,' " moving towards a Keatsian negative capability. This goal, Hurry writes, is realized in *Paterson* (of which he considers only Books I and II) in portraying Paterson as asleep and thus exemplifying a quality of "passivity" which, Freud wrote, is apparent in dreams as "the authority of the self is reduced."

This passivity of the dreamer is accompanied, paradoxically, by an opposing dream condition, "an *expansion* of the self as the [dreamer's] powers of sympathetic identification are released" [DH's italics]. This "expansion" may be realized as "identification" (the dreamer's ego assuming the variant forms of others' identities) or as "composition" (in which the dreamer brings about, through "a combination of the various features of a number of people," "a new unity, a composite figure." The latter process may be seen in the various persona of Paterson in Ws' poem.

As for "identification," Freud argues that one of its main functions in dreams "is to enable the statement of a censored thought or of feelings of guilt or inadequacy, perhaps." Taking this as the text for the last half of his article, Hurry interprets the Cress passages of *Paterson* I and II as evidences of Paterson the poet working through a sense of guilt, inadequacy, and unresponsiveness to "the personal nature of [Cress'] crisis." As the psychic goal of this process "is a direct confrontation with the problem," Hurry is of the opinion that the lyric beginning "On this most voluptuous night of the year" is "the final evasion, a conventional literary love not a felt one," whereas the final, eight-page letter from Cress at the end of Book II is the culmination of the process, the breakthrough to confrontation. The article, which has its merits, thus unhappily concludes as an example of the reductionism of a systemic and external paradigm (in this case, one erected to grapple with psychological phenomena) which limits rather than contributes to a wider frame of reference.

128. Kinoian, Vartkis. "William Carlos Williams: The Storyteller as Humanist." In *The Old Century and the New : Essays in Honor of Charles Angoff.* Ed. Alfred Rosa. Rutherford: Fairleigh Dickinson UP, 1978. Pp. 135-51.

Ws' poetry of the late '20s and early '30s shows "a much deeper sense of place" than had the earlier poems, writes Kinoian. That localizing impulse took as one form Ws' attention to local, working, often minority, people: "As he witnessed their struggles, Williams's efforts in the 1930's can be characterized as a poet's quest and commitment to transform these people into the subjects of his art. Increasingly," writes Kinoian, "in order to pursue that quest, Williams turned to the potentials of the short-story form."

Kinoian addresses himself first to *The Knife of the Times and Other Stories* (1932), a collection which Ws much later characterized as "a product of his deepest concern over the Depression years," but which Kinoian finds to be, in most of its stories, actually "prose versions of Williams' Objectivist poems." The other volume he examines is *Life Along the Passaic River* (1938), a book which "reflects the deeper oppressive atmosphere of the Depression years . . . and [which he designates as] also Williams's most human document." As with *The Knife of the Times*, Kinoian describes and characterizes a number of stories in this collection, giving most attention to five of its stories which were published in *Blast* in 1933 and 1934 and which are "Williams's most revealing works of the 1930s. Together they become his climactic efforts to transform both his emotions and the objects of those emotions—the people he witnessed in their difficult times—into meaningful and significant works of art."

129. Mariani, Paul. " 'Fire of a Very Real Order': Creeley and Williams," *Boundary 2* (Robert Creeley: A Gathering), 6:iii-7:i (1978), 173-90.

Mariani's subject is Ws' influence on the young Creeley and the interactions of the two poets, as charted mainly by their unpublished correspondence and Creeley's responses to Ws' poetry and various critical pieces. Creeley first learned of Ws by reading *The Wedge* in 1945, when he was 18 years old. "Its content was a revelation to me," he later professed. "It proved fire of a very real order." Mariani identifies *The Wedge*, its introductory dicta, other current Ws' critical statements, and Creeley's study of "Williams' line breaks and word breaks, his qualifiers and pronomial indeterminacies, his shifts from a rising to a falling measure and back again" as significantly shaping Creeley's "nascent poetics." In 1950 Creeley initiated a correspondence with Ws, a correspondence which soon gained Charles Olson as a third party and which, in Mariani's account, touches on the importance of Olson's "PROjective Verse" essay to Ws.

Mariani discusses the influence of the poems on love, in *The Desert Music*, on Creeley in the 1950s, and also the "new preoccupation" with poetic measure that appeared in the correspondence in late 1954, a subject that carried over into Ws' interest, in the early '60s, in "the local idiom and the variable foot as the very basis of the new measure." Throughout this essay on the biographical and poetic relationship, Mariani quotes extensively from the Creeley-Ws correspondence, which continued until Ws' death in 1963. "Long before then," he concludes, "Williams' presence—his standards and admonitions—had become ubiquitous touchstones in Creeley's letters, interviews, essays, and—more subtly—in the craft of his fiction and his poems."

130. Nash, Charles C. "Women and the Female Principle in the Works of William Carlos Williams," *Pubs. of the Missouri Philological Assoc.*, 3 (1978), 91-100.

As Nash's title suggests, this is a breakneck, sprinting dash over the huge body of Ws' work, poetry and prose, in illustration of Ws' theme "that women are both victims and survivors of the American past and present"—though that statement of his subject does not prevent Nash from getting off into other loosely suggested subjects: Ws' attitudes towards and symbolic meanings for "the sexual act," beauty generally—because "beauty in Williams' work characterizes the feminine," and Ws' "open admiration for the endurance of the poor." The article throws a negligible glance at the available criticism, and exasperatingly persists in the undefended—probably unrecognized—assumption that the narrators of poems and stories are merely other names for Ws.

131. *A Recognizable Image: William Carlos Williams on Art and Artists.* Ed., with Intro., Bram Dijkstra. N.Y.: New Directions, 1978.
Review by Robert von Hallberg, in *AL*, 52 (1980), 500-502.

Hallberg remarks on Ws' own early yen to be a painter, for one reason because he "earnestly believed that more than any other art painting held the power to change modern culture." But, writes Hallberg, his capacities as an art critic, as shown in these essays, are mixed. There is not much to strike fire in what Ws writes "about particular painters or paintings." Rather,

> the most important essays in this book—"Art and Politics: The Editorship of *Blast*" (1933), "Revolutions Revalued: The Attack on Credit Monopoly from a Cultural Viewpoint" (1936), "Woman as Operator" (1948), and "The Portrait: Emmanuel Romano" (1966)—are focused on issues that go way beyond the techniques of particular painters.

Hallberg observes that Ws, an "enthusiast of experimental painting," shows himself a surprising advocate of "representation in art." "As early as 1928 he claimed that the cubist wish to escape representation was wrong-headed: 'all painting is representation and cannot be anything else' (p. 69) [; and] he finally turned against abstract painting." Hallberg continues,

> The emphasis on representation makes sense from various angles—not least from his sense of the function of art. He was not merely a realist: ". . . it is the degree of understanding about, and not situations themselves, which is of prime importance. . ." (p. 64). The artist should provide not just a representation but "clarity of mind" (p. 196). To some extent, an artist is limited by the Zeitgeist to that understanding which exists, if only potentially, in his or her world. But sometimes there is the potential for great change, and "Revolutions are not won by violence alone but by the accuracy of the thought back of them" (p. 117). Williams understood art in somewhat utilitarian terms: "A 'good' poem is good as it might be successfully used in the organization of an entire social, political, economic [pattern] of its day—or reorganization" (p. 225). He was an experimental poet—no one can question that—but his ideas about the proper subject and function of art, and about the role of the artist were conservative and commonsensical; they are the notions that are frequently designated as "reasonable."

Hallberg concludes that the book will be valuable to students of "Williams's thought" and to those interested in the mutual attraction of poets and painters. He highly commends Dijkstra's editorial work, which required "piecing together various drafts of the pieces included so as to publish the fullest, if not the most authorial, versions of the essays."

132. Saunier-Ollier, Jacqueline. "William Carlos Williams: Deux 'Tableaux d'aprés Brueghel.' " In *Hommage à Emile Gasquet (1920-1979)*. (Annales de la Faculté des Lettres et Sciences Humaines de Nice 34). Paris: Les Belles Lettres, 1978. Pp. 199-208.

Saunier-Ollier writes generally of Ws' interest in and response to Brueghel, beginning with his first seeing the paintings in Vienna in 1924; but she focuses specifically on Brueghel's *Dance of the Peasants* and *The Hunters in the Snow*, and on Ws' poems on those paintings, "The Dance" (1942) and "The Hunters in the Snow" (1960).

In her comparison of the first paired painting and poem, Saunier-Ollier analyzes the visual structure of the painting (its lines, shapes, and colors) and shows Ws' attempt to transform those visual effects into, and in, his poem. She points out that the poem, which omits color images, uses sound imagery and metrical effects to convey what the painting in part conveys by colors. She especially observes that "C'est en effet le mouvement—celui du tableau comme celui du poème—qui a littéralement fasciné Williams et qu'il s'est attaché à rendre." Saunier-Ollier's formal and structural analysis of painting and poem is a fit medium for her interpretation that "The Dance" is "un petit chef-d'oeuvre de subtilité harmonique et rythmique" [sic].

She finds Ws' approach, twenty years later, to the same painter's "Hunters in the Snow" a very different matter. "Chaque détail, chaque mot est choisi en fonction de sa charge poétique et métaphysique," she writes; and her analysis of Ws' poem is thematic and symbolic. She notes, for example, the ambiguity of "a huge bonfire": "des mots tels que 'huge' et 'flares' évoquent plus les flammes dévorantes de l'enfer que la douce chaleur de l'ârte." Essentially, Saunier-Ollier argues, both painting and poem portray a symbolic, allusive reenactment of the Passion of Christ:

> L'essentiel . . . est dans cette enseigne accrochée au-dessus de la porte de l'auberge et que, sane le poète, nous n'aurions peut-être pas remarquée. Elle représente, nous dit Williams—et quels bons yeux il devait avoir!—un cerf portrait un crucifix entre ses bois. "Crucifix", dernier mot de la strophe, placé à la rime et prolongé par un enjambement, est le mot-clé du poeme. Il éclaire d'une lumière tragique et rédemptrice le tableau et le poeme tout entier. En insistant sur ce qui pourrait paraitre un détail insignifiant, Williams souligne le mysticisme profond de Brueghel pour qui les moindres scenes de la vie quotidienne sont autant de répliques des événements bibliques. Pour lui, la Passion de Christ se répète chaque jour et le détail le plus prosaique revêt une signification sacrée.

Saunier-Ollier identifies other allusions to the Passion in pictorial elements of the painting and images of the poem. She concludes, "Williams comme Brueghel nous montre de facon oblique que si tout en ce monde parle de notre mort, tout contient aussi le germe de notre rédemption. Le peintre 'a qui rien n'échappait' et le poete qui voyait en chaque jour 'le premier / (et le dernier) jour du monde' se retrouvent a la fin de leur vie pour faire de l'oeuvre d'art un objet 'd'adoration profonde.' " Illus.

133. Swafford, James. "Temples on the Rock: Religion and the Rhythms of *Paterson*," *Essays in Literature* (Western Ill. Univ.), 5 (1978), 75-84.

> Swafford purports to find in the five books of *Paterson* "structural principles . . . more systematic than Conarroe's [in his *William Carlos Williams' "Paterson"*] admittedly broad outline implies."

> The middle three books of *Paterson* reveal a repeated rhythmic pattern of ascent and descent that grows progressively more exaggerated, while Books I and V represent, respectively, the preparation for ascent and the achievement of the summit, rather than the movement itself. Closely tied to the rhythms of the poem are religious motifs which culminate, along with the ascent/descent pattern, in the triumphant fifth book.

All of this Swafford undertakes to display within nine pages (stopping midway to insert, "After the first two books have revealed a multitude of false religions and true religions now existing only in attenuated forms, Books III and IV show the poet trying to find a true religion of his own and for his own time."). The result becomes a combined scampering commentary on the poem, as directed by these issues, and a surface-action narrative summary. James Breslin in *ALS 1978* writes of this quick runthrough: "brief and schematic, the essay offers little that is fresh." I add only—or interesting.

134. Tapscott, Stephen J. "Williams's Paterson: Doctor and Democrat," *YES*, 8 (1978), 78-94.

Tapscott writes a loosely organized and wide-ranging article. He remarks, for example, that "one of the most startling experiences in reading the manuscripts for *Paterson* [at Yale and SUNY, Buffalo] is to discover Williams's notes and ideas for the poem scrawled on prescription blanks from his medical office"—a fact/ "thing" indicating that "in a sense *Paterson* aspires to be a descriptive diagnosis, a prescriptive cure, and a general treatment of a 'sick' condition in America." He also identifies certain correspondences between Doctor Paterson and Jung's characterization of the doctor in a 1930 *transition* article that "Williams must have read."

Tapscott's thesis is that Paterson's quest is for a socially "redeeming language," the creation of which requires a knowledge of both the world and the mind: "To know the world, Paterson needs to be objective, a doctor, who can glimpse the 'thing' itself. To know the mind, Paterson needs to be an individuated, democratic citizen, with his own prerogatives of internality." Thus,

> Paterson, both giant city and individual person, Doctor and stroller in the park, is Williams's dichotomized figure who assumes both perspectives. Sharing the immediacy of the "local" but looking for the words "with style" which can release men from the imprisonment of habitually limited perception of the local, Williams works to strike both tones simultaneously (especially in the first four books of the poem: the final book abandons the aesthetic or psychic "distance" of the "Doctor" and substitutes the "distance" of Paterson's dreamy old age). The effect of Williams's distance is an increased self-awareness of the objectivity of words as words, as they "build" the city Paterson on the page, and underlying that awareness is a consciousness of the dangers and decadence of democracy in modern practice, as language is debased and used subjectively, cynically, and ineffectually. The effects of Williams's intimacy, by contrast, are the urgent sense of an individual's participation in the local scene itself, and a sense of intimacy with the inner life of the citizens in the city. Frequently in *Paterson* Williams unites these two perspectives, and the results are stunningly clear. Like certain Cezanne paintings which present objects from both a lateral and a disappearing perspective simultaneously, Williams occasionally synthesizes Paterson's perspectives of objective "Doctor" or observer and subjective democratic individual.

Tapscott adds that these syntheses are "the most memorable sections of Williams's 'modern epic.' "

135. Wagner, Linda W., ed. *William Carlos Williams: A Reference Guide*. Boston: G. K. Hall, 1978.
Review by George Monteiro, *WCWR*, 7:i (Spring 1981), 29-31.

> Monteiro writes that his review of such guides as this focuses on the questions, "how useful are they and to whom?" Wagner's guide "will be used by beginning students as well as seasoned veterans," though the latter will find it uneven. Wagner does provide "a brief, knowledgeable introduction" and keeps apparatus "to a minimum." Her bibliography, of 153 pages and covering the years 1909-76, omits certain material, as Wagner indicates:
>
> > This Reference Guide attempts to present a comprehensive listing of only critical materials. Omitted have been personal notes (relating to family, travels, children); inaccessible foreign language publications; and items so fragmentary that they seemed inconsequential when compared with the quantity of available material. (xi)
>
> Monteiro finds that there are annotations of French, German, and Japanese materials, but none of Iberian (e.g., "Paulo Vizioli's important monograph on *Paterson* as a failed attempt at epic" [Brazil, 1965]). He also notes the guide includes items from New York and Chicago newspapers, as well as the *San Francisco Chronicle*, but "nothing from Washington, St. Louis or Newark papers," and finds Wagner's "principle of selection" about such material unclear and unstated. In addition, though Wagner explains that "All entries are annotated with a brief description of the content, not a judgment of it," he finds "on occasion judging, editorializing, evaluating" and proposes such should be supplied for all or none. "The annotations are succinct and informative," though one wishes they were longer; "they run from a fragment of a sentence . . . to two or three short sentences."

136. 1978 Dissertations

A. Hans, James Stuart. "The Return to Origins in the Poetry of Eliot and Williams." Washington University, 1978. Chair: Naomi Lebowitz. *DAI* 39:1549A.

B. Kallet, Marilyn. "Honest Simplicity in the Last Love Poems of Paul Eluard and William Carlos Williams." Rutgers: The State University, 1978. *DAI* 39:4227A.

C. Menides, Laura Jehn. "The Use of the Past in Modern American Poetry: Eliot, Pound, Williams, Crane, Berryman, Olson, Lowell." New York University, 1978. Adviser: Kenneth Silverman.

D. Raaberg, Glora Gwen. "Toward a Theory of Literary Collage: Literary Experimentalism and Its Relation to Modern Art in the Works of Pound, Stein and Williams." University of California-Irvine, 1978. Chairman: Murray Krieger. *DAI* 39:2932A-33A.

E. Stegman, Michael O. "William Carlos Williams and *Paterson*: An Exorcism of Pound and Eliot"; "Wallace Stevens at the *Harmonium*"; "Wallace Stevens and Music." State University of New York at Stony Brook, 1978. *DAI* 39:3587A.

1979

137. Altieri, Charles. "Presence and Reference in a Literary Text: The Example of Williams' 'This Is Just to Say,' " *CritI*, 5 (Spring 1979), 489-510.

Altieri undertakes a refutation of Derrida's "skeptical" view of language with the aid of "the philosophical position of the later Wittgenstein" and by showing that Ws' poetics, specifically in "This Is Just to Say," provide a model "for connecting both the expressive and the denotative aspects of literary language to our understanding of ordinary experience." After a proposed summation of "Derrida's formulation" as, to Altieri's knowledge, "his American disciplines" interpret and use it, Altieri launches his analysis of Ws' poetics.

> If Milton is the grand expositor of human culture as a middle realm, Williams can be seen as in many respects his secular heir, an heir careful to work out how the poetic imagination serves to make man's expulsion from Edenic origins bearable and even invigorating. Williams' poetics begins, as Riddel makes clear, in the awareness that there is no inherent or even recoverable correspondence between words and facts in the world, but Williams then devotes most of his energies to denying the metaphysical alternative to that position—the claim that all language can do is reflect on and play with the emptiness or fictiveness of its signifiers. If words do not copy but produce meanings, then they can be used significantly to focus our attention on the activities of the artist and his constructed characters as they engage in that process of production. The act of producing meanings can be the process by which to achieve another kind of reference, for the act of expression can itself become the focus generating a poem's significance by calling attention to the various ways author and characters station themselves in relation to specific situations. Fiction then is not so much a term describing the ontological status of certain kinds of language (since many utterances in ordinary behavior also do not have referents) but a term characterizing a particular way of using language to reflect upon forms of behavior in which we are not fully conscious of the quality of our activities.

Of these significance-generating powers of language Altieri offers, briefly, the examples of "The Red Wheelbarrow" and, at greater length, "This Is Just to Say." The latter poem "takes as its theme an appropriately minimal, secular version of the loss of origins Milton dramatized. It literally enacts the process of replacing absent objects with words. And like Milton's poem, it does not stop with the metaphysics of loss . . . but asks the reader to reflect on the qualities of mutual understanding that can be constructed from the speech acts in which we compensate for our fallen condition." Finally, Altieri proposes a definition of "measure" that accords with the speech-act theory of language his analysis is grounded in. Ws' "measure" is "a concept he developed in order to reconcile his competing desires to reject mimetic views of art, to stress the constructive act of the artist, and to preserve a sense of poetry as disclosing values and qualities basic to our existential concerns." It is "in short," Altieri writes, "a theoretical means for describing how the production of meaning is also the achievement of meaning."

138. Donley, Carol C. "Relativity and Radioactivity in William Carlos Williams' *Paterson*," *WCWN*, 5:i (Spring 1979), 6-11.

Writing of Ws' interest in Einstein's theory of relativity, Donley states, "His new measure, or variable foot, developed partly from his understanding of relativity." The variable foot she defines, "as it appears in *Paterson*, [as] a tripart line in which the components vary according to contextual relationships: sentence fragments, single words, long phrases—all moving in a changing but 'relatively stable foot.' "

The bulk of Donley's essay, however, concerns Ws' portrait of Mme. Curie and use of the image of radioactivity in *Paterson*. Ws clearly "read Eve Curie's biography of her mother, *Madame Curie*" (1939) and used details of it in his poem, though he also altered it by portraying Mme. Curie as pregnant in order to give "her a sainthood by association with Mary, mother of Christ." The radioactivity, "the radiant gist[,] extracted with great effort from the pitchblend becomes a metaphor in *Paterson* for the poet's search for the beautiful thing—for the meaningful language."

139. Fitch, Noel Riley. "Voyage to Ithaca: William Carlos Williams in Paris," *PULC*, 40 (Spring 1979), 193-214.

Very little has been written of Ws' visits to Paris and his perceptions of it, writes Fitch. She focuses on his six-week visit in 1924, and on his last trip in 1927, giving a history of the other writers he met, of his literary activities there, and of his ambivalence towards Paris. She notes that one result of his 1924 visit was Adrienne Monnier's publication, in her *Le Navire d'Argent*, of "a portion of Williams' *The Great American Novêl*," translated by Auguste Morel, "who had been translating Joyce's *Ulysses*." During his 1927 trip, he met Phillippe Soupault, whose *Last Nights of Paris* Ws and his mother translated in 1928; and he also read and wrote an essay on Joyce's *Work in Progress*, "an essay that was undoubtedly a response to a private criticism by Pound," and which was published in *transition* and, two years later, in *Our Examination Round His Factification for Incamination of Work in Progress*.

Ws' ambivalence towards Paris Fitch finds mainly conveyed in *A Voyage to Pagany* (1928—"Pagany" is "an old Roman term for Europe"), in the *Autobiography*, and in Ws' letters, especially those to Sylvia Beach. His "hostility towards America stemmed both from his hatred of American Puritanism and his love of France," she writes of one pole of Ws' response as shown in *A Voyage*. And his "antipathy for Paris, which was to culminate in the *Autobiography* [thereby raising anger and bruised feelings among past friends in

Paris, including Sylvia Beach] came largely from a sense of literary betrayal by Eliot, and to a lesser extent by Pound." But these derogatory portraits of the *Autobiography* "were uttered in the context of his recurring criticism of the artist-in-exile and with his typical salty frankness. His hostility was less toward Paris or France than toward the Americans who fled there. He had not been accepted by them. Paris did not need him, as America did. And most importantly, Paris, representing the artistic pull of Europe, threatened the development of fresh American forms."

140. Hudgins, Andrew. "*Paterson* and Its Discontents," *ArQ*, 35 (Spring 1979), 25-41.

In the belief that modern "literary landscapes" have a tendency to become psychic landscapes," Hudgins launches a perusal of *Paterson* rooted in the paradigm of id-ego opposition developed in Freud's *Civilization and Its Discontents*. "In Book One," for example, "Williams delineates the conflict between the id and the ego and sets up the problem that he examines in more detail in the next two books, 'Sunday in the Park' focusing on the sensual life, which cannot be sustained, and 'The Library' focusing on the intellectual life, which is sterile." The article proceeds as a running commentary, association reading of selected passages of *Paterson* I-V, as blazed by this thesis. Its possible value is blemished by this posthaste approach as well as by the lack of any references to either criticism of the poem or to Ws' comments on it.

141. MacGowan, Christopher. "William Carlos Williams Material in the Princeton University Library Collection," *WCWN*, 5 :i (Spring 1979), 17-18.

A rigorously itemized listing of the Ws materials at Princeton. Among the "50 items of correspondence" are letters and postcards from Ws (and a few from Floss) to Sylvia Beach, Allen Tate, R. P. Blackmur, Harold Loeb ("the editor of *Broom*"), and Whit Burnett, of *Story* magazine. There are also "many first editions of [Ws'] books and pamphlets," though not of *Poems* 1909.

142. Procopiow, Norma. "The Early Critical Reception of William Carlos Williams," *WCWN*, 5 :i (Spring 1979), 12-16.

In the belief that relative lack of notice (as well as notice bestowed) is a measure of literary repute, Procopiow looks at various "indices of publication" for notices of or/and publications by Ws through 1940. She finds—among "indices which annually compile entries of reviews in magazines and newspapers"—that in the comprehensive *International Index to Periodicals* Ws has no entries until one written by Horace Gregory, in 1940. In the same index, however, Eliot and Pound reap "at least a dozen," one on Pound dating from 1920. In addition, in *The Book Review Digest*, the first Ws entries appear in 1926, in review notices of *In the American Grain*. As for the second index—"prominent magazines of the period"—Ws has a mixed showing. Publications like *Nation, New Republic,* and *Commonweal,* "openly committed to movements and causes both political and artistic[,] . . . took a greater interest in Williams than did others." In American little magazines Ws "had less critical consideration" than did Eliot and Pound, despite the fact that the same magazines published far more of Ws' literature than they did of the writings of his two contemporaries. For example, "Williams published forty-four poems, essays and stories, but there were just three reviews of his work," whereas "Eliot published three essays and no poems, but received eleven reviews or articles." For her third index—contemporary poetry anthologies—Procopiow lists four "major anthologies" (published between 1921 and 1929) which "printed verse by Eliot, Frost, Sandburg, Marianne Moore, Pound, and Stevens, but not Williams." And "book-length studies of contemporary poetry" of the period (her fourth index) are similarly arid regarding Ws. Procopiow's conclusions? The early critics failed to discern the fact as well as the nature of Ws' modernism; and they "were inclined to take Williams more seriously as a prose writer than as a poet." She also gives brief attention to Mariani's and Wagner's coverage of this period of Ws' career, in their reference guides.

143. Rodgers, Audrey T. "William Carlos Williams's 'New World': Images of the Dance," *ArQ*, 35 (Spring 1979), 5-24.

Ws, "more than any other American poet of the twentieth century," Rodgers writes, stresses the importance of dance, especially as the metaphor for the "yoking of those polar worlds" (of "quotidian reality" and the imagination) that "brings about their coexistence in the *third* world of art, where each particular retains an integrity of its own, yet through Invention can 'startle us anew' " [ATR's italics].

After briefly characterizing anthropological, psychological, and sociocultural views of the functions of dance, Rodgers proceeds to some of the functions Ws' literature attributes to dance: "the catharsis of emotions," the "genera[tion of] harmony, balance, oneness," and as "metaphor for the imaginative faculty of art." The remainder of her essay surveys and interprets Ws' "dance" literature, in prose and poetry, from *The Collected Early Poems* through *The Desert Music.*

144. Roulston, Helen H. "The Four Elements of Poetic Consciousness in William Carlos Williams' *Paterson,*" *SDR*, 17:i (Spring 1979), 101-11.

Though Ws' use of "Heraclitis' four elements" to symbolize, in *Paterson,* the complexities of the world [and] his own creative processes" has been noted by "numerous critics," writes Roulston, none has observed that Ws also uses them to chart "the protagonist's journey from his initial sterile perception of the world as ugly, useless chaos to his final understanding of his materials and of the nature of creativity."

Except for Book I, where the elements are depicted in deliberate chaos, Williams' pattern is based on the principle of theme with variations. He initially presents, in each subsequent Book, earth representing the raw poetic materials. Next, he shows the other elements—air (imagination), fire (destructive and creative energy), and water (human community and communication)—interacting in turn with the earth. In each book, this interaction becomes increasingly effective as Paterson comes closer and closer to his artistic goal.

Essentially, Paterson's goal is to become "a truly creative seer and poet"; and his progress towards it, in terms of his relation to the four elements, Roulston discerns as follows. Lacking "comprehension of [and] sympathy for" his townspeople and hobbled by a "sterile" mind, "Paterson's tepid attempts to use his imagination upon his materials are wasted efforts" in Book II. In Book III, the relations among "the elements and their symbolic equivalences . . . result in meaningful destruction"; and the same pattern in Book IV moves toward the "tentatively creative." Book V measures Paterson's distance from his start: "He has journeyed step by step, learning the essential meaning of the four elements—earth (raw materials), air (imagination), fire (creative energy), and water (human understanding)—and how to combine them effectively into a unique creation. . . . He has become 'I, Paterson, the King-self' " and has set forth " 'a complete little universe,' 'the whole life of the poet.' "

145. Sayre, Henry M. "Distancing 'The Rose' from *Roses*," *WCWN*, 5:i (Spring 1979), 18-19.

Bram Dijkastra's assertion [in *The Hieroglyphics of a New Speech* (1969)] that "Williams' poem 'The Rose' was an attempt to realize in poetic terms what Juan Gris had achieved plastically in his 1912 collage *Roses*" has "become an accepted and often reiterated part of the Williams critical canon," writes Sayre, who goes on to argue that the assertion rests on inadequate evidence and that the origin of the poem lies elsewhere. On the basis of the Dadaist organization of *Spring and All* (where 'The Rose' was published), and because he could "discover no reproduction . . . of Gris's *Roses* in any European or American publication before 1930," Sayre believes Gris' painting was unknown to Ws when he wrote the poem. However, Ws almost certainly knew Gris' *The Open Window*, "reproduced in *Broom*, 1 (January 1922)"; and his reference in *Spring and All* to an unspecified Gris "picture which represents 'what the modern trend is' " is very likely to it.

Sayre suggests that Gris created *Roses* "hoping to please [Gertrude] Stein, who was already famous for . . . 'A rose is a rose is a rose,' " and that Ws' poem is of the same genesis. The collage and the poem, "undoubtedly . . . of the same artistic milieu," are very probably offspring of Stein's dictum.

146. Uno, Hiroko. "Two Emily Dickinsons," *WCWN*, 5:i (Spring 1979), 20-22.

This article, Mr. Uno's translation of the 1978 Japanese version, argues that the woman pictured in the frontispiece of Vol. II of

Richard B. Sewall's *The Life of Emily Dickinson* is not the poetess, but rather Ws' maternal grandmother, "born in England about the same time as . . . Emily Dickinson and [of] the name 'Emily Dickenson.' " To illustrate Mr. Uno's comparative analysis, the article reproduces the disputed frontispiece, in addition to "the only authenticated photograph . . . of Emily Dickinson" and two known pictures of Ws' grandmother.

147. Weiland, Steven. "Where Shall We Unearth the Word?: William Carlos Williams and the Aztecs," *ArQ*, 35 (Spring 1979), 42-48.

In this essay on Ws' interests in the Aztecs and the values he identified with their culture, Weiland briefly describes that culture as it emerges in "The Destruction of Tenochtitlan" chapter of *In the American Grain*, and then considers Ws' translations, "near the end of his career," of "three Nahuatl pieces . . . representative of Aztec poems or hymns" and a Spanish poem by Octavio Paz. Ws' "interest in the Aztecs was certainly based on their esthetic devotionalism and real accomplishments in craft and art," he concludes.

148. Williams, William Eric. "The House," *WCWN*, 5:i (Spring 1979), 1-5.

This is basically a physical description of the Williams' house, "a sizable frame structure, clapboard finish, which had a gingerbready front porch that was removed in the 1920's." Located "on the south boundary line of the lot, with ample front, back and north side yards[,] over the years its color has been predominantly a light mustard shade." Williams takes the reader on a tour of the interior of the house, from first floor to attic (a section of which Ws converted in the twenties into "his studio") and into the "full-sized, unfinished cellar," where "winter mornings began between 6 and 7 AM when Dad went down to shake the [coal] furnace." The description includes much of Ws' presence. Williams also notes the pictures in the house, including paintings by Charles Demuth, Charles Sheeler, Marsden Hartley, and "a copy of Ben Shahn's *Paterson*." With illus of the house.

WCWN's editor notes "The Williams house was named to the National Register of Historic Places in July 1973."

149. Levin, Gail. "Wassily Kandinsky and the American Literary Avante-Garde," *Criticism* 21, (Fall 1979), 347-61.

Characterizing Kandinsky, Levin writes that in his essays "he managed to articulate many concepts central to the development of abstract art both in Europe and America" and that his "paintings, particularly the artist's Improvisations of 1909-14, suggested a new freedom of expression." A number of American artists, including Ws' friends Alfred Stieglitz and Marsden Hartley, "were attracted to Kandinsky's art and theory"; and of writers similarly drawn, Levin writes of Gertrude Stein, Ezra Pound, and Ws himself.

Ws had both direct and indirect knowledge of the painter, the indirect through Hartley. Directly, Ws "paid tribute to Wassily Kandinsky in his 'Prologue' to *Kora in Hell: Improvisations*," wherein he "paraphrased Kandinsky's 'axioms for the artist.' " He had also seen, in 1913, the painter's Improvisation No. 27; and there is a possibility that his "The Great Figure" reflects his familiarity with Kandinsky's "poem [titled] 'Anders' or 'Different.' "

150. Williams, William Eric. "Food," *WCWN*, 5:ii (Fall 1979), 1-4.

An at times comic account of Ws' gustatory pleasures and of what is portrayed as his near-Gargantuan appetite. "A seafood dinner of steamers and lobsters was a full symphony. Each clam stripped, washed in the broth, dunked in butter, and engorged, to be followed by the bits of white muscle, painstakingly scraped from each shell, and the last shred chased by the cup of broth, which was drained to the sandy dregs." Everything edible in the lobster was likewise meticulously and entirely consumed. In something of a contrast, walking trips in the country were often refreshed by adventurous taste samplings. "We tasted the buds and twigs of the wild cherry, sassafras, birch and witch hazel. We dug and pulled to obtain the thumb-sized morsel in the heart of the common pasture fern that dots New England's pastures." And more. Williams gives a similarly full account of the good and various spirits at 9 Ridge Road, about which his father's "attitude was that booze was a good ice-breaker and destroyer of inhibitions, but beyond that a poison and a stealer of precious time." With a reproduced photograph of Ws and his mother in October 1940.

151. Zbornik, Richard C. "An Afternoon with Dr. Williams," *WCWN*, 5:ii (Fall 1979), 28-31.

A familiar note on the empathetic attraction of a fellow doctor and aspiring writer to Ws. Dr. Zbornik's first encounter with Ws and "earliest memory of [his] poetry was discovering *Paterson* IV in the fall of 1951." In early 1952 he wrote to Ws; Ws answered; and in the summer of the following year Dr. Zbornik, as "a very young 23" year old, made an impromptu visit to Ws and Flossie and spent the afternoon with them. A kind of poem of homage by the author to Ws accompanies the note, along with a reproduction of Ws' letter (March 10, 1952) to him. Ws wrote, "I write as I do, rightly or wrongly, because I think my way of writing has taken the contours of a way of thought which is essential to the modern world which I know, eminently here."

152. Ziegfeld, Richard E. "Dear God / Dear Bill: The William Carlos Williams-James Laughlin Correspondence," *WCWN*, 5:ii (Fall 1979), 5-20.

Making use of "more than 900 letters between Williams and Laughlin" in the New Directions archive, as well as interviews with James Laughlin, Ziegfeld charts the 30-year long, intimate relationship of author and publisher through five "phases." Regarding Laughlin's goals as a publisher: With his enterprise financed by his inheritance, Laughlin's "primary goal has been to publish literature that, without consideration for profit, [he] deems first rate."

The Ws-Laughlin relationship began in 1934, initiating a three-year period in which "Williams assumed a fatherly tone, as he offered Laughlin poems for his various literary projects" and continuing through the publication of *White Mule* in 1937. In late 1937, Ws, showing he regarded New Directions as an experimental press and that he desired some commercial success, wrote Laughlin that "he might take *Yes, Mrs. Williams* to a commercial press on the assumption that Laughlin would not accept anything except serious verse." This proposal threatened a breach in their relationship, a breach that was quickly repaired when Laughlin wrote Ws, "You are the cornerstone of New Directions." The second phase (1937-1939) was characterized by "a good personal relationship and a satisfactory publishing arrangement . . . [and was a period in which] Laughlin assumed the editorial stance that would prevail until Williams' return after the estrangement in 1960: he published the manuscript with virtually no suggestions for revision (correcting only the numerous misspellings)." In 1940, with "New Directions better established . . . the third phase of the relationship began: neglect on Laughlin's part [as he put others in charge of operating details] and discontent on Williams' part." A new phase of their relationship began in 1950, when Ws wrote Laughlin of his decision to engage David McDowell, who had just gone to Random House, as editor of "his non-poetic works." During Ws' ten years "official" hiatus from New Directions, Ziegfeld writes, he "allowed Laughlin to retain the rights to the poetry," and the two maintained their close "personal friendship." Then, when "the McDowell, Obolensky firm broke up" in 1960, Ws indicated his wish to return entirely to New Directions when he wrote Laughlin that "he was severing his connection with McDowell and wanted to know if Laughlin was interested in *Many Loves and Other Plays*." During this last phase, Laughlin worked patiently and tirelessly in helping Ws to revise and edit his work, labors made doubly difficult after "Williams' second stroke (1958) had caused severe aphasia that seriously affected his diction and his ability to communicate his thoughts logically." Ziegfeld concludes with Laughlin's posthumous tribute to Ws, as man and poet.

153. Baldwin, Neil. "Zukofsky, Williams, and *The Wedge*: Toward a Dynamic of Convergence." In *Louis Zukofsky: Man and Poet*. Ed. Carroll F. Terrell. Orono, Me.: Nat'l Poetry Foundation, 1979. Pp. 129-42.

Noting that, though Ws despaired that his *Spring and All* (1923) "had no circulation at all," he had at the time, in Zukofsky, at least one enthusiastic reader (the book, Baldwin writes, shows "basic affinities shared by these two poets, because it is primarily on and about 'things,' an itemized cataloguing in a condensed Whitman mode"), Baldwin examines Zukofsky's help, 20 years later, in shaping and preparing "another important, threshold collection of poems: *The Wedge.*" Baldwin writes of the developing relationship of the two poets, and then of Zukofsky's editorial advice "and Williams' wholehearted integration" of it into his book.

The two poets were brought together by Pound in 1928, kept abreast of each other's work (especially Zukofsky of the 17-years older Ws'), and with Charles Reznikoff "created the Objectivist atmosphere of the 1930's." Ws began assembling materials for *The Wedge* in 1938; and "the manuscript he sent to Zukofsky for his perusal and commentary in March 1943." Baldwin describes in detail, and also categorizes, Zukofsky's editorial recommendations, which are written in pencil on the MSS. The most recurrent and persistent are suggestions for cutting and tightening; and these were suggestions that Ws acted on: "What began as The (lang) WEDGE, an amorphous, retrospective, wide-ranging collection of 115 pages and 83 titles, was now (more simply) trimmed to *The Language*: 86 pages, 69 titles, in four sections arranged by Zukofsky" and published in 1944. Moreover, a fuller measure of Zukofsky's importance to Ws' career is indicated by Baldwin's claim that "*The Wedge* can be seen as a threshold work, opening the way for Williams to *Paterson I*" (1946).

154. Fischer, Michael. "Rehabilitating Reference: Charles Altieri's 'Presence and Reference in a Literary Text,' " *CritI*, 6, (1979), 343-45.

Fischer applauds Altieri in his attempt to reestablish a referential language, but argues that his analysis is flawed and his position still vulnerable to Derrida's deconstructionism. The flaw exists because Altieri does not dispute Derrida's view that " 'art works primarily do not picture or refer to a world' " and because his attributing to poetry a referential "cultural grounding" is simply, within the Derridean perspective, the assertion of a second arbitrary claim (about culture) as a replacement for the earlier one (about nature) which he had surrendered without argument. "This [procedure] is not to refute Derrida but to give him another target, a societal one whose objectivist pretensions he has successfully dismantled on many occasions."

155. Altieri, Charles. "Culture and Skepticism: A Response to Michael Fischer," *CritI*, 6 (1979), 346-54.

Altieri explains that, regarding his dispute with Derrida, he neither intends to "refute skepticism on metaphysical grounds" nor thinks it possible. "Instead, one evades the skeptic's conclusions in two ways: first, by showing that no practical analysis of behavior requires the kinds of ultimate grounds the skeptic calls into question; and second, by challenging the skeptic to work out the practical consequences of his position." Regarding "Fischer's specific criticisms of my claims about culture," Altieri writes,

> I hope to show that Fischer's concern with ultimate grounds leads him to take too abstract a stance toward culture. He uses terms like "arbitrary," "descriptive and evaluative," and

"outside the self" without making the necessary distinctions which I will argue for shortly. This leads him to a narrow view of reference and to a serious confusion between grounds for interpreting what values a person or culture possesses and those grounds for providing moral imperatives that may dictate values and actions. By demanding certainty rather than probabilistic standards, Fischer risks abstract, inflexible moral standards and seriously reduces the range and quality of the moral distinctions culture can provide.

These goals Altieri pursues with the aid of "the later Wittgenstein." His reply has no references to Ws.

156. Gibbons, Reginald, ed. *The Poet's Work: 29 Masters of 20th Century Poetry on the Origins and Practice of Their Art.* Boston: Houghton Mifflin, 1979.
Review by C. Clausen, in *SewaneeR*, 88 (1980), 497-98.

Gibbons' book includes essays by English, American and foreign poets; included among the Americans are Stevens, Ws, Marianne Moore, Hart Crane, Karl Shapiro, and Gary Snyder. Most of Clausen's brief commentary is given to Stevens' "The Irrational Element in Poetry" and to Karl Shapiro's remarks, in this same collection, on that subject. Clausen detects in these essays a growing wariness of reason, "as if the defenders of poetry . . . have been afraid that the touch of reason might be fatal to their enterprise," and concludes with the precept, "the separation of reason and the imagination impoverishes both."

157. Jackson, Thomas H. "Positivism and Modern Poetics: Yeats, Mallarmé, and William Carlos Williams," *ELH*, 46 (1979), 509-40.

Jackson usefully supplies an abstract of his article:

The following pages propose to restore, at least for the duration of the essay they constitute, the historicality of some specific issues in applied poetic theory. That vigorous school of modern criticism perhaps represented most dramatically at the moment by Joseph Riddel's study of William Carlos Williams, *The Inverted Bell*, centers on a kind of ontological absolutism, presenting itself as a series of attempts to define the absolute essence (or the absolute essencelessness) of the works it focuses on. But it remains profitable to see the various developments in modern poetry in a historical framework, to allow some diachronic blood to flow through the veins of synchronism. What I propose to do is place in relation and in a context the work and theories of Mallarmé, Yeats, and—to a remarkable extent the realizer of their goals, I shall claim—William Carlos Williams. The framework I have in mind, identified broadly, is the cultural struggle over positivism and its offshoots that characterized much of the nineteenth century and which became particularly acute during the latter years of the century. More accurately and inclusively described, it is an entire turn-of-the-century movement toward a philosophical pluralism that comprised work by minds so superficially diverse as Wittgenstein, Whitehead, Mach, Freud, Karl Kraus, Merleau-Ponty, Heidegger, and Husserl.

To this, and before his exposition, he adds "a few general claims":

> I begin with a few general claims. First, among early twentieth-century poets William Carlos Williams was the prime modernist—more a modernist than Pound, than Eliot, than Yeats, more articulately a modernist than Wallace Stevens. Second, his work resolves more powerfully and more elegantly than the *oeuvre* of any other twentieth-century poet the problems posed for imaginative discourse by the sway of Positivist habits of thought about the limits of reason. Third, though in the end he was very different from both of them, he was anticipated in certain important aspects of his endeavors by the early Yeats and by Mallarmé. His accomplishment of what my second claim asserts can be seen both in the practice of his lyric poems and in the theory of the lyric that I think underlies the poems themselves.

158. Lloyd, Margaret Glynne. *William Carlos Williams' "Paterson":
A Critical Reappraisal.* Rutherford: Fairleigh Dickinson UP,
1979.
Review by Hugh Haughton, in *TLS,* 4 December 1981, Pp.
1424-25.

Haughton's review is of both Lloyd's book and Don Byrd's *Charles Olson's "Maximus";* he finds they have much in common and often writes of both in his statements. Haughton honors the tradition of the American epic originating with Whitman, and more specifically of "the long poem in English that has been an almost exclusively American preserve in this century," but finds the two books "so dull and so irrelevant" as to dishonor it. "Both books are nothing if not academic—what Olson curtly called 'professor stuff.' They don't show the first idea of how poetry works or of what reading a poem is like; and the shadow of the Blatant Beast of the PhD thesis falls heavily across them." Another problem is that "Lloyd and Byrd not only do not judge the effectiveness of poetry, but their expositions of Williams's and Olson's 'open' and self-defining theories of poetic composition do not provide any possibility of *falli-bility,* and criterion of *falsifiability* [HH's italics] . . . both in their different ways imply that whatever is (in the poems) is right."

Writing more specifically about Lloyd's book, Haughton lashes it for giving a "caricatured version" of the weaknesses some critics allege to its subject:

> Under Margaret Lloyd's conscientious scrutiny, *Paterson* becomes as dull as ditchwater—a plodding provincial epic based on very vague sociological accounts of the city (by Mumford, Spengler, and others), written in a worthy pedestrian style which is beyond reproach, a modern equivalent of *The Excursion,* perhaps, mixing plain moral reflections with a diffused sense of personal ecstasy. She sums up her argument like this: "Accordingly as we have seen, the content, measure, and overall organisation of *Paterson* is a product of a direct contract and engagement with the factors, the people, and the general dynamics of his environment as well as the new relativistic concepts of reality with which Williams became familiar". She talks about the poem's search for a redeeming language, but hers redeems nothing and is unredeemably blank. She talks about Williams's

"critical thinking in relation to the poem" and concludes it "has much in common with modern genre theory"—as if that meant anything, or could justify the profundity of Williams's conceptions. Her initial world is one in which everything Williams does has "much in common" with what other writers or authorities of some kind have written: she defends Williams by saying he is like X or Y, and she picks her way among the critics, repeating "as X has said", "as Y argued", or "but Z asserted", creating a mosaic of quotations from other people, or from Williams's work, to build up an impression of terrible consistency, even unanimity.

Ws' own voice sounds crystal "real" in the midst of this mélange, Haughton writes (but then one can read/hear him both free of the mélange and in the company of better critics). However, "there is the grave danger at the best of times that Williams will be seen as a dull, 'sincere' poet, or a drastically stupid one (as Winters and Jarrell claimed)—and this pious book does him a profound disservice by making him seem both."

159. Miller, James E., Jr. *The American Quest for a Supreme Fiction/ Whitman's Legacy in the Personal Epic.* Chicago and London: Univ. of Chicago Pr., 1979.
Review by M. L. Rosenthal, *ConL*, 22:iii (1981), 374-76.

Rosenthal declares Miller's thesis is, "very simply,"

Walt Whitman created a peculiarly American form of modern "epic," with confessional elements that make it a "personal epic" as well, and our modern poets of substance have been following through significantly. The modern models discussed are, in order (after the opening chapter on *Leaves of Grass*): Stevens' *Notes toward a Supreme Fiction*, Pound's *Cantos*, Eliot's *The Waste Land*, Williams' *Paterson*, Crane's *The Bridge*, Olson's *The Maximus Poems*, Berryman's *Dream-Songs*, and Ginsberg's *The Fall of America*.

He continues (and let me add that Rosenthal writes so perceptively, precisely, and cogently that I'm loathe to paraphrase his statements),

This is a book full of love for its subject and truly interested in the poetry it discusses. It is full of hurrahs, starting with the always necessary reaffirmation of Whitman's original and indigenous power and his continuous communion with our poets in this century. . . . How pervasive the communion is felt to be is curiously reflected in two passages many pages apart. On page 52 Harold Bloom is quoted as claiming that *Notes toward a Supreme Fiction* is "the *Song of Myself* of our time," and on page 120 Robert Lowell is quoted as claiming that *Paterson* "is our *Leaves of Grass*." Lowell was closer to the mark in seeing the artistic kinship of two earthy improvisers, extremely volatile and projecting their sensuous alertness in every key and context of awareness. The claim for Stevens, on the other hand, is patently forced, despite certain echoes and thematic links. Lowell's remark is a poet's recognition of a special sort of art. The two declarations, Bloom's and Lowell's, are left unexamined and unreconciled. It is characteristic of this study that it provides materials aplenty for relevant contemplation without focusing on the essential idiosyncratic process and achievement of each work it discusses.

Let me labor this point a little. Mr. Miller quotes copiously from his poets, demonstrating connections with Whitman,

intellectual preoccupations, and psychological or sexual resonances, and he makes some general points about style and form.
How good or bad is the poetry quoted? On the whole this is not
a central question of the book. Yet it must be central to thinking
about whether or not a mode of poetry—indeed a proposed
genre—really counts, and whether ideas about it are valid. For
instance, the word "epic" is given great weight, and indeed
there is an "epic" dimension to the great modern sequences. But
the character of the sequence has its own poetics (not quite
that of "long poems," the term used in the opening sentence of
the preface), and that poetics calls for evaluative as well as
thematic description of its models.

Rosenthal concludes that "the book starts all sorts of hares
delightfully, yet leaves its subject companionably open to others"
(which is one effect of another quality Rosenthal earlier cited in
Miller's book—the author's "commendably generous openness of
mind"). "It is a most valuable book in its own right: a wholesome,
highly specific contribution both in its receptivity to the poets'
actual writings and in its human liveliness and directness."

160. Morgan, Richard J. "Chaos and Order: The Cycle of Life
and Art in Williams' *Spring and All*," *Interpretations*, 11
(1979), 35-51.

161. Ober, William B. *Boswell's Clap and Other Essays: Medical
Analyses of Literary Men's Afflictions*. Southern Ill. UP,
1979.
Review by Theodore Ziolkowski, in *SewaneeR*, 89 (Fall
1981), 657-59.

The book's subject, writes Ziolkowski, "as the subtitle specifies,"
is the "medical analyses of literary men's afflictions"—medical
analyses written by a doctor, he hastens to add, who is neither a
writer nor a critic. Ziolowski finds little to praise and much to
berate in both Ober's information and his judgments, a negative
view one readily understands in the shades of Ober's chapter on Ws:

Following a short piece in which he counts the doctors in
Chekhov's works, Ober turns his attention to William Carlos
Williams. If Ober has little patience with critics, he has even less
with physicians so mush-minded that they write poetry in their
spare time. "This may be one reason why Williams went into
general practice, and I became a pathologist. He was willing to
accept the world and people in it as they were; I reserve the right
to review them under the microscope and look daily at their
weaknesses, faults, malformations, and diseases." Ober is no less
stern with Williams's poetry than with his character, objecting
to his "lack of discipline" as well as his "lack of self-criticism."
Paterson is "a defective masterpiece," and the section on Lincoln
in *In the American Grain* is offensive to Ober. "As a doctor,
Williams may have buried his mistakes; as a poet, he published
them."

162. Peterfreund, Stuart. "Vision and Revision in Keats and
Williams," *Lamar Jour. of the Humanities*, 5:ii (1979),
28-39.

Peterfreund writes of the competitive influence (or, in Bloom's term, the "anxiety of influence") that Keats exerted on Ws. He argues that

> Keats is recast by Williams in much the same way that Keats recasts Milton. Williams, in *Paterson*, takes the Keatsian quest for beauty as it is rendered in *Endymion*, and revises it to a quest for "rigor of beauty." The difference of terminology would appear superficial, were we to fail to bear in mind the fact that Keats's poem celebrates the successful attainment of "a thing of beauty," whereas Williams queries: "how will you find beauty when it is locked up in the mind past all remonstrance?" Just as Keats frames the Judeo-Christian quest for salvation in terms of a secular quest for beauty, then, Williams frames the quest for beauty in terms of a quest for rigor of beauty. In both cases the reformulation is necessitated by virtue of the fact that the terms and conditions of a prior world view no longer hold current.

Peterfreund finds reason to believe that "The Wanderer" (said by Ws to be "a reconstruction from memory of my earlier Keatsian *Endymion* imitation that I destroyed") shows Ws "revising Keats a good deal earlier than most commentators have readily granted." Later poems, dating from 1921 to 1955, contain Keatsian "references or allusions": and "all show certain shared characteristics. They are wryly quarrelsome with the purpose of issuing a corrective. And the quarrel and the corrective always concern these three related questions: what takes beauty's place as poetry's subject in the present time, how is it perceived, and how does the poet portray it?" In support of these views Peterfreund compares Ws' "The Nightingales" and Keats' "Ode to a Nightingale." The rest of his article analyzes the competitive influence of *Endymion* on *Paterson*:

> Seen in perspective, Williams' repeated corrections of Keats bear the same relationship to *Paterson* that satire does to epic or prophecy in the classical progression of genres. The repeated emphasis and ridicule of what should not be lead the poet to a comprehensive vision of what should be. And just as for a poet like Blake, satire, a good deal of it literary, must precede the Prophetic Books, so, for a poet like Williams, the satires of Keats are at least in part responsible for the articulation of a comprehensive vision, or revision, if you will, in *Paterson*. The poem's theme, narrative structure, and characterization are all in large measure dependent on raw materials supplied by Keats's *Endymion*. But the dependency, informed by a good deal of revision prior to the composition of *Paterson*, transcends the sort of summative borrowing Williams sees as being the genius of Eliot and those like him.

>> We must value them—the extractors of genius—for what they do: extract. But they are there; we are here. It is not possible for us to imitate them. We are in a different phase—a new language—we are making the mass in which some other later Eliot will dig.

> What Williams does not say in this context is that the makers of the new "mass"—the vision, whole-cloth—must fabricate it in terms of the old, must commit what might be called "the prophetic fallacy," for in order to set forth a holistic and wholly comprehensible vision of present and future, one must needs make analogical links to a wholly understood past. Only by likening his vision of the present in *Paterson* to a corresponding vision in *Endymion*, in other words, can Williams articulate that vision for himself and his audience.

163. Riddel, Joseph. "Decentering the Image: The 'Project' of 'American' Poetics?" In *Textual Strategies/ Perspectives in Post-Structuralist Criticism*. Ed. Josué V. Harani. Ithaca: Cornell UP, 1979. Pp. 322-58.

Riddel's language trills and soars in compositional figures, allusions to tradition, and critical terminology; he can best speak for himself:

I begin by putting the question in quotation marks. "American literature" is an oxymoron—a notion of the belated original, of the immaculate opening of an old closure. "American literature" has always been inscribed in such a questioning parenthesis, because its dream of "making it new," of realizing itself originally, begins with the contradiction inherent in the notion of original or creative "literature," of an original secondariness. What is called the modern, and "American literature" has always been "modern"—that is, inscribed as both an end and a beginning between two notions of history—is always an "event" that is logically anterior yet historically posterior to that literature we call traditional or classical. "American literature" has always played in the paradoxical margins of the "new." One has only to mention the double sense of "tradition" that obsesses our modernist experimenters, the makers of the modern Image, to understand the contradiction Paul de Man finds in the privileged notion of the "modern." To "make it new" means in one sense (for example, T. S. Eliot's) to supplement the tradition, to add something to an already completed whole; but it also means to repeat the moment of some pure origin that has been obscured by history's lengthened shadow, and hence to rewrite the whole. "American literature," we might say, is a search which repeatedly suspends the dream of literature, the dream of totalization, of poetic closure. In this, of course, it simply makes explicit, by repetition, the subversive element in all literature, the "double sense" contained in every "sense of an ending." Once achieved, The Great American Novel would be the end of "American literature"; that is why we have so many of them, and why it is always "to be written."

William Carlos Williams's long poem *Paterson* puts the question of the "American" crisis most directly: how can a new beginning be original? "How to begin to find a shape—to begin to begin again, / turning the inside out: to find one phrase that will / lie married beside another for delight?" In its context this question leads directly to a quotation, a statement once made by the British poet George Barker: "*American poetry is a very easy subject to discuss for the simple reason that it does not exist*" (Book Three, *Paterson*). It is always situated in a borrowed language, and in a tradition that, as Emerson saw, would not close. To "exist," an American poetry would have to write that closure, and repeat an opening that had already always begun. In Emerson's sense, the poet of the present must be the genius: "Next to the originator of a good sentence is the first quoter of it. . . . there are great ways of borrowing. Genius borrows nobly" ("Quotation and Originality"). Williams and his poem compose one figure, one more repetition, in a line of so-called American Adamic poets, running, let us say for historical convenience, from Emerson's call for a purely American idiom to Charles Olson's announcement of the forward thrust of "Projective Verse." This is a somewhat arbitrary line, not a "history" at all, but a metaphor for all the new beginnings that dot the "development" of an "American poetry" which does not yet exist.

As to his subject and thesis:

> Indeed, we might explore one sequence of those repetitions, where the historical possibility of an unbroken, continuous development does seem present, as the measure of the "project." I am referring to what literary history calls the "Imagist movement," obviously an international rather than an American revolution, but a movement nevertheless indirectly tied to Emerson. For Imagism led successively to movements with counternames— Vorticism, Objectivism, even Objectism—and to in-mixtures with continental movements like Dadaism, Surrealism, and Cubism. From Emerson to Olson, there is not a straight line but a movement of appropriations, of decenterings, of repetitions that manage to keep the possibility of an "American" poetry open.

Other than the above original and exemplary elevation, Ws is not mentioned in the essay. Riddel's focus is on Pound and Olson, most especially the latter.

164. Rodgers, Audrey T. *The Universal Drum: Dance Imagery in the Poetry of Eliot, Crane, Roethke and Williams.* University Park: Penn. State UP, 1979.
Review by Jerome Mazzaro, in *AL*, 52 (1980), 503-504.

> Mazzaro finds a number of weaknesses in Rodgers' book. Thematically, it "treats dance imagery as central in the poetry of T. S. Eliot, Hart Crane, Theodore Roethke, William Carlos Williams," arguing that "dance becomes 'one means for expressing a complex set of emotional and intellectual states' wherein 'the spiritual expression' that moves for Isadora Duncan 'into the channels of the body, filling it with vibrating light,' shapes each poet's distinct body of work." Mazzaro finds Rodgers' argument linking dance and poetry as expressive modes lacking adequate development. More seriously, Mazzaro faults her scholarship for being limited. Though one would guess it might be limited because there is little available scholarship and criticism on the dance and literature, the problem extends further: Mazzaro finds chinks in Rodgers' analyses that might have been avoided had the research been adequate. He writes that Rodgers' "own readings provide the bases for the presentations of Roethke and Williams, and . . . the research seems weak." Specifically, errors would have been avoided had she read Bram Dijkstra's *The Hieroglyphics of a New Speech* (1970), and some Brueghel scholarship to clarify the meaning of Kermesse.

165. Salomon, Roger B. "The Mock-Heroics of Desire: Some Stoic Personae in the Work of William Carlos Williams." In *The Stoic Strain in American Literature: Essays in Honor of Marston LaFrance.* Ed. Duane J. MacMillan. Toronto: Univ. of Toronto Pr., 1979. Pp. 97-112.

> Salomon argues that Ws (and Stevens) is a major late romantic. Being of the "later generation of romantics, . . . the transcendental dimension" in which earlier romantics had found a correspondent to the self and its desire "has [for Ws] disappeared completely." What is left is "the continuing claim of the imagination as *the* source of

value, but a claim now in active confrontation with material reality" [RBS's italics]. And the modern late romantic finds that reality to be either "a positive and attractive vehicle for the imaginative tracings of the self," or, in one of Ws' terms, "a pustular scum, a decay, a choking/lifelessness." Salomon's article focuses on the ironic, mock-heroic response in Ws' work to this latter, negative perception of reality, a mock-heroic of a kind for which he finds the prototype in Cervantes:

> In short, the paradoxes of later stoic humanism as explored by Cervantes find striking corroboration in the ambivalent commitments of the modern romantic sensibility. . . . Mock-heroic—as an attitude, a mode of characterization, indeed a form of narrative with its own stylistic determinants—expresses a rich, complex, and continuing tradition. It is to other mock-heroes of Williams that we must now turn for further explorations of this particular sensibility.

With the qualification that "Williams's personae, of course, are quixotic not in their pursuit of abstract, obsolete ideals and social conventions, but, just the opposite, in their equally determined commitment to the new, the fresh, the improvisational, dissonant, and existential," Salomon develops the above ideas as encountered in the texts of *Kora in Hell, In the American Grain, The Great American Novel, Selected Poems, Pictures from Brueghel,* and *Paterson.*

166. Saunier-Ollier, Jacqueline. "Dans le sillage de l'Amory Show: Immaculés et objectivistes," *Revue Française d'Études Américaines,* 7 (1979), 51-65.

167. Saunier-Ollier, Jacqueline. *William Carlos Williams: L'Homme et l'Oeuvre Poétique.* (Publications de la Faculté des Lettres et Sciences Humaines de Nice, XVII) Nice: Les Belles Lettres, 1979.
Review by Marjorie Perloff, *WCWR,* 6:i (Spring 1980), 27-30.

Perloff basically writes that though this study, at 648 pages, is far longer than any critical book in English on Ws, it contains much less. Mme. Saunier-Ollier has done her scholarship. She

> has had access to the Williams archives at Yale and Buffalo, and she seems to have read very widely in the Williams correspondence, the Little Magazines of the period, and the critical commentary on Williams written during his lifetime. Her book also reproduces large chunks of the poet's own writings, especially the *Autobiography,* which appears, a bit here, a bit there, almost *in toto* in the course of the study. Chapter 2, "Une Enfance Lyrique," for example, is made up almost entirely of extracts from the *Autobiography,* with generous helpings from *I Wanted to Write a Poem* and the *Selected Letters.*

As to the biographical part, Saunier-Ollier relies trustingly on the *Autobiography;* and her "narrative of [Ws' life] . . . turns out to be a fairly simplified success story."

Critical quality is largely likewise missing, Perloff writes; Saunier-Ollier "seems to have no real attitude toward her material.

It is initially assumed that Williams is a major modern poet, and the rest simply follows. Accordingly, when Saunier-Ollier turns to the poetry, she is somewhat at a loss." Her loss is mainly evidenced by a critical approach of cataloguing—"trees, flowers, sun, stars, household objects" in addition to more complex and elaborate entities.

The strengths of the book are "two useful chapters on form and versification," the latter of which "has a more detailed account of Williams' verse forms, stress patterns, and habits of lineation than do most Anglo-American studies of the poetry." Perloff adds that "the discussion of the triadic foot [is] especially helpful."

However, the book has exceedingly little information on the subject its author would seem superbly situated for—"Williams reception in France"; her four pages on this subject in *WCWN*, 4 (Fall 1978) is more informative, Perloff finds, than the book's offering. Though the study "is obviously a labor of love," it lacks a "clear sense of audience," Perloff concludes. It is too long and detailed for French readers, and "too naively intentionalist, too doggedly explicative," for Anglo-Americans.

168. Sewell, W. S. "Hans Magnus Enzensberger and William Carlos Williams: Economy, Detail and Suspicion of Doctrine," *GL&L*, 32 (1979), 153-65.

Sewell writes of Ws' influence on the German poet, born in 1929. Enzensberger included five poems by Ws—three of them in his own translation—in "an anthology of international modern poetry, *Museum der modernen Poesie*, which he edited in 1960; and two years later appeared a "bi-lingual volume containing fifty-eight of Williams's poems, both selected and translated by Enzensberger." The two Ws poems analyzed in the article, "Between Walls" and "Pastoral," are included in that selection.

The major forces of influence, Sewell writes, are indicated in the triad of his title: "a highly economical and controlled style of writing; the insight gained from the careful scrutiny of a commonplace object normally taken for granted; and finally an individual frame of mind which insists on change, is always open to doubt, and which cannot be tied down to the abstraction of an inflexible artistic or political creed."

169. Tashjian, Dickran. "New York Dada and Primitivism," in *Dada Spectrum: The Dialectics of Revolt*. Ed. stephen c. foster and rudolf e. kuenzli. Madison, WI: coda press, 1979. Pp. 116-44.

A follow-up of Tashjian's *Skyscraper Primitives: Dada and the American Avant-Garde, 1910-1925* (1975), this article is largely a history of New York Dada and its affinities with primitivism. Tashjian's canvas is copious (covering both visual and verbal arts), and for Ws' students the article mainly provides information on one of Ws' artistic and social environments of the late 1910s and early '20s. Tashjian does touch on Marsden Hartley's and Ws' esthetic commitment to the local, as propounded and realized in their magazine *Contact*. And characterizing Ws' relations to Dada he writes that for Ws

> Dada provided rebellion at closehand, a way to vent one's disgust. And Williams had plenty of disgust—for the stupidity of critics and commercial publishers, for the provincialism of American writers in imitating the English, for the indifference of his neighbors toward his poetry. Dada rebellion might clear a space for fresh art in America. That was precisely what he had to lose with Dada. He had to guard almost jealously the Contact idea against the emblandishments of Dada. How could he create an art of the local through foreign means? The dilemma was complex, and so was his resolution. It took him years to work out Dada on his own terms involving the subterfuge of rejecting Dada while accepting its art/anti-art tensions. The process took place in those works of the early 1920s: *Kora in Hell* (1920), *Sour Grapes* (1921), *Spring and All* (1923), *The Great American Novel* (1923), and *In The American Grain* (1925).

Amply illus.

170. Tashjian, Dickran. *William Carlos Williams and The American Scene, 1920-1940*. Whitney Museum of American Art, New York, in association with the Univ. of California Pr., Berkeley, 1979.
Review by Joel Conarroe, *WCWN*, 5:i (Spring 1979), 23-25.

Conarroe—fortunate man!—was in New York during the two months of the exhibition; and his review is of both the exhibit and the book. He quotes Ws on our need of artists to make us see ("we have to see, be taught to see. We have to be taught to see *here*, because here is everywhere, related to everywhere else.") and adds, "To see *here*: this is what the Whitney show . . . was all about."

The show located Ws "in the context of painters he knew and admired, and of others whose work shares certain characteristics with his own." Included was work by Hartley, Sheeler, Marin, O'Keeffe, Davis, Benton, and Gorky, in addition to "photographs, books, little magazines, a Williams self-portrait, and sculpture." The designated areas/topics of the exhibit included "An American Place," "Proletarian Portrait," "Rural America," "Ethnicity and Folk Identity," "Precisionism," "Perpetuum Mobile: the City," and "America Fantasia," groupings which, though "somewhat arbitrary" and with some "unimpressive" paintings, made a "resonant and instructive" exhibit.

The book, physically, Conarroe describes as "elegant, with good reproductions (several in color) and clear, legible type. The chapters replicate the rooms in the show, so that one can browse through, looking, judging, questioning." But the text he finds less satisfactory:

> Mr. Tashjian's text provides carefully researched information on the individual works as well as material on the historical and aesthetic backgrounds. This commentary, unfortunately, is presented in prose that is frequently graceless. The sentence structure is needlessly tangled; even the syntax and spelling are erratic. It is surprising that anyone intimate with Williams could be on such casual terms with clear writing, or so taken by words like "mechanamorphics," "volumetric," "agribusiness."

171. 1979 Dissertations

A. Holloway, David. "Attitudes to Objectivity: A Contrasting Study of Wallace Stevens and William Carlos Williams." Oxford University, 1979. Supervisor: Charles Tomlinson.

B. Semmler, Iliana Alexandra. "How Deep Is the Water? Sexuality in the Work of William Carlos Williams." State University of New York at Albany, 1979. Chairman: Donald B. Stauffer. *DAI* 40:4600A.

C. Walker, David Lewis. "The Transparent Lyric: Stylistic Strategies in the Poetry of Stevens and Williams."Cornell University, 1979. *DAI* 40:3293A-94A. A study of the fundamental differences which derive from the characteristic premises of Stevens and Williams, two temperamentally at-odds poets.

1980

172. Singleton, Robert R. *"Kora in Hell*: Certain 'Fools' Identified," *AN&Q*, 18 (February 1980), 90-92.

Singleton identifies four "fools" (the allusion is to *Kora*'s opening line: "Fools have big wombs.")–those in I.3, V.2, XVIII.2, and XVI.2 via passages from a letter Ws wrote to Robert Lowell, the *Autobiography*, and the poem "To a Friend" in *Sour Grapes*.

173. Fender, Stephen. "The marriage of flesh and air," *TLS*, 30 May 1980, pp. 617-18.

Though this is listed among the main Williams entries of the 1980 *PMLA Bibliography*, except for its strong rhetoric in the right cause it's unclear why it appears there. Fender writes principally a review of two books, the bulk of it of Doggett's and Buttel's *Wallace Stevens: A Celebration.* Charles Doyle's *William Carlos Williams/ The Critical Heritage* is the Ws' item; but Fender writes little of it.

He instead castigates English teachers and readers for their neglect and indifference to Ws (none of Ws' books were printed in England between "1909, when Ezra Pound arranged publication of *The Tempers*," and an English edition of *Pictures from Brueghel* in 1963), and indicts the English literary establishment–represented by the *Scrutiny* group–for its continuing advocacy of T. S. Eliot, pedantic values, and tepid tastes. He concludes,

> I think that teachers of English have turned their backs not just on modern American poetry but that whole apocalyptic strain in English writing, from *Piers Plowman*, through *The Faerie Queene*, Blake's Prophetic Books, Whitman, Pound's *Cantos* and Olson's *Maximus* Poems, which mimes the abolition of priestly/ poetic mediation between God/author and worshipper/reader, with the result that the work is both synthetic and unclosed. They have rejected it because it is subversive–to tradition, to convention, to all which they are charged with upholding–just as three centuries ago their kingly forebears rejected the experiment of the English Republic.

174. Huberman, Elizabeth. "The First *First President*" (Review-Essay), *WCWR*, 6:i (Spring 1980), 23-26.

> A brief description of the William Carlos Williams Festival at Kean College of New Jersey on May 12, 1979, encompassing readings from his work, scholarly papers, slide shows, films, and a performance of Ws' "one-act play, 'Under the Stars.' " With a lengthier account of the background of Ws' opera *The First President* and a review of the performance at the Festival.

175. Kodolányi, Gyula. "Ideas of the New in Modern Poetry: Notes on the Anglo-American Tradition," *WCWR*, 6:i (Spring 1980), 11-22.

> As the title suggests, G. Kodolányi, of the University of Budapest, writes a wide-ranging, and knowledgeable, essay on Anglo-American modernism as contrasted to "the Continental modernist movements." Artists of the latter group "speaking about the moving forces behind their achievements" refer to "social, psychological, or technological" conditions and theories, whereas, Kodolányi writes, taking Pound's "Imagist Credo" as representative, Anglo-American modernism is focused in "four terms: *rhythm*, the natural object as the natural *symbol, technique, form* [GK's emphases]."
>
> Ws appears basically twice in the essay. First in a description of his encounters with the exiled Hungarian poet, Lajos Kassák, in Vienna in 1924—encounters which, despite the fact the two shared much in temperament, interests, and artistic assumptions, illustrated the basic aesthetic "differences between the Anglo-American and the Continental approach." The other reference, to *Paterson*, characterizes it as showing a modification of the dominant Anglo-American aesthetic that is Kodolányi's subject. Written during a period when Ws "maintained a keen interest in a unifying structural approach to all the phenomena of the world," Ws'
>
>> interest found its way, among other scientific facts, into the poem *Paterson*, which remains the greatest modern attempt in English to fuse in poetry the "trite" historical documents of an industrial city, and our essential emotions, love and hate of each other and of the four primordial elements, that is to say, to fuse extremes of the objective and the subjective, of universal and particular.
>
> As for the dominant Anglo-American modernist aesthetic, Kodolányi concludes,
>
>> it seems that English and American poets have concentrated their efforts more on introducing into the current the new scientific vision of man, the theories of knowledge, communication, and language than the forms of radical social consciousness, of the exploration of the subjective, of the structure of the psyche.

176. Slatin, John M. "The War of the Roses: Williams, Eliot, Moore," *WCWR*, 6:i (Spring 1980), 1-10.

> In Ws' "war" against Eliot, especially after the appearance of *The Waste Land*, he drew upon Marianne Moore's poetry, Slatin writes,

to bolster his attack. Specifically, he argues, "The pages of *Spring and All* are studded with reference to her and her work, [which] references are all of a piece." For in that book, Ws' aim is to free poetry from "the predicament in which . . . the descriptive emphasis of the Imagists had involved it" and to mount "effective native opposition, both theoretical and practical, to Eliot's brilliant, commanding deployment of the forces of tradition." In this campaign, Moore "provided not so much a model as a point of departure, . . . a suggestion which seemed implicit in her procedure, that the word was the focal point of the attack: cut away the 'attachments' and the 'pleasing wraiths' with which the word has been burdened by successive generations of poetic usage, and it can again be used . . . as one of the 'constructive' elements of which a poem is built—as, in Williams' analogy, a house is built of bricks."

After outlining Ws' conception of the relation of word, object, and poem as opposed to Eliot's emphasis (upon tradition for the poet and the poem) and to Harold Bloom's extension of Eliot's poetic ontology, Slatin writes,

> For Williams the poem is continuous neither with Nature nor with Poetry, but is rather contiguous to both, and not to be confused with either. He says in *Spring and All* that the poem and nature exist in simultaneous *opposition* and *apposition* to each other (I, 121), and the same terms may be applied with equal force not only to his conception of the ideal relation between particular poems, but also to his conception of the relation between any given poem and the larger canon of what has already been accepted and legitimized as poetry. His test of poetic strength is thus necessarily at odds with that proposed by Eliot in 1919 and later revised by Bloom: Williams is not so much concerned with the kind of strength which allows one's poetic ancestors to make themselves audible as he is with that strength which enables the poet to "cleave . . . away" from the tradition (I, 101).

Quoting some of Ws' praises of Moore in *Spring and All*, Slatin says that Ws was attracted to "Moore's ability to cut words loose from their conventional or traditional 'attachments.' " He suggests that this is the quality that prompted Ws to respond to her "Roses Only" (1917), but quoted by Slatin from *"Poems* (1921), the collection with which Williams was probably most familiar") by writing the *Spring and All* poem beginning "The rose is absolute." Slatin analyzes each poem to show that Ws, starting his poem "from the point . . . where Moore's poem leaves off," by extension constructed his own poem exemplfying his critical position.

177. Tashjian, Dickran. *"The Little Review* Vers Libre Contest, 1916," *WCWR*, 6:i (Spring 1980), 33.

Williams, with "Helen Holt, and Zoë Aikens, later replaced by Eunice Tietjens," was one of the judges for this contest. "Margaret Anderson published the runners-up [verses] and quoted the judges' reasons for their selections," from both of which Tashjian quotes extracts for what they show of Ws' "poetic criteria in 1917."

178. Schmidt, Peter. "Some Versions of Modernist Pastoral: Williams and the Precisionists," *ConL*, 21 (Summer 1980), 383-406.

      Writing that, though much attention has been given to Ws' relation to the visual arts, most is on the "biographical influences" and little is esthetic analysis, Schmidt undertakes "a reconsideration of Williams' debt to Stieglitz and the Precisionists" by "defin[ing] the premises of their thought, and then consider[ing] how Williams' poems enlarge, complicate, or even refute those ideas even as they give them voice." Including both painters like Georgia O'Keeffe and Charles Sheeler and "straight photographers" like Stieglitz and Paul Strand among the Precisionists, Schmidt lists as their binding premises (1) the conviction "that images ought to be rendered as precisely as possible," (2) at times a projection of the foreground forward, into the picture, (3) the "principle [that] each picture . . . was primarily a portrait of emotion itself—an objective correlative," while maintaining (4) "that the artist's own presence must be impersonal, even invisible," and (5) a strong nationalistic drive: "Declaring their freedom from European academic traditions, the Precisionists sought for an alternative in American culture [and] found it in America's history of technology efficiency."

      "From the early prologue to *Kora in Hell* to the author's introduction to *The Wedge* (1944)" Ws' critical statements "consistently echoed and elaborated the essential ideals of Precisionism" in an unmodified form, writes Schmidt. His poetry, however, even as it reflects and adopts those ideas, shows an awareness of the "differences between the visual arts and literature." Schmidt analyzes poems from *The Collected Earlier Poems* that show Ws' adoption as well as modifications of Precisionist principles, finding, for example, his "Fine Work in Pitch and Copper" to be his "most eloquent portrait of the Precisionists' industrial Arcadia."

      Turning to Ws' "pastoral lyrics," Schmidt writes that they evidence, among other influences, Ws' "extensive knowledge of literary pastoral traditions," and thus "have a still more complex pedigree" than that of his pastoral visions with their evidences of Sheeler, Demuth, Stieglitz, and Strand. "When I Was Younger" (in *Al Que Quiere!*) "begins with a compressed modern version of the traditional pastoral debate between the natural and artificial" and of its convention of "the 'invitation to love.' " On the whole, writes Schmidt, Ws' most important divergence from the Precisionists is his "more acute sense of the gap between [their] pastoral ideals and American reality." He nevertheless promoted those ideals, believing them "the only possible hope for harnessing the accelerating forces of twentieth-century America for human ends."

      Schmidt concludes with a consideration of the title poem of *Spring and All* and a lengthier look at "Burning the Christmas Greens," a poem which, among other significances, he claims is a response to and refutation of the despair of "To Elsie" and a fine demonstration of Ws' skill in "us[ing] the Precisionist techniques tested in his shorter lyrics to construct a longer poem."

      With illus.

179. Bar-Yaacov, Lois. "Driving into the 20th Century/ A Study of Some William Carlos Williams Poems," *Hebrew Univ. Studies in Lit.*, 8 (Autumn 1980), 261-80.

Bar-Yaacov's ostensible and immediate subject is a small group of Ws' poems "written . . . about and from automobiles" and appearing between 1916 and 1944, but she has another, larger subject and thus delivers more than she promises. She begins with a brief survey of the 19th century conflict between an American art dominated by European forms and a native American expression, with attention to the barriers to the growth and recognition of the latter. She relies on John Kouwenhoven's thesis (in *The Arts in Modern American Civilization*) that while the guardians of the genteel were maintaining standards in the accepted literary art of the period, there developed in this country, unremarked and unhindered, a vernacular art, the issue of "the direct interaction of the folk with a technological and democratic civilization [and] marked primarily by the truth of function." This thesis, she proposes, is a light to "the pioneering quality of Williams' work": "It was exactly the greatness of Williams that he did intuitively grasp that it was only out of destruction of established forms and acceptance of the given conditions of American life that a new imaginative encounter with the essential materials of art could take place."

Bar-Yaacov briefly traces Ws' development from the basic romanticism of *Poems* (1909) through his "farewell to romantic transcendentalism" in "The Wanderer," and up to the first of the automobile poems, poems which enable a microcosmic view of "the way in which an artist who chose not to fly from reality met one of the leading revolutionary forces of the 20th century." (One way evident in these poems, she adds, is Ws' use of the experimental presentation of "modern facts" evolved in the visual arts and articulated in its "new theories.")

The earliest poem examined is "The Avenue of Poplars." This poem presents an expression of "one major aspect of the automobile in modern civilization, a symbol and means of expression for the male sexual drive," as well as of "one of Williams' most persistent intuitions, that the individual unconscious . . . is linked to the collective conscious of mankind." Next is "The Young Housewife," wherein "the natural object [again] serves as a vehicle for exploration of the psyche." The poems after these, from Williams' middle period, illustrate what Townley has defined in that period as the "shift from the 'I' to the 'eye.' " Absent is "the 'I' in any other form than that of the objective recorder of experiences" and the poetry "achieves a simultaneity more characteristic of visual than of verbal art." For example, " 'The Right of Way' . . . is one of the earliest and most successful explorations of mechanized movement in American poetry," a poem which "is, in short, the camera eye moving rather than still, an imitation not of painting or still photography, but of the motion picture." The 1935 "View of a Lake," a depression period poem, reflects the style of "ash-can realism"; and " 'The Forgotten City' . . . returns, if only half-heartedly, to the cinematic technique of 'Right of Way.' "

Bar-Yaacov concludes that in these poems "Williams is deeply attuned to that part of the American tradition of art which posits that the raw material of experience is inherently aesthetic. This tradition has always been at war with the genteel custodians of culture in America, who believed that it was necessary to impose beauty, harmony and proportion on a hostile and unregenerate raw reality." More specifically, Ws' contribution to this vernacular tradition is shown in his choice of " 'a strange commonplace,' rather than [an] ideal landscape. . . . But he was able to join this commonplace to its as yet still possible ideal aspects. To allow the minimum to suffice and still not lose the capacity for intuiting an imaginative whole, 'to lift' the commonplace (without falsifying or transcending it) into the world of imagination, this was his peculiar contribution. Like the skyscraper, like jazz, Williams' poetry is a genuinely original American art form."

180. Christensen, Paul. "The New American Romances," *TCL*, 26 (Fall 1980), 269-77.

Christensen's title accurately states his subject; the individual poems (*The Cantos*, "The Waste Land," *The Bridge, Paterson*, and *The Maximus Poems*) are subordinate to his thesis that "some of the long poems written in this century belong in the tradition of European verse romance." He continues,

> Not only are these works technically alike, they are by poets who knew each other and who shared the same basic perspective that something was fundamentally wrong with their society and with the directions of their culture. These long poems are both critical and prospective: each seeks to redeem industrial society by means of a new ideology, a new system of human values, and a new spiritual order, subjects which have traditionally been the concern of romances. It will be my procedure, then, to examine some major characteristics of romance as a genre, as a basis on which to claim these modern works as romances, and to make some distinctions for romance in the twentieth century from its historic antecedents.

The goal of the romance is a new "vision of reality," of "a mythic reality that is meant to penetrate beyond the limited thought structures of the moment." Whereas "epic is the expression of an age that has achieved a philosophy, which a poet articulates with eloquent certainty, . . . romance is the chief expression of an age that has exhausted its philosophy and seeks a new one." In pursuit of that goal, Christensen writes in his only reference to *Paterson*, the poet "attempts to discover the virtue of a New Jersey city, regardless of the squalor and despair he may find in its daily life. [Ws] celebrates what is simple, earthy, unchanging in man even as the violent industrial setting churns around him. The poem is a romance that projects man unchanged and whole in a technologically alien world."

Christensen concludes that "the spirit of romance is essentially the quest for new bearings after the shock of deep social transformation."

181. Frail, David. " 'The Regular Fourth of July Stuff': William Carlos Williams' Colonial Figures as Poets," *WCWR*, 6:ii (Fall 1980), 1-14.

One of Ws' quests, writes Frail, was an exploration of the American past in pursuit of "an American identity," even of "an authentic American form of himself." That "quest led Williams to shape the identities of historical figures to reflect . . . especially his artistic concerns." On the premise, then, that "Williams' figures from the American past . . . can be read as ideograms of the poet," Frail explores Ws' characterization of Cotton Mather in *In the American Grain* and of George Washington in the libretto of *The First President*.

The Puritans, as represented by Mather, are rather like repressed poets psychologically and, to the knowledgeable, suggest inverted poets in the workings of their moral and religious mania. Frail concludes his analysis of Ws' Puritans with

> Mather, then, attributes all creative power to a remote divinity (and his parodic adversary) and none to human beings. By denying the existence of the imagination, he represses the use of his own; therefore, he cannot make the "transposition of the faculties . . . to the world of the imagination" required by the viewer of a work of art. And so the artist's power to transpose ordinary objects and words into "the medium of the imagination" terrifies Mather; he can only theorize that an artist has the power of "*Invisiblizing* . . . the Grossest Bodies."

The Washington portrayed in *The First President* is a contrasting figure, an original American who is analogue for the poet.

> Williams' libretto honors Washington's holding "deep within himself that which refuses to be liberated," for this repression is in service of the imagination. Washington's painful but steadfast sublimination of libido enables him to commit the primal American act of creation, the constitution of the ground out of which an authentic American poem could be written: the nation itself.

In sum, "*The First President* can be read as an allegory of The American Poet, a revolutionary who sublimates his own desires in order to reconstitute the world on 'an abler pattern.' "

Frail goes on to cite "some significant resemblances between the libretto and [*Paterson* which] suggest that the work was a rehearsal of sorts for the latter"—a rehearsal which "must have been helpful [to Ws] both psychologically and formally." For, Frail concludes,

> Writing about the poetics of his opera on the hero of the American Revolution, then, led Williams to draft a version of the constitution of his own revolutionary poetics. That Williams invited his readers to draft such documents from his "colonial" works themselves has been the burden of this essay. Driven by the revolutionary's need for legitimating precedents, Williams searched the American past for such ancestral figures, shaping hostile presences such as Cotton Mather so that he could counter their counter-imaginations, honoring his imaginative forefathers such as Washington by identifying their actions with his style.

182. MacGowan, Christopher J. "Two New Williams Citations,"
    WCWR, 6:ii (Fall 1980), 27-30.

> MacGowan's note records his find of two items missing from Emily
> Wallace's *Bibliography*. A letter in the January 1919 issue of *The
> Little Review*, in the excerpt he quotes, "reflect[s Ws'] apprecia-
> tion of Margaret Anderson and Jane Heap's efforts." And a poem in
> *Dial* (December 1922), " 'When Fresh, It Was Sweet,' records Wil-
> liams' response to a performance of *Katinka* by Nikita Balieff's
> Chauve-Souris, or Bat, Company." MacGowan reproduces Ws' poem
> about this "Moscow troupe [that] appeared in New York through
> much of 1922."

183. Magrid, Barry. "Collecting William Carlos Williams," *WCWR*,
    6:ii (Fall 1980), 15-25.

> Dr. Magrid, a collector of the works of Ws, writes of the ins and outs
> and fine points of such collecting in this article based in his own
> extensive experience. Noting that textual variants between editions
> and printings are not as complex in "the body of Williams' work"
> as in Pound's or Joyce's, he writes that "A Williams poem exists to
> a large extent for the eye, on the page," and that "the format of
> the book itself, its size, paper, and type, all contribute something
> to a Williams poem, which may be conveyed only by the physicality
> of the original edition."
>
> Dr. Magrid gives most of his article to the topics of recent
> market prices, assessibility or rarity of volumes, their dust jackets,
> and the "inscribed, association, or merely signed copies" of Ws'
> early, small press books. He remarks that "beginning with New
> Directions publication of *White Mule* in 1937, the bulk of Williams'
> work began to appear in gradually larger editions, offered by com-
> mercial publishers rather than presses," though he does write of
> individual copies of the later works, and of collecting some, espe-
> cially those from small presses. He concludes "with a listing of the
> market values of Williams' titles over the last five years, obtained
> through catalogue and auction records." With illus. of cover and dust
> jacket designs of three books.

184. Bernstein, Michael André. *The Tale of the Tribe: Ezra Pound
    and the Modern Verse Epic*. Princeton: Princeton UP, 1980.
    Review by C. F. Terrell, *ConL*, 23 (1982), 92-96.

> Noting that Bernstein gives, of his 320-page book, 34 pages to
> "Williams and *Paterson*," Terrell writes that its three chapters
>
> > do useful service early on by sweeping away a mass of critical
> > confusion and clutter which has darkened the poem rather
> > than throwing light upon it. Vlaminck's phrase, "Art is local,"
> > which was much circulated in the twenties, and a Dewey article
> > entitled "Americanism and Localism" (*Dial*, June, 1920), may
> > have led to some of the assumptions of *In the American Grain*
> > which later resulted in enormous problems of structure, realism,
> > and meaning in *Paterson*. These problems were beyond solution
> > by anyone. Romantic notions such as "A man like a city and a
> > woman like a flower" are hard to maintain for one who would

find "no idea but in things." Williams believed a poem such as *Paterson* demanded to be written. New York, Chicago, and Washington were rejected as too big, too special, or too far away, and "a shining city on a hill" as too unreal. Thus, Paterson, N.J. which was on the Passaic River and not far from the Passaic Falls seemed during the twenties and thirties exactly the thing. What happened to it and all its localness might have been the subject of an epic poem, but it was certainly not the subject Williams could or would want to write about. With economy of motion Bernstein sets forth the problem and the delirium of solutions first, so that he can at the end point to the quite extraordinary values to be found in the total work in spite of the difficulties.

185. Berry, Eleanor. "William Carlos Williams's 'The Semblables,' " *NMAL*, 4 (1980), Item 21.

Berry quotes Howard Nemerov's praise of this poem, in *Figures of Thought*: "The poem says almost nothing aloud, limiting itself to rather bare description, yet idea is everywhere radiantly present," and writing that he "regards the poem as something of an apotheosis of Imagism." She finds it "remarkable" that he "says nothing about the form of the poem," which she proceeds to peruse. Basically, she finds "the visual structure of eleven equivalent units (stanzas) belies the syntactical structure, which consists of three remarkable and remarkably disparate sentences." A detailed and particular demonstration of this quality leads her to deduce that "the disparity between the visual-metrical structure of the text and its syntactical structure provokes awareness of the text itself as object. The process of syntactical interpretation is de-automatized by the obstruction to it of the cuts of line- and stanza-divisions." In addition, especially in the second sentence of the poem she finds "an inflationary style undercut by inconsistencies in register and by an arrangement that is persistently at odds with its rhythms." Overall, "The language of the poem is a *tour de force* in the high style, but with its surface disturbed in such a manner as to put it [the high style] in an unkind light"; and she concludes that the parodistic form of the poem contradicts a reading of it "as a work of high seriousness," such as Nemerov presented.

186. Borroff, Marie. "William Carlos Williams: The Diagnostic Eye." In *Medicine and Literature*. Ed. Enid Rhodes Peschel. N.Y.: Neale Watson Academic Pubs., Inc., 1980. Pp. 56-65.

While acknowledging that "Williams's poems tell us less about his day-to-day experiences as a practicing physician than his stories do," Borroff focuses on such poems for her subject. In "his collected short poems [Borroff nowhere refers to the physician passages in *Paterson*] we find only a dozen or so poems" on "doctor and patient," and others which "allude obliquely [sic] to the setting of Williams's professional life." Of this latter group, Borroff looks most fully at the title poem of *Spring and All* in order to specify the qualities of its narrator's consciousness. The poem "presents a [personified] protagonist engaged . . . in an *agon*, a dramatized struggle," which struggle presents itself to the very present "personal consciousness" of the narrator. Through him one senses "that his account of the scene is authentic"—i.e., not only that it is "factual," but that the speaker's consciousness has "an epitomizing, on-target force." The narrator "brings to the experience no distractions or preoccupations; indeed, no self-consciousness"; his mind is entirely focused on "a vital presence engaged in a process of self-definition, . . . [and] he identifies himself with that presence and that process."

Borroff claims and attempts to show that similar states of consciousness are portrayed in other poems (many from *Spring and All*); but as the poems she selects are those having a speaker-in-transit, she disregards her declared focus on physician poems. She then returns to poems of the latter group, making a hodgepodge of wayward observations. See also 193. Paschel.

187. Dotterer, Ronald L. "The Fictive and the Real: Myth and Form in the Poetry of Wallace Stevens and William Carlos Williams," in McCune, Marjorie W. *et al*, eds. *The Binding of Proteus: Perspectives on Myth and the Literary Process.* Lewisburg: Bucknell UP, 1980. Pp. 221-48.

Denoting Stevens and Ws as "the two most influential American poets of their day," Dotterer indicates he writes of them because the two,

> despite endless differences of style, subject, and temperament, show at least one similar progression: the gradual evolution of a long poem that served as the arena and the achievement of the poet's struggle with word and world. A study of the ways in which these poets caused their most important poems "to come into being" points to at least one common element within the diversity of modern American poetry: the centrality of the poem itself in giving order to life.

Continuing the abstract of his article, Dotterer writes,

> Specifically, I shall examine what Williams called "the clouds resolved in a sandy sluice," that is, the five books of *Paterson*: and Stevens's "abstraction blooded;" his *Notes Toward a Supreme Fiction*. In a larger sense, I shall refer also to the gradual complication, expansion, and elucidation of two poetic theories. Both Williams and Stevens sought formal poetic structures that could surpass earlier, more fragmentary visions and could suggest an order that is at once without and within poetry. That ambitious search for a poem with such a structural unity, an essential part of mythopoesis, depends on the making of fictions. For Williams and Stevens, these fictions became respectively the all-inclusive figure of Paterson and the metaphysical figure of a supreme fiction.

Dotterer concludes his abstract by asserting,

> Although these poems may appear at first to contrast as markedly as the diction of their creators, they bear strong similarities in form and substance that illustrate complementary views concerning the relationship of the imagination to the world at large. And although the attitudes and lives of Williams and Stevens may differ, an overriding similarity linking their careers is that the evolution of their literary forms is both a private and an isolating process. The making of these extended poems involves for the authors a distancing not only from earlier poets

but from culture in general—even if there is no permanent
rejection of these traditions. Such making, I shall argue, depends
upon an intentional avoidance of other men's fictions, of setting
out to make or reinterpret societal myths: it relies instead upon
a search for what Stevens at one point calls a "mythology of
self" (*CP*, 28)—a fiction that arises from the self yet ultimately
can exist without the self.

188. Doyle, Charles, ed. *William Carlos Williams: The Critical
Heritage*. London, Boston and Henley: Routledge & Kegan
Paul, 1980.
Review by George Monteiro, *WCWR*, 7:i (Spring 1981),
31-32.

Monteiro writes that "All the volumes of this [Critical Heritage]
series that I have seen are annoying to work with, especially those
covering poets. The volume under review is no exception." Specific
annoyances are the awkward replacement of "the poetry quoted in
the reprinted articles and reviews" with references to "where the
lines or poems can be found in a particular edition of the poet's
work" ("With many such omissions of poetry and the occasional
truncation of essays, it is all rather like having the batteries go dead
in one's hearing aid just as the punch line in a joke is about to be
sprung.") and the rather mundane typeface, "poor quality paper,"
and generally disappointing appearance of the book.

But "the selection of the essays is another matter," writes
Monteiro; and he notes the delights, pleasures, "apercus and fine
touches" of essays and reviews by Yvor Winters, Kenneth Burke,
Randall Jarrell, Hugh Kenner, Kenneth Rexroth, Louis Martz, and
Winfield Townley Scott.

189. Hans, James S. "Presence and Absence in Modern Poetry,"
Criticism, 22 (1980), 320-40.

What differentiates poets like Stevens and Ws is widely recognized,
and criticism has also tried to identify what they and other modernists have in common, be it "a return to 'reality' " or "an emphasis on
self-reflexive poetry." "But," argues Hans, "the reality these poets
see is so various and the reflexivity of their poetry so different that
another approach to their work seems necessary."

> What poets like Eliot and Williams do seem to share is an under-
> standing of the relationship between presence and absence in the
> world, and their understanding of this relationship develops in
> complexity as they mature as poets. One could say that presence
> and absence ultimately come to be defined in terms of the
> relationship between language and reality, but for both Eliot and
> Williams the problem was more profound than that. The impor-
> tant question for both was how human experience could be
> redeemed in a world where absence could no longer be trans-
> cended through a religious commitment, and their changing
> ways of perceiving this difficulty are finally quite similar despite
> the fact that Eliot became an Anglican while Williams continued
> to write from a particularly American perspective.

As for Ws' view of human experience, his own criticism indicates his belief that

all experience begins with the unknown, with our interaction with the undifferentiated flux of life; from this undifferentiated interaction, we differentiate various things and locate them with perishable signs. And since the signs are inadequate renderings of the undifferentiated, being only partial differentiations of it, we can never be content to live simply in the world of our different- ations. We must continually experience the undifferentiated in order to make new differentiations, lest we forget that all differentiations are only partial markers of the unknown which can never be wholly articulated.

In turn, Ws as poet, the early Ws especially, makes of "the differentiations" that embody his experience a poetry "which reflect on the undifferentiated from which the images are derived," whose energy arises not just from the concrete particulars of the poem, "but from the total display of natural energy or desire."

The Williams of this early period does not transform nature into culture; instead, he transforms culture into nature. The cultural edifice of language is not the dominant element here—the natural force of energy/desire is, and language is simply one more expression of that natural energy and desire. And this energy is not an absence or a fiction that the poet makes up to center his world; it is a presence, a mystery that is everywhere, the presence that is marked in man's movements between undifferentiated and differentiated experience, the presence that is marked in precisely the same way in a poem, if it is a good one.

The Ws of *The Collected Later Poems* "holds to the basic movement between undifferentiated experience and its differentia- tion"; but the poetry loses the earlier "intensity of innocent desire" and acquires a violence. "The naive energy of the early work turns into a violent energy that is destructive at the same time it is crea- tive, that leads to death as well as to new life." Absence resides in this world of the later Ws, though not the absence attributed to him by the deconstructionists. Rather, it is an absence "Williams is trying to overcome in his poetry" and which "he finds at the center of only the static world view promulgated by science and the English conti- nental tradition."

In the latest poetry, such as the "descent" passage in *Paterson* and "Asphodel, That Greeny Flower," Ws' poetry presents a more complex, paradoxical conception of experience, one in which "both presence and absence are inseparable aspects of undifferentiated experience, [in which] presence somehow precedes absence, even if they are inseparable."

Hans concludes,

The path of Williams' career, then, proceeds in a dialectical manner, beginning first with a poetry of innocent presence, overturning that into the violence of absence, and finally bring- ing the two together in a paradoxical formulation which stresses the light of presence while conceding the darkness of absence. That such a paradox is ultimately necessary is easy enough to see, for Williams has always been concerned with undifferenti- ated human experience, with experience that is not precategor- ized by the differentiations of language. He always believed that undifferentiated experience was possible, and he always believed that it was the most valuable of human experiences. Thus, he came to write a poetry about this kind of experience and never really wrote a poetry specifically about language. At the most,

> he wrote a poetry about the relationship between language and undifferentiated experience, and since his view of this relationship is one that speaks of presence, one can hardly argue that language and reflexivity dominate the poetry, for only a linguistically oriented universe would make language its primary subject.

In a word, Ws throughout his poetry is of the conviction, argues Hans, that experience in all ways precedes language, that language is either its handmaiden or its warder, and one job of poetry is to lead its audience to see the handmaiden as more attractive.

190. Heinzelman, Kurt. *The Economics of the Imagination.* Amherst, MA: Univ. of Mass. Pr., 1980. Review by Walter Sutton, *WCWR*, 7:i (Spring 1981), 24-25.

"Assuming metaphor and myth to be common properties of economics and literature," writes Sutton,

> Kurt Heinzelman describes his study as an "intersystemic analysis of the language and logic which poetic and economic 'systems' release." Two parts of his book are concerned with, respectively, "Literature and Economics" and "Labor Theory and the Literary Work." In both parts, Mr. Heinzelman conducts parallel and interrelated analyses of the work of economists and poets including, among others, Adam Smith, Ricardo, Malthus, Marx, Spenser, Blake, Wordsworth, Yeats, Frost, and William Carlos Williams.

Heinzelman's main literary subject is "the romantic theory of the imagination . . . as it was carried forward by Blake, Wordsworth, and Williams, the three poets who receive most of his attention." More specifically, Heinzelman looks at the romantic "idea[s] of a 'community' of shared value and of the reader as a 'productive laborer' in his successful imaginative effort to realize the poem," goals difficult to attain in the 20th century, adds Sutton. Nevertheless,

> in his Chapter " 'Getting It' in *Paterson*: The Increment Defended," Mr. Heinzelman sees Williams' main concern as the effort to achieve just such an exchange and, moreover, through his sensitivity to the spoken idiom (and its multitude of voices), to recapture the collective social experience of oral poetry as it developed out of group labor. A far reach.
> The reader's "getting *it*" (grasping the metaphor or poem) is explained by reference to Freud's theory of the dynamics of the joke, Pound's definition of the Image, and Williams' own metaphor of the "radiant gist" of Book Four. In all three, a sudden release of energy is involved. The release of physical energy in fission is metaphorically identified with the economic freeing of credit and with the freeing of the gist of poetic experience through the imaginative labor of reading. (There is an obvious parallel with the earlier revelatory realization of the "Word" in Blake.) Mr. Heinzelman also stresses the necessary variability of the text for both writer and reader—the fact that the labor involved is an ongoing, never-to-be-completed cultural process. These are all good points, though not novel in the criticism of Williams.

In summary, Sutton finds Heinzelman "at his best" when "he reveals unexpected relationships" in economic and literary texts. The weaknesses of his work are "an indulgence in pretentious, turgid prose" and a tendency in his "critical model . . . to assume an autonomy that obscures the complex integrity of the poet's text."

191. Ostrom, Alan. "The Functions of Names in the Mythopeic [sic] Process in William Carlos Williams' *Paterson*," *Literary Onomastics Studies*, 7 (1980), 161-76.

> Using "myth" to mean the creation, by means of "a collection of characters and incidents and environments," of a literature "that transcends mere story and becomes a magnified image and implicit explanation of the intrinsic nature of things," Ostrom proposes to trace Ws' search, in *Paterson*, for the " 'redeeming language' . . . by looking at how he uses names in the poem." He starts with place names in *Paterson* I, quickly moves on to personal names, and—after writing mostly on the first book—catalogues and comments on the names, successively, in the other four books. The article is brief (about 3700 words), prosaic (with little about myth or poetry), and totally, it seems, an individual effort (there are four footnotes, to two texts: *Paterson* and Ws' *Selected Letters*).

192. Perloff, Marjorie. "The Man Who Loved Women: The Medical Fictions of William Carlos Williams," *GaR*, 34 (1980), 840-53.

> Perloff's subject is "the medical stories" published in *Life Along the Passaic River*, all of which are characterized by "a paradigm." Namely, "the patient . . . is always female"; "the doctor-narrator, Williams' projected image of himself, is regularly presented as a no-nonsense, matter-of-fact type"; "although the doctor keeps his distance" and is always portrayed as firmly married, "his references to the treatment of the female patient are regularly couched in sexual language"; the "subliminal erotic response of doctor to patient" seems to evoke, when the "treatment" is successful, "a sense of elation or victory . . . quite in excess of the actual event"; and "the patient is wary of all other doctors, which is to say of men who would or could have similar power over her." Perloff shows the operations and variations of this paradigm in "World's End," "The Girl with a Pimply Face," "A Night in June," "The Venus," and "The Accident"; and she concludes with "some curious changes" it displays "in such later fictions as 'The Farmers' Daughters,' " wherein, with the shift of "the sexual encounter . . . from the realm of fantasy to reality, [there occurs] a curious apathy . . . coupled with a new irritatingly patronizing tone toward women." Perloff's approach, which summons elusive biography to augment and extend the critical analysis, introduces some debatable implications and ambiguities.

193. Peschel, Enid Rhodes, ed. *Medicine and Literature*. N.Y.: Neale Watson Academic Publs., 1980.
Review by Theodore Ziolkowski, in *SewaneeR*, 89 (Fall 1981), 655-57.

> The 25 essays of this collection explore "two areas, the character of the healer-poet and the symbolic nature of disease," with varying

success, writes Ziolkowski. "Measured against the rich possibilities for historical and mythic associations, most of the efforts are disappointing." Among those disappointing efforts seem to be the essay on Ws, one of "nine essays on doctor-writers," as Ziolkowski does not list the Ws' essay in his catalogue of the good ones. Overall, he finds "the volume leads no further than the separate conclusions of the few competent essays that it contains. The lack of focus in most of the pieces coupled with the ignorance of standard sources and broader contexts leads one, at least initially," to rather dismiss the book. See also 186. Borroff.

194. Popović, Dubravka. "Poetika Vilijama Karlosa Wilijamsa ili Problemi novog pocetka," *Letopis Matice Srpske* (Novi Sad, Yugoslavia), 425 (1980), 996-1018.

195. Prichard, William H. *Lives of the Modern Poets*. N.Y.: Oxford UP, 1980.
Review by C. E. Nicholson, in *Journal of American Studies*, 15 (Dec. 1981), 424-26.

Prichard directs his book to a more or less popular audience, an audience that "is literate, at ease with a complicated novel, less so with poetry perhaps." His subject is "the nine most interesting and important poets writing in English in the first part of this century," namely Hardy, Yeats, Robinson, Frost, Pound, Eliot, Stevens, Crane and Ws. The antiquarian title is something of a key to Prichard's approach, which forgoes "recent literary criticism in favour of a nineteenth-century return to a notion of literary appreciation as the journey of a soul through masterpieces."

Nicholson finds the attempt "to make a range of difficult writing available to a non-professional audience involves a relaxation of critical method which is sometimes uncomfortably reductive." He provides several examples, but his last is adequate for illustration: Overall, the book "may be characterized by its author's responses to two major modernist texts," one of which is *Paterson*. Of Ws' epic, Prichard writes, "I don't feel overly guilty at leaving the long poem as mainly a curiosity with some lovely moments in it."

196. Sayre, Henry M. "Ready-Mades and Other Measures: The Poetics of Marcel Duchamp and William Carlos Williams," *JML*, 8:i (1980), 3-22.

Starting with a brief characterization of Duchamp's career and of Ws' changes of opinion about the artist's famous 1917 submission of a urinal to an exhibition in New York, Sayre writes, "Williams believed that he had not only assimilated but overtaken and surpassed the genius of Marcel Duchamp" in that, unlike Duchamp, he had continued his "*work*" [HMS's italics] and "his [lifetime] dedication to the creation of a new American poetry." The rest of Sayre's article sets forth an interesting and important validation of Ws' judgment.

First, as regards poetic form: form was, virtually from the start, Ws' central object, writes Sayre, a priority also selected by modern painters like Cezanne ("the modern painter had defined the experience of form . . . as the quintessential experience of the human mind") and one Ws shared with the American artists, painters, and photographers "with whom [he] associated" (for all their emphasis upon "commonplace objects," all knew the object must be "lift[ed] from its dull bed by force of imagination" to become art). The "best definition of the American extension of European formal exploration" was made by Ws' friend, Charles Sheeler, who said, "a picture could have incorporated in it the structural design implied in abstraction and be presented in a wholly realistic manner." "It is the humanization of the abstract through making the abstract concrete . . . that Williams sees as the major contribution of American Modernism," as he also sees the American branch extending European Modernism by raising the commonplace to art and grounding the esthetic in the mundane. These values are exemplified in "The Red Wheelbarrow" as well as in Duchamp's "urinal *Fountain*."

Sayre finds Ws' poetics to be no less indebted to Duchamp. After briefly tracing his pursuit of a "new measure," Sayre writes, "what Williams needed to discover, and what until 'The Descent' he had despaired of ever discovering, was not only a formal order capable of admitting into itself the flux and change of something like a river—to say nothing of the diversity of the American idiom—but also one which would not deny, in its repetition over the course of a long poem like *Paterson*, the sense of chance and surprise we encounter in the ready-made." The poetics Ws discovered in "The Descent" had been found, in "visual form, by Duchamp in his famous *La Mariée mise à nu par ses célibataires, même*"—"the so-called *Large Glass*," and in "the preliminary works which he later incorporated into it." Sayre describes one of these "early projects," a work called *3 stoppages étalon* (1913-14)" which strikingly portrays the relativism of three meter-length measures, adding that Ws saw *The Large Glass*, into which this project was assimilated, and may also have read Duchamp's own comment on the *stoppages*. Furthermore, a magazine (titled *View*) "with which [Ws] was perhaps most closely associated" during the '40s published a special issue on Duchamp (at that time still "the spiritual and theoretical master of French Modernism") which "was the first comprehensive study of his work ever undertaken, and almost every study [therein] emphasizes the centrality of the *stoppages* and related work to Duchamp's aesthetic."

In addition, Sayre writes, "the thematic concerns of the *Large Glass*, as defined by the *View* articles, are also parallel to Williams' own." Reflecting the theme of divorce in *Paterson*, the *Glass* portrays "bride and bachelors [as] forever relegated to separate domains"; and just as "Williams descends into industrial Paterson, Duchamp descends into a world of mechanized and unfulfilled love," both "seek[ing] in the *descent* the promise of subsequent *ascent*" [HMS's italics].

Sayre concludes by making two points. After describing Duchamp's last ambitious work, *Etant donnés*, he writes of the work's insistence upon the separation of the artist and what he knows from the work's audience and its limited knowledge. "In this sense Duchamp defines art in terms of delay awaiting the completion of active response, and this is in many ways an almost perfect description of Williams' definition of art in *Paterson* V. For Book V is itself a response to 'the delay' of Books I-IV, an admission on Williams' part that the poem had not been finished but had arrived only at a 'state of incompletion.' Book V's theme –art and the survival of art–likewise defines Williams' artistic heritage, from medieval tapestries to Dada, in terms of Williams' own ability and willingness to actively respond to that heritage." Secondly, quoting from late interviews with Ws in which he emphasized his attraction to pictorial art and disaffection from music, Sayre writes, "Williams 'new measure,' then, is a *visual* measure, a design in space. It is a concrete *sign* for the imagination in which . . . Williams takes the abstract side of experience, the imagination which has no concrete reference, and composes a schematic sign which designates it" [HMS's italics]. By such achievements, "Williams solidified his position as an aesthetic theorist and artistic innovator in every way Duchamp's equal. It is no accident that the two of them would assert so much influence on the American painters and poets of the succeeding generation."

197. Tashjian, Dickran. Essay on Ws in *American Writers in Paris, 1920-1939*. Vol. IV of *Dictionary of Literary Biography*, ed. Karen Lane Rood. Detroit: Gale Research Co., 1980. Pp. 415-18.
Announced in *WCWR*, 6:i (Spring 1980), 10.

198. Vendler, Helen. *Part of Nature, Part of Us: Modern American Poets*. Cambridge: Harvard UP, 1980.
Review by Marjorie Perloff, *ConL*, 22:i (1981), 96-103.

Perloff usefully alludes to earlier reviews:

This collection of Helen Vendler's essays and reviews on modern American poets, written over the past decade chiefly for the *New York Times Book Review*, the *New York Review of Books*, and the *New Yorker*, has already received –deservedly, I think– its own rave reviews from a galaxy of critics. among them Irvin Ehrenpreis, William S. Pritchard, and Monroe Spears. The energy and brilliance of Vendler's writing, her sympathy and tact in bringing to the reader's attention the particular qualities that make a given poem memorable, her affinities with Randall Jarrell and R. P. Blackmur—these have been remarked upon.

For her review, Perloff attempts to define "Vendler's critical assumptions, assumptions that are not only unstated but probably quite unconscious." She writes that "Vendler has always avoided theory," has shown "an impatience with history," has "a natural gift for metaphor that makes Vendler herself something of a poet," and "above all, [evinces] a concern for poems as 'stories about human beings,' " particularly the kind of story indicated by "the words of one of her titles, 'Apollo's Harsher Songs.' " The bulk of the review dwells on an examination of this last "assumption."

Basically Perloff criticizes Vendler's humanistic orientation; in her words: "to put it another way, is the moral value of the poem its esthetic value as well?"

More specifically she finds "Vendler's particular moral norms preclude at least the following: (1) religious poetry, the poetry of transcendence . . . ; (2) poetry of intense erotic celebration . . . ; (3) poetry in which the 'private self' . . . becomes just one item in the large mythographic collage of the present" (as in Pound's *Cantos*); (4) "the poetry of play, of intellectual game . . . ; and (5) poetry that subordinates the articulation of detachable meaning to the creation of artful structures" (as in Ws' *Spring and All*—Perloff's only reference to Ws in the review).

In opposition to the above, writes Perloff, Vendler values poetry that places "the private self . . . squarely at the center of the poem," though on even this she is inconsistent, praising Lowell for this quality but criticizing O'Hara. Vendler's outstanding strengths are "in giving her reader the precise graph of a poet's consciousness, his or her successes or failures," with "her finest essays" being those on Stevens and Merrill. Perloff concludes that Vendler conveys, "with astonishing economy, vigor, vividness, and penetration, what she has seen in the poems she has read." Her book "is certainly a remarkable achievement," she writes, despite what she believes is the irrelevance of its "Arnoldian—and ultimately Romantic—norms . . . [to] the *fin de siècle* of our own postmodern age."

199. Woodward, Kathleen. *At Last, the Real Distinguished Thing: The Late Poems of Eliot, Pound, Stevens, and Williams.* Columbus: Ohio State UP, 1980. Review by George F. Butterick, in *AL*, 53 (January 1982), 748-49.

Butterick's first paragraph is worth quoting in full:

> Kathleen Woodward's ultimate concern is wisdom, and the aging which seems to be its prerequisite (she has previously co-edited an anthology called *Aging and the Elderly: Humanistic Perspectives in Gerontology*). She has chosen four definitively modern poets, and by exploring with exactitude their final works, describes how those works fulfill not only a personal life but also a literary age, the final wisdom of Modernism. Her focus is four long meditative poems, spanning what she calls the period of Late Modernism, from 1943 to 1958: Eliot's *Four Quartets*, Pound's *Pisan Cantos*, "To an Old Philosopher in Rome" from Stevens' *The Rock*, and the fifth book of Williams' *Paterson*. She seeks to answer the questions whether aging brings poetic fulfillment and how these poets offer insight into the experience of old age itself. Her dominant concept, taken from "Burnt Norton" (among other places), is the "still point," a state of being in balance, which she finds characteristic of the poems under discussion and, consequently, of wisdom. She seeks to add dimension by invoking thinkers from other arenas than the purely literary, especially that of developmental psychology.

Butterick finds Woodward's competence and conviction especially "evident in her essays on Pound and Stevens. These are superb, among the finest anywhere." His review suggests her chapter on Ws, while good, may be the least interesting in her book. It gives a fine, sound reading of *Paterson* V, but she may have been unfair to choose that poem. "The Descent" is Williams' old-age poem is there ever was one, and is commonly read as such. Or why not the reknowned "Asphodel: That Greeny Flower," which is after all even longer than *Paterson* V and probably more meditative? Among other things it contains a preoccupation with the Bomb, that dire herald of the Postmodern age. She seriously misjudges the delicate but persistent and even irregular beauty of "Asphodel," and thus relegates it to mere "sweetness" and "autobiography."

Butterick roundly commends the book itself, however. "Her study reinforces the meaning of humanistic studies, at the same time broadening their base to include what, demographically at least, will become increasingly a factor in such studies—as War Babies age, as longevity extends, as American graduate education is even more largely shaped by older returnees."

200. Zwicky, Fay. "Seeing and Recording a Local Ambience," *Westerly*, 1 (1980), 91-96.

Zwicky traces, for an Australian audience, a quick capsulization of the initial neglect and then development, in this century, of an American poetry "forge[d in] an indigenous language [and] divorced from the concerns of history and traditional learning that preoccupied Pound and Eliot." She focuses on Ws as exemplar of "The colloquial strain," asserting that he "has had (for better and worse) a great impact on contemporary American and Australian poetry." Her text for illustrating his "seeing and recording" is "The Red Wheel-barrow" [sic], which she analyzes and compares to the Australian poet William Hart Smith's "Kangaroo-Paw."

201. 1980 Dissertations

A. Bartlett, Jeffrey M. "The Advance: William Carlos Williams and Henry Miller, American Modernists." University of Iowa, 1980. Supervisor: Sherman Paul. *DAI* 41:1585A.

B. Bock, Layeh Aronson. "The Birth of Modernism: *Des Imagistes* and the Psychology of William James." Stanford University, 1980.

C. Draper, Jesse Monroe. "The Liberation of William Carlos Williams." University of Virginia, 1980. *DAI* 41:1594A.

D. Grinyer, Mark Allen. "Thought and Language in the Early Works of William Carlos Williams: The Development of His Poetic Terminology through 1917." University of California, Riverside, 1980. Chairman: George Knox. *DAI* 41:1586A-87A.

E. Hodges, Elizabeth Perry. "The Language of Nature: Wordsworth and William Carlos Williams." Columbia University, 1980.

F. Mair, David Clare. "*Paterson* and *The Maximus Poems*: A Comparative Study of the Locale, History and Structure." *DAI* 40:6280A-81A.

G. Marling, William H. "Williams and the Arensberg Circle, 1909-1923." University of California-Santa Barbara, 1980. Director: Allan Stephens. *DAI* 41:3108A-09A.

H. Miki, Roy. "A Preface to William Carlos Williams: The Prepoetics of *Kora in Hell: Improvisations.*" University of British Columbia, 1980. Director: Peter Quartermain. *DAI* 41:4710A.

I. Parisoff, Myra Jane Heinz. "A Study of the Relative Mode of Mind in Pound, Eliot, Stevens, and Williams." University of Tulsa, 1980. Director: Gordon O. Taylor.

J. Richey, Leon Thayer III. "Two Cases of Poetic Influence: William Carlos Williams, Hart Crane, and the Problem of T. S. Eliot." Indiana University, 1980. *DAI* 41:1059A.

K. Schmidt, Peter Jarrett. "Williams and the Visual Arts, 1915-1945." University of Virginia, 1980. Director: J. C. Levenson. *DAI* 41: 4036A.

L. Watson, Douglas Frank. "A Sense of Place in the Poetry of Robert Frost, William Carlos Williams, and Wallace Stevens." Texas Tech University, 1980. Chairman: Warren Walker.

1981

202. Weigl, Bruce. "William Carlos Williams' 'The Yachts,' " *NConL*, 11:i (January 1981), 9-12.

In "The Yachts" Ws opposes "the desirable perfection of the yachts," objectively conveyed in the early part of the poem, to "the misery of humanity struggling below them," characterized "from within" and "in the emotions and language of victims." The "modern, loose blank verse" meter of the poem "is crucial to [its] success," as it "keeps the emotion well within acceptable boundaries, and allows what otherwise would have been indulgence on the poet's part to rise above the cries of the victims and their antagonists."

203. Gallup, Donald. "The William Carlos Williams Collection at Yale," *WCWR*, 7:i (Spring 1981), 1-8.

Drawing upon the Ws-Norman Holmes Pearson letters in the Beinecke Library at Yale, Gallup begins with a chronological account of Pearson's relationship and friendship with Ws, from 1937, when Pearson was a graduate student at Yale, to the year of Ws' death, when they were unfortunately estranged by a misunderstanding on Ws' and Flossie's part. Interleaved into this account is information on Ws' literary materials, now at the Beinecke, that Pearson assiduously obtained from Ws and collected himself over the years. One of those acquisitions was Ws' "own retained copy of the true first edition of his *Poems* (1909)," which Ws had corrected in his own hand. Another, also offered to Pearson by Ws, was, in Ws' words, "a large quantity of the original manuscripts of Paterson 1, 2, 3 & 4 [with] all my scribbled notes on the margins of pages, rejected first draughts, etc such I think you will be anxious to have."

The latter half of the essay is a narrative catalog of the Ws holdings at Yale. After Ws' death, in accord with an agreement between Yale and Ws made in 1955, the library acquired "more than a thousand issues of periodicals, many with Williams' own contributions, and some nine hundred volumes from his library, [which were] mostly first editions, many with presentation inscriptions from their authors." There were also "some two hundred eighty-six manuscripts and typescripts" and a mass of correspondence addressed to Ws. In the list of the number of communications from some 60 or more people, that for Ezra Pound is far and away the most numerous—216 letters and cards. There is a smaller collection of Ws' letters to others and, in addition to assorted other items, Pearson's own "huge Williams collection of some fifty-five first and limited editions," as well as his correspondence with Ws.

204. MacGowan, Christopher J. "William Carlos Williams' 'The Great Figure' and Marsden Hartley," *AL*, 53 (May 1981), 302-305.

Proposing that the association of Marsden Hartley with Ws' poem, "more than the association with [Charles] Demuth, reveals [its] full significance," MacGowan shows that in his *Autobiography* Ws linked his friend Hartley with the poem both expressly and figuratively. In addition, "by [thus] alluding to his painter friend in terms of a numerical figure set against a dynamic, colorful background, Williams matched the strategy of Hartley's 1913-15 canvases [, which are] abstract works, painted in Berlin under the impact of his meeting with Kandinsky and Marc." The "full significance" of the poem, MacGowan deduces, is in " 'The Great Figure' [being] a type of the artist isolated by an America inimical to its vital, creative talents," most immediately, Hartley and Ws himself. "Yet [as recounted by Ws in the *Autobiography*] the poet is about to visit the painter, and the poem [sic] finally affirms the point that America's 'unheeded' artists can support each other."

205. Mahar, William J. "Williams vs. Washington: The Relationship Between the Libretto and History in *The First President*," *WCWR*, 7:i (Spring 1981), 9-22.

Mahar analyzes the problems and weaknesses of Ws' opera. These include significant differences between the view of Washington given in the libretto and that Ws conveys in his "lengthy 'Introduction to the Composer' . . . explaining his views on opera and defending his treatment of Washington." In the libretto itself,

among the most important . . . problems are: (1) the selection of the historical events treated in the individual scenes; (2) the lack of a credible central character; (3) the scissors-and-paste

method by which the major speeches of and about Washington
were assembled; and (4) the apparent misinterpretation of some
of the historical facts of Washington's life which led Williams
into a maze of dramaturgical difficulties.

Mahar concludes, "it is the lack of characterization which
emerges as the central problem in the work," a problem no less
severe in Ws' portrait of the protagonist than among the secondary
characters. In addition, the opera has "flaws which make it a difficult work to set to music. The abrupt shifts in time, the lack of a
clear dramatic pattern, and, above all, the episodic or quasi-improvi-
sational quality of the various scenes may be important features of
Williams' literary style, but they are burdens rather than benefits to
a composer." Overall, Ws fails in his attempt to demonstrate that
Washington had come through the trials of public life with his
spirit unbroken." In order to do that,

> more interpretation was needed, more than Williams was willing
> to give. He saw Washington as a man like himself, as a kind of
> poet perhaps; but Williams could not comprehend the differ-
> ences between himself and the real Washington. In the end, that
> is the reason why he failed to create a strong operatic character
> and why it is unlikely that the libretto will ever be viewed by
> musicians as an "Occasion for Music."

206. Tapscott, Stephen. "Whitman in *Paterson*," *AL*, 53 (May
1981), 291-301.

"Williams uses two related images of Walt Whitman to frame" *Paterson*, writes Tapscott—first as "the slumbering giant who personifies
the unarticulated potential of his place at the start of the poem"
and second as "the swimmer whose return from the sea optimistically closes Book IV." In both, "as if to counter T. S. Eliot's dominant notions of 'tradition,'" "Williams offers Whitman as the
'father' of a paradoxical American tradition of rebelliousness" and
as representative of a tradition which he himself is continuing.

More specifically, Paterson at the start of the poem "modulates from mountain to man to city to giant—just as Whitman in
'Song of Myself' is sometimes a demiurgic voice, sometimes a cor-
porate abstraction, sometimes a passionate single man." However,
whereas Whitman portrays a fruitful equating of society and citizen,
"Williams distinguishes private and public experience; his poem,
accordingly, is less inclusive and associative, more analytic and
formally contained than Whitman's."

As for the end of Book IV, "Williams overtly rouses a Whit-
man-like figure to oppose the momentum of the river's headlong
corrupting rush to the 'generalizing' sea, and to re-direct the motion
of the poem: from distracted waywardness in the sea back inland,
toward a melioristic future." The potential for that redirection and
reenergizing are figured in the scene of the emerged swimmer/Whit-
man as he "absently drops a seed [of a beach plum he has picked
and eaten] and leaves it behind him" to germinate and grow. "The
intervention of the Whitmanian man to achieve that planting [of a
local seed] seems signally important. Implicit in the image is a sense
of the poet's power, for both the poet and his poem are instruments

by which a rescue from the unfruitful divorce of language from its physical reality can be effected." With that finish to his poem, "Williams both salutes Whitman's achievement and acknowledges the continuity of his own modern quest with the difficult beginnings that his image of Whitman represents.

207. Rosenthal, M. L. and Sally M. Gall. "The Modern Sequence and Its Precursors," *ConL*, 22 (Summer 1981), 308-25.

Rosenthal and Gall's subject is "the modern poetic sequence"—"a grouping of mainly lyric poems and passages, rarely uniform in pattern, which tend to interact as an organic whole. It usually includes narrative and dramatic elements, and ratiocinative ones as well, but its structure is finally lyrical. Intimate, fragmented, self-analytical, open, emotionally volatile, the sequence meets the needs of modern sensibility even when the poet aspires to tragic or epic scope." Of Ws' poems it is *Paterson* the authors identify as one of these modern poetic sequences.

After noting some of the barriers to even critical recognition of "this genre, the outgrowth of poets' recognition and pursuit of 'new thresholds, new anatomies,' " the authors write that the first "critical inklings of [this new genre] came early and piecemeal and—naturally—from poets"—specifically Poe in "The Philosophy of Composition," Coleridge in his conception of "organic form," and Emerson in "The Poet." They conclude that

> In short, the modern sequence has evolved out of a serious need for an encompassing poetry, one completely involved with what our lives really mean subjectively. That need reflects the ultimate pressure on modern sensibility to understand itself and to regain what Olson called the "human universe." The pressure, right or wrong, is to reconceive reality in humanly reassuring ways rather than in chillingly impersonal ones. It is felt inescapably by poets, even when they hardly realize why they write as they do, as a pressure to remember and deepen their sense of our human reality while rejecting any hubristic, anthropomorphic self-deception. (See Hart Crane's "Proem: To Brooklyn Bridge" for a very pure projection of this pressure.) The struggle against depression and loss of morale in this context was waged powerfully by great poets in the past in work like Donne's "A Nocturnall upon St. Lucie's Day," Wordsworth's "Tintern Abbey," and Tennyson's *Maud: A Monodrama*. These titles, in their chronological order, will suggest that certain pressures are a constant, cutting across differences of time and poetic genre. At the same time, the poems themselves may suggest an increasing emphasis, as poetry approaches its modern phase, on a complex music of feeling involving a number of radiant centers, progressively liberated from a narrative or thematic framework.

A footnote indicates the article is "excerpted from the opening chapter of *The Modern Poetic Sequence*" which is to be published by Oxford UP.

208. Berry, Eleanor. "Williams' Development of a New Prosodic Form—*Not* the 'Variable Foot,' But the 'Sight Stanza,' " *WCWR*, 7:ii (Fall 1981), 21-30.

Berry's subject is the "sight stanza," Ws' development and use of a visual stanzaic form that is independent of, and commonly in tension with, the syntactic and rhetorical structures of the poem. She traces his progress towards this form from the basically conventional relations of stanza and rhetoric of *Poems* 1909, through "the technique of frequent and arbitrary strong enjambment" found in *Al Que Quiere!* 1917, (Berry analyzes this feature fully in "Canthara") to the emergence of the sight-stanza proper in *Spring and All*. This radically new form, reflecting "Williams' assimilation of the influence of Cubism," functionally "create[s] a sense of order that wins the reader's patience with material at the apparent chaos of which he might otherwise balk," and imposes a "separateness of the words, except as they partake of the quality of thinginess." Berry says Ws returned to the sight-stanza in *Pictures from Brueghel*, though he "does not seem to have recognized—certainly he never discussed—what he was doing by laying poem-shaped grids athwart texts whose syntactical and rhetorical structures were very differently articulated."

209. Cole, Thomas. "Williams and Pound Remembered," *WCWR*, 7:ii (Fall 1981), 5-20.

Thomas Cole was in 1948 the editor of *Imagi* and "an undergraduate at Muhlenberg College." His essay is an affectionate and detailed biographical account of his literary and personal friendship with Williams (beginning in 1948) and with Pound (in the following year). About Ws Cole writes, "We always visited and talked as friends. I was never a great one for attempting deep literary or philosophical themes," though Cole continued as editor, writer, and teacher of poetry as well as companion of poets throughout the 15 years of his and Ws' friendship. Examples of his riches are his accounts of the mid-century issue of *Imagi*, in which appeared "new work" by Ws, Pound, Cummings, Marianne Moore, Stevens, Zukofsky as well as "by twenty new, young poets . . . including William Jay Smith, Charles Olson, Philip Murray, and David Ignatow"; of a visit, in 1950, with Viola Jordan, who "had been an old flame of [Ws and Pound]" in their student days at the University of Pennsylvania"; and of one of his visits to St. Elizabeths, for which he arrived to find Ws also about to visit Pound: "Audrey [a friend] and I sat listening most of the afternoon while the two men reminisced, Pound passing around the goodies that Audrey had brought. Pound was always in control, but it was obvious that he adored Bill and knew how lucky he was to have him there that afternoon." Cole also writes of a number of visits he made to 9 Ridge Road (the last in 1975), as well as of two to Pound at Rapallo. Throughout he quotes at length from the letters Ws wrote him.

210. Coles, Robert. "William Carlos Williams: A Writing Physician," *WCWR*, 7:ii (Fall 1981), 30-31.

While an undergraduate at Harvard, Coles was invited by Ws "to accompany him on his medical rounds," an offer Coles "quickly accepted and soon enough found myself utterly captivated by this brilliant, energetic, many-sided man from Rutherford, NJ, who was known to a whole world of working-class people from Paterson, NJ, as "Doc," and to another world of readers as a writer bravely, even fiercely, determined to develop and retain his own, quite special voice and viewpoint." Such is the origin of this appreciation of Ws, by a physician who writes, "Each year I use his stories and poems in a medical humanities class I teach at Harvard Medical School," and who also gives a fine, rare description of Ws' eyes.

211. Fedo, David A. "*A Dream of Love* and The We Present Production of 1949," *WCWR*, 7:ii (Fall 1981), 32-35.

> "Williams valued *A Dream of Love*" more than any of the other plays printed in *Many Loves and Other Plays,* according to his wife. But, writes Fedo, it "has never been satisfactorily produced on the professional stage." It was produced in New York in July 1949; and, supplemented by a detailed letter from Barbara J. Whiting, the play's director, Fedo describes the intentions and appurtenances of that production. "For its imaginative expressism," the set of the play "won the Obie award for the best off-Broadway set of the season"; and William Saroyan vigorously praised the drama in a piece in the New York *Herald Tribune*. Despite these kudos, the production failed through a combination of inexperienced actors and the descent of "one of New York's worst heat waves" onto the theater lacking air conditioning.

212. Graham, Theodora R. "A New Williams Story: 'Long Island Sound' (1961)," *WCWR*, 7:ii (Fall 1981), 1-3.

> In a headnote Theodora Graham explains this story, "an unrevised autobiographical sketch," was written at James Laughlin's request but, because Floss objected to it, was never published. Aside from "a few editorial changes," Ms. Graham gives us, she adds, "the pure product"—a sketch set during "this first summer at the shore" of a childhood sexual encounter. With a reproduction of a photograph of Ws and his father, "on the Bridgeport Ferry, *circa* 1900."

213. Buckeye, Robert, and Fran Naramore. *William Carlos Williams: Attack from the Present*. Middlebury, Vt.: Middlebury College, 1981.

> The only information available about this is a note in *AL*, 53 (November 1981), 578: "A 20-page catalogue of an exhibit; also, a bibliography of the Williams manuscript materials in the Abernethy Library of American Literature."

214. Mariani, Paul. *William Carlos Williams/ A New World Naked*. N.Y.: McGraw Hill, 1981.
Review by Gilbert Sorrentino, in *The New York Times Book Review*, 22 Nov. 1981, pp. 1, 34-36.

"The most laudable aspect of Paul Mariani's critical biography of William Carlos Williams is that it largely succeeds in placing him, in his biographer's words, as 'the single most important American poet of the twentieth century.' " So Sorrentino begins his review, much of which depicts the critical and academic neglect of Ws during his lifetime and tallies Ws' poetic strengths that were myopically missed by the critics. Sorrentino writes,

> Paul Mariani is relentless in detailing the shabby critical treatment accorded Williams throughout the whole of his career, a record of intellectual misprision that invented a Williams who was, and still is—with endemic regularity—thought of as a kind of amiable primitive, an unsophisticated scribbler, a simple small-town doctor who wrote on the side, but wrote, mind you, without quite knowing what he was doing: the literary equivalent of Grandma Moses or the New Jersey version of *vers libre*'s gift to the world, Carl Sandburg. Mr. Mariani shatters these idiocies by a careful examination of Williams's work in poetry, fiction and criticism, setting it against the general somnambulism of the time. In a sense, this book may be read as a kind of graph of the reactionary shoddiness of the American critical mind in the face of a modern master, and I half suspect that Mr. Mariani intends us to read it this way because of the attention he has paid to this facet of Williams's career.

Sorrentino notes that, "paradoxically," the cause of Ws' neglect "might be laid at [his own] door": neither the critics, nor even other English and American poets, were ready to consider the possibility of "a vernacular American poetry" as early as 1917, when Ws discerned the potential; and when Ws published in 1920 "Portrait of a Lady"—his "first wholly successful demonstration that there was an American idiom, that its rhythms might be formally controlled, and that it could be turned to metrical patterns that are not those of the 'natural' English iambic"—"Mariani does not note that it occasioned any comment." Instead, Ws' achievement was overshadowed by "The Love Song of J. Alfred Prufrock" "and would soon be eclipsed by 'The Waste Land,' the poem that enraged him because it seemed a betrayal of a new American poetry in gestation, as well as a portent of the return of poetry, as he put it, 'to the classroom.' He was, of course, right."

Not only did the critics fail to give Ws the attention he merited; they misperceived him when they did attend. Randall Jarrell was asked, despite Ws' misgivings, to write the introduction to his *Selected Poems* (1949), "the book that was to have served to broaden his audience. It was a mistake":

> This introduction petrified, for the rest of Williams's lifetime, and well beyond his death in 1963, the general critical attitude toward his work. In effect, what Jarrell's unenthusiastic introduction did for Williams was to present him as unlettered but well-meaning, and lacking in poetic intelligence and craft: in short, a good-hearted rube, not to be mentioned in the same breath as Eliot, Frost or Stevens. Mariani continues, "the sense one was left with [was] that one was dealing here with a circumscribed and minor talent."

Sorrentino gives other examples of critics' hatchetings prompted by the critical biases of the time. Mariani explains in his preface that the biography issued "out of the work that he did in the early '70's 'in an attempt to determine why the critics had for so long either

dismissed or tried actually to destroy Williams' poetic reputation.' "
Sorrentino finds "the 'why' is made explicit throughout" the book:

> Williams himself gave, unwittingly, one of the reasons when he
> wrote, early on: "The goal of writing is to keep a beleaguered
> line of understanding which has movement from breaking down
> and becoming a hole into which we sink decoratively to rest."
> Writing is almost always most admired when it is decoratively
> resting—in our time, the more comatose, the more static a
> mirror image of "reality" the better—and at least three-quarters
> of the writers of any era employ language and techniques inade-
> quate to deal with that era; they are, in effect, decorators.
> Williams was a troublesome artist who was always starting anew,
> and in the despised language that he found, as he said, "in the
> mouths of Polish mothers." The critics, bemused by "deep
> thoughts" that shuffled along in stale iambics with the occa-
> sional tinkle of rhyme to wake them up, were having none of it.
> What could they have possibly said of a man who wrote, in
> 1950: "To me all sonnets say the same thing of no importance.
> What does it matter what the line 'says'? There is no poetry of
> distinction without formal invention."

The rest of Sorrentino's review is a sketch of Ws' life and
career, interspersed with further ironies and incongruities. Regarding
the value Ws placed on the local: "This 'localism'—in which Williams insisted that one would discover the universal—coupled with
his radical disruption of outworn forms and a consistent sabatoging
of 'content' as meaningless was to carry the innovations of the
European avant-garde into the American climate. These innovations
were seen by most of his readers as provincial and inarticulate."
Even as late as the 1950s the literary environment had little tolerance for Ws' achievement: "Robert Creeley, referring to the literary
climate of the '50's, wrote that its arbiters 'were dominant in their
insistence upon an idea of form extrinsic to the given instance . . .
Auden [was] the measure of competence.' "
Sorrentino observes that Ws might have been better received
and understood "had he found a commercial publisher earlier than
1934"; because his "enormously important early books" were not
kept in print, "there was little opportunity for the creation of a
body of intelligent critical discourse to be built up around this
work." As it is,

> Mr. Mariani calls his life one of "complex tragedy and brilli-
> ance." How complex, how tragic and how brilliant, his biog-
> raphy fully explores. Had he not been a man of such stamina
> and courage, such stubbornness, or had he not had, perhaps,
> what Pound called in a 1917 letter, "enough Spanish blood to
> muddy up [his] mind," he would have been silent by the mid-
> 30's. As it was, he persisted.

215. Perloff, Marjorie. *The Poetics of Indeterminacy: Rimbaud to
Cage*. Princeton: Princeton UP, 1981.
Review by Wendy Steiner, *Criticism*, 24 (Winter 1982), 64-70.

> Perloff, writes Steiner, "sets out to do nothing less than recast the
> modernist canon," attempting to unseat the High Modernists and to
> make the case for Rimbaud, Stein, Apollinaire, Ashbery, Cage,
> Antin and claiming a place for Ws, Pound and Beckett as their
> "heirs or coevals." Steiner rather praises the intention but finds

problems in the execution. Indeterminacy itself, which Steiner defines generally as "the presence in a work of conflicting, undecidable interpretations," changes in Perloff's usage during the course of the book. Most dubious, Steiner finds, is Perloff's equating indeterminancy with opaqueness, and in addition attributing the opaqueness innately to the work rather than to the limits of the historical—or even of the individual critic's—context for the reading. Other problems of Perloff's presentation are "the naïveté of [her] stance," her use of "imprecise semiotics" ("perhaps the single most disheartening feature of the book"), and her neglect of Derrida.

On the positive side, the book (though it "seems to be only a first stage in the critical reception of the difficult poets it treats") "is extremely useful in delineating the issues in that reception: the model of the visual arts, the concepts of modernism and post-modernism, the influence of romanticism, the importance of continental, especially French, influence, and the need for (an accurate) semiotics for understanding the complex semantics of such art."

Steiner's review indicates that Perloff writes of Ws' *Spring and All, Kora in Hell,* and *Paterson.* Steiner's reference to the last is: Perloff's "claim that Williams's symbolism in *Paterson* was a mode that he was uncomfortable with, his earlier indeterminacy being instead his native element, is belied by his vehemently symbolist history, *In the American Grain.*"

216. Revell, Peter. *Quest in Modern American Poetry.* London: Vision Press, and Totowa, N.J.: Barnes and Noble, 1981. Review by Richard Crowder, *AL,* 54 (October 1982), 458-59.

Crowder writes,

> Revell's book describes how five American poets looked for restored harmony in a world made chaotic by science and philosophy. Following a banal but serviceable theme, the author writes of Aiken, Pound, Eliot, H.D., and Williams, who, though in rather close contact throughout sixty years, followed different roads to recovery. Revell recounts to what extent, for example, they relied (or did not) on F. H. Bradley, Henri Bergson, Freud, "pagan" myth, and Christianity. He lays the foundation for his discussions by reviewing Whitman's voyage motif and his determination to be free of dogma.

Crowder characterizes Revell's readings of "the long poem" by each poet (Aiken's *The Divine Pilgrim,* Pound's *Cantos,* Eliot's *Four Quartets,* H.D.'s *Trilogy,* and Ws' *Paterson*). In contrast to H.D.'s "fable of spiritual renewal," Ws "dived into the temporal, the 'filthy Passaic,' in his quest for ultimate significance. *Paterson* presents the unadorned details of urban living. Opposed especially to Eliot, Williams was dead set against tradition as the source of ultimate harmony." Crowder concludes, ambiguously (and in the light of his description of the book, generously), "The value of this book is the bringing together of these points of view, which most of us have recognized for years (possibly outside Revell's scheme)."

217. Spencer, Benjamin T. *Patterns of Nationality: Twentieth-Century Literary Versions of America.* N.Y.: Burt Franklin, 1981.
Review by Walter B. Rideout, *AL*, 54 (December 1982), 602-604.

> Rideout's review says little about Ws, but his characterization of Spencer's book will broadly indicate Spencer's interest in Ws. *Patterns of Nationality* is in part a continuation of Spencer's *The Quest for National Identity*, a history of American literature up to "the last decade of the nineteenth century." His subject in *Patterns* is "the evolving concepts of an American literature," a subject explored in two parts. The first part is made up of three essays, one on the period 1892-1912, one on the literature of the 1920s and 30s, and a third, which Rideout finds "the most interesting," that "examines the theoretical question of what 'a national American literature' actually is." It is not, Spencer claims, a literature that "emphasizes the American scene," events, or character, but is rather to be found at " 'the metaphorical and the symbolic' level of reading: 'Literature may become American, then, on this plane not by seeking to express a new experience, but by expressing or exploring the far reaches of human consciousness through objects primarily American in memory, through "felt objects," and by eschewing objects foreign to the recurring associations of the American people.' "
>
> The second, longer part is composed of eight essays on "Americanism" in the work of Stein, Pound, Williams, Anderson, Fitzgerald, Crane, Edward Dahlberg, and Mailer. Though Rideout finds unclear Spencer's limiting his exploration to these eight authors, he writes that "in reading any of these essays one feels the constant presence of a fine scholarly-critical mind, a mind acute and sensitive in its insights, discriminating in its interpretation of evidence."

218. *William Carlos Williams: Poèmes / Poems.* A bilingual ed. Trans. with intro. and notes by Jacqueline Saunier-Ollier. Paris: Éditions Aubier-Montaigne, 1981.
No review available. The book was announced in *WCWR*, 8:ii (Fall 1982), 32.

219. 1981 Dissertations

A. Bar-yaacov, Lois. "Some Aspects of American Modernism: William Carlos Williams and Marianne Moore—The 'In-Patriots.' " Hebrew University, 1981.

B. Berry, Eleanor. "Syntactical and Metrical Structures in the Poetry of William Carlos Williams." University of Toronto, 1981. Supervisor: Eric Domville. *DAI* 42:4449A.

C. Dunn, Allen Roy. "The Self-Authenticating Stance in the Poetry of Wallace Stevens and William Carlos Williams." University of Washington, 1981. Chairperson: Leroy Searle. *DAI* 42:2669A.

D. Fisher, Ann W. "The Autobiographies of William Carlos Williams." Claremont Graduate School, 1981. Adviser: William C. Spengemann. *DAI* 42:214A.

E. Fredman, Stephen Albert. "Sentences: Three Works of American Prose Poetry." *DAI* 41:3579A.

F. Parisoff, Myra Jane Heinz. "A Study of the Relative Mode of Mind in Pound, Eliot, Stevens, and Williams." *DAI* 41:3574A.

G. Stewart, Patrick Leonard, Jr. "Charles Sheeler, William Carlos Williams and the Development of the Precisionist Aesthetic, 1917-1931." University of Delaware, 1981. Supervisor: William Innes Homer. *DAI* 42:1834A.

1982

220. Di Piero, W. S. "Notes on Memory and Enthusiasm," *SoR*, 18 (Winter 1982), 1-24.

> In this meditation and essay (in the older sense, of attempt or weighing) Ws is called forth to illustrate the pole of enthusiasm. "For Williams," writes Di Piero, "a poem need be nothing more than an act of enthusiastic noticing, a spelling out of the lyric imperative 'O look!'" When such "an aesthetic govern[s] the entire progress of a career it is quite narrow and limiting, since it does not allow for the passionate interrogations of history and memory which one finds throughout Yeats and Crane. In a sense, Williams' career is a demonstration of the values and limitations of the two modes, noticing and interrogation." Thus, the enthusiastic mode determined that "Williams was a devouring presence, and if his manner is not as boisterous as Whitman's and Pound's, his impulse is the same: welcome the plentitude of the world, junk and jewels alike, take it all in, get it down, register it." In that approach, "beauty is reduced to that which is for whatever reason interesting, and inevitably the poem . . . becomes an exercise in solipsism disguised by affectionate descriptive language." In contrast, "in the longer poems at the end of *Pictures* [from which Di Piero takes all his examples for the discussion of Ws], the literalist strain is absorbed and enriched by another, more luxurious, in which patterns of recollection converge on the moment of telling, the past intricated in the argumentative present." Especially is this true of "Asphodel, That Greeny Flower": "In its reckoning with memory and imagination, with nature's plentitude as it reflects the honeycombing of private life, with the value of metaphor and correspondences ('Are facts not flowers/ and flowers facts?'), 'Asphodel' must have been the poem Williams wrote to thank the Muse."

221. Wallace, Emily Mitchell. "Musing in the Highlands and Valleys: The Poetry of Gratwick Farm," *WCWR*, 8:i (Spring 1982), 8-41.

The Gratwick Farm Emily Wallace writes of was an idyllic natural retreat—dating from the Gratwick family's building of "a summer residence there in 1900 when servants were plentiful and income tax non-existent"—at which Professor Charles Abbott and his wife Theresa Gratwick Abbott entertained the Williams's during "eleven visits [they made] to the farm, the first time in 1940, the second in 1946, and the last time in 1958." Wallace writes of "two aspects of Gratwick Farm, as an extraordinary country retreat and as a place for intense literary labor that challenged Williams to explore and express affinities he otherwise might not have brought to fruition." Her characterization of the Gratwicks and the Abbotts portrays them as industrious, intelligent, hospitable, and convivial, qualities which, in conjunction with the summer beauty of Gratwick Farm, constituted a fertile seedbed for poems Ws wrote there. Of those poems, Wallace in her discussion of "The Yellow Tree Peony" admirably demonstrates the fullness and density of its mythological resonances ("The poem does not prefigure Demeter as the goddess of grain and corn . . . , for the emphasis is on the power of the 'Lady of the Wild Things,' ruler of the kingdoms of life and death, and early matriarchal goddess 'altogether noble and womanly.' "); and she increases knowledge about and appreciation of the poem by writing of William Gratwick's painstaking, lengthy, and professional attempts to hybridize tree peonies in order to create a long-sought yellow variety, thereby showing Ws' poem has additionally a rigorous horticultural genesis. The two other poems he wrote during the 1946 visit have a joint title, "Two Deliberate Exercises," and are jointly influenced by Ws' readings of Valéry on "Consciousness and Nature." "Rogation Sunday" and "The Intelligent Sheepman and the New Cars" are more briefly explored. Observing that "the true audacity for Williams was in making his own versions of two Greek poems," Wallace describes in detail the circumstances of Ws' translations of "Theocritus: Idyl I" and of the Sappho "love-ode" incorporated into *Paterson* V. For the translation of the Sappho, Abbott's help in introducing Ws to a Greek scholar and in expediting Ws' interest and efforts "appears to have been quietly indispensable," writes Wallace. And of Theocritus: "Temperamentally, Williams was as close to Theocritus as to any other poet, including his triple father Shakespeare-Keats-Whitman." In the midst of all this, Wallace proposes a functional definition of the "variable foot" [to quote the core, "A flexible or variable foot is a unit of poetic language that is the length appropriate to its overall intensity (stress) of sound, sense, typographical appearance, and the 'something else' that comes from the tension of the units in relation to one another."] and, apropos Ws and his critics, observes pithily that "Critics who attack Williams for his inconsistencies in whatever realm of thought might find more excitement in trying to comprehend the scope of his mind." In sum, this is a knowledgeable, perceptive, fully researched, skillfully composed, and thoroughly valuable essay. With illus.

222. Williams, William Eric. "The Physical," *WCWR*, 8:i (Spring 1982), 1-7.

The "physical" of the title refers first to Ws' appearance and physique and then to the range of physical activities his son recalls him vigorously pursuing. These include Ws' marathon walks, especially with his brother Edgar and his father, working, especially farming and gardening, baseball, which he pursued "as a player and spectator," fishing (a passion of his sons about which Williams writes, "I guess his kicks came from being with us boys and sharing in our triumph with each catch."), and fencing.

The latter half of the essay describes the Williams' visits, in the 1940s, with Charles and Theresa Abbott "on the Gratwick estate," and concludes with a tribute to Ws' energetic, generous humanity. "Few other than close intimates realized what boundless energy he possessed and how generous he was in spending it on his patients, his art and his fellow artists." Williams writes, he was "a human guy who had something for everyone."

Illus., and with photographs of Ws, in 1910 and 1916.

223. Cox, Don. "Two Glimpses of Williams," *WCWR*, 8:ii (Fall 1982), 29-30.

Mr. Cox, a fellow resident of Rutherford born "over a generation later than the poet," and also an author, writes of his appreciation of Ws' writings ("I was particularly impressed with the raw and down-to-earth portrayals in *Life Along the Passaic River*") and of two encounters with Ws. The first, on an "evening in the late '40's," was at a meeting of a food coop to which Ws belonged and of which Mr. Cox was then president. "Williams attended and surprised us all by reading a newly composed poem on the meaning and importance of the cooperative movement," a poem Mr. Cox believes was lost. The second encounter, on the street in early 1960, occurred just after the publication of an article by Mr. Cox "featured on the cover" of the *Saturday Review*, for which Ws congratulated him and urged him to keep writing: "It's what in you that counts and if you have something to say, say it, even if you can't find a publisher right away."

224. Cushman, Stephen. "Williams Revising: The Worksheets of 'Threnody,'" *WCWR*, 8:ii (Fall 1982), 23-28.

Referring to Ws' often-noted "view of revision as compromise, and . . . loss," Cushman notes that the poet did nonetheless revise, often repeatedly; and he meticulously examines the ten drafts of Ws' 18-line "Threnody," in "the Williams Collection at Buffalo." Evidences of "the pains Williams often took to hone the fleeting presence into a finished poem," more pragmatically the drafts show that "he added, cancelled, sharpened images, altered diction and syntax, adjusted line arrangements, enhanced acoustic patterns, and experimented with visual format."

225. Kolich, Augustus M. "Introduction to an Unpublished Williams' Manuscript: 'Let us order our world:'" *WCWR*, 8:ii (Fall 1982), 15-17.

In view of some references to the war in this MSS and also of the dates of a literary controversy that seems to have sparked Ws to write it, Kolich (in correction of Baldwin and Meyer's dating the MSS c. 1941) deduces it "was written either very late in 1941 or perhaps early in 1942." Ws' note of *"Paterson"* on the first page indicates he intended it for his epic.

The controversy was mainly between Van Wyck Brooks, who in a talk at Columbia in late 1941 classified writers as either "Primary (those who were 'great' and dealt with 'great themes') [or] Coterie [which] included the expatriates and most of the Modernists" and, opposing Brooks, Dwight Macdonald, who in a *Partisan Review* essay accused Brooks of "acting *'in Defense* of bourgeoise-Philistine values' [DM's italics] and in support of a national 'drift towards totalitarianism.' " In addition to writing a letter to *PR* "in support of Macdonald," Ws wrote this essay. "In response to the patriotic demand for order and tradition," Williams answered: " 'Order has meant too often no more than to maim.' [and] Men in 'established positions' lived for 'the perpetuation of traditions' which allowed for the digging of 'the graveyards of the imagination.' " Ws' essay follows, on pp. 17-22.

226. Schmidt, Peter. "Dada, *Paterson*, and Epic Tradition," *WCWR*, 8:ii (Fall 1982), 1-14.

Schmidt first considers the Dada documents Ws saw (notably, a translation from Hugo Ball's 1916-1917 diary, published in 1936, and Tzara's "Dada Souleve Tout," in French in 1921) and may have seen, citing them as "precedents for . . . the jumble of broken sentences in *Paterson* III.iii [that] represent[s] the flood debris of dead words," as well as for "the library burning episode in III.ii." "Disordering syntax and linear reading," the *Paterson* passage and the Dada pieces all "spit out a flood of things once known and believed but now thrown up in disgust and despair."

Then, to address the issue of the impact of Dada upon "the overall architecture" of the poem, Schmidt argues that one first needs to consider "how the structure of Williams' epic compares with those of the past." Whereas traditional epic embodies two points of view, the one "prospective and dramatic" and the other "retrospective and (relatively) static," Romantic and modern epics tend to conflate these viewpoints and to make "the growth of the poet's mind the norm for the epic," with a concomitant result that the form, forging traditional closure, is often "unfinished and unfinishable." As regards "Dr. Paterson's own struggle to change and [his] many successes and reversals," Schmidt posits that Books I-IV represent a version of the Romantic-modern epic, whereas Ws' addition of Book V moves the poem towards the classical epic form. Dr. Paterson's quest is, by the end of Book IV, essentially tragic, his "descent . . . consistent with both the topography of the Passaic River Valley" and with the Dadaist maxim "that art and ideas petrify, and therefore have to be discarded soon after they are invented" (one consequence of which is that "Dada thus made artists martyrs to the impossible ideal of perpetual self-renewal"). With the addition of Book V, "the poem ends classically, with the hero

returning to the Falls, to a world where the eternal and the time-
bound, the creative and the decadent, may be held in balance." "In
creating two endings for his long poem," Schmidt concludes, "Williams fashioned an agitated equilibrium between the impulses toward
closure and exposure, retrospection and progression, which have
informed epics from *The Iliad* on."

227. Doyle, Charles. *William Carlos Williams and the American
Poem*. N.Y.: St. Martin's Pr., 1982.

> No review available. Doyle's book covers the range of Ws' career,
> from *Poems* (1909) to *Pictures from Brueghel* (1962), with five of
> its 14 chapters given to *Paterson*.

228. Fedo, David A. "The Meaning of Love in William Carlos
Williams' *A Dream of Love*," *ConL*, 23 (1982), 169-90.

> Fedo first writes of various accolades the play has received and of
> Ws' estimate of it: he not only valued it above his other plays but
> "even ranked it 'in importance' with his major poem *Paterson*."
> Fedo writes of its origins ("the conception of the play grew from the
> suggestion of adultery"), its composition (drawing on Ws' notes for
> it at Yale), and about the play itself. In the characterization of Doc
> Thurber and his wife, Myra, the play closely considers the nature of
> the love each has for the other, the role of the other woman, Dotty
> Randall, in Doc's life and in the marriage (as well as her character
> and situation), and provides "the audience extraordinary insights"
> in the meeting, after Doc Thurber's death, of Myra and Dotty. Fedo
> ends on "the question of the autobiographical implications of *A
> Dream of Love*" (which are posed by Ws creating for his male lead
> a character with a "double career as poet and physician") and on
> certain dramatic and characterizational problems that seem to follow
> from Ws' failure of objective distance.

229. Marling, William. *William Carlos Williams and the Painters,
1909-1923*. Ohio UP, 1982.
No review available. The book was announced in *WCWR*,
8:ii (Fall 1982), 32.

230. Soupault, Phillippe. *Last Nights of Paris*, trans. William Carlos
Williams. N.Y.: Full Court Pr., 1982.
Review by Neil Baldwin, *WCWR*, 8:ii (Fall 1982), 31-32.

> Ws and Soupault met in Paris in 1924, and later Ws read his *Les
> Dernières Nuits de Paris* (1928) while on a summer vacation. He
> wrote to Pound that same summer, " 'The first few pages of Soupault
> are delightful reading. Easy, deceptive, accurate to the rules of con-
> versation. . . . Perhaps it will grow foolishly fantastic later in the
> book. . . .' Soupault's fanciful, surrealistic, yet graphic style took
> hold," writes Baldwin; "and Williams collaborated with his mother,

Elena, on translating the book, published in 1929." Of the book itself, Baldwin writes,

> It is a magical book, a chiaroscuro portrait of odd, Night-town characters caught in a wandering odyssey through the Left Bank, observed all the while by a narrator who is more a floating eye than a real person. The story rests loosely on the activities of a prostitute, Georgette; her brother, Octave; a kind of master-mind, Volpe; and on occasional appearances by a mysterious sailor with a sinister canvas bag and other denizens of Parisian nightlife who seem to appear and fade with the fog that hangs heavily along the quais.

He adds that the novel "attracts by its evocation of Paris in the '20's," and that "the characters of *Last Nights of Paris* are embodiments of sensations, rather than attempts to portray individuals. As such, although they bewilder us, they do not perplex, because it is easy to accept the artifice laid like a thin veneer over every page. This is a tribute to the translation, which does not draw too much attention to itself. You can hear the French beneath the American diction." At "the end of the book, after an endless parade of days and nights, the narrator concedes, 'I was simply an ambulatory theater in which they [the characters] were playing an improvised comedy,' " as indeed this novel is a comedy, Baldwin affirms.

Soupault has written a preface for this edition, which is translated by the publisher, Rod Padgett.

231. 1982 Dissertations

A. Cushman, Stephen. "William Carlos Williams and the Meanings of Measure." Yale University, 1982. Director: Thomas R. Whitaker.

B. Flackmann, Josephine Marschel. "From Counterpoint to Harmony: A Stylistic Analysis of William Carlos Williams' Poetry." *DAI* 43: 1971A.

C. Horner, John Edward. "The Attenuated Vision: Images of Man in the Poetry of Edwin Arlington Robinson, William Carlos Williams, and Randall Jarrell." *DAI* 43:1972A.

D. Knight, Christopher John. "The Disparate Vision: Modern Empiricism in Gertrude Stein, Ernest Hemingway, William Carlos Williams and Marianne Moore." New York University, 1982. Adviser: John Kuehl. *DAI* 43:446A.

STEPHEN BOARDWAY

INDEX OF PEOPLE, BOOKS, AND THINGS

The items indexed include the names of people, the titles of books, plays, or musical compositions and most other capitalized words or concepts, except for the names of cities and publishing companies in bibliographical notes. Works by William Carlos Williams are indexed alphabetically by title. Where variants occur, the latest form adopted by Williams himself has been considered standard. Stephen Boardway, who did most of the work, was directed by the precept: "if in doubt, put it in." Both Steve and I are pleased with the occasional help of Dirk Stratton and the tireless assistance of Kate Woznik.

CFT

‡‡‡‡‡

A